ENGLISH ▶

HOW TO USE THE SIGNS

❶ OPEN THIS FLAP

❷ TURN TO THE COUNTRY IN WHICH YOU ARE INTERESTED

❸ COMPARE THE SIGNS FOR EXPLANATION

FRANÇAIS ▶

COMMENT INTERPRETER LES SYMBOLES

① OUVRIR CE VOLET

② REPORTEZ-VOUS AU PAYS QUI VOUS INTERESSE

③ COMPAREZ LES SIGNES POUR EN AVOiR L'EXPLICATION

DEUTSCH ▶

ANLEITUNG ZUR BENUTZUNG DER ZEICHEN

❶ ÖFFNEN SIE DIESES FALTBLATT

❷ SUCHEN SIE DAS LAND ÜBER WELCHES SIE AUSKÜNFTE HABEN MÖCHTEN

❸ VERGLEICHEN SIE DIE ZEICHEN AUF DER KLAPPE MIT DENEN DES LANDES

ESPAÑOL ▶

COMO UTILIZAR LOS SIMBOLOS

① ABRA ESTA SOLAPA

② BUSQUE EL PAIS QUE LE INTERESA

③ COMPARE LOS SIMBOLOS PARA OBTENER SU EXPLICACION

Cover Design and Hostelling International advertisements by Big Design, London.
Inside Front Cover, pages 1-32 & "We want to hear from you" pages by Elanders (UK) Limited.

IYHF acknowledges the help of Member Associations in providing photographs for pages 1-32.

In pursuance of the Environmental Charter adopted by IYHF's 39th International Conference,
this book has been produced using only paper from environment-friendly sources. The Nordic
Council of Ministers decided in November 1989 to introduce common Nordic environmental
labelling of products. Today, the 'Swan' is the only existing environmental label for printed
matter in Europe. The criteria is set with this main target area:

    The effect on the environment is minimised within the production process.

The product itself:

    This product is 100% recyclable.

    The ink, varnish and glue does not contain chemicals classified as environmentally
hazardous according to EU directives.

    The paper used is produced with low environmental impact (emissions) not with
chemicals classified as environmentally hazardous according to EU directives.

Published in 2000 by
International Youth Hostel Federation
Secretariat, 1st Floor, Fountain House, Parkway, Welwyn Garden City,
Hertfordshire, AL8 6JH, England
Registered under the Charity Act in England.

Distributed in the United Kingdom by World Leisure Marketing
... and through Hostelling International outlets worldwide.
"Hostelling International" is the brand name of Youth Hostelling Worldwide

Europe 2001

HOSTELLING INTERNATIONAL

Welcome
Bienvenue
Willkommen
Bienvenido

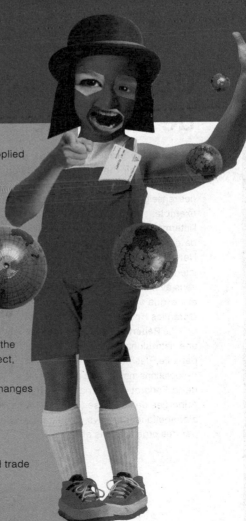

The information in this Guide has been supplied by the Youth Hostel Associations of each country represented. Hostels are listed alphabetically by country and city, and symbols indicate hostel opening times, prices, facilities etc. - these are explained in the fold-out section at the front of this Guide. For further information about hostels worldwide either contact your local Youth Hostel Association (YHA) or visit our Internet home page at www.iyhf.org.

Every effort has been made to ensure that the information contained in this Guide is correct, and Hostelling International can accept no responsibility for any inaccuracies or for changes subsequent to publication.

ISBN 0 901496 56 1

English

Français

Deutsch

Español

How to use this Guide

Fiesch Youth Hostel - Switzerland

This guide is organized in two parts - the Introduction and the Hostel Directory. See Contents (inside front cover) for full details.

In the **Introduction** you will find general information such as: how to make advance bookings using the International Booking Network (IBN), international emergency telephone numbers, member discounts, and Hostelling International Assured Standards.

The **Hostel Directory** is an alphabetical listing, by country and town, of hostels belonging to full members of the International Youth Hostel Federation. At the end of the directory you will find an alphabetical listing, by country, of supplementary accommodation provided by affiliate organizations.

Comment se servir de ce guide

Ce guide se présente en deux parties - l'introduction et le répertoire des auberges. Voir l'Index (verso de la couverture du devant) pour en savoir plus.

Dans **l'Introduction**, vous trouverez des renseignements généraux sur, par exemple, les réservations par l'intermédiaire du système informatisé de réservation, IBN (International Booking Network), les numéros d'urgence internationaux, les remises auxquelles vous avez droit en tant que membre, et ce que veulent dire les Normes Garanties Hostelling International.

Le **Répertoire des Auberges** est une liste alphabétique, par pays et par ville, des auberges affiliées aux associations membres (à part entière) de la Fédération Internationale des Auberges de Jeunesse (IYHF). A la fin du répertoire, vous trouverez une autre liste alphabétique, par pays, contenant la liste des hébergements secondaires proposés par des organisations affiliées.

Marbella Youth Hostel - Spain

Wie Sie diesen Führer benutzen

Nürnberg Youth Hostel - Germany

Der Führer besteht aus zwei Teilen - die Einführung und das internationale Herbergsverzeichnis. Siehe Inhaltsverzeichnis (innere Titelseite) für Einzelheiten.

In der **Einführung** finden Sie allgemeine Informationen, z.B. wie man über das "International Booking Network" (IBN) Betten im Voraus buchen kann, internationale Notrufnummern, Mitgliederrabatte und "Hostelling International Assured Standards".

Das **Herbergsverzeichnis** ist eine alphabetisch, nach Ländern und Orten eingeteilte Übersicht aller Herbergen von Vollmitgliedern der Internationalen Jugendherbergsföderation (IYHF). Am Ende des Verzeichnis befindet sich eine Liste mit zusätzlichen Übernachtungsangeboten von angegliederten Organisationen.

Cómo utilizar esta Guía

Armagh City Youth Hostel - Northern Ireland

Esta guía ha sido elaborada en dos partes: la introducción y las listas de albergues. En el Indice (ver el reverso de la portada) se especifican las diferentes secciones.

En la **Introducción** usted encontrará información general, por ejemplo: cómo realizar reservas con antelación a través de nuestra red internacional de reservas IBN (International Booking Network), los números de teléfono de emergencia internacionales, los descuentos que usted, en su calidad de miembro, puede conseguir y la definición de las Normas Garantizadas de Hostelling International.

En las **Listas de Albergues** están catalogados alfabéticamente por país y por ciudad los albergues afiliados a las Asociaciones miembros de pleno derecho de la Federación Internacional de Albergues Juveniles (IYHF). Al final de dichas listas, en una sección aparte, se relacionan alfabéticamente por país alojamientos suplementarios administrados por otras organizaciones afiliadas.

Introduction to Hostelling International

Welcome to the world of Hostelling International - a unique network of accommodation centres where you can enjoy a good night's sleep in friendly surroundings at an affordable price.

Hostelling International is the brand name of the International Youth Hostel Federation, the organization representing Youth Hostel Associations, worldwide. Hostelling International is the largest, most experienced network dedicated to travellers of all ages, young and old. Only in Bavaria, Germany is access limited to guests aged under 27. You can find out more by visiting our website www.iyhf.org. **For budget accommodation you can trust, look for the blue triangle symbol.**

Felicien Rops Youth Hostel - Namur, Belgium

RAIL PASS DIRECT,
for all your Inter-Rail needs!!

Hitting the rails in Europe this year?

If so, you need to call Rail Pass Direct on **01733 502808** for all your Inter-Railing needs. Whether you are under or over 26, we have the pass for you.

We can also supply you with not only the Thomas Cook European Timetable, which is essential for anyone who is planning an Inter-Rail trip, but also with a wide range of books and maps with which to plan your journey more effectively.

Order your Inter-Rail Pass from RAIL PASS DIRECT on 01733 502808 **and we can supply you with an Inter-Rail Survival Kit worth £41.00, for an amazing £28.00 which includes postage and packing. The kit comprises: The Thomas Cook European Timetable, Europe 2001: an Inter-Railer's and Eurailer's Guide, the Thomas Cook Rail Map of Europe, a European Travel Phrasebook and a bumbag.***

All the Thomas Cook publications can be bought separately at a special IYHF offer of £2.00 off each publication and FREE postage and packing. Please quote IYHF01 when placing your order.

Benefits of Membership

To stay at a Youth Hostel, you must become a member of your national Youth Hostel Association. If there is no national YHA in your country, you can purchase a Hostelling International Card or a Welcome Stamp on arrival at your chosen hostel.

Membership offers a wide range of benefits - including:

- 4,200 **accommodation** centres in more than 60 countries worldwide - open to people of **all ages**, and offering a choice of single, double and dormitory rooms.

- Participation in all Hostelling International **activities**, programmes and events.

- Thousands of **discounts** worldwide - from travel and sports activities, to restaurants, museums and entertainment! A selection of discounts is listed at the back of this Guide. For the full story, check out www.iyhf.org.

- Advance **reservations** up to 6 months ahead using the International Booking Network (IBN) system - **see page 10** for further information.

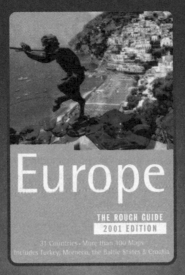

Quality Standards You Can Count On

Hostelling International's Assured Standards Scheme means you can rely on a consistent level of services and facilities wherever you stay.

- **Welcome** - hostels are open to all. You can join if you are not already a member, and you can make advance reservations. Plus you will have access to essential facilities if the hostel closes for a period during the day.

- **Comfort** - a good night's sleep (including the hire of freshly-laundered linen if it is not included in the overnight charge), and sufficient washing/ shower facilities. Meals are generally available, along with self-catering facilities and a food store close by.

- **Cleanliness** - the highest standards of hygiene wherever you travel.

- **Security** - for you and your possessions, including lockers for luggage and valuables.

- **Privacy** - in showers, washing areas and toilets. Most hostels provide single sex dormitories - although if requested, a mixed sex dormitory may be offered to people travelling together.

Standards are monitored by Hostelling International and by you, the user. **There are Comment Cards at the back of this Guide - tell us what you think!**

HOSTEL GRADES

▲ **Standard:** applies to the majority of hostels

△ **Simple:** applies to smaller hostels, or those in remote locations with simple facilities - you may find limited staffing and shorter opening hours.

Some hostels listed in this Guide are outside the Assured Standards Scheme - these provide accommodation in areas where it would not otherwise be available.

TRAVELLERS WITH DISABILITIES ♿

Hostelling International welcomes travellers with disabilities - hostels suitable for wheelchair access display the ♿ symbol in this Guide.

ENVIRONMENTAL CHARTER

Hostels adhere to the IYHF Environmental Charter. This lays down criteria for the consumption and conservation of resources, waste disposal and recycling, nature conservation and the provision of environmental education.

Whitepark Bay Youth Hostel - Northern Ireland

9

Bookings & Reservations

BOOK AHEAD THROUGH [IBN]

Our computerized booking system offers simple, low-cost booking up to 6 months in advance for nearly 300 key hostels in 40 countries worldwide. In this Guide, hostels accepting advance bookings display the [IBN] symbol and are highlighted in blue.

IBN is unique in the budget accommodation sector - benefits include:

- Pay when you book, using local currency.

- Make reservations during your travels - **see pages 39 - 49 for [IBN] global booking centres.**

- You can often pay by credit card - see opposite.

- In many countries, one call to the Central Reservations Office reserves a series of overnight stays in several hostels.

OTHER BOOKING INFORMATION

- Advance booking isn't essential during low season, but at busy times or in key cities, it is advisable to avoid disappointment - family rooms are soon occupied, and groups should book ahead of time.

- Book by fax or letter to your chosen hostel - if booking by letter, enclose an international postal reply coupon and a self-addressed envelope.

- If you make an advance booking without paying a deposit you will usually be required to arrive at the hostel by 1800 hours, unless a different time is agreed.

We know you will enjoy the hostel experience. You will certainly be able to afford it. We look forward to meeting you.

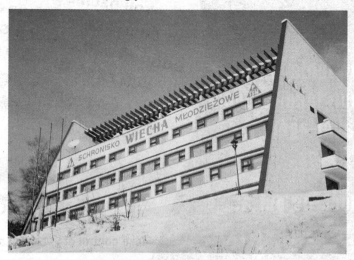

Wiecha Youth Hostel - Ustrón-Jaszowiec, Poland

MAKE YOUR CREDIT CARD BOOKINGS AT THESE CENTRES		
Australia	☎	(2) 9261 1111
Canada	☎	(1) 800 663 5777
England & Wales	☎	(1629) 581 418
France	☎	(1) 44 89 87 27
Northern Ireland	☎	(28) 9032 4733
Republic of Ireland	☎	(1) 830 1766
New Zealand	☎	(3) 379 9808
Scotland	☎	(8701) 553 255
Switzerland	☎	(1) 360 1414
USA	☎	(202) 783 6161

Bienvenue à Hostelling International

Bienvenue au monde d'Hostelling International - un réseau unique d'hébergement où vous pouvez passer une bonne nuit de sommeil dans un milieu accueillant et à des prix abordables.

Hostelling International est la marque de la Fédération Internationale des Auberges de Jeunesse (International Youth Hostel Federation), l'organisation qui représente les Associations d'Auberges de Jeunesse à travers le monde. Hostelling International est le plus grand réseau d'hébergement et celui qui a la plus longue expérience du service des voyageurs de tous les âges, qu'ils soient jeunes ou moins jeunes. La seule exception concerne en Bavière, en Allemagne, où seuls les usagers de moins de 27 ans sont admis dans les auberges. Pour en savoir plus, consultez notre site Internet à www.iyhf.org. **Pour un hébergement économique auquel vous pouvez vous fier, suivez le triangle bleu.**

Villa Camerata Youth Hostel - Florence, Italy

Les Avantages que vous apporte l'Adhésion

Afin d'être admis à séjourner dans une auberge de jeunesse, il vous faudra devenir membre de l'Association d'Auberges de Jeunesse de votre pays. S'il n'existe pas d'Association nationale dans votre pays, vous pouvez acheter une carte ou un Timbre de Bienvenue (*Welcome Stamp*) à votre arrivée à l'auberge.

La qualité d'adhérent HI vous permet de bénéficier d'un grand nombre de privilèges, parmi lesquels citons:

- 4200 **établissements** dans plus de 60 pays du monde - ils sont ouverts aux jeunes de **tous les âges** et proposent un choix d'hébergements de capacité variable: des chambres individuelles ou pour deux personnes ou bien encore des dortoirs.

- La possibilité de participer aux **activités** et manifestations en tout genre organisées par Hostelling International.

- Des milliers de **réductions** à travers le monde, sur tout: voyages, activités sportives, restaurants, musées, divertissements! Nous vous en donnons un avant-goût **à la fin de ce guide** mais pour la liste complète, faites un tour sur www.iyhf.org.

- La possibilité de **réserver** jusqu'à six mois à l'avance par IBN - **voir page 16** pour plus de détails.

Yitzhak Rabin Youth Hostel - Jerusalem, Israel

Des Normes de Qualité qui vous sont garanties

Le Plan pour la Garantie des Normes en Auberges a été mis en place par Hostelling International pour vous assurer une qualité constante dans nos prestations et nos installations, quelle que soit l'auberge où vous séjournez.

- **Accueil** - les auberges sont ouvertes à tous. Vous pourrez y acquérir une adhésion si vous n'êtes pas encore membre et y effectuer des réservations. De plus, l'accès à certaines parties de l'auberge vous est garanti, lorsque celle-ci ferme dans la journée.

- **Confort** - une bonne nuit de sommeil (ainsi que la possibilité de louer des draps propres, s'ils ne sont pas déjà compris dans le prix de la nuitée) et des douches/lavabos en nombre suffisant. Une forme ou une autre de restauration est généralement disponible, ainsi qu'une cuisine équipée pour préparer ses propres repas et un magasin d'alimentation à l'auberge ou à proximité.

- **Propreté** - un haut degré d'hygiène et de propreté où que vous vous rendiez.

- **Sécurité** - de votre personne et de vos biens (consignes pour bagages et objets de valeur).

- **Intimité** - dans les douches, les blocs sanitaires et les toilettes. La plupart des auberges proposent un hébergement dans des dortoirs non-mixtes, bien que certains établissements pourront offrir, sur demande, des chambres ou dortoirs mixtes à des groupes voyageant ensemble.

La présence de ces normes dans les auberges sera contrôlée par Hostelling International et par vous, les usagers. **Il y a des fiches-commentaires à la fin de ce guide - Dites-nous ce que vous en pensez!**

CATEGORIES D'AUBERGES

▲ **Standard:** s'applique à la majorité des auberges

△ **Simple:** s'applique aux établissements plus petits ou à ceux qui sont situés dans des lieux reculés et qui proposent donc des prestations plus simples: entre autre, le personnel y sera limité ainsi que les heures d'ouverture.

Quelques-unes des auberges listées dans ce guide ne font pas partie du Plan de Garantie des Normes en Auberge. Celles-ci ont toutefois été inclues dans le guide parce qu'elles permettent de fournir un hébergement là où il y aurait eu une absence totale de structures économiques d'accueil.

VOYAGEURS HANDICAPPES &

Hostelling International accueille les voyageurs handicappés - les auberges qui disposent d'installations facilitant l'accès aux fauteuils roulants sont indiquées par le symbole &.

CHARTE SUR L'ENVIRONNEMENT

Les auberges s'engagent à adhérer à la Charte sur l'Environnement de l'IYHF. Celle-ci dicte les critères de consommation et de préservation des ressources, d'élimination des déchets et de recyclage, de défense de l'environnement et prévoit également que les auberges devront jouer un rôle dans l'éducation écologique.

Don't let anyone tell you where to go.

EUROPRAIL INTERNATIONAL
is your one stop station for:

- Eurailpass
- Eurailpass/Drive
- Europass
- BritRail Pass
- BritRail/Drive
- Europass/Drive

RAIL PASSES
for most European countries:

Austria / Belgium / Finland / France / Germany
Hungary / Italy / Luxembourg / Netherlands
Norway / Spain / Sweden / Switzerland

Visit our award winning website
www.europrail.net

Call for more information about
Europrail International SPECIALS

- Receive a Free Eurail Guide Book
- Free Reservations (trains w/supplements not included)
- Free Pass Security
- Free Shipping
- Free Eurail Map and Travelers Guide
- Draws for Free Eurailpass

Specials are offered at designated times of the year, call for details.

Go where you want with...

EUROPRAIL INTERNATIONAL

Fax 519.645.0682 • Toll Free 1.888.667.9734 • email: europrail@eurail.on.ca
Visit us on the web: www.europrail.net

15

Réservations

RESERVEZ A L'AVANCE GRACE A **IBN**

Notre réseau international de réservation (IBN) vous offre une solution simple et économique pour réserver à l'avance, dans plus de 300 sites-clés, répartis dans 40 pays à travers le monde. Dans notre listing, les auberges proposant ce service de réservation apparaissent sur fond bleu et sont indiquées par le symbole **IBN**.

IBN est unique dans le secteur de l'hébergement économique - les avantages sont nombreux:

- Réglez à la réservation, dans la devise de votre pays ou du pays dans lequel vous vous trouvez.

- Réservez tout au long de votre voyage - **voir pages 39 - 49 pour les centres de réservation IBN**.

- Vous pourrez souvent régler par carte de crédit - voir ci-contre.

- Dans de nombreux pays, un seul coup de téléphone à une centrale de réservation vous permettra de réserver une série de nuitées dans plusieurs auberges.

AUTRES POINTS A NOTER SUR LES RESERVATIONS

- Hors saison, il n'est pas toujours nécessaire de réserver à l'avance, mais pendant les périodes de forte demande ou dans les grandes villes touristiques, nous vous conseillons vivement de le faire pour vous éviter une déception. Il est à noter que les chambres familiales sont très demandées et que les groupes doivent toujours réserver avant de se présenter.

- Il est possible de réserver par fax ou par courrier - si vous le faites par courrier, n'oubliez pas de joindre un coupon-réponse international, ainsi qu'une enveloppe à vos nom et adresse.

- Si vous réservez sans verser d'arrhes, vous devrez normalement arriver à l'auberge avant 18h, à moins d'avoir convenu avec l'auberge d'une heure différente pour votre arrivée.

Nous sommes sûrs que votre expérience des auberges sera agréable. Elle sera de toutes façons abordable. Nous sommes impatients de faire votre connaissance.

Hotel Beta Youth Hostel - Praha, Czech Republic

RESERVEZ PAR CARTE DE CREDIT AUPRES DES CENTRES SUIVANTS		
Angleterre & Pays de Galles	☎	(1629) 581 418
Australie	☎	(2) 9261 1111
Canada	☎	(1) 800 663 5777
Ecosse	☎	(8701) 553 255
Etats-Unis	☎	(202) 783 6161
France	☎	(1) 44 89 87 27
Irlande du Nord	☎	(28) 9032 4733
Nouvelle Zélande	☎	(3) 379 9808
République d'Irlande	☎	(1) 830 1766
Suisse	☎	(1) 360 1414

Catalazete Youth Hostel - Lisbon, Portugal

Einführung zu Hostelling International

Willkommen in der Welt von Hostelling International - ein unvergleichliches Netz von Unterkünften, wo Sie in einem gastfreundlichen Umfeld gut und preiswert übernachten können.

Hostelling International ist der Markenname der Internationalen Jugendherbergsföderation (IYHF), eine Organisation, die Jugendherbergen weltweit vertritt. Hostelling International ist das größte und erfahrenste Netzwerk, das sich für Reisende jeden Alters - jung und alt - engagiert. Nur in Bayern, Deutschland, liegt die Altersgrenze für Gäste unter 27 Jahre. Mehr darüber erfahren Sie auf unserer Website www.iyhf.org. **Für preisgünstige und bewährte Unterkünfte, schauen Sie nach dem blauen Dreieck-Symbol.**

Heiligenblut Youth Hostel - Austria

Vorteile der Mitgliedschaft

Um in einer Jugendherberge zu übernachten, müssen Sie Mitglied Ihres nationalen Jugendherbergsverbands (JHV) werden. Sollte Ihr Land keinen JHV haben, können Sie bei Ankunft in der Herberge eine "Hostelling International Card" oder "Welcome Stamps" erwerben.

Die Mitgliedschaft bietet eine breite Palette an Leistungen - inklusive:

- 4,200 **Unterkünfte** weltweit in über 60 Ländern - für **alle Altersgruppen** - mit einer Auswahl an Einzel-, Doppel- und Mehrbettzimmern.

- Teilnahme an allen Hostelling International **Aktivitäten**, Programmen und Veranstaltungen.

- Tausende von **Rabatten** weltweit - für Reise- und Sportaktivitäten bis zu Restaurants, Museen und Unterhaltung! Eine Auswahl an Rabatten finden Sie **im hinteren Teil dieses Führers.** Für einen ausführlichen Bericht checken Sie unter www.iyhf.org.

- Mit dem "International Booking Network" (IBN) können **Reservierungen** bis zu 6 Monate im Voraus gebucht werden - **siehe Seite 22** für weitere Informationen.

Basel Youth Hostel - Switzerland

Gesicherte Qualitätsstandards

"Hostelling International Assured Standards Scheme " heißt, Sie können sich in unseren Herbergen auf einen gleichbleibenden Service- und Ausstattungsstandard verlassen - wo immer Sie auch übernachten.

- **Empfang** - Herbergen sind für alle Altersgruppen geöffnet. Sie können, wenn Sie es noch nicht sind, Mitglied werden und Reservierungen im Voraus buchen. Wenn die Herberge für einen Teil des Tages geschlossen ist, haben Sie trotzdem Zugang zu allen notwendigen Einrichtungen.

- **Komfort** - eine gute Nachtruhe (inklusive Verleih frischer Bettwäsche, falls nicht im Übernachtungspreis enthalten) und genügend Wasch-/Dusch-Einrichtungen. Mahlzeiten sowie Selbstversorgungsausstattungen werden generell angeboten. Nahrungsmittelgeschäfte befinden sich meistens in Herbergsnähe.

- **Sauberkeit** - die höchsten Hygienestandards wo immer Sie reisen.

- **Sicherheit** - für Sie und Ihr Eigentum, inklusive Schließfächer für Gepäck und Wertsachen.

- **Privatsphäre** - in Duschen, Waschräumen und Toiletten. In unseren Herbergen gibt es überwiegend nach Geschlecht getrennte Schlafräume - aber auf Anfrage können auch gemeinsame Schlafräume für Gruppenreisende gebucht werden.

Standards werden von Hostelling International und von Ihnen überwacht. **Im hinteren Teil dieses Führers finden Sie Kommentarkarten - sagen Sie uns Ihre Meinung!**

HERBERGSKATEGORIEN

▲ **Standard:** Gilt für den größten Teil der Herbergen.

△ **Einfach:** Gilt für kleinere oder sich in abgelegenen Gegenden befindende Herbergen, in denen Sie einfache Einrichtungen, wenig Personal und beschränkte Öffnungszeiten vorfinden könnten.

Einige Herbergen in diesem Führer entsprechen nicht den Richtlinien des "Assured Standards Scheme" - dies sind Unterkünfte in Gebieten, wo es sonst keine geben würde.

REISENDE MIT BEHINDERUNGEN &

Hostelling International heißt Reisende mit Behinderungen willkommen - Jugendherbergen für Rollstuhlfahrer sind im Verzeichnis mit & gekennzeichnet.

UMWELTCHARTA

Herbergen befolgen die Richtlinien der IYHF Umweltcharta. Diese schreibt die Kriterien für Verbrauch und Sparen von Ressourcen, Abfallbeseitigung und Recycling, Umweltschutz und Förderung der Umweltschutzerziehung vor.

Buchungen & Reservierungen

BUCHEN IM VORAUS DURCH [IBN]

Unser computergestütztes Reservierungssystem bietet einfache und preisgünstige Reservierungen bis zu 6 Monaten im Voraus für fast 300 Schlüsselherbergen in 40 Ländern weltweit. Alle angeschlossenen Herbergen, die Vorausreservierungen akzeptieren, sind in diesem Führer mit dem [IBN] Symbol gekennzeichnet und in blau hervorgehoben.

IBN ist im preisbewussten Unterkunftssektor einzigartig - Leistungen umfassen:

- Zahlen Sie in der Landeswährung wenn Sie buchen.

- Reservierungen während Ihrer Reise - **siehe Seiten 39 - 49 für** [IBN] **Internationale Buchungszentren.**

- Sie können oft auch mit Kreditkarten zahlen - siehe gegenüber.

- In vielen Ländern reicht ein Anruf beim Zentralen Reservierungsbüro, um mehrere Übernachtungen in verschiedenen Herbergen zu buchen.

WEITERE BUCHUNGSINFORMATIONEN

- Vorausbuchungen sind in der Nebensaison nicht unbedingt notwendig, aber in Hauptreisezeiten oder in beliebten Städten sind sie zu empfehlen, damit Enttäuschungen vermieden werden. Familienzimmer sind schnell vergeben, und Gruppen sollten immer im Voraus buchen.

- Buchen Sie per Fax oder Brief bei der ausgewählten Herberge. Bei schriftlicher Buchung bitte einen internationalen Antwortschein plus selbst adressierten und frankierten Briefumschlag beilegen.

- Bei Vorausbuchungen ohne Anzahlung sollten Sie vor 18.00 Uhr in der Herberge eintreffen, sofern keine andere Zeit vereinbart wurde.

Wir sind sicher, ein Herbergsaufenthalt wird Ihnen viel Freude machen. Auf jeden Fall können Sie sich diesen leisten. Wir freuen uns auf Ihren Besuch.

Málaga Youth Hostel - Spain

KREDITKARTEN-RESERVIERUNGEN BEI DIESEN ZENTREN

Australien	☎	(2) 9261 1111
England & Wales	☎	(1629) 581 418
Frankreich	☎	(1) 44 89 87 27
Kanada	☎	(1) 800 663 5777
Neuseeland	☎	(3) 379 9808
Nordirland	☎	(28) 9032 4733
Republik Irland	☎	(1) 830 1766
Schottland	☎	(8701) 553 255
Schwelz	☎	(1) 360 1414
USA	☎	(202) 783 6161

Hostelling International - Introducción

Bienvenido al mundo de Hostelling International - una red de alojamientos sin igual, en los que usted pasará una buena noche, en un ambiente acogedor y a precios asequibles.

Hostelling International es la marca de la Federación Internacional de Albergues Juveniles (IYHF), la organización que representa a las Asociaciones de Albergues Juveniles de todo el mundo. Hostelling International es la red más extensa y con más experiencia del servicio a los viajeros de todas las edades, tanto los jóvenes como los menos jóvenes (sólo en Bavaria, Alemania, se aplica un límite máximo de edad de 26 años en los albergues). Para más información, visite nuestra página Internet www.iyhf.org. **Si desea alojamiento económico de confianza, busque el triángulo azul.**

Dublin International Youth Hostel - Republic of Ireland

Ventajas de la Afiliación

Para alojarse en un albergue juvenil, es necesario hacerse miembro de la Asociación de Albergues Juveniles del país en que uno viva. Si no existe una Asociación de Albergues Juveniles en su país, usted tendrá la oportunidad de adquirir una tarjeta Hostelling International o un "sello de bienvenida" (*Welcome Stamp*) a su llegada al albergue elegido.

Su afiliación a Hostelling International le brinda toda una serie de ventajas, a saber:

- 4.200 **establecimientos** repartidos por más de 60 países del mundo - abiertos a personas **de todas las edades** y ofreciendo alojamiento en habitaciones individuales, dobles y múltiples.

- La posibilidad de participar en las **actividades**, los programas y los acontecimientos de todo tipo organizados por Hostelling International.

- Miles de **descuentos**, a nivel mundial y en todo: viajes, deportes, restaurantes, museos, diversiones, etc. Al final de esta Guía encontrará una selección de descuentos - pero, para verlos todos, consulte nuestra página *web* www.iyhf.org.

- La oportunidad de realizar **reservas** con un máximo de 6 meses de antelación a través de nuestra red internacional de reservas (IBN) - **ver pág. 28** para más información.

Den Haag Youth Hostel - Netherlands

Normas de Calidad Garantizadas

El Plan de las Normas Garantizadas ha sido instituido por Hostelling International para asegurarle un nivel de calidad uniforme en nuestras instalaciones y prestaciones, sea cual sea el albergue en el que usted se aloje.

- **Recibimiento** - Los albergues están abiertos a todos. Usted podrá hacerse miembro en el albergue mismo si no lo es aún y realizar reservas con antelación en otros albergues. Además, aunque el establecimiento cierre durante parte del día, usted tendrá acceso a las zonas más imprescindibles del mismo.

- **Comodidad** - Una buena noche (así como la posibilidad de alquilar sábanas recién lavadas si no se incluyen en el precio de la pernoctación) y suficientes lavabos/duchas. Normalmente se sirven comidas en los albergues y suele haber, además, una cocina para uso de los huéspedes. Asimismo, hay generalmente una tienda de comestibles cerca del albergue.

- **Limpieza** - Las más rigurosas normas de higiene dondequiera que usted se aloje.

- **Seguridad** - Personal y de sus pertenencias, que incluye la disponibilidad de consignas de equipaje y casillas con llave para los objetos de valor.

- **Intimidad** - En las duchas, los lavabos y los aseos. En la mayoría de los albergues, el alojamiento consiste en dormitorios múltiples separados para hombres y mujeres, aunque es posible que algunos de ellos dispongan de habitaciones mixtas para quienes viajen juntos y las soliciten.

La aplicación de estas normas en los albergues es objeto de un seguimiento por parte de Hostelling International, pero también por parte de usted, el usuario. **Al final de la guía encontrará unos impresos en los que puede enviarnos sus comentarios - ¡díganos lo que opina!**

Saint-Brieuc Youth Hostel - France

CLASIFICACIÓN DE LOS ALBERGUES

▲ **Categoría Normal:** se aplica a la mayoría de los albergues.

△ **Categoría Sencilla:** se aplica a los albergues más pequeños y a los situados en lugares remotos, cuyas instalaciones y prestaciones son sólo básicas - por ejemplo, es posible que el personal y el horario de apertura sean limitados.

Algunos de los albergues relacionados en esta Guía no pertenecen al Plan de las Normas Garantizadas - han sido incluidos en ella porque están situados en lugares en los que no nos es posible ofrecer otro tipo de alojamiento.

VIAJEROS MINUSVÁLIDOS &

Los disminuidos físicos son bienvenidos en los albergues de Hostelling International - los establecimientos que disponen de acceso para sillas de ruedas llevan el símbolo & en la Guía.

NORMAS MEDIOAMBIENTALES

Los albergues deben cumplir con las Normas Medioambientales de IYHF. Estas establecen los criterios relativos al consumo y conservación de recursos, a la eliminación de residuos y su reciclaje, a la protección de la naturaleza y a la provisión de educación medioambiental.

af Chapman/Skeppsholmen Youth Hostel - Stockholm, Sweden

NORMAS DE CALIDAD GARANTIZADAS

Reservas

RESERVE CON ANTELACIÓN A TRAVÉS DE [IBN]

Nuestro sistema informatizado de reservas constituye una forma sencilla y económica de reservar con un máximo de 6 meses de antelación, en casi 300 albergues claves repartidos por 40 países del mundo. En nuestra Guía, los establecimientos que disponen de este servicio llevan el símbolo [IBN] y se destacan de los demás por su fondo azul.

IBN es único en el sector del alojamiento económico - las ventajas que presenta son numerosas:

- Pague al reservar en la moneda del país en el que se encuentre.

- Haga reservas a lo largo de todo su viaje - **ver pág. 39 - 49: Centros de Reservas [IBN] del mundo.**

- Podrá generalmente pagar con tarjeta de crédito - ver el recuadro en la página contigua.

- En muchos países, una sola llamada a la Central de Reservas le permitirá reservar varias pernoctaciones en diferentes albergues.

RESERVAS - OTROS PUNTOS IMPORTANTES

- No es imprescindible reservar con antelación durante la temporada baja, pero en temporada alta y en las grandes ciudades es recomendable hacerlo para no llevarse desilusiones - las habitaciones familiares, en particular, se ocupan con rapidez y los grupos también deben reservar con tiempo.

- Reserve por fax o por carta dirigiéndose directamente al albergue deseado - si reserva por correo, adjunte un cupón internacional de respuesta pagada y un sobre con su nombre y dirección.

- Si reserva con antelación pero sin abonar un depósito, normalmente deberá llegar al albergue antes de las 18 h., a menos que haya concertado previamente otra hora de llegada.

Estamos seguros de que disfrutará de su estancia en nuestros albergues y de que no le saldrá cara la experiencia. Esperamos tener el agrado de su visita.

Bunnik Youth Hostel - Netherlands

RESERVE CON TARJETA DE CRÉDITO EN LAS SIGUIENTES CENTRALES:		
Australia	☎	(2) 9261 1111
Canadá	☎	(1) 800 663 5777
Escocia	☎	(8701) 553 255
Estados Unidos	☎	(202) 783 6161
Francia	☎	(1) 44 89 87 27
Inglaterra y Gales	☎	(1629) 581 418
Irlanda del Norte	☎	(28) 9032 4733
Nueva Zelanda	☎	(3) 379 9808
República de Irlanda	☎	(1) 830 1766
Suiza	☎	(1) 360 1414

Carbisdale Castle Youth Hostel - Scotland

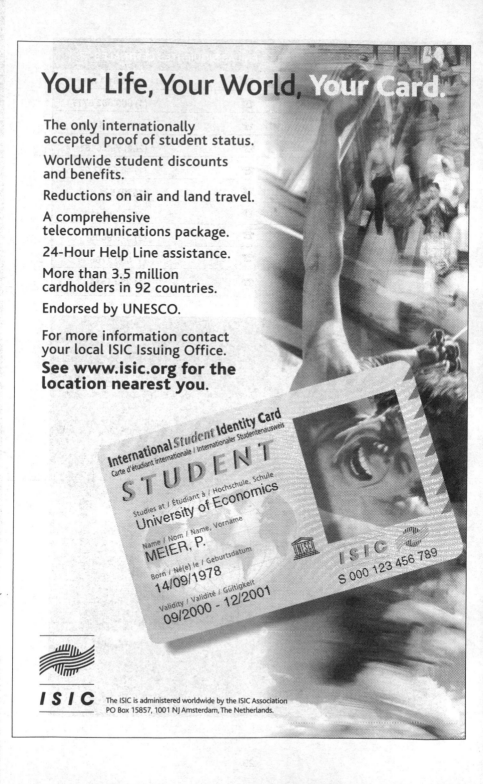

Money From Home In Minutes.

If you're stuck for cash on your travels, don't panic. Millions of people trust Western Union to transfer money in minutes to 176 countries and over 78,000 locations worldwide. Our record of safety and reliability is second to none. For more information, call Western Union: USA 1-800-325-6000, Canada 1-800-235-0000. Wherever you are, you're never far from home.

www.westernunion.com

WESTERN UNION | MONEY TRANSFER

The fastest way to send money worldwide.

HOSTELLING INTERNATIONAL

Do it the HI way!

For HI quality accommodation at the best prices. Visit one of our 4200 hostels in over 60 countries.

www.iyhf.org

AMERICAS, AFRICA, ASIA, PACIFIC

Youth Hostels outside of Europe are listed in the Hostelling International Guide - Americas, Africa, Asia and the Pacific. The addresses of the full member Associations are given below:

Les Auberges de jeunesse en dehors de l'Europe figurent dans le Hostelling International Guide - Amériques, Afrique, Asie et le Pacifique. Les adresses des Associations membres à part entière sont données ci-dessous:

Die Jugendherbergen ausserhalb von Europa werden im Hostelling International Guide - Amerika, Afrika, Asien und der Pazifik, aufgeführt. Die Adressen der vollberechtigten Mitgliedsverbände sind unten angegeben:

Los albergues juveniles de los países no europoes figuran en nuestra Guía de Africa, Américas, Asia y el Pacífico. A continuación se encuentran las direcciones de las Asociaciones miembros de pleno derecho de Hostelling International de dichos países:

ALGERIA:

Fédération Algérienne des Auberges de Jeunesse, Camp de Jeunes et de Loisirs, Zeralda, Gouvernat du Grand Alger 16320.
☏ (2) 329011 ✆ (2) 329024

AUSTRALIA:

YHA Australia, PO Box 314, Camperdown, New South Wales 1450.
☏ (2) 9565 1699 ✆ (2) 9565 1325
✉ yha@yha.org.au
🖳 www.yha.com.au

BAHRAIN:

Bahrain Youth Hostels Society, PO Box 2455, H No. 1105 R No. 4225 Block 342, Manama.
☏ 727170 ✆ 729919

BRAZIL:

Federação Brasileira dos Albergues da Juventude, Rua General Dionisio 63, Botafogo, CEP: 22271-050, Rio de Janeiro.
☏ (21) 2860303 ✆ (21) 2865652
✉ info@hostel.org.br
🖳 www.hostel.org.br

CANADA:

Hostelling International - Canada, 205 Catherine St, Suite 400, Ottawa, Ontario K2P 1C3.
☏ (613) 237-7884 ✆ (613) 237-7868
✉ info@hostellingintl.ca
🖳 www.hostellingintl.ca

CHILE:

Asociación Chilena de Albergues Turísticos Juveniles, Hernando de Aguirre 201 Of 602, Santiago.
☏ (2) 2333220 ✆ (2) 2332555
✉ hostelling@hostelling.cl
🖳 www.hostelling.co.cl

CHINA (People's Republic of):

Beijing, Shanghai and Guangdong Youth Hostel Associations , c/o Guangdong YHA 185 Huanshi Xi Road, 510010, Guangzhou.
☏ (20) 86666889 ✆ (20) 86665039
✉ gdyhac@public.guangzhou.gd.cn

Hong Kong Youth Hostels Association,
Room 225, Block 19, Shek Kip Mei Estate,
Sham Shui Po, Kowloon, Hong Kong.
t 27881638 **f** 27883105
e hkyha@datainternet.com
w www.yha.org.hk

COSTA RICA:

Red Costarricense de Albergues Juveniles,
PO Box 1355-1002 P E, Ave Central,
Calles 29 y 31, San José.
t 2348186 **f** 2244085
e recajhi@sol.racsa.co.cr
w www.hostelling-costarica.com

EGYPT:

Egyptian Youth Hostels Association,
1 El-Ibrahimy St, Garden City, Cairo.
t (2) 7940527, 7961448 **f** (2) 7950329
e eyhamo@usa.net

INDIA:

Youth Hostels Association of India,
5 Nyaya Marg, Chanakyapuri, New Delhi 110 021.
t (11) 6871969, 6110250 **f** (11) 6113469
e yhostel@del2.vsnl.net.in
w www.yhaindia.org

JAPAN:

Japan Youth Hostels Inc,
Suidobashi Nishiguchi Kaikan, 2-20-7
Misaki-cho, Chiyoda-ku, Tokyo 101-0061.
t (3) 3288-1417 **f** (3) 3288 1248
e info@jyh.or.jp
w www.jyh.or.jp

KENYA:

Kenya Youth Hostels Association,
Ralph Bunche Road, PO Box 48661, Nairobi.
t (2) 721765 **f** (2) 724862
e kyha@africaonline.co.ke

S. KOREA:

Korea Youth Hostels Association,
Rm 408, Juksun Hyundai Bldg 80,
Juksun-Dong, Jongro-Ku, Seoul 110-052.
t (2) 7253031 **f** (2) 7253113
e inform@kyha.or.kr
w www.kyha.or.kr

LIBYA:

Libyan Youth Hostel Association,
69 Amr Ben Al-Aas Street, PO Box 10322,
Tripoli, Al-Jamahiriya.
t (21) 4445171 **f** (21) 3330118

MALAYSIA:

Malaysian Youth Hostels Association,
KL International Youth Hostel, 21 Jalan Kg.
Attap, 50460 Kuala Lumpur.
t (3) 22736870/71 **f** (3) 22741115
e myha@pd.jaring.my

MOROCCO:

*Fédération Royale Marocaine des Auberges de
Jeunes,* Parc de la Ligue Arabe, BP 15998,
Casa Principale, Casablanca 21000.
t (2) 470952 **f** (2) 227677

NEW ZEALAND:

Youth Hostels Association of New Zealand Inc,
PO Box 436, 193 Cashel St, 3rd Floor, Union
House, Christchurch.
t (3) 3799970 **f** (3) 3654476
e info@yha.org.nz
w www.yha.org.nz

PAKISTAN:

Pakistan Youth Hostels Association,
Shaheed-e-Millat Rd, (near Akhbar Market)
Aabpara, Sector G-6/4, Islamabad.
t (51) 2826899 **f** (51) 2826899
e pyha@comsats.net.pk

PERU:

Asociación Peruana de Albergues Turísticos Juveniles, Avda Casimiro Ulloa 328, San Antonio, Miraflores, Lima 18.
☏ (1) 2423068 ✆ (1) 4448187
✉ hostell@terra.com.pe

PHILIPPINES:

Youth & Student Hostel Foundation of the Philippines, 4227-9 Tomas Claudio St, Baclaran, Parañaque 1700, Metro Manila.
☏ (2) 8320680, 8322112 ✆ (2) 8322263
✉ yshfp@i-next.net

QATAR:

Qatar Youth Hostels Association, PO Box 9660, Doha.
☏ 4867180, 4866402 ✆ 4863968

SAUDI ARABIA:

Saudi Arabian Youth Hostels Association, Alshehab Alghassni St, Alnmouzajiyah District, North Almurabb'h, Riyadh 11451.
☏ (1) 4055552, 4051478 ✆ (1) 4021079
✉ sayha@zajil.net
🖥 www.sayha.org

SOUTH AFRICA:

South African Youth Hostels Association, 3rd Floor St Georges House, 73 St Georges Mall, Cape Town 8001.
☏ (21) 4242511 ✆ (21) 4244119
✉ info@hisa.org.za
🖥 www.hisa.org.za

SUDAN:

Sudanese Youth Hostels Association, House No 66, Street No 47 Khartoum East, PO Box 1705, Khartoum.
☏ (11) 722087 ✆ (11) 780308

THAILAND:

Thai Youth Hostels Association, 25/14 Phitsanulok Road, Se-Sao Thewet, Dusit, Bangkok 10300.
☏ (2) 628-7413, 7414, 7415 ✆ (2) 628-7416
✉ bangkok@tyha.org
🖥 www.tyha.org

TUNISIA:

Association Tunisienne des Auberges et Tourisme de Jeunesse, 10 Ruc Ali Bach Hamba, BP 320, 1015 Tunis RP.
☏ (1) 339408 ✆ (1) 241387
✉ ataj@planet.tn
🖥 www.cybertunisia.com/ataj

UNITED ARAB EMIRATES:

United Arab Emirates Youth Hostel Association, Al Qusaiss Road, Near Al Ahli Club, PO Box 19536, Dubai.
☏ (4) 2988151 ✆ (4) 2988141

USA:

American Youth Hostels, Inc, 733 15th Street N.W, Suite 840, Washington DC 20005.
☏ (202) 7836161 ✆ (202) 7836171
✉ hiayhserv@hiayh.org
🖥 www.hiayh.org

URUGUAY:

Asociación de Alberguistas del Uruguay, Pablo de María 1583/008, CP 11200, PO Box 10680, Montevideo.
☏ (2) 4004245, 4000581 ✆ (2) 4001326
✉ aau@adinet.com.uy
🖥 www.internet.com.uy/aau

INTERNATIONAL TELEPHONE CODES AND EMERGENCY CONTACT NUMBERS
INDICATIFS TÉLÉPHONIQUES INTERNATIONAUX ET NUMÉROS D'URGENCE

Country	GMT	Int Code	Country Code	Medical	Police	Fire
Algeria	+1	00	+213		17	14
Argentina	-4	00	+5411	107	101	100
Australia	+8/+10	0011	+61	000	000	000
Austria	+1	00	+43	144	133	122
Bahrain	+3	0	+973	999	999	999
Bangladesh	+6	00	+880	500121-5, 5050525-29	8322501-8	9556666-7 9555555-7
Belgium	+1	00	+32	100	101	100
Brazil	-2/-5	00	+55	192	190	193
Bulgaria	+2	00	+359	150	166	160.
Canada	-3/-11	00	+1	911	911	911
Chile	-6	00	+56	131	133	132
China	+8	00	+86	120	110	119
China - Hong Kong	+8	00	+852	999	999	999
Colombia	-5	009/007/005	+57	132	112	119
Costa Rica	-6	00	+506	911	117	118
Croatia	+1	00	+385	94	92	93
Czech Republic	+1	00	+420	155	158	150
Denmark	+1	00	+45	112	112	112
Egypt	+2	00	+20	123	122	125
Estonia	+2	800	+372	112	112/110	112
Faeroe Islands	GMT	00	+298	000	000	000
Finland	+2	999	+358	112	10022	112
France	+1	00	+33	15	17	18
Germany	+1	00	+49	112	110	112
Greece	+2	00	+30	166	100	199
Guatemala	-6	00	+502	125/128	120/110	123/122
Hungary	+1	00	+36	104	107	105
Iceland	GMT	00	+354	112	112	112
India	+5.5	00	+91	102	100	101
Indonesia	+7/+9	001 or 008	+62	118	110	113
Ireland - Republic	GMT	00	+353	999	999	999
Israel	+2	00	+972	101	100	102
Italy	+1	00	+39	118	112	115
Japan	+9	001	+81	119	110	119
Kenya	+3	0196	+254	999	999	999
Latvia	+1	00	371	03	02	01
Lebanon	+2	00	961	140	112	175
Libya	+2	00	+218	191	193	190
Lithuania	+1	8-10	+370	03	02	01
Luxembourg	+1	00	+352	112	113	112

INTERNATIONALE TELEFONKODES UND NOTRUFNUMMERN
PREFIJOS TELEFÓNICOS INTERNACIONALES Y TELÉFONOS DE EMERGENCIA

Country	GMT	Int Code	Country Code	Medical	Police	Fire
Macedonia	+1	99	+389	94	92	93
Malaysia	+8	00	+60	999	999	994
Malta	+1	00	+356	196	191	191
Mexico	-6/8	00	+52	080	080	080
Morocco	GMT	00	+212	15	19	15
Nepal	+5.45	00	+977	102	100	101
Netherlands	+1	00	+31	112	112	112
New Caledonia	+10	00	+687	15	17	18
New Zealand	+12	00	+64	111	111	111
Nicaragua	+6	001	+505	128	118	115
Norway	+1	00	+47	113	112	110
Pakistan	+5	00	+92	15	15	16
Peru	-5	00	+51	105	105	116
Philippines	+8	00	+63	00632-8319 731	117	00632-8269 131
Poland	+1	0	+48	999	997	998
Portugal	+1	00	+351	112	112	112
Qatar	+3	0	+974	999	999	999
Romania	+2	00	40	961	955	981
Russia	+2/+12	8-10	+7	02	01	03
Saudi Arabia	+3	00	+966	977	999	998
Singapore	+8	001	+65	995	999	995
Slovakia	+1	00	+421	155	158	150
Slovenia	+1	00	+386	112	113	112
South Africa	+2	01	+27	10177	10111	10111
South Korea	+9	001/002	+82	119	112	119
Spain	+1	00	+34	061	091	
Sudan	+3	00	+249	779500	780751	774444
Sweden	+1	00	+46	112	112	112
Switzerland	+1	00	+41	144	117	118
Taiwan	+8	00	+886	119	110	119
Thailand	+7	001	+66	1155	191	199
Tunisia	+1	00	+216	190	197	198
Turkey	+2	00	+90	112	155	110
UAE	+4	00	+971	999	292222	669999
United Kingdom	GMT	00	+44	999	999	999
Uruguay	-3	00	+598	105	109	104
USA	-6/9	011	+1	911	911	911
Venezuela	-4	00	+58	171	171	171
Yugoslavia	+1	99	+381	94	92	93

INTERNATIONAL BOOKING NETWORK IBN BOOKING CENTRES

The International Booking Network (IBN) enables you to book a bed up to 6 months in advance of your stay (depending on availability) at nearly 300 key hostels around the world. The locations listed below all offer outward bookings by IBN. The hostels in the network are listed within each of the country sections and highlighted in blue. They are also indicated with the symbol IBN .

CENTRES DE RESERVATION IBN (INTERNATIONAL BOOKING NETWORK)

Le réscau international de réservation (International Booking Network - IBN) vous permet de réserver un lit jusqu'à six mois à l'avance (selon les disponibilités), dans près de 300 auberges à travers le monde. Les sites listés ci-dessous vous offrent tous la possibilité d'effectuer des réservations par le biais d'IBN. Les auberges appartenant au réseau IBN sont indiquées en bleu dans le listing des auberges de chaque pays et également par le symbole IBN .

INTERNATIONAL BOOKING NETWORK IBN BUCHUNGSZENTREN

International Booking Network (IBN) ermöglicht Ihnen das Buchen einer Unterkunft bis zu 6 Monaten im voraus (je nach Verfügbarkeit) in ca. 300 der wichtigsten Jugendherbergen rund um den Globus. In den unten aufgelisteten Buchungszentren können internationale Buchungen durch IBN vorgenommen werden. Die im Netzwerk zusammengeschlossenen Jugendherbergen sind innerhalb jeder Ländersektion aufgeführt und blau hervorgehoben. Sie sind auch mit dem Symbol IBN gekennzeichnet.

INTERNATIONAL BOOKING NETWORK IBN CENTROS DE RESERVAS

La Red Internacional de Reservas IBN le permite reservar una cama hasta 6 meses antes de su estancia (siempre y cuando haya camas disponibles) en casi 300 albergues claves del mundo. Los centros relacionados a continuación ofrecen todos ellos la posibilidad de realizar reservas a través de IBN. Los albergues que pertenecen a la red IBN aparecen impresos en color azul en las listas de albergues de cada país y llevan, además, el símbolo IBN .

IBN

ARGENTINA

Red Argentina de Alojamiento para Jóvenes
Buenos Aires – National Office
Florida 835, 3rd Floor Of.319, C1005AAQ
Buenos Aires
☎ (54) (11) 4511-8712
✆ (54) (11) 4312-0089
✉ raaj@hostels.org.ar

AUSTRALIA

Australian Youth Hostels Association
Adelaide – YHA South Australia
38 Sturt Street, Adelaide, South Australia 5000
☎ (61) (8) 8231-5583
✆ (61) (8) 8231-4219
✉ yhasa@ozemail.com.au

Brisbane – YHA Queensland
154 Roma Street, Brisbane, Queensland 4000
☎ (61) (7) 3236-1680
✆ (61) (7) 3236-1702
✉ membership@yhaqld.org

Cairns – YHA Queensland
20-24 McLeod Street, Cairns, Queensland 4870
☎ (61) (7) 4051-0772
✆ (61) (7) 4031-3158
✉ cnsyha@yhaqld.org

Canberra – YHA New South Wales
191 Dryandra Street, O'Connor, Canberra, ACT 2602
☎ (61) (2) 6248-9155
✆ (61) (2) 6249-1731
✉ canberra@yhansw.org.au

Darwin - YHA Northern Territory
69 Mitchell Street, Darwin, NT 0801
☎ (61) (8) 8981-6344
✆ (61) (8) 8981-6674
✉ yhant@yhant.org.au

Melbourne – YHA Victoria
Level 1, 377 Little Lonsdale Street,
Melbourne, Victoria 3000
☎ (61) (3) 9670-7991
✆ (61) (3) 9670-9840
✉ yha@yhavic.org.au

Perth – YHA Western Australia
236 William Street, Northbridge, Perth,
Western Australia 6003
☎ (61) (8) 9227-5122
✆ (61) (8) 9227-5123
✉ enquiries@yhawa.com.au

Sydney – YHA New South Wales
GPO Box 5276, 422 Kent St, Sydney,
New South Wales 2001
☎ (61) (2) 9261-1111
✆ (61) (2) 9261-1969
✉ yha@yhansw.org.au

Sydney - travel.com.au
80 Clarence Street, Sydney 2000
☎ (61) (2) 9290-1500
✆ (61) (2) 9262-2774
✉ ibn@travel.com.au

AUSTRIA

Österreichischer Jugendherbergsverband
Graz – ÖJHV YGH
Idlhofgasse 74, A-8020 Graz
☎ (43) (316) 7083
✆ (43) (316) 7083-88
✉ jgh-graz@jgh.at

Graz –Logo Youth Information Service
Karmeliterplatz1, A-8010 Graz
☎ (43) (316) 1799
✆ (43) (316) 877 4900
✉ info@logo.at

Klagenfurt – ÖJHV Regional Office
Neckheimgasse 6, 9020 Klagenfurt
☎ (43) (463) 230019
✆ (43) (463) 230022
✉ oejhv-kaernten@oejhv.or.at

Salzburg –
Kaigasse 24, A5020 Salzburg
☎ (43) (662) 841165
📠 (43) (662) 840164
✉ jhw.sbg@aon.at

Vienna – ÖJHV National Office
1010 Wien, Gonzagag.22
☎ (43) (1) 5335353
📠 (43) (1) 5350861
✉ oejhv-wien-travel-service@oejhv.or.at,
oejhv@chello.at

Österreichisches Jugendherbergswerk
Vienna – ÖJHW National Office
1010 Wien, Helferstorferstrasse 4
☎ (43) (1) 5331833
📠 (43) (1) 533183385
✉ oejhw@oejhw.or.at, travel@supertramp.co.at

BELGIUM

Belgium - Les Auberges de Jeunesse
Brussels – Les AJ National Office
Rue de la Sablonnière 28, B-1000 Bruxelles
☎ (32) (2) 219 5676
📠 (32) (2) 219 1451
✉ info@laj.be

Belgium - Vlaamse Jeugdherbergcentrale
Antwerp – VJH National Office
Van Stralenstraat 40, B-2060 Antwerpen
☎ (32) (3) 232 7218
📠 (32) (3) 231 8126
✉ vjh@vjh.be

BRAZIL

Federaçao Brasiliera dos Albergues da Juventude
Curitiba – Regional Office
Rua Padre Agostinho 645, Mercês, Curitiba,
Paraná CEP - 80430-050
☎ (55) (21) 233-2746
📠 (55) (21) 233-2834
✉ ajcwb@uol.com.br

Porto Alegre – Regional Office
Rua Dos Andradas, 1137 S. 214,
Centro - Porto Alegre, RS CEP: 90020-008
☎ (55) (51) 226-5380
📠 (55) (51) 226-5380
✉ turjovem@zaz.com.br

Rio de Janeiro – Regional Office
Rua da Assembleia No 10, Sala 1616,
Centro-CEP:20011-000, Rio de Janeiro
☎ (55) (21) 5312234
📠 (55) (21) 5312234
✉ albergue@microlink.com.br

São Paulo – Regional Office
Rua Sete de Abril, 386 Cj. 22, CEP 01044-908,
Sao Paulo - SP
☎ (55) (11) 2580388
📠 (55) (11) 2580388
✉ info@alberguesp.com.br

CANADA

Canadian Hostelling Association
Edmonton – Travel Shop
10926 - 88 Avenue, Edmonton, Alberta T6G 0Z1
☎ (1) (780) 439-3089
📠 (1) (780) 433-7781
✉ travelshop@hostellingintl.ca

Montréal – Boutique Tourisme Jeunesse
4008 Rue St Denis, Montréal, Québec H2W 2M4
☎ (1) (514) 844-0287
📠 (1) (514) 844-5246
✉ boutiquetjmtl@videotron.net

Montréal – Tourisme Jeunesse
4545 Pierre de Coubertin, C P 1000,
Succursale M, Montréal, Québec H1V 3R2
☎ (1) (514) 252-3117
📠 (1) (514) 252-3119
✉ info-tj@tourismejeunesse.org

Ottawa – National Office
400-205 Catherine Street, Ottawa, Ontario, K2P 1C3
☎ (1) (613) 237-7884
📠 (1) (613) 237-7868
✉ info@hostellingintl.ca

IBN

Québec City – Boutique Tourisme Jeunesse
94 Boulevard René-Lévesque Ouest, Québec City,
Québec G1R 2A4
☎ (1) (418) 522-2552
✆ (1) (418) 522-2455
✉ boutiquetjqc@vidoetron.net

Toronto – International Travel
56 Church Street, Toronto, Ontario M5C 2G1
☎ (1) (416) 363-0697 ext.15
✆ (1) (416) 368-6499
✉ ressale@hostellingint-gl.on.ca

Vancouver – Regional Office
134 Abbott Street, Suite 402, Vancouver,
British Colombia, V6B 2K4
☎ (1) (604) 684-7101
✆ (1) (604) 684-7181
✉ info@hihostels.bc.ca

CHILE

*Asociación Chilena de Albergues Turísticos
Juveniles*
Santiago – National Office
Hernando de Aguirre 201,OF 602, Providencia
☎ (56) (2) 2333220
✆ (56) (2) 2333220
✉ hostelling@hostelling.cl

CHINA

*Beijing, Shanghai and Guangdong Youth
Hostel Associations of China*
Guangzhou – c/o National Office
185 Huanshi Xi Road, Guangzhou,
Guangdong Province.
☎ (86) (20) 86677422
✆ (86) (20) 86665039
✉ gdyhac@public.guangzhou.gd.cn

Hong Kong Youth Hostels Association
Hong Kong – National Office
Room 225, Block 19, Shek Kip Mei Estate,
Shamshuipo, Kowloon, Hong Kong
☎ (852) 27881638
✆ (852) 27883105
✉ hkyha@datainternet.com

CROATIA

Croatian Youth Hostel Association
Zagreb – National Office
Dezmanova 9, 10000 Zagreb
☎ (385) (1) 484-7474
✆ (385) (1) 484-7472
✉ hfhs-cms@zg.tel.hr

CZECH REPUBLIC

KMC Club of Young Travellers
Prague – National Office
KMC - Travel Service Booking Centre, Praha 1,
Karolíny Svetlé 30, 110 00 Prague
☎ (420) (2) 22220347
✆ (420) (2) 22220347
✉ kmc@kmc.cz

DENMARK

Danhostel
Copenhagen – National Office
Hostelling International Denmark,
Vesterbrogade 39, DK1620, Copenhagen V
☎ (45) 33313612
✆ (45) 33313626
✉ ldv@danhostel.dk

ECUADOR

Idiomas s.a.
Guayaquil –
Junin 203 y Panama, Floor 2, Office 4, Guayaquil.
☎ (593) (4) 56-4488
✆ (593) (4) 56-6939
✉ idiomas@idiomas.com.ec

ENGLAND & WALES

Youth Hostels Association (England & Wales)
Credit/Debit Card Reservations only –
PO Box 67, Matlock, Derbyshire DE4 3YX
t (44) (1629) 581418
f (44) (1629) 581062
e ibnreservations@yha.org.uk

1st Western Air Travel
Totnes –
1st Western Air Travel, Bickham, Totnes,
Devon, TQ9 7NJ
t (44) (870) 3301100
f (44) (870) 3301133
e info@westernair.co.uk

London - Overseas Visitors Club
OVC House, 41 Longridge Road, Earls Court,
London SW5 9SD
t (44) 20 7244 8055
f (44) 20 7259 2323
e ovclondon@excite.co.uk

ESTONIA

Estonian Youth Hostels Association
Tallin – National Office
Tatari 39-310, EE0001 Tallinn
t (372) 6461455
f (372) 6461595
e eyha@online.ee

FINLAND

Suomen Retkeilymajajärjestö-SRM
Helsinki – National Office
Yrjönkatu 38 B 15, 00100 Helsinki
t (358) (9) 565 7150
f (358) (9) 565 7150
e info@srm.inet.fi

FRANCE

Fédération Unie des Auberges de Jeunesse
Paris – National Office
27 Rue Pajol, 75018 Paris
t (33) (1) 44898727
f (33) (1) 44898710
e fuaj@fuaj.org

Paris – FUAJ Beaubourg
9 Rue Brantome, 75003 Paris
t (33) (1) 48047040
f (33) (1) 42770329
e fuajbeau@caramail.com

GERMANY

Deutsches Jugendherbergswerk
Berlin – Brandenburg Regional Office
Tempelhofer Ufer 32, D-10963 Berlin
t (49) (30) 2649520
f (49) (30) 2620437
e djh-berlin-brandenburg@jugendherberge.de

Detmold – National Office
Deutsches Jugendherbergswerk, Service GmbH,
32754 Detmold
t (49) (5231) 7401-1
f (49) (5231) 740149
e ibn@djh.de

Dresden - Sachsen Regional Office
Maternistrasse 22, 01067 Dresden
t (49) (351) 4942211
f (49) (351) 4942213
e servicecenter@djh-sachsen.de

Düsseldorf – Rheinland Regional Office
Postfach 110301, 40503 Düsseldorf
t (49) (211) 5770321
f (49) (211) 5770350
e service-center@djh-rheinland.de

Hamburg – Nordmark Regional Office
Rennbahnstrasse 100, 22111 Hamburg
t (49) (40) 65599529
f (49) (40) 65599552
e loewel@djh-nordmark.de

IBN

Munich – YH München Booking Center
Wendl-Dietrich-Strasse 20, 80634 München
☎ (49) (89) 131156
✆ (49) (89) 1678745
✉ jhmuenchen@djh-bayern.de

HUNGARY

Magyarországi Ifjúsági Szállások
Budapest – Mellow Mood
1134 Budapest, Dorzsa Gyorgy ut 152
☎ (36) (1) 3408585
✆ (36) (1) 3208425
✉ travel@hostels.hu

INDIA

Youth Hostels Association of India
New Delhi - International Hostel
5 Nyaya Marg, Chanakyapuri, New Delhi 110021.
☎ (91) (11) 6116285
✆ (91) (11) 4676349
✉ yhostel@del2.vsnl.net.in

IRELAND - NORTHERN

Hostelling International - Northern Ireland
Belfast – National Office
22 Donegall Road, Belfast, BT12 5JN
☎ (44) (28) 32315435
✆ (44) (28) 32439699
✉ info@hini.org.uk

IRELAND - REPUBLIC

An Oige
Dublin – Booking Centre
61 Mountjoy Street, Dublin 7
☎ (353) (1) 830 4555
✆ (353) (1) 830 5808
✉ mailbox@anoige.ie

ISRAEL

Israel Youth Hostels Association
Jerusalem – National Office
Jerusalem 1 Shazar St, International Convention
Center, PO Box 6001, Jerusalem 91060
☎ (972) (2) 655-8406, 8442
✆ (972) (2) 655-8432
✉ iyhytb@iyha.org.il

ITALY

Assoc Italiana Alberghi per la Gioventu
Bologna – Regional Office
Via dell' Unione n.6/a, 40126 Bologna
☎ (39) (051) 224913
✆ (39) (051) 224913
✉ aig_bo@iperbole.bologna.it

Catania – Local Office
Via Andrea Costa 34/B, 95127 Catania, Sicily
☎ (39) (095) 539853
✆ (39) (095) 539853
✉ aigcatania@iol.it

Florence – Regional Office
Viale Augusto Righi 2/4, 50137 Florence
☎ (39) (055) 600315
✆ (39) (055) 610300

Genoa – Regional Office
Salita Salvatore Viale n 1, Genova
☎ (39) (010) 586407
✆ (39) (010) 586407

Naples – Regional Office
Salita della Grotta a Piedigrotta 23, 80122 Naples
☎ (39) (081) 7612346, 7611215
✆ (39) (081) 7612391

Palermo – Regional Office
Via Houel 5, 90138 Palermo, Sicily
☎ (39) (091) 336595
✆ (39) (091) 336595

Rome – National Office
Via Cavour 44, 00184 Rome
📞 (39) (06) 4871152
📠 (39) (06) 4880492
📧 aig@uni.net

Venice – Regional Office
Calle Castelforte S. Rocco, 3101 San Polo,
30125 Venezia
📞 (39) (041) 5204414
📠 (39) (041) 5204034
📧 hostel@libero.it

JAPAN

Japan Youth Hostels Inc
Kyoto – Kyoto Youth Hostel Association
29 Uzumasa-Nakayama-cho, Ukyo-ku,
Kyoto 616-8191
📞 (81) (75) 462-9185
📠 (81) (75) 462-2289
📧 utano-yh@mbox.kyoto-inet.or.jp

Nagoya-Aichi – Aichi Youth Hostel Association
Aichiken Seinen Kaikan, 18-8 Sakae 1 chome,
Naka-ku, Nagoya 460-0008
📞 (81) (52) 221-6080
📠 (81) (52) 221-6057

Osaka – Osaka Youth Hostel Association
Nankai-Nipponbashi Building 2F, 1-3-19,
Nipponbashi-nishi, Naniwa ku,
Osaka 556-0004
📞 (81) (6) 6633-8621
📠 (81) (6) 6634-0751
📧 yhaosaka@osk3.3web.ne.jp

Tokyo – National Office (JYH)
Suidobashi Nishiguchi Kaikan, 2-20-7,
Misaki-cho, Chiyoda-ku, Tokyo 101-0061
📞 (81) (3) 3288-1417
📠 (81) (3) 3288-1248
📧 info@jyh.or.jp

Tokyo – Tokyo Youth Hostels Association
Saiwai Building, 4 Goban-cho, Chiyoda-Ku,
Tokyo 102-0076
📞 (81) (3) 3261-0191
📠 (81) (3) 3261-0190
📧 tyh@aggre.co.jp

Tokyo-Yoyogi – Tokyo-Yoyogi Youth Hostel
3-1 Yoyogi-Kamizono-cho, Shibuya-ku,
Tokyo 151-0052
📞 (81) (3) 3467-9163
📠 (81) (3) 3467-9417
📧 yoyogi@jyh.gr.jp

KOREA - SOUTH

Korea Youth Hostels Association
Seoul – National Office
Rm 408, Juksun Hyundai Bldg 80, Juksun-Dong,
Jongro-Ku, Seoul 110-052
📞 (82) (2) 725-3031
📠 (82) (2) 725-3113
📧 inform@kyha.or.kr

LITHUANIA

Lithuanian Youth Hostels
Vilnius – National Office
Filaretai Youth Hostel
Filaretu Street 17, 2007 Vilnius
📞 (370) (2) 254627 / 262660
📠 (370) (2) 220149
📧 filaretai@post.omnitel.net

MALAYSIA

Malaysian Youth Hostels Association
Kuala Lumpur – MSL Travel Centre
66, Jalan Putra, 50350 Kuala Lumpur
📞 (60) (3) 4424722
📠 (60) (3) 4433707
📧 msl@po.jaring.my

IBN

MALTA

NSTS Student & Youth Travel
Valletta –
220 St Paul Street, Valletta VLT07
t (356) 244983
f (356) 230330
e nsts@nsts.org

MEXICO

Guadalajara – Mundo Joven Travel Shop
Av. Patria 600 local 13-E, Plaza Amistad,
Guadalajara, Jalisco 45110
t (52) (36) 730936
f (52) (36) 733656

Mexico City – Mundo Joven Travel Shop
Insurgentes sur 1510-D, Mexico City DF 03920
t (52) (5) 6613233
f (52) (5) 6631556
e hostellingmexico@remaj.com,
productos@mundojoven.com.mx

Mexico City – Viajes Educativos
Insurgentes sur 421 Loc. B-10, Col. H Condesa
c.p. 06170 Mexico DF.
t (52) (5) 5740899 / 5740896
f (52) (5) 5743521
e ve@ve.com.mx

NEW ZEALAND

Auckland – USIT Beyond Travel Centre
18 Shortland Street, Auckland
t (64) (9) 379-4224
f (64) (9) 366-6275
e enquiries@usitbeyond.co.nz

Youth Hostels Association of New Zealand
Christchurch - National Office
P O Box 436, Level 3, Union House,
193 Cashel Street, Christchurch
t (64) (3) 379-9970
f (64) (3) 365-4476
e info@yha.org.nz

NORWAY

Norske Vandrerhjem
Oslo – National Office
Dronningensgate 26, PB 364 Sentrum, N-0102 Oslo
t (47) (23) 139300
f (47) (23) 139350
e hostels@online.no

PERU

Asociación Peruana de Albergues Turísticos Juveniles
Lima – National Office
AJ Turistico Internacional,
Av Casimiro Ulloa 328, Lima 18
t (51) (1) 2423068
f (51) (1) 4448187
e hostell@terra.com.pe

PORTUGAL

Movijovem
Lisbon – National Office
Av Duque de Avila 137, 1069-017 Lisbon
t (351) 213596000
f (351) 213596001
e movijovem@movijovem.pt,
reservas@movijovem.pt

RUSSIA

St Petersburg – Russian Youth Hostels,
Sindbad Travel
3rd Sovetskaya Ulitsa 28, St Petersburg
t (7) (812) 327-8384
f (7) (812) 329-8019
e ryh@ryh.ru

Moscow – Blue Chip Travel
Chistoprudny Blvd. 12A, Suite 628, 101000 Moscow
t (7) (095) 916-9364
f (7) (095) 924-4968
e info@world4u.ru

Moscow – STAR Travel
Leningradskypr. 80/21, 3rd Floor,
125178 Moscow
☏ (7) (095) 797-9555
✆ (7) (095) 797-9554
✉ star@glasnet.ru

SCOTLAND

Scottish Youth Hostels Association
Stirling – National Office
7 Glebe Crescent, Stirling, FK8 2JA
☏ (44) (541) 553255
✆ (44) (1786) 891350
✉ reservations@syha.org.uk

SINGAPORE

Singapore – STA Travel Pte Ltd
33A Cuppage Road, Cuppage Terrace,
Singapore 229458
☏ (65) 7377188
✆ (65) 7372591
✉ osu@statravel.com.sg

SLOVAKIA

CKM SYTS
Bratislava – CKM 2000 Travel
Vysoka 32, 814 45 Bratislava
☏ (421) (7) 52731024
✆ (421) (7) 52731025
✉ ckm2000@ckm.sk

SOUTH AFRICA

Hostels Association of South Africa
Cape Town – National Office
3rd Floor, St Georges House, 73 St Georges Mall,
Cape Town, 8001
☏ (27) (21) 242511
✆ (27) (21) 244119
✉ info@hisa.org.za

Durban – Africa Wonderland Tours
19 Smith Street, Durban 4001, Natal
☏ (27) (31) 3324944
✆ (27) (31) 3324551
✉ wonderland.durban@pixie.co.za

Johannesburg – Africa Wonderland Tours
Inchanga Ranch, Inchanga Road, Witkoppen,
4 Ways, Johannesburg
☏ (27) (11) 708-1459
✆ (27) (11) 708-1464
✉ wonderland@pixie.co.za

SPAIN

Red Española de Albergues Juveniles
Alicante – IVAJ
Pl. San Cristobal, 8-10, 03002 Alicante
☏ (34) (965) 144789
✆ (34) (965) 144789
✉ turivaj@ivaj.gva.es

Barcelona – ICSJ Youth Tourism
Passeig De Mare De Deu Del Coll 41-51, 08023
Barcelona, Catalunya
☏ (34) (93) 2105151
✆ (34) (93) 2100798
✉ tujcom@usa.net

Barcelona/TUJUCA
c/Rocafort 116-122, 08015 Barcelona
☏ (34) (93) 4838363
✆ (34) (93) 4838347
✉ atencio_@tujuca.com

Madrid – TIVE Office
C/Fernando el Catolico 88, 28015 Madrid
☏ (34) (91) 5437412
✆ (34) (91) 5440062
✉ tive.juventud@comadrid.es

Valencia – Turivaj
c/ Del Hospital, 11, 46001 Valencia
☏ (34) (96) 3869952
✆ (34) (96) 3869903
✉ turivaj@ivaj.gva.es

IBN

SWEDEN

Swedish Touring Club
Stockholm – National Office
Box 25, 101 20 Stockholm
☎ (46) (8) 4632100
✆ (46) (8) 6781958
✉ info@stfturist.se

SWITZERLAND

Schweizer Jugendherbergen
Zurich – National Office
Schaffhauserstrasse 14, Postfach, CH-8042 Zurich
☎ (41) (1) 360-1414
✆ (41) (1) 360-1460
✉ bookingoffice@youthhostel.ch

TAIWAN

Kaohsiung City –
Kaohsiung International Youth Hostel
120 Wen wu First Street, Kaohsiung
☎ (886) (7) 2012477
✆ (886) (7) 2156322
✉ kokiyh@ms57.hinet.net

Taipei – Chinese Taipei Youth Hostel Association
12F-2, 50 Chung Hsiao West Road, Sec 1, Taipei
☎ (886) (2) 23317272
✆ (886) (2) 23317272
✉ aabc@ms8.hinet.net

Taipei – Federal Vacation
7F, 41 Tung-Hsin Rd, Taipei 110
☎ (886) (2) 87681133
✆ (886) (2) 87681515
✉ tci@tptsl.seed.net.tw

Taipei –
Kang Wen Culture & Education Foundation
1208A/12F, 142, Chung-Hsiao E Rd, Sec 4, Taipei
☎ (886) (2) 27751138
✆ (886) (2) 27212784
✉ gftours@tptsl.seed.net.tw

THAILAND

Thai Youth Hostels Association
Bangkok – National Office
25/14 Phitsanulok Road, Se-Sao Thewet, Dusit,
BKK 10300
☎ (66) (2) 628-7413, 7414, 7415
✆ (66) (2) 628-7416
✉ bangkok@tyha.org

TURKEY

Instanbul – Gençtur Tourism & Travel
Istiklai Cad. Zambak Sok. 15/5,
Taksim 80080, Istanbul
☎ (90) (212) 2492515
✆ (90) (212) 2492554
✉ ibn@genctur.com

UNITED STATES

Hostelling International – American Youth Hostels
Boston –
Eastern New England Council Travel Centre
1105 Commonwealth Avenue, Boston, MA 02215
☎ (1) (617) 719-0900 ext. 10
✆ (1) (617) 719-0904
✉ travelctr_hienec@juno.com

Boulder –
Rocky Mountain Council Travel Centre
1310 College Avenue, Suite 315, Boulder,
Colorado 80302
☎ (1) (303) 442-1166
✆ (1) (303) 442-4453
✉ hi-rocky@indra.com

Los Angeles – Los Angeles Council Travel Centre
1434 Second Street, Santa Monica, CA 90401
☎ (1) (310) 393-3413
✆ (1) (310) 393-1769
✉ hiayhla@aol.com

New York – HI-New York Hostel Shop
891 Amsterdam Avenue, New York, NY 10025
☎ (1) (212) 932-2300
✆ (1) (212) 932-2574
✉ reserve@hinewyork.org

Philadelphia –
Delaware Valley Council Travel Centre
624 South 3rd Street, Philadelphia, PA 19147
☎ (1) (215) 925-6004
✆ (1) (215) 925-4874
✉ hidvc@hi-dvc.org

San Francisco –
Golden Gate Council Travel Centre
425 Divisadero Street, Suite 307, San Francisco,
CA 94117-2242
☎ (1) (415) 701-1320
✆ (1) (415) 863-3865
✉ travelsf@norcalhostels.org

St Louis – Gateway Council Travel Centre
7187 Manchester Road, St Louis, MO 63143-2450
☎ (1) (314) 644-4660
✆ (1) (314) 644-6192
✉ info@gatewayhiayh.org

Washington DC – HI-AYH National Office
☎ (1) (202) 783-6161
✆ (1) (202) 783-6171
✉ hiayhserv@hiayh.org

URUGUAY

Asociacion de Alberguistas del Uruguay
Montevideo – National Office
Pablo del Maria 1583/008, 11200 Montevideo
☎ (598) (2) 400-4245
✆ (598) (2) 400-1326
✉ aau@adinet.com.uy

"The tourist who moves about to see and hear and open himself to all the influences of the places which condense centuries of human greatness is only a man in search of excellence."

"Le touriste qui voyage pour voir et entendre et s'ouvrir à toutes les influences des lieux qui condensent des siècles de grandeur humaine est tout simplement un homme à la recherche de l'excellence."

„Der Tourist, der unterwegs ist, um zu schauen und zu hören und sich den Einflüssen der Orte zu eröffnen, die Jahrhunderte menschlicher Größe zusammenfassen, ist einfach ein Mensch auf der Suche nach Großartigem."

"El turista que se desplaza para ver y oír y abrirse a todas las influencias de los lugares en que se condensan siglos de grandeza humana es simplemente un hombre en busca de excelencia."

Max Lerner

Welcome to the HI world!

HOSTELLING INTERNATIONAL

The HI world offers you

4200 hostels.

Internet booking

Thousands of discounts.

Quality accommodation.

www.iyhf.org

Austria

AUTRICHE
ÖSTERREICH
AUSTRIA

Ⓥ **Österreichischer Jugendherbergsverband,
Hauptverband, 1010 Wien, Schottenring 28, Austria.**

☏ (43) (1) 5335353, 5335354
🖷 (43) (1) 5350861
e oejhv@chello.at
🖳 www.oejhv.or.at

Office Hours: Monday-Thursday, 09.00-17.00hrs, Friday 09.00-15.00hrs

Travel Service, GmbH: Österreichischer Jugendherbergsverband,
Gonzagagasse 22, 1010 Wien, Austria.

☏ (43) (1) 5321660
🖷 (43) (1) 5350861
e oejhv-travelservice@chello.at

Ⓦ **Österreichisches Jugendherbergswerk,
Helferstorferstrasse 4, A 1010 Wien, Austria.**

☏ (43) (1) 5331833
🖷 (43) (1) 5331833 Ext 85
e oejhw@oejhw.or.at
🖳 www.oejhw.or.at

Office Hours: Monday-Friday 09.30-18.00hrs

Travel Section: Supertramp, 1010 Wien,
Helferstorferstrasse 4, Austria.

☏ (43) (1) 5335137
🖷 (43) (1) 5331833 Ext 81
e travel@supertramp.co.at
🖳 www.supertramp.co.at

A copy of the Hostel Directory for Ⓥ & Ⓦ can be obtained from:
Hauptverband, 1010 Wien, Schottenring 28, Austria.

Capital:	Vienna	**Population:**	8,025,000
Language:	German	**Size:**	83,849 sq km
Currency:	AS (schilling)	**Telephone Country Code:**	43

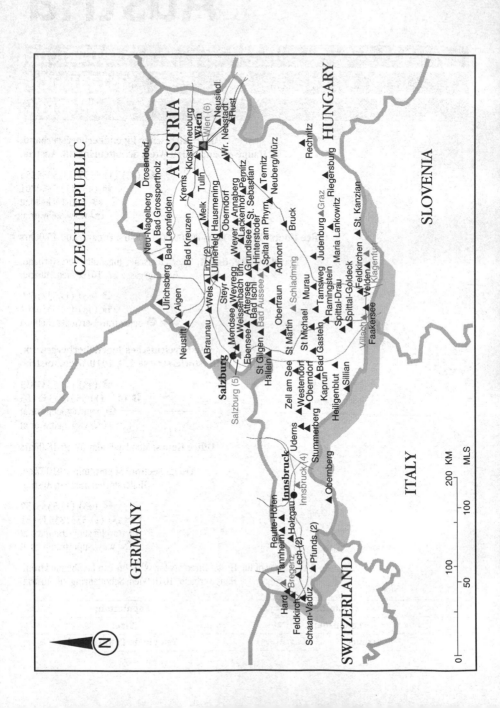

English

Youth Hostels in Austria are controlled by two Associations which operate independently, ÖJHV (Ⓥ) and ÖJHW (Ⓦ). Hostels are located in cities, in the countryside and on hills/mountains.

Price range

Price range AS 150-250. € 10.88-18.14. ⒝⒝inc ⌷.

Rooms and Reservations

Ⓡ ⒓ (All Rooms). Reservations via ⒤⒝⒩ ⌕ National Booking Centre, Hostel or National Office by ❶ ❻ ❺. (Reservation charges may apply). Smoking is limited - please check.

Guests

Membership Card and Passport/Photo ID are required. ♦♦♦ welcome. Group bookings via Hostel or National Office by ❶ ❻ ❺ (Reservation charges may apply).

Open times

Main hostels: open ⒓, Resident manager. **Other hostels:** open ⒓, Resident manager. **Seasonal hostels** are generally open Jan-Mar, Jul, Aug, Nov, Dec.

Meals

⍢ B Ⓡ For individuals & for ♦♦♦.

Discounts

HI Member Discounts available - see discounts section and www.iyhf.org.

Travelling around

For ease of travel use ✈ ⛟ Self-Drive.

Passports and Visas

Passport, Photo ID and Visa required.

Health

Medical insurance is recommended. EU Nationals require Form E111 to obtain treatment within EU countries.

Français

Les auberges de jeunesse autrichiennes sont administrées par deux Associations indépendantes l'une de l'autre, l'ÖJHV (Ⓥ) et ÖJHW (Ⓦ). Les auberges sont situées dans les villes, à la campagne et à la montagne.

Tarifs des nuitées

Tarifs des nuitées 150-250 AS. € 10.88-18.14. ⒝⒝inc ⌷.

Chambres et réservations

Ⓡ ⒓ (Toutes chambres). Réservations via ⒤⒝⒩ ⌕ le Centre National de Réservation, l'auberge ou le Bureau National par ❶ ❻ ❺. (Des frais de réservation pourront vous être facturés). Il est permis de fumer dans certaines chambres - veuillez vérifier.

Usagers

La carte d'adhérent ainsi que le passeport/pièce d'identité avec photo sont à présenter. Accueil des ♦♦♦. Réservations pour groupes via l'auberge et le Bureau National par ❶ ❻ ❺ (Des frais de réservation pourront vous être facturés).

Horaires d'ouverture

Grandes auberges: ouvertes ⒓, Gérant réside sur place. **Autres auberges:** ouvertes ⒓, Gérant réside sur place. **Auberges saisonnières** ouvertes généralement jan-mar, juil, août, nov, déc.

Repas

⍢ B Ⓡ Pour individuels & pour ♦♦♦.

Remises

Remises pour les adhérents HI - voir la section "Remises" et notre site: www.iyhf.org.

Déplacements

Modes de transport recommandés ✈ 🚂 Voiture.

Passeports et visas

Passeport, pièce d'identité avec photo et visa obligatoires.

Santé

Une assurance médicale de voyage est conseillée. Les ressortissants de l'Union Européenne doivent se munir du formulaire E111 pour bénéficier de soins médicaux dans les états de l'UE.

Deutsch

Für Jugendherbergen gibt es in Österreich zwei unabhängige Vereine, den ÖJHV (Ⓥ) und das ÖJHW (Ⓦ). Herbergen befinden sich in Städten, auf dem Land und in Bergen/Gebirgen.

Preisspanne

Preisspanne 150-250 AS. € 10.88-18.14. BB inc.

Zimmer und Reservierungen

R 12 (Alle Zimmer). Reservierungen über IBN Nationales Buchungszentrum, Herberge oder Landesverband per t f e. (Reservierungskosten könnten anfallen). Rauchen ist begrenzt - bitte checken.

Gäste

Mitgliedsausweis und Reisepass/ Personalausweis sind erforderlich. 👪 willkommen. Gruppenbuchungen über Herberge oder Landesverband per t f e (Reservierungskosten könnten anfallen).

Öffnungszeiten

Hauptherbergen: Zugang 12, Herbergsmanager wohnt im Haus. **Andere Herbergen:** Zugang 12, Herbergsmanager wohnt im Haus. **Saison-Herbergen** sind normalerweise Jan-Mär, Jul, Aug, Nov, Dez geöffnet.

Mahlzeiten

🍴 B R Für Einzelreisende & für 👪.

Ermäßigungen

HI-Mitgliedsrabatt ist erhältlich – siehe Teil für Rabatte und Ermäßigungen und www.iyhf.org.

Reisen im Land

Reisen ist einfach mit ✈ 🚂 Selbstfahrer.

Reisepässe und Visa

Reisepass, Personalausweis und Einreisevisum erforderlich.

Gesundheit

Unfall-/Krankenversicherung wird empfohlen. EU Staatsangehörige benötigen Formular E111 für ärztliche Behandlungen innerhalb der EU Länder.

Español

Los albergues juveniles austriacos están administrados por dos asociaciones que funcionan independientemente la una de la otra, ÖJHV (Ⓥ) y la ÖJHW (Ⓦ). Los albergues están situados en las ciudades, el campo y la montaña.

Tarifas mínima y máxima

Tarifas mínima y máxima 150-250 AS. € 10.88-18.14. BB inc.

Habitaciones y Reservas

R 📠 (todas las habitaciones). Reservas por **IBN** 🖰 o a través de la Central Nacional de Reservas, el albergue o la Asociación Nacional por ❶ ❷ ❸. (Es posible que se aplique un suplemento en concepto de gastos de reserva). Está permitido fumar sólo en algunas salas/habitaciones - infórmese.

Huéspedes

Los huéspedes deben presentar su Carnet de Alberguista y su pasaporte o carnet de identidad. Se admiten 👪. Reservas de grupo a través del albergue o la Asociación Nacional por ❶ ❷ ❸ (Es posible que se aplique un suplemento en concepto de gastos de reserva).

Horarios y fechas de apertura

Albergues principales - abiertos 📠, Gerente residente. **Otros albergues** - abiertos 📠, Gerente residente. **Albergues de temporada** suelen abrir: ene-mar, jul, ago, nov, dic.

Comidas

🍽 B **R** Para individuales y para 👪.

Descuentos

Se conceden descuentos a los miembros de Hostelling International – véase la sección sobre descuentos y nuestra página Internet en www.iyhf.org.

Desplazamientos

Transportes recomendados: ✈ 🚂 Automóvil.

Pasaportes y Visados

Pasaporte o carnet de identidad y visado obligatorios.

Información Sanitaria

Seguro médico recomendado. Los ciudadanos procedentes de países pertenecientes a la UE necesitan el impreso E111 para obtener asistencia médica en dichos países.

"He who would travel happily must travel light."

"Celui qui veut voyager joyeusement doit voyager légèrement."

„Wer glücklich reisen will, sollte nur wenig Gepäck mitnehmen."

"El que quiera viajar feliz debe viajar ligero de equipaje."

Antoine de Saint-Exupéry

Bad Gastein ⓦ

5640 Bad Gastein,
Ederplatz 2,
Salzburg.
ⓣ (6434) 2080
ⓕ (6434) 50688
ⓔ hostel.badgastein@salzburg.co.at

Open Dates:	🗓
Open Hours:	07.00-11.00hrs; 17.00-22.00hrs
Reservations:	Ⓡ ꞋCCꞌ
Price Range:	AS 165.00-205.00 € 13.80-16.70 BBinc 🍴
Beds:	150 - 10x² 43x⁴
Facilities:	♦♦♦ 53x ♦♦♦ 🍽 (BD) 🛏 📺 📖 ✎ 2 x 🍷 ☎ 📷 🅿 🛈 ♿ ⚠ ♨ 🔥 🍳 🏠

Directions:	
✈	Salzburg Wolfgang Amadeus 80km
🚇	Bad Gastein 400m
Attractions:	⛳ ⛰ 🚵 ⛷ 🏂 🏃 ∪5km 🎿4km 🏊400m

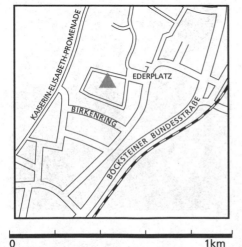

Bregenz ⓥ

Mehrerauerstraße 3-5,
6900 Bregenz,
Vorarlberg.
ⓣ (5574) 42867
ⓕ (5574) 42867-88
ⓔ jghbregenz@jgh.at

Open Dates:	🗓
Open Hours:	07.00-22.00hrs
Reservations:	Ⓡ ⟨IBN⟩ ꞋCCꞌ
Price Range:	AS 200.00-290.00 € 14.53-21.08 BBinc 🍴
Beds:	130 - 4x² 4x⁴ 4x⁵ 14x⁶ 1x⁶
Facilities:	♦♦♦ ♦♦♦ 🍽 🛏 📺 4 x 🍷 ☎ ⬆ 🛈 🍳 ♿ ⚠ 🔥 🎡

Directions:	
✈	Altenrhein CH 20km
A🚌	20m
🚇	300m
Attractions:	⛰ 🎡300m 🏃 🎿 🏊200m

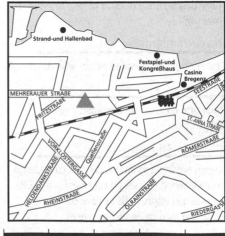

Graz Ⓥ

A-8020 Graz,
Idlhofgasse 74,
Styria.
t (316) 714876
f (316) 714876-88
e jgh.graz@jgh.at

Open Dates:	12
Open Hours:	Mon-Fri. 07.00-22.00hrs; Weekend. 07.00-10.00hrs; 17.00-22.00hrs
Reservations:	R IBN CC
Price Range:	AS 230.00-275.00 € 16.71-19.99 BB inc
Beds:	96 - 9x2 15x4 1x6 2x6+
Facilities:	TV 4 x 8 P
Directions:	2 SW from city centre
✈	Thalerhof 7km
A 🚌	500m
🚂	Hauptbahnhof Graz 500m
🚌	#31,32,33,50 150m
🚋	300m
Attractions:	5km 4km 3km

Innsbruck Ⓦ - Jugendherberge Innsbruck

6020 Innsbruck,
Reichenauerstrasse 147,
Tirol.
t (512) 346179; (512) 346180
f (512) 346179 Ext 12
e yhibk@tirol.com

Open Dates:	01.01-23.12; 27-31.12
Open Hours:	07.00-10.00hrs; 17.00-23.00hrs
Reservations:	R IBN
Price Range:	AS 155.00-260.00 € 11.26 - 18.89 BB inc
Beds:	178 - 5x1 5x2 6x4 24x6
Facilities:	6x (BD) TV 2 x 8 P i
Directions:	2 NE from city centre
✈	Innsbruck 5km
A 🚌	Innsbruck Hauptbahnhof 2km
🚌	Bus O, 2km ap König Laurinstrasse
Attractions:	3000m 500m 50m 1km

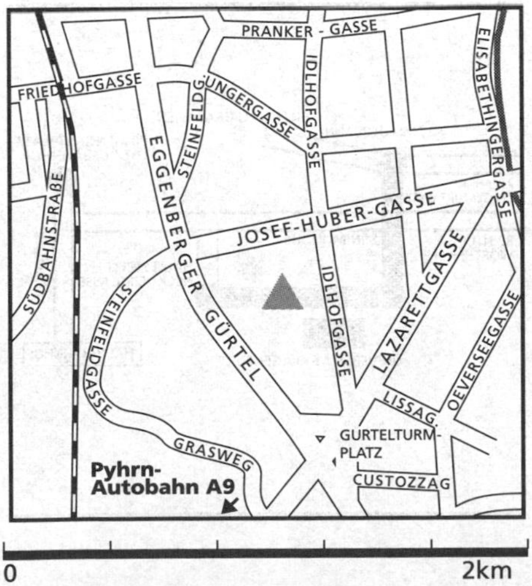

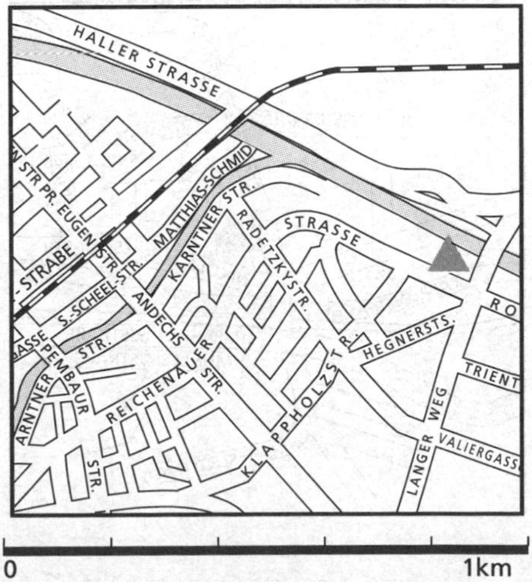

Kaprun ⓥ

A-5710 Kaprun,
Nikolaus Gassnerstrasse 448,
Salzburg.
📞 (6547) 8507
📠 (6547) 8507 Ext 3
📧 jgh.kaprun@jgh.at

Open Dates:	🗓
Open Hours:	07.00-10.00hrs; 17.00-22.00hrs
Reservations:	Ⓡ ⒸⒸ
Price Range:	AS 200.00-300.00 € 13.45-19.99 BB inc 🍴
Beds:	150 - 2x¹🛏 4x²🛏 4x³🛏 9x⁴🛏 13x⁶🛏 2x⁶🛏
Facilities:	🏃 9x 🏃 🍽 🛋 📺 3 x🍴 🚰 🅿 ℹ 🛒 ♿ ⚠ ☉ ☕ 🖥 🏠

Directions:

🚂	Zell am See 6km
Attractions:	🎋 ⛰ 📷 🏊 2000m ⛷ 🏃 ⛷ 🚣 700m

Klagenfurt ⓥ

JGH,
A-9020 Klagenfurt,
Universitätsviertel,
Neckheimg. 6.
📞 (463) 230020
📠 (463) 230020 Ext: 20
📧 jgh.klagenfurt@oejhv.or.at

Open Dates:	🗓
Open Hours:	06.00-10.00hrs; 17.00-23.00hrs
Reservations:	Ⓡ ⒾⒷⓃ ⒸⒸ
Price Range:	AS 215 € 15.62 BB inc 🍴
Beds:	3x²🛏 35x⁴🛏
Facilities:	♿ 🏃 35x 🏃 🍽 (LD) 🛋 🖥 📺 4 x🍴 🔲 📷 🅿 ℹ 🛒 ♿

Directions:

✈	Klagenfurt-Wörthersee 8km
🚂	Klagenfurt 4km
🚌	#10 or #12 200m
Attractions:	🎋 📷 1km 🚲 🏊 1500-2000m ⛵5km 🚣100m ⛷1km

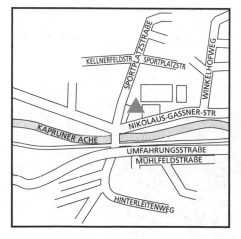

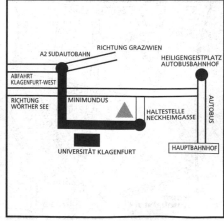

Linz [⊙] - Stanglhofweg

4020 Linz,
Stanglhofweg 3,
Oberösterreich: (near the stadium,
1km to centre).
☎ (732) 664434
🖷 (732) 664434 Ext. 75
📧 jgh.linz@oejhv.or.at

Open Dates:	08.01-21.12
Open Hours:	08.00-16.00hrs (Mon-Thur); 08.00-13.00hrs (Fri); 18.00-21.00hrs (daily)
Reservations:	R
Price Range:	AS 198.00-328.00 € 14.38-23.83 BB inc
Beds:	172 - 24x² 4x³ 28x⁴
Facilities:	28x ⁴⁴⁴ ⁴⁴⁴ 🍽 🚺 📺 4x 🍴 📷 🔒 🅿 ℹ 🎿 ⛰ 🔍 🍴 ⛪

Directions:

✈	Linz 10km
⛴	Linz-Schiffsanlegestelle 4km
🚂	Linzer 2km
🚌	#17 500m, #19 500m, #45 500m ap Leondingerstr
🚃	#1 2km, #3 2km ap Goethekreuzung

Attractions: ⚲ 🏊 3km

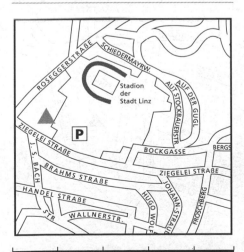

Salzburg [⊙]

JGH,
A-5020 Salzburg Nonntal,
Josef-Preis Allee 18.
☎ (662) 8426700
🖷 (662) 841101
📧 jgh.salzburg@jgh.at

Open Dates:	🗓
Open Hours:	07.00-24.00hrs
Reservations:	R IBN CC
Price Range:	AS 175.00, € 12.14 (8 Bed/room), AS 230.00, € 15.77 (4 Bed/room), AS 267.00, € 19.41 (2 Bed/room) BB inc
Beds:	390 - 21x² 5x³ 19x⁴ 2x⁵ 32x⁶
Facilities:	♿ ⁴⁴⁴ 19x ⁴⁴⁴ 🍽 🚺 📺 🎿 5 x 🍴 🔒 📷 ♨ 🔒 ⬆ 🅿 ℹ 🎿 ⛰ 🔍 🍴

Directions: 1SW from city centre

✈	Salzburg Maxglan 5km
A🚌	#77 to station, #5 to Justizgebäude
🚂	Salzburg 3km
🚌	#5, #55 ap Justizgebäude
🚃	#5 150m

Attractions: ⚘ ⛰ 🚴 ⛷ 1400m 🎣 🎿 ⟳1km ⚲1.5km 🏊1.5km

Salzburg [Ⓦ] -
Eduard Heinrich Haus

5020 Salzburg-Josefiau,
Eduard-Heinrich Str 2.
☏ (662) 625976
✆ (662) 627980
e hostel.eduard-heinrich@salzburg.co.at

Open Dates:	🗓12
Open Hours:	07.00-10.00hrs; 17.00-24.00hrs
Reservations:	**Ⓡ** **IBN** **CC**
Price Range:	AS 180.00-220.00 € 13.10 - 16.00 BB inc 🍴
Beds:	120 - 4x² 4x³ 1x⁴ 16x⁶
Facilities:	ⅲ 21x ⅲ ⅼⓄⅼ (BD) ♨ 📺 📖 🎮 2 x🍷 ▭ 🖼 🅿 ⅈ ♻ ⚠ 🔍 ▦ 🏠
Directions:	3SW from city centre
✈	Salzburg Wolfgang Amadeus 6km
🚂	Salzburg 4km
🚌	500m ap Bundespolizeidirektion 1km
Attractions:	🌳 ⛰ 🚴 ⛷ 🚶 ∪2km ॐ2km 🏊2km

Schladming [Ⓥ]

8970 Schladming,
Coburgstrasse 253,
Styria.
☏ (3687) 24531
✆ (3687) 24531-88
e jgh.schladming@jgh.at

Open Dates:	01.01-31.10; 26-31.12
Open Hours:	08.00-13.00hrs; 17.00-22.00hrs
Reservations:	**Ⓡ** **IBN** **CC**
Price Range:	AS 180.00-315.00 € 13.08 - 22.89 BB inc 🍴
Beds:	215 - 2x¹ 10x² 3x³ 20x⁴ 1x⁵ 16x⁶
Facilities:	ⅲ 8x ⅲ ⅼⓄⅼ ♨ 📺 🎮2 x🍷 🖼 ⅲ 🅱 🅿 ⅈ 💱 ♻ ⚠ 🔍 ▦
Directions:	
✈	Salzburg 89km
🚂	Schladming 1.5km
🚌	Rathausplatz 100m
Attractions:	🌳 ⛰ ⛷ ⛸ 🚶 ∪1km ॐ500m 🏊500m

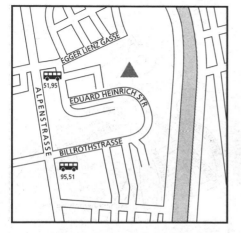

St Gilgen ⓥ -
JGH Schafbergblick

YGH,
5340 St Gilgen,
Mondseerstraße 7-11,
Salzburg.
☏ (6227) 2365
🖷 (6227) 2365 Ext 75
🖃 jgh.stgilgen@oejhv.or.at

Open Dates:	29.01-22.12
Open Hours:	08.00-13.00hrs(Mon-Fri), 17.00-19.00hrs(daily)
Reservations:	Ⓡ
Price Range:	AS 170-290 € 12.35-21.07 BB inc 🗟
Beds:	128 - 12x²🛏 26x⁴🛏
Facilities:	� 26x � 🍽 🖳 📺2 x🍴 🔒 🅿 ⓘ 🖥 ☕ ⛰ 🎿 🔍 🏡

Directions:

✈	Salzburg 40km
🚂	Salzburg 30km
🚌	ap St. Gilgen 500m
Attractions:	🏕 ⛰ 🔍 🎿 1522m 🚶 🏃 ↻20km 🔍300m 🛶

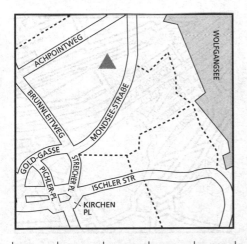

Villach ⓥ

9500 Villach,
St Martin,
Dinzlweg 34,
Kärnten.
☏ (4242) 56368
🖷 (4242) 56368-20
🖃 jgh.villach@oejhv.or.at

Open Dates:	🗓
Open Hours:	06.00-10.00hrs; 17.00-22.00hrs
Reservations:	Ⓡ ⟨IBN⟩ ⟨CC⟩
Price Range:	AS 195.00 € 14.17 BB inc 🗟
Beds:	144 - 3x²🛏 28x⁵🛏
Facilities:	� 28x � 🍽 🖳 📺 🍴3 x🍴 🅿 ⓘ 🖥 ☕ ⛰ 🛢 🎿 🔍

Directions:

✈	Klagenfurt Wörthersee 45km
🚂	Villach 1.5km
🚌	St. Martin 300m
Attractions:	🏕 ⛰ 🔍2.5km 🚴 🏃 🔍 🛶2.5km 🚡 🎿 1000-2000m

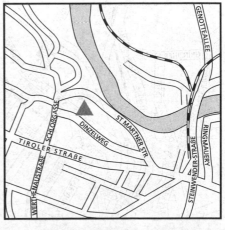

Wien ⓥ - Brigittenau

1200 Wien,
Friedrich Engelsplatz 24.
☏ (1) 33282940; (1) 3300598
🖷 (1) 3308379
📧 jgh.1200wien@chello.at

Open Dates:	01.01-04.02; 18.02-31.12
Open Hours:	🕐
Reservations:	Ⓡ IBN CC
Price Range:	AS 185-230 € 13.44-16.71 BBinc 🍴
Beds:	434 - 103x² 12x³ 36x⁴ 4x⁶ 1x⁶
Facilities:	♿ ♗ 155x ♗ 🍽 🖳 🏢 📺 🖵4 x 🍷 🖼 🏠 8 🎯 ✨
Directions:	4NW from city centre
✈	Wien-Schwechat 20km
A🚌	ap Südbahnhof, then S1, S2 or S3. Westbahnhof, then U6 ap Handelskai
⛴	Wien-Reichsbrücke 2.5km
🚂	W 6km, S 7km, Handelskai 500m
🚌	11A, 5A ap Friedrich Engels Platz 50m
🚋	N, 31, 33 ap Friedrich Engels Platz 50m
Ⓤ	U6 Handelskai 500m
Attractions:	🎡1.5km ⚲ ⚲1km ⚓1km

Wien ⓥ - Hütteldorf

1130 Wien,
Schlossberggasse 8.
☏ (1) 8771501; (1) 8770263
🖷 (1) 8770263 Ext 2
📧 jgh@wigast.com

Open Dates:	🗓
Open Hours:	07.00-00.00hrs
Reservations:	Ⓡ IBN CC
Price Range:	AS 160.00-215.00 € 11.63-15.63 BBinc 🍴
Beds:	295 - 4x¹ 11x² 2x³ 11x⁴ 1x⁵ 24x⁶ 7x⁶
Facilities:	♗ 23x ♗ 🍽 (BD) 🏢 📺 🖵 🖳 🖼 8 ⬍ 🅿 ⓘ 🎯 ✨ 🎢 ⚲ 🏠
Directions:	10W from city centre
✈	Vienna International 30km
🚂	Wien Hütteldorf 500m
🚌	53B 20m
Ⓤ	U4 Hütteldorf 500m
Attractions:	🎡 ⚲ ⚲500m ⚓1km

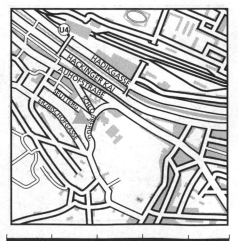

0   4.5km   0   1.2km

Wien ⓦ - Myrthengasse

1070 Wien,
Myrthengasse 7.
☎ (1) 52363160
🖷 (1) 5235849
✉ hostel@chello.at

Open Dates:	🗓
Open Hours:	⏱
Reservations:	ⓡ (IBN) ⒸⒸ
Price Range:	AS 185-230 € 13.44-16.71 BBinc 🍽
Beds:	260 - 17x²🛏 1x³🛏 41x⁴🛏 1x⁵🛏 9x⁶🛏
Facilities:	♿ ♦♦♦ 41x ♦♦♦ 🍽 🛁 📺 📷 1 x 🍴 🖸 🖼 ♨ ⬆ ℹ 🧺 🏤
Directions:	2W from city centre
✈	Wien-Schwechat 20km
A🚌	Vienna ✈ lines 20km
🚆	Westbahnhof 3km, Südbahnhof 8km
🚌	#48A 500m; #13A 500m
Ⓤ	U2, U3 Volkstheater; U6 Burggasse

Zell am See ⓦ

5700 Zell am See,
Haus der Jugend,
Seespitzstrasse 13,
Salzburg.
☎ (6542) 57185
🖷 (6542) 571854
✉ hostel.zell-see@salzburg.co.at

Open Dates:	01.12-31.10
Open Hours:	07.00-10.00hrs; 16.00-22.00hrs
Reservations:	ⓡ ⒸⒸ
Price Range:	AS 165.00-175.00 € 11.30-14.20 BBinc 🍽
Beds:	106 - 7x²🛏 17x⁴🛏 4x⁶🛏
Facilities:	♦♦♦ 28x ♦♦♦ 🍽 🛁 📺 ⬆ 📷 🖼 🅿 ℹ ♨ ⬛ 🔍 🏤
Directions:	
✈	Salzburg Wolfgang Amadeus 100km
🚆	Zell am See 2km
Attractions:	⚘ ⛰ ⬅ 🚴 ⛷ 🎣 🚶 ⚲ U1km 🔍1km ⚓2km

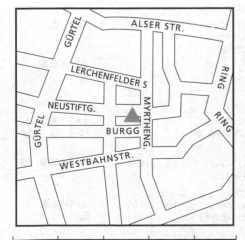

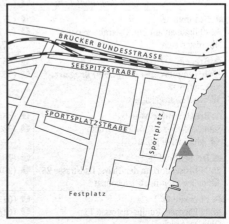

Location/Address	Telephone No. Fax No.	Beds	Opening Dates	Facilities
▲ **Admont** ⓦ 8911 Admont-Schloss Röthelstein, Aigen 32 Steiermark. ⓔ jgh.admont@jgh.at	☎ (3613) 2432 🖷 (3613) 279583	104	01.05–30.09	♛♛ ⽧ⓡ ⌷cc⌷ 🅿
▲ **Aigen** ⓥ 4160 Aigen im Mühlkreis, Adalbert-Stifter-Landesjugendherberge, Oberösterreich.	☎ (7281) 6283 🖷 (7281) 6283-4	80	01.01–31.08; 23.09–31.12	⽧ⓡ 🅿
▲ **Annaberg** ⓦ 3222 Annaberg, Annarotte 77, Niederösterreich. ⓔ jugendherberge-annaberg@aon.at	☎ YH (2728) 8496 🖷 (2728) 8496-4	116	🗓12	♛♛ ⽧ⓡ 🅿
▲ **Bad Aussee** ⓥ ⌊IBN⌋ A-8990 Bad Aussee, Jugendherbergsstr 148, Styria. ⓔ jgh.badaussee@jgh.at	☎ (3622) 52238 🖷 (3622) 52238-88	158	01.01–31.10; 25–31.12	♛♛ ⽧ⓡ ⌷cc⌷ 🅿 🗍
▲ **Bad Gastein** ⓦ **5640 Bad Gastein, Ederplatz 2, Salzburg.** ⓔ hostel.badgastein@salzburg.co.at	☎ (6434) 2080 🖷 (6434) 50688	150	🗓12	♛♛ ⽧ⓡ ⌷cc⌷ 🅿 🗍
▲ **Bad Großpertholz** ⓦ 3972 Bad Großpertholz, Bad Großpertholz 177, Niederösterreich. ⓔ oejhw-wien-noe@telecom.at	☎ (2857) 2965 🖷 (2857) 2965	52	15.04–15.10	♛♛ ⽧ⓡ 🅿
▲ **Bad Ischl** ⓥ - JGH Bad Ischl YGH 4820 Bad Ischl, Am Rechensteg 5, Oberösterreich. ⓔ jgh.badischl@oejhv.or.at	☎ (6132) 26577 🖷 (6132) 26577 Ext 75	122	27.12.00–06. 01.01; 21.01–07.12	♛♛ ⽧ ♿ 🅿
△ *Bad Kreuzen* ⓦ *Oberösterreich, 4362 Bad Kreuzen,* *Neuaigen 14, Burg.*	☎ *(7266) 6686*	*45*	*01.04–31.10*	⽧ ✁ 🅿
△ *Bad Leonfelden* ⓦ *Passauer Strasse 3, 4190 Bad Leonfelden.*	☎ *(7213) 8109* 🖷 *(7213) 634213*	*44*	🗓12	⽧ ✁
▲ **Braunau** ⓥ 5280 Braunau am Inn, Osternbergerstr 57, Oberösterreich.	☎ (7722) 81638 🖷 (7722) 81638; (7722) 6313614	52	01.03–31.10	ⓡ ♿
▲ **Bregenz** ⓥ ⌊IBN⌋ **Mehrerauerstraße 3-5, 6900 Bregenz,** **Vorarlberg.** ⓔ jghbregenz@jgh.at	☎ (5574) 42867 🖷 (5574) 42867-88	130	🗓12	♛♛ ⽧ⓡ ⌷cc⌷ 🗍
▲ **Bruck an der Mur** ⓥ Stadtwaldstrasse 1, A-8600 Bruck. ⓔ jgh.bruck@jgh.at	☎ (3862) 58448 🖷 (3862) 58448-88	92	🗓12	♛♛ ⽧ⓡ ♿ ⌷cc⌷ 🅿 🗍 ☕
▲ **Drosendorf** ⓦ 2095 Drosendorf an der Thaya, Badstrasse 25. ⓔ oejhw-wien-noe@telecom.at	☎ (2915) 2257 🖷 (2915) 2257	63	15.04–15.10	♛♛ ⽧ⓡ 🅿
▲ **Ebensee** ⓦ 4802 Ebensee, Rindbachstrasse 15, Oberösterreich. ⓔ ebensee@jutel.at	☎ (6133) 6698 🖷 (6133) 669885	80	01.04–31.10	♛♛ ⽧ⓡ ♿ 🅿

Location/Address	Telephone No. Fax No.	Beds	Opening Dates	Facilities
△ *Faak - See - Scheiber* ⓦ *9583 Faak - See - Scheiber Nr.12.*	(4254) 2301 (4254) 4620	51	🔟₁₂	¶◎ ⬚ 🅿
△ *Feldkirch* ⓦ *6805 Feldkirch-Levis, Reichstrasse 111,* *Vorarlberg.*	(5522) 73181 (5522) 79399	80	01.01–19.11; 09.12–31.12	♦♦ ◎ Ⓡ ⅙ 🅿 ⊡
△ *Feldkirchen* ⓥ *9560 Kärnten, Briefelsdorf 7,* *Am Maltschachersee.*	(4277) 2644	38	10.05–30.09	◎ 🅿 ⊡
▲ Fürstenfeld ⓥ - Jugend & Familiengästehaus Thermenland/Fürstenfeld Burgenlandstraße 15-17, A-8280 Fürstenfeld.	(316) 7083-0 (316) 7083-88	135	Opening June 2001– 31.12.01; 🔟₁₂.02	♦♦ ◎ Ⓡ 0.5E ⅙ ⌐CC⌐ 🅿
▲ Graz ⓥ ⒾⒷⓃ **A-8020 Graz, Idlhofgasse 74, Styria.** e jgh.graz@jgh.at	(316) 714876 (316) 714876-88	96	🔟₁₂	♦♦ ◎ Ⓡ 2SW ⌐CC⌐ 🅿 ⊡ ♥
▲ Grundlsee ⓥ A-8993 Grundlsee, Wienern-Gössl 149. e bookingcenter@jgh.at	(3622) 8629 (3622) 8629-88	60	01.05–31.10	◎ Ⓡ 🅿
▲ Hallein ⓥ A-5400 Hallein, Schloss Wispach-Esterhazy, Salzburg. e jgh.hallein@jgh.at	(6245) 80397 (6245) 80397 Ext 3	112	01.04–30.09	◎ 🅿
△ *Hard* ⓥ - *"JH Elke Vonach"* *6971 Hard, Allmendstr. 87,* *Vorarlberg (1,5km from Bregenz).*	(5574) 73435 (5574) 73435	24	🔟₁₂	Ⓡ 🅿
▲ Heiligenblut ⓥ 9844 Heiligenblut, Hof 36, Kärnten. e jgh.heiligenblut@oejhv.or.at	(4824) 2259 (4824) 2259-19	93	08.12.00– 15.10.01	♦♦ ◎ 🅿
▲ Hinterstoder ⓦ 4573 Hinterstoder 33, Oberösterreich. e hinterstoder@jutel.at	(7564) 5227 (7564) 522711	96	🔟₁₂	♦♦ ◎ Ⓡ 🅿
▲ Holzgau ⓦ Holzgauerhof 6654 Holzgau 66. e holzgauer-hof@aon.at	(5633) 5250 (5633) 20031	53	15.12–15.05; 15.06–01.11	♦♦ ◎ Ⓡ 🅿 ♥
▲ Innsbruck ⓦ - Jugendherberge Innsbruck ⒾⒷⓃ **6020 Innsbruck,** **Reichenauerstrasse 147, Tirol.** e yhibk@tirol.com	(512) 346179; (512) 346180 (512) 346179 Ext 12	178	01.01–23.12; 27–31.12	◎ Ⓡ 2NE 🅿 ⊡ ⚲
▲ Innsbruck ⓦ - Studentenheim Reichenauerstrasse 147, 6020 Innsbruck. e yhibk@tirol.com	(512) 346179; (512) 346180 (512) 346179-12	112	01.07–31.08	◎ Ⓡ 2E 🅿 ⊡ ⚲
▲ Innsbruck ⓦ - "Fritz Prior - Schwedenhaus" 6020 Innsbruck, Rennweg 17b, Tirol. e youth.hostel@tirol.com	(512) 585814 (512) 585814-4	75	01.07–31.08	♦♦ ◎ 2NE 🅿
▲ Innsbruck ⓥ 6020 Innsbruck, Volkshaus, Radetzkystr. 47.	(512) 395882; (663) 9156214 (512) 395882/ 4	52	🔟₁₂	🅿

Location/Address	Telephone No. Fax No.	Beds	Opening Dates	Facilities
▲ **Judenburg** Ⓥ YGH Judenburg, Kaserngasse 22, A-8750 Judenburg, STYRIA. ⓔ jgh.judenburg@jgh.at	☎ (3572) 87355 🖷 (3572) 87355-88	102	01.01–31.10; 25–31.12	♟ ⵁ Ⓡ ♿ ᶜᶜ Ⓟ ⊚ ☕
▲ **Kaprun** Ⓥ A-5710 Kaprun, Nikolaus Gassnerstrasse 448, Salzburg. ⓔ jgh.kaprun@jgh.at	☎ (6547) 8507 🖷 (6547) 8507 Ext 3	150	▥12	♟ ⵁ Ⓡ ᶜᶜ Ⓟ
▲ **Klagenfurt** Ⓥ 〔ⅠⒷⓃ〕 JGH, A-9020 Klagenfurt, Universitätsviertel, Neckheimg. 6. ⓔ jgh.klagenfurt@oejhv.or.at	☎ (463) 230020 🖷 (463) 230020 Ext: 20		▥12	♟ ⵁ Ⓡ ♿ ᶜᶜ ☞ Ⓟ ⊚
▲ **Klagenfurt** Ⓦ - Kolping JGH 9020 Klagenfurt, Enzenbergstrasse 26, Kärnten.	☎ (463) 56965 🖷 (463) 56965-632	200	10.07–10.09	ⵁ Ⓟ
△ *Klosterneuburg* Ⓦ *3400 Klosterneuburg-Gugging, Hüttersteig 8,* *Niederösterreich.*	☎ *(2243) 83501* 🖷 *(2243) 83501*	*65*	*01.05–01.09*	ⵁ ☞ Ⓟ
▲ **Krems** Ⓥ - Radfahrer Jugendherberge 3500 Krems an der Donau, Ringstrasse 77, Niederösterreich. ⓔ oejhv-noe@oejhv.or.at	☎ (2732) 83452 🖷 (2732) 83452	52	01.04–31.10	♟ ⵁ Ⓡ Ⓟ 🚲
▲ **Lackenhof** Ⓦ 3295 Lackenhof am Ötscher, Ötscherweg 3, Niederösterreich. ⓔ oejhw-wien-noe@telecom.at	☎ (7480) 5251 🖷 (7480) 5338	137	▥12	♟ ⵁ Ⓡ
▲ **Lech** Ⓥ 6764 Vorarlberg, Arlberger Taxizentrale, Lech 428. ⓔ info@taxi-lech.at	☎ (5583) 2501 🖷 (5583) 32586	45	15.06–15.09	♟ ☞
▲ **Lech-Stubenbach** Ⓦ Jugendheim Lech-Stubenbach, A-6764 Lech am Arlberg, Stubenbach 244. ⓔ holger.schatzmann@cable.vol.at	☎ (5583) 2419 🖷 (5583) 24194	64	01.01–30.04; 01.07–04.09; 01.12–31.12	♟ ⵁ Ⓡ
▲ **Linz** Ⓥ - Stanglhofweg **4020 Linz, Stanglhofweg 3, Oberösterreich:** **(near the stadium, 1km to centre).** ⓔ jgh.linz@oejhv.or.at	☎ (732) 664434 🖷 (732) 664434 Ext. 75	172	08.01–21.12	♟ ⵁ Ⓡ Ⓟ
▲ **Linz** Ⓥ - Blütenstr Landesjugendherberge Linz im Lentia 2000, 4040 Linz, Blütenstr 23.	☎ (732) 737078 🖷 (732) 737078-15	106	01.01–22.12; 26–31.12	ⵁ Ⓟ
▲ **Maria Lankowitz** Ⓥ A 8591 Maria Lankowitz, Am See 2. ⓔ jgh.marialankowitz@jgh.at	☎ (3144) 71700 🖷 (3144) 71700-88	124	01.01–31.10; 25–31.12	♟ Ⓡ ♿ ᶜᶜ Ⓟ ☕
▲ **Melk** Ⓦ 3390 Melk an der Donau, Abt-Karl-Strasse 42, Niederösterreich. ⓔ oejhw-wien-noe@telecom.at	☎ (2752) 52681 🖷 (2752) 54257	104	15.03–31.10	♟ ⵁ Ⓡ Ⓟ

Location/Address	Telephone No. Fax No.	Beds	Opening Dates	Facilities
▲ **Mondsee** ⓥ - "JGH Mondsee" 5310 Mondsee, Krankenhausstrasse 9, Oberösterreich. ⓔ jgh.mondsee@oejhv.or.at	❶ (6232) 2418 ❻ (6232) 2418 Ext 75	80	01.02–15.12	♦♦♦ ¶◎¶ 🄿
▲ **Murau** ⓦ 8850 Murau, St. Leonhardsplatz 4 Steiemark. ⓔ jgh.murau@jgh.at	❶ (3532) 2395 ❻ (3532) 2395	136	01.05–31.12	♦♦♦ ¶◎¶ ⒭ ♿ ⒸⒸ 🄿 ☕
▲ **Neuberg** ⓥ 8692 Neuberg an der Mürz, Kaplanweg 8, Styria. ⓔ bookingcenter@jgh.at	❶ (3857) 8495 ❻ (3857) 8495-88	50	01.01–31.03; 01.05–31.10; 25–31.12	¶◎¶ ⒭ 🄿
▲ **Neu-Nagelberg** ⓥ - "Hans Czettel JH" 3871 Neu-Nagelberg 114. ⓔ oejhv-noe@oejhv.or.at	❶ (2859) 7476 ❻ (2859) 7476	39	11.01–23.12	¶◎¶ ⒭ 🄿
▲ **Neusiedl** ⓦ 7100 Neusiedl am See, Herbergsgasse 1, Burgenland.	❶ (2167) 2252 ❻ (2167) 2252	86	01.03–30.11	♦♦♦ ¶◎¶ ⒭ 🄿 🚲
△ *Neustift* ⓦ *4143 Neustift im Mühlkreis 71, Rannahof, Oberösterreich.* ⓔ *jugendherberge@vpn.ut*	❶ *(7284) 8196* ❻ *(7284) 8396*	*100*	🗓	♦♦♦ ¶◎¶ 🄿
▲ **Obernberg** ⓦ - Jugendheim am Brenner Obernberg 49, 6156 Obernberg. ⓔ spot.obernberg@alpenverein.at	❶ (5274) 87475 ❻ (5274) 87475	85	01.01–15.04; 01.06–30.09; 27–31.12 (♦♦♦ Only)	¶◎¶ 🄿
▲ **Oberndorf** ⓥ 6372 Oberndorf, bei Kitzbühel/Tirol, Eberharting 1.	❶ (05352) 63651 ❻ (05352) 65201	104	01.01–31.10; 15–31.12	♦♦♦ ¶◎¶ 6N 🄿 ⓓ
▲ **Obertraun** ⓦ 4831 Obertraun, Winkl 26, Oberösterreich. ⓔ obertraun@jutel.at	❶ (6131) 360 ❻ (6131) 3604	140	🗓	♦♦♦ ¶◎¶ ⒭ 🄿
△ *Pernitz* ⓦ *2763 Pernitz, Hauptstr 79, Niederösterreich.*	❶ *(2632) 72373*	*45*	*01.04–31.10*	☞
▲ **Pfunds** ⓥ JGH Dangl, A-6542 Pfunds 347, Tirol.	❶ (5474) 5244 ❻ (5474) 5244-4	60	01.05–20.10; 15.12–20.04	♦♦♦ ¶◎¶ ⒭ ☞ 🄿
▲ **Pfunds** ⓥ 6542 Pfunds, Dorf 92. ⓔ info@post-pfunds.com	❶ (5474) 5711 ❻ (5474) 5711-34	54	15.05–20.10; 15.12–20.04	♦♦♦ ¶◎¶ ⒭ ☕
△ *Ramingstein* ⓥ - *Burg Finstergrün* *5591 Ramingstein, Wald 65.*	❶ *(06475) 228* ❻ *(06475) 228*	*176*	*01.05–15.10*	¶◎¶ 🄿
△ *Rechnitz* ⓥ *Burgenland, 7471 Rechnitz, Hochstrasse 1.*	❶ *(3363) 79245* ❻ *(3363) 79245*	*56*	🗓	¶◎¶ ☞ 🄿
▲ **Reutte-Höfen** ⓥ 6600 Reutte, JGH am Graben 1, Tirol. ⓔ jgh-hoefen@tirol.com	❶ (5672) 626440 ❻ (5672) 626444	51	01.01–02.11; 15–31.12	♦♦♦ ¶◎¶ ⒭
▲ **Rust** ⓦ - JGH Rust 7071 Rust, Conradplatz 1.	❶ (2685) 591 ❻ (2685) 591-4	58	🗓	♦♦♦ ¶◎¶ ⒭ ⒸⒸ 🄿 ☕

Location/Address	Telephone No. Fax No.	Beds	Opening Dates	Facilities
▲ **Salzburg** Ⓥ ⒾⒷⓃ JGH, A-5020 Salzburg Nonntal, Josef-Preis Allee 18. 🅔 jgh.salzburg@jgh.at	🅣 (662) 8426700 🅕 (662) 841101	390	📅	ḧ 🍴 Ⓡ 1 SW ♿ cc 🅿 📺
△ *Salzburg* Ⓦ *- Aigner Strasse* *5026 Salzburg, Aigner Strasse 34.* 🅔 *hostel.aigen@salzburg.co.at*	🅣 *(662) 623248* 🅕 *(662) 623248-13*	*105*	*01.07–31.08*	ḧ 🍴 2 NW 🅿
▲ **Salzburg** Ⓦ *-* Eduard Heinrich Haus ⒾⒷⓃ 5020 Salzburg-Josefiau, Eduard-Heinrich Str 2. 🅔 hostel.eduard-heinrich@salzburg.co.at	🅣 (662) 625976 🅕 (662) 627980	120	📅	ḧ 🍴 Ⓡ 3 SW cc 🅿 📺
▲ **Salzburg** Ⓦ *- Haunspergstrasse* 5020 Salzburg, Haunspergstrasse 27.	🅣 (662) 875030 🅕 (662) 883477	105	01.07–26.08	ḧ Ⓡ 🚲
△ *Salzburg* Ⓦ *- Walserfeld* *5071 Salzburg-Walserfeld, Schulstrasse 18.*	🅣 *(662) 851377* 🅕 *(662) 853301*	*156*	*01.07–25.08*	ḧ 🍴 🅿
▲ **Schladming** Ⓥ ⒾⒷⓃ **8970 Schladming, Coburgstrasse 253,** **Styria.** 🅔 jgh.schladming@jgh.at	🅣 (3687) 24531 🅕 (3687) 24531-88	215	01.01–31.10; 26–31.12	ḧ 🍴 Ⓡ cc 🅿
▲ **Sillian** Ⓦ 9920 Sillian-Arnbach 37, Tirol.	🅣 (4842) 6321 🅕 (4842) 6321-20	37	01.05–31.10	☛
▲ **Spital am Pyhrn** Ⓦ 'Lindenhof', 4582 Spital am Pyhrn 77, Oberösterreich.	🅣 (7563) 214	140	01.01–31.10; 01–31.12	ḧ 🍴 🅿
▲ **Spittal an der Drau** Ⓥ 9800 Spittal an der Drau, Stadiongelände, zur Seilbahn 2 neben Goldecktalstation, Kärnten.	🅣 (4762) 3252 🅕 (4762) 3252 Ext 4	69	📅	🍴 🅿
▲ **Spittal/Goldeck** Ⓦ 9800 Spittal/Goldeck, Kärnten. 🅔 goldeck@gmx.at	🅣 (4762) 2701	45	22.12.00– 15.04.01; 20.06–20.09	ḧ 🍴 Ⓡ
△ *Steyr* Ⓥ *4400 Steyr, Josef Hafnerstrasse 14,* *Oberösterreich.*	🅣 *(7252) 45580* 🅕 *(7252) 45580*	*45*	*06.01–22.12*	☛ 🅿
▲ **Stummerberg** Ⓦ 6272 Kaltenbach/Stumm, Zillertal, Stummerberg 68, Tirol.	🅣 (5283) 3577	40	📅	ḧ 🍴 ☛ 🅿
▲ **St Gilgen** Ⓥ *- JGH Schafbergblick* **YGH, 5340 St Gilgen,** **Mondseerstraße 7-11, Salzburg.** 🅔 jgh.stgilgen@oejhv.or.at	🅣 (6227) 2365 🅕 (6227) 2365 Ext 75	128	29.01–22.12	ḧ 🍴 Ⓡ 🅿
▲ **St. Kanzian, Unterburg** Ⓥ *-* Klopeiner See 9122 St. Kanzian, Lerchenweg 2. 🅔 jgh.klopeinersee@oejhv.or.at	🅣 (4239) 40160 🅕 (4239) 40160-20	72	01.03–31.10	ḧ 🍴 Ⓡ 2.3 E 🅿 🚲

Location/Address	Telephone No. Fax No.	Beds	Opening Dates	Facilities
▲ **St Martin am Tennengebirge** Ⓥ JH Sonnrain, A-5522 St Martin Nr 100, Salzburg. ⓔ jgh.stmartin@jgh.at	☏ (6463) 7318 🖷 (6463) 7318 Ext 3	126	01.01–17.04; 11.05–30.09; 16–31.12	ᵻᵻᵻ ⑩ 4SE Ⓟ
▲ **St Michael im Lungau** Ⓥ A-5582 Herbergsgasse 348, Salzburg. ⓔ jgh.stmichael@jgh.at	☏ (6477) 8630 🖷 (6477) 8630-3	188	01.01–17.04; 11.05–30.09; 16–31.12	ᵻᵻᵻ ⑩ 4SE ♂ Ⓟ
▲ **St Sebastian/Mariazell** Ⓥ - Sportzentrum Mariazellerland Erlaufseestraße 49, A-8630 St. Sebastian/ Mariazell. ⓔ jgh.mariazellerland@jgh.at	☏ (3882) 2669 🖷 (3882) 2669-88	140	⑫	& ⒸⒸ ⊡ ☕
▲ **Tamsweg** Ⓦ - "Haus Hatheyerbühel" 5580 Tamsweg, Hatheyergasse 512.	☏ (6474) 2199 🖷 (6474) 2195	44	01.07–31.08	ᵻᵻᵻ ⑩ Ⓡ Ⓟ ⊡ ⚲
▲ **Tannheim** Ⓦ - "Haus Zobl" Tannheim 25, 6675 Tannheim.	☏ (5675) 6341 🖷 (5675) 6341	48	⑫	ᵻᵻᵻ ⑩ Ⓡ ♂ Ⓟ ⊡ ☕ ⚲ ⚙
△ *Ternitz* Ⓥ *2630 Ternitz, Straße des 12. Februar 38.*	☏ (2630) 38483 🖷 (2630) 38483-4	*32*	*01.01–31.01; 15.02–15.10; 15.11–31.12*	⑩ Ⓟ
▲ **Tulln** Ⓦ - Jugend-und Familiengästehaus Tulln Marc Aurel-Park, 3430 Tulln. ⓔ oejhw-wien-noe@telecom.at	☏ (1) 5237158-0 🖷 (1) 523715822	126	⑫	ᵻᵻᵻ ⑩ Ⓡ & Ⓟ ⊡ ☕ ⚲
▲ **Uderns** Ⓥ 6271 Uderns, Finsing 73, YGH "Finsingerhof". ⓔ finsingerhof@utanet.at	☏ (5288) 62010; (6644) 109514 🖷 (5288) 62866	89	⑫	ᵻᵻᵻ ⑩ Ⓡ Ⓟ
▲ **Ulmerfeld-Hausmening** Ⓥ - "JH Schlosz Ulmerfeld" 3363 Ulmerfeld-Hausmening Burgweg 1 Schloss, Niederösterreich. ⓔ oejhv-noe@oejhv.or.at	☏ (7475) 54080	62	01.04–31.10	ᵻᵻᵻ ⑩ Ⓡ Ⓟ ⊡
▲ **Ulrichsberg** Ⓦ 4161 Ulrichsberg, Falkensteinstr.1.	☏ (7288) 7046 🖷 (7288) 7046-20	34	⑫	ᵻᵻᵻ ⑩ Ⓡ &
▲ **Velden** Ⓥ - Cap Wörth 9220 Velden, Seecorso 37-39. ⓔ jgh.capwoerth@oejhv.or.at	☏ (463) 230019 🖷 (463) 230019-13	220	⑫	ᵻᵻᵻ ⑩ Ⓡ 0.8E & ⒸⒸ Ⓟ ⊡ ☕

Vienna/Vienne/Viena ☞Wien

Location/Address	Telephone No. Fax No.	Beds	Opening Dates	Facilities
▲ **Villach** Ⓥ **IBN** **9500 Villach, St Martin, Dinzlweg 34, Kärnten.** ⓔ jgh.villach@oejhv.or.at	☏ (4242) 56368 🖷 (4242) 56368-20	144	⑫	ᵻᵻᵻ ⑩ Ⓡ ⒸⒸ Ⓟ
△ *Weissenbach am Attersee* Ⓥ - *Europacamp Franz von Schönthanallee 42, 4854 Weissenbach, Oberösterreich.*	☏ (7663) 220 🖷 (7663) 8905-14	*173*	*01.06–31.08*	⑩ Ⓟ ⊡ ☕

Location/Address	Telephone No. Fax No.	Beds	Opening Dates	Facilities
▲ **Wels** Ⓥ 4600 Wels, Dragonerstr.22.	☎ (7242) 235757; (7242) 67284 ❺ (7242) 235756	50	07.01–23.12	P
▲ **Westendorf** Ⓥ - Funpark Westendorf/Burgweghof Vorderwindau 15, 6363 Westendorf. ⓔ funpark.westerndorf@netway.at	☎ (5334) 6460 ❺ (5334) 6460	60	⓬	⁙ ⓞ Ⓡ 2.5 SW P ⌷ ☕ 🚲
▲ **Weyer** Ⓦ 3335 Weyer, Mühlein 56, Oberösterreich. ⓔ weyer@jutel.at	☎ (7355) 6284 ❺ (7355) 62844	136	⓬	⁙ ⓞ Ⓡ ♿ P
▲ **Weyregg/Attersee** Ⓦ Weyregg/Attersee 3, Oberösterreich. ⓔ weyregg@jutel.at	☎ (7664) 2780 ❺ (7664) 27804	42	01.05–31.10	⁙ ⓞ Ⓡ P
▲ **Wien** Ⓥ - "Hostel Ruthensteiner" Ruthensteiner JH, 1150 Wien, Robert Hamerling 24. ⓔ hostel.ruthensteiner@telecom.at	☎ (1) 8934202; (1) 8932796 ❺ (1) 8932796	77	⓬	⁙ ⓞ 5 W CC ⌀ ⌷
▲ **Wien** Ⓥ IBN Schloßherberge am Wilhelminenberg, 1160 Wien, Savoyenstrasse 2. ⓔ shb@wigast.com	☎ (1) 4858503700 ❺ (1) 4858503702	164	⓬	⁙ ⓞ Ⓡ 10 W CC P ⌷
▲ **Wien** Ⓥ - Brigittenau IBN **1200 Wien, Friedrich Engelsplatz 24.** ⓔ jgh.1200wien@chello.at	☎ (1) 33282940; (1) 3300598 ❺ (1) 3308379	434	01.01–04.02; 18.02–31.12	⁙ ⓞ Ⓡ 4 NW ♿ CC 🚲
▲ **Wien** Ⓥ - Hütteldorf IBN **1130 Wien, Schlossberggasse 8.** ⓔ jgh@wigast.com	☎ (1) 8771501; (1) 8770263 ❺ (1) 8770263 Ext 2	295	⓬	⁙ ⓞ Ⓡ 10 W CC P ⌷
▲ **Wien** Ⓦ - Myrthengasse IBN **1070 Wien, Myrthengasse 7.** ⓔ hostel@chello.at	☎ (1) 52363160 ❺ (1) 5235849	260	⓬	⁙ ⓞ Ⓡ 2 W ♿ CC ⌷
△ *Wien* Ⓦ - *Turmherberge Don Bosco* *1030 Wien, Lechnerstrasse 12.*	☎ *(1) 7131494*	*53*	*01.03–30.11*	3 SE
▲ **Wiener Neustadt** Ⓥ - "Europahaus" 2700 Wiener Neustadt, Europahaus, Promenade 1, Niederösterreich. (50km SE of Wien). ⓔ oejhv-noe@oejhv.or.at	☎ (2622) 29695 ❺ (2622) 29695	36	01.07–31.08	⁙ Ⓡ P
▲ **Zell am See** Ⓦ **5700 Zell am See, Haus der Jugend, Seespitzstrasse 13, Salzburg.** ⓔ hostel.zell-see@salzburg.co.at	☎ (6542) 57185 ❺ (6542) 571854	106	01.12–31.10	⁙ ⓞ Ⓡ CC P

Belgium

BELGIQUE
BELGIEN
BELGICA

Ⓥ **Vlaamse Jeugdherbergcentrale,
Van Stralenstraat 40,
B-2060 Antwerp, Belgium.**

📞 (32) 03 2327218
📠 (32) 03 2318126
📧 info@vjh.be
🖥 www.vjh.be

Office Hours: Monday-Friday 09.00-18.00hrs. Saturday (Easter-15.09) 09.00-13.00hrs.

Ⓛ **Les Auberges de Jeunesse,
Rue de la Sablonnière 28 B-1000, Brussels, Belgium.**

📞 (32) 02 2195676
📠 (32) 02 2191451
📧 info@laj.be
🖥 www.laj.be

Office Hours: Monday-Friday 09.00-12.30hrs/13.00-17.00hrs

A copy of the Hostel Directory for this Country can be obtained from:
The National Office

Capital:	Brussels	**Population:**	10,000,100
Language:	Dutch, French, German	**Size:**	30,515 sq km
Currency:	BEF (Belgian franc)	**Telephone Country Code:**	32

English

The Vlaamse Jeugdherbergcentrale (Ⓥ) runs hostels in the northern region and Les Auberges de Jeunesse (Ⓛ) operates in the southern part of the country. Hostels are located in cities, in the countryside and on the coast.

Price range

Price range BEF 430-510. € 10,66-12,64. BB inc ⊠.

Rooms and Reservations

Ⓡ ⬚ (All Rooms). Reservations via ⃝IBN National Booking Centre or Hostel by ➊ ➍ ℮ . Smoking is limited - please check.

Guests

Membership Card and Passport/Photo ID are required. ♦♦♦ welcome. Group bookings via National Booking Centre or Hostel by ➊ ➍ ℮ .

Open times

Main hostels: open ⊕. Reception open: 07:30-23:00hrs. Resident manager. **Other**

hostels: open 07:30-10:00hrs, 17:00-22:00hrs. Reception open: 07:30-10:00hrs, 17:00-22:00hrs. Resident manager.

Meals

🍽 BLD **R** For individuals & for ♦♦♦.

Discounts

HI Member Discounts available - see discounts section and www.iyhf.org.

Travelling around

For ease of travel use 🚌 🚂 Self-Drive.

Travel/Activity Packages

Tours/sightseeing, cycling/mountain biking and walking/trekking packages available. Package bookings via National Booking Centre or Hostel by ❶ ❶ ❷.

Passports and Visas

Passport, Photo ID and Visa required.

Health

Medical insurance is recommended. EU Nationals require Form E111 to obtain treatment within EU countries.

Français

La Vlaamse Jeugdherbergcentrale (Ⓥ) gère les auberges de la région nord tandis que Les Auberges de Jeunesse (Ⓛ) gère celles de la partie sud du pays. Les auberges sont situées dans les villes, à la campagne et sur le littoral.

Tarifs des nuitées

Tarifs des nuitées 430-510 BEF. € 10,66-12,64. BB inc ⌘.

Chambres et réservations

R 🖾 (Toutes chambres). Réservations via IBN le Centre National de Réservation ou

l'auberge par ❶ ❶ ❷. Il est permis de fumer dans certaines chambres - veuillez vérifier.

Usagers

La carte d'adhérent ainsi que le passeport/pièce d'identité avec photo sont à présenter. Accueil des ♦♦♦. Réservations pour groupes via le Centre National de Réservation ou l'auberge par ❶ ❶ ❷.

Horaires d'ouverture

Grandes auberges: ouvertes ⌚. Accueil ouvert entre 7h30-23h. Gérant réside sur place. **Autres auberges:** ouvertes entre 7h30-10h, 17h-22h. Accueil ouvert entre 7h30-10h, 17h-22h. Gérant réside sur place.

Repas

🍽 BLD **R** Pour individuels & pour ♦♦♦.

Remises

Remises pour les adhérents HI - voir la section "Remises" et notre site: www.iyhf.org.

Déplacements

Modes de transport recommandés 🚌 🚂 Voiture.

Forfaits Voyages/Activités

Forfaits circuits touristiques, cyclotourisme/VTT et randonnées pédestres disponibles. Réservations des forfaits via le Centre National de Réservation ou l'auberge par ❶ ❶ ❷.

Passeports et visas

Passeport, pièce d'identité avec photo et visa obligatoires.

Santé

Une assurance médicale de voyage est conseillée. Les ressortissants de l'Union Européenne doivent se munir du formulaire E111 pour bénéficier de soins médicaux dans les états de l'UE.

Deutsch

Die Vlaamse Jeugdherbergcentrale (Ⓥ) betreibt Herbergen in den nördlichen Regionen und Les Auberges de Jeunesse (Ⓛ) im südlichen Teil des Landes. Herbergen befinden sich in Städten, auf dem Land und an der Küste.

Preisspanne

Preisspanne 430-510 BEF. € 10,66-12,64. BB inc 🏧.

Zimmer und Reservierungen

Ⓡ 🖾 (Alle Zimmer). Reservierungen über IBN Nationales Buchungszentrum oder Herberge per ❶ ❶ ❸. Rauchen ist begrenzt - bitte checken.

Gäste

Mitgliedsausweis und Reisepass/ Personalausweis sind erforderlich. ♦♦♦ willkommen. Gruppenbuchungen über Nationales Buchungszentrum oder Herberge per ❶ ❶ ❸.

Öffnungszeiten

Hauptherbergen: Zugang ♘. Rezeption zwischen 07:30-23:00Uhr. Herbergsmanager wohnt im Haus. **Andere Herbergen:** Zugang zwischen 07:30-10:00Uhr, 17:00-22:00Uhr. Rezeption zwischen 07:30-10:00Uhr, 17:00-22:00Uhr. Herbergsmanager wohnt im Haus.

Mahlzeiten

🍽 BLD Ⓡ Für Einzelreisende & für ♦♦♦.

Ermäßigungen

HI-Mitgliedsrabatt ist erhältlich – siehe Teil für Rabatte und Ermäßigungen und www.iyhf.org.

Reisen im Land

Reisen ist einfach mit 🚃 🚐 Selbstfahrer.

Reise-/Aktivitäten-Packages

Touren/sightseeing, Fahrrad/Mountainbiking und wandern/Trekking-Packages erhältlich. Package-Buchungen über Nationales Buchungszentrum oder Herberge per ❶ ❶ ❸.

Reisepässe und Visa

Reisepass, Personalausweis und Einreisevisum erforderlich.

Gesundheit

Unfall-/Krankenversicherung wird empfohlen. EU Staatsangehörige benötigen Formular E111 für ärztliche Behandlungen innerhalb der EU Länder.

Español

La "Vlaamse Jeugdherbergcentrale" (albergues con el símbolo Ⓥ), es responsable de los albergues de la región norte. Les "Auberges de Jeunesse" (albergues con el símbolo Ⓛ) administran los albergues del sur del país. Los albergues están situados en las ciudades, el campo y la costa.

Tarifas mínima y máxima

Tarifas mínima y máxima 430-510 BEF. € 10,66-12,64. BB inc 🏧.

Habitaciones y Reservas

Ⓡ 🖾 (todas las habitaciones). Reservas por IBN o a través de la Central Nacional de Reservas o el albergue por ❶ ❶ ❸. Está permitido fumar sólo en algunas salas/habitaciones - infórmese.

Huéspedes

Los huéspedes deben presentar su Carnet de Alberguista y su pasaporte o carnet de identidad. Se admiten ♦♦♦. Reservas de grupo a través de la Central Nacional de Reservas o el albergue por 🛈 🛈 🄴.

Horarios y fechas de apertura

Albergues principales - abiertos 🕐. Horario de recepción: 07:30-23:00h. Gerente residente.
Otros albergues - abiertos: 07:30-10:00h, 17:00-22:00h. Horario de recepción: 07:30-10:00h, 17:00-22:00h. Gerente residente.

Comidas

🍴 BLD 🆁 Para individuales y para ♦♦♦.

Descuentos

Se conceden descuentos a los miembros de Hostelling International – véase la sección sobre descuentos y nuestra página Internet en www.iyhf.org.

Desplazamientos

Transportes recomendados: 🚂 🚌 Automóvil.

Viajes Combinados con Actividades

Viajes combinados con visitas turísticas, cicloturismo/bicicleta de montaña y senderismo. Reserva de viajes combinados a través de la Central Nacional de Reservas o el albergue por 🛈 🛈 🄴.

Pasaportes y Visados

Pasaporte o carnet de identidad y visado obligatorios.

Información Sanitaria

Seguro médico recomendado. Los ciudadanos procedentes de países pertenecientes a la UE necesitan el impreso E111 para obtener asistencia médica en dichos países.

Antwerpen ⓥ -
Op Sinjoorke

**2020 Antwerpen,
Eric Sasselaan 2.**
🛈 **(03) 2380273**
🅕 **(03) 2481932**

Open Dates:	08.01-15.12
Open Hours:	07.00-10.00hrs; 16.00-24.00hrs (Night access)
Reservations:	(IBN) (CC)
Price Range:	BEF 430 € 10.66 (BB) inc 🏠
Beds:	131 - 2x1🛏 4x2🛏 8x4🛏 8x6🛏 5x6🛏
Facilities:	♿ ♦♦♦ 8x ♦♦♦ 🍴 🍺 ♨ 🛏 📺 📖2 x🍴 ▣ 💼 8 🅿 🚐 ♣ ⚠ 🔔
Directions:	4S from city centre
✈	Brussels 45km; Antwerp 5km
🚂	Antwerp Central 5km, Antwerp South 500m
🚌	27 Central Station, 25 Groenplaats (direction Bouwcentrum) 100m
Ⓤ	2 Central Station (direction Hoboken Ⓤ Bouwcentrum) 100m

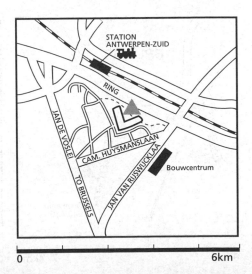

STATION ANTWERPEN-ZUID

RING

JAN DE VOSEI

CAM. HUYSMANSLAAN

TO BRUSSELS

JAN VAN RIJSWIJCKLAAN

Bouwcentrum

0   6km

Brugge ⓥ - Europa

8310 Brugge 4/Assebroek,
Baron Ruzettelaan 143.
☎ (050) 352679
f (050) 353732

Open Dates:	08.01-15.12
Open Hours:	07.30-10.00hrs; 13.00-23.00hrs (Night access)
Reservations:	[IBN] [CC]
Price Range:	BEF 430-510 € 10.66-12.64 [BB]inc 🛏
Beds:	212 - 4x¹ 22x⁴ 20x⁶
Facilities:	♿ 22x ⚇ ⑪ 🍴 🚿 🏢 📺 2 x 🍽 🖥 🔒 🅿 ✉ ⚽ 🎣
Directions:	[2SE] from city centre
✈	Brussels 85km
🚂	Brugge 1.5km
🚌	2 300m; 749 100m

Brussels ⓛ -

Generation Europe

4 Rue de l'Eléphant,
1080 Bruxelles.
☎ (02) 4103858
f (02) 4103905
e brussels.europe@laj.be

Open Dates:	16.01-30.12
Open Hours:	07.30-01.00hrs
Reservations:	[IBN] [CC]
Price Range:	BEF 430-820 € 10.66-20.32 [BB]inc 🛏
Beds:	160 - 10x² 24x⁴ 2x⁶ 4x⁶⁺
Facilities:	♿ ⚇ 26x ⚇ 🍴 🏢 📺 🖥 💻 4 x 🍽 🖥 🖼 🔒 💲 🅿 ℹ ✉ 🎣 🚿 ⏰ ⚽ 🏨 🏛
Directions:	
✈	Zaventem 15km
⛴	Zeebrugge 125km
🚂	South Station 2km
🚋	18 500m ap Porte de Flandres
Ⓤ	Comte de Flandre 300m

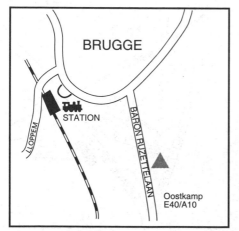

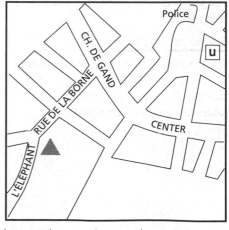

Brussels Ⓛ - Jacques Brel

Rue de la Sablonnière 30,
1000 Bruxelles.
☎ (02) 2180187
🖷 (02) 2172005
✉ brussels.brel@laj.be

Open Dates:	02.01-15.12
Open Hours:	07.30-01.00hrs
Reservations:	(IBN) (CC)
Price Range:	BEF 430-820 € 10.66-20.32 BBinc ⃞
Beds:	173 - 2x¹ 21x² 5x³ 11x⁴ 6x⁶ 3x⁶ᵗʰ
Facilities:	♿ ♂♀ 16x ♂♀ ⍾ 🖥 📱 ⎘ 4 x 🍴 ⬜ 🖼 ♨ ⊜ ⛨ 🔲 🔍 🏠
Directions:	[NE] from city centre
✈	Brussels 20km
A🚌	BH, BZ 200m
⛴	Zeebrugge 125km
🚂	Gare Bruxelles Nord 2km
🚌	61 200m ap Botanique
🚋	92, 93, 94 200m ap Botanique
U	Madou 200m; Botanique 200m

Brussels Ⓥ - Bruegel

1000 Brussels,
Heilig Geeststraat 2. (Corner:
Keizerslaan-Kapellekerk/Eglise de la
Chapelle).
☎ (02) 5110436
🖷 (02) 5120711

Open Dates:	🗓
Open Hours:	07.00-01.00hrs
Reservations:	(CC)
Price Range:	BEF 430-820 € 10.66-20.33 BBinc ⃞
Beds:	137 - 6x¹ 21x² 2x³ 9x⁴ 1x⁵ 1x⁶ 3x⁶ᵗʰ
Facilities:	♿ ♂♀ 31x ♂♀ ⍾ 🖥 💬 📱 📺 3 x 🍴 🖼 🔲 🔍 🐾 ⚠ ⊙
Directions:	[S] from city centre
✈	Brussels 15km
🚂	Central Station 300m
🚌	20 Midi Station 50m ap Chapelle
U	Central Station 300m

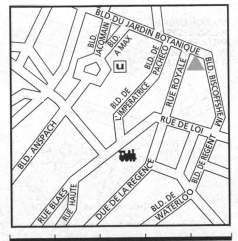

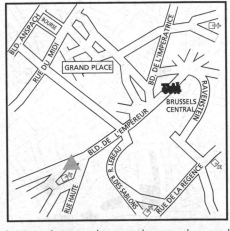

Gent [Ⓥ] - De Draecke

9000 Gent,
St Widostraat 11.
☎ (09) 2337050
🖷 (09) 2338001
✉ youthhostel.gent@skynet.be

Open Dates:	01.01-30.12
Open Hours:	07.00-23.00hrs (Night access)
Reservations:	Ⓡ ⒾⒷⓃ ⒸⒸ
Price Range:	BEF 510-600 € 12.64-14.87 BB^{inc} 🍲
Beds:	106 - 6x² 3x³ 10x⁴ 3x⁵ 5x⁶
Facilities:	♦♦♦ 27x ♦♦♦ 🍽 🍺 🚲 ☼ 🏔 TV 🗄 1 x🍴 📷 🔒 ⓲ 🚼

Directions:

✈	Brussel 65km
⛴	Oostende 55km
🚆	Gent St Pieters 4km
🚋	No. 1, 10, 11, 13 200m ap Gravensteen (Castle)

Liège [Ⓛ] - Georges Simenon

Rue Georges Simenon 2,
4020 Liège.
☎ (04) 3445689
🖷 (04) 3445687
✉ liege@laj.be

Open Dates:	01-06.01; 09.02-31.12
Open Hours:	07.30-01.00hrs
Reservations:	ⒾⒷⓃ ⒸⒸ
Price Range:	BEF 510-820 € 12.64-20.32 BB^{inc} 🍲
Beds:	204 - 16x⁴ 12x⁵ 4x⁶
Facilities:	♿ ♦♦♦ 40x ♦♦♦ 🍽 🔒 🏔 TV 📖 4 x🍴 🗄 📷 🔒 ⬆ ⓲ 🚼 ⛺

Directions: [0.5 SE] from city centre

✈	Brussels 100km
🚆	Liège Guillemins 2km
🚌	No. 4 300m

Attractions: 🏊 500m

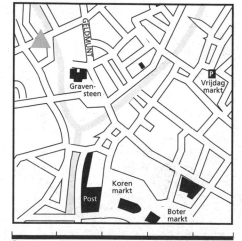

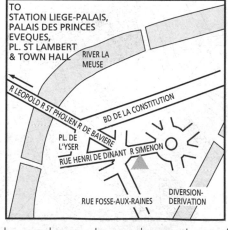

Namur [Ⓛ] - Felicien Rops

Felicien Rops,
Ave Félicien Rops,
8-5000 Namur.
☎ (081) 223688
✆ (081) 224412
✉ namur@laj.be

Open Dates:	01-06.01; 09.02-31.12
Reservations:	(IBN) (CC)
Price Range:	BEF 430-820 € 10.66-20.32 BB|ino
Beds:	100
Facilities:	♿ ††† ††† ⑩ ⛺ 🍴 🚲 ✿ 📺 📖1 x🍷 ⓪ Ⓟ ⓘ 💬 🌺

Directions:

🚂	Namur 3km
🚌	3, 4 300m
Attractions:	🚴 🏃

Oostende [Ⓥ] - De Ploate

8400 Oostende,
Langestraat 82.
☎ (059) 805297
✆ (059) 809274
✉ deploate@travel.to

Open Dates:	02.01-01.12; 15-22.12; 25-30.12
Open Hours:	07.30-24.00hrs (Night access)
Reservations:	(CC)
Price Range:	BEF 510 € 12.64 BB|inc
Beds:	124 - 3x³🛏 4x⁴🛏 3x⁵🛏 2x⁶🛏 9x⁶🛏
Facilities:	††† 21x ††† 🍴 🍺 🚌 📺 📖 🧺 1 x🍷 📷 ⑧ ⓘ 🏠

Directions:

✈	Oostende 5km
A🚌	Line 6 Airport 5km
⛴	Oostende 2km
🚂	Oostende 2km

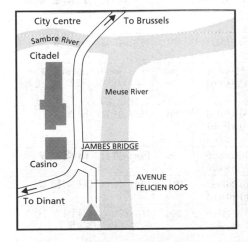

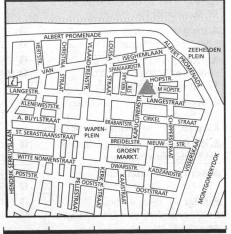

Location/Address	Telephone No. Fax No.	Beds	Opening Dates	Facilities
▲ Antwerpen Ⓥ - Op Sinjoorke (IBN) 2020 Antwerpen, Eric Sasselaan 2.	☎ (03) 2380273 🖷 (03) 2481932	131	08.01–15.12	⍨ �🍽 4S ♿ CC P ⬚ ☕ ⚲
▲ Blankenberge Ⓥ - De Wullok 8370 Blankenberge, Ruitersstraat 9. ⓔ jeugdherberg.de wullok@blankenberge.be	☎ (050) 415307 🖷 (050) 426014	79	12	⍨ ⍨ 🍽 R ♿ CC ☞ P ☕
▲ Bokrijk/Genk Ⓥ - De Roerdomp 3600 Bokrijk/Genk, Boekrakelaan 30.	☎ (089) 356220 🖷 (089) 303980	104	27.02–05.11	⍨ ⍨ 🍽 ♿ P ☕
▲ Bouillon Ⓛ - Sur La Hauteur Chemin du Christ 16, 6830 Bouillon. ⓔ bouillon@laj.be	☎ (061) 468137 🖷 (061) 467818	136	01–06.01; 09.02–31.12	⍨ 🍽 R CC ☞ P ⬚ ☕ ⚲
▲ Brugge Ⓥ - Europa (IBN) 8310 Brugge 4/Assebroek, Baron Ruzettelaan 143.	☎ (050) 352679 🖷 (050) 353732	212	08.01–15.12	⍨ 🍽 2SE ♿ CC P ☕ ⚲
▲ Brugge Ⓥ - Brugge/Dudzele "Herdersbrug" 8380 Dudzele/Brugge, Louis Coiseaukaai 46. ⓔ vjh.herdersbrug@yucom.be	☎ (050) 599321 🖷 (050) 599349	106	15.01–15.12	⍨ 🍽 ♿ P ⬚ ☕
▲ Brussels Ⓛ - Generation Europe (IBN) 4 Rue de l'Eléphant, 1080 Bruxelles. ⓔ brussels.europe@laj.be	☎ (02) 4103858 🖷 (02) 4103905	160	16.01–30.12	⍨ 🍽 ♿ CC P ⬚
▲ Brussels Ⓛ - Jacques Brel (IBN) Rue de la Sablonnière 30, 1000 Bruxelles. ⓔ brussels.brel@laj.be	☎ (02) 2180187 🖷 (02) 2172005	173	02.01–15.12	⍨ 🍽 1NE ♿ CC ⬚
▲ Brussels Ⓥ - Bruegel 1000 Brussels, Heilig Geeststraat 2. (Corner: Keizerslaan-Kapellekerk/ Eglise de la Chapelle).	☎ (02) 5110436 🖷 (02) 5120711	137	12	⍨ 🍽 1S ♿ CC ☕
▲ Champlon Ⓛ - Barriere De Champlon Rue de la Gendarmerie 6, Barrière de Champlon, 6971 Champlon. ⓔ champlon@laj.be	☎ (084) 455294 🖷 (084) 457045	72	01–06.01; 09.02–31.12	🍽 R CC ☞ P ⬚ ☕ ⚲
▲ Diest Ⓥ - Den Drossaard 3290 Diest, St. Jansstraat 2A (Warande).	☎ (013) 313721 🖷 (013) 313721	70	15.02–15.11	⍨ 🍽 ☕ ⚲
▲ Gent Ⓥ - De Draecke (IBN) 9000 Gent, St Widostraat 11. ⓔ youthhostel.gent@skynet.be	☎ (09) 2337050 🖷 (09) 2338001	106	01.01–30.12	⍨ 🍽 R CC ☕ ⚲ ⚙
▲ Geraardsbergen Ⓥ - 'T Schipke 9500 Geraardsbergen, Kampstraat 59. (Recreatiedomein 'De Gavers').	☎ (054) 416189 🖷 (054) 419461	104	23.02–05.11	⍨ ♿ ☞
▲ Huizingen Ⓥ - 'T Golvende Brabant 1654 Huizingen, Prov Domein.	☎ (02) 3830026 🖷 (02) 3830026	58	15.02–30.11	⍨ R ☞
▲ Kortrijk Ⓥ - Groeninghe 8500 Kortrijk, Passionistenlaan 1A.	☎ (056) 201442 🖷 (056) 204663	96	17.01–22.12	⍨ 🍽 P ☕
▲ Liège Ⓛ - Georges Simenon (IBN) Rue Georges Simenon 2, 4020 Liège. ⓔ liege@laj.be	☎ (04) 3445689 🖷 (04) 3445687	204	01–06.01; 09.02–31.12	⍨ 🍽 ♿ CC ☞ ⬚

Location/Address	Telephone No. Fax No.	Beds	Opening Dates	Facilities
▲ **Maldegem** Ⓥ - Die Loyale 9990 Maldegem, Gentsesteenweg 124.	☎ (050) 713121 📠 (050) 719070	74	15.02–15.11	� 🍴 ♿ 🅿 🚲
▲ **Malmédy** Ⓛ - Hautes Fagnes 4960 Malmédy, Bévercé 8a. ✉ malmedy@laj.be	☎ (080) 338386 📠 (080) 770504	178	01.01–26.08; 17.09–23.11; 30.11–31.12	♦ 🍴 Ⓡ 1N ♿ CC ✂ 🅿 🔲 ☕ 🚲
▲ **Mechelen** Ⓥ - De Zandpoort Zandpoortvest, 2800 Mechelen.		120	Open from 01.05	♦ 🍴 ♿ 🅿 ☕ 🚲
▲ **Mons** Ⓛ Rampe Du Chateau, 7000 Mons. ✉ info@laj.be	☎ (02) 2195676 📠 (02) 2191451	146	01.03–31.12	♦ 🍴 Ⓡ 0.1N ♿ CC ✂ 🅿 🔲 ☕ 🚲
▲ **Namur** Ⓛ - Felicien Rops (IBN) **Felicien Rops, Ave Félicien Rops, 8-5000 Namur.** ✉ namur@laj.be	☎ (081) 223688 📠 (081) 224412	100	01–06.01; 09.02–31.12	♦ 🍴 ♿ CC ✂ 🅿 🔲 ☕ 🚲 ☼
▲ **Nijlen** Ⓥ - 'T Pannenhuis 2560 Nijlen, Wijngaardberg 42.	☎ (03) 4110733 📠 (03) 4110725	64	15.02–15.11	♦ 🍴 ✂ ☕
▲ **Oostduinkerke** Ⓥ - De Peerdevisser 8670 Oostduinkerke, Duinparklaan 41.	☎ (058) 512649 📠 (058) 522880	135	01.02–15.12	♦ 🍴 ♿ 🅿 ☕ 🚲
▲ **Oostende** Ⓥ - De Ploate **8400 Oostende, Langestraat 82.** ✉ deploate@travel.to	☎ (059) 805297 📠 (059) 809274	124	02.01–01.12; 15–22.12; 25–30.12	♦ 🍴 CC ☕
▲ **Sankt-Vith** Ⓥ - Ardennen-Eifel 4780 St Vith, Rodterstrasse 13A.	☎ (080) 229331 📠 (080) 229332	90	01.01–23.12; 27–31.12	♦ 🍴 ♿ 🅿 ☕ 🚲
▲ **Tilff** Ⓛ - Ferme du Château 4130 Tilff, Esplanade de l'abeille 9. ✉ tilff@laj.be	☎ (04) 3445689 📠 (04) 3445687	35	01–06.01; 09.02–31.12 (♦ only)	Ⓡ ✂ 🅿 🚲
▲ **Tongeren** Ⓥ - Begeinhof 3700 Tongeren, St Ursulastraat 1.	☎ (012) 391370 📠 (012) 391348	82	🔲	♦ 🍴 ♿ 🅿 ☕
▲ **Tournai** Ⓛ 7500 Tournai, Rue Saint-Martin 64. ✉ tournai@laj.be	☎ (069) 216136 📠 (069) 216140	100	01–06.01; 09.02–31.12	♦ 🍴 Ⓡ ♿ CC ✂ ☕
▲ **Voeren** Ⓥ - De Veurs 3790 St Martens Voeren, Comberg 29B.	☎ (04) 3811110 📠 (04) 3811313	90	23.02–11.11; 21–31.12	♦ 🍴 ☕ 🚲
▲ **Westerlo** Ⓥ - Boswachtershuis 2260 Westerlo, Papedreef 1.	☎ (014) 547938 📠 (014) 547938	82	01.03–13.11 (For ♦ 01.03–23.12)	♦ 🍴 🅿 ☕ 🚲
▲ **Zoersel** Ⓥ - Gagelhof 2980 Zoersel, Gagelhoflaan 18. ✉ zoersel@vjh.be	☎ (03) 3851642 📠 (03) 3851642	62	01.06–30.09 (For ♦ 🔲 Ⓡ)	♦ 🍴 Ⓡ ✂ 🅿 🔲 ☕ 🚲

HOSTELLING INTERNATIONAL

Make your credit card bookings at these centres
Réservez par cartes de crédit aux centres suivants
Reservieren Sie per Kreditkarte bei diesen Zentren
Reserve con tarjeta de crédito en los siguientes centros

English

Australia	☎ (2) 9261 1111
Canada	☎ (800) 663 5777
England & Wales	☎ (1629) 581 418
France	☎ (1) 44 89 87 27
Northern Ireland	☎ (28) 9032 4733
Republic of Ireland	☎ (1) 830 1766
New Zealand	☎ (3) 379 9808
Scotland	☎ (8701) 553 255
Switzerland	☎ (1) 360 1414
USA	☎ (202) 783 6161

Français

Angleterre & Pays de Galles	☎ (1692) 581 418
Australie	☎ (2) 9261 1111
Canada	☎ (800) 663 5777
Écosse	☎ (8701) 553 255
États-Unis	☎ (202) 783 6161
France	☎ (1) 44 89 87 27
Irlande du Nord	☎ (28) 9032 4733
Nouvelle-Zélande	☎ (3) 379 9808
République d'Irlande	☎ (1) 830 1766
Suisse	☎ (1) 360 1414

Deutsch

Australien	☎ (2) 9261 1111
England & Wales	☎ (1629) 581 418
Frankreich	☎ (1) 44 89 87 27
Irland	☎ (1) 830 1766
Kanada	☎ (800) 663 5777
Neuseeland	☎ (3) 379 9808
Nordirland	☎ (28) 9032 4733
Schottland	☎ (8701) 553 255
Schweiz	☎ (1) 360 1414
USA	☎ (202) 783 6161

Español

Australia	☎ (2) 9261 1111
Canadá	☎ (800) 663 5777
Escocia	☎ (8701) 553 255
Estados Unidos	☎ (202) 783 6161
Francia	☎ (1) 44 89 87 27
Inglaterra y Gales	☎ (1629) 581 418
Irlanda del Norte	☎ (28) 9032 4733
Nueva Zelanda	☎ (3) 379 9808
República de Irlanda	☎ (1) 830 1766
Suiza	☎ (1) 360 1414

IBN INTERNATIONAL BOOKING NETWORK

Croatia

CROATIE

KROATIEN

CROACIA

Hrvatski Ferijalni i Hostelski Savez
(Croatian Youth Hostel Association),
Savska cesta 5/1
10000 Zagreb, Croatia.

t (385) 4829294
f (385) 4829296
e hfhs@zg.tel.hr
www.ncomp.com/hfhs

Office Hours: Mon-Fri 08.00-16.00hrs

Travel Section: HFHS Travel Section,
Dežmanova 9, 10000 Zagreb, Croatia.

t (385) (1) 4847474
f (385) (1) 4847472
e hfhs-cms@zg.tel.hr

Office Hours: Mon-Fri 08.00-16.00hrs

A copy of the Hostel Directory for this Country can be obtained from:
The National Office

Capital:	Zagreb	**Population:**	4,784,265
Language:	Croatian	**Size:**	56,538 sq km
Currency:	Kuna (Kn)	**Telephone Country Code:**	385

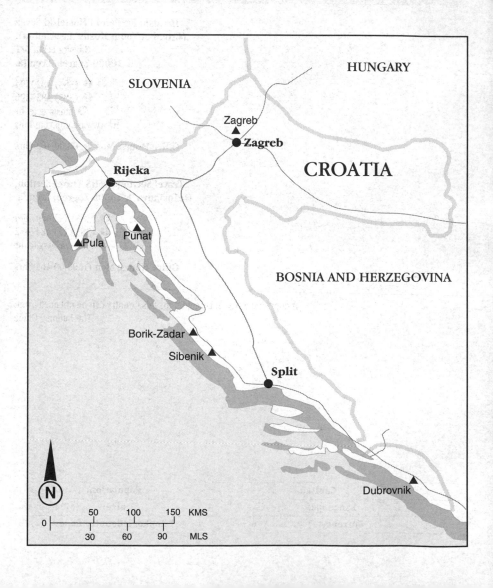

English

Hostels are located in cities and on the coast.

Price range

Price range Kunas 58-80. $\boxed{BB}^{inc}$ 🛏.

Rooms and Reservations

R during May-Sep. (2🛏 3🛏 4🛏).
Reservations via National Booking Centre or
Hostel by ❶ ❷. Smoking is limited - please
check.

Guests

Membership Card and Passport/Photo ID are
required. ♦♦♦ welcome. Group bookings via
National Booking Centre or Hostel by ❶ ❷.

Open times

Main hostels: open 🗓, 🕔. Reception open:
08:00-20:00hrs. **Other hostels:** open Jun-Sep,
🕔. Reception open: 08:00-20:00hrs. **Seasonal
hostels** are generally open Jun-Sep.

Meals

🍴 BLD **R** For individuals & for ♦♦♦.

Travelling around

For ease of travel use ✈ 🚄 ⛴ 🚌.

Travel/Activity Packages

Tours/sightseeing, water sports and
accommodation/transport packages available.
Package bookings via National Booking Centre
or Hostel by ❶ ❷.

Passports and Visas

Passport and Visa required.

Health

Emergency medical treatment is free.

Français

Les auberges sont situées dans les villes et sur le
littoral.

Tarifs des nuitées

Tarifs des nuitées 58-80 Kunas. $\boxed{BB}^{inc}$ 🛏.

Chambres et réservations

R mai-sep. (2🛏 3🛏 4🛏). Réservations via
le Centre National de Réservation ou l'auberge
par ❶ ❷. Il est permis de fumer dans
certaines chambres - veuillez vérifier.

Usagers

La carte d'adhérent ainsi que le passeport/pièce
d'identité avec photo sont à présenter. Accueil
des ♦♦♦. Réservations pour groupes via le Centre
National de Réservation ou l'auberge par ❶ ❷.

Horaires d'ouverture

Grandes auberges: ouvertes 🗓, 🕔. Accueil
ouvert entre 8h-20h. **Autres auberges:**
ouvertes juin-sept, 🕔. Accueil ouvert entre
8h-20h. **Auberges saisonnières** ouvertes
généralement juin-sep.

Repas

🍴 BLD **R** Pour individuels & pour ♦♦♦.

Déplacements

Modes de transport recommandés ✈ 🚄
⛴ 🚌.

Forfaits Voyages/Activités

Forfaits circuits touristiques, sports aquatiques
et hébergement/transport disponibles.
Réservations des forfaits via le Centre National
de Réservation ou l'auberge par ❶ ❷.

Passeports et visas

Passeport et visa obligatoires.

Santé

Soins d'urgence gratuits.

Deutsch

Herbergen befinden sich in Städten und an der Küste.

Preisspanne

Preisspanne 58-80 Kunas. [BB]inc 🛏.

Zimmer und Reservierungen

R während Mai-Sept. (2🐷 3🐷 4🐷).
Reservierungen über Nationales Buchungszentrum oder Herberge per ❶ ❸.
Rauchen ist begrenzt - bitte checken.

Gäste

Mitgliedsausweis und Reisepass/Personalausweis sind erforderlich. ††† willkommen. Gruppenbuchungen über Nationales Buchungszentrum oder Herberge per ❶ ❸.

Öffnungszeiten

Hauptherbergen: Zugang 🔟, ⏲. Rezeption zwischen 08:00-20:00Uhr. **Andere Herbergen:** Zugang zwischen Jun-Sep, ⏲. Rezeption zwischen 08:00-20:00Uhr. **Saison-Herbergen** sind normalerweise Jun-Sept geöffnet.

Mahlzeiten

🍽 BLD **R** Für Einzelreisende & für †††.

Reisen im Land

Reisen ist einfach mit ✈ 🚐 ⛴ 🚌.

Reise-/Aktivitäten-Packages

Touren/sightseeing, Wassersport und Unterkunft/Transport-Packages erhältlich. Package-Buchungen über Nationales Buchungszentrum oder Herberge per ❶ ❸.

Reisepässe und Visa

Reisepass/Einreisevisum erforderlich.

Gesundheit

Nur im Notfall sind medizinische Behandlungen kostenlos.

Español

Los albergues están situados en las ciudades y la costa.

Tarifas mínima y máxima

Tarifas mínima y máxima 58-80 Kunas. [BB]inc 🛏.

Habitaciones y Reservas

R en may-sep. (2🐷 3🐷 4🐷). Reservas a través de la Central Nacional de Reservas o el albergue por ❶ ❸. Está permitido fumar sólo en algunas salas/habitaciones - infórmese.

Huéspedes

Los huéspedes deben presentar su Carnet de Alberguista y su pasaporte o carnet de identidad. Se admiten †††. Reservas de grupo a través de la Central Nacional de Reservas o el albergue por ❶ ❸.

Horarios y fechas de apertura

Albergues principales - abiertos 🔟, ⏲. Horario de recepción: 08:00-20:00h. **Otros albergues** - abiertos jun-sep, ⏲. Horario de recepción: 08:00-20:00h. **Albergues de temporada** suelen abrir: jun-sep.

Comidas

🍽 BLD **R** Para individuales y para †††.

Desplazamientos

Transportes recomendados: ✈ 🚐 ⛴ 🚌.

Viajes Combinados con Actividades

Viajes combinados con visitas turísticas, deportes náuticos y alojamiento/transporte. Reserva de viajes combinados a través de la Central Nacional de Reservas o el albergue por ❶ ❸.

Pasaportes y Visados

Pasaporte y visado obligatorios.

Información Sanitaria

Asistencia médica de urgencia gratuita.

Dubrovnik

Bana Jelačića 15-17,
20000 Dubrovnik.
📞 (20) 423241
📠 (20) 412592
📧 hfhs-du@du.hinet.hr

Open Dates: 🗓

Open Hours: 🕐

Reservations: **R**

Price Range: $10-12 BB inc 🍽

Beds: 80 - 1x 14x 4x

Facilities: 🚻 2x 🚻 🍴 🛁 🛋 📺 1 x 🍽
🖼 ✏ 🎱

Directions:

✈ Dubrovnik 10km

A🚌 Gruž Station 500m

⛴ Gruž-Luka 1km

🚌 #4 & 5 100m ap Montovijerna

Attractions: ⚓ 300m

"Travel only with thy equals or thy betters; if there are none, travel alone."

"Ne voyage qu'avec tes égaux ou tes supérieurs; si tu n'en as pas, voyage tout seul."

„Reise nur mit deinesgleichen oder Höherstehenden; wenn es keine gibt, reise allein."

"Viaja solamente con tus iguales o con tus superiores; si no tienes ninguno, viaja solo."

The Dhammapada

[Map]

Gruž Harbour

JADRANSKA CESTA
GORNJI KONO
OD REPUBLIKE
VLADIMIRI NAZORA
NIKOLE TESLE
BANA JELACICA
SV. MIHAJLA
VOJNOVICA
IVA
DR. ANTE STARCEVICA
Boninovo Beach
GORICA
SV. VLAHA

0   1.5km

Location/Address	Telephone No. Fax No.	Beds	Opening Dates	Facilities
▲ **Borik-Zadar** YH Borik, Obala Kneza Trpimira 76, 23 000 Zadar.	☎ (23) 331145 🖷 (23) 331190	330	01.04–30.11	††† 🍽 Ⓡ P
▲ **Dubrovnik** **Bana Jelačića 15-17, 20000 Dubrovnik.** 🅴 hfhs-du@du.hinet.hr	☎ (20) 423241 🖷 (20) 412592	80	🗓	††† 🍽 Ⓡ ♂
▲ **Pula** Zaljev Valsaline 4, 52 000 Pula. 🅴 hfhs-pula@pu.tel.hr	☎ (52) 210002 (52) 210003 🖷 (52) 212394	145	🗓	††† 🍽 Ⓡ P
Zadar ☞**Borik-Zadar**				

YOUTH HOSTEL ACCOMMODATION
OUTSIDE THE ASSURED STANDARDS SCHEME

Punat, Island KRK YH Punat 51 521 Punat, Otok KRK.	☎ (51) 854037 🖷 (51) 4841269	125	01.06–30.09	††† 🍽 Ⓡ P
Šubićevac-Šibenik YH Šubićevac, Put Luguša 1, 22 000 Šibenik.	☎ (22) 216410 🖷 (22) 216410	40	01.04–31.10	††† Ⓡ P
Zagreb Petrinjska 77, 10 000 Zagreb.	☎ (1) 4841261 🖷 (1) 4841269	210	🗓	††† Ⓡ P

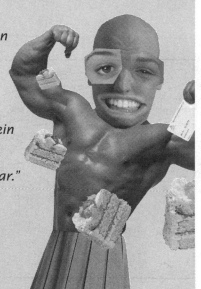

"To travel hopefully is a better thing than to arrive."

"Voyager avec espoir est mieux que d'arriver."

„Mit Hoffnung zu reisen ist besser, als sein Ziel zu erreichen."

"Viajar con esperanza es mejor que llegar."

Robert Louis Stevenson

Czech Republic

LA REPUBLIQUE TCHEQUE
DIE TSCHECHISCHE REPUBLIK
LA REPUBLICA CHECA

**KMC Club of Young Travellers,
Karolíny Světle 30, 11000 Praha 1,
Czech Republic**

ⓣ (420) (2) 22220081
(420) (2) 22220347
(420) (2)22221328
ⓕ (420) (2) 22220347
(420) (2) 22221328
ⓔ kmc@kmc.cz
🖳 http://www.kmc.cz

Office Hours: Monday-Friday, 09.00-17.00hrs

A copy of the Hostel Directory for this Country can be obtained from:
The National Office

Capital:	Prague		**Population:**	10,500,000
Language:	Czech		**Size:**	78,864 sq km
Currency:	Kč (Czech Koruna)		**Telephone Country Code:**	420

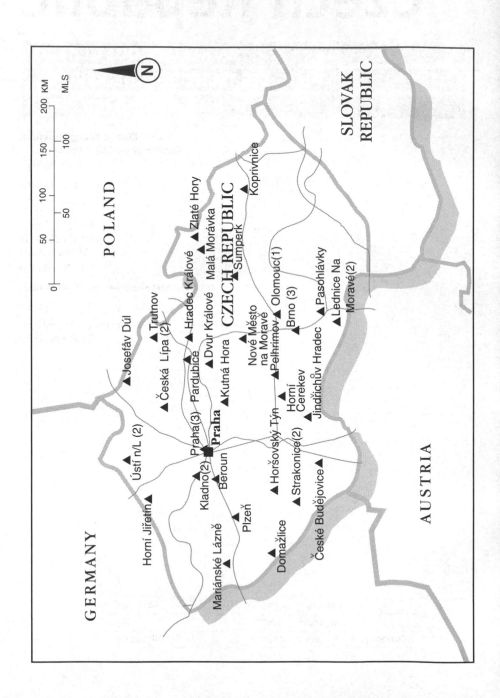

LA REPUBLIQUE TCHEQUE • CZECH REPUBLIC 91

English

Hostels are located in cities, in the countryside and on hills/mountains.

Price range

Price range CSK 200-600. [BB]inc 🛄.

Rooms and Reservations

R 🖳 (All Rooms). Reservations via 🖳 National Booking Centre, Hostel or National Office by ❶ ❷ ❸. (Reservation charges may apply). Smoking is limited - please check.

Guests

Membership Card and Passport/Photo ID are required. Pets are allowed - check with hostel. ♚♚♚ welcome. Group bookings via 🖳 National Booking Centre, Hostel or National Office by ❶ ❷ ❸ (Reservation charges may apply).

Open times

Main hostels: open 🖳, 14:00-20:00hrs. Reception open: ⊙. Resident manager. **Other hostels:** open 🖳, 14:00-20:00hrs. Reception open: 07:00-10:00hrs, 14:00-22:00hrs. Resident manager. **Seasonal hostels** are generally open May-Sep.

Meals

🍽 BD **R** For individuals & for ♚♚♚. ✇ Not all utensils provided - check with hostel.

Discounts

HI Member Discounts available - see discounts section and www.iyhf.org.

Travelling around

For ease of travel use ✈ 🚋 🚐 Self-Drive.

Travel/Activity Packages

Tours/sightseeing and accommodation/transport packages available. Package bookings

via 🖳 National Booking Centre or National Office by ❶ ❷ ❸.

Passports and Visas

Passport and Visa required.

Health

Medical insurance is recommended.

Français

Les auberges sont situées dans les villes, à la campagne et à la montagne.

Tarifs des nuitées

Tarifs des nuitées 200-600 CSK. [BB]inc 🛄.

Chambres et réservations

R 🖳 (Toutes chambres). Réservations via 🖳 le Centre National de Réservation, l'auberge ou le Bureau National par ❶ ❷ ❸. (Des frais de réservation pourront vous être facturés). Il est permis de fumer dans certaines chambres - veuillez vérifier.

Usagers

La carte d'adhérent ainsi que le passeport/pièce d'identité avec photo sont à présenter. Les animaux domestiques sont autorisés mais vérifiez lesquels auprès de l'auberge. Accueil des ♚♚♚. Réservations pour groupes via 🖳 le Centre National de Réservation, l'auberge ou le Bureau National par ❶ ❷ ❸ (Des frais de réservation pourront vous être facturés).

Horaires d'ouverture

Grandes auberges: ouvertes 🖳, entre 14h-20h. Accueil ouvert ⊙. Gérant réside sur place. **Autres auberges:** ouvertes 🖳, entre 14h-20h. Accueil ouvert entre 7h-10h, 14h-22h. Gérant réside sur place. **Auberges saisonnières** ouvertes généralement mai-sep.

Repas

🍴 BD **R** Pour individuels & pour 👥. ⚲
Pas tous les ustensils sont fournis - à vérifier
auprès de l'auberge.

Remises

Remises pour les adhérents HI - voir la section
"Remises" et notre site: www.iyhf.org.

Déplacements

Modes de transport recommandés ✈ 🚆
🚌 Voiture.

Forfaits Voyages/Activités

Forfaits circuits touristiques et hébergement/
transport disponibles. Réservations des forfaits
via 🖥 le Centre National de Réservation ou le
Bureau National par ❶ ❷ ❸.

Passeports et visas

Passeport et visa obligatoires.

Santé

Une assurance médicale de voyage est
conseillée.

Deutsch

Herbergen befinden sich in Städten, auf dem
Land und in Bergen/Gebirgen.

Preisspanne

Preisspanne 200-600 CSK. [BB]inc 🍴.

Zimmer und Reservierungen

R 🛏 (Alle Zimmer). Reservierungen über
🖥 Nationales Buchungszentrum, Herberge
oder Landesverband per ❶ ❷ ❸.
(Reservierungskosten könnten anfallen).
Rauchen ist begrenzt - bitte checken.

Gäste

Mitgliedsausweis und Reisepass/
Personalausweis sind erforderlich. Haustiere
sind erlaubt - in der Herberge nachfragen.
👥 willkommen. Gruppenbuchungen über 🖥
Nationales Buchungszentrum, Herberge oder
Landesverband per ❶ ❷
❸ (Reservierungskosten könnten anfallen).

Öffnungszeiten

Hauptherbergen: Zugang 🛏,
14:00-20:00Uhr. Rezeption ☺.
Herbergsmanager wohnt im Haus. **Andere
Herbergen:** Zugang 🛏, 14:00-20:00Uhr.
Rezeption zwischen 07:00-10:00Uhr,
14:00-22:00Uhr. Herbergsmanager wohnt im
Haus. **Saison-Herbergen** sind normalerweise
Mai-Sept geöffnet.

Mahlzeiten

🍴 BD **R** Für Einzelreisende & für 👥. ⚲
Nicht alle Utensilien werden bereitgestellt - in
der Herberge nachfragen.

Ermäßigungen

HI-Mitgliedsrabatt ist erhältlich – siehe Teil für
Rabatte und Ermäßigungen und www.iyhf.org.

Reisen im Land

Reisen ist einfach mit ✈ 🚆 🚌
Selbstfahrer.

Reise-/Aktivitäten-Packages

Touren/sightseeing und Unterkunft/Transport-
Packages erhältlich. Package-Buchungen über
🖥 Nationales Buchungszentrum oder
Landesverband per ❶ ❷ ❸.

Reisepässe und Visa

Reisepass/Einreisevisum erforderlich.

Gesundheit

Unfall-/Krankenversicherung wird empfohlen.

Español

Los albergues están situados en las ciudades, el campo y la montaña.

Tarifas mínima y máxima

Tarifas mínima y máxima 200-600 CSK. BB inc ▯.

Habitaciones y Reservas

R ▯ (todas las habitaciones). Reservas por ▯ o a través de la Central Nacional de Reservas, el albergue o la Asociación Nacional por ❶ ❶ ❷. (Es posible que se aplique un suplemento en concepto de gastos de reserva). Está permitido fumar sólo en algunas salas/habitaciones - infórmese.

Huéspedes

Los huéspedes deben presentar su Carnet de Alberguista y su pasaporte o carnet de identidad. Se admiten animales - consulte con el albergue. Se admiten ▯. Reservas de grupo por ▯ o a través de la Central Nacional de Reservas, el albergue o la Asociación Nacional por ❶ ❶ ❷ (Es posible que se aplique un suplemento en concepto de gastos de reserva).

Horarios y fechas de apertura

Albergues principales - abiertos ▯, 14:00-20:00h. Horario de recepción: ▯. Gerente residente. **Otros albergues** - abiertos ▯, 14:00-20:00h. Horario de recepción: 07:00-10:00h, 14:00-22:00h. Gerente residente. **Albergues de temporada** suelen abrir: may-sep.

Comidas

▯ BD R Para individuales y para ▯. ▯ La cocina no dispone de todos los utensilios - consulte con el albergue.

Descuentos

Se conceden descuentos a los miembros de Hostelling International – véase la sección sobre descuentos y nuestra página Internet en www.iyhf.org.

Desplazamientos

Transportes recomendados: ▯ ▯ ▯ Automóvil.

Viajes Combinados con Actividades

Viajes combinados con visitas turísticas y alojamiento/transporte. Reserva de viajes combinados por ▯ o a través de la Central Nacional de Reservas o la Asociación Nacional por ❶ ❶ ❷.

Pasaportes y Visados

Pasaporte y visado obligatorios.

Información Sanitaria

Seguro médico recomendado.

"Everywhere is nowhere. When a person spends all his time in foreign travel, he ends by having many acquaintances, but no friends."

"Partout est nulle part. Lorsque quelqu'un passe son temps à voyager à l'étranger, il finit avec beaucoup de connaissances, mais sans amis."

„Überall ist nirgendwo. Wenn jemand ständig fremde Länder bereist, hat er letztendlich viele Bekannte, aber keine Freunde."

"Todas partes es ninguna parte. Cuanda una persona dedica todo su tiempo a viajar al extranjero, acaba teniendo muchos conocidos, pero ningún amigo."

Seneca

Praha - Hotel Beta

Roškotova 1225/I,
14700 Praha 4 - Krč.
📞 (2) 41445252
📠 (2) 41445090
✉ beta@alphanet.cz

Open Dates: 01.01-22.12; 26-31.12

Open Hours: 🕓

Reservations: **R** ⌐CC⌐

Price Range: CSK 400-450   BB inc 🍴

Beds: 250 - 40x² 30x³ 20x⁴

Facilities: ♿ ♦♦♦ 5x ♦♦♦ 🍽 ▥ 📺 🖼 ♨
            🅿 ⓘ

Directions:

✈   Praha-Ruzyně 20km

🚃   Praha-Hlavní nádraží 9km

🚌   124,205 50m ap U Statku

U   U-Line - Budějovická

Attractions: ⚲2km ⚓3km

"Though we travel the world over to find the beautiful, we must carry it with us or we find it not."

"Bien que nous parcourons le monde pour trouver ce qui est beau, nous devons le porter en nous ou nous ne le trouvons pas."

„Obwohl wir die ganze Welt bereisen, um das Schöne zu finden, müssen wir es in uns selber tragen, sonst werden wir es nicht finden."

"Aunque demos la vuelta al mundo buscando la belleza, tenemos que llevarla dentro de nosotros mismos o no la encontraremos"

Ralph Waldo Emerson

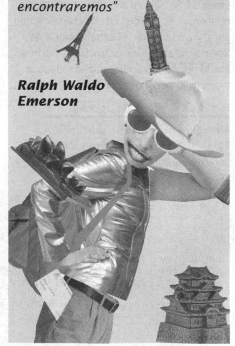

PRAGUE CENTRE

JEREMENKEVA   OLBRACHT

Kovarovicova

RUDECKOVA

PANUSKOVA

Ra-Rado

Roškotova

Bus Stop
205,
124

ZELENÝ PRUH

ANTALA STAŠKA

Budejovicka
M-METRO C

Tocita

ROZARCINA

TOCITA

NA ST. VINICI

NAD OBCL L

BRANICKA

0   2km

Location/Address	Telephone No. Fax No.	Beds	Opening Dates	Facilities
△ **Beroun** - Hotel Barbora Garni Na Podolí 740, Beroun.	☎ (311) 25442 🖷 (311) 612500	26	🔲12	👫 🍽 ℝ ♿ 🅿 ☕
▲ **Brno** - Koleje Jana Taufera MZLU Jana Babáka 3/5, 61600 Brno.	☎ (5) 41321335 🖷 (5) 41248966	30	🔲12	👫 🍽 ℝ ♿ ♂ 🅿
▲ **Brno** - Penzion Palacký Kolejní 2, 61200 Brno.	☎ (5) 41641111 🖷 (5) 41210409	80	🔲12	👫 🍽 ℝ ♿ 🅿 ☕
▲ **Česká Lípa** - Student Hotel Lípa Ul. 28. října 2707, 47006 Česká Lípa. 🅴 hotel.lipa@cinet.cz	☎ (425) 22966 🖷 (425) 22966	210	🔲12	👫 🍽 ℝ 1N ♿ 🅿 📷 🚲 ⚡
△ **Česká Lípa** - Vila Adéla Česká Lípa, 47001 Česká Lípa, Děčínská 1414.	☎ (425) 52786, (425) 52831	26	🔲12	👫 ℝ ♂
▲ **České Budějovice** - Junior Hostel Dobrovodská 120/762, 37000 České Budějovice.	☎ (38) 7412382	40	🔲12	👫 🍽 ℝ 4NE ♿ ♂ 🅿 🚲
△ **Domažlice** - Domov mládeže Obchodníakademie 34401 Domažlice, Boženy Němcové 116.	☎ (189) 722386	96	🔲12	👫 🍽 ℝ ♂
▲ **Dvůr Králové nad Labem** - Hostel Student E. Krásnohorské 2069, 54401 Dvůr Králové nad Labem.	☎ (437) 820184 🖷 (437) 820194	200	🔲17	👫 🍽 ℝ ♿ ♂ 🅿
△ **Horní Jiřetín** - Zámek 43543 Horní Jiřetín, Zámek Jezeří.	☎ (35) 93338	15	🔲12	👫 ℝ ♂ 🅿
△ **Horšovský Týn** - Domov mládeže SZŠ 34601 Horšovský Týn, Nádražní ulice 43.	☎ (188) 2319, (188) 2432	45	🔲12	👫 🍽 ℝ ♂
△ **Hříběci.u Horní Cerekve** - Ubytovna Domu Dětí a Mládeže 39403 Horní Cerekev.	☎ (366) 26411 🖷 (366) 26411	38	01.06–15.09	👫 🍽 🅿
▲ **Hradec Králové** - Hotel Garni Na Kotli 1147, 50296 Hradec Králové. 🅴 hotel.garni@worldoneline.cz	☎ (49) 5763600 🖷 (49) 5262591	67	🔲12	👫 🍽 🅿
▲ **Jindřichův Hradec** - Pension uTkadlen, Pod Hradem 7/IV., Jindřichův Hradec.	☎ (331) 321348 🖷 (331) 326076	20	🔲12	👫 🍽 ℝ 🅿
▲ **Josefův Důl** - Sportcentrum Peklo 46844 Josefův Důl 960.	☎ (428) 381068 🖷 ((428) 381103	126	🔲12	👫 🍽 ℝ ♿ 🅿 ☕
△ **Kladno** - Domov mládeže SOŠ, SOU a U 27201 Kladno 2, ul 5, května 1870.	☎ (312) 623165 🖷 (312) 623166	80	🔲12	👫 🍽 ℝ
△ **Kladno** - Domov mládeže SOŠ, SOU a U K Nemocnici 2007, 27203 Kladno, Dubská.	☎ (312) 627416 🖷 (312) 628598	130	🔲12	👫 🍽 ℝ ♿ ♂ 🅿
△ **Kopřivnice** - Turistická ubytovna Pod lesem Komenského 622, 74221 Kopřivnice.	☎ (656) 721357 🖷 (656) 811064	150	🔲12	👫 🍽 ℝ ♿ ♂ 🅿
△ **Kutná Hora** - O-KČT TJ Turista Národního odboje 56, 28401 Kutná Hora.	☎ (327) 512960 🖷 (327) 514961	36	🔲12	👫 ℝ ♿ ♂ 🅿
▲ **Lednice na Moravě** - Koleje MZLU Petra Bezruče Valtická 538, 69144 Lednice na Moravě.	☎ (627) 340161 🖷 (627) 340983	220	🔲12	👫 🍽 ℝ ♿

Location/Address	Telephone No. Fax No.	Beds	Opening Dates	Facilities
▲ **Malá Morávka - Karlov** - Student Penzion Zámeček, 79336 Malá Morávka - Karlov. ℮ petrsenk@volny.cz	☏ (603) 335308 ℻ (603) 335308	60	🗐	♔ 🅾 Ⓡ ♿ ♂ 🅿 🚲
▲ **Mariánské Lázně** - Hotel Krakonos 35334 Mariánské Lázně. ℮ krankonoš.ml@iol.cz	☏ (165) 622624 ℻ (165) 622383	250	🗐	🅾 Ⓡ
▲ **Nové Město na Moravě** - Hotelová ubytovna DUO 59231 Nové Město na Moravě, Masarykova 1493.	☏ (616) 916245	150	🗐	♔ 🅾 Ⓡ ♂
▲ **Olomouc** - Univerzita Palackého Šmeralova 12, 77111 Olomouc.	☏ (608) 5226057 ℻ (608) 5226057	66	🗐	♔ 🅾 Ⓡ ♿ ♂ 🅿
▲ **Pardubice** - Harmony Club Hotely Bělehradská 458, 53009 Paradubice.	☏ (40) 6435020 ℻ (40) 6435025	90	🗐	♔ 🅾 Ⓡ ♿ 🆑 ♂ 🅿 🍴
△ *Pasohlávky - Turist Unimo 69122 Pasohlávky 60.*	☏ *(626) 427712* ℻ *(626) 427712*	*90*	🗐	♔ 🅾 Ⓡ ♿ ♂ 🅿 🍴
△ *Pelhřimov - JENA Ubytovna Pražská 1541, 39301 Pelhřimov.*	☏ *(366) 22045*	*66*	🗐	♔ 🅾 Ⓡ ♿ ♂
▲ **Plzeň** - Hostel SOU č.4 Vejprnická 56, 31802 Plzeň.	☏ (19) 286443 ℻ (19) 286443	80	🗐	♔ 🅾 Ⓡ 3W 🅿
▲ **Praha** - Hostel Advantage Sokolská 11-13, 12000 Praha 2.	☏ (2) 24914062 ℻ (2) 24914067	96	🗐	♔ 🅾 Ⓡ ♿ 🍴
▲ **Praha** - Hotel Beta **Roškotova 1225/I, 14700 Praha 4 - Krč.** ℮ beta@alphanet.cz	☏ (2) 41445252 ℻ (2) 41445090	250	🗐	♔ 🅾 Ⓡ ♿ 🆑 🅿
△ *Praha - Hotel Standart Vodní Stavby, 17000 Praha 7 - Holešovice, Přístavní 2.*	☏ *(2) 875258 or (2) 875674* ℻ *(2) 806752*	*150*	🗐	♔ 🅾 Ⓡ
▲ **Strakonice** - Domov mládeže Želivského 291, 38642 Strakonice.	☏ (342) 23281	70	🗐	♔ 🅾 Ⓡ ♿ ♂ 🅿
△ *Strakonice - Hotel Garnet Dr.J.Fifky 186, 38602 Strakonice.*	☏ *(342) 321984* ℻ *(342) 28231*	*104*	🗐	♔ 🅾 Ⓡ ♿ 🅿 🍴
▲ **Trutnov** - Pension Ùsvit M.Gorkého 421, 54101 Trutnov.	☏ (439) 811405 ℻ (439) 826406	200	🗐	♔ 🅾 Ⓡ 🅿
△ *Ústí n/L - Ubytovna Junior 40000 Ústí n/L, Kosmonautù 571/1.*	☏ *(47) 62215*	*15*	🗐	♔ 🅾 Ⓡ
▲ **Ústí nad Labem-Nestěmice** - Hotel Český Lev Sibiřská 560, 40331 Ústí nad Labem-Nestěmice.	☏ (47) 5507063 ℻ (47) 5507098	150	🗐	♔ 🅾 Ⓡ ♿ 🅿 🍴
▲ **Zlaté Hory** - Areál Bohema Travel Market, Areál Bohema, 79376 Zlaté Hory.	☏ (645) 425177 ℻ (645) 425069	520	🗐	♔ 🅾 Ⓡ ♿ 🆑 🅿 🍴

Denmark

DANEMARK

DÄNEMARK

DINAMARCA

DANHOSTEL Danmarks Vandrerhjem
Vesterbrogade 39, DK-1620 Copenhagen V,
Denmark

☏ (45) 33313612
🖷 (45) 33313626
✉ ldv@danhostel.dk
🖳 www.danhostel.dk

Office Hours: Monday-Thursday 09.00-16.00hrs, Friday 09.00-15.00hrs

A copy of the Hostel Directory for this Country can be obtained from:
The National Office and all hostels.

Capital:	Copenhagen		**Population:**	5,170,000
Language:	Danish		**Size:**	43,069 sq km
Currency:	kr (1 Krone = 100 øre)		**Telephone Country Code:**	45

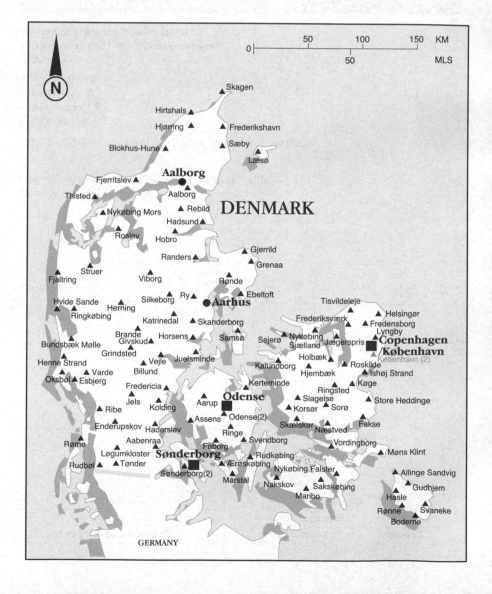

English

Hostels are located in cities, in the countryside and on the coast.

Price range

Price range DKR 75-100. 🖾.

Rooms and Reservations

R 🖾 (All Rooms). Reservations via **IBN** 🖼 or Hostel by ❶ ❷ ❸. Smoking is limited - please check.

Guests

Membership Card is required. Pets are allowed - check with hostel. ♦♦♦ welcome. Group bookings via 🖼 Hostel or National Office by ❶ ❷ ❸.

Open times

Main hostels: open 🖾, ⏱. Reception open: 08:00-12:00hrs, 16:00-20:00hrs Jun-Aug; 08:00-10:00hrs, 16:00-18:00hrs Sep-May. Resident manager. **Other hostels:** open Mar-Oct. **Seasonal hostels** are generally open Apr-Sep.

Meals

🍴 B **R** For ♦♦♦. ☞ Not all utensils provided - check with hostel.

Discounts

HI Member Discounts available - see discounts section and www.iyhf.org.

Travelling around

For ease of travel use 🚂 🛥 🚌 Self-Drive.

Passports and Visas

Passport required.

Health

Medical insurance is recommended. EU Nationals require Form E111 to obtain treatment within EU countries.

Français

Les auberges sont situées dans les villes, à la campagne et sur le littoral.

Tarifs des nuitées

Tarifs des nuitées 75-100 DKR. 🖾.

Chambres et réservations

R 🖾 (Toutes chambres). Réservations via **IBN** 🖼 ou l'auberge par ❶ ❷ ❸. Il est permis de fumer dans certaines chambres - veuillez vérifier.

Usagers

La carte d'adhérent est à présenter. Les animaux domestiques sont autorisés mais vérifiez lesquels auprès de l'auberge. Accueil des ♦♦♦. Réservations pour groupes via 🖼 l'auberge et le Bureau National par ❶ ❷ ❸.

Horaires d'ouverture

Grandes auberges: ouvertes 🖾, ⏱. Accueil ouvert entre 8h-12h, 16h-20h juin-août; 8h-10h, 16h-18h sep-mai. Gérant réside sur place. **Autres auberges:** ouvertes mar-oct. **Auberges saisonnières** ouvertes généralement avril-sep.

Repas

🍴 B **R** Pour ♦♦♦. ☞ Pas tous les ustensils sont fournis - à vérifier auprès de l'auberge.

Remises

Remises pour les adhérents HI - voir la section "Remises" et notre site: www.iyhf.org.

Déplacements

Modes de transport recommandés 🚂 ⛴
🚌 Voiture.

Passeports et visas

Passeport obligatoire.

Santé

Une assurance médicale de voyage est
conseillée. Les ressortissants de l'Union
Européenne doivent se munir du formulaire
E111 pour bénéficier de soins médicaux dans
les états de l'UE.

Deutsch

Herbergen befinden sich in Städten, auf dem
Land und an der Küste.

Preisspanne

Preisspanne 75-100 DKR. 🈷.

Zimmer und Reservierungen

R 🈁 (Alle Zimmer). Reservierungen über
(IBN) 🖳 oder die Herberge per ❶ ❷ ❸.
Rauchen ist begrenzt - bitte checken.

Gäste

Mitgliedsausweis ist erforderlich. Haustiere sind
erlaubt - in der Herberge nachfragen.
❶❶❶ willkommen. Gruppenbuchungen über 🖳
Herberge oder Landesverband per ❶ ❷ ❸.

Öffnungszeiten

Hauptherbergen: Zugang 🈁, ⊙. Rezeption
zwischen 08:00-12:00Uhr, 16:00-20:00Uhr
Jun-Aug; 08:00-10:00Uhr, 16:00-18:00Uhr
Sept-Mai. Herbergsmanager wohnt im Haus.
Andere Herbergen: Zugang zwischen
Mär-Okt. **Saison-Herbergen** sind
normalerweise Apr-Sept geöffnet.

Mahlzeiten

🍽 B **R** Für ❶❶❶. ☝ Nicht alle Utensilien
werden bereitgestellt - in der Herberge
nachfragen.

Ermäßigungen

HI-Mitgliedsrabatt ist erhältlich – siehe Teil für
Rabatte und Ermäßigungen und www.iyhf.org.

Reisen im Land

Reisen ist einfach mit 🚂 ⛴ 🚌
Selbstfahrer.

Reisepässe und Visa

Reisepass erforderlich.

Gesundheit

Unfall-/Krankenversicherung wird empfohlen.
EU Staatsangehörige benötigen Formular E111
für ärztliche Behandlungen innerhalb der EU
Länder.

Español

Los albergues están situados en las ciudades, el
campo y la costa.

Tarifas mínima y máxima

Tarifas mínima y máxima 75-100 DKR. 🈷.

Habitaciones y Reservas

R 🈁 (todas las habitaciones). Reservas por
(IBN) 🖳 o a través del albergue por ❶ ❷
❸. Está permitido fumar sólo en algunas
salas/habitaciones - infórmese.

Huéspedes

Los huéspedes deben presentar su Carnet de
Alberguista. Se admiten animales - consulte con
el albergue. Se admiten ❶❶❶. Reservas de grupo
por 🖳 o a través del albergue o la Asociación
Nacional por ❶ ❷ ❸.

Horarios y fechas de apertura

Albergues principales - abiertos 🔟, 🕐.
Horario de recepción: 08:00-12:00h,
16:00-20:00h jun-ago; 08:00-10:00h,
16:00-18:00h sep-may. Gerente residente.
Otros albergues - abiertos mar-oct.
Albergues de temporada suelen abrir:
abr-sep.

Comidas

🍽 B **R** Para 👪. 🍴 La cocina no dispone
de todos los utensilios - consulte con el
albergue.

Descuentos

Se conceden descuentos a los miembros de
Hostelling International – véase la sección
sobre descuentos y nuestra página Internet en
www.iyhf.org.

Desplazamientos

Transportes recomendados: 🚂 🚢 🚌
Automóvil.

Pasaportes y Visados

Pasaporte obligatorio.

Información Sanitaria

Seguro médico recomendado. Los ciudadanos
procedentes de países pertenecientes a la UE
necesitan el impreso E111 para obtener
asistencia médica en dichos países.

Aalborg -
DANHOSTEL Aalborg

Skydebanevej 50,
9000 Aalborg.
☎ 98116044
📠 98124711
📧 aalborg@danhostel.dk

Open Dates:	20.01-15.12
Open Hours:	08.00-12.00hrs; 16.00-21.00 hrs
Reservations:	**R**
Price Range:	DKK 100.00 (Rooms 398.00 DKK) 💷
Beds:	140 - 35x🛏
Facilities:	♿35x 👪 🍽 (B) 🍴 🛏 📺 📱2 x🍸 🔒 🅿 🅰 ⛰ 🔍

Directions:

✈	Aalborg 10km
A🚌	4km
🚂	3km
🚌	#8 200m

Attractions: ⛳600m 🎿500m 🏊500m

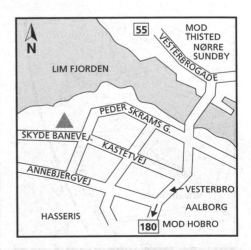

Århus -
DANHOSTEL Århus

Marienlundsvej 10,
8240 Risskov.
🕿 86167298
📠 86105560
✉ danhostel.aarhus@get2net.dk

Open Dates:	20.01-15.12
Open Hours:	07.00-11.00hrs; 16.00-22.00 hrs
Reservations:	**R**
Price Range:	DKK 90.00
	(Rooms 270.00-400.00 DKK) 🏠
Beds:	150 - 20x⁴🛏 2x⁵🛏 12x⁶🛏
Facilities:	♿ 🛏 20x 🛏 🍽 (B) ✎ 🛋 📺
	🗄 🍴 🔒 🅿 🖊 🖥 🏊 ⛰
Directions:	③N from city centre
✈	Tirstrup - Aarhus 30km
⛴	Aarhus 3km
🚌	1 - 6 - 9 - 56 to Marienlund

Billund -
DANHOSTEL Billund

Ellehammers Alle 2,
7190 Billund.
🕿 75332777
📠 75332877
✉ billund@danhostel.dk

Open Dates:	🗓
Open Hours:	08.00-12.00hrs; 15.00-20.00 hrs
Reservations:	**R** **CC**
Price Range:	DKK 100
	(Rooms 325-450 DKK) 🏠
Beds:	228 - 22x⁴🛏 22x⁵🛏 2x⁶🛏
Facilities:	♿ 🛏 44x 🛏 🍽 ✎ 🛋 📺 🖥
	🖥5 x 🍴 🗄 🖼 🍴 🔒 🅿 🖊 🖥
	🏊 ⛰ ☎
Directions:	
✈	Billund 500m
A🚌	Billund 500m
⛴	Esbjerg 60km
🚂	Vejle 25km
🚌	44 & 912F 500m

Attractions: 🏌 🚴 ∪ ᖇ500m ⚓500m

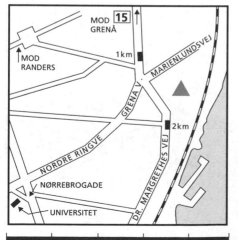

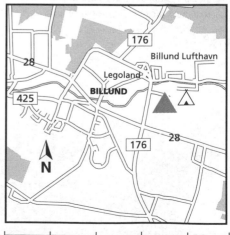

Copenhagen -
DANHOSTEL
Copenhagen Amager

Vejlands Allé 200,
2300 København S.
☎ 32522908
🖷 32522708
📧 copenhagen@danhostel.dk

Open Dates:	15.01-01.12
Open Hours:	☾
Reservations:	® IBN ⌐CC⌐
Price Range:	DKK 95.00-125.00 ▦
Beds:	528 - 64x² 80x⁵
Facilities:	♿ ⅲ 144x ⅲ ⁞⊙⁞ ☞ ⌂ TV 2 x ⊤ ▣ ♨ P ⅰ 🎿 ⚓
Directions:	4SE from city centre
✈	Copenhagen 4km
A🚌	100S + 250S
⛴	Copenhagen 4km
🚂	Copenhagen Central Station 5km
🚌	37, 46, 100S & 250S
Attractions:	⌖ ⌃ 2km

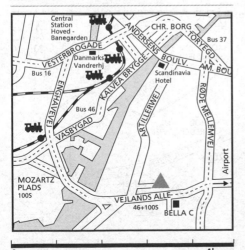

Copenhagen -
DANHOSTEL
Copenhagen Bellahøj

Herbergvejen 8,
2700 Brønshøj.
☎ 38289715
🖷 38890210
📧 bellahoej@danhostel.dk

Open Dates:	01.03-15.01
Open Hours:	☾
Reservations:	® IBN
Price Range:	DKK 95.00 (Rooms 260.00-570.00 DKK) ▦
Beds:	252 - 7x⁴ 31x⁶ 3x⁶⁺
Facilities:	ⅲ 7x ⅲ ⁞⊙⁞ ☞ ⌂ TV ☯3 x ⊤ ▣ ▣ ♨ 8 P 🎿 ⚓
Directions:	5NW from city centre
✈	Kastrup-Copenhagen 15km
A🚌	250S 800m
⛴	Copenhagen 5km
🚂	Copenhagen Central 4km
🚌	11 or 2 200m ap Bellahøj or Brønshøj
Ⓤ	Grøndal 500m
Attractions:	⌃ 500m

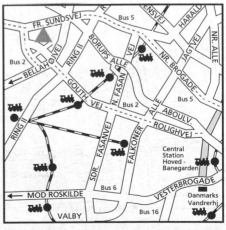

Fjerritslev -
DANHOSTEL Fjerritslev

Brøndumvej 14-16,
9690 Fjerritslev.
☎ 98211190
✆ 98212522

Open Dates: 🗓

Open Hours: 07.00-22.00 hrs

Reservations: ⓡ ⒸⒸ

Price Range: DKK 100.00
(Rooms 200-500 DKK) 🖳

Beds: 178 - 2x² 2x³ 38x⁴ 3x⁶

Facilities: ♿ ⅲ 40x ⅲ 🍽 ☞ 📺 🎦
3 x🍴 🖼 🎱 ☺ 🅿 ℹ 🧺 ⚡
🎢 ♻ 🔍 🏢

Directions:

✈ Aalborg 45km
🚌 A 200m
⛴ 10km
🚂 50km
🚌 100m

Attractions: ⚑ 📷 5km 🚴 🚶 ∪2km 🏊 🚣

Helsingør -
DANHOSTEL Helsingør

Ndr Strandvej 24,
3000 Helsingør.
☎ 49211640
✆ 49211399
✉ helsingor@danhostel.dk

Open Dates: 01.02-30.11

Open Hours: 08.00-12.00hrs; 15.00-21.00hrs
(01.05-30.09); 08.00-12.00hrs;
15.00-20.00hrs (01.10-30.04)

Reservations: ⓡ

Price Range: DKK 95.00
(Rooms 250.00-550.00 DKK) 🖳

Beds: 180 - 3x² 2x³ 19x⁴ 7x⁵
3x⁶ 6x⁶

Facilities: ♿ ⅲ 38x ⅲ 🍽 (B) ☞ 🚹 📺
🖼 🎦3 x🍴 🖼 ⛪ 🅿 ℹ 🧺 ⚡
🎢 🔍 🏛

Directions: 1.5NW from city centre

✈ Copenhagen 60km
⛴ Helsingborg-Helsingør 2km
🚂 Helsingør 2km
🚌 340 200m ap Højstrup 200m
🚋 Højstrup 200m ap Højstrup 200m

Attractions: ⚑ 📷 🚶 ∪2km 🏊100m 🚣

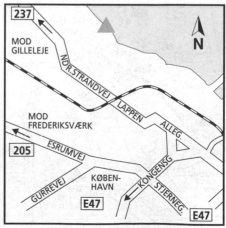

Odense -
DANHOSTEL Odense

Kragsbjergvej 121,
5230 Odense M.
📞 66130425
📠 65912863
✉ odensehostel@mailhost.net

Open Dates:	15.02-01.12
Open Hours:	08.00-12.00hrs; 16.00-20.00hrs
Reservations:	**R** **CC**
Price Range:	DKK 95.00 (Rooms DKK 299.00-376.00) 🏧
Beds:	170 - 4x² 15x⁴ 1x⁵ 12x⁶
Facilities:	👪 32x 👪 🍽 (B) 🛆 🚲 ⚑ 📺 🧺3 x 🍴 🔒 🖼 ♨ P ℹ 🔌 ♻ 🎢 🔍 🛝 🎪
Directions:	2SE from city centre
✈	Billund 75km
A🚌	2.5km
🚂	Odense 2.5km
🚌	61; 62; 63, 64 200m ap Munkebjerg Plads
Attractions:	🚲 🏊 2.5km

There are 2 hostels in Odense. See following pages.

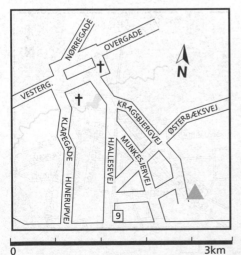

Ribe -
DANHOSTEL Ribe

Sct Pedersgade 16,
6760 Ribe.
📞 75420620
📠 75424288
✉ ribe@danhostel.dk

Open Dates:	01.02-30.11
Open Hours:	08.00-12.00hrs; 16.00-18.00hrs
Reservations:	**R**
Price Range:	DKK 100.00-250.00 🏧
Beds:	140 - 4x² 18x⁴ 12x⁵
Facilities:	♿ 👪 34x 👪 🍽 (B) 🛆 ⚑ 📺 🍴 🧺4 x 🍴 🔒 🖼 🎱 P ℹ 🔌 ♻ 🔍 🛝 🎪
Directions:	
✈	Billund 55km
⛴	Esbjerg 35km
🚂	Ribe 500m
🚌	Ribe 500m ap Ribe Bus Station
Attractions:	🎭 🚲 🎿 ∪2km ⚲1km 🏊1km

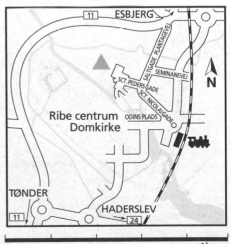

Svendborg -
DANHOSTEL Svendborg

Vestergade 45,
5700 Svendborg.
☎ 62216699
📠 62202939
✉ danhostel.svendborg@get2net.dk

Open Dates:	04.01-17.12
Open Hours:	08.00-20.00hrs
Reservations:	R CC
Price Range:	DKK 100.00-400.00 🔟
Beds:	268 - 7x^1🛏 30x^2🛏 31x^3🛏 16x^4🛏
Facilities:	👪 84x 👬 🍽 (BD) ☕ 👥 📺 🎮10 x🍴 🔥 📷 🔢 🅿 ℹ 👶 ✿ ⚠ 🔍 👨‍👩‍👧

Directions:

✈	42km
⛴	1km
🚂	800m
🚌	800m

Attractions: 🍀 🏛3km 🚴 🏊2km 🚣2km

Sæby -
DANHOSTEL Sæby

Sæbygaardsvej 32,
9300 Sæby.
☎ 98463650
📠 98467630
✉ sabyfri@internord.dk

Open Dates:	🗓12
Open Hours:	08.00-22.00hrs
Reservations:	R
Price Range:	DKK 70.00-170.00 🔟
Beds:	156 - 2x^2🛏 13x^4🛏 3x^5🛏 15x^6🛏 2x^6🛏
Facilities:	👪 32x 👬 🍽 ☕ 📺 📷 🎮3 x🍴 🔥 🔢 🅿 👶 ⚠ 🌀 🔍 🏢
Directions:	0.8W from city centre
✈	Aalborg 50km
A🚌	500m
⛴	Frederikshavn 12km
🚂	Frederikshavn 12km
🚌	73 200m
Attractions:	🍀 🏛1.5km ∪5km 🏊400m 🚣12km

There is 1 hostel in Sæby. See following pages.

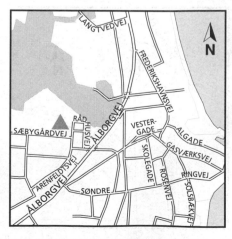

Sønderborg -
DANHOSTEL Sønderborg

Kærvej 70,
6400 Sønderborg.
☎ 74423112
✆ 74425631
✉ sonderborg@danhostel.dk

Open Dates:	01.02-30.11
Open Hours:	08.00-12.00hrs; 16.00-20.00hrs
Reservations:	Ⓡ
Price Range:	DKK 100.00-400.00 💷
Beds:	200 - 38x⁴ 6x⁶
Facilities:	♿ ♟ 44x ♟ 🍽 ✈ ♨ 📺 ♒ 4x🍴 📮 📷 🏧 8 💲 Ⓟ ⓘ 🎮 ♣ ⛺ ⚡ 🔍 🍴

Directions:

✈	Sønderborg 5km
⛴	Fynshav 14km
🚌	Sønderborg 1km
🚍	1km

Attractions: 🏞 🎡 🚲 ⚓1.5km ⛵500m

Tisvildeleje -
DANHOSTEL Tisvildeleje

Bygmarken 30,
3220 Tisvildeleje.
☎ 48709850
✆ 48709897
✉ sch@helene.dk

Open Dates:	🗓
Open Hours:	08.00-21.00hrs
Price Range:	DKK 100.00-450.00 💷
Beds:	160 - 40x⁴
Facilities:	♿ ♟ 40x ♟ 🍽 ✈ ♨ 📺 📷 5x🍴 📮 📷 🏧 Ⓟ ⓘ 🎮 ♣ ⛺ 🔍 🍴 🏇

Directions:

✈	Copenhagen-Kastrup 60km
⛴	Elsinore (Helsingør) 28km
🚌	Tisvildeleje 500m

Attractions: 🏞 🎡500m 🚲 🎿 ⛳400m ⚓ ⛵9km

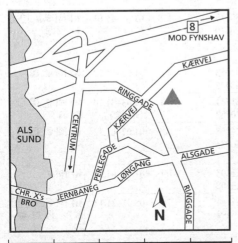

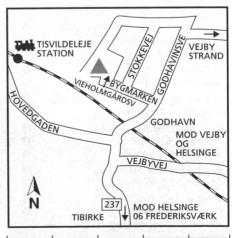

Location/Address	Telephone No. Fax No.	Beds	Opening Dates	Facilities
▲ **Aabenraa** - DANHOSTEL Aabenraa Sønderskovvej 100, 6200 Aabenraa.	☎ 74622699 ✆ 74622939	102	01.03–31.10	ⅲ ⍥ & ⚲ 🅿 ⊡
▲ **Aalborg** - DANHOSTEL Aalborg **Skydebanevej 50, 9000 Aalborg.** ℮ aalborg@danhostel.dk	☎ 98116044 ✆ 98124711	140	20.01–15.12	ⅲ ⍥ Ⓡ & ⚲ 🅿 ⊡
▲ **Århus** - DANHOSTEL Århus **Marienlundsvej 10, 8240 Risskov.** ℮ danhostel.aarhus@get2net.dk	☎ 86167298 ✆ 86105560	150	20.01–15.12	ⅲ ⍥ Ⓡ 3N & ⚲ 🅿 ⊡
▲ **Årup** - DANHOSTEL Årup Skolegade 3, 5560 Årup. ℮ aarupdanhostel@mail.tele.dk	☎ 64431328 ✆ 64432034	54	15.01–15.12	ⅲ ⍥ ⚲ 🅿
▲ **Assens** - DANHOSTEL Assens Adelgade 26, 5610 Assens. ℮ assensvandrerhjem@post.tele.dk	☎ 64711357 ✆ 64715657	54	01.03–31.10	ⅲ ⍥ ⚲ 🅿
▲ **Billund** - DANHOSTEL Billund **Ellehammers Alle 2, 7190 Billund.** ℮ billund@danhostel.dk	☎ 75332777 ✆ 75332877	228	⌸	ⅲ ⍥ Ⓡ & ⼕ ⚲ 🅿 ⊡
▲ **Blokhus-Hune** - DANHOSTEL Blokhus-Hune Kirkevej 26, 9492 Blokhus. ℮ blokvhj@post9.tele.dk	☎ 98249180 ✆ 98209005	100	01.03–01.11 (ⅲ ⌸)	ⅲ ⍥ Ⓡ & ⚲ 🅿 ☕
▲ **Boderne** - DANHOSTEL Boderne Bodernevej 28, 3720 Aakirkeby. ℮ danhostel@rosengaarden.dk	☎ 56974950 ✆ 56974948	75	⌸	ⅲ ⍥ ⚲ 🅿 ⊡
▲ **Brande** - DANHOSTEL Brande Dr Arendsvej 2, 7330 Brande.	☎ 97182197 ✆ 97182199	54	01.03–30.11 (ⅲ 01.01–20.12)	ⅲ ⍥ Ⓡ ⚲ 🅿
▲ **Copenhagen** - DANHOSTEL Copenhagen Amager 【IBN】 **Vejlands Allé 200, 2300 København S.** ℮ copenhagen@danhostel.dk	☎ 32522908 ✆ 32522708	528	15.01–01.12	ⅲ ⍥ Ⓡ 4SE & ⼕ ⚲ 🅿 ⊡
▲ **Copenhagen** - DANHOSTEL Copenhagen Bellahøj 【IBN】 **Herbergvejen 8, 2700 Brønshøj.** ℮ bellahoej@danhostel.dk	☎ 38289715 ✆ 38890210	252	01.03–15.01	ⅲ ⍥ Ⓡ 5NW ⚲ 🅿 ⊡
▲ **Ebeltoft** - DANHOSTEL Ebeltoft Søndergade 43, 8400 Ebeltoft.	☎ 86342053 ✆ 86342077	72	01.02–31.12	ⅲ ⍥ ⚲ 🅿
▲ **Enderupskov** - DANHOSTEL Enderupskov Ribelandevej, 30, 6510 Gram.	☎ 74821711 ✆ 74820782	50	01.03–31.10 (ⅲ ⌸)	ⅲ ⍥ ⚲ 🅿 ⊡ ☕ ⚲
▲ **Esbjerg** - DANHOSTEL Esbjerg Vardevej 80, 6700 Esbjerg. ℮ esbjerg@danhostel.dk	☎ 75124258 ✆ 75136833	124	01.02–01.12	ⅲ ⍥ ⚲ 🅿 ⊡ ⚲
▲ **Fåborg** - DANHOSTEL Fåborg Grønnegade 72, 5600 Fåborg.	☎ 62611203 ✆ 62613508	69	01.04–01.10	ⅲ ⍥ ⚲
▲ **Fakse** - DANHOSTEL Fakse Østervej 4, 4640 Fakse. ℮ fvh@faksevandrerhjem.stam.dk	☎ 56714181 ✆ 56715492	70	08.01–21.12	ⅲ ⍥ Ⓡ 0.1S & ⚲ 🅿 ⊡ ☕ ⚲

Location/Address	Telephone No. Fax No.	Beds	Opening Dates	Facilities
▲ Fjaltring - DANHOSTEL Fjaltring Kjeldbjergvej 7, Fjaltring, 7620 Lemvig. ℮ johsa@post10.tele.dk	☎ 97887700 ✆ 97887274	24	⌆	⅋ ⑩ ℞ ♂ Ⓟ
▲ Fjerritslev - DANHOSTEL Fjerritslev **Brøndumvej 14-16, 9690 Fjerritslev.**	☎ 98211190 ✆ 98212522	178	⌆	⅋ ⑩ ℞ ♿ ⌘ ♂ Ⓟ
▲ Fredensborg - DANHOSTEL Fredensborg Østrupvej 3, 3480 Fredensborg. ℮ danhostel@mail.dk	☎ 48480315 ✆ 48481656	94	05.01–15.12	⅋ ⑩ ℞ ♂ Ⓟ ⑩ ☕
▲ Fredericia - DANHOSTEL Fredericia Vestre Ringvej 98, 7000 Fredericia.	☎ 75921287 ✆ 75932905	135	15.01–15.12	⅋ ⑩ ℞ 2SE ♿ ⌘ ♂ Ⓟ ⑩ ⚲
▲ Frederikshavn - DANHOSTEL Frederikshavn Buhlsvej 6, 9900 Frederikshavn.	☎ 98421475 ✆ 98426522	130	01.02–19.12	⅋ ⑩ ℞ 1NW ♿ ♂ Ⓟ
▲ Frederiksværk - DANHOSTEL Frederiksværk Strandgade 30, 3300 Frederiksværk. ℮ strandbo@image.dk	☎ 47770725 ✆ 47720766	100	01.02–30.11	⅋ ⑩ ♿ ♂ Ⓟ ⑩
▲ Givskud - DANHOSTEL Givskud Løveparkvej 2, 7323 Givskud. ℮ danhostel@aof-rejser.dk	☎ 75730500 ✆ 75730530	128	01.01–30.11	⅋ ⑩ ℞ ♿ ⌘ ♂ Ⓟ ⑩ ⚲
▲ Gjerrild - DANHOSTEL Gjerrild Dyrehavevej 9, Gjerrild, 8500 Grenå. ℮ djursvold@post.tele.dk	☎ 86384199 ✆ 86384302	92	01.04–30.09	⅋ ⑩ ♿ ♂ Ⓟ ⑩
▲ Grenå - DANHOSTEL Grenå Ydesvej 4, 8500 Grenå. ℮ danhostel-grenaa-sportel-vandrerhjem@ worldonline.dk	☎ 86326622 ✆ 86321248	108	05.01–20.12	⅋ ⑩ ♿ ⌘ ♂ Ⓟ ⑩ ⚲
▲ Grindsted - DANHOSTEL Grindsted Morsbøl Skolevej 24, Morsbøl 7200 Grindsted. ℮ gvh@image.dk	☎ 75322605 ✆ 75310905	80	01.04–30.09 (⅋ 01.02–30.11)	⅋ ⑩ ℞ 5SW ♿ ♂ Ⓟ ⑩ ⚲
▲ Gudhjem - DANHOSTEL Gudhjem Ejner Mikkelsens Vej 14, 3760 Gudhjem. ℮ danhostel-gudhjem@bornholm.net	☎ 56485035 ✆ 56485635	220	⌆	⅋ ⑩ ♂ Ⓟ
▲ Haderslev - DANHOSTEL Haderslev Erlevvej 34, 6100 Haderslev. ℮ bh-had@post12.tele.dk	☎ 74521347 ✆ 74521364	102	01.02–30.11	⅋ ⑩ ℞ ♿ ♂ Ⓟ ⑩ ⚲
▲ Hadsund - DANHOSTEL Hadsund Stadionvej 33, 9560 Hadsund. ℮ hadsund@get2net.dk	☎ 98574345 ✆ 98574356	48	01.04–30.09	⅋ ⑩ ℞ ⌘ ♂ Ⓟ ⑩ ☕
▲ Hasle - DANHOSTEL Hasle Fælledvej 28, 3790 Hasle.	☎ 56964175 (01.11-01.04, 56966434) ✆ 56964175	100	01.05–30.10	⅋ ⑩ ♂ Ⓟ
▲ Helsingør - DANHOSTEL Helsingør **Ndr Strandvej 24, 3000 Helsingør.** ℮ helsingor@danhostel.dk	☎ 49211640 ✆ 49211399	180	01.02–30.11	⅋ ⑩ ℞ 1.5NW ♿ ♂ Ⓟ

Location/Address	Telephone No. Fax No.	Beds	Opening Dates	Facilities
▲ **Henne St** - DANHOSTEL Henne Strand Strandvejen 458, 6854 Henne Strand. ⊖ hennestrand@danhostel.dk	☏ 75255075 ⨍ 75255075	44	12.04–14.10	� ⑩ ⓡ ♿ ⌀ Ⓟ
▲ **Herning** - DANHOSTEL Herning Holingknuden 2, Holing, 7400 Herning.	☏ 97123144 ⨍ 97216169	112	01.02–30.11	� ⑩ ⓡ 3NW ♿ ⌀ Ⓟ ⑩
▲ **Hirtshals** - DANHOSTEL Hirtshals Kystvejen 53, 9850 Hirtshals. ⊖ danhostel.hirtshals@adr.dk	☏ 98941248 ⨍ 98945655	72	01.03–01.11	� ⑩ ⓡ ⓒⓒ ⌀ Ⓟ 🚲
▲ **Hjembæk** - DANHOSTEL Hjembæk Tornbrinken 2, Hjembæk, 4450 Jyderup. ⊖ vandrerhjem@svp.dk	☏ 59268181 ⨍ 59268033	50	⑫	� ⑩ ⓡ ⌀ ⑩
▲ **Hjørring** - DANHOSTEL Hjørring Thomas Morildsvej, 9800 Hjørring. ⊖ danhostel.hjoerring@adr.dk	☏ 98926700 ⨍ 98901550	140	01.03–01.10	� ⑩ ⓡ ♿ ⌀ Ⓟ ⑩ 🚲
▲ **Hobro** - DANHOSTEL Hobro Amerikavej 24, 9500 Hobro. ⊖ danhostel.hobro@adr.dk	☏ 98521847 ⨍ 98511847	108	15.01–15.12	� ⑩ ♿ ⌀ Ⓟ ⑩
▲ **Holbæk** - DANHOSTEL Holbæk Ahlgade 1B, 4300 Holbæk. ⊖ vandrehjem@vestnet.dk	☏ 59442919 ⨍ 59439485	90	04.01–20.12	� ⑩ ⓡ ♿ ⓒⓒ Ⓟ ⑩
▲ **Horsens** - DANHOSTEL Horsens Flintebakken 150, 8700 Horsens. ⊖ horsens@danhostel.dk	☏ 75616777 ⨍ 75610871	108	15.01–15.12	� ⑩ ♿ ⓒⓒ Ⓟ ⑩
▲ **Hvide Sande** - DANHOSTEL Hvide Sande Numitvej 5, 6960 Hvide Sande. ⊖ danhostel@hvidesande.dk	☏ 97312105 ⨍ 97312196	88	⑫	� ⑩ ⌀ Ⓟ ⑩
▲ **Ishøj** - DANHOSTEL Ishøj Strand Ishøj Strandvej 13, 2635 Ishøj. ⊖ ishoj@danshostel.dk	☏ 43535015 ⨍ 43535045	191	⑫	� ⑩ ⓡ 0.8W ♿ ⓒⓒ ⌀ Ⓟ ⑩ 🚲
▲ **Jels** - DANHOSTEL Jels Ørstedvej 10, Jels, 6630 Rødding. ⊖ jelsdanh@post10.tele.dk	☏ 74552869 ⨍ 74553107	98	⑫	� ⑩ ♿ ⓒⓒ ⌀ Ⓟ ⑩
▲ **Juelsminde** - DANHOSTEL Juelsminde Rousthøj Alle 1, 7130 Juelsminde. ⊖ jlc@juelsmindekom.dk	☏ 75693313, 75693066 ⨍ 75693130, 75693957	68	01.05–01.10 (� ⑫)	� ⑩ ♿ ⌀ Ⓟ ⑩
▲ **Jægerspris** - DANHOSTEL Jægerspris Skovnæsvej 2, 3630 Jægerspris.	☏ 47311032 ⨍ 47312832	90	01.02–15.12	� ⑩ ⓒⓒ ⌀ Ⓟ ⑩
▲ **Kalundborg** - DANHOSTEL Kalundborg Stadion Alle 5, 4400 Kalundborg. ⊖ kalundborg@danhostel.dk	☏ 59561366 ⨍ 59564626	118	⑫	� ⑩ ⓡ 1W ♿ ⓒⓒ ⌀ Ⓟ ⑩
▲ **Katrinedal** - DANHOSTEL Katrinedal Vellingvej 53, 8654 Bryrup. ⊖ katrinedal@get2net.dk	☏ 75756146 ⨍ 75757810	64	01.05–01.09 (� 01.01–01.12)	� ⑩ ⓡ ⌀ Ⓟ
▲ **Kerteminde** - DANHOSTEL Kerteminde Skovvej 46, 5300 Kerteminde. ⊖ info@dkhostel.dk	☏ 65323929 ⨍ 65323924	90	03.01–15.12	� ⑩ ♿ ⌀ Ⓟ ⑩

Location/Address	Telephone No. Fax No.	Beds	Opening Dates	Facilities
▲ **Kolding** - DANHOSTEL Kolding Ørnsborgvej 10, 6000 Kolding. 📧 kolding@danhostel.dk	☏ 75509140 🖷 75509151	92	01.02–01.12	👪 🍴 ♂ Ⓟ 🅾
▲ **Korsør** - DANHOSTEL Korsør Tovesvej 30F, 4220 Korsør. 📧 korsoer@turisme.dk	☏ 58371022 🖷 58356870	80	07.01–15.12	👪 🍴 Ⓡ 2.5NE ♿ ɛ꞊ᴄᴄ꞊ɜ ♂ Ⓟ 🅾 ♻
▲ **Køge** - DANHOSTEL Køge Lille Køgegaard, Vamdrupvej 1, 4600 Køge.	☏ 56651474 🖷 56660869	80	01.04–15.12	👪 🍴 Ⓡ 2.5W ♂ Ⓟ 🅾
▲ **Lyngby** - DANHOSTEL Lyngby Rådvad 1, 2800 Lyngby.	☏ 45803074 🖷 45803032	94	01.04–25.10 (👪 10.01–15.12)	👪 🍴 7NE ♂ Ⓟ
▲ **Læsø** - DANHOSTEL Læsø Lærkevej 6, 9940 Vesterø Havn, Læsø. 📧 ts@laesoe-vandrerhjem.dk	☏ 98499195 🖷 98499160	90	15.04–01.10	👪 🍴 ♂ Ⓟ
▲ **Løgumkloster** - DANHOSTEL Løgumkloster Vænget 28, 6240 Løgumkloster.	☏ 74743618 🖷 74743619	42	06.04–13.12	👪 🍴 ♂ Ⓟ
▲ **Maribo** - DANHOSTEL Maribo Sdr Boulevard 82B, 4930 Maribo.	☏ 54783314 🖷 54783265	96	03.01–26.12	👪 🍴 Ⓡ ɛ꞊ᴄᴄ꞊ɜ ♂ Ⓟ
▲ **Marstal** - DANHOSTEL Marstal Færgestræde 29, 5960 Marstal. 📧 mav@adr.dk	☏ 62531064 🖷 62531057	82	01.05–31.08	👪 🍴 ♂
▲ **Møn** - DANHOSTEL Møn Langebjergvej 1, 4791 Borre. 📧 danhostel-mons-klint@post.tele.dk	☏ 55812030 🖷 55812818	105	01.05–01.09	👪 🍴 ♂ Ⓟ
▲ **Nakskov** - DANHOSTEL Nakskov Branderslevvej 11, 4900 Nakskov.	☏ 54922434 🖷 54923367	60	🔲12	👪 🍴 ♿ ♂ Ⓟ 🅾
▲ **Næstved** - DANHOSTEL Næstved Frejasvej 8, 4700 Næstved. 📧 nstvh@post4.tele.dk	☏ 55722091 🖷 55725645	87	15.03–15.11 (👪 01.02–30.11)	👪 🍴 1SE ♂ Ⓟ
▲ **Nykøbing Falster (Falster)** - DANHOSTEL Nykøbing Falster Østre Alle 110, 4800 Nykøbing Falster. 📧 nyk.f@danhostel.dk	☏ 54856699 🖷 54823242	94	15.01–15.12	👪 🍴 ♿ ♂ Ⓟ 🅾 ♻
▲ **Nykøbing Mors (Jutland)** - DANHOSTEL Nykøbing Mors Østerstrand, 7900 Nykøbing Mors. 📧 danhostel.nyk.mors@adr.dk	☏ 97720617 🖷 97720776	129	01.02–20.12	👪 🍴 Ⓡ ♿ ♂ Ⓟ 🅾 ☕
▲ **Nykøbing Sjælland (Sealand)** - DANHOSTEL Nykøbing Sjælland Egebjergvej 162, 4500 Nykøbing Sj. 📧 vandrerhjem@odsherred-naturkole.dk	☏ 59930062 🖷 59930162	44	08.01–16.12	👪 🍴 ɛ꞊ᴄᴄ꞊ɜ ♂ Ⓟ 🅾
▲ **Odense** - DANHOSTEL Odense **Kragsbjergvej 121, 5230 Odense M.** 📧 odensehostel@mailhost.net	☏ 66130425 🖷 65912863	170	15.02–01.12	👪 🍴 Ⓡ 2SE ɛ꞊ᴄᴄ꞊ɜ ♂ Ⓟ 🅾 ♻
▲ **Odense** - DANHOSTEL Odense City Østre Stationvej 31, 5000 Odense.	☏ 63110425 🖷 63113520	140	🔲12	👪 🍴 Ⓡ ♂ Ⓟ 🅾 ☕

Location/Address	Telephone No. Fax No.	Beds	Opening Dates	Facilities
▲ **Oksbøl** - DANHOSTEL Oksbøl Præstegårdsvej 21, 6840 Oksbøl. e danhostel@post.tele.dk	☏ 75271877 🖷 75272544	100	15.01–15.12	⑈ ⑀ ♿ ☌ P ⑄
▲ **Randers** - DANHOSTEL Randers Gethersvej 1, 8900 Randers. e randers.danhostel@adr.dk	☏ 86425044 🖷 86419854	136	15.02–30.11	⑈ ⑀ ® 0.5 NW ♿ ☌ P ⑄
▲ **Rebild** - DANHOSTEL Rebild Rebildvej 23, Rebild, 9520 Skørping. e rebild@vandrerhjem.dk	☏ 98391340 🖷 98392740	100	20.01–30.11	⑈ ⑀ ♿ ☌ P ⑄
▲ **Ribe** - DANHOSTEL Ribe **Sct Pedersgade 16, 6760 Ribe.** e ribe@danhostel.dk	☏ 75420620 🖷 75424288	140	01.02–30.11	⑈ ⑀ ® ♿ ☌ P ⑄
▲ **Ringe** - DANHOSTEL Ringe Søvej 34, 5750 Ringe.	☏ 62622151 🖷 62622154	46	04.01–18.12	⑈ ⑀ ♿ ☌ P ⑄
▲ **Ringkøbing** - DANHOSTEL Ringkøbing Kirkevej 26, 6950 Ringkøbing. e rofi@rofi.dk	☏ 97322455 🖷 97324959	120	🔲₁₂	⑈ ⑀ ® 1.5 SW ♿ ☌ P ⑄
▲ **Ringsted** - DANHOSTEL Ringsted St Bendtsgade 18, 4100 Ringsted.	☏ 57611526 🖷 57613426	84	02.01–15.12	⑈ ⑀ ☌ P
▲ **Roskilde** - DANHOSTEL Roskilde Vindeboder 7, 4000 Roskilde. e danhostel.roskilde@post.tele.dk	☏ 46352184 🖷 46326690	152	🔲₁₂	⑈ ⑀ ® ♿ CC ☌ P ⑄ ⑄
▲ **Roslev** - DANHOSTEL Roslev Viumvej 8, 7870 Roslev. e roslevva@post11.tele.dk	☏ 97571385 🖷 97572052	92	🔲₁₂	⑈ ⑀ ☌ P ⑄ ⑄
▲ **Rudbøl** - DANHOSTEL Rudbøl Rudbølvej 19-21, Rudbøl, 6280 Højer. e danhostelrudb@mail.tele.dk	☏ 74738298 🖷 74738035	54	15.03–31.10	⑈ ⑀ ® ☌ P ⑄ ⑄
▲ **Rudkøbing** - DANHOSTEL Rudkøbing Engdraget 11, 5900 Rudkøbing. e rudkobing@danhostel.dk	☏ 62511830 🖷 62511830	66	15.03–31.10 (⑈ 🔲₁₂)	⑈ ⑀ ® ♿ ☌ P ⑄
▲ **Ry** - DANHOSTEL Ry Randersvej 88, 8680 Ry. e mail@danhostel-ry.dk	☏ 86891407 🖷 86892870	130	01.01–31.11	⑈ ⑀ ♿ CC ☌ P ⑄
▲ **Rømø** - DANHOSTEL Rømø Lyngvejen 7, 6792 Rømø. e romo@danhostel.dk	☏ 74755188 🖷 74755187	91	15.03–15.10	⑈ ⑀ ☌ P
▲ **Rønde** - DANHOSTEL Rønde Grenåvej 10B, 8410 Rønde. e roende@danhostel.dk	☏ 86371108 🖷 86371128	70	🔲₁₂	⑈ ⑀ ® ♿ CC ☌ P ⑄ ⑄
▲ **Rønne** - DANHOSTEL Rønne Arsenalvej 12, 3700 Rønne. e rvh@post4.tele.dk	☏ 56951340 🖷 56950132	140	01.03–01.11	⑈ ⑀ CC ☌ P ⑄
▲ **Sakskøbing** - DANHOSTEL Sakskøbing Saxe's alle 10, 4990 Sakskøbing. e pless@post.tele.dk	☏ 54706045 🖷 54706041	78	03.01–19.12	⑈ ⑀ ® ♿ CC ☌ P ⑄
▲ **Samsø** Klintevej 8, Ballen, 8305 Samsø.	☏ 86592044 🖷 86592343	100	15.03–01.11	⑈ ⑀ ☌ P ⑄

Location/Address	Telephone No. Fax No.	Beds	Opening Dates	Facilities
▲ **Sandvig** - DANHOSTEL Sandvig Hammershusvej 94, 3770 Allinge. ℮ danhostel.sandvig@get2net.dk	☎ 56480362 ✆ 56481862	100	01.04–31.10	♦♦♦ ⑩ ☞ Ⓟ
△ *Sejerø - DANHOSTEL Sejerø Sejerbyvej 4, Sejerby, 4592 Sejerø.*	☎ 59590290, 44980504 (02.08-22.06)	*35*	*23.06–04.08*	♦♦♦ ⑩ Ⓡ ☞ Ⓟ
▲ **Silkeborg** - DANHOSTEL Silkeborg Åhavevej 55, 8600 Silkeborg.	☎ 86823642 ✆ 86812777	93	01.03–30.11	♦♦♦ ⑩ ♿ ☞ Ⓟ ⓖ
▲ **Skagen NY** - DANHOSTEL Skagen NY Rolighedsvej 2, 9990 Skagen. ℮ danhostel.skagen@adr.dk	☎ 98442200 ✆ 98442255	112	15.02–30.11	♦♦♦ ⑩ Ⓡ ♿ ☞ Ⓟ ⓖ
▲ **Skanderborg** - DANHOSTEL Skanderborg Dyrehaven 9, 8660 Skanderborg. ℮ skanderborg@danhostel.dk	☎ 86511966 ✆ 86511334	138	01.05–01.10	♦♦♦ ⑩ 3N ☞ Ⓟ ⓖ
▲ **Skjern** - DANHOSTEL Bundsbæk Mølle Bundsbækvej 25, 6500 Skjern. ℮ museum@skjern-egvad-museum.dk	☎ 97362343 ✆ 97362480	28	🔟	♦♦♦ ⑩ Ⓡ ☞ Ⓟ
▲ **Skælskør** - DANHOSTEL Skælskør Lystskov, Slagelsevej 48, 4230 Skælskør. ℮ vandrerhjem@lystskoven.dk	☎ 58160980 ✆ 58160989	100	01.02–10.12	♦♦♦ ⑩ ♿ ☞ Ⓟ ⓖ
▲ **Slagelse** - DANHOSTEL Slagelse Bjergbygade 78, 4200 Slagelse.	☎ 58522528 ✆ 58522540	125	15.01–10.12	♦♦♦ ⑩ ☞ Ⓟ
▲ **Sorø** - DANHOSTEL Sorø Skælskørvej 34, 4180 Sorø. ℮ info@kkfg.dk	☎ 57849200 ✆ 57849201	77	01.04–30.09	♦♦♦ ⑩ ♿ CC☞ Ⓟ ⓖ
▲ **Store Heddinge** - DANHOSTEL Store Heddinge Ved Munkevænget 1, 4660 Store Heddinge.	☎ 56502022 ✆ 56502022	63	30.03–30.09 (♦♦♦ 🔟)	♦♦♦ ⑩ ☞ Ⓟ
▲ **Struer** - DANHOSTEL Struer Fjordvejen 12, Bremdal, 7600 Struer.	☎ 97855313 ✆ 97840950	90	01.02–30.11	♦♦♦ ⑩ Ⓡ 1.5 SE ♿ ☞ Ⓟ ⓖ
▲ **Svaneke** - DANHOSTEL Svaneke Reberbanevej 9, 3740 Svaneke. ℮ danhostel-svaneke@bornholm.net	☎ 56496242 ✆ 56497383	152	01.04–01.11	♦♦♦ ⑩ Ⓡ ☞ Ⓟ ⓖ
▲ **Svendborg** - DANHOSTEL Svendborg **Vestergade 45, 5700 Svendborg.** ℮ danhostel.svendborg@get2net.dk	☎ 62216699 ✆ 62202939	268	04.01–17.12	♦♦♦ ⑩ Ⓡ CC☞ Ⓟ ⓖ
▲ **Sæby** - DANHOSTEL Sæby **Sæbygaardsvej 32, 9300 Sæby.** ℮ sabyfri@internord.dk	☎ 98463650 ✆ 98467630	156	🔟	♦♦♦ ⑩ Ⓡ 0.8 W ☞ Ⓟ ⓖ
▲ **Sønderborg-Vollerup** - DANHOSTEL Vollerup Mommarkvej, 17+22, 6400 Sønderborg. ℮ vollerup@post1.tele.dk	☎ 74423990 ✆ 74425290	200	🔟	♦♦♦ ⑩ Ⓡ 1E ♿ CC☞ ☞ Ⓟ ⓖ ☕
▲ **Sønderborg** - DANHOSTEL Sønderborg **Kærvej 70, 6400 Sønderborg.** ℮ sonderborg@danhostel.dk	☎ 74423112 ✆ 74425631	200	01.02–30.11	♦♦♦ ⑩ Ⓡ ♿ ☞ Ⓟ ⓖ

Location/Address	Telephone No. Fax No.	Beds	Opening Dates	Facilities
▲ Thisted - DANHOSTEL Thisted Skinnerup, Kongemøllevej 8, 7700 Thisted. ⓔ danhostel.thisted@adr.dk	☎ 97925042 ✆ 97925150	88	01.03–31.10	⁙ ⑩ 4N ⊂CC⊃ ☞ P ⓖ
▲ Tisvildeleje - DANHOSTEL Tisvildeleje Bygmarken 30, 3220 Tisvildeleje. ⓔ sch@helene.dk	☎ 48709850 ✆ 48709897	160	⒓	⁙ ⑩ & ☞ P ⓖ
▲ Tønder - DANHOSTEL Tønder Sønderport 4, 6270 Tønder. ⓔ danhostel@tonder-net.dk	☎ 74723500 ✆ 74722797	124	01.02–20.12	⁙ ⑩ ☞ P ⓖ
▲ Varde - DANHOSTEL Varde Ungdomsgården, Pramstedvej 10, 6800 Varde. ⓔ varde@danhostel.dk	☎ 75221091 ✆ 75223338	48	15.03–01.10	⁙ ⑩ ☞ P
▲ Vejle - DANHOSTEL Vejle Gl Landevej 80, 7100 Vejle. ⓔ info@vejle-danhostel.dk	☎ 75825188 ✆ 75831783	120	15.01–01.12	⁙ ⑩ 3SE ☞ P ⓖ
▲ Viborg - DANHOSTEL Viborg Vinkelvej 36, 8800 Viborg. ⓔ viborg@danhostel.dk	☎ 86671781 ✆ 86671788	112	01.03–30.11	⁙ ⑩ 2SE ☞ P ⓖ
▲ Vordingborg - DANHOSTEL Vordingborg Præstegaardsvej 18, 4760 Vordingborg. ⓔ vandrerhjem@videnscentret.dk	☎ 45 55 360800 ✆ 45 55 360801	112	04.01–20.12	⁙ ⑩ Ⓡ 2.5SW & ⊂CC⊃ ☞ P ⓖ ⦿ ⚙
▲ Ærøskøbing - DANHOSTEL Ærøskøbing Smedevejen 15, 5970 Ærøskøbing. ⓔ stormaeroe@mail.tele.dk	☎ 62521044 ✆ 62521644	87	01.04–31.10	⁙ ⑩ 0.5S & ☞ P ⓖ ⚙

"*Certainly, travel is more than the seeing of sights; it is a change that goes on, deep and permanent, in the ideas of living.*"

"*Il est certain que le voyage, c'est plus que la simple visite des sites touristiques; c'est un changement en continu, profond et permanent, sur l'idée que nous nous faisons de la vie.*"

„*Gewiss ist Reisen mehr als Sehenswürdigkeiten anschauen; es findet eine tiefe und bleibende Veränderung der Lebensansichten statt.*"

"*No cabe duda que viajar es más que hacer turismo; es un cambio continuo, profundo y permanente, en el concepto que tenemos de la vida*"

Miriam Beard

FAROE ISLANDS HOSTELS

All the hostels listed here are Simple Standard

Ferõamannaheimiõ Á - Gilijanes

FO-360 Sandavágur
☏ (298) 333465
🖷 (298) 332901
✉ giljanes@post.olivant.fo

La Caretta

FO-350 Vestmanna
☏ (298) 424610
🖷 (298) 424708
✉ carreta@post.olivant.fo

Gjáargarõur
FO-476 Gjógv
☏ (298) 423171
🖷 (298) 423505
✉ trygvisivertsen@email.dk

Fjalsgarõur
FO-690 Oyndarfjøõur
☏ (298) 444522
🖷 (298) 444570
✉ giljanes@post.olivant.fo

Youth Hostel Íbúo
Garõavegur 31, FO-700 Klaksvik
☏ (298) 457555
☏ (298) 287965
🖷 (298) 457555
✉ ibudkl@post.olivant.fo

Áargarõur
FO-827 Øravik
☏ (298) 371302
🖷 (298) 372057

Bládýpi
Dr. Jakobsensgøta 14-16 FO-100 Tórshavn
☏ (298) 311951
🖷 (298) 319451

Scout Centre Selatraõ
c/o Hoydalsvegur 6
Postboks 1080
FO-110 Tórshavn
☏ (298) 311075/288950
☏ (298) 448950
🖷 (298) 310775
✉ kfumskfo@post.olivant.fo

Vallaraheimiõ Tórshavn
Viõ Oyggjarvegin
FO-100 Tórshavn
☏ (298) 318900
🖷 (298) 315707
✉ booking@smyril-line.fo

International Booking Network

The advantages are cle[ar]

www.iyhf.org

HOSTELLING INTERNATIONAL

IBN INTERNATIONAL BOOKING NETWORK

England & Wales

ANGLETERRE & PAYS DE GALLES

ENGLAND & WALES

INGLATERRA Y GALES

YHA (England & Wales) Limited,
Trevelyan House, 8 St. Stephen's Hill,
St. Albans, Hertfordshire, AL1 2DY, England.

Customer Services
t (44) 870 870 8808
f (44) (1727) 844126
e customerservices@yha.org.uk
WWW www.yha.org.uk

Office Hours: Monday-Friday, 09.00-18.30hrs

Central London Booking Service

t (44) (20) 73733400
f (44) (20) 73733455
e lonres@yha.org.uk

Office Hours: Monday, 09.00-17.00hrs Tues-Fri, 09.00-19.00hrs Saturday, 09.00-17.00hrs

A copy of the Hostel Directory for this Country can be obtained from:
The National Office

Capital:	London	**Population:**	52,211,175
Language:	English	**Size:**	151,207 sq km
Currency:	£ Sterling (Pound)	**Telephone Country Code:**	44

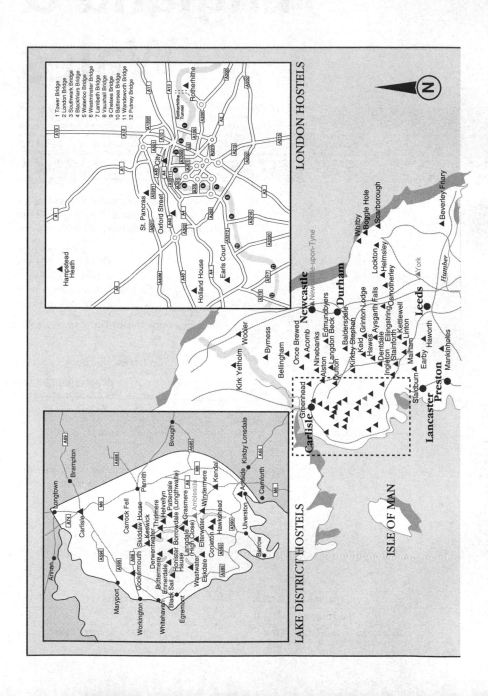

LONDON HOSTELS

1 Tower Bridge
2 London Bridge
3 Southwark Bridge
4 Blackfriars Bridge
5 Waterloo Bridge
6 Westminster Bridge
7 Lambeth Bridge
8 Vauxhall Bridge
9 Chelsea Bridge
10 Battersea Bridge
11 Wandsworth Bridge
12 Putney Bridge

Rotherhithe
Rotherhithe Tunnel

St. Pancras
Oxford Street
Earls Court
Holland House
Hampstead Heath

LAKE DISTRICT HOSTELS

Brough
Brampton
Longtown
Penrith
Kirkby Lonsdale
Orton
Kendal
Carrock Fell
Skiddaw House
Keswick
Helvellyn
Thirlmere
Patterdale
Ambleside
Grasmere
Windermere
Sedbergh
Carlisle
Dentwentwater
Buttermere
Langdale
Borrowdale (Longthwaite)
Hawkshead
Honister Hause
Elterwater
Ullverston
Hawkshead
Ennerdale
Black Sail
Wastwater (High Close)
Copeland
Camforth
Whitehaven
Eskdale
Barrow
Cockermouth
Workington
Egremont
Maryport
Aira
Aspatria

Wooler
Kirk Yetholm
Byrness
Bellingham
Once Brewed
Acomb
Ninebanks
Alston
Edmundbyers
Langdon Beck
Dufton
Kirkby Stephen
Baldersdale
Keld
Grinton Lodge
Hawes
Aysgarth Falls
Dentdale
Ellingstring
Stainforth
Ingleton
Linton
Kettlewell
Malham
Earby
Haworth
Stainburn
Mankinholes

Newcastle-upon-Tyne
Newcastle
Durham
Greenhead
Carlisle
Lancaster
Preston
Leeds
York
Humber
Whitby
Boggle Hole
Scarborough
Lockton
Helmsley
Osmotherley
Beverley Friary

ISLE OF MAN

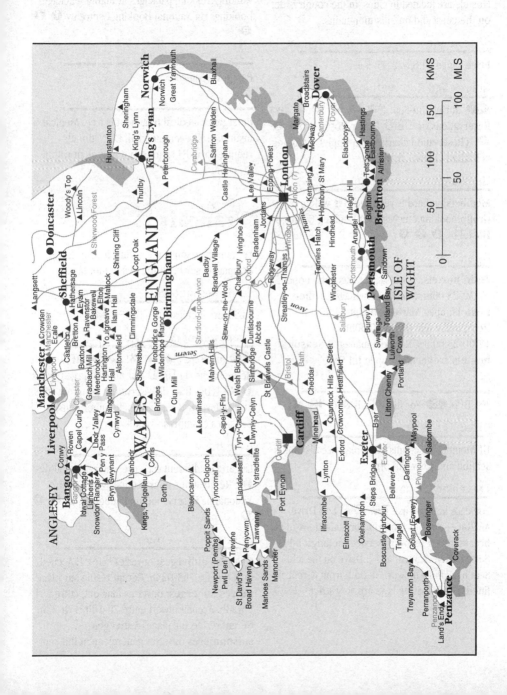

English

Hostels are located in cities, in the countryside, on the coast and on hills/mountains.

Price range

Price range £6.65-22.95. 🔲.

Rooms and Reservations

R during Jun-Sep. (¹🛏 ²🛏 ³🛏 ⁴🛏 ⁵🛏 👪).
Reservations via **IBN** 🖳 or Hostel by **t** **f**
e. (Reservation charges may apply). Smoking is limited - please check.

Guests

Membership Card is required. 👪 welcome.
Group bookings via National Booking Centre or Hostel by **t** **f** **e**.

Open times

Main hostels: open 🔲, ᗪ. Reception open:
07:30-23:00hrs. Resident manager. **Other hostels:** open Mar-Oct, 07:00-23:00hrs.
Reception open: 07:00-10:00hrs,
17:00-23:00hrs. Resident manager. **Seasonal hostels** are generally open Jul-Sep.

Meals

🍽 BLD **R** For individuals & for 👪. 🍴.

Discounts

HI Member Discounts available - see discounts section and www.iyhf.org.

Travelling around

For ease of travel use 🚌 🚐 Self-Drive.
AA/RAC + various motoring organisations offer breakdown & recovery services amongst other things. Drivers must be 17. Drive on the left.
Seat belts must be worn in both front & rear if fitted. Drink-driving laws are very strict.

Travel/Activity Packages

Water sports, cycling/mountain biking and walking/trekking packages available. Package bookings via National Booking Centre by **t** **f** **e**.

Passports and Visas

Passport required.

Health

Emergency medical treatment is free. Medical insurance is recommended. EU Nationals require Form E111 to obtain treatment within EU countries.

Français

Les auberges sont situées dans les villes, à la campagne, sur le littoral et à la montagne.

Tarifs des nuitées

Tarifs des nuitées 6.65-22.95£. 🔲.

Chambres et réservations

R juin-sep. (¹🛏 ²🛏 ³🛏 ⁴🛏 ⁵🛏 👪).
Réservations via **IBN** 🖳 ou l'auberge par **t**
f **e**. (Des frais de réservation pourront vous être facturés). Il est permis de fumer dans certaines chambres - veuillez vérifier.

Usagers

La carte d'adhérent est à présenter. Accueil des 👪. Réservations pour groupes via le Centre National de Réservation ou l'auberge par **t** **f** **e**.

Horaires d'ouverture

Grandes auberges: ouvertes 🔲, ᗪ. Accueil ouvert entre 7h30-23h. Gérant réside sur place.
Autres auberges: ouvertes mar-oct, entre 7h-23h. Accueil ouvert entre 7h-10h, 17h-23h.
Gérant réside sur place. **Auberges saisonnières** ouvertes généralement juil-sep.

Repas

'◎' BLD **R** Pour individuels & pour ⅲ. ✂.

Remises

Remises pour les adhérents HI - voir la section "Remises" et notre site: www.iyhf.org.

Déplacements

Modes de transport recommandés 🚂 🚐 Voiture. Les organisations automobiles AA/RAC offrent, entre autres, des services de dépannage et de recouvrement de véhicule. Si vous voulez conduire en Grande-Bretagne, il vous faudra avoir au moins 17 ans. La conduite est à gauche. Le port des ceintures de sécurité à l'avant et à l'arrière du véhicule, s'il en est équipé, est obligatoire. Les lois concernant l'alcool au volant sont très strictes.

Forfaits Voyages/Activités

Forfaits sports aquatiques, cyclotourisme/VTT et randonnées pédestres disponibles. Réservations des forfaits via le Centre National de Réservation par ❶ ❷ ❸.

Passeports et visas

Passeport obligatoire.

Santé

Soins d'urgence gratuits. Une assurance médicale de voyage est conseillée. Les ressortissants de l'Union Européenne doivent se munir du formulaire E111 pour bénéficier de soins médicaux dans les états de l'UE.

Deutsch

Herbergen befinden sich in Städten, auf dem Land, an der Küste und in Bergen/Gebirgen.

Preisspanne

Preisspanne 6.65-22.95 £. ▣.

Zimmer und Reservierungen

R während Jun-Sept. (¹🛏 ²🛏 ³🛏 ⁴🛏 ⁵🛏 ⅲ). Reservierungen über IBN 🖥 oder die Herberge per ❶ ❷ ❸. (Reservierungskosten könnten anfallen). Rauchen ist begrenzt - bitte checken.

Gäste

Mitgliedsausweis ist erforderlich. ⅲ willkommen. Gruppenbuchungen über Nationales Buchungszentrum oder Herberge per ❶ ❷ ❸.

Öffnungszeiten

Hauptherbergen: Zugang 🗄, ☲. Rezeption zwischen 07:30-23:00Uhr. Herbergsmanager wohnt im Haus. **Andere Herbergen:** Zugang zwischen Mär-Okt, 07:00-23:00Uhr. Rezeption zwischen 07:00-10:00Uhr, 17:00-23:00Uhr. Herbergsmanager wohnt im Haus. **Saison-Herbergen** sind normalerweise Jul-Sept geöffnet.

Mahlzeiten

'◎' BLD **R** Für Einzelreisende & für ⅲ. ✂.

Ermäßigungen

HI-Mitgliedsrabatt ist erhältlich – siehe Teil für Rabatte und Ermäßigungen und www.iyhf.org.

Reisen im Land

Reisen ist einfach mit 🚂 🚐 Selbstfahrer. AA/RAC sowie verschiedene andere Automobil-vereine bieten u. a. Reparatur- und Abschleppdienste an. Fahrer müssen mindestens 17 J. sein; links fahren; Sicherheitsgurte müssen sowohl vorne als auch hinten, falls vorhanden, getragen werden. Sehr strenge Gesetze für Alkohol am Steuer.

Reise-/Aktivitäten-Packages

Wassersport, Fahrrad/Mountainbiking und wandern/trekking-Packages erhältlich.

Package-Buchungen über Nationales
Buchungszentrum per ❶ ❷ ❸.

Reisepässe und Visa

Reisepass erforderlich.

Gesundheit

Nur im Notfall sind medizinische Behandlungen
kostenlos. Unfall-/Krankenversicherung wird
empfohlen. EU Staatsangehörige benötigen
Formular E111 für ärztliche Behandlungen
innerhalb der EU Länder.

Español

Los albergues están situados en las ciudades, el
campo, la costa y la montaña.

Tarifas mínima y máxima

Tarifas mínima y máxima 6.65-22.95£. 🗐.

Habitaciones y Reservas

❶ en jun-sep. (¹🛏 ²🛏 ³🛏 ⁴🛏 ⁵🛏 👫).
Reservas por (IBN) 🖰 o a través del albergue
por ❶ ❷ ❸. (Es posible que se aplique un
suplemento en concepto de gastos de reserva).
Está permitido fumar sólo en algunas
salas/habitaciones - infórmese.

Huéspedes

Los huéspedes deben presentar su Carnet de
Alberguista. Se admiten 👫. Reservas de grupo
a través de la Central Nacional de Reservas o el
albergue por ❶ ❷ ❸.

Horarios y fechas de apertura

Albergues principales - abiertos 🗓, ⏱.
Horario de recepción: 07:30-23:00h. Gerente
residente. **Otros albergues** - abiertos mar-oct,
07:00-23:00h. Horario de recepción:
07:00-10:00h, 17:00-23:00h. Gerente residente.
Albergues de temporada suelen abrir:
jul-sep.

Comidas

🍽 BLD ❶ Para individuales y para 👫. ☝.

Descuentos

Se conceden descuentos a los miembros de
Hostelling International – véase la sección
sobre descuentos y nuestra página Internet en
www.iyhf.org.

Desplazamientos

Transportes recomendados: 🚌 🚐
Automóvil. La AA, el RAC y otras organizaciones
de automovilismo ofrecen, entre otras
prestaciones, servicios de asistencia en
carretera y de grúa. La edad minima para los
conductores es de 17 años. Se circula por la
izquierda. Es obligatorio llevar los cinturones
de seguridad abrochados tanto en los asientos
delanteros como en los traseros, si el automóvil
tiene estos últimos instalados. La legislación en
materia de conducción bajo la influencia del
alcohol es muy estricta.

Viajes Combinados con Actividades

Viajes combinados con deportes náuticos,
cicloturismo/bicicleta de montaña y
senderismo. Reserva de viajes combinados a
través de la Central Nacional de Reservas por
❶ ❷ ❸.

Pasaportes y Visados

Pasaporte obligatorio.

Información Sanitaria

Asistencia médica de urgencia gratuita. Seguro
médico recomendado. Los ciudadanos
procedentes de países pertenecientes a la UE
necesitan el impreso E111 para obtener
asistencia médica en dichos países.

Ambleside -
Waterhead

Ambleside,
Cumbria LA22 0EU.
☏ (15394) 32304
🖶 (15394) 34408
✉ ambleside@yha.org.uk

Open Dates:	🗓
Open Hours:	🕐
Reservations:	IBN CC
Price Range:	£9.50-13.50 💶
Beds:	245 - 12x² 17x³ 9x⁴ 5x⁵ 4x⁶ 12x⁶
Facilities:	👥 47x 👥 🍴 🚿 🚲 ☼ ⛺ 📺 🎮 🖥 💼 ⚒ 8 P ℹ 🧺 🐾 🏠
Directions:	1.5 S from city centre
✈	Manchester 145km
🚢	Stranraer/Belfast 97km
🚂	Windermere 6.5km
🚌	555 500m ap Waterhead Pier
Attractions:	🏞 ⛰ 🚴 🚶 U2km 🔍1.5km 🏊4km

Bath -
Bathwick Hill

Bath,
BA2 6JZ.
☏ (1225) 465674
🖶 (1225) 482947
✉ bath@yha.org.uk

Open Dates:	🗓
Open Hours:	🕐
Reservations:	R IBN CC
Price Range:	£7.75-11.00 💶
Beds:	124 - 3x² 12x⁴ 2x⁵ 4x⁶ 4x⁶
Facilities:	👥 🍴 🚿 🚲 ☼ ⛺ 📺 🎮 🖥 💼 ℹ 🧺 🐾 🏛
Directions:	1 E from city centre
🚂	Bath Spa 1.5km
🚌	18 1.5km ap Outside Hostel
Attractions:	🔍1km 🏊1km

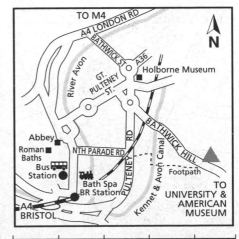

Cambridge

97 Tenison Rd,
Cambridge CB1 2DN.
☎ (1223) 354601
fax (1223) 312780
e cambridge@yha.org.uk

Open Dates:	📅
Open Hours:	🕐
Reservations:	IBN CC
Price Range:	£8.50-12.50 🍴
Beds:	100 - 7x² 1x³ 8x⁴ 1x⁵ 5x⁶ 2x⁶
Facilities:	ⅲ 🍽 ⚲ 🛏 📺 ▢ 🖼 8 ♿ ♻
Directions:	2 SE from city centre
✈	Stansted 32km
A🚌	Cambridge 1.6km
🚌	Cambridge 400m
🚌	No.1 400m ap Cambridge Railway Station
Attractions:	⚓ 800m

Canterbury - Ellerslie

54 New Dover Rd,
Canterbury,
Kent CT1 3DT.
☎ (1227) 462911
fax (1227) 470752
e canterbury@yha.org.uk

Open Dates:	01.02-31.12
Open Hours:	07.30-10.00hrs; 13.00-23.00hrs
Reservations:	IBN CC
Price Range:	£7.75-11.00 🍴
Beds:	85 - 1x¹ 1x² 1x⁴ 5x⁶ 4x⁶
Facilities:	ⅲ 🍽 ⚲ 🛏 📺 ▢ 🎱 ▢ 🖼 ♨ 8 P ℹ ♿ ♻ 🏢 🏠 🏡
Directions:	1 SE from city centre
✈	Gatwick 107.2km
⛴	Dover 22.4km
🚌	Canterbury East 1km; Canterbury West 2km
Attractions:	🎿 ∪ 5km ⚲ 3km ⚓ 2km

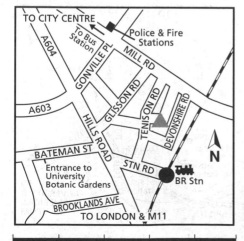

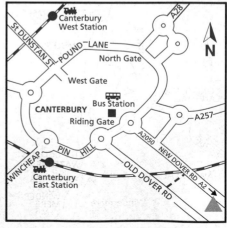

Dover

306 London Rd,
Dover,
Kent CT17 0SY.
☏ (1304) 201314
🖷 (1304) 202236
📧 dover@yha.org.uk

Open Dates:	🗓
Open Hours:	07.00-10.00hrs; 13.00-23.00hrs
Reservations:	IBN CC
Price Range:	£7.75-11.00 💷
Beds:	132 - 6x^2 1x^4 2x^6 12x^{6+}
Facilities:	♂♂♂ ♂♂ 🍴 🚿 🚪 📺 🧺 ♨ ℹ 🖥 ♿ ♿
Directions:	0.5 NW from city centre

🚢	Dover 2km
🚂	Dover Priory 1km

Attractions: 🔍1km 🚴 🚶 ⌚5km ⚓500m 🏊1km

Liverpool

25 Tabley St (off Wapping),
Liverpool,
L1 8EE.
☏ (151) 7098888
🖷 (151) 7090417
📧 liverpool@yha.org.uk

Open Dates:	🗓
Open Hours:	🕐
Reservations:	IBN CC
Price Range:	£13.50-18.00 BB inc 💷
Beds:	110 - 2x^3 17x^4 6x^6
Facilities:	♿ ♂♂♂ ♂♂ 🍴 🚿 🚪 📺3 x 🍷 🖥 🖼 🔟 🅿 ℹ
Directions:	1 SW from city centre

✈	Liverpool 8km, Manchester 44km
🚢	Liverpool 1km
🚂	Lime Street 1.5km
Ⓤ	James Street 600m

Attractions: 🚴

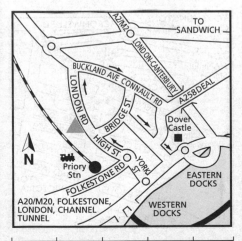

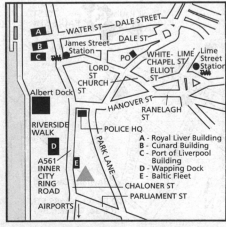

A - Royal Liver Building
B - Cunard Building
C - Port of Liverpool Building
D - Wapping Dock
E - Baltic Fleet

London -
City of London

36 Carter Lane,
London EC4V 5AB.
📞 (20) 72364965
📠 (20) 72367681
✉ city@yha.org.uk

Open Dates:	🗓12
Open Hours:	🕐
Reservations:	Ⓡ IBN -CC-
Price Range:	£19.90-23.50 BB inc 🍴
Beds:	193 - 3x1🛏 6x2🛏 7x3🛏 8x4🛏 7x5🛏 6x6🛏 7x6🛏
Facilities:	5x ♔ 🍴 🛏 📺 ⛾1 x 🍴 🖿 ⊞ 🔢 ⓘ 🎦 🏫
Directions:	2NE from city centre
✈	Heathrow 12.8km; Gatwick 19.2km
🚌	Blackfriars 300m; St Pauls 500m
🚐	ap St. Pauls 500m
Ⓤ	Blackfriars 300m; St Pauls 274m
Attractions:	🚲 ⛵1km

London -
Earls Court

38 Bolton Gardens,
London,
SW5 0AQ.
📞 (20) 73737083
📠 (20) 78352034
✉ earlscourt@yha.org.uk

Open Dates:	🗓12
Open Hours:	🕐
Reservations:	Ⓡ IBN -CC-
Price Range:	£16.50-18.50 🍴
Beds:	159 - 3x2🛏 3x3🛏 9x4🛏 3x6🛏 10x6🛏
Facilities:	🍴 (B) 🖿 🚿 🛏 📺 ⛾ 🔟 🖿 ⊞ 🔢 ⓘ 🎦 🐾 🏫
Directions:	6SW from city centre
✈	Heathrow 12km
🚌	Waterloo 3.5km
🚐	31; C1; C3; N31; N1; 6HT 100m
Ⓤ	Earl's Court 500m

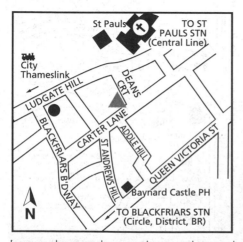

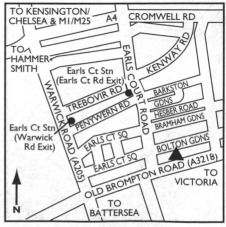

London - Hampstead Heath

4 Wellgarth Rd,
Golders Green,
London NW11 7HR.
☎ (20) 84589054
f (20) 82090546
e hampstead@yha.org.uk

Open Dates: ▢12

Open Hours: ◷

Reservations: ⓡ ⓘⒷⓝ ⒸⒸ

Price Range: £17.70-19.90 ⒷⒷ inc ▢

Beds: 200 - 14x²⚏ 9x³⚏ 14x⁴⚏ 9x⁵⚏ 4x⁶⚏ 2x⁶⚏

Facilities: ♜ 10x ♜ ⵑⵀ ✆ ⛬ 📺 ▦ ⵠ ▣ ◨ ⛫ ⑧ Ⓟ Ⓘ ⛻ ⚘ ⛩

Directions: ⑨ⓃⓌ from city centre

✈ Gatwick 76.8km; Heathrow 48km

🚂 Kings Cross/St. Pancras 4km

🚌 210 & 268 400m ap North End Road Ⓤ

Ⓤ Northern; Golder's Green 1km

Attractions: ⵚ

London - Holland House

Holland House,
Holland Walk,
Kensington,
London W8 7QU.
☎ (20) 79370748
f (20) 73760667
e hollandhouse@yha.org.uk

Open Dates: ▢12

Open Hours: ◷

Reservations: ⓡ ⓘⒷⓝ ⒸⒸ

Price Range: £18.50-20.50 ⒷⒷ inc ▢

Beds: 201 - 1x¹⚏ 1x²⚏ 1x³⚏ 1x⁴⚏ 1x⁶⚏ 13x⁶⚏

Facilities: ♜ ⵑⵀ ✆ ⛬ 📺 ▦ ⵠ 1 x ⛫ ◨ ▣ ⛫ ⑧ Ⓘ ⛻ ⚘ ⛩

Directions: ⑥ⓈⓌ from city centre

✈ Heathrow 48km; Gatwick 76.8km

A🚌 Airbus

🚂 Paddington 3.2km; Waterloo 14.4km

🚌 9 & 10 500m ap Kensington High Street Ⓤ

Ⓤ Holland Park; Circle Line 400m; High Street, Kensington 400m

Attractions: ⵚ ⚲400km

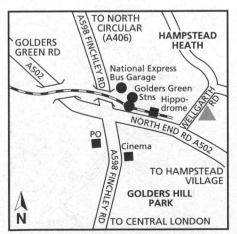

London - Oxford Street

14 Noel St,
London W1V 3PD.
- ☎ (20) 77341618
- 📠 (20) 77341657
- ✉ oxfordst@yha.org.uk

Open Dates:	🗓
Open Hours:	🕐
Reservations:	Ⓡ IBN CC
Price Range:	£17.50-21.50
Beds:	75 - 24x² 5x³ 4x⁴
Facilities:	

Directions:

✈	Heathrow 48km; Gatwick 76.8km
A🚐	A2 Kings Cross & Marblearch 1.5km
🚂	Victoria 3km; Waterloo 3km; Kings Cross 1.5km
🚐	10, 8, 73, 25, 55, 176 200m; 6, 12, 13, 15, 23, 94, 139, 113 400m ap Oxford Street; Regent Street
Ⓤ	Central, Bakerloo and Victoria Lines to Oxford Circus 400m, or Northern and Central Lines to Tottenham Court Road 500m

London - Rotherhithe

20 Salter Rd,
London SE16 5PR.
- ☎ (20) 72322114
- 📠 (20) 72372919
- ✉ rotherhithe@yha.org.uk

Open Dates:	🗓
Open Hours:	🕐
Reservations:	Ⓡ IBN CC
Price Range:	£19.90-23.50 BBinc
Beds:	320 - 22x² 12x⁴ 33x⁶ 3x⁶
Facilities:	

Directions:

✈	Heathrow 40km; Gatwick 50km
⛴	Dover 125km
🚂	Waterloo 6km
🚐	381, N381 ap Outside Hostel
Ⓤ	Rotherhithe 400m

Attractions: 🏊 2km

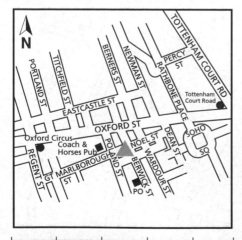

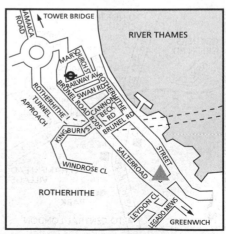

London - St Pancras

**79-81 Euston Rd,
London NW1 2QS.**
☎ (20) 73889998
🖷 (20) 73886766
✉ stpancras@yha.org.uk

Open Dates: ▣
Open Hours: ◷
Reservations: Ⓡ ⒾⒷⓃ ⒸⒸ
Price Range: £19.90-23.50 BB inc 🖵
Beds: 152 - 10x🛏 1x🛏 18x🛏 3x🛏 5x🛏
Facilities: ♦♦♦ 🍽 (BD) 🚿 🏛 📺 🖥 ▣ 🎒 ⑧ ⊜ ⊠ ⓘ 🚲

Directions:

✈	Heathrow 48km; Gatwick 76.8km
A🚌	Airbus 48km
🚇	St Pancras, Kings Cross 200m
🚌	73
Ⓤ	Kings Cross; St Pancras 200m

Attractions: 🚴

Manchester

**Potato Wharf,
Castlefield,
Manchester M3 4NB.**
☎ (161) 8399960
🖷 (161) 8352054
✉ manchester@yha.org.uk

Open Dates: ▣
Open Hours: ◷
Reservations: Ⓡ ⒾⒷⓃ ⒸⒸ
Price Range: £13.50-18.00 BB inc 🖵
Beds: 140 - 1x🛏 33x🛏 4x🛏
Facilities: ♿ ♦♦♦ ♦♦ 🍽 🚿 ⚙ 🏛 📺 🖥 3 x 🍴 ▣ 🏧 ⑧ ⊠ Ⓟ ⓘ 🚲

Directions:

✈	Manchester 16km
⛴	Liverpool 44km
🚇	Manchester Piccadilly 1.5km
🚌	33 500m ap Liverpool Road
🚊	GMEX 500m ap G-Mex
Ⓤ	Metro Link GMEX 500m

Attractions: 🏊 100m

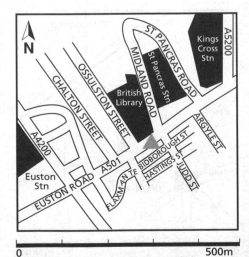

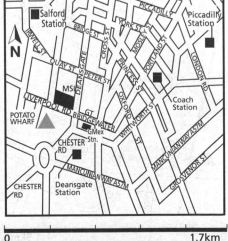

Oxford - New Oxford

2a Botley Rd,
Oxford OX2 0AB.
t (1865) 727275
f (1865) 769402
e oxford@yha.org.uk

Open Dates: 🗓

Open Hours: 🕓

Reservations: (IBN) (CC)

Price Range: £13.50-18.00 BB inc 🗂

Beds: 184 - 8x² 12x⁴ 20x⁶

Facilities: ♿ ♀♀♀ 20x ♀♀♀ ⊙ ☕ 🚲 ✲ 🏠 📺 📱 🗄2 x❚ 🅾 🖼 ⚒ 8 ⬍ 🖼 🌿

Directions: 3NE from city centre

✈ Heathrow 80km; Gatwick 176km

🚢 Portsmouth 136km

NB: This hostel will open in April 2001. In the meantime, please make your enquiries/bookings at the current Oxford site:

32 Jack Straw's Lane, Oxford OX3 0DW
t (1865) 762997, **f** (1865) 769402
e oxford@yha.org.uk

Stratford-upon-Avon - Hemmingford House

Alveston,
Stratford-upon-Avon,
Warwickshire CV37 7RG.
t (1789) 297093
f (1789) 205513
e stratford@yha.org.uk

Open Dates: 🗓

Open Hours: 🕓

Reservations: (IBN) (CC)

Price Range: £11.50-15.50 BB inc 🗂

Beds: 130 - 8x² 6x⁴ 1x⁵ 8x⁶ 5x⁶

Facilities: ♀♀♀ 6x ♀♀♀ ⊙ 🅾 🏠 📺 🗄2 x❚ 🅾 ⚒ 🅿 ℹ 🖼 🌿

Directions:

✈ Birmingham 32km

🚌 National Express 3.5km

🚂 Stratford Upon Avon 4.5km

🚌 18 ap Youth Hostel Front Gate

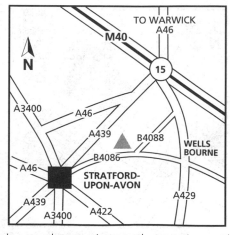

York

York International,
Water End,
Clifton,
York,
Yorkshire YO30 6LP.
☎ (1904) 653147
📠 (1904) 651230
✉ york@yha.org.uk

Open Dates:	🗓
Open Hours:	🕐
Reservations:	IBN CC
Price Range:	£11.50-15.50 BB inc 📖
Beds:	150 - 1x¹ 7x² 1x³ 21x⁴ 4x⁶ 3x⁶
Facilities:	ⅲ 21x ⅲ 🍽 📷 ⚙ 🏨 📺 📄 🎱 1x 🍴 🔲 🖼 ♨ 8 P ℹ ♿ 🎿 ⚠ 🔍 🏪 🏠 🏘
Directions:	1.5 NW from city centre
✈	Leeds-Bradford 40km
⛴	Hull 80km
🚃	York 2km
🚌	32-19 500m ap Clifton Green
Attractions:	⚓ 1.5km

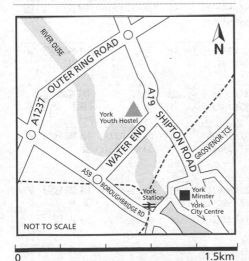

Location/Address	Telephone No. Fax No.	Beds	Opening Dates	Facilities
△ *Acomb* *Main St, Acomb, Hexham,* *Northumberland NE46 4PL.*	☏ *(1434) 602864*	*36*	📅	⊟CC⊟ ☛ 🅿
▲ Alfriston Frog Firle, Alfriston, Polegate, East Sussex BN26 5TT. ℯ alfriston@yha.org.uk	☏ (1323) 870423 ℻ (1323) 870615	68	09.02–15.12; 28–31.12	¶⊙ ® ⊟CC⊟ ☛ 🅿
▲ Alston The Firs, Alston, Cumbria CA9 3RW.	☏ (1434) 381509 ℻ (1434) 382401	30	06.04–31.10	¶⊙ ⊟CC⊟ ☛ 🅿 ▣
▲ Alstonefield Gypsy Lane, Alstonefield, Derbyshire DE6 2FZ.	☏ (1335) 310206 ℻ (1335) 310206	20	12.04–30.08	††† ☛
▲ Ambleside - Waterhead ⟨IBN⟩ **Ambleside, Cumbria LA22 0EU.** ℯ ambleside@yha.org.uk	☏ (15394) 32304 ℻ (15394) 34408	245	📅	††† ¶⊙ ⟨1.5S⟩ ⊟CC⊟ ☛ 🅿 ▣ 🚲 ✿
▲ Arnside Oakfield Lodge, Redhills Rd, Arnside, Carnforth, Lancashire LA5 0AT. ℯ arnside@yha.org.uk	☏ (1524) 761781 ℻ (1524) 762589	72	09.02–03.11; 09.11–24.11; 28–31.12	††† ¶⊙ ® ⊟CC⊟ ☛ 🅿 ▣ ✿
▲ Arundel Warningcamp, Arundel, West Sussex BN18 9QY.	☏ (1903) 882204 ℻ (1903) 882776	60	05.01–26.12	††† ¶⊙ ⊟CC⊟ ☛ 🅿 ✿
▲ Aysgarth Falls Aysgarth, Leyburn, North Yorkshire DL8 3SR. ℯ aysgarth@yha.org.uk	☏ (1969) 663260 ℻ (1969) 663110	67	01.02–02.12	††† ¶⊙ ⊟CC⊟ ☛ 🅿
▲ Badby Church Green, Badby, Daventry, Northamptonshire NN11 3AS.	☏ / ℻ (1327) 703883	30	12.04–01.09; 04.09–27.10	⊟CC⊟ ☛
▲ Bakewell Fly Hill, Bakewell, Derbyshire DE45 1DN. ℯ bakewell@yha.org.uk	☏ (1629) 812313 ℻ (1629) 812313	32	02.01–26.12	¶⊙ ⊟CC⊟ ☛ 🅿 ✿
▲ Baldersdale Blackton, Baldersdale, Barnard Castle, Co Durham DL12 9UP.	☏ (1833) 650629 ℻ (1833) 650629	39	06.04–31.10	¶⊙ ⊟CC⊟ ☛ 🅿
▲ Bangor ⟨IBN⟩ Tan-y-Bryn, Bangor, Gwynedd Wales LL57 1PZ. ℯ bangor@yha.org.uk	☏ (1248) 353516 ℻ (1248) 371176	84	📅	††† ¶⊙ ⊟CC⊟ ☛ 🅿 ▣
▲ Bath - Bathwick Hill ⟨IBN⟩ **Bath, BA2 6JZ.** ℯ bath@yha.org.uk	☏ (1225) 465674 ℻ (1225) 482947	124	📅	¶⊙ ® ⟨1E⟩ ⊟CC⊟ ☛ ▣ 🚲 ✿
▲ Beer Bovey Combe, Townsend, Beer, Seaton, Devon EX12 3LL. ℯ beer@yha.org.uk	☏ (1297) 20296 ℻ (1297) 23690	40	05.03–02.09; 04.09–31.10	††† ¶⊙ ⊟CC⊟ ☛ 🅿
▲ Bellever Postbridge, Yelverton, Devon PL20 6TU.	☏ (1822) 880227 ℻ (1822) 880302	38	09.04–31.10	††† ¶⊙ ⊟CC⊟ ☛ 🅿 ✿
△ *Bellingham* *Woodburn Rd, Bellingham, Hexham,* *Northumberland NE48 2ED.*	☏ *(1434) 220313*	*28*	*01.04–27.10*	††† ☛ 🅿

Location/Address	Telephone No. Fax No.	Beds	Opening Dates	Facilities
▲ **Beverley** - Beverley Friary The Friary, Friar's Lane, Beverley, East Yorkshire HU17 0DF.	☎ (1482) 881751 🖷 (1482) 880118	34	12.04–01.09; 04.09–27.10	⍤ & CC ⍩ P
▲ **Blackboys** Uckfield, East Sussex TN22 5HU.	☎ (1825) 890607 🖷 (1825) 890104	29	12.04–08.09	⍩ P 🗔 ☼
△ *Black Sail* *Black Sail Hut, Ennerdale, Cleator,* *Cumbria CA23 3AY.*	☎ *(411) 108450* 🖷 *(411) 159472*	*16*	*01.04–27.10*	⍤ R CC ⍩ ☼
△ *Blaencaron* *Tregaron, Ceredigion, Wales SY25 6HL.*	☎ *(1629) 581399*	*16*	*13.04–29.09*	⍩ P
▲ **Blaxhall** Heath Walk, Blaxhall, Woodbridge, Suffolk IP12 2EA.	☎ (1728) 688206 🖷 (1728) 689191	40	10.04–01.09; 04.09–30.10	⍤ CC ⍩ P 🗔
▲ **Boggle Hole** Mill Beck, Fylingthorpe, Whitby, North Yorkshire YO22 4UQ. 🄴 bogglehole@yha.org.uk	☎ (1947) 880352 🖷 (1947) 880987	80	16.02–01.12; 30–31.12	⍥ ⍤ R CC ⍩ P
▲ **Borrowdale (Longthwaite)** Longthwaite, Borrowdale, Keswick, Cumbria CA12 5XE. 🄴 borrowdale@yha.org.uk	☎ (17687) 77257 🖷 (17687) 77393	88	01.01–28.12	⍥ ⍤ CC ⍩ P 🗔 ☼
▲ **Borth** Morlais, Borth, Ceredigion, Wales SY24 5JS. 🄴 borth@yha.org.uk	☎ (1970) 871498 🖷 (1970) 871827	60	02.04–27.10	⍥ ⍤ CC ⍩ P
▲ **Boscastle Harbour** Palace Stables, Boscastle, Cornwall PL35 0HD.	☎ (1840) 250287 🖷 (1840) 250615	25	12.04–31.10	⍤ CC ⍩ ☼
▲ **Boswinger** Gorran, St Austell, Cornwall PL26 6LL.	☎ (1726) 843234 🖷 (1726) 843234	38	09.04–31.10	⍥ ⍤ CC ⍩ P 🗔 ☼
▲ **Bradenham** Bradenham, High Wycombe, Buckinghamshire HP14 4HF. 🄴 bradenham@yha.org.uk	☎ (1494) 562929 🖷 (1494) 564743	16	01.03–08.04; 13.04–03.11	R CC ⍩ P ☼
▲ **Bradwell Village** Vicarage Rd, Bradwell, Milton Keynes, Buckinghamshire MK13 9AJ.	☎ (1908) 310944 🖷 (1908) 310944	38	10.04–06.09	CC ⍩ P
△ *Bretton* *Nether Bretton, Derbyshire.*	☎ *(1433) 631856* 🖷 *(1433) 631856*	*18*	*12.04–10.11*	⍩ P ☼
△ *Bridges Long Mynd* *Ratlinghope, Shrewsbury,* *Shropshire SY5 0SP.*	☎ *(1588) 650656* 🖷 *(1694) 650531*	*37*	🗓12	⍩ P
▲ **Brighton** Patcham Place, London Rd, Brighton, Sussex BN1 8YD. 🄴 brighton@yha.org.uk	☎ (1273) 556196 🖷 (1273) 509366	84	01–03.01; 01–28.02; 01.03–31.10	⍤ 6NW CC ⍩ P 🗔 🚲 ☼
▲ **Bristol** IBN International YHA, Hayman House, 14 Narrow Quay, Bristol BS1 4QA. 🄴 bristol@yha.org.uk	☎ (117) 9221659 🖷 (117) 9273789	92	🗓12	⍥ ⍤ 1SW CC ⍩ 🗔 🚲 ☼

Location/Address	Telephone No. Fax No.	Beds	Opening Dates	Facilities
▲ **Broad Haven** Broad Haven, Haverfordwest, Pembrokeshire, Wales SA62 3JH. ⓔ broadhaven@yha.org.uk	☎ (1437) 781688 ⓕ (1437) 781100	75	09.02–03.11	ᵻᵻᵼ ⵏⵑ ⴲ ⴺCCⴲ ⵣ 🅿 🔟
▲ **Broadstairs** 3 Osborne Rd, Broadstairs, Kent CT10 2AE. ⓔ broadstairs@yha.org.uk	☎ (1843) 604121 ⓕ (1843) 604121	34	02–31.01; 01.04–18.10	ᵻᵻᵼ 0.5W ⴺCCⴲ ⵣ ✿
▲ **Bryn Gwynant** Nantgwynant, Caernarfon, Gwynedd, Wales LL55 4NP. ⓔ bryngwynant@yha.org.uk	☎ (1766) 890251 ⓕ (1766) 890479	77	05.01–24.02; 02.03–27.10	ᵻᵻᵼ ⵏⵑ ⴺCCⴲ ⵣ 🅿
▲ **Burley** Cott Lane, Burley, Ringwood, Hampshire BH24 4BB.	☎ (1425) 403233 ⓕ (1425) 403233	36	02.04–03.09; 06.09–08.10	ⵏⵑ ⴺCCⴲ ⵣ 🅿 ✿
▲ **Buttermere** King George VI Memorial Hostel, Buttermere, Cockermouth, Cumbria CA13 9XA. ⓔ buttermere@yha.org.uk	☎ (17687) 70245 ⓕ (17687) 70231	70	01.01–28.12	ᵻᵻᵼ ⵏⵑ ⴺCCⴲ ⵣ 🅿 ✿
▲ **Buxton** Sherbrook Lodge, Harpur Hill Rd, Buxton, Derbyshire SK17 9NB.	☎ (1298) 22287 ⓕ (1298) 22287	56	04.02–26.12	ⵏⵑ ⴺCCⴲ ⵣ 🅿 ✿
△ *Byrness* *7 Otterburn Green, Byrness, Newcastle-upon-Tyne, Northumberland NE19 1TS.*	☎ *(1830) 520425* ⓕ *(1830) 520425*	*22*	*08.04–06.10*	ⴺCCⴲ ⵣ 🅿 🔟
▲ **Cambridge** [IBN] **97 Tenison Rd, Cambridge CB1 2DN.** ⓔ cambridge@yha.org.uk	☎ (1223) 354601 ⓕ (1223) 312780	100	🔓	ⵏⵑ 2SE ⴺCCⴲ ⵣ 🔟
▲ **Canterbury** - Ellerslie [IBN] **54 New Dover Rd, Canterbury, Kent CT1 3DT.** ⓔ canterbury@yha.org.uk	☎ (1227) 462911 ⓕ (1227) 470752	85	01.02–31.12	ⵏⵑ 1SE ⴺCCⴲ ⵣ 🅿 🔟
▲ **Capel Curig** Plas Curig, Capel Curig, Betws-y-Coed, Wales LL24 0EL. ⓔ capelcurig@yha.org.uk	☎ (1690) 720225 ⓕ (1690) 720270	52	09.02–27.10; 02.11–22.12; 28–31.12	ᵻᵻᵼ ⵏⵑ ⴺCCⴲ ⵣ 🅿
△ *Capel-y-Ffin* *Capel-y-Ffin, Llanthony, Nr. Abergavenny, Wales, NP7 7NP.*	☎ *(1873) 890650*	*40*	*01.04–03.10*	ⵏⵑ ⴺCCⴲ ⵣ 🅿 ✿
▲ **Cardiff** [IBN] 2 Wedal Rd, Roath Park, Cardiff, Wales CF14 3QX. ⓔ cardiff@yha.org.uk	☎ (2920) 462303 ⓕ (2920) 464571	68	🔓	ⵏⵑ ⴲ ⴺCCⴲ ⵣ 🅿 🔟 ✿
▲ **Carlisle** The University of Northumbria, The Old Brewery Residences, Bridge Lane, Caldewgate, Carlisle, Cumbria CA2 5SW. ⓔ dee@carruthers@unn.ac.uk	☎ (1228) 597352 ⓕ (1228) 597352	56	07.07–08.09	Ⓡ ⴲ ⵣ 🅿 🔟

Location/Address	Telephone No. Fax No.	Beds	Opening Dates	Facilities
▲ **Carrock Fell** High Row Cottage, Haltcliffe, Hesket Newmarket, Wigton, Cumbria CA7 8JT.	☏ (16974) 78325 ☎ (16974) 78325	20	01.04–27.10	⊟CC⊟ ☞ ℙ
▲ **Castle Hedingham** 7 Falcon Square, Castle Hedingham, Halstead, Essex CO9 3BU. @ castlehed@yha.org.uk	☏ (1787) 460799 ☎ (1787) 461302	50	09.02–03.11	♦♦ ⵁⵁ Ⓡ ⊟CC⊟ ☞ ✿
▲ **Castleton** Castleton Hall, Castleton, Hope Valley S33 8WG. @ castleton@yha.org.uk	☏ (1433) 620235 ☎ (1433) 621767	150	04.02–23.12	♦♦ ⵁⵁ Ⓡ ⊟CC⊟ ☞ ℙ ✿
▲ **Charlbury** The Laurels, The Slade, Charlbury, Oxfordshire OX7 3SJ @ charlbury@yha.org.uk	☏ (1608) 810202 ☎ (1608) 810202	51	09.02–01.09; 04.09–10.11	♦♦ ⵁⵁ ⅋ ☞ ℙ ▣ ✿
▲ **Cheddar** Hillfield, Cheddar, Somerset BS27 3HN. @ cheddar@yha.org.uk	☏ (1934) 742494 ☎ (1934) 744724	53	28.01–10.11; 16.11–22.12	♦♦ ⵁⵁ ⊟CC⊟ ☞ ℙ ▣ ✿
▲ **Chester** [IBN] Hough Green House, 40 Hough Green, Chester CH4 8JD. @ chester@yha.org.uk	☏ (1244) 680056 ☎ (1244) 681204	117	12.01–15.12	♦♦ ⵁⵁ Ⓡ 2SW ⊟CC⊟ ☞ ℙ ▣ ⟲ ✿
▲ **Clun Mill** The Mill, Clun, Nr Craven Arms, Shropshire SY7 8NY.	☏ (1588) 640582 ☎ (1588) 640582	24	12.04–30.08	⊟CC⊟ ☞ ℙ
▲ **Cockermouth** Double Mills, Cockermouth, Cumbria CA13 0DS.	☏ (1900) 822561 ☎ (1900) 822561	28	01.04–27.10	⊟CC⊟ ☞ ℙ ✿
▲ **Coniston (Holly How)** Holly How, Far End, Coniston, Cumbria LA21 8DD.	☏ (15394) 41323 ☎ (15394) 41803	60	12.01–25.11	♦♦ ⵁⵁ Ⓡ ⊟CC⊟ ☞ ℙ ▣ ✿
▲ **Coniston Coppermines** Coppermines House, Coniston, Cumbria LA21 8HP.	☏ (15394) 41261 ☎ (15394) 41261	28	01.04–27.10	ⵁⵁ ⊟CC⊟ ☞ ℙ ✿
▲ **Conwy** Larkhill, Sychnant Pass Rd, Conwy, Wales, LL32 8AJ. @ conwy@yha.org.uk	☏ (1492) 593571 ☎ (1492) 593580	80	09.02–27.10; 02.11–22.12; 28–31.12	♦♦ ⵁⵁ ⅋ ⊟CC⊟ ☞ ℙ ▣ ✿
▲ **Copt Oak** Whitwick Rd, Copt Oak, Markfield, Leicestershire LE67 9QB.	☏ (1530) 242661 ☎ (1530) 242661	16	12.04–30.08	⊟CC⊟ ☞ ℙ
▲ **Corris** Old School, Old Rd, Corris, Machynlleth, Powys SY20 9QT.	☏ (1654) 761686 ☎ (1654) 761686	46	🗓	♦♦ ⵁⵁ ☞ ℙ
▲ **Coverack** Parc Behan, School Hill, Coverack, Helston, Cornwall TR12 6SA.	☏ (1326) 280687 ☎ (1326) 280119	38	09.04–31.10	♦♦ ⵁⵁ ⊟CC⊟ ☞ ℙ

Location/Address	Telephone No. Fax No.	Beds	Opening Dates	Facilities
▲ **Crowcombe Heathfield** Denzel House, Crowcombe Heathfield, Taunton, Somerset TA4 4BT.	☎ (1984) 667249 🖷 (1984) 667249	50	09.04–06.09	ⅲ ᴄᴄ ⌁ P 🗗
△ *Crowden-in-Longdendale* *Peak National Park Hostel, Crowden,* *Glossop, Derbyshire SK13 1HZ.*	☎ *(1457) 852135* 🖷 *(1457) 852135*	*38*	*02.04–18.11*	ⅼ⊙ⅼ ᴄᴄ ⌁ P
△ *Cynwyd* *The Old Mill, Cynwyd, Corwen, Denbighshire,* *Wales LL21 0LW.*	☎ *(1490) 412814* 🖷 *(1490) 412814*	*30*	*12.04–29.09*	ᴄᴄ ⌁ P
▲ **Dartington** Lownard, Dartington, Totnes, Devon TQ9 6JJ.	☎ (1803) 862303 🖷 (1803) 865171	30	12.04–30.09	ⅲ ᴄᴄ ⌁ P 🗗
▲ **Dentdale** Cowgill, Dent, Sedbergh, Cumbria LA10 5RN.	☎ (15396) 25251 🖷 (15396) 25068	38	26.01–09.12; 31.12	ⅼ⊙ⅼ ᴄᴄ ⌁ P
▲ **Derwentwater** Barrow House, Borrowdale, Keswick, Cumbria CA12 5UR. ✉ derwentwater@yha.org.uk	☎ (17687) 77246 🖷 (17687) 77396	88	05.01–31.12	ⅲ ⅼ⊙ⅼ Ⓡ ᴄᴄ ⌁ P 🗗 ✿
▲ **Dimmingsdale** Little Ranger, Dimmingsdale, Oakamoor, Stoke-on-Trent, Staffordshire ST10 3AS.	☎ (1538) 702304 🖷 (1538) 702304	20	12.04–01.09; 04–20.09	ᴄᴄ ⌁ P
▲ **Dolgoch** Tregaron, Ceredigion SY25 6NR.	☎ (1629) 581399	22	09–21.04; 25.05–01.09	⌁ P
▲ **Dover** ⒤ⒷⓃ **306 London Rd, Dover, Kent CT17 0SY.** ✉ dover@yha.org.uk	☎ (1304) 201314 🖷 (1304) 202236	132	🔟	ⅲ ⅼ⊙ⅼ 0.5NW ᴄᴄ ⌁
▲ **Dufton** 'Redstones', Dufton, Appleby, Cumbria CA16 6DB.	☎ (17683) 51236 🖷 (17683) 53798	36	06.04–03.10	ⅼ⊙ⅼ ᴄᴄ ⌁ P 🗗
△ *Earby* *Katherine Bruce Glasier Memorial Hostel,* *Glen Cottage, 9-11 Birch Hall Lane, Earby,* *Barnoldswick, Lancashire BB18 6JX.*	☎ *(1282) 842349* 🖷 *(1282) 842349*	*22*	*01.04–27.10*	ᴄᴄ ⌁ P
▲ **Eastbourne** East Dean Rd, Eastbourne, East Sussex BN20 8ES.	☎ (1323) 721081 🖷 (1323) 721081	32	12.04–30.09	ⅲ ᴄᴄ ⌁ P ✿
▲ **Edale** Hostel and Activity Centre, Rowland Cote, Edale, Hope Valley S33 7ZH. ✉ edale@yha.org.uk	☎ (1433) 670302 🖷 (1433) 670243	141	🔟	ⅼ⊙ⅼ Ⓡ ᴄᴄ ⌁ P 🗗 ✿
▲ **Edmundbyers** Low House, Edmundbyers, Consett, Co Durham DH8 9NL.	☎ (1207) 255651 🖷 (1207) 255651	33	01.04–27.10	♿ ᴄᴄ ⌁ P
▲ **Ellingstring** Lilac Cottage, Ellingstring, Masham, nr Ripon, North Yorks HG4 4PW.	☎ (1677) 460132 🖷 (1677) 460132	18	13–15.04; 04–06.05; 25–27.05; 23.07–30.08	⌁ P
▲ **Elmscott** Hartland, Bideford, Devon EX39 6ES.	☎ (1237) 441367 🖷 (1237) 441910	32	12.04–08.09	ᴄᴄ ⌁ P

Location/Address	Telephone No. Fax No.	Beds	Opening Dates	Facilities
▲**Elterwater** - Langdale Ambleside, Cumbria LA22 9HX. e elterwater@yha.org.uk	t (15394) 37245 f (15394) 37120	45	05.01–22.12; 28–31.12	R CC P
▲**Elton** Elton Old Hall, Main St, Elton, Matlock, Derbyshire DE4 2BW.	t (1629) 650394 f (1629) 650394	32	12.04–01.09; 04.09–27.10	CC P
▲**Ennerdale (Gillerthwaite)** Cat Crag, Ennerdale, Cleator, Cumbria CA23 3AX.	t (1946) 861237	24	01.04–27.10	CC P
▲**Epping Forest** Wellington Hill, High Beach, Loughton, Essex IG10 4AG. e epping@yha.org.uk	t (20) 85085161 f (20) 85085161	36	12.04–30.11	CC P
▲**Eskdale** Boot, Holmrook, Cumbria CA19 1TH. e eskdale@yha.org.uk	t (19467) 23219 f (19467) 23163	50	04.03–31.10	CC P
▲**Exeter** IBN 47 Countess Wear Rd, Exeter, Devon EX2 6LR. e exeter@yha.org.uk	t (1392) 873329 f (1392) 876939	88	13.01–23.12; 29–31.12	R 3SE CC P
▲**Exford** Exe Mead, Exford, Minehead, Somerset TA24 7PU.	t (1643) 831288 f (1643) 831650	51	12.02–31.10	CC P
▲**Eyam** Hawkhill Rd, Eyam, Hope Valley S32 5QP. e eyam@yha.org.uk	t (1433) 630335 f (1433) 639202	60	09.02–08.12; 28–31.12	R CC P
▲**Golant** Penquite House, Golant, Fowey, Cornwall PL23 1LA. e golant@yha.org.uk	t (1726) 833507 f (1726) 832947	94	09.02–03.11; 22–27.12	R CC P
▲**Gradbach Mill** Gradbach, Quarnford, Buxton, Derbyshire SK17 0SU. e gradbach@yha.org.uk	t (1260) 227625 f (1260) 227334	87	09.02–02.12	R CC P
▲**Grasmere** - Butterlip How Butterlip How, Easedale Rd, Grasmere, Cumbria LA22 9QG. e grasmerebh@yha.org.uk	t (15394) 35316 f (15394) 35798	128	05.01–16.12	CC P
▲**Great Yarmouth** 2 Sandown Rd, Great Yarmouth, Norfolk NR30 1EY.	t (1493) 843991 f (1493) 856600	40	13–28.04; 25.05–02.09	CC
▲**Greenhead** Station Rd, Greenhead, Brampton, Cumbria CA8 7HG.	t (16977) 47401 f (16977) 47401	40	06.04–31.10	CC
▲**Grinton Lodge** Grinton Lodge, Grinton, Richmond, North Yorkshire DL11 6HS. e grinton@yha.org.uk	t (1748) 884206 f (1748) 884876	69	09.02–24.11; 28–31.12	R CC P

Location/Address	Telephone No. Fax No.	Beds	Opening Dates	Facilities
▲ **Hartington** Hartington Hall, Hartington, Buxton, Derbyshire SK17 0AT. ⓔ hartington@yha.org.uk	☎ (1298) 84223 🖷 (1298) 84415	140	07.05–31.12	♦♦ ⦿ & ⌷ ⌷ P ⊡ ⚘
▲ **Hastings** Guestling Hall, Rye Rd, Guestling, Hastings, East Sussex TN35 4LP.	☎ (1424) 812373 🖷 (1424) 814273	52	02.04–30.09	♦♦ ⦿ ⓡ ⌷ ⌷ P ⚘
▲ **Hathersage** Castleton Rd, Hathersage, Hope Valley S32 1EH.	☎ (1433) 650493 🖷 (1433) 650493	40	02.04–28.10; 31.12	⦿ ⌷ ⌷ P ⚘
▲ **Hawes** Lancaster Terrace, Hawes, North Yorkshire DL8 3LQ.	☎ (1969) 667368 🖷 (1969) 667723	58	09.02–18.12; 22–26.12	⦿ ⌷ ⌷ ⊡ ⚘
▲ **Hawkshead** Esthwaite Lodge, Hawkshead, Ambleside, Cumbria LA22 0QD. ⓔ hawkshead@yha.org.uk	☎ (15394) 36293 🖷 (15394) 36720	109	09.02–03.11; 09.11–15.12; 28–31.12	♦♦ ⦿ ⓡ ⌷ ⌷ P ⊡ ⚘
▲ **Haworth** Longlands Hall, Longlands Drive, Lees Lane, Haworth, Keighley, West Yorkshire BD22 8RT. ⓔ haworth@yha.org.uk	☎ (1535) 642234 🖷 (1535) 643023	100	09.02–03.11; 09.11–15.12; 28–31.12	⦿ ⓡ ⌷ ⌷ P ⊡ ⚘
▲ **Helmsley** Carlton Lane, Helmsley, York YO62 5HB.	☎ (1439) 770433 🖷 (1439) 770433	40	06.04–31.10	⦿ ⌷ ⌷
▲ **Helvellyn** Greenside, Glenridding, Penrith, Cumbria CA11 0QR. ⓔ helvellyn@yha.org.uk	☎ (17684) 82269 🖷 (17684) 82009	64	01.01–01.12; 28–31.12	⦿ ⌷ ⌷ P ⚘
High Close ☞**Langdale**				
▲ **Hindhead** Devils Punchbowl, off Portsmouth Rd, Thursley, Nr Godalming, Surrey GU8 6NS.	☎ (1428) 604285 🖷 (1428) 604285	16	04.04–07.05; 25–28.05; 20.07–03.09	⌷ ⌷ P ⊡
Holford ☞**Quantock Hills**				
▲ **Holmbury St Mary** Radnor Lane, Holmbury St Mary, Dorking, Surrey RH5 6NW. ⓔ holmbury@yha.org.uk	☎ (1306) 730777 🖷 (1306) 730933	52	09.02–03.11	⦿ ⓡ ⌷ ⌷ P
▲ **Honister Hause** Seatoller, Keswick, Cumbria CA12 5XN.	☎ (17687) 77267 🖷 (17687) 77267	26	01.04–27.10	⦿ ⌷ ⌷ P ⚘
▲ **Hunstanton** 15 Ave Rd, Hunstanton, Norfolk PE36 5BW.	☎ (1485) 532061 🖷 (1485) 532632	46	10.04–03.11	♦♦ ⦿ ⌷ ⌷ P ⊡
▲ **Idwal Cottage** Nant Ffrancon, Bethesda, Bangor, Gwynedd, Wales LL57 3LZ. ⓔ idwal@yha.org.uk	☎ (1248) 600225 🖷 (1248) 602952	43	05.01–01.09; 07.09–22.12; 28–31.12	⌷ ⌷ P
▲ **Ilam** Ilam Hall, Ashbourne, Derbyshire DE6 2AZ. ⓔ ilam@yha.org.uk	☎ (1335) 350212 🖷 (1335) 350350	135	09.02–03.11	♦♦ ⦿ ⓡ & ⌷ ⌷ P ⊡ ⚘

Location/Address	Telephone No. Fax No.	Beds	Opening Dates	Facilities
▲ **Ilfracombe** Ashmour House, 1 Hillsborough Terrace, Ilfracombe, Devon EX34 9NR. ✉ ilfracombe@yha.org.uk	☎ (1271) 865337 🖷 (1271) 862652	50	16.02–04.11; 28–31.12	♦♦♦ �🍽 CC ✂ P
▲ **Ingleton** Greta Tower, Sammy Lane, Ingleton, Carnforth, Lancashire LA6 3EG.	☎ (15242) 41444 🖷 (15242) 41854	58	09.02–16.12; 21–31.12	♦♦♦ �🍽 CC ✂ P
▲ **Ironbridge Gorge** John Rose Building, High St, Coalport, Telford, Shropshire TF8 7HT. ✉ ironbridge@yha.org.uk	☎ (1952) 588755 🖷 (1952) 588722	165	09.02–03.11; 22–27.12	♦♦♦ �🍽 R ⚇ CC ✂ P ✿
▲ **Ivinghoe** The Old Brewery House, High St, Ivinghoe, Leighton Buzzard, Buckinghamshire LU7 9EP.	☎ (1296) 668251 🖷 (1296) 662903	50	28.01–02.09; 18.09–16.12; 24–27.12	⏹🍽 CC ✂ P
▲ **Jordans** Welders Lane, Jordans, Beaconsfield, Buckinghamshire HP9 2SN.	☎ (1494) 873135 🖷 (1494) 875907	22	06.04–31.10	CC ✂ P ✿
▲ **Keld** Keld Lodge, Upper Swaledale, Keld, Richmond, North Yorkshire DL11 6LL.	☎ (1748) 886259 🖷 (1748) 886013	38	03.04–31.10	⏹🍽 CC ✂
▲ **Kemsing** Church Lane, Kemsing, Sevenoaks, Kent TN15 6LU. ✉ kemsing@yha.org.uk	☎ (1732) 761341 🖷 (1732) 763044	50	02.02–27.10; 02.11–22.12	♦♦♦ ⏹🍽 CC ✂ P ✿
▲ **Kendal** 118 Highgate, Kendal, Cumbria LA9 4HE. ✉ kendal@yha.org.uk	☎ (1539) 724066 🖷 (1539) 724906	54	01–02.01; 19.01–31.12	CC ✂ P ✿
▲ **Keswick** Station Rd, Keswick, Cumbria CA12 5LH. ✉ keswick@yha.org.uk	☎ (17687) 72484 🖷 (17687) 74129	91	🔳	⏹🍽 CC ✂ P ⏺ ✿
▲ **Kettlewell** Whernside House, Kettlewell, Skipton, North Yorkshire BD23 5QU.	☎ (1756) 760232 🖷 (1756) 760402	51	09.02–16.12; 24–26.12	♦♦♦ ⏹🍽 CC ✂ P
▲ **Kings, Dolgellau** Kings, Penmaenpool, Dolgellau, Gwynedd, Wales LL40 1TB. ✉ kings@yha.org.uk	☎ (1341) 422392 🖷 (1341) 422477	56	12.04–01.09	♦♦♦ 6SW CC ✂ P
▲ **King's Lynn** Thoresby College, College Lane, King's Lynn, Norfolk PE30 1JB.	☎ (1553) 772461 🖷 (1553) 764312	35	12.04–03.09	♦♦♦ CC ✂ ✿
Kirk Yetholm ☞Scotland				
▲ **Kirkby Stephen** Fletcher Hill, Market St, Kirkby Stephen, Cumbria CA17 4QQ.	☎ (17683) 71793 🖷 (17683) 71793	44	06.04–31.10	♦♦♦ ⏹🍽 CC ✂ P ⏺
▲ **Land's End** Letcha Vean, St Just in Penwith, Penzance, Cornwall TR19 7NT. (7km N of Land's End).	☎ (1736) 788437 🖷 (1736) 787337	43	02.03–31.10	♦♦♦ ⏹🍽 CC ✂ P

Location/Address	Telephone No. Fax No.	Beds	Opening Dates	Facilities
▲ **Langdale** - High Close High Close, Loughrigg, Ambleside, Cumbria LA22 9HJ. 🅔 langdale@yha.org.uk	☎ (15394) 32304 🖷 (15394) 34408	80	04.04–28.10	⦿ Ⓡ Ⓒㄷㄷ ぢ Ⓟ ✿
▲ **Langdon Beck** Forest-in-Teesdale, Barnard Castle, Co Durham DL12 0XN. 🅔 langdonbeck@yha.org.uk	☎ (1833) 622228 🖷 (1833) 622372	34	09.02–01.12	⸙⸙ ⦿ ㄷㄷ ぢ Ⓟ ▣
△ *Langsett* *Stockbridge, Sheffield, S36 4GY.*	☎ *(1226) 761548* 🖷 *(1226) 761548*	*27*	🄵	ぢ Ⓟ
△ *Lawrenny* *Millenium YH, Lawrenny, Kilgetty,* *Pembrokeshire, Wales SA68 0PN.*	☎ *(1646) 651270* 🖷 *(1646) 651856*	*24*	🄵	ぢ Ⓟ
▲ **Lee Valley** Lee Valley Park, Cheshunt, Hertfordshire. 🅔 ionres@yha.org.uk	☎ (20) 7373 3400 🖷 (20) 7373 3455	112	05.01–23.12	⸙⸙ ⦿ Ⓡ 1E ㄜ ㄷㄷ ぢ Ⓟ ▣ ⮝
▲ **Leominster** - Leominster Priory The Old Priory, Leominster, Herefordshire HR6 8EQ.	☎ (1568) 620517 🖷 (1568) 620517	30	12.04–27.10	0.2 NE ぢ Ⓟ ▣
▲ **Lincoln** 77 South Park, Lincoln LN5 8ES. 🅔 lincoln@yha.org.uk	☎ (1522) 522076 🖷 (1522) 567424	45	05.02–03.11	⸙⸙ ⦿ 2SE ㄷㄷ ぢ Ⓟ ▣
▲ **Linton** The Old Rectory, Linton-in-Craven, Skipton, North Yorkshire BD23 5HH.	☎ (1756) 752400 🖷 (1756) 753159	38	06.04–28.10	⦿ ㄷㄷ ぢ Ⓟ
▲ **Litton Cheney** Dorchester, Dorset DT2 9AT.	☎ (1308) 482340 🖷 (1308) 482636	24	12.04–03.09	⸙⸙ ㄷㄷ ぢ ▣
▲ **Liverpool** Ⓘ̲ᴮ̲ᴺ̲ **25 Tabley St (off Wapping), Liverpool,** **L1 8EE.** 🅔 liverpool@yha.org.uk	☎ (151) 7098888 🖷 (151) 7090417	110	🄵	⸙⸙ ⦿ 1SW ㄜ ㄷㄷ ぢ Ⓟ ▣
▲ **Llanbedr** Plas Newydd, Llanbedr, Barmouth, Gwynedd, Wales LL45 2LE. 🅔 llanbedr@yha.org.uk	☎ (1341) 241287 🖷 (1341) 241389	42	12.04–27.10	⸙⸙ ⦿ ㄷㄷ ぢ Ⓟ
▲ **Llanberis** Llwyn Celyn, Llanberis, Caernarfon, Gwynedd, Wales LL55 4SR. 🅔 llanberis@yha.org.uk	☎ (1286) 870280 🖷 (1286) 870936	60	05.01–24.02; 02.03–07.04; 10.04–27.10; 02.11–22.12	⦿ ㄷㄷ ぢ Ⓟ
△ *Llanddeusant* *The Old Red Lion, Llanddeusant, Llangadog,* *Carmarthenshire, Wales SA19 6UL.*	☎ *(1550) 740619*	*28*	*13.04–06.09*	⦿ ぢ Ⓟ
▲ **Llangollen** Tyndwr Hall, Tyndwr Rd, Llangollen, Denbighshire, Wales LL20 8AR. 🅔 llangollen@yha.org.uk	☎ (1978) 860330 🖷 (1978) 861709	134	🄵	⸙⸙ ⦿ ㄷㄷ ぢ Ⓟ ▣ ✿

Location/Address	Telephone No. Fax No.	Beds	Opening Dates	Facilities
▲ **Lledr Valley Betws-y-Coed** Lledr House, Pont-y-Pant, Dolwyddelan, Wales LL25 0DQ.	☎ (1690) 750202 ✆ (1690) 750410	60	13.04–27.08	ⵁ 7SW ⵁ ⵁ P
▲ **Llwyn y Celyn** Libanus, Brecon, Powys, Wales LD3 8NH. ⊜ llwynycelyn@yha.org.uk	☎ (1874) 624261 ✆ (1874) 625916	42	10.02–03.09; 06.09–29.10; 01.11–31.12	ⵁ ⵁ ⵁ P
△ *Lockton* *The Old School, Lockton, Pickering,* *North Yorkshire YO18 7PY.*	☎ *(1751) 460376* ✆ *(1751) 460376*	*22*	*12.04–01.09;* *04–20.09*	ⵁ ⵁ P
▲ **London** - City of London ⓘⒷⓃ **36 Carter Lane, London EC4V 5AB.** ⊜ city@yha.org.uk	☎ (20) 72364965 ✆ (20) 72367681	193	ⵁ	ⵁ ⵁ Ⓡ 2NE ⵁ
▲ **London** - Earls Court ⓘⒷⓃ **38 Bolton Gardens, London, SW5 0AQ.** ⊜ earlscourt@yha.org.uk	☎ (20) 73737083 ✆ (20) 78352034	159	ⵁ	ⵁ Ⓡ 6SW ⵁ ⵁ ⵁ
▲ **London** - Hampstead Heath ⓘⒷⓃ **4 Wellgarth Rd, Golders Green,** **London NW11 7HR.** ⊜ hampstead@yha.org.uk	☎ (20) 84589054 ✆ (20) 82090546	200	ⵁ	ⵁ ⵁ Ⓡ 9NW ⵁ ⵁ P ⵁ
▲ **London** - Holland House ⓘⒷⓃ **Holland House, Holland Walk,** **Kensington, London W8 7QU.** ⊜ hollandhouse@yha.org.uk	☎ (20) 79370748 ✆ (20) 73760667	201	ⵁ	ⵁ Ⓡ 6SW ⵁ ⵁ ⵁ
▲ **London** - Oxford Street ⓘⒷⓃ **14 Noel St, London W1V 3PD.** ⊜ oxfordst@yha.org.uk	☎ (20) 77341618 ✆ (20) 77341657	75	ⵁ	Ⓡ ⵁ ⵁ ⵁ
▲ **London** - Rotherhithe ⓘⒷⓃ **20 Salter Rd, London SE16 5PR.** ⊜ rotherhithe@yha.org.uk	☎ (20) 72322114 ✆ (20) 72372919	320	ⵁ	ⵁ ⵁ Ⓡ ♿ ⵁ ⵁ P ⵁ
▲ **London** - St Pancras ⓘⒷⓃ **79-81 Euston Rd, London NW1 2QS.** ⊜ stpancras@yha.org.uk	☎ (20) 73889998 ✆ (20) 73886766	152	ⵁ	ⵁ ⵁ Ⓡ ⵁ ⵁ ⵁ
Longthwaite ▨**Borrowdale**				
▲ **Lulworth Cove** School Lane, West Lulworth, Wareham, Dorset BH20 5SA.	☎ (1929) 400564 ✆ (1929) 400640	34	02.03–08.09; 11.09–08.11	ⵁ ⵁ ⵁ ⵁ P ✿
▲ **Lynton** Lynbridge, Lynton, Devon EX35 6AZ.	☎ (1598) 753237 ✆ (1598) 753305	36	09.04–31.10	ⵁ ⵁ ⵁ ⵁ P ⵁ ✿
▲ **Malham** John Dower Memorial Hostel, Malham, Skipton, North Yorkshire BD23 4DE. ⊜ malham@yha.org.uk	☎ (1729) 830321 ✆ (1729) 830551	82	01.01–16.12; 28–31.12	ⵁ ⵁ Ⓡ ⵁ ⵁ P ⵁ
▲ **Malvern Hills** 18 Peachfield Rd, Malvern Wells, Malvern, Worcestershire WR14 4AP. ⊜ malvern@yha.org.uk	☎ (1684) 569131 ✆ (1684) 565205	59	05.01–22.12	ⵁ ⵁ Ⓡ ⵁ ⵁ P

Location/Address	Telephone No. Fax No.	Beds	Opening Dates	Facilities
▲ **Manchester** (IBN) Potato Wharf, Castlefield, Manchester M3 4NB. e manchester@yha.org.uk	☎ (161) 8399960 ✆ (161) 8352054	140	🗓	††† � ℝ ♿ ᴄᴄ ☞ ℙ ⊡ ☀
▲ **Mankinholes** Todmorden, Lancashire OL14 6HR.	☎ (1706) 812340 ✆ (1706) 812340	32	12.04–27.10	ᴄᴄ ☞ ℙ
▲ **Manorbier** Nr Tenby, Pembrokeshire, Wales SA70 7TT. e manorbier@yha.org.uk	☎ (1834) 871803 ✆ (1834) 871101	71	02.03–31.10	††† ⟨⟩ ♿ ᴄᴄ ☞ ℙ ⊡ ☀
▲ **Margate** The Beachcomber, 3-4 Royal Esplanade, Westbrook Bay, Margate, Kent CT9 5DL. e margate@yha.org.uk	☎ (1843) 221616 ✆ (1843) 221616	54	06–21.04; 04–06.05; 25.05–30.09	††† [0.7 W] ᴄᴄ ☞ ☀
▲ **Marloes Sands** Runwayskiln, Marloes, Haverfordwest, Pembrokeshire, Wales SA62 3BH.	☎ (1646) 636667 ✆ (1646) 636667	30	13.04–27.10	☞ ℙ
▲ **Matlock** 40 Bank Rd, Matlock, Derbyshire DE4 3NF. e matlock@yha.org.uk	☎ (1629) 582983 ✆ (1629) 583484	53	19.01–15.12; 24–27.12	††† ⟨⟩ ℝ ♿ ᴄᴄ ☞ ℙ ⊡ ☀
▲ **Maypool** Maypool House, Galmpton, Brixham, Devon TQ5 0ET.	☎ (1803) 842444 ✆ (1803) 845939	65	12.02–31.10	⟨⟩ ᴄᴄ ☞ ℙ ☀
▲ **Meerbrook** Old School, Meerbrook, Leek, Staffordshire ST13 8SJ.	☎ (1538) 300174 ✆ (1538) 300174	22	13.04–27.10	☞ ℙ
Milton Keynes ☞Bradwell Village				
▲ **Minehead** Alcombe Combe, Minehead, Somerset TA24 6EW.	☎ (1643) 702595 ✆ (1643) 703016	36	09.04–02.09	††† ⟨⟩ ᴄᴄ ☞ ℙ
▲ **Newport** - Trefdraeth Lower St Mary St, Newport, Pembrokeshire, Wales SA42 0TS.	☎ (1239) 820080 ✆ (1239) 820080	28	10.04–04.09	††† ♿ ☞ ℙ ☀
▲ **Newcastle upon Tyne** (IBN) 107 Jesmond Rd, Newcastle upon Tyne NE2 1NJ. e newcastle@yha.org.uk	☎ (191) 2812570 ✆ (191) 2818779	60	01.01–20.12	⟨⟩ ℝ ᴄᴄ ☞ ℙ ᘓᘓ ☀
△ *Ninebanks* *Orchard House, Mohope, Ninebanks, Hexham, Northumberland NE47 8DO.*	☎ *(1434) 345288* ✆ *(1434) 345288*	*26*	*01.01–30.09*	ᴄᴄ ☞ ℙ
▲ **Norwich** 112 Turner Rd, Norwich NR2 4HB. e norwich@yha.org.uk	☎ (1603) 627647 ✆ (1603) 629075	63	01.04–21.12	⟨⟩ ℝ [2 W] ᴄᴄ ☞ ℙ ⊡ ᘓᘓ ☀
▲ **Okehampton** Klondyke Rd, Okehampton, Devon EX20 1EW. e okehampton@yha.org.uk	☎ (1837) 53916 ✆ (1837) 53965	102	01.02–30.11	††† ⟨⟩ [0.5 SW] ᴄᴄ ☞ ℙ ⊡ ☀

Location/Address	Telephone No. Fax No.	Beds	Opening Dates	Facilities
▲ **Once Brewed** Military Rd, Bardon Mill, Hexham, Northumberland NE47 7AN. 📧 oncebrewed@yha.org.uk	☎ (1434) 344360 📠 (1434) 344045	90	09.02–24.11	††† ⑩ Ⓡ CC 🗗 P 🖬
▲ **Osmotherley** Cote Ghyll, Osmotherley, Northallerton, North Yorkshire DL6 3AH. 📧 osmotherley@yha.org.uk	☎ (1609) 883575 📠 (1609) 883715	72	02.02–03.11; 28–31.12	††† ⑩ Ⓡ CC 🗗 P
▲ **Oxford** - New Oxford [IBN] **2a Botley Rd, Oxford OX2 0AB.** 📧 oxford@yha.org.uk	☎ (1865) 727275 📠 (1865) 769402	184	🛏	††† ⑩ 3 NE ♿ CC 🖬 ☕ 🚲 ❄
▲ **Patterdale** Goldrill House, Patterdale, Penrith, Cumbria CA11 0NW. 📧 patterdale@yha.org.uk	☎ (17684) 82394 📠 (17684) 82034	82	26.01–31.12	⑩ CC 🗗 P 🖬 ❄
▲ **Penycwm (Solva)** Solva, Whitehouse, Penycwm, Nr Solva, Haverfordwest, Pembrokeshire, Wales SA61 6LA. 📧 penycwm@yha.org.uk	☎ (1437) 721940 📠 (1437) 720959	26	🛏	††† ⑩ 4 SE 🗗 P
▲ **Pen-y-Pass** Nantgwynant, Caernarfon, Gwynedd, Wales LL55 4NY. 📧 penypass@yha.org.uk	☎ (1286) 870428 📠 (1286) 872434	84	01–03.01; 09.02–06.05; 25.05–03.06; 20.07–28.10; 28–31.12	††† ⑩ ♿ CC 🗗 P
▲ **Penzance** [IBN] Castle Horneck, Alverton, Penzance, Cornwall TR20 8TF. 📧 penzance@yha.org.uk	☎ (1736) 362666 📠 (1736) 362663	80	01.02–23.12	⑩ Ⓡ 1 W CC 🗗 P 🖬 🚲 ❄
▲ **Perranporth** Droskyn Point, Perranporth, Cornwall TR6 0GS.	☎ (1872) 573812 📠 (1872) 573319	26	10.04–08.09	CC 🗗
▲ **Peterborough** - Nene Park Millennium Youth Hostel Thorpe Meadows, Peterborough, PE3 6GA. 📧 peterborough@yha.org.uk	☎ (1629) 825850 for information 📠 (1629) 824571	40	10.04–27.10	††† ⑩ 1.5 W 🗗 P
▲ **Plymouth** [IBN] Belmont House, Belmont Place, Stoke, Plymouth PL3 4DW. 📧 plymouth@yha.org.uk	☎ (1752) 562189 📠 (1752) 605360	62	01.01–30.12	††† ⑩ 3 W CC 🗗 P 🖬
▲ **Poppit Sands** 'Sea View', Poppit, Cardigan, Cardiganshire, Wales SA43 3LP. 📧 poppit@yha.org.uk	☎ (1239) 612936 📠 (1239) 612936	40	10.04–07.07; 10.07–01.09; 04.09–27.10	††† CC 🗗 P ❄
▲ **Port Eynon** The Old Lifeboat House, Port Eynon, Swansea, Wales SA3 1NN.	☎ (1792) 390706 📠 (1792) 391540	30	10.04–07.07; 09.07–01.09; 04.09–27.10	CC 🗗

Location/Address	Telephone No. Fax No.	Beds	Opening Dates	Facilities
▲ **Portland** Hardy House, Castletown, Portland, Dorset DT5 1BJ. ℮ portland@yha.org.uk	☏ (1305) 861368 ✆ (1305) 861568	28	25.03–30.09	☞
▲ **Portsmouth** (IBN) Wymering Manor, Old Wymering Lane, Cosham, Portsmouth, Hampshire PO6 3NL. ℮ portsmouth@yha.org.uk	☏ (23) 92375661 ✆ (23) 92214177	64	01.02–22.12	¶◎¶ 6NE CC ☞ P ♺ ✿
▲ **Pwll Deri** Castell Mawr, Tref Asser, Goodwick, Pembrokeshire, Wales SA64 0LR.	☏ (1348) 891385 ✆ (1348) 891385	30	13.04–28.10	CC ☞ P
▲ **Quantock Hills** Sevenacres, Holford, Bridgwater, Somerset TA5 1SQ.	☏ (1278) 741224 ✆ (1278) 741224	34	12.04–07.05; 25–28.05; 20.07–03.09	CC ☞ P
▲ **Ravenstor** Millers Dale, Buxton, Derbyshire SK17 8SS. ℮ ravenstor@yha.org.uk	☏ (1298) 871826 ✆ (1298) 871275	83	09.02–15.12; 28–31.12	¶¶¶ ◎¶ R CC ☞ P ✿
▲ **Ridgeway** Ridgeway Centre, Courthill, Wantage, Oxfordshire OX12 9NE.	☏ (12357) 60253 ✆ (12357) 68865	59	14.01–08.09; 11.09–24.11; 30.11–22.12; 28–31.12	¶¶¶ ◎¶ ♿ CC ☞ P ▣
▲ **Rochester** - Medway Capstone Farm (Rochester) YH, Capstone Rd, Gillingham, Kent ME7 3JE. ℮ medway@yha.org.uk	☏ (1634) 400788 ✆ (1634) 400794	40	09.02–03.11; 09.11–15.12; 24–27.12	¶¶¶ ◎¶ ♿ CC ☞ P ▣ ✿
△ *Rowen* *Rhiw Farm, Rowen, Conwy, Wales LL32 8YW.*	☏ *(1492) 593571*	*24*	*12.04–01.09*	☞ P
▲ **Saffron Walden** 1 Myddylton Place, Saffron Walden, Essex CB10 1BB.	☏ (1799) 523117 ✆ (1799) 520840	40	10.04–27.10	◎¶ CC ☞ P
▲ **St Briavels Castle** The Castle, St Briavels, Lydney, Gloucestershire GL15 6RG. ℮ stbriavels@yha.org.uk	☏ (1594) 530272 ✆ (1594) 530849	70	06.04–01.09; 02–20.09; 19.10–03.11	◎¶ R CC ☞ P
△ *St David's* *Llaethdy, St David's, Haverfordwest,* *Pembrokeshire, Wales SA62 6PR.*	☏ *(1437) 720345* ✆ *(1437) 721831*	*40*	*13.04–30.10*	CC ☞ P
▲ **Salcombe** 'Overbecks', Sharpitor, Salcombe, Devon TQ8 8LW.	☏ (1548) 842856 ✆ (1548) 843865	51	09.04–31.10	¶¶¶ ◎¶ CC ☞ P
▲ **Salisbury** (IBN) Milford Hill House, Milford Hill, Salisbury, Wiltshire SP1 2QW. ℮ salisbury@yha.org.uk	☏ (1722) 327572 ✆ (1722) 330446	70	▭	◎¶ CC ☞ P ▣ ♺ ✿
▲ **Sandown** The Firs, Fitzroy St, Sandown, Isle of Wight PO36 8JH.	☏ (1983) 402651 ✆ (1983) 403565	47	22.03–10.09; 13.09–11.10	¶¶¶ ◎¶ CC ☞ P ✿

Location/Address	Telephone No. Fax No.	Beds	Opening Dates	Facilities
▲ **Scarborough** The White House, Burniston Rd, Scarborough, North Yorkshire YO13 0DA. ⓔ scarborough@yha.org.uk	❶ (1723) 361176 ❺ (1723) 500054	50	06.04–31.10	❖❖ ⑩ ⒸⒸ ✂ P ⑥
▲ **Sheringham** 1 Cremer's Drift, Sheringham, Norfolk NR26 8HX. ⓔ sheringham@yha.org.uk	❶ (1263) 823215 ❺ (1263) 824679	109	16.02–01.12	❖❖ ⑩ Ⓡ ♿ ⒸⒸ ✂ P
▲ **Sherwood Forest** ⒾⒷ⒩ Forest Corner, Edwinstowe, Nottinghamshire, NG21 9RN. ⓔ sherwood@yha.org.uk	❶ (1623) 825794 ❺ (1623) 825796	39	01.02–22.12; 31.12	❖❖ ⑩ ♿ ⒸⒸ ✂ P
△ *Shining Cliff* *Shining Cliff Woods, Jackass Lane,* *near Ambergate, Derbyshire DE56 2RE.*	❶ *(7788) 725938* ❺ *(1629) 760827*	*20*	*13–15.04;* *04–06.05;* *25–27.05;* *23.07–30.08*	✂ P
▲ **Shrewsbury** The Woodlands, Abbey Foregate, Shrewsbury, Shropshire SY2 6LZ. ⓔ shrewsbury@yha.org.uk	❶ (1743) 360179 ❺ (1743) 357423	54	02.03–27.10	⑩ ⒸⒸ ✂ P ⑥
△ *Skiddaw House* *Skiddaw Forest, Bassenthwaite, Keswick,* *Cumbria, CA12 4QX.*	❶ *(16974) 78325* ❺ *(16974) 78325*	*20*	*30.03–27.10*	✂ ✿
▲ **Slaidburn** King's House, Slaidburn, Clitheroe, Lancashire BB7 3ER.	❶ (1200) 446656	31	01.04–29.09	ⒸⒸ ✂ P
▲ **Slimbridge** Shepherd's Patch, Slimbridge, Gloucestershire GL2 7BP. ⓔ slimbridge@yha.org.uk	❶ (1453) 890275 ❺ (1453) 890625	56	09.02–03.11; 28–31.12	❖❖ ⑩ Ⓡ ⒸⒸ ✂ P ⑥ ✿
▲ **Snowdon Ranger** Rhyd Ddu, Caernarfon, Gwynedd, Wales LL54 7YS. ⓔ snowdon@yha.org.uk	❶ (1286) 650391 ❺ (1286) 650093	66	09.02–28.10; 02.11–02.12	⑩ ⒸⒸ ✂ P ✿
Solva ☞**Penycwm**				
▲ **Stainforth** Taitlands, Stainforth, Settle, North Yorkshire BD24 9PA. ⓔ stainforth@yha.org.uk	❶ (1729) 823577 ❺ (1729) 825404	48	02.02–15.12	❖❖ ⑩ Ⓡ ⒸⒸ ✂ P
△ *Steps Bridge* *Dunsford, Exeter, Devon EX6 7EQ.*	❶ *(1647) 252435* ❺ *(1647) 252948*	*24*	*12.04–03.09*	ⒸⒸ ✂ P
▲ **Stow-on-the-Wold** The Square, Stow on the Wold, Cheltenham, Gloucestershire GL54 1AF.	❶ (1451) 830497 ❺ (1451) 870102	50	01.02–10.11; 17.11–22.12; 28–31.12	❖❖ ⑩ ⒸⒸ ✂ P ⑥
▲ **Stratford-upon-Avon -** Hemmingford House ⒾⒷ⒩ **Alveston, Stratford-upon-Avon,** **Warwickshire CV37 7RG.** ⓔ stratford@yha.org.uk	❶ (1789) 297093 ❺ (1789) 205513	130	▢	❖❖ ⑩ ⒸⒸ ✂ P ⑥

Location/Address	Telephone No. Fax No.	Beds	Opening Dates	Facilities
▲ **Streatley-on-Thames** Hill House, Reading Rd, Streatley, Reading, Berks RG8 9JJ. e streatley@yha.org.uk	☎ (1491) 872278 ✆ (1491) 873056	51	02.02–08.12; 28–31.12	⁙ ⁞⊙⁞ ⊂CC⊃ ☞ P
▲ **Street** The Chalet, Ivythorn Hill, St, Somerset BA16 0TZ.	☎ (1458) 442961 ✆ (1458) 442738	28	12.04–30.09	⁙ ⊂CC⊃ ☞ P ❂
▲ **Swanage** Cluny, Cluny Crescent, Swanage, Dorset BH19 2BS. e swanage@yha.org.uk	☎ (1929) 422113 ✆ (1929) 426327	104	09.02–03.11	⁙ ⁞⊙⁞ ®️ ⊂CC⊃ ☞ P ⊡ ❂
△ *Tanners Hatch* *Polesden Lacey, Dorking, Surrey RH5 6BE.* e *tanners@yha.org.uk*	☎ *(1306) 877964* ✆ *(1306) 877964*	*25*	*05.01–31.12*	⊂CC⊃ ☞
△ *Telscombe* *Bank Cottages, Telscombe, Lewes, East Sussex BN7 3HZ.*	☎ *(1273) 301357* ✆ *(1273) 301357*	*22*	*12.04–03.09*	⊂CC⊃ ☞ ❂
△ *Thirlmere* *The Old School, Stanah Cross, Keswick, Cumbria CA12 4TH.*	☎ *(17687) 73224* ✆ *(17687) 73224*	*28*	*30.03–30.09*	⊂CC⊃ ☞ P ❂
△ *Thurlby* *16 High St, Thurlby, Bourne, Lincolnshire PE10 0EE.*	☎ *(1778) 425588* ✆ *(1778) 425588*	*24*	*12.04–20.09*	⁙ ♿ ⊂CC⊃ ☞ P
▲ **Tintagel** Dunderhole Point, Tintagel, Cornwall PL34 0DW.	☎ (1840) 770334 ✆ (1840) 770733	24	10.03–30.09	⊂CC⊃ ☞ P ❂
▲ **Totland Bay** Hurst Hill, Totland Bay, Isle of Wight PO39 0HD.	☎ (1983) 752165 ✆ (1983) 756443	62	01.03–01.11	⁙ ⁞⊙⁞ ⊂CC⊃ ☞ P ❂
▲ **Trevine** Fford-yr-Afon Trevine, Haverfordwest, Pembrokeshire, Wales SA62 5AU.	☎ (1348) 831414 ✆ (1348) 831414	26	11.04–07.07; 10.07–01.09	⁙ ⊂CC⊃ ☞ P
▲ **Treyarnon Bay** Tregonnan, Treyarnon, Padstow, Cornwall PL28 8JR.	☎ (1841) 520322 ✆ (1841) 520464	41	09.04–31.10	⁙ ⁞⊙⁞ ⊂CC⊃ ☞ P ❂
▲ **Truleigh Hill** Tottington Barn, Truleigh Hill, Shoreham-by-Sea, West Sussex BN43 5FB.	☎ (1903) 813419 ✆ (1903) 812016	56	02.04–11.10	⁙ ⁞⊙⁞ ⊂CC⊃ ☞ P ❂
△ *Tyncornel* *Llanddewi-Brefi, Tregaron, Ceredigion, Wales SY25 6PH.*	☎ *(1629) 581399*	*16*	*13.04–22.09*	®️ ☞ P
▲ **Ty'n-y-Caeau** Groesffordd, Brecon, Powys, Wales LD3 7SW. e tynycaeau@yha.org.uk	☎ (1874) 665270 ✆ (1874) 665278	54	04.02–01.09; 03.09–27.10; 01.11–27.12; 31.12	⁙ ⁞⊙⁞ ⊂CC⊃ ☞ P
▲ **Wastwater** Wasdale Hall, Wasdale, Seascale, Cumbria CA20 1ET. e wastwater@yha.org.uk	☎ (19467) 26222 ✆ (19467) 26056	50	01.01–22.12; 28–31.12	⁙ ⁞⊙⁞ ⊂CC⊃ ☞ P ❂

Location/Address	Telephone No. Fax No.	Beds	Opening Dates	Facilities
▲ **Welsh Bicknor** The Rectory, Welsh Bicknor, Nr Goodrich, Ross-on-Wye, Herefordshire HR9 6JJ. ℮ welshbicknor@yha.org.uk	☎ (1594) 860300 🖷 (1594) 861276	78	01.02–24.03; 30.03–01.09; 03.09–27.10; 29.10–22.12; 28–31.12	♦♦♦ ᵀᴼᶦ ⸢CC⸣ ⚲ P ▯
▲ **Whitby** East Cliff, Whitby, North Yorkshire YO22 4JT.	☎ (1947) 602878 🖷 (1947) 825146	58	01.02–10.12; 30–31.12	♦♦♦ ᵀᴼᶦ ⸢CC⸣ ⚲ P
Wight, Isle of ☞ **Sandown and Totland Bay**				
▲ **Wilderhope Manor** The John Cadbury Memorial Hostel, Longville in the Dale, Much Wenlock, Shropshire TF13 6EG. ℮ wilderhope@yha.org.uk	☎ (1694) 771363 🖷 (1694) 771520	70	09.02–03.11; 22–27.12	ᵀᴼᶦ Ⓡ ⸢CC⸣ ⚲ P
▲ **Winchester** The City Mill, 1 Water Lane, Winchester, Hampshire SO23 0EJ.	☎ (1962) 853723 🖷 (1962) 855524	31	01.03–28.04; 01.05–30.06; 02.07–08.09; 11.09–03.11	ᵀᴼᶦ ⸢CC⸣ ⚲ ✳
▲ **Windermere** High Cross, Bridge Lane, Troutbeck, Windermere, Cumbria LA23 1LA. ℮ windermere@yha.org.uk	☎ (15394) 43543 🖷 (15394) 47165	69	01.01–28.12	♦♦♦ ᵀᴼᶦ ⸢CC⸣ ⚲ P ▯ ✳
▲ **Windsor** ⟨IBN⟩ Edgeworth House, Mill Lane, Windsor, Berkshire SL4 5JE. ℮ windsor@yha.org.uk	☎ (1753) 861710 🖷 (1753) 832100	67	02.01–24.12	♦♦♦ ᵀᴼᶦ ⸢CC⸣ ⚲ P ▯ ☙ ✳
▲ **Woody's Top** Ruckland, near Louth, Lincs LN11 8RQ.	☎ (1529) 413421 🖷 (1529) 413421	22	12.04–15.09	♦♦♦ ⸢CC⸣ ⚲ P
▲ **Wooler** - Cheviot 30 Cheviot St, Wooler, Northumberland NE71 6LW.	☎ (1668) 281365 🖷 (1668) 282368	52	01.03–31.10	ᵀᴼᶦ ♿ ⸢CC⸣ ⚲ P ▯
▲ **York** ⟨IBN⟩ **York International, Water End, Clifton, York, Yorkshire YO30 6LP.** ℮ york@yha.org.uk	☎ (1904) 653147 🖷 (1904) 651230	150	🗓	♦♦♦ ᵀᴼᶦ ⟨1.5 NW⟩ ⸢CC⸣ ⚲ P ▯ ✳
▲ **Youlgreave** Fountain Square, Youlgreave, Bakewell, Derbyshire DE45 1UR.	☎ (1629) 636518 🖷 (1629) 636518	42	16.02–23.12; 31.12	♦♦♦ ᵀᴼᶦ ⸢CC⸣ ⚲ ✳
△ *Ystradfellte* *Tai'r Heol, Ystradfellte, Aberdare, Wales CF44 9JF.*	☎ *(1639) 720301* 🖷 *(1639) 720301*	*28*	*13.04–10.07; 13.07–04.09; 07.09–30.10*	⚲ P

YOUTH HOSTEL ACCOMMODATION
OUTSIDE THE ASSURED STANDARDS SCHEME

| Duntisbourne Abbots
 Cirencester, Gloucestershire GL7 7JN. | ☎ (1285) 821682
 🖷 (1285) 821697 | 47 | 06.04–03.11 | ᵀᴼᶦ Ⓡ ⸢CC⸣ ⚲ P ▯ |

HOSTELLING
INTERNATIONAL

Take the HI way!

For HI quality accommodation at the best prices.

Visit one of our 4200 hostels in over 60 countries.

www.iyhf.org

Finland

FINLANDE
FINNLAND
FINLANDIA

Suomen Retkeilymajajärjestö-SRM ry,
Yrjönkatu 38 B 15, FIN-00100 Helsinki,
Finland.

t (358) (9) 565 7150
f (358) (9) 565 71510
e info@srm.inet.fi
w www.srmnet.org

Office Hours: Monday-Friday, 09.00-16.00hrs

A copy of the Hostel Directory for this Country can be obtained from:
The National Office

Capital:	Helsinki	**Population:**	5,200,000
Language:	Finnish and Swedish	**Size:**	338,145 sq km
Currency:	FIM (markka)	**Telephone Country Code:**	358

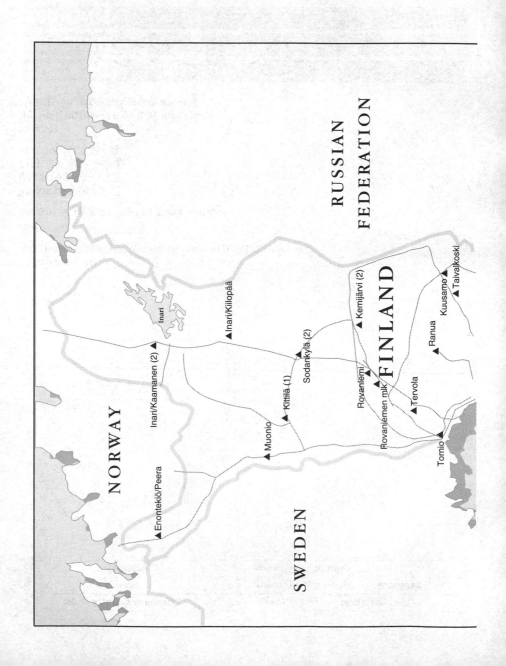

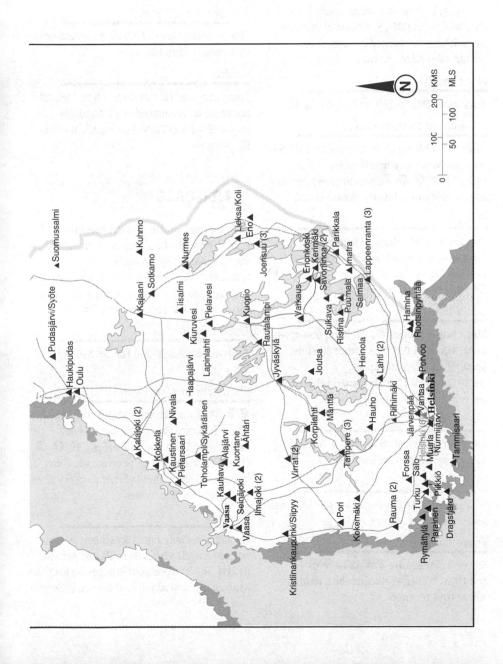

English

Many hostels are closed 24-26 Dec (Christmas). Most hostels have a sauna. Hostelling International Membership Cardholders get FIM 15 discount on normal rates. Hostels are located in cities, in the countryside and on the coast.

Price range

Price range FIM 50-260. € 8.41-43.73. 🔟.

Rooms and Reservations

R 🔟 (All Rooms). Reservations via (IBN) National Booking Centre, Hostel or National Office by ❶ ❶ ❷. (Reservation charges may apply). Smoking is limited - please check.

Guests

Pets are allowed - check with hostel. ⅢⅢ welcome. Group bookings via National Booking Centre, Hostel or National Office by ❶ ❷ (Reservation charges may apply).

Open times

Main hostels: open 🔟, ☉. Reception open: 06/07:00hrs-24/02:00hrs, **Other hostels:** open 🔟, ☉. Reception open: 08/09:00hrs-21/23:00hrs. **Seasonal hostels** are generally open Jun-Aug.

Meals

🍽 B For individuals & for ⅢⅢ. ☞ Not all utensils provided - check with hostel.

Discounts

HI Member Discounts available - see discounts section and www.iyhf.org.

Travelling around

For ease of travel use 🚂 🚢 🚌 Self-Drive. Winter weather can be hazardous, winter tyres required.

Travel/Activity Packages

Accommodation/transport packages available. Package bookings via National Booking Centre or National Office by ❶ ❷.

Passports and Visas

Please contact Finnish Embassy or Consulate in your country of residence.

Health

Emergency medical treatment is free. Medical insurance is recommended. EU Nationals require Form E111 to obtain treatment within EU countries.

Français

De nombreuses auberges ferment entre le 24 et le 26 déc (Noël). La plupart sont équipées d'un sauna. Les adhérents Hostelling International bénéficient d'une remise de 15 FIM sur les tarifs normaux. Les auberges sont situées dans les villes, à la campagne et sur le littoral.

Tarifs des nuitées

Tarifs des nuitées 50-260 FIM. € 8.41-43.73. 🔟.

Chambres et réservations

R 🔟 (Toutes chambres). Réservations via (IBN) le Centre National de Réservation, l'auberge ou le Bureau National par ❶ ❶ ❷. (Des frais de réservation pourront vous être facturés). Il est permis de fumer dans certaines chambres - veuillez vérifier.

Usagers

Les animaux domestiques sont autorisés mais vérifiez lesquels auprès de l'auberge. Accueil des ⅢⅢ. Réservations pour groupes via le Centre National de Réservation, l'auberge ou le Bureau

National par ❶ ❷ (Des frais de réservation pourront vous être facturés).

Horaires d'ouverture

Grandes auberges: ouvertes 🄸, Ꭳ. Accueil ouvert entre 6/7h-24/2h. **Autres auberges:** ouvertes 🄸, Ꭳ. Accueil ouvert entre 8/9h-21/23h. **Auberges saisonnières** ouvertes généralement juin-août.

Repas

🍴 B Pour individuels & pour ⅲ. ☞ Pas tous les ustensils sont fournis - à vérifier auprès de l'auberge.

Remises

Remises pour les adhérents III - voir la section "Remises" et notre site: www.iyhf.org.

Déplacements

Modes de transport recommandés 🚌 ⛴ 🚗 Voiture. En hiver les conditions climatiques peuvent être hasardeuses et les pneus-neige sont nécessaires.

Forfaits Voyages/Activités

Forfaits hébergement/transport disponibles. Réservations des forfaits via le Centre National de Réservation ou le Bureau National par ❶ ❷.

Passeports et visas

Veuillez contacter l'ambassade ou le consulat finlandais de votre pays de résidence.

Santé

Soins d'urgence gratuits. Une assurance médicale de voyage est conseillée. Les ressortissants de l'Union Européenne doivent se munir du formulaire E111 pour bénéficier de soins médicaux dans les états de l'UE.

Deutsch

Viele Herbergen sind vom 24.-26. Dez. (Weihnachten) geschlossen. Die meisten Herbergen haben eine Sauna. Inhaber von Hostelling International Mitgliedskarten erhalten einen 15 FIM-Rabatt auf Standardsätze. Herbergen befinden sich in Städten, auf dem Land und an der Küste.

Preisspanne

Preisspanne 50-260 FIM. € 8.41-43.73. 🏧.

Zimmer und Reservierungen

Ⓡ 🄸 (Alle Zimmer). Reservierungen über ⒤⒝⒩ Nationales Buchungszentrum, Herberge oder Landesverband per ❶ ❶ ❷. (Reservierungskosten könnten anfallen). Rauchen ist begrenzt - bitte checken.

Gäste

Haustiere sind erlaubt - in der Herberge nachfragen. ⅲ willkommen. Gruppenbuchungen über Nationales Buchungszentrum, Herberge oder Landesverband per ❶ ❷ (Reservierungskosten könnten anfallen).

Öffnungszeiten

Hauptherbergen: Zugang 🄸, Ꭳ. Rezeption zwischen 06/07:00Uhr-24/02:00Uhr. **Andere Herbergen:** Zugang 🄸, Ꭳ. Rezeption zwischen 08/09:00Uhr-21/23:00Uhr. **Saison-Herbergen** sind normalerweise Jun-Aug geöffnet.

Mahlzeiten

🍴 B Für Einzelreisende & für ⅲ. ☞ Nicht alle Utensilien werden bereitgestellt - in der Herberge nachfragen.

Ermäßigungen

HI-Mitgliedsrabatt ist erhältlich – siehe Teil für Rabatte und Ermäßigungen und www.iyhf.org.

Reisen im Land

Reisen ist einfach mit 🚂 🛳 🚌
Selbstfahrer. Winterwetter kann gefahrvoll sein,
Winterreifen erforderlich.

Reise-/Aktivitäten-Packages

Unterkunft/Transport-Packages erhältlich.
Package-Buchungen über Nationales
Buchungszentrum oder Landesverband per ❻
❺.

Reisepässe und Visa

Bitte erkundigen Sie sich vor der Abreise bei
der finnischen Botschaft oder dem finnischen
Konsulat in Ihrem Land.

Gesundheit

Nur im Notfall sind medizinische Behandlungen
kostenlos. Unfall-/Krankenversicherung wird
empfohlen. EU Staatsangehörige benötigen
Formular E111 für ärztliche Behandlungen
innerhalb der EU Länder.

Español

Muchos albergues cierran en Navidad del 24 al
26 de diciembre. La mayoría tienen sauna. A los
titulares del carnet de socio de Hostelling
International se les concede 15 mk de
descuento. Los albergues están situados en las
ciudades, el campo y la costa.

Tarifas mínima y máxima

Tarifas mínima y máxima 50-260 FIM.
€ 8.41-43.73. 🈺.

Habitaciones y Reservas

🅡 🈺 (todas las habitaciones). Reservas por
[IBN] o a través de la Central Nacional de
Reservas, el albergue o la Asociación Nacional
por ❶ ❻ ❺. (Es posible que se aplique un
suplemento en concepto de gastos de reserva).

Está permitido fumar sólo en algunas
salas/habitaciones - infórmese.

Huéspedes

Se admiten animales - consulte con el albergue.
Se admiten ♦♦♦. Reservas de grupo a través de la
Central Nacional de Reservas, el albergue o la
Asociación Nacional por ❻ ❺ (Es posible que
se aplique un suplemento en concepto de
gastos de reserva).

Horarios y fechas de apertura

Albergues principales - abiertos 🈺, 🕐.
Horario de recepción: 06/07:00h-24/02:00h.
Otros Albergues - abiertos 🈺, 🕐. Horario
de recepción: 08/09:00h-21/23:00h.
Albergues de temporada suelen abrir:
jun-ago.

Comidas

🍽 B Para individuales y para ♦♦♦. 🍴 La cocina
no dispone de todos los utensilios - consulte
con el albergue.

Descuentos

Se conceden descuentos a los miembros de
Hostelling International – véase la sección
sobre descuentos y nuestra página Internet en
www.iyhf.org.

Desplazamientos

Transportes recomendados: 🚂 🛳 🚌
Automóvil. En invierno las condiciones
climáticas pueden ser muy peligrosas, son
necesarios los neumáticos para la nieve.

Viajes Combinados con Actividades

Viajes combinados con alojamiento y
transporte. Reserva de viajes combinados a
través de la Central Nacional de Reservas o la
Asociación Nacional por ❻ ❺.

Pasaportes y Visados

Infórmese en la embajada o consulado finlandeses de su país.

Información Sanitaria

Asistencia médica de urgencia gratuita. Seguro médico recomendado. Los ciudadanos procedentes de países pertenecientes a la UE necesitan el impreso E111 para obtener asistencia médica en dichos países.

"The true traveler is he who goes on foot, and even then, he sits down a lot of the time."

"Le vrai voyageur est celui qui va à pied, et encore, il s'assoit une grande partie du temps."

„Der wahre Reisende ist derjenige, der zu Fuß geht, und selbst dann setzt er sich sehr häufig nieder."

"El verdadero viajero es el que va a pie, y aun así pasa mucho tiempo sentado."

Colette

Helsinki - Eurohostel

Linnankatu 9,
00160 Helsinki.
t (9) 6220470
f (9) 655044
e eurohostel@eurohostel.fi

Open Dates:	🗓
Open Hours:	🕐
Reservations:	**R** (IBN) (CC)
Price Range:	FIM 125-205 € 21.02-34.48 📖
Beds:	305 - 25x^1🛏 100x^2🛏 10x^3🛏
Facilities:	♿ ♟ 135x ♟ 🍽 🛋 ☕ ⚙ 📺 🧺 🔲 🖼 8️⃣ 🔁
Directions:	2SE from city centre
✈	Helsinki-Vantaa 20km
A🚌	2km
⛴	Viking Line & Finnjet Terminal 500m
🚊	2km
🚃	#4 ap 100m
U	Railway Station 2km

There are 6 hostels in Helsinki. See following pages.

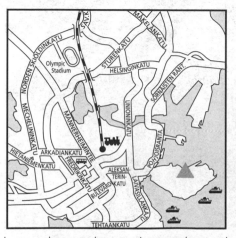

Helsinki - Stadion Hostel

Pohj Stadiontie 3 B,
00250 Helsinki.
t (9) 4778480
f (9) 47784811
e stadion@hostel.inet.fi

Open Dates:	01.01-24.12; 26-31.12
Reservations:	**R** (IBN) (CC)
Price Range:	FIM 80-155 € 13.46-26.07 📖
Beds:	168 - 2x^1🛏 3x^2🛏 1x^3🛏 2x^4🛏 1x^5🛏 13x^6🛏
Facilities:	♟ 7x ♟ 🍽 (B) 🛋 ♿ ⚙ 🛏 📺 🧺 🔲 🖼 8️⃣ 🅿 🏧
Directions:	2N from city centre
✈	Helsinki-Vantaa 18km
A🚌	Finnair Bus ap Opera House
⛴	5km
🚊	Helsinki 2km
🚃	3B, 7 500m
Attractions:	⛷

There are 6 hostels in Helsinki. See following pages.

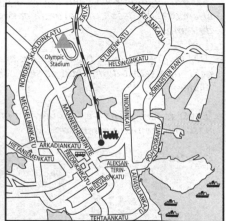

0   4.2km

Tampere -
Hostel Uimahallin Maja

Pirkank 10-12,
33230 Tampere.
❶ (3) 2229460
❷ (3) 2229940
❸ aris@sci.fi

Open Dates: 🗓

Open Hours: 07.00 (06.30)-22.30 (24.00)hrs
(Reception will close on winter sundays at 11.00hrs)

Reservations: **Ⓡ**

Price Range: FIM 110-220 € 18.50-37.00 📖

Beds: 103 - 35x¹🛏 10x²🛏 3x⁴🛏 2x⁶🛏

Facilities: 👭 15x 👭 🍽 ☞ 📺 🖼 ⬍ 🅿

Directions:

✈ Tampere 17km

🚂 Tampere 1.5km

🚌 50m ap Pyynikintori

Attractions: ⚐ ⚲ 1.3km ⚓ 1.3km

There are 3 hostels in Tampere. See following pages.

Turku -
Hostel Turku

Linnankatu 39,
20100 Turku.
❶ (2) 2627680
❷ (2) 2627675
❸ hosteltk@saunalahti.fi

Open Dates: 🗓 (Closed for renovation 01.12.00-01.03.01)

Open Hours: 06.00-10.00hrs; 15.00-24.00hrs

Price Range: FIM 60-120 € 10.09-20.18 📖

Beds: 120 - 2x²🛏 10x⁴🛏 2x⁶🛏 5x⁶🛏

Facilities: ♿ 👫 12x 👫 🍽 (B) ☞ 🛏 📺
🐾 1 x 🍴 🗄 🖼 🅿

Directions: ②Ⓢ from city centre

✈ Turku 10km

⛴ Turku 2km

🚌 ap Boren Puisto 100m

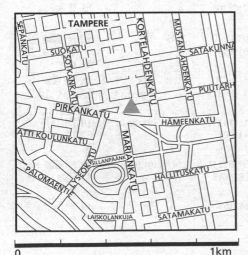

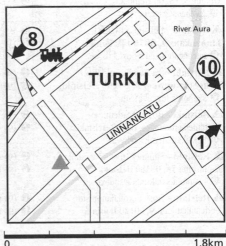

Location/Address	Telephone No. Fax No.	Beds	Opening Dates	Facilities
▲ **Ähtäri** - Hostel Ouluvesi Ähtärintie, 63700 Ähtäri. Postal address: Koulutie 16, 63700 Ähtäri.	☎ (6) 5337482 📠 (6) 5337479	60	01–31.07	⁂ ⍾ R ☞ P ⚙
▲ **Alajärvi** - Kuusiniemi Camp and Course Centre Heikinkankaantie 44, 62900 Alajärvi. ℮ kuusiniemi@japo.fi	☎ (6) 5574542, (6) 55777242	50	01.06–31.08	⁂ ⍾ 6W ☞ P ⚙
▲ **Dragsfjärd** - Dragsfjärds vandrarhotell Kulla, 25870 Dragsfjärd.	☎ (2) 424553 📠 (2) 424553	41	03.04–31.10	⁂ ⍾ R ☞ P
▲ **Eno** - Jokipirtin Majatalo Uimaharjuntie 751, 81270 Paukkaja.	☎ (13) 774607 📠 (13) 774607	44	[2]	⁂ ⍾ 8N ☞ P ⚙
▲ **Enonkoski** - Kievari Enonhovi Urheilukentäntie 1, 58175 Enonkoski.	☎ (15) 479431 📠 (15) 479435	30	[2]	⁂ ⍾ CC ☞ P ⚙
△ *Enontekiö / Peera* - *Peeran Retkeilykeskus Kilpisjärventie 12413, 99490 Kilpisjärvi.*	☎ *(16) 532659* 📠 *(16) 532659*	*53*	*20.02–31.10; 15.12–15.01*	⁂ ⍾ R 90NW CC ☞ P ⚙
▲ **Forssa** - Summer Hostel Forssa Saksankatu 25, 30100 Forssa. ℮ hostel@fai.fi	☎ (3) 414 0270 📠 (3) 414 0270	52	01.06–31.07	⁂ ⍾ ☞ P
▲ **Haapajärvi** - Haapajärven retkeilymaja Erkkiläntie 1, 85800 Haapajärvi.	☎ (8) 7699223 📠 (8) 7699200	40	05.06–07.08	⁂ ⍾ 1SE ☞ P
▲ **Hamina** - Kesähotelli Anna Annankatu 1, 49400 Hamina.	☎ (400) 433561 📠 (5) 3541600	80	01.06–15.08	⍾ 1S CC P ⚙
▲ **Hauho** - Hostel Miekka Häränvattantie 67, 14700 Hauho.	☎ (3) 6545112 📠 (3) 6545321	35	15.05–31.08	⁂ ⍾ R 6W ☞ P ⚙
▲ **Haukipudas** - Hostel Virpiniemi Hiihtomajantie 27, 90820 Kello. ℮ virpiniemi@mail.suomi.net	☎ (8) 5614200 📠 (8) 5614224	101	[2]	⁂ ⍾ 12SW ☞ P ⚙
▲ **Heinola** - Finnhostel Heinola Opintie 3, 18200 Heinola. ℮ gasthaus@sci.fi	☎ (3) 7141655 📠 (3) 7188103	76	03.06–06.08	⁂ ⍾ 1.2N ☞ P ⚙
▲ **Helsinki** - Eurohostel [IBN] **Linnankatu 9, 00160 Helsinki.** ℮ eurohostel@eurohostel.fi	☎ (9) 6220470 📠 (9) 655044	305	[2]	⁂ ⍾ R 2SE CC ☞ ⚙
▲ **Helsinki** - Stadion Hostel [IBN] **Pohj Stadiontie 3 B, 00250 Helsinki.** ℮ stadion@hostel.inet.fi	☎ (9) 4778480 📠 (9) 47784811	168	01.01–24.12; 26–31.12	⁂ ⍾ R 2N CC ☞ P ⚙
▲ **Helsinki** - Hostel Academica Hietaniemenkatu 14, 00100 Helsinki. ℮ hostel.academica@hyy.fi	☎ (9) 13114334 📠 (9) 441201	66	01.06–01.09	⁂ ⍾ 1W CC ☞ P ⚙
▲ **Helsinki** - Summer Hostel Satakunta Lapinrinne 1Λ, 00180 Helsinki. ℮ ravintola.satakunta@sodexho.fi	☎ (9) 69585231 📠 (9) 6854245	147	01.06–31.08	⁂ ⍾ R 1SW CC ☞ ⚙
▲ **Helsinki** - Hostel Erottajanpuisto Uudenmaankatu 9, 00120 Helsinki.	☎ (9) 642169 📠 (9) 6802757	54	[2]	⁂ ⍾ 0.3S CC ☞ ⚙

Location/Address	Telephone No. Fax No.	Beds	Opening Dates	Facilities
▲ **Helsinki** - Hostel Karavaani Rastila Camping, Karavaanikatu 4, 00980 Helsinki. 🄴 rastilacamping@rastilacamping.fi	❶ (9) 31015779 ❸ (9) 3441578	74	04.06–03.08	▐▌▐ **R** 12E & ⧼CC⧽ ☞ **P** ◙ ❀
▲ **Iisalmi** - Iisalmen NMKY:n hostel (YMCA) Sarvikatu 4C, 74120 Iisalmi.	❶ (17) 823940 ❸ (17) 823940	46	01.06–31.07	▐▌▐ ☞ **P** ◙
▲ **Ilmajoki** - Hostel Viitala Ristimäentie 207, 61350 Huissi.	❶ (6) 4227657	20	01.06–31.08	▐▌▐ ⭠⊙⭢ 10W ☞ **P** ◙
▲ **Ilmajoki** - Hostel Palonkortteeri Kauppatie 26, 60800 Ilmajoki. 🄴 artrockcafe@artrockcafe.fi	❶ (6) 4240000 ❸ (6) 4240057	120	12	▐▌▐ ⭠⊙⭢ ⧼CC⧽ ☞ **P** ◙ ☕
▲ **Imatra** - Ukonlinna Lciritic 8, 55420 Imatra.	❶ (5) 4321270 ❸ (5) 4321270	22	12	▐▌▐ ⭠⊙⭢ 3SE ☞ **P**
▲ **Inari/Kaamanen** - Kaamasen Kievari 99910 Kaamanen. 🄴 kaamanen@na.netppl.fi	❶ (16) 672713 ❸ (16) 672786	97	12	▐▌▐ ⭠⊙⭢ 28N ⧼CC⧽ ☞ **P** ◙ ☕
▲ **Inari/Kaamanen** - Hostel Jokitörmä 99910 Kaamanen. 🄴 lomakyla@jokitorma.inet.fi	❶ (16) 672725 ❸ (16) 672745	50	12	▐▌▐ ⭠⊙⭢ 27N ⧼CC⧽ ☞
▲ **Inari/Kiilopää** - Hostel Ahopää Fell Resort Kiilopää, 99830 Saariselkä. 🄴 kiilopaa@suomenlatu.fi	❶ (16) 6700700 ❸ (16) 667121	36	12	▐▌▐ ⭠⊙⭢ **R** 45S ⧼CC⧽ ☞ **P** ◙ ☕
▲ **Järvenpää** - Järvenpään Matkailukeskus Stålhanentie, 04400 Järvenpää.	❶ (9) 74255200 ❸ (9) 74255250	21	12	▐▌▐ ⭠⊙⭢ **R** 2.5S ⧼CC⧽ ☞ **P** ◙ ☕
▲ **Joensuu** - Finnhostel Joensuu The Eastern Finland Sport College, Kalevankatu 8, 80110 Joensuu. 🄴 finnhostel@islo.jns.fi	❶ (13) 2675076 ❸ (13) 2675075	84	12	▐▌▐ ⭠⊙⭢ 0.5W ☞ **P** ◙
▲ **Joensuu** - Joensuun Elli Länsikatu 18, 80110 Joensuu. 🄴 hotel.elli@kolumbus.fi	❶ (13) 225927 ❸ (13) 225763	53	01.06–26.08	▐▌▐ ⭠⊙⭢ ⧼CC⧽ ☞ **P** ◙ ☕
△ *Joensuu - Partiotalo* *Vanamokatu 25, 80130 Joensuu.*	❶ *(13) 123381*	44	*01.06–31.08*	▐▌▐ **R** 1S & ☞ **P**
▲ **Joutsa** - Vaihelan tila Vaihelantie 24, 19920 Pappinen. 🄴 vaihelan.tila@co.inet.fi	❶ (14) 889107 ❸ (14) 889197	14	12	▐▌▐ ⭠⊙⭢ 16NW ☞ **P**
▲ **Jyväskylä** - Finnhostel Laajari Laajavuorentie 15, 40740 Jyväskylä. 🄴 kristiina.enkenberg@jkl.fi	❶ (14) 624885 ❸ (14) 624888	89	01.01–23.12; 26–31.12	▐▌▐ ⭠⊙⭢ **R** 4W ⧼CC⧽ ☞ **P** ◙ ☕
▲ **Kajaani** - Hostel Huone ja Aamiainen Pohjolankatu 4, 87100 Kajaani.	❶ (8) 622254 ❸ (8) 622254	46	12	▐▌▐ ⭠⊙⭢ **R** 0.6SE ⧼CC⧽ **P**
▲ **Kalajoki/Hiekkasärkät** - Tapion Tupa Hiekkasärkät, 85100 Kalajoki. 🄴 tapiontupa@tapiontupa.com	❶ (8) 466622 ❸ (8) 466699	36	12	▐▌▐ ⭠⊙⭢ 4S ☞ **P** ☕
▲ **Kalajoki** - Hostel Retkeilijä Opintie 2, 85100 Kalajoki.	❶ (400) 510303 ❸ (8) 463431	55	15.06–31.07	▐▌▐ ⭠⊙⭢ ☞ **P**

Location/Address	Telephone No. Fax No.	Beds	Opening Dates	Facilities
▲ **Kauhava** - Tuppiroska Yrittäjäopisto, Kauppatie 109, 62200 Kauhava.	☎ (6) 4315350 🖷 (6) 4315352	200	01.06–15.08	ⅲ ⏻ ⋵CC⋴ ♂ 🅿 ⊡ ☕
▲ **Kaustinen** - Koskelan Lomatalo Känsäläntie 123, 69600 Kaustinen. 🅴 koskelan.lomatalo@kaustinen.fi	☎ (6) 8611338	31	▣	ⅲ ⏻ 5W ♂ 🅿 ⊡
▲ **Kemijärvi** - Matkatupa A725 Ulkuniemi PL, 98100 Kemijärvi.	☎ (16) 888517	74	01.05–31.10	ⅲ ⏻ 26S ♂ 🅿 ⊡ ☕
▲ **Kemijärvi** - Hostel Kemijärvi Lohelankatu 1, 98100 Kemijärvi.	☎ (16) 813253, (16) 813341; (40) 5812007 🖷 (16) 813342	35	▣	ⅲ ⏻ 0.3W ⋵CC⋴ ♂ 🅿 ☕
▲ **Kerimäki** - Korkeamäen Majatalo Ruokolahdentie 545, 58200 Kerimäki.	☎ (50) 5215817; (15) 442186	47	20.06–20.08	ⅲ ⏻ 6S ♂ 🅿 ⊡ ☕
▲ **Kittilä** - Hostel Majari Valtatie 5, 99100 Kittilä.	☎ (16) 648508, (400) 410592 🖷 (16) 642259	59	10.06–05.08	ⅲ ⏻ ♂ 🅿
▲ **Kiuruvesi** - Matkamaja Kiurusoppi Museokatu 17, 74700 Kiuruvesi.	☎ (17) 754444 🖷 (17) 753286	32	01.06–10.08	ⅲ ⏻ ♂ 🅿 ⊡
▲ **Kokemäki** - Kesähotelli Tyrni Kauvatsantie 189, 32800 Kokemäki. 🅴 hannu.pihkala@huittinen.fi	☎ (50) 3366996, (2) 5604711 🖷 (2) 5604703	96	01.06–31.07	ⅲ ⏻ 1.9N ♿ ♂ 🅿 ⊡
▲ **Kokkola** - Hostel Tankkari Vanhansatamanlahti, 67100 Kokkola.	☎ (6) 8314006 🖷 (6) 8310306	23	01.06–31.08	ⅲ ⏻ 2.5N ♂ 🅿 ☕
▲ **Korpilahti** - Matkailutila Surkeenjärvi Surkeejärventie, 41800 Korpilahti.	☎ (14) 827437 🖷 (14) 827437	38	01.05–30.09	ⅲ ⏻ Ⓡ 20W ♂ 🅿
▲ **Kristiinankaupunki** - Hostel Kilstrand/Kiilinranta Kiilintie 90, 64490 Siipyy.	☎ (6) 2225611 🖷 (6) 2225615	60	01.06–16.08	ⅲ ⏻ Ⓡ 30S ♿ ♂ 🅿 ⊡ ☕
▲ **Kuhmo** - Kuhmon retkeilymaja Piilolan koulu, 88900 Kuhmo.	☎ (8) 6556245 🖷 (8) 6556384	33	01–31.07	ⅲ ♂ 🅿
▲ **Kuopio** - Hostel Puijon Maja Puijontie, 70300 Kuopio. 🅴 hotelli.puijo@pspt.fi	☎ (17) 2555250 🖷 (17) 2555266	42	▣	ⅲ ⏻ Ⓡ 2NW ⋵CC⋴ 🅿 ☕ ☕ ⚙
▲ **Kuortane** - Finnhostel Virtaniemen Lomatila Virtala (Virtaniementie 35) 63100 Kuortane. 🅴 pirjo.virtaniemi@lomatila.inet.fi	☎ (6) 5256689 🖷 (6) 5256694	70	▣	ⅲ ⏻ Ⓡ 14SE ♿ ⋵CC⋴ ♂ 🅿 ☕ ☕
▲ **Kuusamo** - Kuusamon Kansanopisto Kitkantie 35, 93600 Kuusamo.	☎ (8) 8522132 🖷 (8) 8521134	110	25.06–31.08	ⅲ ⏻ ♂ 🅿 ⊡
▲ **Lahti** - Lahden Kansanopisto Harjukatu 46, 15100 Lahti. 🅴 lahden.kansanopisto@lahdenko.sci.fi	☎ (3) 8781181 🖷 (3) 8781234	72	04.06–12.08	ⅲ ⏻ ⋵CC⋴ 🅿
▲ **Lahti** - Mukkulan kesähotelli Ritaniemenkatu 10, 15240 Lahti. 🅴 kesahotelli.mukkula@saunalahti.fi	☎ (3) 8823602; (3) 8823521 🖷 (3) 8823603; (3) 8823522	120	01.06–15.08	4N ⋵CC⋴ ♂ 🅿

Location/Address	Telephone No. Fax No.	Beds	Opening Dates	Facilities
▲ **Lapinlahti** - Hostel Portaanpää 73100 Lapinlahti. ❷ toimisto@portaanpaa.fi	❶ (17) 768860 ❺ (17) 731998	93	03.06–06.08	♦♦ ⵁ 2S ᵭ P ▣
▲ **Lappeenranta** - Finnhostel Lappeenranta Kuusimäenkatu 18, 53810 Lappeenranta. ❷ huhtiniemi@loma-oksa.inet.fi	❶ (5) 4515555 ❺ (5) 4515558	80	15.01–15.12	♦♦ ⵁ 2W ᵭ ⨑ P ☕
△ *Lappeenranta - Huhtiniemi Kuusimäenkatu 18, 53810 Lappeenranta.* ❷ *huhtiniemi@loma-oksa.inet.fi*	❶ *(5) 4515555* ❺ *(5) 4515558*	*24*	*01.06–15.08*	ⵁ 2W ⨑ ᵭ P ▣
▲ **Lappeenranta** - Karelia Park Korpraalinkuja 1, 53810 Lappeenranta. ❷ kari.nalli@armpa.inet.fi	❶ (5) 675211, (5) 4530405 ❺ (5) 4528454	50	01.06–31.08	♦♦ ⵁ 2W ⨑ P ▣ ☕
▲ **Lieksa/Koli** - Kolin retkeilymaja Niinilahdentie 47, 83960 Koli.	❶ (13) 673131 ❺ (13) 673131	47	🄵₁₂	♦♦ ⵁ 96 W ᵭ P ☕
▲ **Mänttä** - Mäntän retkeilymaja Koulukatu 6, 35800 Mänttä.	❶ (3) 4888641; (50) 3705246 ❺ (3) 4888500	53	01.06–12.08	♦♦ ᵭ ᵭ P ▣ ⚲
▲ **Muonio** - Lomamaja Pekonen Lahenrannantie 10, 99300 Muonio. ❷ loma.maja@pekonen.inet.fi	❶ (16) 532237 ❺ (16) 532236	28	01.04–30.09	♦♦ 0.5W ᵭ P
▲ **Muurla** - Kesähostelli Muurlan Evankelinen Opisto Muurlantie 365, 25130 Muurla. ❷ toimisto@muurlanopisto.org	❶ (2) 7320511 ❺ (2) 7320533	58	01.06–31.08	♦♦ ⵁ ᵭ ᵭ P ▣ ☕
▲ **Nivala** - Hostel Nivala Maliskyläntie 2, 85500 Nivala.	❶ (8) 443171 ❺ (8) 442555	112	01–31.07	♦♦ ⵁ Ⓡ ᵭ P ▣
▲ **Nurmes** - Hyvärilän Matkailukeskus Lomatie 75500 Nurmes. ❷ matkailu@nurmes.fi	❶ (13) 481770 ❺ (13) 481775	70	🄵₁₂	♦♦ ⵁ 4E ⨑ ᵭ P ▣ ☕
▲ **Nurmijärvi** - Lomakoti Kotoranta Kotorannantie 74, 05250 Kiljava. ❷ marja.weckstrom@kotoranta.fi	❶ (9) 2765879, (9) 2765255; (40) 7605212 ❺ (9) 2765928	34	🄵₁₂	♦♦ ⵁ 15N ᵭ ᵭ P ☕
▲ **Oulu** - Summer Uni Hostel Välkkylä Kajaanintie 36, 90100 Oulu.	❶ (8) 8803311 ❺ (8) 8803754	160	02.06–29.08	♦♦ Ⓡ 1.5E ⨑ ᵭ P ▣
▲ **Parainen** - Hostel Norrdal Solliden Camping, Norrby, 21600 Parainen.	❶ (2) 4585955 ❺ (2) 4585955	14	🄵₁₂	ⵁ 1.5N ⨑
▲ **Parikkala** - Karjalan Lomahovi 59100 Parikkala. ❷ lomahovi@lomayhtyma.fi	❶ (5) 6577700 ❺ (5) 470597	20	01.06–31.08	♦♦ ⵁ 4S ⨑ P ▣ ☕ ⚲
▲ **Pielavesi** - Pielavesi Hostelli Laurinpurontie 23, 72400 Pielavesi.	❶ (17) 862970 ❺ (17) 861327	22	04.06–12.08	♦♦ ⵁ 0.5E ᵭ P ▣ ☕
▲ **Pietarsaari** - Svanen/Joutsen Luodontie 50, 68660 Pietarsaari. ❷ svanen@multi.fi	❶ (6) 7230660 ❺ (6) 7810008	20	15.05–31.08	♦♦ ⵁ 4N ᵭ ⨑ ᵭ P ▣ ☕

Location/Address	Telephone No. Fax No.	Beds	Opening Dates	Facilities
▲ **Piikkiö** - Hostel Tuorla Country College of South Western Finland, Tuorlantie 1, 21500 Piikkiö. 🅔 toimisto.tuorla@tuorla.com	☎ (2) 2731672, (50) 3039803 🕿 (2) 2731672	84	🏠	♠♠ ⏚ ® 4W ⏛ P ⭕ ☎
▲ **Pori** - Hostel Tekunkorpi Tekniikantie 4, 28600 Pori.	☎ (2) 6348400 🕿 (2) 6348408	160	15.05–15.08	♠♠ 5W -CC- ⏛ P ⭕
▲ **Porvoo** - Porvoon retkeilymaja Linnankoskenkatu 1-3, 06100 Porvoo.	☎ (19) 5230012 🕿 (19) 5230012	33	02.01–20.12	♠♠ ⏛ P 🚲
▲ **Pudasjärvi/Syöte** - Hostel Syöte Pikku-Syöte tunturi, 93280 Syöte.	☎ (8) 838172 🕿 (8) 838173	52	🏠	♠♠ ⏚ 55NE -CC- ⏛ P ⭕ ☎
▲ **Puumala** - Hostel Reissumaja Koskenseläntie 98, 52200 Puumala. 🅔 koskenselka@lomavinkki-oy.inet.fi	☎ (15) 4681119 🕿 (15) 4681809	21	🏠	♠♠ 2NW -CC- ⏛ P ⭕ ☎
▲ **Ranua** - Pikku Ilves Keskustie 10, 97700 Ranua. 🅔 hotelli.ilveslinna@pp.inet.fi	☎ (16) 3551201 🕿 (16) 3551284	36	🏠	♠♠ ⏚ ® ♿ -CC- ⏛ P ⭕ ☎ 🚲 ⚙
▲ **Rauma** - Hostel Poroholma Camping Site, 26100 Rauma. 🅔 poroholma@kalliohovi.fi	☎ (2) 83882500 🕿 (2) 83882400	38	15.05–31.08	♠♠ ⏚ 2N -CC- ⏛ P ⭕ ☎
▲ **Rauma** - Summer Hostel Rauma Satamakatu 20, 26100 Rauma.	☎ (2) 8240130	195	01.06–31.08	♠♠ ⏚ -CC- ⏛ P ☎
▲ **Rautalampi** - Korholan Kartano Korholantie 111, 77700 Rautalampi.	☎ (17) 530320	50	01.01–21.12	♠♠ ® 2N ♿ ⏛ P ⭕
▲ **Riihimäki** - Riihimäen Retkeilyhotelli Merkuriuksenkatu 7, 11130 Riihimäki.	☎ (400) 876169	139	01.06–31.07	♠♠ ⏚ ⏛ P ⭕
▲ **Ristiina** - Löydön Kartano Kartanontie 151, 52300 Ristiina.	☎ (15) 664101 🕿 (15) 664109	58	🏠	♠♠ ⏚ 6N ⏛ P ⭕
▲ **Rovaniemen maalaiskunta** - TH-Kievari Gasthaus Kemintie 1956, 97130 Hirvas.	☎ (16) 382017 🕿 (16) 382191	50	🏠	♠♠ ⏚ 3N -CC- P ⭕ ☎ 🚲
▲ **Rovaniemi** - Hostel Tervashonka Hallituskatu 16, 96100 Rovaniemi.	☎ (16) 344644 🕿 (16) 344644	58	🏠	♠♠ ⏚ ⏛ P
▲ **Rymättylä** - Hostel Päiväkulma Kuristentie 225, 21140 Rymättylä. 🅔 hostelp@saunalahti.fi	☎ (2) 2521894 🕿 (2) 2521794	50	01.05–30.09	♠♠ ⏚ 3SE -CC- ⏛ P ⭕
▲ **Ruotsinpyhtää** - Finnhostel Krouvinmäki Ruotsinpyhtään Ruukkialue Oy, 07970 Ruotsinpyhtää. 🅔 ruotsinpyhtaan.ruukkialue@co.inet.fi	☎ (19) 618474 🕿 (19) 618475	18	🏠	♠♠ ⏚ ® ♿ ⏛ P ⭕ ☎
▲ **Salo** - Laurin koulu Venemestarinkatu 37, 24240 Salo. 🅔 helja.karjalainen@salo.fi	☎ (2) 7784409 🕿 (2) 7784810	60	04.06–10.08	♠♠ ® ⏛ P
▲ **Savonlinna** - Malakias Pihlajavedenkuja 6, 57170 Savonlinna. 🅔 casino.myynti@svlkylpylaitos.fi	☎ (15) 533283 🕿 (15) 533283	30	02.07–05.08	♠♠ ⏚ 2W -CC- ⏛ P ⭕

Location/Address	Telephone No. Fax No.	Beds	Opening Dates	Facilities
▲ **Savonlinna** - Vuorilinna Kylpylaitoksentie, 57130 Savonlinna. ℮ casino.myynti@svlkylpylaitos.fi	☎ (15) 7395495 🖷 (15) 272524	30	04.06–26.08	♦♦♦ ⑩ ♿ ⊡ ♂ P ⑥ ♥
▲ **Seinäjoki** - Marttilan Kortteeri Puskantie 38, 60100 Seinäjoki.	☎ (6) 4204817 🖷 (6) 4234226	157	01.06–09.08	♦♦♦ ⑩ ⬚1N⬚ ⊡ ♂ P ⑥ ♥
▲ **Sodankylä** - Lapin opisto Kansanopistontie 5, 99600 Sodankylä. ℮ kanslia@lapinopisto.fi	☎ (16) 612181 🖷 (16) 611503	27	01.06–14.08	♦♦♦ ⑩ ⬚2E⬚ ⊡ ♂ P ♥
▲ **Sodankylä/Raudanjoki** - Hostel Visatupa Seipäjärventie 409, 99510 Raudanjoki. ℮ skangas@iki.fi	☎ (16) 634133 🖷 (16) 634101	45	⬚12⬚	♦♦♦ ⑩ ⬚56S⬚ ♿ ♂ P ⑥
▲ **Sotkamo** - Hostel Tikkanen Kainuuntie 31, 88600 Sotkamo.	☎ (8) 6660541	32	⬚12⬚	♦♦♦ ♂ P ⑥ ☍
▲ **Sulkava/Kaartilankoski** - Partalansaaren Lomakoti Hirviniementie 5, 58720 Kaartilankoski.	☎ (15) 478850 🖷 (15) 478850	50	⬚12⬚	♦♦♦ ⑩ Ⓡ ⬚16S⬚ ♂ P ⑥ ♥ ☍
▲ **Suomussalmi/Kuivajärvi** - Domnan Pirtti Kuivajärventie 195, 89840 Ylivuokki.	☎ (8) 723179 🖷 (8) 711189	31	01.04–30.09	♦♦♦ ⑩ ⬚75SE⬚ P ♥
▲ **Taivalkoski** - Jokimutka Parviaisentie 64, 93420 Jurmu.	☎ (8) 845762	34	10.06–31.07	♦♦♦ ⑩ Ⓡ ⬚25 3E⬚ ♂ P ⑥ ♥
▲ **Tammisaari** - Ekenäs Vandrarhem/ TammisaarenRetkeilymaja Höijerintie 10, 10600 Tammisaari.	☎ (19) 2416393 🖷 (19) 2413917	88	16.05–20.08	♦♦♦ ⑩ ♂ P ⑥
▲ **Tampere** - Hostel Uimahallin Maja **Pirkank 10-12, 33230 Tampere.** ℮ aris@sci.fi	☎ (3) 2229460 🖷 (3) 2229940	103	⬚12⬚	♦♦♦ ⑩ Ⓡ ♂ P
▲ **Tampere** - Hostel Tampere YWCA Tuomiokirkonkatu 12 A, 33100 Tampere.	☎ (3) 2544020 🖷 (3) 2544022	70	01.06–25.08	♦♦♦ ⑩ ♂ P
▲ **Tampere** - Summer Hotel Härmälä Nuolialantie 50, 33900 Tampere. ℮ myyntipalvelu@lomaliitto.fi	☎ (3) 2651355 🖷 (3) 2660365	35	01.06–31.08	♦♦♦ ⑩ ⬚4S⬚ ⊡ ♂ P ⑥
▲ **Tervola** - Wild Lapland Kätkävaara, Tervola, 97140 Muurola. ℮ lapin.elamyslomat@co.inet.fi	☎ (16) 439116 🖷 (16) 439116	40	01.03–30.09	♦♦♦ ⑩ Ⓡ ⬚20N⬚ ⊡ P ⑥ ♥ ☍ ⚙
▲ **Toholampi** - Hirvikosken kurssikeskus Tornikoskentie 50, 69410 Sykäräinen. ℮ hirvikoski@toholampi.fi	☎ (6) 8623086 🖷 (6) 8623080	84	⬚12⬚	♦♦♦ ⑩ ⬚24W⬚ ♿ ⊡ ♂ P ⑥ ♥ ☍
▲ **Tornio** - Hostel Tornio Kivirannantie 13-15, 95410 Tornio. ℮ pptoimisto@ppopisto.fi	☎ (16) 2119244 🖷 (16) 2119222	90	28.05–17.08	♦♦♦ ⑩ ⬚25N⬚ ♿ ♂ P ⑥
▲ **Turku** - Hostel Turku **Linnankatu 39, 20100 Turku.** ℮ hosteltk@saunalahti.fi	☎ (2) 2627680 🖷 (2) 2627675	120	⬚12⬚ (Closed for renovation 01.12.00– 01.03.01)	♦♦♦ ⑩ ⬚2S⬚ ♿ ♂ P ⑥
▲ **Vaasa** - Hostel Tekla Palosaarentie 58, 65200 Vaasa.	☎ (6) 3276411 🖷 (6) 3213989	160	⬚12⬚	♦♦♦ ⑩ Ⓡ ⬚3N⬚ ⊡ ♂ P ⑥ ♥

Location/Address	Telephone No. Fax No.	Beds	Opening Dates	Facilities
▲ Vantaa/Tikkurila - Tikkurilan Retkeilyhotelli Valkoisenlähteentie 52, 01300 Vantaa.	☏ (9) 83628620 🖷 (9) 8720068	100	🖾	♄ ⎰ & ᴄᴄ ☞ P 🗓 🍲
▲ Varkaus - Varkauden Retkeilymaja Kuparisepänkatu 5, 78870 Varkaus. ✉ linnea.ihalainen@vrk.varkaus.fi	☏ (17) 5795700 🖷 (17) 5795700	73	01.06–13.08	♄ 2W ☞ P 🗓 🍲
▲ Virrat - Domus Virrat Sipiläntie 3, 34800 Virrat.	☏ (3) 4755600 🖷 (3) 4755605	78	01.06–15.08	♄ ⎰ & ☞ P 🗓 🍲
▲ Virrat/Vaskivesi - Finnhostel Haapamäki 34710 Vaskivesi.	☏ (3) 4758845; (400) 627854 🖷 (3) 4758811	100	01.05–30.09	♄ ⎰ Ⓡ 20S & ☞ P 🗓

"Sloth makes all things difficult, but industry, all things easy. He that rises late must trot all day, and shall scarce overtake his business at night, while laziness travels so slowly that poverty soon overtakes him."

"La paresse rend tout difficile alors que l'industrie tout facile. Celui qui se lève tard doit courir partout, et aura du mal à dépasser son travail en fin de journée, tandis que la paresse voyage si lentement que la pauvreté aura tôt fait de le dépasser."

„Trägheit macht alle Dinge schwierig, aber Fleiß alle Dinge einfach. Derjenige, der spät aufsteht, muss den ganzen Tag traben und wird selten seine Aufgaben bis zum Abend erledigt haben, wobei Faulheit sich so langsam bewegt, dass Armut ihn bald überholt."

"La indolencia lo hace todo difícil, mientras que la industria, todo fácil. El que se levanta tarde tiene que pasarse todo el día corriendo, y apenas si ha logrado adelantar su trabajo por la noche, en tanto que la pereza viaja tan lentamente que la pobreza tarda poco en adelantarle."

Benjamin Franklin

France

FRANCE

FRANKREICH

FRANCIA

**Fédération Unie des Auberges de Jeunesse (FUAJ),
27 rue Pajol, 75018 Paris, France.**

☎ (33) (0) 1 44898727
(33) (0) 836 688698 (2,23 Francs per min)
🖷 (33) (0) 1 44898710
🖳 www.fuaj.org

Office Hours: Monday-Friday, 09.30-18.00hrs
Saturday, 10.00-17.00hrs.

**Travel Section: Groups and individuals, Fédération Unie des Auberges de Jeunesse,
27 rue Pajol, 75018 Paris, France.**

☎ (33) (0) 1 44898727
🖷 (33) (0) 1 44898749

A copy of the Hostel Directory for this Country can be obtained from:
The National Office

Capital:	Paris	**Population:**	58,256,000
Language:	French	**Size:**	550,000 sq km
Currency:	F (franc)	**Telephone Country Code:**	33

France

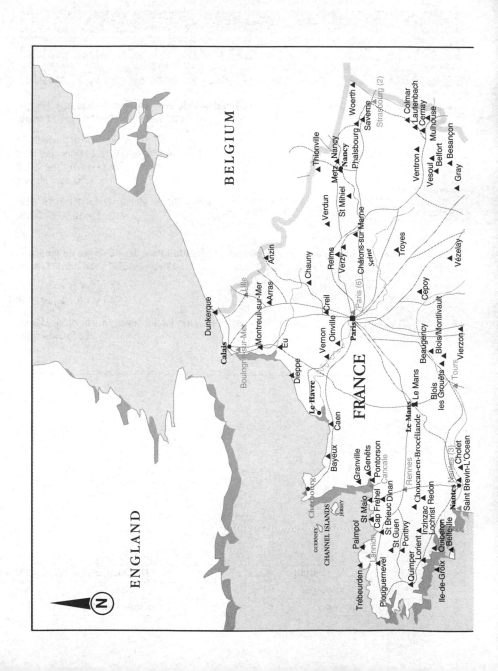

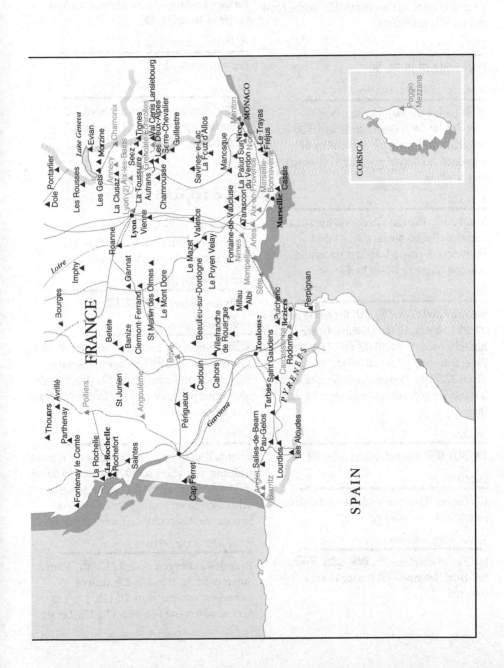

English

Book beds and not bedrooms. Hostels are located in cities, in the countryside, on the coast and on hills/mountains.

Price range

Price range FF 45-74. 🔲.

Rooms and Reservations

R during Jan-Mar, Jul, Aug, Dec. (¹🐄 ²🐄 ³🐄 ⁴🐄). Reservations via **IBN** National Booking Centre or Hostel by ❶. (Reservation charges may apply). All hostels are non-smoking.

Guests

Membership Card and Passport/Photo ID are required. The maximum stay is 3 days. ♦♦♦ welcome. Group bookings via National Booking Centre or Hostel by ❶.

Open times

Main hostels: open 🔲, ◔. Reception open: 07:00-10:00hrs, 17:00-22:00hrs, **Other hostels:** open 07:00-10:00hrs, 17:00-22:00hrs. Reception open: 07:00-10:00hrs, 17:00-22:00hrs. Resident manager. **Seasonal hostels** are generally open Jan-Apr, Jul, Aug, Dec.

Meals

🍽 BLD **R** For individuals & for ♦♦♦. 🐚.

Discounts

HI Member Discounts available - see discounts section and www.iyhf.org.

Travelling around

For ease of travel use ✈ 🚂 ⛴ 🚌 Self-Drive. International Driving Licence required.

Travel/Activity Packages

Winter sports, water sports, cycling/mountain biking and walking/trekking packages available. Package bookings via 🖰 National Booking Centre or Hostel by ❶.

Passports and Visas

Passport required.

Health

Medical insurance is recommended. EU Nationals require Form E111 to obtain treatment within EU countries.

Français

Réserver des lits et non des chambres. Les auberges sont situées dans les villes, à la campagne, sur le littoral et à la montagne.

Tarifs des nuitées

Tarifs des nuitées 45-74 FF. 🔲.

Chambres et réservations

R jan-mar, juil, août, déc. (¹🐄 ²🐄 ³🐄 ⁴🐄). Réservations via **IBN** le Centre National de Réservation ou l'auberge par ❶. (Des frais de réservation pourront vous être facturés). Toutes les auberges sont non-fumeurs.

Usagers

La carte d'adhérent ainsi que le passeport/pièce d'identité avec photo sont à présenter. La durée maximale du séjour est de 3 jours. Accueil des ♦♦♦. Réservations pour groupes via le Centre National de Réservation ou l'auberge par ❶.

Horaires d'ouverture

Grandes auberges: ouvertes 🔲, ◔. Accueil ouvert entre 7h-10h, 17h-22h. **Autres auberges:** ouvertes entre 7h-10h, 17h-22h. Accueil ouvert entre 7h-10h, 17h-22h. Gérant réside sur place. **Auberges saisonnières** ouvertes généralement jan-avril, juil, août, déc.

Repas

🍽 BLD Ⓡ Pour individuels & pour ⅲ. ☝.

Remises

Remises pour les adhérents HI - voir la section "Remises" et notre site: www.iyhf.org.

Déplacements

Modes de transport recommandés ✈ 🚆 🚢 🚌 Voiture. Permis de conduire international obligatoire.

Forfaits Voyages/Activités

Forfaits sports d'hiver, sports aquatiques, cyclotourisme/VTT et randonnées pédestres disponibles. Réservations des forfaits via 📠 le Centre National de Réservation ou l'auberge par ❸.

Passeports et visas

Passeport obligatoire.

Santé

Une assurance médicale de voyage est conseillée. Les ressortissants de l'Union Européenne doivent se munir du formulaire E111 pour bénéficier de soins médicaux dans les états de l'UE.

Deutsch

Reserviert Betten, keine Zimmer. Herbergen befinden sich in Städten, auf dem Land, an der Küste und in Bergen/Gebirgen.

Preisspanne

Preisspanne 45-74 FF. 🏨.

Zimmer und Reservierungen

Ⓡ während Jan-Mär, Jul, Aug, Dez. (1🚆 2🚆 3🚆 4🚆). Reservierungen über ⒾⒷⓃ Nationales Buchungszentrum oder Herberge per ❸. (Reservierungskosten könnten anfallen). Rauchen ist in allen Herbergen NICHT gestattet.

Gäste

Mitgliedsausweis und Reisepass/Personalausweis sind erforderlich. Der maximale Aufenthalt beträgt 3 Tage. ⅲ wlllkommen. Gruppenbuchungen über Nationales Buchungszentrum oder Herberge per ❸.

Öffnungszeiten

Hauptherbergen: Zugang 🏨, ⏰. Rezeption zwischen 07:00-10:00Uhr, 17:00-22:00Uhr, **Andere Herbergen:** Zugang zwischen 07:00-10:00Uhr, 17:00-22:00Uhr. Rezeption zwischen 07:00-10:00Uhr, 17:00-22:00Uhr. Herbergsmanager wohnt im Haus. **Saison-Herbergen** sind normalerweise Jan-Apr, Jul, Aug, Dez geöffnet.

Mahlzeiten

🍽 BLD Ⓡ Für Einzelreisende & für ⅲ. ☝.

Ermäßigungen

HI-Mitgliedsrabatt ist erhältlich – siehe Teil für Rabatte und Ermäßigungen und www.iyhf.org.

Reisen im Land

Reisen ist einfach mit ✈ 🚆 🚢 🚌 Selbstfahrer. Internationaler Führerschein erforderlich.

Reise-/Aktivitäten-Packages

Wintersport, Wassersport, Fahrrad/Mountainbiking und Wandern/Trekking -Packages erhältlich. Package-Buchungen über 📠 Nationales Buchungszentrum oder Herberge per ❸.

Reisepässe und Visa

Reisepass erforderlich.

Gesundheit

Unfall-/Krankenversicherung wird empfohlen.
EU Staatsangehörige benötigen Formular E111
für ärztliche Behandlungen innerhalb der EU
Länder.

Español

Se reservan camas, no habitaciones. Los
albergues están situados en las ciudades, el
campo, la costa y la montaña.

Tarifas mínima y máxima

Tarifas mínima y máxima 45-74 FF. 🖳.

Habitaciones y Reservas

🅡 en ene-mar, jul, ago, dic.
(¹🛏 ²🛏 ³🛏 ⁴🛏). Reservas por [IBN] o a
través de la Central Nacional de Reservas o el
albergue por ❶. (Es posible que se aplique un
suplemento en concepto de gastos de reserva).
Está prohibido fumar en todos los albergues.

Huéspedes

Los huéspedes deben presentar su Carnet de
Alberguista y su pasaporte o carnet de
identidad. La estancia máxima es de 3 días. Se
admiten ⅲ. Reservas de grupo a través de la
Central Nacional de Reservas o el albergue por
❶.

Horarios y fechas de apertura

Albergues principales - abiertos 🖳, ⊙.
Horario de recepción: 07:00-10:00h,
17:00-22:00h, **Otros albergues** - abiertos:
07:00-10:00h, 17:00-22:00h. Horario de
recepción: 07:00-10:00h, 17:00-22:00h.
Gerente residente. **Albergues de temporada**
suelen abrir: ene-abr, jul, ago, dic.

Comidas

🍽 BLD 🅡 Para individuales y para ⅲ. 🍴.

Descuentos

Se conceden descuentos a los miembros de
Hostelling International – véase la sección
sobre descuentos y nuestra página Internet en
www.iyhf.org.

Desplazamientos

Transportes recomendados: ✈ 🚅 ⛴
🚌 Automóvil. Es necesario un permiso de
conducir internacional.

Viajes Combinados con Actividades

Viajes combinados con deportes de invierno,
deportes náuticos, cicloturismo/bicicleta de
montaña y senderismo. Reserva de viajes
combinados por 🖳 o a través de la Central
Nacional de Reservas o el albergue por ❶.

Pasaportes y Visados

Pasaporte obligatorio.

Información Sanitaria

Seguro médico recomendado. Los ciudadanos
procedentes de países pertenecientes a la UE
necesitan el impreso E111 para obtener
asistencia médica en dichos países.

Aix-les-Bains

Promenade du Sierroz,
73100 Aix-les-Bains (Savoie).
☎ 0479883288
✆ 0479611405
✉ aix-les-bains@fuaj.org

Open Dates:	23.12-03.01; 03.02-04.11
Open Hours:	18.00-10.00hrs (low season); 14.00-10.00hrs (high season)
Reservations:	**R** **IBN** **CC**
Price Range:	74 FF € 11.28
Beds:	92 - 2x³ 18x⁴ 1x⁵ 1x⁶
Facilities:	♿ ♦♦♦ 20x ♦♦♦ ⌑ ⌑ ⌑ 📺 ▨ ✎ 4 x ⌑ ⌑ ⌑ ⌑ 🅿 ℹ ✿ ⚠ ⌑ ⌑
Directions:	3NW from city centre
✈	Genève 80km
🚂	Aix-les Bains TGV 3km
🚌	2 Plage Aix 200m ap Camping
Attractions:	⛲ ⌑ ⌑ ⌑ 1550m ⌑ ⌑ ⌑ 5km ⌑ 200m

Angoulême

Parc de Bourgines,
16000 Angoulême (Charente).
☎ 0545924580
✆ 0545959071
✉ angouleme@fuaj.org

Open Dates:	03.01-15.12
Open Hours:	07.30-14.00hrs (01.04-01.10 Mon-Sat; 08.00-10.00hrs Sun); 07.30-23.00hrs (01.10-21.04 Mon-Sat; 08.00-10.00; 18.00-23.00hrs Sun)
Reservations:	**IBN** **CC**
Price Range:	70 FF € 10.68 **BB** inc ⌑
Beds:	85 - 2x² 11x⁶ 2x⁶
Facilities:	♦♦♦ 15x ♦♦♦ ⌑ ⌑ ⌑ 📺 🅿 ℹ ⌑ ✿ ✿ ⌑
Directions:	2S from city centre
🚂	Angoulême 2km
🚌	7, 9 ap Port de l'houmeau 200m
Attractions:	⛲ 🚴 ⌑ ⌑300m ⌑100m

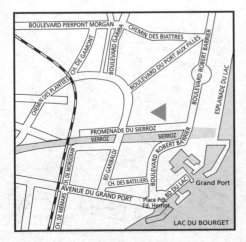

Annecy

4 Route du Semnoz,
74000 Annecy (Haute-Savoie).
☎ 0450453319
✆ 0450527752

Open Dates: 02.01-30.11
Open Hours: ◔
Reservations: (IBN) (CC)
Price Range: 74 FF € 11.28 [BB]inc [SH]
Beds: 117 - 1x¹🛏 2x²🛏 2x³🛏 19x⁴🛏 6x⁵🛏
Facilities: ♿ ♂♂ 30x ♂♂ ⛷🍴 🛒 🚲 ⚙ 🏨 📺 2 x 🍴 📷 💼 8️⃣ 🅿 ℹ️ ❀ ⟑ ☕
Directions: [1W] from city centre
✈ Genève 40km
🚂 Annecy 3km
🚌 #1 1km ap Hôtel de Police
Attractions: ⛳ ⛰ 🎣 🏊 1700m ⛸ 🎿 ⇲ 1km

Arles

20 Ave Foch,
13200 Arles (Bouches-du-Rhône).
☎ 0490961825
✆ 0490963126

Open Dates: 05.02-20.12
Open Hours: 07.00-10.00hrs; 17.00-24.00hrs (Summer), 07.00-10.00; 17.00-23.00hrs (Winter)
Reservations: (IBN) (CC)
Price Range: 50 FF € 7.62 [SH]
Beds: 108 - 2x²🛏 2x⁴🛏 12x⁶🛏
Facilities: ♂♂ 🍴 🍷 🏨 📺 💼 1 x 🍴 8️⃣ ℹ️ ❀ ☕
Directions: [1S] from city centre
✈ Nîmes 26km
⛴ Marseille 95km
🚂 Arles 2km
🚌 2 ap Fournier
Attractions: 🚴 ∪ 10km ⚲ ⇲

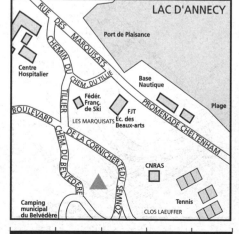

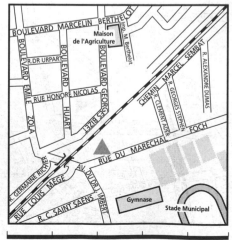

Biarritz -
Aintziko Gazte Etxea

8 Rue Chiquito de Cambo,
64200 Biarritz (Pyrénées Atlantiques).
☏ 0559417600
🖷 0559417607
e biarritz@fuaj.org

Open Dates: 03.01-20.12

Open Hours: ⏰

Reservations: **R** **IBN** **CC**

Price Range: 74 FF € 11.28 BB|inc ⌂

Beds: 96 - 6x² 6x³ 18x⁴

Facilities: ⚴ 👪 👪 ⍩ 💊 ⛂ 🏛 TV 🗋
🍴3 x 🖪 📦 8 P 𝑖 🌼 ⚘

Directions: 3S from city centre

✈ Biarritz Parme 2km

🚂 Biarritz 500m

🚌 #2, 9 ap Bois de Boulogne 300m

Attractions: 🏛 🔍1.5km 🚲 🏃 ∪3.5km
🔍3.5km 🏊

Boulogne-sur-Mer

Place Rouget de Lisle,
62200 Boulogne-sur-Mer (Pas-de-Calais).
☏ 0321991530
🖷 0321991539
e boulogne-sur-mer@fuaj.org

Open Dates: 01.02-22.12

Open Hours: 08.00-01.00hrs (low season
08.00-24.00hrs)

Reservations: **IBN** **CC**

Price Range: 74 FF € 11.28 BB|inc ⌂

Beds: 135 - 2x² 29x³ 11x⁴

Facilities: ⚴ 👪 11x 👪 🍴 💊 💊 ⚙ 🏛
TV 🗋 🍴2 x 🖪 📦 ⬍ P 𝑖
🌼 🏠

Directions: 0.5S from city centre

✈ Lille Lesquin 120km

⛴ Seacat Boulogne

🚂 Boulogne 100m

🚌 6, 7, 10, 11, 15, 19, 20 Boulogne,
Outreau ap Gare SNCF

Attractions: 🔍 🏃 ∪11km 🔍3km 🏊2km

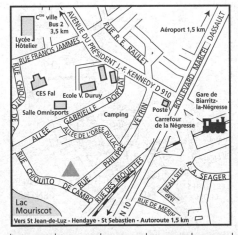

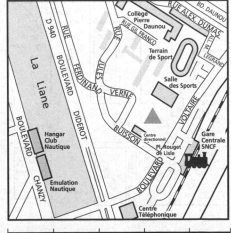

Cadouin

Place de l'Abbaye,
24480 Cadouin (Dordogne).
☎ 0553732878
🖷 0553732879
✉ cadouin@fuaj.org

Open Dates:	01.02-15.12
Open Hours:	08.00-23.00hrs
Reservations:	®
Price Range:	70 FF € 10.68 BB inc 🏠
Beds:	80 - 6x² 1x³ 10x⁵ 1x⁶ 2x⁶
Facilities:	♿ ††† 10x ††† 🍽 ☛ 🚲 👥 📺 🍴 2 x🍷 🔒 🅿 ℹ 🧺 ♦ ⚠ 🔍 🎞 🏮

Directions:

✈	Bergerac 35km
⛴	Bordeaux 120km
🚂	Le Buisson 5km
Attractions:	🏞 🚲 🚶 ↻10km ⚓5km 🏊15km

Cancale

Port Picain,
35260 Cancale (Ille et Vilaine).
☎ 0299896262
🖷 0299897879
✉ cancale@fuaj.org

Open Dates:	04.02-02.01
Open Hours:	🕐
Reservations:	® IBN CC
Price Range:	53 FF € 8.08 🏠
Beds:	82 - 2x¹ 13x² 1x³ 7x⁴ 2x⁵ 1x⁶
Facilities:	♿ ††† 5x ††† 🍽 ☛ ☕ 🚲 👥 📺 🧹 2 x🍷 🔒 🖼 🏧 8 🅿 ℹ ♦ ⚠ 🧺 🏠

Directions:	2N from city centre
✈	Rennes/Dinard 70km
⛴	Port Picain
🚂	St. Malo 15km
🚌	500m ap Cancale - Port Picain
Attractions:	🏞 🔍 🚲 🚶 ↻10km

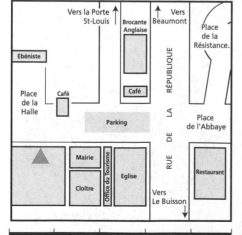

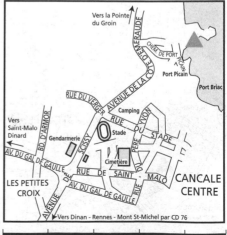

Carcassonne

Rue Vicomte de Trencavel,
Cité Médiévale,
11000 Carcassonne (Aude).
☎ 0468252316
✆ 0468711484
✉ carcassonne@fuaj.org

Open Dates:	01.02-15.12
Open Hours:	◷
Reservations:	[IBN] [CC]
Price Range:	74 FF € 11.28 [BB]inc [⌂]
Beds:	120 - 2x² 8x⁴ 12x⁶ 2x⁶
Facilities:	♔♔♔ 4x ♔♔♔ ⛄ ⛄ ☕ 🖤 ⛄ ⛺ TV ▤ 🛏 1 x⟟ ⧠ ▣ ☑ ⛴ ✂ ⛪ ⌂
Directions:	1E from city centre
✈	Toulouse 100km
🚊	Carcassonne 2km
🚌	#2 500m
Attractions:	⛺ 2km ⚹ ⛵ 2km

Chamonix Mont-Blanc

127 Montée J Balmat,
Les Pélerins d'en Haut,
74400 Chamonix Mont-Blanc
(Haute-Savoie).
☎ 0450531452
✆ 0450559234
✉ chamonix@fuaj.org

Open Dates:	02.12-10.05; 25.05-30.09 (🏠₁₂ ♔♔♔)
Open Hours:	◷
Reservations:	[IBN] [CC]
Price Range:	74 FF € 11.28 [BB]inc [⌂]
Beds:	120 - 12x² 15x⁴ 6x⁶
Facilities:	♿ ♔♔♔ 21x ♔♔♔ ☕ 🖤 ⛄ ⛺ TV ▤ 🛏 3 x⟟ ⧠ ▣ ♒ 8 P ☑ ⛴ ⛰ ◷ ⚲ ⛺
Directions:	
✈	Genève 90km
🚊	Les Pelerins 700m
🚌	ap Pelerins Ecole 300m
Attractions:	⛵ ⛰ ⛷ ⛸ 1085m ⚹ 🚶 ⛯ 10km ⛷ 3km ⛵ 3km

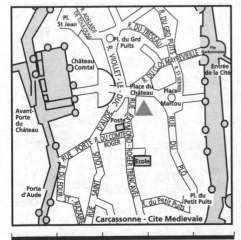

Carcassonne - Cite Medievale

0 _____ 600m

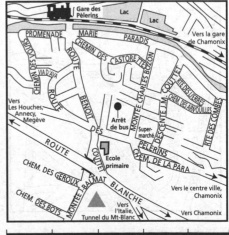

0 _____ 400m

Cherbourg

55 Rue de L'Abbaye,
50100 Cherbourg (Manche).
📞 0233781515
📠 0233781516

Open Dates:	04.01-21.12
Reservations:	(IBN) (ECC)
Price Range:	74 FF € 11.28 📖
Beds:	99 - 3x²🛏 3x³🛏 16x⁴🛏 4x⁵🛏
Facilities:	♿ 👬 26x 👬 🅾 🚿 ☕ 🚲 🛋 📺 🍴3 x🍴 🖼 🅿 ℹ

Directions:

⛴	Cherbourg 3km
🚉	Cherbourg 3km
🚌	#3 & #5 100m ap "Chantier"

Attractions: ⛳ 🎡 🚲 🏃 ∪5km ⚓ 🏊

Lille

12 Rue Malpart,
59800 Lille (Nord).
📞 0320570894
📠 0320639893
📧 lille@fuaj.org

Open Dates:	29.01-15.12
Open Hours:	06.30-02.00hrs (Mar-Oct); 07.00-01.00hrs (Nov-Feb)
Reservations:	(IBN) (ECC)
Price Range:	74 FF € 11.28 (BB)inc 🍴
Beds:	165 - 1x¹🛏 3x²🛏 14x³🛏 5x⁴🛏 12x⁵🛏 6x⁶🛏
Facilities:	♿ 👬 13x 👬 🅾 🚿 ☕ 🛋 📺 1 x🍴 🗄 🖼 🔢 ⬆ 🅿 ℹ 🚍

Directions:

0.5 SW	from city centre
✈	Roissy 180km
⛴	Calais 140km
🚉	Lille-Flandres 500m
🚌	#13 200m ap Hôtel de Ville
Ⓤ	Mairie de Lille #1 & 2 300m

Attractions: ∪6km ⚓2km 🏊2km

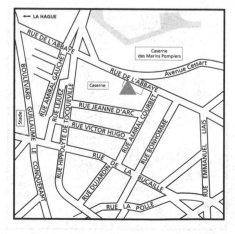

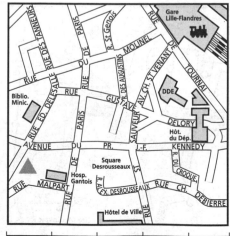

Lyon - AJ du Vieux Lyon

**41-45 Montée du Chemin Neuf,
69005 Lyon (Rhône).**
☎ 0478150550
🖷 0478150551
🄴 lyon@fuaj.org

Open Dates:	🗓
Open Hours:	07.00-13.00hrs; 14.00-01.00hrs
Reservations:	(IBN) ECC
Price Range:	74 FF € 11.28 BBinc 🈺
Beds:	180 - 1x² 9x⁴ 2x⁵ 17x⁶ 2x⁶ᵁ
Facilities:	♿ ††† 4x ††† ⦿ ☕ 🛏 TV 🔌 ▣ 🖼 8 ⓘ 🅿 ✂

Directions:

✈	Satolas, St Exupery 25km
A🚌	Satobus 2km
🚂	Part-Dieu, Perrache 3km
🚌	Funiculaire St Jean-St Just ap Funiculaire, Minimes Station 200m
Ⓤ	Minimes 200m

Attractions: 🎠 ⛰ 📷 🚶 ⚓

There are 2 hostels in Lyon. See following pages.

Nîmes

**La Cigale - 257 Chemin de l'Auberge de Jeunesse,
30900 Nîmes (Gard).**
☎ 0466680320
🖷 0466680321
🄴 nimes@fuaj.org

Open Dates:	🗓
Open Hours:	🕐
Reservations:	Ⓡ (IBN) ECC
Price Range:	74 FF € 11.28 🈺
Beds:	80 - 5x² 11x⁴ 2x⁶ 2x⁶
Facilities:	♿ ††† 11x ††† ⦿ ☕ 🛏 ⦿ 🔌 1x 🍽 ▣ 🖼 🏧 8 🅿 ⓘ 🅿 ✂ 🎿 ☀ ⚲ 🏠

Directions:	2 NW from city centre
✈	10km
🚂	Nimes 4km
🚌	2 ap Stade 400m

Attractions: 🚲 ⚓

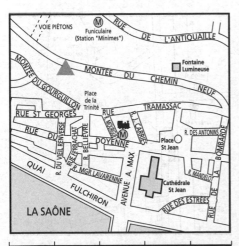

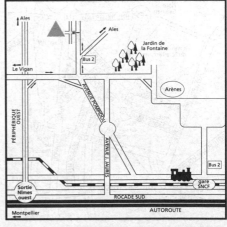

Paris - Le d'Artagnan

80 rue Vitruve,
75020 Paris.
☎ 0140323456
🖷 0140323455
✉ paris.le-dartagnan@fuaj.org

Open Dates:	🗓
Open Hours:	🕐
Reservations:	**R** IBN CC
Price Range:	115 FF until 28.02.01; 118 FF from 01.03.01 € 17.53 until 28.02.01; € 17.99 from 01.03.01 BB inc 🛏
Beds:	439 - 20x² 77x³ 28x⁴ 7x⁶
Facilities:	♿ ⅲ ⅰ◎ℓ 🍴 🖥 📺 🗄 📺 3 x 🍽 🔲 🖼 ♿ 🔢 ◉ 🧺 ℹ 🚼 ⊙
Directions:	5E from city centre
✈	Roissy 25km
🚐	Porte de Bagnolet #351
🚆	Gare de Lyon 1km, Gare du Nord, Gare de L'Est 5km
🚌	26: ap "Pyrénées/Bagnolet"; 351: ap "Porte de Bagnolet"; PC2 ap "Virtruve"
Ⓤ	Porte de Bagnolet - Line 3 800m

There are 4 hostels in Paris. See following pages.

Poggio Mezzana

"L'Avillanella",
20230 Poggio Mezzana (Corse).
☎ 0495385010
🖷 0495385011

Open Dates:	01.04-28.10
Open Hours:	08.00-20.00hrs
Reservations:	**R** IBN
Price Range:	53 FF € 8.08 🈺
Beds:	117 - 4x¹ 6x² 2x³ 4x⁴ 11x⁵ 3x⁶
Facilities:	ⅲ 3x ⅰ◎ ◎ℓ 🍴 🚿 🛏 📺 2 x🍽 🔲 🖼 🅿 ℹ 🚼 ♨ ⚠ �◦ 🎰
Directions:	2N from city centre
✈	Bastia Poretta 20km
⛴	Bastia 40km
🚆	Casamozza 18km
🚌	ap "Lotissement" St Michel 100m

Attractions: ⛺ 🎡 🚴 🏃 ⟳18km ♨

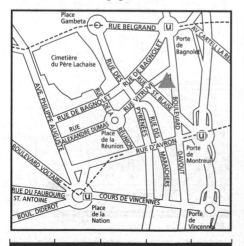

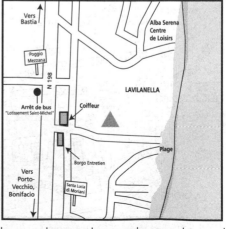

Saint-Brieuc

Manoir de la Ville Guyomard,
Les Villages,
22000 St-Brieuc (Côtes-d'Armor).
☎ 0296787070
✆ 0296782747
✉ saint-brieuc@fuaj.org

Open Dates:	🗓[12]
Open Hours:	⏰ (07.00-22.00hrs low season)
Reservations:	**R** **CC**
Price Range:	74 FF € 11.28 [BB]inc
Beds:	125 - 5x¹⚏ 15x³⚏ 12x⁴⚏
Facilities:	♿ ♦♦♦ 27x ♦♦♦ 🍴 ☕ 🚿 🛏 📺 📖
	6 x🍷 🖨 🖼 🏧 🔒 Ⓟ ☂ ✿
	⚟ ☎ 🛒 🏠
Directions:	[3W] from city centre
⛴	St Malo, Roskof 110km
🚄	St Brieuc 3km
🚌	#3 300m
Attractions:	⚘ 🚴 🚶 ∪4km ⚲3km 🏊2km

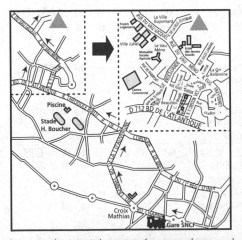

Strasbourg -
Parc du Rhin

Rue des Cavaliers,
BP 58,
67017 Strasbourg Cedex (Bas-Rhin).
☎ 0388455420
✆ 0388455421
✉ strasbourg.parc-du.rhin@fuaj.org

Open Dates:	01.01-31.10; 01.12-20.12
Open Hours:	⏰
Reservations:	**IBN** **CC**
Price Range:	74 FF € 11.28 [BB]inc 🍽
Beds:	246 - 18x³⚏ 43x⁴⚏ 4x⁵⚏
Facilities:	♿ ♦♦♦ 66x ♦♦♦ 🍴 ☕ 🚿 🛏 📺
	🛏3 x🍷 🖨 🖼 🔒 Ⓟ ☂ 🎮 ✿
	⚟ ☎ 🛒 🏠
Directions:	[4NE] from city centre
✈	Entzheim 25km
🚄	Strasbourg 4km
🚌	21, 2 ap Parc du Rhin 1km
Attractions:	⚘

There are 2 hostels in Strasbourg. See following
pages.

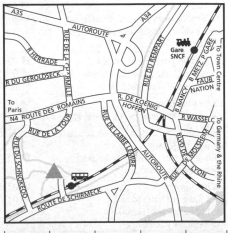

Location/Address	Telephone No. Fax No.	Beds	Opening Dates	Facilities
▲ Aix-en-Provence (IBN) Le Jas de Bouffan, 3 Ave Marcel-Pagnol, 13090 Aix-en-Provence (Bouches-du-Rhône).	☏ 0442201599 🖷 0442593612	60	01.06–20.12	††† ¶◎| (R) [2W] ﬆ ⊦CC⊣ P ◙ ♨
▲ Aix-les-Bains (IBN) Promenade du Sierroz, 73100 Aix-les-Bains (Savoie). ✉ aix-les-bains@fuaj.org	☏ 0479883288 🖷 0479611405	92	23.12–03.01; 03.02–04.11	††† ¶◎| (R) [3NW] ﬆ ⊦CC⊣ ﬃ P ◙ ♨
△ Albi (Assoc) AJ MJC, 13 Rue de la Republique, 81000 Albi (Tarn).	☏ 0563545365 🖷 0563546155	36	[12]	††† ¶◎| [0.5NE] ﬃ P ◙
▲ Anglet (IBN) "Gazte Etxea", 19 Route des Vignes, 64600 Anglet (Pyrénées Atlantiques). ✉ biarritz@fuaj.org	☏ 0559587000 🖷 0559587007	96	15.11–15.02	††† ¶◎| [2E] ﬆ ⊦CC⊣ ﬃ P ☕ ♨
▲ Angoulême (IBN) Parc de Bourgines, 16000 Angoulême (Charente). ✉ angouleme@fuaj.org	☏ 0545924580 🖷 0545959071	85	03.01–15.12	¶◎| [2S] ⊦CC⊣ P ☕
▲ Annecy (IBN) 4 Route du Semnoz, 74000 Annecy (Haute-Savoie).	☏ 0450453319 🖷 0450527752	117	02.01–30.11	††† ¶◎| [1W] ﬆ ⊦CC⊣ ﬃ P ◙ ♨ ✿
△ Anzin (Assoc) Auberge du Parc Mathieu, 43 rue des Martyrs, 59410 Anzin (Nord).	☏ 0327282100 🖷 0327282101	40	[12]	††† [0.5N] ﬃ P
▲ Arles (IBN) 20 Ave Foch, 13200 Arles (Bouches-du-Rhône).	☏ 0490961825 🖷 0490963126	108	05.02–20.12	¶◎| [1S] ⊦CC⊣ ☕
△ Arras 59 Grand-Place, 62000 Arras (Pas-de-Calais). ✉ arras@fuaj.org	☏ 0321227002 🖷 0321074615	53	01.02–31.11	††† ¶◎| ﬃ ♨ ✿
△ Autrans Auberge de Jeunesse "Les Hirondelles", Les Gaillards, 38880 Autrans (Isère). ✉ autrans@fuaj.org	☏ 0476947715 🖷 0476947789	55	01.01–12.05; 04.06–14.10; 29.10–11.11; 03.12–31.12	††† ¶◎| (R) [0.2S] P ☕ ♨
△ Avrillé-Langeais (Assoc) "Pause-Gâtines", Rue des Tilleuls, 37340 Avrillé (Indre et Loire).	☏ 0247249600 (R) 0247251445 🖷 0247482659	35	01.07–31.08 ([12] †††)	††† ¶◎| (R) ﬆ ﬃ P ◙ ♨
△ Banize (Assoc) Centre d'Hébergement Lou Pélélé, Puy-Joint, 23120 Banize (Creuse).	☏ 0555660063 🖷 0555660207 (Mairie)	29	[12]	††† (R) ﬃ P ☕ ♨
▲ Bayeux (Assoc) "Family Home", 39 Rue Gal de Dais, 14400 Bayeux (Calvados).	☏ 0231921522 🖷 0231925572	140	[12]	††† ¶◎| ﬆ ⊦CC⊣ ﬃ P ◙ ♨
▲ Beaugency 152 route de Châteaudun, 45190 Beaugency (Loiret). ✉ beaugency@fuaj.org	☏ 0238446131 🖷 0238441473	110	01.03–31.12	††† ¶◎| [2N] ﬆ ﬃ P

Location/Address	Telephone No. Fax No.	Beds	Opening Dates	Facilities
▲ **Beaulieu-sur-Dordogne** 'La Riviera Limousine', Place du Monturu, 19120 Beaulieu-sur-Dordogne (Corrèze). 🄴 beaulieu@fuaj.org	☎ 0555911382 🖷 0555912606	28	01.04–31.10	�りゃ ⦿l 0.3 NE ☞ P ⦿ 🚲
▲ **Belfort (Assoc)** Résidence Madrid, FJT, 6 rue de Madrid, 90000 Belfort (Territoire de Belfort).	☎ 0384213916 🖷 0384285895	20	▯12	♦♦♦ ⦿l ® 0.8 NW ⦅CC⦆ P ⦿ 🚲
▲ **Belle-Ile en Mer** Haute Boulogne, Belle Ile, 56360 Le Palais (Morbihan). 🄴 belle-ile@fuaj.org	☎ 0297318133 🖷 0297315838	93	03.01–30.09; 01.11–24.12	⦿l 1.5 NW ৬ ⦅CC⦆ ☞ P ⦿
▲ **Besançon (Assoc)** FJT/AJ "Les Oiseaux", 48 rue des Cras, 25000 Besançon (Doubs).	☎ 0381403200 🖷 0381403201	20	▯12	⦿l 3 F ⦅CC⦆ P ⦿ ⦿
△ *Betete* *AJ-Centre d'Animation de l'Abbaye de* *Prebenoit, 23270 Betete (Creuse).*	☎ 0555807891 🖷 0555808680	50	01.04–01.11	♦♦♦ ⦿l ® 4.5 SW ☞ P ⦿
▲ **Biarritz** - Aintziko Gazte Etxea ⦅IBN⦆ **8 Rue Chiquito de Cambo,** **64200 Biarritz (Pyrénées Atlantiques).** 🄴 biarritz@fuaj.org	☎ 0559417600 🖷 0559417607	96	03.01–20.12	♦♦♦ ⦿l ® 3 S ৬ ⦅CC⦆ P ⦿ 🚲
▲ **Boulogne-sur-Mer** ⦅IBN⦆ **Place Rouget de Lisle, 62200** **Boulogne-sur-Mer (Pas-de-Calais).** 🄴 boulogne-sur-mer@fuaj.org	☎ 0321991530 🖷 0321991539	135	01.02–22.12	♦♦♦ ⦿l 0.5 S ৬ ⦅CC⦆ ☞ P ⦿ ✿
▲ **Bourges** "Jacques Coeur", 22 rue Henri Sellier, 18000 Bourges (Cher). 🄴 bourges@fuaj.org	☎ 0248245809 🖷 0248655146	86	08.01–14.12	♦♦♦ ⦿l ® 1 SW ☞ P ⦿ ⦿ 🚲
▲ **Brive La Gaillarde** ⦅IBN⦆ **56 Av Maréchal Bugeaud,** **19100 Brive La Gaillarde (Corrèze).** 🄴 brive@fuaj.org	☎ 0555243400 🖷 0555848280	93	15.01–15.12	♦♦♦ ⦿l 0.4 E ⦅CC⦆ ☞ P 🚲
▲ **Cadouin** **Place de l'Abbaye,** **24480 Cadouin (Dordogne).** 🄴 cadouin@fuaj.org	☎ 0553732878 🖷 0553732879	80	01.02–15.12	♦♦♦ ⦿l ® ৬ ☞ P ⦿ 🚲
▲ **Caen (Assoc)** FJT "Robert Rême", 68 rue Eustache Restout, 14000 Caen (Calvados).	☎ 0231521996 🖷 0231842949	58	01.06–30.09	♦♦♦ ⦿l ® ৬ ☞ P ⦿ ⦿ 🚲
△ *Cahors (Assoc)* *Espace Frédéric Suisse, 20 Rue F Suisse,* *46000 Cahors (Lot).*	☎ 0565356471, 0565539702 🖷 0565359592	50	▯12	⦿l ☞ ⦿ 🚲 ✿
▲ **Cancale** ⦅IBN⦆ **Port Picain,** **35260 Cancale (Ille et Vilaine).** 🄴 cancale@fuaj.org	☎ 0299896262 🖷 0299897879	82	04.02–02.01	♦♦♦ ⦿l ® 2 N ৬ ⦅CC⦆ ☞ P ⦿ ⦿ 🚲

Cannes ☞**Le Trayas**

Location/Address	Telephone No. Fax No.	Beds	Opening Dates	Facilities
△ *Cap Fréhel* *Kérivet-la ville Hardrieux-Plevenon,* *22240 Fréhel (Côtes-d'Armor).*	☎ *0296414898* 🖷 *0296414898*	*44*	*01.04–30.09*	♟ ⑩ Ⓡ 2NE ♿ ☞ P ⬛ 🛵
▲ **Carcassonne** IBN **Rue Vicomte de Trencavel,** **Cité Médiévale, 11000 Carcassonne** **(Aude).** 🄴 carcassonne@fuaj.org	☎ 0468252316 🖷 0468711484	120	01.02–15.12	♟ ⑩ 1E ⅏CC⅏ ☞ ⬛ 🍵 🛵
△ *Cassis* *La Fontasse,* *13260 Cassis (Bouches-du-Rhône).*	☎ *0442010272*	*60*	*06.03–05.01*	4W ☞ P
▲ **Cepoy-Montargis** 25 Quai du Port, 45120 Cepoy (Loiret): (Montargis 6km N). 🄴 cepoy@fuaj.org	☎ 0238932545 🖷 0238931106	115	01.02–20.12	♟ ⑩ 0.5N ⅏CC⅏ ☞ P ⬛ 🍵 🛵
▲ **Cernay (Assoc)** MJC/Auberge Internationale de la Jeunesse 16a, Faubourg de Colmar, 68700 Cernay (Haut-Rhin).	☎ 0389754459 🖷 0389758748	55	02.01–16.12	♟ ⑩ 0.5NE ☞ P ⬛ 🛵
Chambord ☞**Blois-Montlivault**				
▲ **Chamonix Mont-Blanc** IBN **127 Montée J Balmat,** **Les Pélerins d'en Haut, 74400** **Chamonix Mont-Blanc (Haute-Savoie).** 🄴 chamonix@fuaj.org	☎ 0450531452 🖷 0450559234	120	02.12–10.05; 25.05–30.09 (🗓12 ♟)	♟ ⑩ ♿ ⅏CC⅏ P ⬛ 🍵 🛵
▲ **Chamrousse** Le Recoin, 38410 Chamrousse (Isère). 🄴 chamrousse@fuaj.org	☎ 0476899131 🖷 0476899666	80	01.12–01.05; 10.06–10.09	♟ ⑩ 0.4SW ⅏CC⅏ P ⬛ 🛵 ❄
▲ **Chaumont (Assoc)** FJT/AJ, 1 rue de Carcassonne, 52000 Chaumont (Haute Marne).	☎ 0325032277	12	🗓12	♟ ⑩ 1SW ☞ P ⬛ 🛵
▲ **Chauny** Bd Bad-Kostritz, 02300 Chauny (Aisne).	☎ 0323520996 🖷 0323399092	39	🗓12	♟ ⑩ 1N ♿ ☞ P 🛵
▲ **Cherbourg** IBN **55 Rue de L'Abbaye,** **50100 Cherbourg (Manche).**	☎ 0233781515 🖷 0233781516	99	04.01–21.12	♟ ⑩ ♿ ⅏CC⅏ ☞ P ⬛ 🛵
▲ **Cholet** - Les Pâquerettes (Assoc) FJT, 5 rue de la Casse, BP 316, 49303 Cholet Cedex (Maine et Loire).	☎ 0241713636 🖷 0241626222	12	15.06–15.09 and school holidays	♟ ⑩ Ⓡ 0.8E ♿ P ⬛ ⬛ 🛵
△ *Clermont-Ferrand* *"Auberge du Cheval Blanc", 55 Ave de l'URSS,* *63000 Clermont-Ferrand (Puy-de-Dôme).*	☎ *0473922639* 🖷 *0473929996*	*58*	*01.04–31.10*	♟ ⑩ 1.5NW ☞ P 🛵
△ *Colmar (Assoc)* *AJ "Mittelhart", 2 Rue Pasteur,* *68000 Colmar (Haut-Rhin).*	☎ *03 89805739* 🖷 *0389807616*	*110*	*15.01–15.12*	♟ Ⓡ 1W ⅏CC⅏ P 🛵

Location/Address	Telephone No. Fax No.	Beds	Opening Dates	Facilities
▲ **Creil (Assoc)** Centre des Cadres Sportifs, 1 rue du Général Leclerc, 60100 Creil (Oise). ✉ cadres.sportifs@wanadoo.fr	☎ 0344646220 📠 0344646229	138	🗓	♥♥♥ 🍴 ℝ 1S ℂℂ ✂ 🅿 🖥 ⊛ ✿
△ *Dieppe* *48 Rue Louis Fromager, Quartier Janval de Dieppe, 76550 Saint Aubin/Scie (the YH is in Dieppe) (Seine-Maritime).* ✉ *dieppe@fuaj.org*	☎ *0235848573* 📠 *0235848962* *(call before)*	*42*	*Call the Youth Hostel*	♥♥♥ 🍴 3S ✂ 🅿 ⊛
▲ **Dinan** Moulin de Méen, Vallée de la Fontaine des Eaux, 22100 Dinan (Côtes d'Armor). ✉ dinan@fuaj.org	☎ 0296391083 📠 0296391062	70	01.02–31.12	♥♥♥ 🍴 2NE ✂ 🅿 🖥 ⊛
▲ **Dole (Assoc)** "Association Le St Jean", Place Jean XXIII, BP 164, 39101 Dole Cedex (Jura). ✉ lestjean@wanadoo.fr	☎ 0384823674 📠 0384791769	60	🗓	🍴 1S ✂ 🅿 🖥
▲ **Dunkerque** Place Paul Asseman, 59140 Dunkerque (Nord).	☎ 0328633634 📠 0328632454	120	02.01–23.12	♥♥♥ 🍴 ℝ 3NW 🅿 ⊛
▲ **Eu (Assoc)** Centre des Fontaines, rue des Fontaines, BP 123, 76260 Eu (Seine Maritime). ✉ centre-des-fontaines@wanadoo.fr	☎ 0235860503 📠 0235864512	55	03.01–22.12	♥♥♥ 🍴 ℂℂ 🅿 ☕ ⊛
▲ **Evian (Assoc)** Centre International de Séjour, ave de Neuvecelle, BP 31, 74500 Evian les Bains Cedex (Haute Savoie). ✉ jptreil@mjc.hautesavoie.net	☎ 0450753587 📠 0450754567	50	🗓	♥♥♥ 🍴 ℝ 1S ℂℂ ✂ 🅿 🖥 ☕ ⊛
△ *Fontaine-de-Vaucluse* *Chemin de la Vignasse, 84800 Fontaine-de-Vaucluse (Vaucluse).*	☎ *0490203165* 📠 *0490202620*	*50*	*01.02–15.11*	♥♥♥ 🍴 ℝ 0.8S ✂ 🅿 🖥
▲ **Fontenay-le-Comte (Assoc)** "Les Trois Portes", Foyer Sud Vendée/AJ, 16 Rue des Gravants, BP 347, 85206 Fontenay le Comte Cedex (Vendée).	☎ 0251691344 📠 0251690423	50	🗓	♥♥♥ 🍴 ℝ 0.5E ♿ ℂℂ ✂ 🅿 🖥 ☕ ⊛
▲ **Fréjus** Chemin du Counillier, 83600 Fréjus (Var).	☎ 0494531875 📠 0494532586	120	01.02–30.12	♥♥♥ 🍴 ℝ 1.7NE ✂ 🅿 ⊛ ✿
▲ **Gannat (Assoc)** Maison du Folklore - Centre des cultures et Traditions, Route de St Priest, 03800 Gannat. ✉ maison.du.folklore@wanadoo.fr	☎ 0470902829 📠 0470906636	52	01.04–31.10	♥♥♥ 🍴 ℝ 1W 🅿 ☕
▲ **Granville (Assoc)** Centre Régional de Nautisme, Bd des Amiraux, 50400 Granville (Manche). ✉ crng@dial.oleane.com	☎ 0233912262 📠 0233505199	160	04.01–21.12	🍴 0.2S ℂℂ 🅿 🖥 ☕ ⊛

Location/Address	Telephone No. Fax No.	Beds	Opening Dates	Facilities
▲ **Gray (Assoc)** "Le Foyer", 2 Rue André Maginot, 70100 Gray (Haute Saône). ✉ lefoyer@wanadoo.fr	☏ 0384649920 🕾 0384649929	10	🔟	�01 ❤️ ECC ☐ P 🔲 💧 ✿
▲ **Grenoble-Echirolles** (IBN) 10 Ave du Grésivaudan, 38130 Echirolles (Isère). ✉ grenoble-echirolles@fuaj.org	☏ 0476093352 🕾 0476093899	130	🔟	�01 ❤️ 5SW ♿ ECC ☐ P 🔲 💧 🐾 ✿
▲ **Guillestre (Assoc)** les Quatre Vents, "La Rochette", BP22, 05600 Guillestre (Hautes Alpes).	☏ 0492450432 🕾 0492450432	80	01.02–30.09	�01 ❤️ R 1.5SW ♿ P 🔲 💧 🐾 ✿
△ *Ile-de-Groix* *Fort du Méné,* *56590 Ile de Groix (Morbihan).*	☏ *0297868138* 🕾 *0297865243*	*50*	*01.04–15.10*	�01 1.2NE ☐ P 🔲
▲ **Imphy (Assoc)** Résidence Georges Bouqueau, 8 Rue Jean Sounié, 58160 Imphy (Nièvre).	☏ 0386909520 🕾 0386383187	20	🔟	❤️ 1SE ☐ P 🔲 💧 🐾
▲ **Inzinzac-Lochrist** Ferme du Gorée, 56650 Inzinzac-Lochrist (Morbihan).	☏ 0297360808 🕾 0297369083	35	01.03–31.10; (R 01.11–28.02)	�01 ❤️ 1N ♿ ☐ P
▲ **La Clusaz** Route du Col de Croix Fry, "Les Etages", BP47, 74220 La Clusaz Cedex (Haute-Savoie). ✉ laclusaz@fuaj.org	☏ 0450024173 🕾 0450026585	85	16.12–23.09 (R �01 23.09–16.12)	❤️ R 3SE ♿ ECC P 💧
▲ **La Foux d'Allos** Neige et soleil, 04260 La Foux d'Allos (Alpes-de-Haute-Provence). ✉ la-foux-allos@fuaj.org	☏ 0492838108 🕾 0492838370	69	01.12–25.04; 10.06–15.09	�01 ❤️ 0.2N ☐ 💧 🐾
△ *La Palud-sur-Verdon* *"L'immense Botte de Paille",* *Départementale 23, 04120 La Palud-sur-* *Verdon (Alpes-de-Haute-Provence).*	☏ *0492773872* 🕾 *0492773872*	*68*	*01.03–31.10*	❤️ 0.5S ☐ P 🔲 🐾
▲ **La Rochelle** Ave des Minimes, BP 3045, 17013 La Rochelle Cedex (Charente-Maritime).	☏ 0546444311 🕾 0546454148	224	03.01–22.12	�01 ❤️ 2SW ♿ P 🔲 💧 ✿
▲ **La Toussuire** La Toussuire - Foncouverte, 73300 St Jean de Maurienne (Savoie).	☏ 0479567204 🕾 0479830093	72	01.12–30.04	�01 ❤️ R 1SW ECC P 💧 🐾
△ *Lannion - Beg Leguer* *Plage de Goalagorn, Beg Leguer,* *22300 Lannion (Côtes d'Armor).*	☏ *0296472486* 🕾 *0296370206*	*14*	*01.04–15.09*	�01 ❤️ 8W ☐
▲ **Lannion** - Les Korrigans (IBN) Rive Gauche - 6, Rue du 73e Territorial, 22300 Lannion (Côtes D'Armor). ✉ lannion@fuaj.org	☏ 0296379128 🕾 0296370206	65	🔟	�01 ❤️ 0.3SW ♿ ☐ P 🔲 💧 🐾 ✿

Location/Address	Telephone No. Fax No.	Beds	Opening Dates	Facilities
▲ **Le Mans (Assoc)** AJ-FJT le Flore, 23 rue Maupertuis, 72000 le Mans (Sarthe). **e** florefjt@cybercable.tm.fr	**t** 0243812755 **f** 0243810610	28	02.01–15.12	0.2 NE
△ *Le Mazet St Voy (Assoc)* *"Ferme du Besset", La Bataille,* *43520 Le Mazet St Voy (Haute Loire).*	**t** *0471650035* **f** *0471650544*	*30*		4 NW
▲ **Le Mont-Dore** "Chalet Le Grand Volcan", Route du Sancy 63240 Le Mont-Dore (Puy-de-Dome). **e** le-mont-dore@fuaj.org	**t** 0473650353 **f** 0473652639	84	01.01–30.09; 01.12–31.12	3 S
△ *Le Puy en Velay (Assoc)* *Centre Pierre Cardinal, 9 Rue Jules Vallès,* *43000 Le Puy en Velay (Haute Loire).*	**t** *0471055240* **f** *0471056124*	*70*	*01.10–01.04* *(except* *weekends);* *01.04–31.06*	0.2 SE
▲ **Le Trayas/Théoule-sur-Mer** 9 Av de la Véronèse, Le Trayas, 06590 Théoule-sur-Mer (Alpes-Maritimes).	**t** 0493754023 **f** 0493754345	100	15.02–20.12	8 W
△ *Les Aldudes (Assoc)* *Urtxintxenea,* *64430 Les Aldudes (Pyrénées Atlantiques).* **e** urtintx@aol.com	**t** *0559375658* **f** *0559375552*	*80*		0.4 S
▲ **Les Deux Alpes** "Les Brûleurs de Loups", 38860 Les Deux Alpes (Isère). **e** les-deux-alpes@fuaj.org	**t** 0476792280 **f** 0476792615	57	01.12–02.05; 16.06–02.09	0.15 S
▲ **Les Gets** "Les Farfadets", Le Poncet, 74160 Les Gets (Haute Savoie).	**t** 0450791486 (Morzine) **f** 0450791486 (Morzine)	67		2.5 W
▲ **Les Rousses** 2400 Le Bief de la Chaille, 39220 Les Rousses (Jura).	**t** 0384600280 **f** 0384600967	48	23.12 15.04; 20.05–30.09	3 S
▲ **Lille** (IBN) **12 Rue Malpart, 59800 Lille (Nord).** **e** lille@fuaj.org	**t** 0320570894 **f** 0320639893	165	29.01–15.12	0.5 SW
▲ **Lorient** AJ du Ter - 41 rue Victor Schoelcher, 56100 Lorient (Morbihan). **e** lorient@fuaj.org	**t** 0297371165 **f** 0297879549	104	05.01–20.12	4 SW
▲ **Lourdios/Ichère (Assoc)** AJ, Estivade d'Aspe Pyrénées, "Maison Pelou", 64570 Lourdios Ichère (Pyrénées Atlantiques).	**t** 0559344639 **f** 0559344804	23		3 N
▲ **Lyon** - AJ du Vieux Lyon (IBN) **41-45 Montée du Chemin Neuf,** **69005 Lyon (Rhône).** **e** lyon@fuaj.org	**t** 0478150550 **f** 0478150551	180		

Location/Address	Telephone No. Fax No.	Beds	Opening Dates	Facilities
▲ **Lyon-Sud** ⟨IBN⟩ 51 rue Roger Salengro, 69200 Vénissieux (Rhône). 📧 lyon-sud@fuaj.org	☎ 0478763923 🖷 0478775111	120	17.01–23.12	⁙ ⴵⱺⵏ 5SE ✂ P ▣ ☕
△ *Manosque* *Parc de la Rochette,* *04100 Manosque (Alpes de Haute-Provence).*	☎ *0492875744* 🖷 *0492724391*	*57*	*01.01–15.12*	⁙ ⴵⱺⵏ 1N ✂ P 🚲
▲ **Marseille** - Bonneveine ⟨IBN⟩ (Impasse du Dr Bonfils) Av J Vidal, 13008 Marseille (Bouches-du-Rhône). 📧 marseille_bonneveine@fuaj.org	☎ 0491176330 🖷 0491739723	150	05.02–21.12	ⴵⱺⵏ 5SE ⦃CC⦄ P ▣ ☕
▲ **Marseille** - Château de Bois-Luzy Allée des Primevères, 13012 Marseille (Bouches-du-Rhône).	☎ 0491490618 🖷 0491490618	90	🗓12	⁙ ⴵⱺⵏ ⓡ 4NE ✂ P ▣
△ *Martinique* - Morne Rouge *Av Jean Jaurés, Hauts du Bourg,* *97260 Morne Rouge (Martinique).*	☎ *0596523981* 🖷 *0596523981*	*43*	🗓12	ⴵⱺⵏ ⓡ 1N ♿ ✂ P ▣
▲ **Menton** ⟨IBN⟩ Plateau St-Michel, 06500 Menton (Alpes-Maritimes). 📧 menton@fuaj.org	☎ 0493359314 🖷 0493359307	80	01.02–30.11	ⴵⱺⵏ 1.5NW ⦃CC⦄ ▣
▲ **Metz (Assoc)** - Carrefour 6 rue Marchant, 57000 Metz (Moselle). 📧 ascarrefour@wanadoo.fr	☎ 0387750726 🖷 0387367144	60	🗓12	⁙ ⴵⱺⵏ ⦃CC⦄ P ▣ 🚲
▲ **Metz (Assoc)** - Plage 1 Allée de Metz Plage, 57000 Metz (Moselle). 📧 aubjeumetz@ad.com	☎ 0387304402 🖷 0387331980	62	🗓12	⁙ ⴵⱺⵏ 0.3N ⦃CC⦄ ✂ P ▣ 🚲 ❄
▲ **Millau (Assoc)** FJT Sud Aveyron Accueil, 26 rue Lucien Costes, 12100 Millau (Aveyron).	☎ 0565612774 🖷 0565619058	60	🗓12	⁙ ⴵⱺⵏ ⓡ 0.8NW ✂ P ▣ 🚲
Montargis ☞**Cepoy**				
△ *Montpellier* ⟨IBN⟩ *Rue des Ecoles Laïques (Impasse Petite Corra terie), 34000 Montpellier (Hérault).* 📧 *montpellier@fuaj.org*	☎ *0467603222* 🖷 *0467603230*	*90*	*15.01–16.12*	⁙ ⴵⱺⵏ ⦃CC⦄ ☕ 🚲
▲ **Morzine/Avoriaz** Holiday Campus, La Coutettaz, BP 74 74110 Morzine (Haute-Savoie).	☎ 0450791486 🖷 0450791486	76	20.12–28.04; 01.06–30.09	⁙ ⴵⱺⵏ ⓡ 0.3E ⦃CC⦄ P ▣ ☕ 🚲 ❄
▲ **Mulhouse** 37 Rue de l'Illberg, 68200 Mulhouse (Haut-Rhin).	☎ 0389426328 🖷 0389597495	106	01.04–30.12	ⴵⱺⵏ ⓡ 2W ♿ ⦃CC⦄ ✂ P ☕
△ *Nancy (Assoc)* *"Château de Remicourt", 149,* *Rue de Vandoeuvre, 54600 Villers les* *Nancy (Meurthe et Moselle).*	☎ *0383277367* 🖷 *0383414135*	*60*	*02.01–23.12*	ⴵⱺⵏ 4SW ♿ ⦃CC⦄ P ☕ 🚲

Location/Address	Telephone No. Fax No.	Beds	Opening Dates	Facilities
▲ **Nantes** - La Manu (IBN) 2 Place de la Manu, 44000 Nantes (Loire-Atlantique). @ nanteslamanu@fuaj.org	☏ 0240292920 ✆ 0251124842	83	🗓	♂♀ ⑩ R 2E ♿ CC ⬦ ♨ 🚲
▲ **Nantes** - Porte Neuve (Assoc) 1 place Ste Elisabeth, 44042 Nantes Cedex (Loire Atlantique).	☏ 0240206363 ✆ 0240206379	50	🗓	♂♀ ⑩ R 0.5NW CC ⬦ P 🔲
▲ **Nantes** - Port Beaulieu (Assoc) FJT, 9 Bd Vincent Gâche, 44200 Nantes (Loire Atlantique).	☏ 0240122400 ✆ 0251820005	66	01.06–31.08	♂♀ ⑩ 3S ♿ CC ⬦ P 🔲 ♨ 🚲
▲ **Nice** (IBN) Route Forestière du Mont Alban, 06300 Nice (Alpes-Maritimes).	☏ 0493892364 ✆ 0492040310	56	02.01–31.10	4E ⬦ 🔲
▲ **Nîmes** (IBN) **La Cigale - 257 Chemin de l'Auberge de J eunesse, 30900 Nîmes (Gard).** @ nimes@fuaj.org	☏ 0466680320 ✆ 0466680321	80	🗓	♂♀ ⑩ R 2NW ♿ CC ⬦ P 🔲 ♨ 🚲
▲ **Nouméa** City Hostel, 51 bis rue Olry, BP 767, 98845 Nouméa Cedex (New Caledonia).	☏ 0687275879 ✆ 0687254817	96	🗓	♂♀ R CC ⬦ P 🔲 🚲 ✿
▲ **Paimpol** Château de Kerraoul, 22500 Paimpol (Côtes-d'Armor). @ paimpol@fuaj.org	☏ 0296208360 ✆ 0296209646	80	🗓	⑩ 2W CC ⬦ P
▲ **Paris** - Cité des Sciences (IBN) 24, Rue des Sept Arpents, 93310 Le Pré St Gervais (Seine Saint Denis). @ paris.cite-des-sciences@fuaj.org	☏ 0148432411 ✆ 0148432682	184	🗓	3NE ♿ CC ⬦ 🔲 🚲
▲ **Paris** - Le d'Artagnan (IBN) **80 rue Vitruve, 75020 Paris.** @ paris.le-dartagnan@fuaj.org	☏ 0140323456 ✆ 0140323455	439	🗓	⑩ R 5E ♿ CC ⬦ 🔲 ♨
▲ **Paris** - Jules Ferry 8 Boulevard Jules Ferry, 75011 Paris. @ paris.jules-ferry@fuaj.org	☏ 0143575560 ✆ 0143148209	99	🗓	CC ⬦ 🔲
▲ **Paris** - Clichy (IBN) "Léo Lagrange", 107 Rue Martre, 92110 Clichy (Hauts de Seine). @ paris.clichy@fuaj.org	☏ 0141272690 ✆ 0142705263	338	🗓	⑩ R CC P 🔲 ♨ 🚲
△ *Parthenay* *Périscope, 16, Rue Blaise Pascal, 79200 Parthenay (Deux Sèvres).* @ *periscope@district-parthenay.fr*	☏ *0549954689* ✆ *0549946485*	*105*	🗓	⑩ 0.5SW ♿ ⬦ P 🔲 ♨
▲ **Pau-Gelos** (Assoc) FJT, Logis des Jeunes, Base de Plein Air, 64110 Gelos (Pyrénées Atlantiques). @ fjt@ldj.pau.org	☏ 0559065302 ✆ 0559110520	40	🗓	3SE ⬦ 🔲 ♨ 🚲

Location/Address	Telephone No. Fax No.	Beds	Opening Dates	Facilities
▲ **Périgueux (Assoc)** FJT, Rue des Thermes Prolongés, 24000 Périgueux (Dordogne). 🄴 fjtdordogne@wanadoo.fr	☎ 0553068140 🖷 0553068149	16	🔲12	⑪ Ⓟ 🖻 🍴 🚲
△ *Perpignan* *Allée Marc Pierre, Parc de la Pépinière,* *Av de Grande-Bretagne,* *66000 Perpignan (Pyrénées-Orientales).*	☎ *0468346332* 🖷 *0468511602*	*49*	*21.01–19.12*	♂
▲ **Phalsbourg (Assoc)** Centre Européen de Rencontres, 6 Rue de Général Rottembourg, 57370 Phalsbourg (Moselle).	☎ 0387243737 🖷 0387241356	76	🔲12	�119 ⑪ Ⓡ 0.5SE ♿ ECC Ⓟ 🍴 🚲
△ *Plouguernevel (Assoc)* *Village Vacances de Kermarc'h, 22110* *Plouguernevel (Côtes d' Armor).*	☎ *0296291095*	*25*	🔲12	♂ Ⓟ
▲ **Poggio Mezzana** (IBN) **"L'Avillanella",** **20230 Poggio Mezzana (Corse).**	☎ 0495385010 🖷 0495385011	117	01.04–28.10	�119 ⑪ Ⓡ 2N Ⓟ 🖻 🍴 🚲
▲ **Poitiers** (IBN) 1 Allée Roger Tagault, 86000 Poitiers (Vienne). 🄴 poitiers@fuaj.org	☎ 0549300970 🖷 0549300979	140	15.01–31.12	⑪ Ⓡ 3SW ♿ ECC ♂ Ⓟ 🍴 🚲 ⚙
△ *Pontarlier* *2 rue Jouffroy, 25300 Pontarlier (Doubs).* 🄴 *pontarlier@fuaj.org*	☎ *0381390657* 🖷 *0381390657*	*72*	*26.12–10.11*	�119 ⑪ 0.2N ♂ Ⓟ 🍴 🚲
▲ **Pontivy** Ile des Récollets, 56300 Pontivy (Morbihan).	☎ 0297255827 🖷 0297257648	65	04.01–22.12 (Ⓡ low season).	�119 ⑪ Ⓡ ♂ Ⓟ
△ *Pontorson (Assoc)* *Centre Duguesclin, 21 bd Patton,* *50170 Pontorson (Manche).* 🄴 *aj@ville-pontorson.fr*	☎ *0233601865* 🖷 *0233601865*	*57*	🔲12	�119 0.5NW ♿ ♂ Ⓟ
△ *Quimper (Assoc)* *Auberge de Jeunesse, 6 ave des Oiseaux,* *29000 Quimper (Finistère).*	☎ *0298649797* 🖷 *0298553837*	*54*	*08.01–20.12*	�119 ⑪ 1.5W ♂ 🚲
▲ **Redon (Assoc)** Maison d'Accueil du Pays de Redon, 2, Rue Chantebel, BP 101, 35603 Redon Cedex (Ille et Vilaine). 🄴 mapar-redon@wanadoo.fr	☎ 0299721439 🖷 0299721653	20	01.06–31.08	�119 ⑪ 0.5N ECC ♂ Ⓟ 🍴 🚲
▲ **Reims (Assoc)** Centre International de Séjour, Chaussée Bocquaire, Parc Léo Lagrange, 51100 Reims (Marne). 🄴 centre.international.reims@wanadoo.fr	☎ 0326405260 🖷 0326473570	150	🔲12	⑪ Ⓡ 0.5SW ♿ ECC ♂ Ⓟ 🖻 🚲 ⚙
Reims ☞**Verzy**				
▲ **Rennes** (IBN) 10-12 Canal Saint-Martin, 35700 Rennes (Ille-et-Vilaine).	☎ 0299332233 🖷 0299590621	96	02.01–22.12	�119 ⑪ 1.5N ♿ ECC ♂ Ⓟ 🖻 🍴

Location/Address	Telephone No. / Fax No.	Beds	Opening Dates	Facilities
▲ **Roanne** AJ "Centre Jeunesse Pierre Bérégovoy", 4 Rue Fontenille, 42300 Roanne (Loire).	☎ 0477725211 🖷 0477706628	57		⑫ ...
△ *Rochefort-sur-Mer (Assoc)* *Logis Etape/AJ, 20 rue de la République,* *17300 Rochefort-sur-Mer* *(Charente Maritime).* @ *rochefort.omj1@libertysurf.fr*	☎ *0546997462 (in July & August), 0546821040* 🖷 *0546992125, 0546997462 (in July & August)*	45		
▲ **Rodez (Assoc)** AJ/FJT, "Les Quatre Saisons", 26 Bd des Capucines, Onet le Chateau 12034 Rodez Cedex 9 (Aveyron) @ assoc.fjt.gd.rodez@wanadoo.fr	☎ 0565775105 🖷 0565673797	60		3N ... CC P
△ *Rodome (Assoc)* *Ferme Équestre H'Val,* *11140 Rodome (Aude).* @ *b_val@club-internet.fr*	☎ *0468203222* 🖷 *0468207610*	24	*31.03–15.11*	P
▲ **Saintes** 2 Place Geoffroy Martel, 17100 Saintes (Charente-Maritime). @ saintes@fuaj.org	☎ 0546921492 🖷 0546929782	70		P
▲ **Saint-Brévin les Pins** "La Pinède", 1 Allée de la Jeunesse, 44250 St-Brévin Les Pins (Loire Atlantique).	☎ 0240272527 🖷 0240644877	59	01.02–07.10; 29.10–31.12	0.3N P
▲ **Saint-Brieuc** **Manoir de la Ville Guyomard,** **Les Villages, 22000** **St-Brieuc (Côtes-d'Armor).** @ saint-brieuc@fuaj.org	☎ 0296787070 🖷 0296782747	125		3W CC P
▲ **Saint-Gaudens (Assoc)** "Le Venasque", 3 Rue de la Résidence, 31804 Saint-Gaudens Cedex (Haute Garonne).	☎ 0561947273 🖷 0561947274	20	02.01–31.12	0.5W P
△ *Saint-Guen* *10, Rue du Sénéchal, 22530 St Guen* *(Côtes d'Armor).*	☎ *0296285434* 🖷 *0296260156*	40	*01.05–30.09*	P
▲ **Saint-Junien** Auberge de St. Amand, 13 rue de St. Amand, 87200 St. Junien (Haute-Vienne).	☎ 0555022279 🖷 0555022279	54		1 NW P
▲ **Saint-Malo (Assoc)** CRI Patrick Varangot, 37 av du RP Umbricht, BP 108, 35407 St-Malo (Ille et Vilaine). @ fjt.ajcri.patrick.varangot@wanadoo.fr	☎ 0299402980 🖷 0299402902	248		1.5 NE CC P
△ *Saint-Martin des Olmes (Assoc)* *"Auberge de Saint Martin" Le Bourg,* *St Martin des Olmes 63600* *Ambert (Puy de Dome).*	☎ *0473820138* 🖷 *0473820138*	48	*15.02–15.11* *(⑫)*	6E P

Saint-Raphaël ☞ **Fréjus**

Location/Address	Telephone No. Fax No.	Beds	Opening Dates	Facilities
△ *Saverne* *Château des Roban,* *67700 Saverne (Bas-Rhin).* @ *saverne@fuaj.org*	☎ *0388911484* 🖷 *0388711597*	*86*	*01.02–31.12*	ⅲ ⑩ Ⓟ 🛵
△ *Savines-le-Lac* *"Les Chaumettes",* *05160 Savines-le-Lac (Hautes-Alpes).*	☎ *0492442016* 🖷 *0492442454*	*50*	*01.05–15.09*	ⅲ ⑩ 0.8 SW ☞ Ⓟ ⓞ 🍵 🛵 ☀
▲ **Seez Les Arcs** "La Verdache", 73700 Seez (Savoie). @ seez-les-arcs@fuaj.org	☎ 0479410193 🖷 0479410336	80	01.01–30.09; 17.12–31.12	ⅲ ⑩ Ⓡ ♿ ECC Ⓟ 🍵 🛵
▲ **Serre-Chevalier** Le Bez, BP 2, 05240 Serre-Chevalier 1400 (Hautes-Alpes). @ serre-chevalier@fuaj.org	☎ 0492247454 🖷 0492248339	129	20.12–30.10	ⅲ ⑩ Ⓡ 0.5 NW ECC ☞ Ⓟ 🍵 🛵 ☀
▲ **Sète** IBN "Villa Salis", rue du Général Revest, 34200 Sète (Hérault).	☎ 0467534668 🖷 0467513401	96	15.01–15.12	ⅲ ⑩ Ⓡ ECC Ⓟ 🍵 🛵
▲ **Strasbourg** - Parc du Rhin IBN **Rue des Cavaliers, BP 58,** **67017 Strasbourg Cedex (Bas-Rhin).** @ strasbourg.parc-du.rhin@fuaj.org	☎ 0388455420 🖷 0388455421	246	01.01–31.10; 01.12–20.12	ⅲ ⑩ 4 NE ♿ ECC Ⓟ ⓞ 🍵 🛵
▲ **Strasbourg** - René Cassin IBN 9 rue de l'Auberge de Jeunesse, 67200 Strasbourg (Bas-Rhin).	☎ 0388302646 🖷 0388303516	286	🗓12	⑩ 2 W ♿ ☞ Ⓟ 🍵 🛵
△ *Tarascon* *31 Boulevard Gambetta,* *13150 Tarascon (Bouches-du-Rhône).* @ *tarascon@fuaj.org*	☎ *0490910408* 🖷 *0490915417*	*65*	*01.03–15.12*	ⅲ ⑩ 0.5 NE Ⓟ 🛵
▲ **Tarbes (Assoc)** 88 Rue Alsace Lorraine, 65000 Tarbes (Hautes Pyrénées). @ fjttarbes@wanadoo.fr	☎ 0562389120 🖷 0562376981	58	🗓12	ⅲ ⑩ 2 N ♿ ☞ Ⓟ ⓞ 🍵 🛵
Théoule-sur-Mer ☞**Le Trayas**				
▲ **Thionville (Assoc)** Centre Européen de Séjour/"Salvador Allende" AJ, 3 Place de la Gare, 57100 Thionville (Moselle). @ auberge.jeunesse.thionville@wanadoo.fr	☎ 0382563214, 0382561606	60	🗓12	ⅲ ⑩ 0.5 S ☞ Ⓟ 🛵
▲ **Thouars (Assoc)** F.J.T./AJ "Hector Etoubleau", 5 Boulevard du 8 Mai, 79100 Thouars (Deux Sevres).	☎ 0549662240 🖷 0549661074	38	🗓12	⑩ 1 N ♿ Ⓟ ⓞ ☀
▲ **Tignes** "Les Clarines", 73320 Tignes (Savoie). @ tignes@fuaj.org	☎ 0479063507; 0479410193 Ⓡ 🖷 0479410336	66	01.01–01.05; 25.06–17.09; 01.10–31.12	ⅲ ⑩ Ⓡ 5 E ECC Ⓟ 🍵
△ *Tours* IBN *1 Ave D'Arsonval, Parc de Grandmont,* *37200 Tours (Indre-et-Loire).*	☎ *0247251445* 🖷 *0247482659*	*170*	🗓12	ⅲ ⑩ Ⓡ 4 S ♿ ECC ☞ Ⓟ ⓞ 🛵

Location/Address	Telephone No. Fax No.	Beds	Opening Dates	Facilities
△ *Trébeurden* *Le Toëno, 60 Route de la Corniche,* *22560 Trébeurden (Côtes-d'Armor).*	☎ *0296235222* 🖷 *0296144434*	*56*	*01.02–30.11*	⋔ ⵘ 1N P (ℝ ⋔ 🗒) ▫ ⌖
▲ **Troyes-Rosières** Chemin Ste Scholastique 10430, Rosières (Aude). ✉ troyes-rosieres@fuaj.org	☎ 0325820065 🖷 0325729378	104	🗒	ⵘ ℝ 0.2S ♿ ⚲ P ☕ ⌖
▲ **Valence (Assoc)** Vacanciel l'Epervière, Chemin de l'Epervière, 26000 Valence (Drome).	☎ 0475423200 🖷 0475562067	84	19.01–31.12	⋔ ⵘ 2.5S ♿ ꞔCCꞕ P ☕
▲ **Val Cenis Lanslebourg** Hameau des Champs, 73480 Lanslebourg/Mont-Cenis (Savoie). ✉ valcenis@fuaj.org	☎ 0479059096 🖷 0479058252	76	10.12–25.09 (ℝ only for ⋔ 01.05–15.06)	ⵘ 1E ꞔCCꞕ P ☕ ⌖ ⚙
▲ **Vesoul** Ave des Rives du Lac, 70000 Vaivre Montoille (Haute Saone).	☎ 0384764855, 0384762286 🖷 0384757493	72	🗒	⋔ ℝ 2.5W P ⚙
Vénissieux ☞**Lyon-Sud**				
△ *Ventron* *"Les Roches", 8 Chemin de Fondronfaing,* *88310 Ventron (Vosges).*	☎ *0329241956*	*36*	🗒	⋔ ℝ 2.5S ⚲ P ▫ ⌖
▲ **Verdun** AJ Centre Mondial de la Paix, Place Monseigneur Ginisty, 55100 Verdun (Meuse).	☎ 0329862828 🖷 0329862882	103	01.02–31.12	⋔ ⵘ ℝ 0.2SW ♿ ⚲ P ☕
△ *Vernon (Assoc)* *Centre d'Hebergement Ile de France,* *28 Av de l'Ile-de-France,* *27200 Vernon (Eure).*	☎ *0232516648* 🖷 *0232212341*	*24*	*01.04–30.09*	⋔ ℝ 1.5W ⚲ P
△ *Verzy* *16 Rue du Bassin, 51380 Verzy (Marne).*	☎ *0326979010*	*48*	🗒	ⵘ 0.25W ♿ ⚲ P ▫ ⌖
Vaivre ☞**Vesoul**				
△ *Vienne (Assoc)* *11 Quai Riondet, 38200 Vienne (Isère).*	☎ *0474532197* 🖷 *0474319893*	*50*	Closed Sat–Sun 16.09–15.05	⋔ ⵘ 0.2S ⚲ P ⌖
△ *Vierzon* *1 rue François Mitterrand,* *18100 Vierzon (Cher).* ✉ *vierzon@fuaj.org*	☎ *0248753062* 🖷 *0248711903*	*84*	*01.03–15.02*	⋔ ⵘ 0.5SW ⚲ P ▫ ☕ ⌖
△ *Villefranche de Rouergue (Assoc)* *FJT du Rouergue, 23 rue Lapeyrade,* *Cour de La Gare, 12200* *Villefranche de Rouergue (Aveyron).*	☎ *0565450968* 🖷 *0565458282*	*6*	🗒	⋔ ⵘ 0.5S ♿ ⚲ ▫ ☕
△ *Woerth* *10 rue du Moulin, 67360 Woerth (Bas-Rhin).* ✉ *woerth@fuaj.org*	☎ *0388540330* 🖷 *0388095832*	*62*	*01.03–22.12*	⋔ ⵘ ℝ 0.2NE ⚲ P ▫ ⌖

Location/Address	Telephone No. Fax No.	Beds	Opening Dates	Facilities

YOUTH HOSTEL ACCOMMODATION
OUTSIDE THE ASSURED STANDARDS SCHEME

Location/Address	Telephone No. / Fax No.	Beds	Opening Dates	Facilities
Blois - Les Grouëts 18 rue de l'Hôtel Pasquier, Les Grouëts, 41000 Blois (Loir-et-Cher). ⓔ blois@fuaj.org	☎ 0254782721 🖷 0254782721	48	01.03–15.11	5W ☞ P 🚲
Blois - Montlivault Levée de la Loire, Cedex 181, Montlivault, 41350 Vineuil (Loir-et-Cher). ⓔ blois@fuaj.org	☎ 0254782721 🖷 0254782721	31	01.07–31.08	1SW ☞ P
Cap Ferret AJ, 87 Ave de Bordeaux, 33970 Ferret (Gironde).	☎ 0556606462	60	01.07–31.08	⍾ⓄⓁ Ⓡ 0.5E ☞
Châlons en Champagne "L'Embellie"."Square Antral", 6 rue Kellermann, 51000 Châlons-en-Champagne (Marne).	☎ 0326681356	40	🖷	1E ☞ P 🖻
Choucan Paimpont Choucan, Paimpont, 35380 Plélan-le-Grand (Ille-et-Vilaine).	☎ 0297227675	24	01.05–30.09	4NW ☞ P 🖻
Lautenbach "Dynamo", La Schellimatt, 68610 Lautenbach (Haut-Rhin).	☎ 0389742681	30	Weekends + School holidays	Ⓡ ☞
Maël-Pestivien (Assoc) "Ferme-Manoir de Kérauffret", 22160 Maël Pestivien (Côtes d' Armor).	☎ 0296457528	20	01.05–31.10	⍾⍾ ⍾ⓄⓁ Ⓡ 3E ☞ P 🖻 🚲
Montreuil-Sur-Mer (Assoc) "La Hulotte", Citadelle, rue Carnot, 62170 Montreuil-Sur-Mer (Pas de Calais).	☎ 0321061083 🖷 0321061083	43	01.03–30.10	⍾⍾ 0.2W ☞ P
Oinville "Relais Randonnée", Impasse 10 bis rue de Gournay, 78250 Oinville sur Montcient (Yvelines).	☎ 0134753391 🖷 0134753391	19	🖷	⍾⍾ 0.5NW ☞ 🖻 🚲
Puicheric 2 rue Marcellin Albert, 11700 Puicheric (Aude).	☎ 0468437381 🖷 0468437184	20	🖷	⍾⍾ ⓄⓁ Ⓡ ♿ ☞ 🖻 🚲
Quiberon "Les Filets Bleus", 45 rue du Roch Priol, 56170 Quiberon (Morbihan).	☎ 0297501554	60	01.04–30.09	⍾⍾ 1E ☞ P ⚘
Saint-Mihiel 12 rue sur Meuse, 55300 St-Mihiel (Meuse).	☎ 0329891506 🖷 0329891506	60	03.04–30.11 (⍾⍾ 🖷)	⍾⍾ ⓄⓁ ☞ P
Salies-de-Béarn AJ, Route du Padu, 64270 Salies-de-Béarn (Pyrénées-Atlantiques).	☎ 0559650696 🖷 0559650696	16	🖷	0.4W ☞ P
Vézelay (Assoc) Route de l'Etang, 89450 Vézelay (Yonne).	☎ 0386332418 🖷 0386332418	40	31.03–01.12 (Ⓡ ⍾⍾ 🖷)	⍾⍾ Ⓡ 0.6SE ☞ P 🖻 🚲
Yvetot 6 rue de la Briqueterie, 76190 Yvetot (Seine Maritime).	☎ 0235953701	8	01.04–30.10	⍾⍾ ☞ P

Germany

ALLEMAGNE
DEUTSCHLAND
ALEMANIA

Deutsches Jugendherbergswerk,
Hauptverband für Jugendwandern
und Jugendherbergen e.V.,
Bad Meinberger Str. 1,
D-32760 Detmold, Germany.

☏ (49) (5231) 9936-0
🖷 (49) (5231) 9936-66,
(49) (5231) 9995-90
e info@djh.org
www.djh.de

Office Hours: Monday-Thursday, 08.00-16.30hrs, Friday 08.00-14.30hrs.

Travel Section:
DJH Service GmbH
Postfach 1462
D-32704 Detmold, Germany.

☏ (49) (5231) 7401-0
🖷 (49) (5231) 7401-49
e service@djh.de
www.djh.de

Office Hours: Monday-Thursday, 08.00-16.30hrs, Friday 08.00-14.30hrs.

Capital:	Berlin	**Population:**	82,057,000
Language:	German	**Size:**	357,021 sq km
Currency:	DM (Deutsche Mark)	**Telephone Country Code:**	49

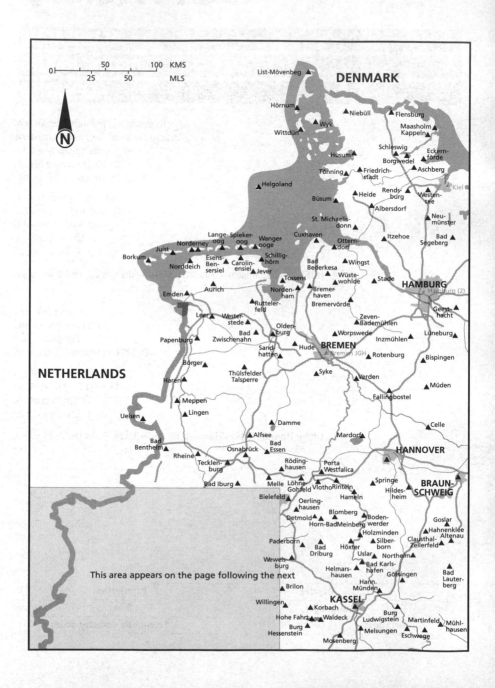

50   100   KMS
0
     25   50   MLS

N

List-Mövenberg

DENMARK

Hörnum
Niebüll   Flensburg
Wyk   Maasholm
Wittdün   Kappeln
Schleswig   Eckern-
Husum   Borgwedel   förde
Aschberg
Tönning   Friedrich-
stadt
Helgoland   Kiel
Büsum   Rends-   Westen-
Heide   burg   see
Albersdorf
St. Michaelis-   Neu-
donn   münster
Lange- Spieker-   Cuxhaven
Norderney oog   oog Wanger-   Otter-   Itzehoe   Bad
Juist   ooge   dorf   Segeberg
Borkum   Esens-   Schillig-   Bad   Wingst
Norddeich Ben-   hörn   Bederkesa   Wüste-
sersiel Carolin-   Jever   Tossens   wohlde   Stade
ensiel   Norden-   Bremer-   **HAMBURG**
Emden   Aurich   ham   haven   Hamburg (2)
Rüttelar-   Bremervörde   Geest-
feld   Zeven-   hacht
Leer   Wester-   Bademühlen   Lüneburg
stede   Bad   Olden-   Worpswede   Inzmühlen
Papenburg   Zwischenahn burg   Sand-   Hude Bremen JGH Rotenburg   Bispingen
hatten   **BREMEN**
Börger   Thülsfelder   Syke   Verden   Müden
Haren   Talsperre
Fallingbostel
Meppen
Celle
Uelsen   Lingen
Damme   Mardorf
Alfsee
Bad   **HANNOVER**
Bad   Osnabrück Essen   Röding-   Porta
Bentheim   hausen   Westfalica
Rheine Tecklen-   **BRAUN-**
burg   Melle Löhne   Springe Hildes-   **SCHWEIG**
Bad Iburg   Gohfeld Vlotho Rinteln   heim
Bielefeld   Hameln
Oerling-   Goslar
hausen   Blomberg   Boden-   Hahnenklee
Detmold   werder   Clausthal- Altenau
Horn-Bad Meinberg   Holzminden   Zellerfeld
Paderborn   Bad   Silber-   Uslar Northeim
Druburg   Höxter born   Bad Karls-   Bad
Wewels-   Helmars-   hafen   Göttingen   Lauter-
burg   hausen   berg
Hann.
Brilon   Münden   Martinfeld Mühl-
Willingen   **KASSEL**   hausen
Korbach   Burg
Hohe Fahrt Waldeck Ludwigstein Melsungen Eschwege
Burg   Mosenberg
Hessenstein

This area appears on the page following the next

NETHERLANDS

50 100 KMS
0 |
25 50 MLS

N

Schönberg · Burg · Iben horst · Zingst · Binz
Kiel · Oldenburg · Graal-Müritz · Barth · Stralsund
Malente · Warne-münde · Ribnitz-Damgarten · S.-Devin
Plön · Schön-walde · Kühlungsborn
Eutin
Scharbeutz-Klingberg · Trave-münde · Bad Doberan · Rostock · Greifswald · Heringsdorf
Bad Segeberg · Lübeck · Beckerwitz · Wismar · Güstrow · Demmin · Murchin
Bad Oldesloe · Dassow-Holm · Flessenow · Teterow · Uckermünde-Bellin
Ratze-burg · Schwerin · Dahmen
Mölln · Malchow
Geesthacht · Waren/Müritz · Burg Stargard
Lauenburg · Plau · Zielow
Lüneburg · Grabow · Mirow · Feldberg
Hitzacker · Prebelow
Uelzen · Bad Freienwalde
Hankens-büttel · POLAND
Wandlitz · Liepnitzsee
Gardelegen · Milow · Ernst Reuter · Buckow
Wolfsburg · Berlin, GH · Münchehofe
BRAUN-SCHWEIG · Wannsee · BERLIN
Haldensleben · Braunsdorf · Bad Saarow
Magdeburg · Köriser See
Schöningen · Gommern · Köthener See · Bremsdorfer Mühle
Goslar · Hahnenklee · Wernigerode · Dessau · Lutherstadt Wittenberg · Lübben/Spreewald · Chossewitz
Altenau · Torfhaus · Quedlinburg
Schierke · Thale · Bernburg · Burg/Spreewald · Cottbus
Braunlage · Meisdorf · Radis
Bad Lauterberg
Bad Sachsa · Nord-hausen · Gorenzen
Halle
Heldrungen
Mühlhausen · Nebra · Naumburg
Bad Kösen

This area appears on the page following the next

This area appears on the page following the next

KASSEL
Steinberg-haus
Willingen
Korbach
Hohe Fahrt
Waldeck
Burg
Ludwigstein
Martinfeld
Mühl-hausen
Burg
Hessen-stein
Melsungen
Eschwege
Mosenberg
Rotenburg
a.d. Fulda

Eisenach
Insels-berg
Rurberg
Nideggen
Bonn
Marburg
Bad
Münster-eifel
Bad
Honnef
Monschau
Gemünd
Bad Salzungen
Brotte-rode
Hellenthal
Blanken-heim
Altenahr
Ahrweiler
Wetzlar
Gießen
Lauterbach
Fulda
Hilders
Montabaur
Prüm
Gerolstein
Mayen
Diez
Weilburg
Laubach
Hoherods-kopf
Ober-bernhards
Daun
Limburg
a.d.
Grävenwiesbach
Gersfeld
Bischofsheim
Manderscheid
Cochem
Broden-bach
Bad Ems
Ober-reifenberg
Bad
Homburg
Büdingen
St. Goar
Traben-Trabach
Oberwesel
Bacharach
Wiesbaden
FRANK-FURT
Bollendorf
Bernkastel-Kues
Bingen
Rüdes-heim
Frankfurt
Linsen-gericht
Königs-berg
Sargen-roth
Mainz
Schweinfurt
Trier
Morbach
Hermes-keil
Idar-Oberstein
Bad
Kreuznach
Darmstadt
Aschaf-fenbug
Lohr
Rothenfels
Würzburg
Saarburg
Weis-kirchen
Burg
Lichtenberg
Steinbach
Worms
Breuberg
Zwingenberg
Wertheim
Dreisbach
Tholey
Wolfstein
Heppenheim
Erbach
Amorbach
Tauber-bischofs-heim
Ochsenfurt
Altleiningen
Weinheim
Walldürn
Hochspeyer
Mannheim
Heidelberg
Igersheim
Weikersheim
Creglingen
Saarbrücken
Homburg
Neckargemünd
Mosbach
Rothenburg-Tauber
Merzalben
Neustadt
Speyer
Kirchberg
Dahn
Bad Berg-zabern
Heilbronn
Feuchtwangen
Karlsruhe
Schwäbisch
Hall
Rechen-berg
Gunzen-hausen
Pforzheim
Ludwigs-burg
Murrhardt
Dinkelsbühl
Baden-Baden
Bad
Herrenalb
STUTTGART
Aalen
Ellwangen
Nördlingen
Herrenwies
Esslingen
Hohen-staufen
Königsbronn
FRANCE
Kehl
Forbach
Heidenheim
Donauwörth
Zuflucht
Dornstetten-Hallwangen
Tübingen
Bad
Urach
Freuden-stadt
Günzburg
Alpirsbach
Erpfingen
Ulm
Blaubeuren
Balingen
Lochen
Breisach
Freiburg
Villingen
Sigmaringen
Biberach
Todtnau-berg
Titisee-
Burg
Wildenstein
Wieden
Neustadt
Memmingen
Feldberg
Bonndorf
Ottobeuren
Platzhof
Menzen-schwand
Schluchsee
Seebrugg
Singen
Über-lingen
Ravensburg
Isny
Kempten
Lörrach
Konstanz
Friedrichs-hafen
Lindau
Füssen
Oberstdorf-Kornau

N

0   50   100 KMS
   25   50   MLS

SWITZERLAND

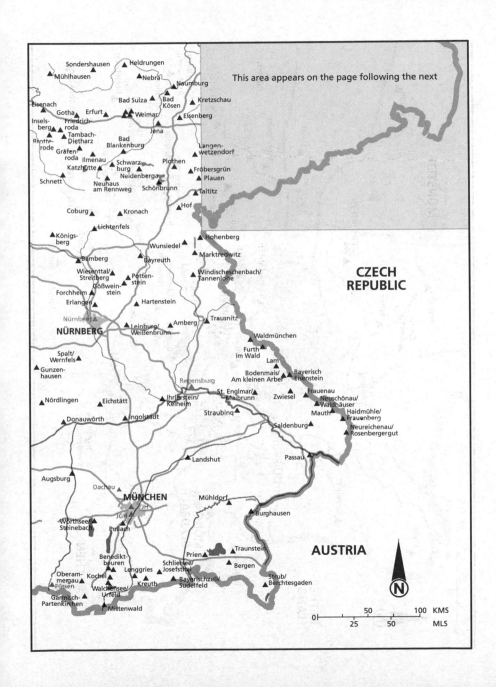

This area appears on the page following the next

Sondershausen Heldrungen
Mühlhausen Nebra Naumburg
Bad Sulza Bad Kretzschau
Kösen
Eisenach
Gotha Erfurt Weimar Eisenberg
Inselsberg Friedrich-
roda
Jena
Tambach- Bad
Blotterode Dietharz Blankenburg Langen-
Gräfen- wetzendorf
roda Ilmenau Schwarz Plothen
Katzhütte burg Fröbersgrün
Neidenberga Plauen
Schnett Neuhaus Schönbrunn
am Rennweg Taltitz

Coburg Kronach Hof
Lichtenfels
Königs- Hohenberg
berg Wunsiedel
Bamberg Bayreuth Marktredwitz
Wiesenttal/ Windischeschenbach/
Streitberg Pötten- Tannenlohe
Gößwein- stein
Forchheim stein
Erlangen Hartenstein

CZECH
REPUBLIC

Nürnberg Amberg Trausnitz
NÜRNBERG Leinburg/
Weißenbrunn
Waldmünchen
Spalt/ Furth
Wernfels im Wald
Gunzen- Lam
hausen Bodenmais/ Bayerisch
Am kleinen Arber Eisenstein
Regensburg
Nördlingen Eichstätt Ihrlerstein/ St. Englmar/ Zwiesel Frauenau
Kelheim Maibrunn Neuschönau/
Straubing Waldhäuser
Donauwörth Ingolstadt Mauth Haidmühle/
Saldenburg Frauenberg
Neureichenau/
Rosenbergergut

Landshut Passau

Augsburg
Dachau
MÜNCHEN Mühldorf
JH
Wörthsee Burghausen
Steinebach JGB
Pullach

Benedikt- Prien Traunstein
beuren Schliersee/ Bergen
Oberam- Kochel Lenggries Josefsthal
mergau Bayerischzell/ Strub/
Füssen Walchensee Kreuth Sudelfeld Berchtesgaden
Garmisch- Urfeld
Partenkirchen Mittenwald

AUSTRIA

N

50 100 KMS
0
25 50 MLS

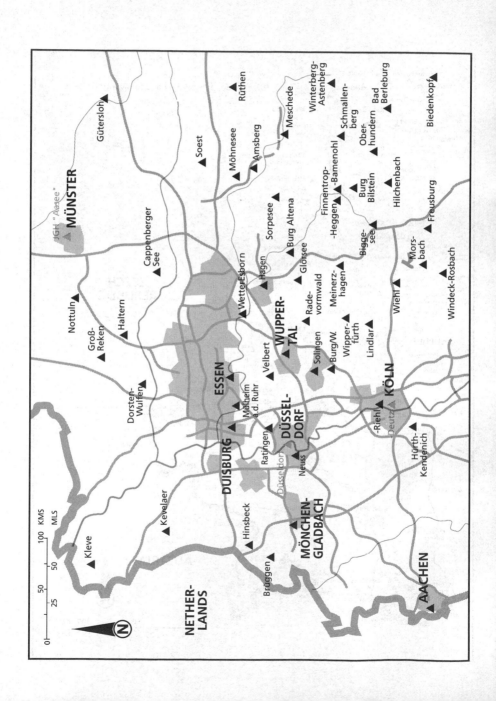

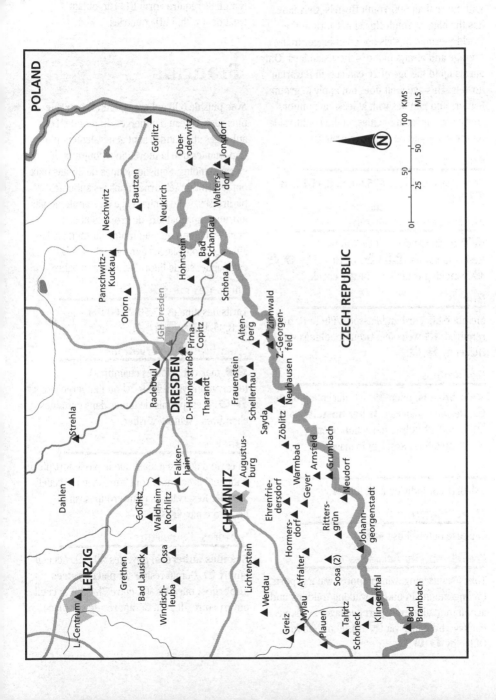

English

With more than 600 Youth Hostels, Germany has the biggest Youth Hostel network in the world. German hostels are often bigger than average and always of the highest standard. Only guests up to the age of 26 can stay in Bavarian hostels. This age limit does not apply to group leaders and families with at least one minor. Hostels are located in cities, in the countryside, on the coast and on hills/mountains.

Price range

Price range DM 17.50-25.00. € 8,95-12,78. BB|inc ⌘.

Rooms and Reservations

R during Mar-Oct. (All Rooms). Reservations via IBN ⌨ or Hostel by ☎ ⓕ ⓔ. Smoking is limited - please check.

Guests

Membership Card and Passport/Photo ID are required. ⋔⋔⋔ welcome. Group bookings via Hostel by ⓕ ⓔ.

Open times

Main hostels: open 🗒, �. Reception open: �. Resident manager. **Other hostels:** open 🗒, 07:00-22:00hrs. Reception open: 07:00-20:00hrs. Resident manager.

Meals

🍽 BLD For individuals & for ⋔⋔⋔.

Travelling around

For ease of travel use 🚌.

Travel/Activity Packages

Tours/sightseeing, winter sports, waters sports, cycling/mountain biking, walking/trekking and accommodation/transport packages available. Package bookings via ⌨ Hostel or National Office by ⓕ ⓔ.

Health

Medical insurance is recommended. EU Nationals require Form E111 to obtain treatment within EU countries.

Français

Avec plus de 600 auberges, l'Allemagne a le plus vaste réseau d'auberges du monde. Les auberges allemandes sont généralement plus importantes que la moyenne et toujours de grand standing. Seuls les jeunes de 26 ans max ont le droit de séjourner dans les auberges bavaroises. Cette limite d'âge ne s'applique pas aux accompagnateurs de groupes ni aux familles comprenant au moins un mineur. Les auberges sont situées dans les villes, à la campagne, sur le littoral et à la montagne.

Tarifs des nuitées

Tarifs des nuitées 17.50-25.00 DM. € 8,95-12,78. BB|inc ⌘.

Chambres et réservations

R mar-oct. (Toutes chambres). Réservations via IBN ⌨ ou l'auberge par ☎ ⓕ ⓔ. Il est permis de fumer dans certaines chambres - veuillez vérifier.

Usagers

La carte d'adhérent ainsi que le passeport/pièce d'identité avec photo sont à présenter. Accueil des ⋔⋔⋔. Réservations pour groupes via l'auberge par ⓕ ⓔ.

Horaires d'ouverture

Grandes auberges: ouvertes 🗒, �. Accueil ouvert �. Gérant réside sur place. **Autres auberges:** ouvertes 🗒, entre 7h-22h. Accueil ouvert entre 7h-20h. Gérant réside sur place.

Repas

🍴 BLD Pour individuels & pour ♦♦♦.

Déplacements

Modes de transport recommandés 🚌.

Forfaits Voyages/Activités

Forfaits circuits touristiques, sports d'hiver, sports aquatiques, cyclotourisme/VTT, randonnées pédestres et hébergement/transport disponibles. Réservations des forfaits via 🖥 l'auberge ou le Bureau National par ❶ ❷.

Santé

Une assurance médicale de voyage est conseillée. Les ressortissants de l'Union Européenne doivent se munir du formulaire E111 pour bénéficier de soins médicaux dans les états de l'UE.

Deutsch

Mit über 600 Jugendherbergen hat Deutschland das größte Jugendherbergsnetz der Welt. Die deutschen Herbergen sind oft überdurchschnittlich groß und immer von allerbestem Niveau. In den bayerischen Jugendherbergen beträgt die obere Altersgrenze 26 Jahre. Diese Altersbegrenzung gilt nicht für Gruppenleiter und Familien mit mindestens einem minderjährigen Kind. Herbergen befinden sich in Städten, auf dem Land, an der Küste und in Bergen/Gebirgen.

Preisspanne

Preisspanne 17.50-25.00 DM. € 8,95-12,78. BB inc 🍴.

Zimmer und Reservierungen

🅡 während Mär-Okt. (Alle Zimmer). Reservierungen über IBN 🖥 oder die Herberge per ❶ ❶ ❷. Rauchen ist begrenzt - bitte checken.

Gäste

Mitgliedsausweis und Reisepass/Personalausweis sind erforderlich. ♦♦♦ willkommen. Gruppenbuchungen über Herberge per ❶ ❷.

Öffnungszeiten

Hauptherbergen: Zugang 🖥, ◔. Rezeption ◔. Herbergsmanager wohnt im Haus. **Andere Herbergen:** Zugang 🖥, 07:00-22:00Uhr. Rezeption zwischen 07:00-20:00Uhr. Herbergsmanager wohnt im Haus.

Mahlzeiten

🍴 BLD Für Einzelreisende & für ♦♦♦.

Reisen im Land

Reisen ist einfach mit 🚌.

Reise-/Aktivitäten-Packages

Touren/sightseeing, Wintersport, Wassersport, Fahrrad/Mountainbiking, wandern/trekking und Unterkunft/Transport-Packages erhältlich. Package-Buchungen über 🖥 Herberge oder Nationalverband per ❶ ❷.

Gesundheit

Unfall-/Krankenversicherung wird empfohlen. EU Staatsangehörige benötigen Formular E111 für ärztliche Behandlungen innerhalb der EU Länder.

Español

Alemania disfruta de la red de albergues juveniles más extensa del mundo, con más de 600 establecimientos. Los albergues suelen ser más grandes de lo normal y son siempre de primera calidad. En Bavaria, el límite máximo de edad es de 26 años, aunque éste no se aplica a los jefes de grupo ni a las familias con por lo menos un niño menor de edad. Los albergues están situados en las ciudades, el campo, la costa y la montaña.

Tarifas mínima y máxima

Tarifas mínima y máxima 17.50-25.00 DM. € 8,95-12,78. [BB]^{inc} [SH].

Habitaciones y Reservas

R en mar-oct. (Todas las habitaciones). Reservas por [IBN] 🖥 o a través del albergue por ❶ ❻ ❸. Está permitido fumar sólo en algunas salas/habitaciones - infórmese.

Huéspedes

Los huéspedes deben presentar su Carnet de Alberguista y su pasaporte o carnet de identidad. Se admiten ⅲ. Reservas de grupo a través del albergue por ❻ ❸.

Horarios y fechas de apertura

Albergues principales - abiertos [12], ⌚. Horario de recepción: ⌚. Gerente residente. **Otros albergues** - abiertos [12], 07:00-22:00h. Horario de recepción: 07:00-20:00h. Gerente residente.

Comidas

🍽 BLD Para individuales y para ⅲ.

Desplazamientos

Transportes recomendados: 🚆.

Viajes Combinados con Actividades

Viajes combinados con visitas turísticas, deportes de invierno, deportes náuticos, cicloturismo/bicicleta de montaña, senderismo y alojamiento/transporte. Reserva de viajes combinados por 🖥 o a través del albergue o la Asociación Nacional por ❻ ❸.

Información Sanitaria

Seguro médico recomendado. Los ciudadanos procedentes de países pertenecientes a la UE necesitan el impreso E111 para obtener asistencia médica en dichos países.

"A wise traveller never despises his own country."

"Le voyageur sage ne méprise jamais son propre pays."

„Ein weiser Reisender verachtet nie das eigene Land."

"El viajero sabio nunca desprecia su propio país."

Carlo Goldoni

Bad Homburg

Mühlweg 17,
61348 Bad Homburg.
☎ (6172) 23950
✆ (6172) 22312
✉ bad-homburg@djh-hessen.de

Open Dates:	01.01-23.12; 27-31.12
Open Hours:	07.00-01.00hrs
Price Range:	31.00-36.00 DM € 16.00-18.50 BB inc SH
Beds:	201 - 1x¹ 12x² 41x⁴ 2x⁶
Facilities:	& 56x 8 x
Directions:	0.5 SW from city centre
✈	Frankfurt Rhein-Main 20km
🚂	Bad Homburg 2km
Attractions:	2km

Berlin -
JH Ernst Reuter

Hermsdorfer Damm 48-50,
13467 Berlin.
☎ (30) 4041610
✆ (30) 4045972
✉ jh-ernst-reuter@jugendherberge.de

Open Dates:	01.01-02.12; 27-31.12
Open Hours:	🕐
Reservations:	R
Price Range:	28.00-35.00 DM € 14.32 17.90 BB inc
Beds:	111 - 16x⁶
Facilities:	
Directions:	15N from city centre
✈	Tegel (TXL) 5km
🚂	Berlin-Zoo 15km
🚌	125 5m ap Jugendherberge
🚋	(S-Bahn) S 25 Tegel 2km
U	U 6 ALT-Tegel 2km
Attractions:	

There are 3 hostels in Berlin. See following
pages.

R > 2 weeks ☎ (30) 2623024
✆ (30) 2629529

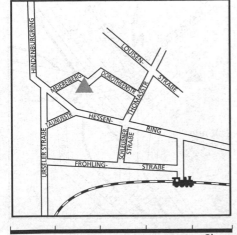

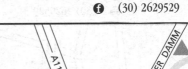

Berlin - JGH Berlin

Kluckstr. 3,
10785 Berlin.
- ☎ (30) 2611097
- 🖶 (30) 2650383
- ✉ jh-berlin@jugendherberge.de

Open Dates:	📅
Open Hours:	◷
Reservations:	Ⓡ ⒤ⒷⓃ
Price Range:	36.00-52.00 DM € 18.41-26.59 BBinc 🍽
Beds:	350
Facilities:	♂♂♂ ♀♀♀ 🍴 ☕ 🛏 📺 ∿3 x 🍷 💼 🅿 ℹ 🛝 🌺 🔍
Directions:	3W from city centre
✈	Berlin Tegel 10km
A🚌	129 30m, 109 500m
🚂	Zoologischer Garten 2km
🚌	129 ap Gedenkstätte
🚃	Potsdamer Platz 1km
Ⓤ	U 1 Kurfürstenstrasse 0.8km, U 2 Bülowstrasse 1.2km
Attractions:	🚵 ⛵5km

Ⓡ   > 2 weeks   ☎   (30) 2623024
  🖶   (30) 2629529

Berlin - JGH am Wannsee

Badeweg 1,
Ecke Kronprinzessinnenweg,
14129 Berlin.
- ☎ (30) 8032034
- 🖶 (30) 8035908
- ✉ jh-wannsee@jugendherberge.de

Open Dates:	01.01-01.12; 27-31.12
Open Hours:	◷
Reservations:	Ⓡ
Price Range:	35.00-43.00 DM € 17.90-21.99 BBinc 🍽
Beds:	288 - 72x 🛏
Facilities:	♿ ♂♂♂ ♀♀♀ 🍴 🛏 📺 🔲 📷 🅿 🛝 🌺 🔍
Directions:	20SW from city centre
✈	Tegel 25km
🚂	Berlin-Wannsee 1.5km
🚌	118 Badeweg 30m
🚃	(S-Bahn) S1, S7, Nikolassee 500m
Attractions:	🎡 🏛2km ⛵1km

Ⓡ   > 2 weeks   ☎   (30) 2623024
  🖶   (30) 2629529

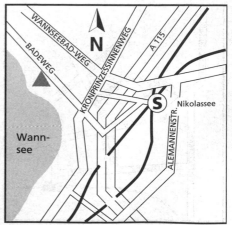

Bremen

JGH,
Kalkstr 6,
28195 Bremen.
☎ (421) 171369
🖷 (421) 171102
✉ jh-bremen@djh-unterweser-ems.de

Open Dates:	02.01-23.12
Open Hours:	◷
Reservations:	┣CC┫
Price Range:	31.50-39.00 DM € 16.11-19.94 BB inc ▯
Beds:	172 - 11x² 32x⁴ 5x⁶
Facilities:	♿ ⋔⋔⋔ 6x ⋔⋔ ⵏ◯⵿ ᪲ TV ▯2 x ▮ 🖾 ⌂ P ◑ ⚲
Directions:	1NW from city centre
✈	Bremen 5km
🚆	Bremen Central 3km
🚌	26 200m ap Brill
🚋	1, 8 200m ap Brill
Attractions:	⚘ ⚲1km

Dresden - JGH

Maternistraße 22,
01067 Dresden.
☎ (351) 492620
🖷 (351) 4926299
✉ jghdresden@djh-sachsen.de

Open Dates:	⊟12
Open Hours:	◷
Reservations:	Ⓡ ⁅IBN⁆
Price Range:	33.00-45.00 DM € 16.87-23.01 BB inc ▯
Beds:	450 - 149x² 38x⁴
Facilities:	♿ ⋔⋔⋔ 38x ⋔⋔ ⵏ◯⵿ (BD) ᪲ TV ⵏ◯⵿7 x ▮ 🖾 ▤ ⚲
Directions:	
✈	Dresden 10km
A🚌	Airport-Cityliner & S-Bahn 12km
⛴	Dresden-City 2km
🚆	Dresden Central 1km
🚋	7, 9, 10, 26 200m
Attractions:	⚵ ⚲50m

There are 2 hostels in Dresden. See following pages.

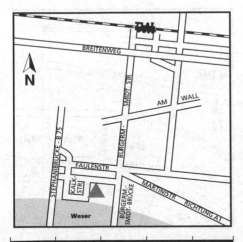

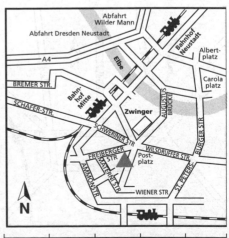

Düsseldorf

Düsseldorfer Str 1,
40545 Düsseldorf.
t (211) 557310
f (211) 572513
e jh-duesseldorf@djh-rheinland.de

Open Dates:	08.01-21.12
Open Hours:	06.00-01.00hrs
Reservations:	IBN
Price Range:	39.00-48.00 DM € 19.94-24.54 BBinc
Beds:	272 - 9x1 27x2 10x3 37x4 1x5 4x6 3x6+
Facilities:	37x (BD) TV 8 x P
Directions:	3 W from city centre
✈	Düsseldorf 12km
Train	Düsseldorf Central 6km
U	70, 74, 75, 76, 77, Luegplatz 1km
Attractions:	3km

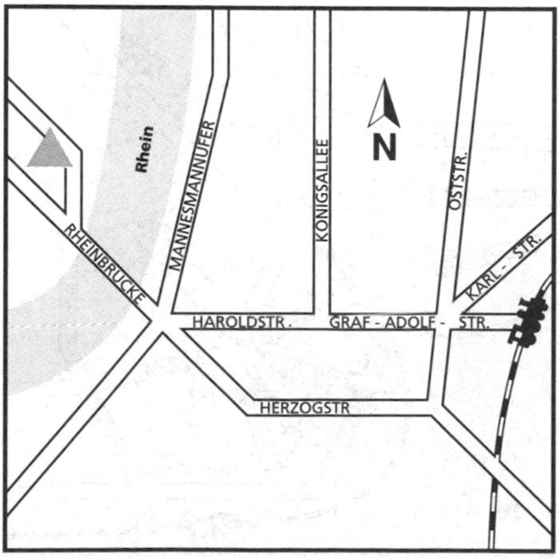

0 6km

Frankfurt

"Haus der Jugend" Deutschherrnufer 12,
60594 Frankfurt.
t (69) 6100150
f (69) 61001599
e jugendherberge_frankfurt@t-online.de

Open Dates:	02.01-22.12
Open Hours:	06.30-02.00hrs
Reservations:	R IBN CC
Price Range:	27.50-55.00 DM € 14.00-28.00 BBinc
Beds:	470 - 15x2 2x3 36x4 4x6 32x6+
Facilities:	TV 1 x 8
Directions:	1 SE from city centre
✈	Frankfurt 12km
A Bus	61 South, then tram 14 to Bornheim, stop "Frankensteiner Platz"
Train	Frankfurt 3km
Tram	16 or S-Bahn 2-6 ap Lokalbahnhof
U	S-Bahn 2-6 to Lokalbahnhof
Attractions:	800m

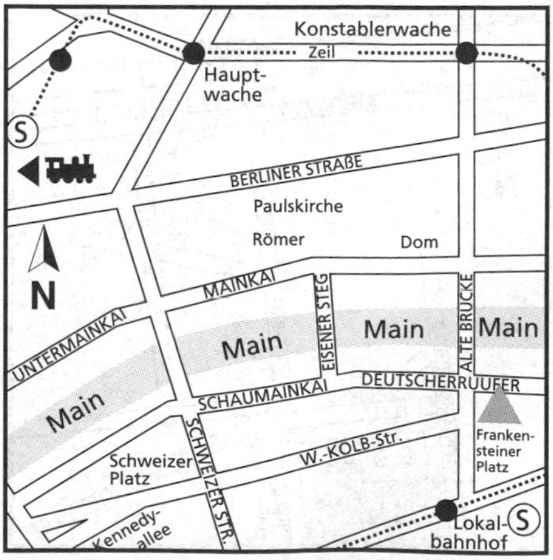

0 3km

Freiburg

Kartäuserstr 151,
79104 Freiburg.
📞 (761) 67656
📠 (761) 60367
✉ jh-freiburg@t-online.de

Open Dates:	27.12.00-22.12.01
Open Hours:	07.00-23.30hrs
Reservations:	Ⓡ
Price Range:	28.00-33.00 DM € 14.32-16.87
	BB inc 🏠
Beds:	405 - 8x² 30x⁴ 30x⁶
Facilities:	♿ ♦♦♦ 4x ♦♦♦ 🍽 ♨ 📺 11 x 🍴 🖿 🅿 🛈 ⚡ ⚠ ☀ 🔍 ⚏ ⛪
Directions:	6E from city centre
✈	Strassburg 70km
🚋	L1 500m ap Römerhof
Attractions:	🎣 ⛰ 🏊 ⛸ 🚶 ⛎5km ☂3km ⛵2km

Güstrow-Schabernack

Heidberg 33,
18273 Güstrow.
📞 (3843) 840044
📠 (3843) 840045
✉ jh-guestrow@t-online.de

Open Dates:	18.01-20.12
Open Hours:	07.00-22.00hrs
Reservations:	Ⓡ
Price Range:	29.00-37.00 DM € 14.83-18.92
	BB inc
Beds:	110 - 4x¹ 9x² 4x³ 8x⁴ 4x⁵ 4x⁶
Facilities:	♦♦♦ ♦♦♦ 🍽 ♨ ♨ 📺 2 x 🍴 🖿 🅿 🛈 ⚡ 🔍 ⚏
Directions:	6SE from city centre
🚌	Güstrow Central 6km
🚌	ap in front of hostel
Attractions:	🎣 🔍1.5km 🚴 🚶 ⛎1.5km ☂1.5km ⚓1km

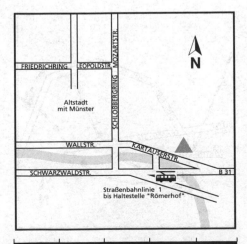

N

FRIEDRICHRING LEOPOLDSTR. MOZARTSTR.
SCHLOBBERGRING
Altstadt mit Münster
WALLSTR. KARTÄUSERSTR.
SCHWARZWALDSTR. B 31
Straßenbahnlinie 1 bis Haltestelle "Römerhof"

0 1.5km

Halle

**August-Bebel-Str 48a,
06108 Halle.**
t (345) 2024716
f (345) 2025172
e jh-halle@djh-sachsen-anhalt.de

Open Dates:	01.01-23.12; 28-31.12
Open Hours:	07.00-10.00hrs; 17.00-23.00hrs
Price Range:	24.00 DM € 12.27 BB inc
Beds:	72 - 1x² 3x 4x 4x
Facilities:	††† 3x ††† ¹⁰¹ ☺ 2 x 🍸 🔘 P 🔍

Directions:

✈	Halle-Schkeuditz 25km
🚆	Halle 1.5km
🚊	5, 7, 9

Attractions: 🚴 🏃 ∪6km ⚓1km ⚓1.5km

Hamburg -
Auf dem Stintfang

**Alfred-Wegener-Weg 5,
20459 Hamburg.**
t (40) 313488; ††† **R** (40) 3191037
f (40) 315407
e jh-stintfang@t-online.de

Open Dates:	05.02-23.12; 27-31.12
Open Hours:	06.30-09.30hrs; 11.30-01.00hrs
Reservations:	**R** **IBN**
Price Range:	from 28.00 DM € from 14.32 BB inc
Beds:	332 - 15x² 14x⁴ 21x⁶ 15x⁶
Facilities:	♿ ††† 14x ††† ¹⁰¹ ☺ 🚲 ☺ 📺 1 x🍸 🔘 🖼 ⬆ 📋 🔍

Directions: 2SW from city centre

✈	Hamburg-Airport 10km
⛴	Hamburger Hafen 200m
🚆	Hauptbahnhof 2km
🚌	112 200m
Ⓤ	S1, S3, U3 Landungsbrücken 200m

Attractions: ⚓1km

There are 2 hostels in Hamburg. See following pages.

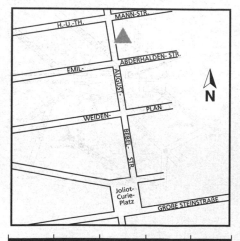

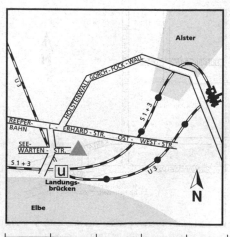

Hannover

Ferdinand-Wilhelm-Fricke-Weg 1,
30169 Hannover.
☎ (511) 1317674
✆ (511) 18555
✉ jh-hannover@djh-hannover.de

Open Dates:	27.12.00-23.12.01
Open Hours:	⏱
Price Range:	28.00-38.00 DM € 14.32-19.43 RR inc
Beds:	317 - 1x¹ 39x² 22x⁴ 24x⁶ 1x⁶
Facilities:	♿ ♦♦♦ 26x ♦♦♦ �|O| (BD) ☕ 🛏 📺 6 x ▤ 📷 8 ⚡ P 🐾 ⚒ ▦
Directions:	2S from city centre
✈	Hannover
🚂	Hannover Hauptbahnhof 5km
🚃	3, 7 1km ap Fischerhof
Attractions:	🚶 🔍 🏊

Heidelberg

Tiergartenstr 5,
69120 Heidelberg.
☎ (6221) 412066
✆ (6221) 402559
✉ jh-heidelberg@t-online.de

Open Dates:	01.01-23.12; 27-31.12
Open Hours:	07.00-23.30hrs
Reservations:	Ⓡ
Price Range:	25.00-30.00 DM € 12.78-15.34 BB inc
Beds:	440 - 1x¹ 3x² 19x⁴ 34x⁶ 17x⁶
Facilities:	♦♦♦ ♦♦♦ �|O| 🛏 📺 🛍 5 x ▤ 6 📷 8 P ℹ 🐾 ⚠ ⚒ ▦
Directions:	4NW from city centre
✈	Frankfurt 80km
A🚌	bis Heidelberg
🚂	Heidelberg 15km
🚌	33 10m ap YH
Attractions:	🚴 🚶 🔍1km 🏊500m

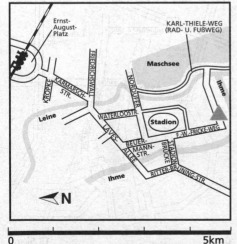

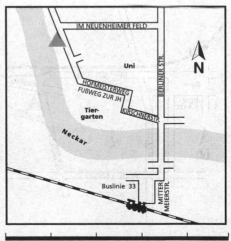

Köln - Deutz

Siegesstr 5a,
50679 Köln.
t (221) 814711
f (221) 884425
e jh-koeln-deutz@djh-rheinland.de

Open Dates:	01.01-23.12; 27-31.12
Open Hours:	🕓
Reservations:	(IBN)
Price Range:	33.00-38.00 DM € 16.87-19.43 BB inc 🍴
Beds:	320 - 4x^1🛏 4x^2🛏 20x^3🛏 3x^4🛏 39x^6🛏 8x^6🛏
Facilities:	♿ 🚻 10x 🚻 🍽 (BD) 🛋 📺 5 x 🍴 🔲 ⬆ 🅿 🔍
Directions:	3E from city centre
✈	Köln-Bonn 12km
🚇	Köln Central 600m
Attractions:	⛵ 5km

Köln - Riehl

An der Schanz 14,
50735 Köln.
t (221) 767081
f (221) 761555
e jh-koeln-riehl@djh-rheinland.de

Open Dates:	01.01-23.12; 27-31.12
Open Hours:	🕓
Price Range:	40.00-65.00 DM € 20.45-33.23 BB inc 🍴
Beds:	366 - 15x^1🛏 21x^2🛏 6x^3🛏 52x^4🛏 12x^6🛏
Facilities:	♿ 🚻 52x 🚻 🍽 (BD) ☕ 🛋 📺 📷 1 x 🍴 🔲 ⬆ 🅿 🟠 🔍
Directions:	6NE from city centre
✈	14km
🚇	Köln 3km
Ⓤ	16,18

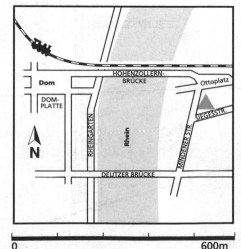

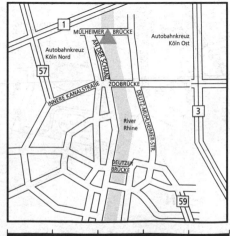

Lübeck

Am Gertrudenkirchhof 4,
23568 Lübeck.
- ☎ (451) 33433
- 🖷 (451) 34540
- 🅴 jhluebeck@djh-nordmark.de

Open Dates:	01.01-23.12; 27-31.12
Open Hours:	07.30-24.00hrs
Reservations:	(IBN)
Price Range:	from 28.00 DM € from 14.32 BB inc 🛏
Beds:	217 - 1x¹🛏 16x²🛏 8x⁴🛏 4x⁵🛏 22x⁶🛏
Facilities:	♿ 👯 12x 👯 🍽 🛌 1 x 🍴 📺 💼 ♿ 🅿 ❸ 🔍
Directions:	2NE from city centre
✈	Hamburg Airport 60km
⛴	Travemuende 10km
🚂	Hauptbahnhof 2km
🚌	1,3,11,12 200m ap Gustav-Radbruch-Platz
Attractions:	🚴 🏊

There are 2 hostels in Lübeck. See following
pages.

Mainz - Rhein-Main-Jugendherberge

Jugendgästehaus Mainz
Otto-Brunfels-Schneise 4,
55130 Mainz.
- ☎ (6131) 85332
- 🖷 (6131) 82422
- 🅴 jh-mainz@djh-info.de

Open Dates:	01.01-23.12; 27-31.12
Open Hours:	06.30-00.00hrs
Reservations:	ⓡ (CC)
Price Range:	29.90-39.40 DM € 15.28-20.14 BB inc 🛏
Beds:	166 - 22x²🛏 27x⁴🛏
Facilities:	♿ 👯 👯 🍽 ☕ 🛌 📺 💷 5 x 🍴 ♿ 🅿 ♿ ⚠ 🔍 🛏
Directions:	5SE from city centre
🚂	Mainz Central 3.5km
🚌	62, 63 ap Jugendgästehaus Mainz 400m
Attractions:	🏃 🏊 3km

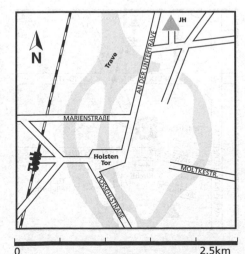

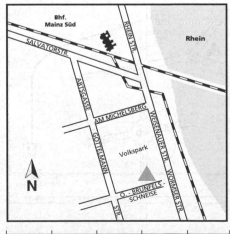

München - Neuhausen

Wendl-Dietrich Str 20,
80634 München (Bavaria).
📞 (89) 131156
📠 (89) 1678745
✉ jhmuenchen@djh-bayern.de

Open Dates: 01.01-30.11

Open Hours: 🕐

Reservations: Ⓡ ⒾⒷⓃ ⒸⒸ

Price Range: 33.00 DM € 16.87 ᴮᴮⁱⁿᶜ 🍺

Beds: 385 - 5x¹ 17x² 24x⁴ 36x⁶
         1x⁶

Facilities: � 🍴 ☕ 🛏 📺 2 x 🍷 ⌾ 💼 ⚥
               🔒 📋 🌱

Directions:

✈   München 30km

🚊   Hauptbahnhof 3km

🚃   12, 17 5 minutes

Ⓤ   1 Rotkreuzplatz 500m

Attractions: 🚴 🚶 🏊 5km

München - JGH Thalkirchen

Miesingstr 4,
81379 München (Bavaria).
📞 (89) 7236550; (89) 7236560
📠 (89) 7242567
✉ jghmuenchen@djh-bayern.de

Open Dates: 🗓

Open Hours: 🕐

Reservations: Ⓡ ⒾⒷⓃ ⒸⒸ

Price Range: 35.50 DM € 18.15 ᴮᴮⁱⁿᶜ 🍺

Beds: 352 - 58x² 11x³ 42x⁴
         6x⁶

Facilities: ♂♀ ♂♀ 🍴 🛏 📺 2 x 🍷 ⌾ 💼
               🔒 Ⓟ 🛏 ♿ ⚠ 🔔

Directions:

✈   München, 40 minutes by public
     transport

🚊   10km

Ⓤ   3 Thalkirchen 350m

Attractions: 🚴 🚶 🏊

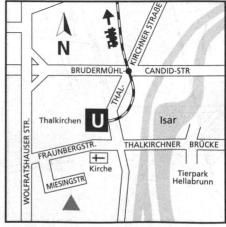

Münster - Aasee

"JGH",
Bismarckallee 31,
48151 Münster.
☎ (0251) 5302810
📠 (0251) 5302850
✉ jgh-muenster@djh-wl.de

Open Dates: 01.01-23.12; 27-31.12

Open Hours: 07.00-01.00hrs

Reservations: **ⓡ** **(IBN)**

Price Range: 40.50-50.50 DM € 20.71-25.82

Beds: 208 - 22x² 41x⁴

Facilities: ♿ ††† 41x ††† ⑂ 🍺 🛗 📺 🍴
8 x🍴 🖥 📷 🛏 🔒 ⬆ 🅿 ⓘ ✆
🌳

Directions: [2W] from city centre

🚂 Münster 2km

🚌 10, 34 500m Hoppendamm

Attractions: 🚲 ⚓3km

Nürnberg - JGH

Burg 2,
90403 Nürnberg (Bavaria).
☎ (911) 2309360
📠 (911) 23093611

Open Dates: 01.01-23.12; 27-31.12

Open Hours: 07.00-01.00hrs

Reservations: **ⓡ** **(IBN)** **⌐CC⌐**

Price Range: 33.00 DM € 16.87 **BB**inc 🍴

Beds: 320 - 10x² 2x³ 33x⁴
13x⁵ 15x⁶

Facilities: ♿ ††† ††† 🍴 🛏 📺 4 x🍴 📷
🔒 ⬆ ⓘ ✆ 🏢

Directions:

✈ Nürnberg 6km

🚂 Nürnberg Central 1.5km

🚋 9 to Krelingstraße

Ⓤ 1 Lorenzkirche 700m

Attractions: ⚓5km

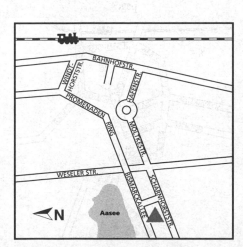

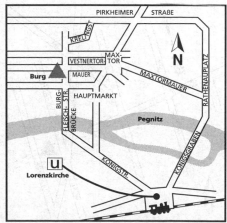

Stuttgart

Haußmannstr 27,
70188 Stuttgart (enter via Werastr,
corner Kernerstr).
☎ (711) 241583
📠 (711) 2361041
✉ jh-stuttgart@t-online.de

Open Dates:	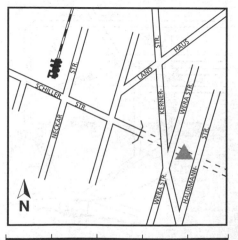
Open Hours:	07.00-00.00hrs
Price Range:	25.00-30.00 DM € 12.78-15.34 [BB] inc 🏠
Beds:	285 - 1x¹ 7x² 42x⁴ 15x⁶
Facilities:	♦♦♦ 42x ♦♦♦ 🍴 🛏 📺 🛢5 x 🍸 🍷
Directions:	[1 SE] from city centre
🚂	Stuttgart 500m
🚌	42 200m ap Eugensplatz
🚎	15 200m ap Eugensplatz
Attractions:	🏃 ⚲ 🏊3km

Weimar -
JGH "Maxim Gorki"

Zum Wilden Graben 12,
99425 Weimar.
☎ (3643) 850750
📠 (3643) 850749
✉ jgh-weimar@gmx.de

Open Dates:	28.12.00-20.12.01
Open Hours:	🕐
Reservations:	**R** ⊂CC⊃
Price Range:	26.00-31.00 DM € 13.29-15.85 [BB] inc 🏠
Beds:	60 - 2x¹ 3x² 4x⁴ 4x⁵ 3x⁶
Facilities:	♦♦♦ 10x ♦♦♦ 🍴 🍷 🛏 📺 🛢 1 x 🍸 📷 P ♿ ⊙ 🍷
Directions:	
✈	Erfurt 30km
🚂	Weimar Central 4km
🚌	8 ap Rainer-Maria-Rilke Str
Attractions:	⚲2km 🏊2km

There are 4 hostels in Weimar. See following
pages.

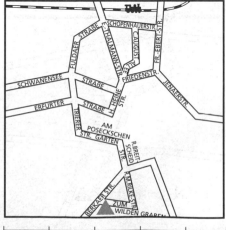

Location/Address	Telephone No. Fax No.	Beds	Opening Dates	Facilities
▲ **Aachen** - Euregionales JGH Aachen Maria-Theresia-Allee 260, 52074 Aachen. ✆ jh-aachen@djh-rheinland.de	☎ (241) 711010 ✆ (241) 7110120	180	01.01–23.12; 27–31.12	⁆⁆ ⍤ Ⓡ 5SW ⓰ ▣ ⓰
▲ **Aalen** - Schubart-Jugendherberge Stadionweg 8, 73430 Aalen.	☎ (7361) 49203 ✆ (7361) 44682	125	01.01–19.11; 27–31.12	⁆⁆ ⍤ ▣
▲ **Affalter** Weg zur Jugendherberge 4, 08294 Lößnitz.	☎ (3771) 33940 ✆ (3771) 33951	35	⍚	⁆⁆ ⍤ ▣
▲ **Albersdorf** Bahnhofstraße 19, 25767 Albersdorf. ✆ jhalbersdorf@djh-nordmark.de	☎ (4835) 642 ✆ (4835) 8462	114	06.01–22.12	⁆⁆ ⍤ ⓰ ▣ ⍟
▲ **Alfsee** Westerfeldstr., 49597 Rieste. ✆ jh-alfsee@djh-unterweser-ems.de	☎ (05464) 9208-0 ✆ (05464) 9208-55	154	⍚	⁆⁆ ⍤ 2E ⓰ ▣ ⍟ ⓰ ⍥
▲ **Alpirsbach** Reinerzauer Steige 80, 72275 Alpirsbach.	☎ (7444) 2477 ✆ (7444) 1304	124	03.01–22.12	⍤ ▣
▲ **Altena** "Burg Altena", Fritz-Thomee-Straße 80, 58762 Altena. ✆ jh-burg.altena@djh-wl.de	☎ (2352) 23522 ✆ (2352) 26330	59	27.12.00–28.01.01; 19.02–23.12	⍤ Ⓡ ▣
▲ **Altenahr** - Naturschutz-Jugendherberge Langfigtal 8, 53505 Altenahr. ✆ jh-altenahar@djh-info.de	☎ (2643) 1880 ✆ (2643) 8136	98	01.01–23.12; 27–31.12	⍤ ⒸⒸ ▣
▲ **Altenau** Auf der Rose 11, 38707 Altenau. ✆ jh-altenau@djh-hannover.de	☎ (5328) 361 ✆ (5328) 8276	164	27.12.00–23.12.01	⁆⁆ ⍤ 0.5SE ▣
▲ **Altenberg** Dresdener Str 70, 01773 Altenberg.	☎ (35056) 32318 ✆ (35056) 32707	115	⍚	⁆⁆ ⍤ ▣
▲ **Altleiningen** - Burg-Jugendherberge, Jugendgästehaus Burg, 67317 Altleiningen. ✆ jh-altleiningen@djh-info.de	☎ (6356) 1580 ✆ (6356) 6364	160	01.01–23.12; 27–31.12	⁆⁆ ⍤ ⓰ ⒸⒸ ▣ ⓰
Am Kleinen Arber ☞**Bodenmais**				
▲ **Amberg** Fronfestgasse 22, 92224 Amberg (Bavaria).	☎ (9621) 10369 ✆ (9621) 10369	36	04.01–23.12	⁆⁆ ⍤
▲ **Amorbach** Kniebreche 4, 63916 Amorbach (Bavaria).	☎ (9373) 1366 ✆ (9373) 7140	92	16.01–30.11	⁆⁆ ⍤
▲ **Arnsfeld** - Naturfreundenhaus"Rauschenbachmühle" Jugendherbergsstr. 1, 09477 Arnsfeld.	☎ (37343) 88670 ✆ (37343) 88670	42	⍚	⁆⁆ ⍤
▲ **Arnsberg** Rumbecker Höhe 1, 59821 Arnsberg. ✆ jh-arnsberg@djh-wl.de	☎ (2931) 10627 ✆ (2931) 13589	122	14.01–16.12	⍤ ▣
▲ **Aschaffenburg** Beckerstraße 47, 63739 Aschaffenburg (Bavaria).	☎ (6021) 930763 ✆ (6021) 970694	110	21.01–19.12	⁆⁆ ⍤
▲ **Ascheffel-Aschberg** 24358 Ascheffel.	☎ (4353) 307 ✆ (4353) 815	36	13.04–31.10	⁆⁆ ⍤ ⓰ ▣

Location/Address	Telephone No. Fax No.	Beds	Opening Dates	Facilities
▲ **Augsburg** Beim Pfaffenkeller 3, 86152 Augsburg (Bavaria).	☎ (821) 33909 🖷 (821) 151149	144	31.01–20.12	ᴙ ⱺ
▲ **Augustusburg** 'Schloss Augustusburg', 09573 Augustusburg.	☎ (37291) 20256 🖷 (37291) 6341	104	🗓	ᴙ ⱺ Ⓡ Ⓟ
▲ **Aurich** Am Ellernfeld, 26603 Aurich.	☎ (4941) 2827 🖷 (4941) 67482	90	01.03–31.10	ᴙ ⱺ 1SW ⅖ Ⓟ
▲ **Bacharach** "Burg Stahleck", 55422 Bacharach. ✉ jh-bacharach@djh-info.de	☎ (6743) 1266 🖷 (6743) 2684	166	01.01–23.12; 27–31.12	ᴙ ⱺ ⅽⅽ ☕
▲ **Bad Bederkesa** Margaretenweg 2, 27624 Bad Bederkesa. ✉ jugendherberge-bad-bederkesa@t-online.de	☎ (4745) 406 🖷 (4745) 8058	70	01.03–31.10	ᴙ ⱺ 1W
▲ **Bad Bentheim** Am Wasserturm 34, 48455 Bad Bentheim.	☎ (5922) 2480 🖷 (5922) 6043	122	🗓	ᴙ ⱺ 1E ⅖ Ⓟ
▲ **Bad Bergzabern** Altenbergweg, 76887 Bad Bergzabern. ✉ jh-bad-bergzabern@djh-info.de	☎ (6343) 8383 🖷 (6343) 5184	141	01.01–23.12; 27–31.12	ⱺ ⅽⅽ Ⓟ
▲ **Bad Berleburg** Goetheplatz 1, 57319 Bad Berleburg. ✉ jh-bad.berleburg@djh-wl.de	☎ (2751) 7340 🖷 (2751) 2076	61	02.01–30.11	ᴙ ⱺ Ⓟ
▲ **Bad Blankenburg** Am Kesselberg 1, 07422 Bad Blankenburg.	☎ (36741) 2528 🖷 (36741) 47625	141	28.12.00– 22.12.01	ⱺ Ⓡ Ⓟ
▲ **Bad Brambach** Röthenbach 4, 08648 Bad Brambach.	☎ (37438) 20541	34	🗓	ᴙ ⱺ Ⓟ
▲ **Bad Doberan** - Tempelberg Tempelberg 1a, 18209 Bad Doberan. ✉ jugendherberge-tempelberg@t-online.de	☎ (38203) 62439 🖷 (38203) 62228	116	01.02–31.10	ⱺ Ⓡ
▲ **Bad Driburg** "Kulturstudienplatz", Schirrmannweg 1, 33014 Bad Driburg. ✉ jh-bad.driburg@djh-wl.de	☎ (5253) 2570 🖷 (5253) 3882	124	16.01–14.12	ᴙ ⱺ Ⓟ
▲ **Bad Ems** Alte Kemmenauer Str 41, 56130 Bad Ems. ✉ jh-bad-ems@djh-info.de	☎ (2603) 2680 🖷 (2603) 50384	120	01.01–23.12; 27–31.12	ᴙ ⱺ ⅽⅽ Ⓟ ☕
▲ **Bad Essen** Schledehauser Str 81, 49152 Bad Essen. ✉ jh-badessen@djh-unterwesen-ems.de	☎ (5472) 2123 🖷 (54?2) 6233	140	🗓	ᴙ ⱺ Ⓟ
▲ **Bad Freienwalde** Hammerthal 3, 16259 Bad Freienwalde. ✉ jh-bad-freienwalde@jugendherberge.de	☎ (3344) 3875 🖷 (3344) 31598	48	01.03–31.10	ᴙ ⱺ Ⓡ 2W
▲ **Bad Herrenalb** - Ev. Ferienheim Aschenhüttenweg 44, 76332 Bad Herrenalb.	☎ (7083) 2430 🖷 (7083) 51031	118	27.12.00– 22.12.01	ᴙ ⱺ ⅖ Ⓟ
▲ **Bad Homburg** **Mühlweg 17, 61348 Bad Homburg.** ✉ bad-homburg@djh-hessen.de	☎ (6172) 23950 🖷 (6172) 22312	201	01.01–23.12; 27–31.12	ᴙ ⱺ 0.5SW ⅖

Location/Address	Telephone No. Fax No.	Beds	Opening Dates	Facilities
▲ **Bad Honnef** Selhoferstr 106, 53604 Bad Honnef. e jh-bad-honnef@djh-rheinland.de	☏ (2224) 71300 ✆ (2224) 79226	210	02.01–07.12	♔♔ ⵏⵐ ☞ 🅿
▲ **Bad Iburg** Offenes Holz, 49186 Bad Iburg. e jh-badiburg@djh-unterweser-ems.de	☏ (5403) 74220 ✆ (5403) 9770	142	🛏12	♔♔ ⵏⵐ 1.5N 🅿
▲ **Bad Karlshafen** Winnefelder Str 7, 34385 Bad Karlshafen. e bad-karlshafen@djh-hessen.de	☏ (5672) 338 ✆ (5672) 8361	86	27.12.00– 23.12.01	♔♔ ⵏⵐ 0.5N 🅿
▲ **Bad Kösen** Bergstr 3, 06628 Bad Kösen.	☏ (34463) 27597	114	01.01–23.12; 28–31.12	♔♔ ⵏⵐ 🅿 ⓕ
▲ **Bad Kreuznach** Auf dem Kuhberg, 55543 Bad Kreuznach. e jh-bad-kreuznach@djh-info.de	☏ (671) 62855 ✆ (671) 75351	136	01.01–23.12; 27–31.12	♔♔ ⵏⵐ ♿ ᶜᶜ 🅿 ☕ 🚲
▲ **Bad Lausick** Herbergsweg 2, 04651/ Bad Lausick/OT Buchheim. e jhbadlausick@djh-sachsen.de	☏ (34345) 7270 ✆ (34345) 72723	146	01.01–19.12; 30–31.12	♔♔ ⵏⵐ 3E ♿ 🅿 ⓕ
▲ **Bad Lauterberg** Flösswehrtal 25, 37431 Bad Lauterberg. e jh-lauterberg@djh-hannover.de	☏ (5524) 3738 ✆ (5524) 5708	131	27.12.00– 23.12.01	♔♔ ⵏⵐ 🅿
Bad Mergentheim ☞Igersheim				
▲ **Bad Münstereifel-Rodert** Herbergsweg 1-5, 53902 Bad Münstereifel-Rodert. e jh-bad-muenstereifel@djh-rheinland.de	☏ (2253) 7438 ✆ (2253) 7483	164	01.01–23.12	♔♔ ⵏⵐ ♿ ☞ 🅿
▲ **Bad Neuenahr-Ahrweiler -** Jugendgästehaus St Pius-Str 7, 53474 Bad Neuenahr-Ahrweiler. e jh-bad-neuenahr-ahrweiler@djh-info.de	☏ (2641) 34924 ✆ (2641) 31574	140	01.01–23.12; 27–31.12	♔♔ ⵏⵐ ♿ ᶜᶜ 🅿 ☕ 🚲
▲ **Bad Oldesloe** Konrad- Adenauer-Ring 2, 23843 Bad Oldesloe. e jhbadoldesloe@djh-nordmark.de	☏ (4531) 5945 ✆ (4531) 67574	110	06.01–02.12	♔♔ ⵏⵐ ♿ 🅿 🚲
▲ **Bad Sachsa** Jugendherbergsstr 9-11, 37441 Bad Sachsa.	☏ (5523) 8800 ✆ (5523) 7163	121	27.12.00– 23.12.01	♔♔ ⵏⵐ 🅿
▲ **Bad Salzungen** Kaltenborner-Str-70, 36433 Bad Salzungen.	☏ (3695) 622208 ✆ (3695) 628833	63	28.12.00– 23.12.01	♔♔ ⵏⵐ Ⓡ 🅿
▲ **Bad Saarow-Pieskow** Dorfstr. 20, 15526 Bad Saarow. e jh-bad-saarow@jugendherberge.de	☏ (33631) 2664 ✆ (33631) 59023	92	🛏12 (Ⓡ 01.11–28.02)	♔♔ ⵏⵐ
▲ **Bad Schandau-Ostrau** Dorfstr 14, 01814 Bad Schandau-Ostrau. e jhbadschandau@djh-sachsen.de	☏ (35022) 42408 ✆ (35022) 42409	101	🛏12	♔♔ ⵏⵐ Ⓡ 3NE 🅿
▲ **Bad Segeberg** Kastanienweg 1, 23795 Bad Segeberg. e jhbadsegeberg@djh-nordmark.de	☏ (4551) 2531 ✆ (4551) 4518	152	06.01–22.12	♔♔ ⵏⵐ ♿ 🅿 ⓕ 🚲

Location/Address	Telephone No. Fax No.	Beds	Opening Dates	Facilities
▲ Bad Sulza August-Bebel-Str 27, 99518 Bad Sulza.	☎ (36461) 20567 ✆ (36461) 20963	74	28.12.00– 23.12.01	♦♦♦ ⦿ R P ☐
▲ Bad Urach Burgstr 45, 72574 Bad Urach.	☎ (7125) 8025 ✆ (7125) 40358	123	17.01–18.12	♦♦♦ ⦿ P ☐
▲ Bad Zwischenahn Schirrmannweg 14, 26160 Bad Zwischenahn.	☎ (4403) 2393 ✆ (4403) 64588	115	01.12–31.10	⦿ P
▲ Baden-Baden - Werner-Dietz JH Hardbergstr 34, 76532 Baden-Baden.	☎ (7221) 52223 ✆ (7221) 60012	151	01–09.01; 12.01–23.12; 27–31.12	♦♦♦ ⦿ 2NW P
▲ Balingen Schloßstr 5, 72336 Balingen.	☎ (7433) 20805 ✆ (7433) 5911	46	01.01–10.12; 28–31.12	♦♦♦ ⦿
Balingen ☞ Lochen				
▲ Bamberg - JH "Wolfsschlucht" Oberer Leinritt 70, 96049 Bamberg (Bavaria).	☎ (951) 56002 ✆ (951) 55211	84	01.02–14.12	♦♦♦ ⦿
▲ Balingen-Lochen Auf der Lochen 1, 72336 Balingen-Lochen.	☎ (7433) 37383 ✆ (7433) 382296	102	01.01–10.12; 27–31.12	♦♦♦ ⦿ P
▲ Barth - Donnerberg Donnerberg, 18356 Barth. ✉ jh-barth@t-online.de	☎ (38231) 2843 ✆ (38231) 2090	155	01.04–31.10	♦♦♦ ⦿ R & P
▲ Bautzen Am Zwinger 1, 02625 Bautzen.	☎ (3591) 40347 ✆ (3591) 40348	50	🖥	♦♦♦ ⦿
▲ Bayerisch-Eisenstein Brennesstr 23, 94252 Bayerisch-Eisenstein (Bavaria).	☎ (9925) 337 ✆ (9925) 730	142	01.01–14.11; 27–31.12	♦♦♦ ⦿ ☞ ☐
▲ Bayreuth Universitätsstr 28, 95447 Bayreuth (Bavaria).	☎ (921) 764380 ✆ (921) 512805	150	01.02–14.12	♦♦♦ ⦿ ☞ ☐
▲ Bayrischzell - JH Sudelfeld Unteres Sudelfeld 9, 83735 Bayrischzell (Bavaria).	☎ (8023) 675 ✆ (8023) 274	94	01.01–14.11; 28–31.12	♦♦♦ ⦿
▲ Beckerwitz Haus Nr 21, 23968 Gramkow OT. Beckerwitz.	☎ (38428) 60362 ✆ (38428) 61986	100	01.04–30.09	♦♦♦ ⦿ R P
▲ Benediktbeuern - "Don-Bosco-JH" Don-Bosco-Str 3, 83671 Benediktbeuern (Bavaria). ✉ lichtenstern@don-bosco-jh.de	☎ (8857) 88350 ✆ (8857) 88351	170	11.01–14.12	♦♦♦ ⦿ R &
▲ Benediktbeuern - "JH Miriam der Don Bosco-Schwestern" Bahnhofstr 58, 83671 Benediktbeuern (Bavaria). ✉ djh-miriam.bb@t-online.de	☎ (8857) 9050 ✆ (8857) 694680	130	16.01–14.12	♦♦♦ ⦿ R P
Berchtesgaden ☞ Strub				
▲ Bergen Hochfellnstr 18, 83346 Bergen (Bavaria).	☎ (8662) 48830 ✆ (8662) 48838	40	01.01–14.11; 26–31.12	⦿ P
▲ Berlin - JH Ernst Reuter **Hermsdorfer Damm 48-50, 13467 Berlin.** ✉ jh-ernst-reuter@jugendherberge.de	☎ (30) 4041610 ✆ (30) 4045972	111	01.01–02.12; 27–31.12	⦿ R 15N ☐

Location/Address	Telephone No. Fax No.	Beds	Opening Dates	Facilities
▲ Berlin - JGH Berlin (IBN) Kluckstr. 3, 10785 Berlin. ⓔ jh-berlin@jugendherberge.de	☎ (30) 2611097 ✆ (30) 2650383	350	🔄	♦♦ ⦿ Ⓡ 3W P ☞
▲ Berlin - JGH am Wannsee Badeweg 1, Ecke Kronprinzessinnenweg, 14129 Berlin. ⓔ jh-wannsee@jugendherberge.de	☎ (30) 8032034 ✆ (30) 8035908	288	01.01–01.12; 27–31.12	♦♦ ⦿ Ⓡ 20SW �> P 🔄
▲ Bernburg Krumbholzallee 2, 06406 Bernburg. ⓔ jh_bbg@t-online.de	☎ (3471) 352027 ✆ (3471) 352027	65	01.01–23.12; 27–30.12	♦♦ ⦿ ⅚ P 🔄
▲ Bernkastel-Kues Jugendherbergsstr 1, 54470 Bernkastel-Kues. ⓔ jh-bernkastel-kues@djh-info.de	☎ (6531) 2395 ✆ (6531) 1529	96	01.01–23.12; 27–31.12	⦿ ЕСС P
▲ Biberach Heusteige 40, 88400 Biberach.	☎ (7351) 21885 ✆ (7351) 21315	139	01–09.01; 07.02–31.12	♦♦ ⦿ P
▲ Biedenkopf Am Freibad 15, 35216 Biedenkopf. ⓔ biedenkopf@djh-hessen.de	☎ (6461) 5100; (6461) 6569 ✆ (6461) 2425	207	27.12.00– 23.12.01	♦♦ ⦿ 0.5W P
▲ Bielefeld - "JGH" Hermann-Kleinewächter-Str. 1, 33602 Bielefeld. ⓔ jgh-bielefeld@djh-wl.de	☎ (521) 522050 ✆ (521) 52205110	160	01.01–23.12; 27–31.12	♦♦ ⦿ Ⓡ 0.5W ⅚ P 🔄 ☞ 🚲
▲ Biggesee Auf dem Mühlenberg, 57462 Olpe-Stade. ⓔ jh-biggesee@djh-wl.de	☎ (2761) 6775 ✆ (2761) 64714	240	27.12.00– 23.12.01	♦♦ ⦿ P
▲ Bilstein "Burg Bilstein", Von-Gevore-Weg 10, 57368 Lennestadt. ⓔ jh-burg.bilstein@djh-wl.de	☎ (2721) 81217 ✆ (2721) 83016	227	01.01–23.12; 27–31.12	⦿ P
▲ Bingen-Bingerbrück Herterstr 51, 55411 Bingen. ⓔ jh-bingen-bingerbrueck@djh-info.de	☎ (6721) 32163 ✆ (6721) 34012	176	01.01–23.12; 27–31.12	⦿ ЕСС
▲ Binz Strandpromenade 35, 18609 Ostseebad Binz/Rügen. ⓔ jh-binz@t-online.de	☎ (38393) 32597 ✆ (38393) 32596	143	29.12.00– 12.12.01	♦♦ ⦿ Ⓡ
▲ Bispingen Töpinger Str 42, 29646 Bispingen.	☎ (5194) 2375 ✆ (5194) 7743	108	27.12.00– 23.12.01	⦿ P
▲ Blankenheim - JH Burg-Blankenheim Burg 1, 53945 Blankenheim. ⓔ jh-burg-blankenheim@djh-rheinland.de	☎ (2449) 95090 ✆ (2449) 950910	164	01.01–23.12	♦♦ ⦿ Ⓡ P ☞
▲ Blaubeuren Auf dem Rucken 69, 89143 Blaubeuren.	☎ (7344) 6444 ✆ (7344) 21416	128	01–09.01; 24.01–05.11; 27.11–31.12	♦♦ ⦿ P 🔄
▲ Blomberg Ulmenallee 15, 32825 Blomberg. ⓔ jh-blomberg@djh-wl.de	☎ (5235) 7255 ✆ (5235) 2130	163	27.12.00– 23.12.01	⦿ P

Bockswiese ☞Hahnenklee

Location/Address	Telephone No. Fax No.	Beds	Opening Dates	Facilities
▲ **Bodenmais** - JH Am Kleinen Arber 94249 Bodenmais (Bavaria).	☎ (9924) 281 ✆ (9924) 850	71	Closed for the present	††† ⑪
▲ **Bodenwerder** Richard-Schirrmann-Weg, 37619 Bodenwerder.	☎ (5533) 2685 ✆ (5533) 6203	124	27.12.00– 23.12.01	††† ⑪ ċ ℗
▲ **Bollendorf** Südeifel-Jugendherberge, Auf der Ritschlay 1, 54669 Bollendorf. @ jh-bollendorf@djh-info.de	☎ (6526) 200 ✆ (6526) 1204	156	01.01–23.12; 27–31.12	⑪ ㏄ ℗ ☕ ⚲
▲ **Bonn** - JGH Bonn-Venusberg,Kulturstudienplatz ⒾⒷⓃ Haager Weg 42, 53127 Bonn. @ jh-bonn@djh-rheinland.de	☎ (228) 289970 ✆ (228) 2899714	249	01.01–23.12; 27–31.12	⑪ 4SW ċ ㏄ ℗ ⑥ ☕
▲ **Bonndorf/Schw** Waldallee 27, 79848 Bonndorf.	☎ (7703) 359 ✆ (7703) 1686	214	27.12.00– 23.12.01	††† ⑪ 1W ℗ ⑥
▲ **Börger** Herbergsweg 2, 26904 Börger.	☎ (5953) 228	62	01.04–31.10	††† ⑪ 1NW
▲ **Borgwedel** Kreisstr 17, 24857 Borgwedel. @ jhborgwedel@djh-nordmark.de	☎ (4354) 219 ✆ (4354) 1305	281	06.01–22.12	††† ⑪ ċ ℗ ⑥
▲ **Borkum** Reedestr.231, 26757 Borkum, (North Sea). @ jh-borkim@djh-unterweser-ems.de	☎ (4922) 579 ✆ (4922) 7124	530	⓬	⑪ Ⓡ 7SE ℗
▲ **Born-Ibenhorst** Im Darßer Wald, 18375 Born-Ibenhorst. @ jh-born@t-online.de	☎ (38234) 229 ✆ (38234) 231	180	01.03–31.10	††† ⑪ Ⓡ ċ ℗ ⑥
▲ **Braunlage** Von-Langen-Str 28, 38700 Braunlage.	☎ (5520) 2238 ✆ (5520) 1569	130	27.12.00– 23.12.01	††† ⑪ ℗
▲ **Braunschweig** Salzdahlumer Str. 170, 38126 Braunschweig.	☎ (531) 264320 ✆ (531) 2643270	160	27.12.00– 23.12.01	††† ⑪ ċ ℗
▲ **Braunsdorf** Dorfstr 17, 15518 Braunsdorf.	☎ (33633) 635 ✆ (33633) 65630	54	⓬	††† ⑪ Ⓡ
▲ **Breisach** Rheinuferstr 12, 79206 Breisach.	☎ (7667) 7665 ✆ (7667) 1847	158	27.12.00– 22.12.01	⑪ ℗ ⑥
▲ **Bremen** JGH, Kalkstr 6, 28195 Bremen. @ jh-bremen@djh-unterweser-ems.de	☎ (421) 171369 ✆ (421) 171102	172	02.01–23.12	††† ⑪ 1NW ċ ㏄ ℗
▲ **Bremerhaven** YH + YGH Gaußstr 54-56, 27580 Bremerhaven. @ info@jgh-bremerhaven.nordcom.net	☎ (471) 982080 ✆ (471) 87426	170	⓬	⑪
▲ **Bremervörde** Feldstr 9, 27432 Bremervörde.	☎ (4761) 1275 ✆ (4761) 70701	122	⓬	††† ⑪ ℗
▲ **Bremsdorfer Mühle** 15890 Bremsdorf. @ jh-bremsdorfer-muehle@jugendherberge.de	☎ (33654) 272 ✆ (33654) 49044	140	⓬ (Ⓡ 01.11–28.02)	††† ⑪

Location/Address	Telephone No. Fax No.	Beds	Opening Dates	Facilities
▲ **Breuberg, Burg** 64747 Breuberg. 📧 burgbreuberg@djh-hessen.de	☎ (6165) 3403 📠 (6165) 6469	129	03.01–23.12	ℝ 3E 🅿
▲ **Brilon** "EURO-Umweltstudienplatz", Hölsterloh 3, 59929 Brilon. 📧 jh-brilon@djh-wl.de	☎ (2961) 2281 📠 (2961) 51731	165	16.01–14.12	ⅲ ⑩ 🅿
▲ **Brodenbach** Moorkamp 7, 56332 Brodenbach. 📧 jh-brodenbach@djh-info.de	☎ (2605) 3389 📠 (2605) 4244	105	01.01–23.12; 27–31.12	⑩ ECC 🅿
▲ **Brotterode** Am Zainhammer 4, 98599 Brottcrode.	☎ (36840) 32125 📠 (36840) 32125	65	28.12.00– 23.12.01	ⅲ ⑩ ℝ 🅿
▲ **Brüggen** Auf dem Eggenberg 1, 41379 Brüggen. 📧 jh-brueggen@djh-rheinland.de	☎ (2163) 5161 📠 (2163) 59967	134	15.03–23.12; 27–31.12	ⅲ ⑩ ☞ 🅿
Buchheim ☞**Bad Lausick**				
▲ **Buckow** Berliner Str 36, 15377 Buckow. 📧 jh-buckow@jugendherberge.de	☎ (33433) 286 📠 (33433) 56274	106	▦(ℝ 01.11.00– 28.02.01)	ⅲ ⑩ ℝ 1.5S
▲ **Büdingen** Jugendherberge 1, 63654 Büdingen. 📧 buedingen@djh-hessen.de	☎ (6042) 3697 📠 (6042) 68178	121	27.12.00– 23.12.01	ⅲ ⑩ 2NE 🅿
▲ **Burg auf Fehmarn** Mathildenstr 34, 23769 Burg auf Fehmarn. 📧 jhburg@djh-nordmark.de	☎ (4371) 2150 📠 (4371) 6680	188	06.01–22.12	⑩ ♿ 🅿 ▣ 🚲
▲ **Burg an der Wupper** An der Jugendherberge 11, 42659 Solingen. 📧 jh-burg-wupper@djh-rheinland.de	☎ (212) 41025 📠 (212) 49449	118	01.01–23.12; 27–31.12	ⅲ ⑩ 🅿
▲ **Burg/Spreewald** JII 'Tricdrich-Ludwig-Jahn', Jugendherbergsweg 8, 03096 Burg/Spreewald. 📧 jh-burg@jugendherbcrge.de	☎ (35603) 225 📠 (35603) 13248	203	▦(ℝ ⅲ 01.11.00– 28.02.01)	ⅲ ⑩ ℝ
▲ **Burg Stargard** Dewitzer Chausse 07, 17094 Burg Stargard. 📧 jh-burg-stargard@t-online.de	☎ (39603) 20207 📠 (39603) 20255	126	01.02–02.01	ⅲ ⑩ ℝ 🅿
Burg Wildenstein ☞**Wildenstein**				
▲ **Burghausen** Kapuzinergasse 235, 84489 Burghausen (Bavaria). 📧 jhburghaus@aol.com	☎ (8677) 4187 📠 (8677) 911318	110	01.01–30.11	ⅲ ⑩ 0.5S ♿ ☞ 🅿 ▣
▲ **Büsum** Dr Martin-Bahr-Str 1, 25761 Büsum. 📧 jhbuesum@djh-nordmark.de	☎ (4834) 93371 📠 (4834) 93376	206	01.02–22.12	ⅲ ⑩ ♿ 🅿
▲ **Cappenberger See** Richard-Schirrmann-Weg 7, 44534 Lünen. 📧 jh-cappenberger.see@djh-wl.de	☎ (2306) 53546 📠 (2306) 73000	122	15.01–22.12	ⅲ ⑩ 🅿
▲ **Carolinensiel** Herbergsmense 13, 26409 Wittmund.	☎ (4464) 252 📠 (4464) 655	123	01.01–30.11	⑩ ℝ 0.5W 🅿

Location/Address	Telephone No. Fax No.	Beds	Opening Dates	Facilities
▲ **Celle** Weghausstr 2, 29223 Celle.	☎ (5141) 53208 ᖴ (5141) 53005	128	27.12.00– 23.12.01	⚄ ⓧ P
▲ **Chemnitz** Augustusburger Str 369, 09127 Chemnitz. ℯ jhchemnitz@djh-sachsen.de	☎ (371) 71331 ᖴ (371) 73331	88	01.01–19.12; 28–31.12	⚄ ⓧ 5E P
▲ **Chossewitz** Weichensdorfer Str 3, 15848 Chossewitz. ℯ jh-chossewitz@jugendherberge.de	☎ (33673) 5757 ᖴ (33673) 55100	58	ⓡ (R 01.11.00– 28.02.01)	⚄ ⓧ R
▲ **Clausthal-Zellerfeld** Altenauer Str 55, 38678 Clausthal-Zellerfeld.	☎ (5323) 84293 ᖴ (5323) 83827	122	27.12.00– 23.12.01	⚄ ⓧ P
▲ **Coburg** Parkstr 2, 96450 Coburg (Bavaria).	☎ (9561) 15330 ᖴ (9561) 28653	145	16.01–14.12	⚄ ⓧ
▲ **Cochem** Klottener Str 9, 56812 Cochem. ℯ jh-cochem@djh-info.de	☎ (2671) 8633 ᖴ (2671) 8568	146	01.01–23.12; 27–31.12	ⓧ CC P
▲ **Colditz** Haingasse 42, 04680 Colditz.	☎ (34381) 43335	41	ⓡ	⚄ ⓧ P
Cologne ☞**Köln**				
▲ **Cottbus** Klosterplatz 2/3, 03046 Cottbus.	☎ (355) 22558 ᖴ (355) 23798	40	ⓡ	⚄ ⓧ ♂
▲ **Creglingen** Erdbacher Str 30, 97993 Creglingen.	☎ (7933) 336 ᖴ (7933) 1326	153	01.01–23.01; 03.02–31.12	⚄ ⓧ ♿ P
▲ **Cuxhaven-Duhnen** Schlensenweg 2, 27476 Cuxhaven. ℯ jhcuxhaven@djh-nordmark.de	☎ (4721) 48552 ᖴ (4721) 45794	277	16.01–14.12	⚄ ⓧ ♿ P 🚲
▲ **Dachau - JGH** IBN Rosswachtstrasse 15, 85221 Dachau (Bavaria). ℯ jghdachau@djh-bayern.de	☎ (8131) 322950 ᖴ (8131) 3229550	110	ⓡ	⚄ ⓧ ♿ P ☕
▲ **Dahlen** Belgernsche Str 25, 04774 Dahlen. ℯ jhdahlen@djh-sachsen.de	☎ (34361) 55002 ᖴ (34361) 55003	125	ⓡ	⚄ ⓧ 1 NE P
▲ **Dahmen** Dorfstr 14, 17166 Dahmen.	☎ (39933) 70552 ᖴ (39933) 70650	237	16.01–30.11	⚄ ⓧ R P 🅾
▲ **Dahn** Am Wachtfelsen 1, 66994 Dahn. ℯ jh-dahn@djh-info.de	☎ (6391) 1769 ᖴ (6391) 5122	108	01.01–23.12; 27–31.12	⚄ ⓧ CC P ☕
▲ **Damme** Steinfelder Str 57, 49401 Damme. ℯ jh-damme@djh-unterweser-ems.de	☎ (5491) 96720 ᖴ (5491) 967229	164	ⓡ	⚄ ⓧ 1.5 NW ♿ P ☕
▲ **Darmstadt** Landgraf-Georg-Str 119, 64287 Darmstadt. ℯ darmstadt@djh-hessen.de	☎ (6151) 45293 ᖴ (6151) 422535	122	27.12.00– 23.12.01	ⓧ 0.8E P
▲ **Dassow-Holm** An der B 105, 23942 Dassow.	☎ (38826) 80614 ᖴ (38826) 80614	122	01.05–30.09	⚄ ⓧ R ♿ P
▲ **Daun** Maria-Hilf-Str. 21, 54550 Daun. ℯ jh-daun@djh-info.de	☎ (6592) 2884 ᖴ (6592) 1506	147	01.01–23.12; 27–31.12	⚄ ⓧ CC P ☕

Location/Address	Telephone No. Fax No.	Beds	Opening Dates	Facilities
▲ **Demmin** R-Breitscheid-Str, Postfach 1201, 17102 Demmin.	☎ (3998) 223388 ✆ (3998) 223388	32	01.04–31.10	⊙ ℝ
▲ **Dessau** Waldkaterweg 11, 06846 Dessau. ✉ jh-dessau@djh-sachsen-anhalt.de	☎ (340) 619452 ✆ (340) 619452	63	01.01–23.12; 28–31.12	⫟ ⊙ Ⓟ
▲ **Detmold** Schirrmannstr 49, 32756 Detmold. ✉ jh-detmold@djh-wl.de	☎ (5231) 24739 ✆ (5231) 28927	126	16.01–13.12	⫟ ⊙ Ⓟ
▲ **Diez** Schloss, 65582 Diez. ✉ jh-diez@djh-info.de	☎ (6432) 2481 ✆ (6432) 4504	91	01.01–31.10	⊙ ⒺⒸⒸ
▲ **Dinkelsbühl** Koppengasse 10, 91550 Dinkelsbühl (Bavaria).	☎ (9851) 9509 ✆ (9851) 4874	148	01.03–30.09	⫟ ⊙
▲ **Donauwörth** Goethestr 10, 86609 Donauwörth (Bavaria).	☎ (906) 5158 ✆ (906) 243817	95	Closed for renovation until May 2001	⫟ ⊙
▲ **Dornstetten** - Pfahlberg Auf dem Pfahlberg 39, 72280 Dornstetten-Hallwangen.	☎ (7443) 6469 ✆ (7443) 20212	125	01.01–10.12; 27–31.12	⫟ ⊙ ♿ Ⓟ
▲ **Dorsten-Wulfen** Im Schöning 83, 46286 Dorsten-Wulfen. ✉ jh-dorsten@djh-wl.de	☎ (2369) 8722 ✆ (2369) 23867	102	08.01–20.12	⫟ ⊙ Ⓟ
▲ **Dreisbach** - Jugendherberge an der Saarschleife, Jugendgästehaus, Herbergstr 1, 66693 Dreisbach-Mettlach. ✉ jh-dreisbach@djh-info.de	☎ (6868) 270 ✆ (6868) 556	122	01.01–23.12; 27–31.12	⫟ ⒃ ♿ ⒺⒸⓄ Ⓟ ⬤ 🚲
▲ **Dresden** - "Rudi Arndt" Hübnerstr 11, 01069 Dresden.	☎ (351) 4710667 ✆ (351) 4728959	81	⬚12	⊙ 3S ⬚
▲ **Dresden** - Radebeul Weintraubenstr 12, 01445 Radebeul.	☎ (351) 8382880 ✆ (351) 8382881	82	⬚12	⊙ 10W Ⓟ
▲ **Dresden** - JGH ⒾⒷⓃ **Maternistraße 22, 01067 Dresden.** ✉ jghdresden@djh-sachsen.de	☎ (351) 492620 ✆ (351) 4926299	450	⬚12	⫟ ⊙ ℝ ♿
▲ **Duisburg** Kalkweg 148E, 47279 Duisburg. ✉ jh-duisburg-wedau@djh-rheinland.de	☎ (203) 724164 ✆ (203) 720834	134	07.01–23.12	⫟ ⊙ 4.5W Ⓟ ⬚
▲ **Düsseldorf** ⒾⒷⓃ **Düsseldorfer Str 1, 40545 Düsseldorf.** ✉ jh-duesseldorf@djh-rheinland.de	☎ (211) 557310 ✆ (211) 572513	272	08.01–21.12	⫟ ⊙ 3W ♿ Ⓟ ⬚
▲ **Eckernförde** Sehestedter Str 27, 24340 Eckernförde. ✉ jheckernfoerde@djh-nordmark.de	☎ (4351) 2154 ✆ (4351) 3604	164	06.01–22.12	⫟ ⊙ Ⓟ ⬚ 🚲
▲ **Ehrenfriedersdorf** Greifensteinstr 46, 09427 Ehrenfriedersdorf.	☎ (37346) 1253	41	01.01–31.10; 01–31.12 (⫟01.11– 30.11)	⫟ ⊙ 4SW Ⓟ

Location/Address	Telephone No. Fax No.	Beds	Opening Dates	Facilities
▲ **Eichstätt** Reichenaustr 15, 85072 Eichstätt (Bavaria). ✉ jheichstaett@djh-bayern.de	☎ (8421) 980410 🖷 (8421) 980415	112	01.02–30.11	♂♀ ⊚
▲ **Eisenach** - Artur Becker "Artur Becker", Mariental 24, 99817 Eisenach.	☎ (3691) 743259 🖷 (3691) 743260	102	28.12.00– 23.12.01	♂♀ ⊚ R ♿ P
▲ **Eisenberg** - "Froschmühle" JH "Froschmühle", Mühltal 5, 07607 Eisenberg.	☎ (36691) 43462 🖷 (36691) 60034	130	28.12.00– 23.12.01	♂♀ R P
▲ **Ellwangen** Schloß ob Ellwangen, 73479 Ellwangen.	☎ (7961) 53880 🖷 (7961) 55331	65	27.12.00– 22.12.01	♂♀ ⊚
▲ **Emden** An der Kesselschleuse 5, 26725 Emden. ✉ jh-emden@t-online.de	☎ (4921) 23797 🖷 (4921) 32161	90	01.02–30.11	♂♀ ⊚ P
▲ **Erbach** Eulbacher Str 33, 64711 Erbach. ✉ erbach@djh-hessen.de	☎ (6062) 3515 🖷 (6062) 62848	156	27.12.00– 23.12.01	♂♀ ⊚ 1.5NE P
▲ **Erfurt** Hochheimerstr 12, 99094 Erfurt. ✉ jugendherberge-erfurt@t-online.de	☎ (361) 5626705 🖷 (361) 5626706	201	28.12.00– 23.12.01	♂♀ ⊚ R ♿ P ☕
▲ **Erlangen** - JH Frankenhof Südliche Stadtmauerstr 35, 91054 Erlangen (Bavaria).	☎ (9131) 862274; 862555 🖷 (9131) 862119	66	03.01–22.12	⊚
▲ **Erpfingen** Auf der Reute 1, 72820 Sonnenbühl.	☎ (7128) 1652 🖷 (7128) 3370	149	01.01–03.12; 27–31.12	♂♀ ⊚ P ⊚
▲ **Esborn** Wacholderstr 11, 58300 Wetter. ✉ jh-esborn@djh-wl.de	☎ (2335) 7718 🖷 (2335) 73519	60	15.01–14.12	⊚ P
▲ **Eschwege** Fritz-Neuenroth-Weg 1, 37269 Eschwege. ✉ eschwege@djh-hessen.de	☎ (5651) 60099 🖷 (5651) 70916	175	27.12.00– 23.12.01	♂♀ ⊚ 0.3NE ♿
▲ **Esens-Bensersiel** - "Ewald-Neemann - JH" Grashauser Flage 2, 26427 Esens.	☎ (4971) 3717 🖷 (4971) 659	146	01–31.01; 01.03–31.12	♂♀ ⊚ R 1N ♿ P
▲ **Essen-Werden** Pastoratsberg 2, 45239 Essen-Werden. ✉ jh-essen@djh-rheinland.de	☎ (201) 491163 🖷 (201) 492505	130	01.01–23.12; 27–31.12	♂♀ ⊚ 10N P
▲ **Esslingen** Neuffenstr 65, 73734 Esslingen.	☎ (711) 381848 🖷 (711) 388886	104	03.01–03.12	♂♀ ⊚ P
▲ **Eutin** Jahnhöhe 6, 23701 Eutin. ✉ jheutin@djh-nordmark.de	☎ (4521) 2109 🖷 (4521) 74602	172	06.01–22.12	♂♀ ⊚ P ⊚ ⚓
▲ **Falkenhain** An der Talsperre Kriebstein, 09648 Mittweida. ✉ jhfalkenhain@djh-sachsen.de	☎ (3727) 2952 🖷 (3727) 600050	220	01.05–30.09	♂♀ ⊚ 6NE P ⊚ ☕
▲ **Fallingbostel** Liethweg 1, 29683 Fallingbostel. ✉ jh-fallingbostel@djh-hannover.de	☎ (5162) 2274 🖷 (5162) 5704	92	27.12.00– 23.12.01	♂♀ ⊚ P

Location/Address	Telephone No. Fax No.	Beds	Opening Dates	Facilities
▲ **Feldberg** Klinkecken 6, 17258 Feldberg.	☎ (39831) 20520 🖷 (39831) 22178	87	01.03–31.10	ⅲ ⅼⓞⅼ ⓡ 🅿
▲ **Feldberg/Schw** - Hebelhof Passhöhe 14, 79868 Feldberg.	☎ (7676) 221 🖷 (7676) 1232	270	27.12.00– 22.12.01	ⅲ ⅼⓞⅼ ⓡ 🅿
▲ **Feuchtwangen** Dr.-Hans-Güthlein-Weg 1, 91555 Feuchtwangen (Bavaria).	☎ (9852) 670990 🖷 (9852) 6709920	74	03.01–19.12	ⅲ ⅼⓞⅼ 🅿
▲ **Finnentrop-Bamenohl** "Jupp- Schöttler-Jugendherberge", Herbergsweg 1, 57413 Finnentrop-Bamenohl.	☎ (2721) 7293 🖷 (2721) 5486	30	27.12.00– 23.12.01	ⅼⓞⅼ 🅿
▲ **Finnentrop-Heggen** Ahauser Str 22-24, 57405 Finnentrop-Heggen. ⊜ jh-finnentrop.heggen@djh-wl.de	☎ (2721) 50345 🖷 (2721) 79460	223	27.12.00– 23.12.01	ⅲ ⅼⓞⅼ ♿ 🅿
▲ **Flensburg** Fichtestr 16, 24943 Flensburg. ⊜ jhflensburg@djh-nordmark.de	☎ (461) 37742 🖷 (461) 312952	198	29.01–21.12; 28.12.01- 02.01.02	ⅲ ⅼⓞⅼ 4NE 🅿 ⟲
▲ **Flessenow** Am Schweriner See 1B, 19067 Rubow OT. Flessenow. ⊜ jugendherberge.flessenow@t-online.de	☎ (3866) 82400 🖷 (3866) 82401	123	01.05–30.09	ⅲ ⅼⓞⅼ ⓡ 🅿
▲ **Forbach** - "Heinrich-Kastner-JH" Birket 1, Postfach 1175, 76594 Forbach.	☎ (7228) 2427 🖷 (7228) 1551	78	27.12.00– 23.12.01	ⅲ ⅼⓞⅼ 2E 🅿
▲ **Forbach** - Environmental Study Centre, Franz-Köbele-JH OT Herrenwies, Haus Nr 33, 76596 Forbach.	☎ (7226) 257 🖷 (7226) 1318	143	27.12.00– 22.12.01	ⅲ ⅼⓞⅼ 🅿
▲ **Forchheim** - "Don-Bosco-JH" Don-Bosco-Str. 4, 91301 Forchheim (Bavaria).	☎ (9191) 70710 🖷 (9191) 707111	108	07.01–22.12	ⅲ ⅼⓞⅼ ⓡ 1.5E ♂ 🅿 ⟲
▲ **Frankfurt** [IBN] **"Haus der Jugend" Deutschherrnufer 12,** **60594 Frankfurt.** ⊜ jugendherberge_frankfurt@t-online.de	☎ (69) 6100150 🖷 (69) 61001599	470	02.01–22.12	ⅲ ⅼⓞⅼ ⓡ 1SE ♿ -CC- 🖥 ☕ ⟲
▲ **Frauenau** Hauptstr 9a, 94258 Frauenau (Bavaria).	☎ (9926) 735 🖷 (9926) 735	24	01.01–30.11	ⅼⓞⅼ ♂
Frauenberg ☞**Haidmühle**				
▲ **Frauenstein** - Kulturstudienplatz Walkmühlenstr 13, 09623 Frauenstein. ⊜ jhfrauenstein@djh-sachsen.de	☎ (37326) 1307 🖷 (37326) 84400	91	🈚12	ⅲ ⅼⓞⅼ 1SW 🅿 🖥
▲ **Freiburg** **Kartäuserstr 151, 79104 Freiburg.** ⊜ jh-freiburg@t-online.de	☎ (761) 67656 🖷 (761) 60367	405	27.12.00– 22.12.01	ⅲ ⅼⓞⅼ ⓡ 6E ♿ 🅿 🖥
▲ **Freudenstadt** Eugen-Nägele-Str 69, 72250 Freudenstadt.	☎ (7441) 7720 🖷 (7441) 85788	132	01–10.11; 27–31.12	ⅲ ⅼⓞⅼ 🅿 🖥
▲ **Freusburg** Burgstrasse 46, 57548 Kirchen-Freusburg. ⊜ jh-freusburg@djh-wl.de	☎ (2741) 61094 🖷 (2741) 63135	219	27.12.00– 23.12.00	ⅲ ⅼⓞⅼ 🅿

Location/Address	Telephone No. Fax No.	Beds	Opening Dates	Facilities
▲ **Friedrichroda** Waldstrasse 25, 99894 Friedrichroda. ⊖ jugendherberge_friedrichroda@t-online.de	☏ (3623) 304410 ✆ (3623) 305003	125	28.12.00– 23.12.01	۱۰۱ Ⓡ Ⓟ
▲ **Friedrichshafen** - Graf-Zeppelin-JH Lindauer Str 3, 88046 Friedrichshafen.	☏ (7541) 72404 ✆ (7541) 74986	235	01.01–10.12; 27–31.12	۱۰۱ Ⓡ 2E Ⓟ ⬚ ൟ
▲ **Friedrichstadt** Ostdeutsche Str 1, 25840 Friedrichstadt.	☏ (4881) 7984 ✆ (4881) 7984	65	16.01–30.11	۱۱۱ ۱۰۱ Ⓟ
▲ **Fröbersgrün** - Umweltstudienplatz Ortsstr 17, 08548 Syrau, Ortsteil Fröbersgrün. ⊖ jhfroebersgruen@djh-sachsen.de	☏ (37431) 3256 ✆ (37431) 88963	98	01.02–31.10 (۱۱۱01.11– 30.01)	۱۱۱ ۱۰۱ 3N Ⓟ ⬚
▲ **Fulda** Schirrmannstr 31, 36041 Fulda. ⊖ fulda@djh-hessen.de	☏ (661) 73389 ✆ (661) 74811	122	27.12.00– 23.12.01	۱۱۱ ۱۰۱ 2SW Ⓟ
▲ **Furth im Wald** Daberger Str 50, 93437 Furth im Wald (Bavaria).	☏ (9973) 9254 ✆ (9973) 2447	128	01.01–14.11; 27–31.12	۱۱۱ ۱۰۱
▲ **Füssen** (IBN) Mariahilferstr 5, 87629 Füssen (Bavaria).	☏ (8362) 7754 ✆ (8362) 2770	138	01.01–14.11; 27–31.12	۱۱۱ ۱۰۱ ⬚
▲ **Gardelegen** - Otto-Reutter-Haus Waldschnibbe, 39638 Gardelegen. ⊖ jh-gardelegen@djh-sachsen-anhalt.de	☏ (3907) 712629 ✆ (3907) 712629	90	01.01–23.12; 28–31.12	۱۱۱ ۱۰۱ Ⓟ
▲ **Garmisch-Partenkirchen** Jochstr 10, 82467 Garmisch-Partenkirchen (Bavaria).	☏ (8821) 2980 ✆ (8821) 58536	200	01.01–14.11; 27–31.12	۱۱۱ ۱۰۱ ⬚
▲ **Geesthacht** Berliner Str 117, 21502 Geesthacht. ⊖ jhgeesthacht@djh-nordmark.de	☏ (4152) 2356 ✆ (4152) 77918	127	06.01–09.12	۱۱۱ ۱۰۱ ઙ Ⓟ ൟ
Gehringswalde ☞Warmbad				
▲ **Gerolstein** Zur Büschkapelle 1, 54568 Gerolstein. ⊖ jh-gerolstein@djh-info.de	☏ (6591) 4745 ✆ (6591) 7243	184	01.01–23.12; 27–31.12	۱۱۱ ۱۰۱ ઙ [CC]
▲ **Gersfeld** Jahnstr 6, 36129 Gersfeld. ⊖ gersfeld@djh-hessen.de	☏ (6654) 340 ✆ (6654) 7788	107	27.12.00– 23.12.01	۱۱۱ ۱۰۱ 0.5SE Ⓟ
▲ **Geyer** Anton-Günther-Weg 3, 09468 Geyer. ⊖ jhgeyer@djh-sachsen.de	☏ (37346) 1364 ✆ (37346) 1770	93	☍	۱۱۱ ۱۰۱ Ⓡ 2W Ⓟ
▲ **Gießen** Richard-Schirrmann-Weg 53, 35398 Giessen. ⊖ giessen@djh-hessen.de	☏ (641) 65879 ✆ (641) 9605502	75	27.12.00– 23.12.01	۱۱۱ ۱۰۱ 3W Ⓟ
▲ **Glörsee** 58339 Breckerfeld. ⊖ jh-gloersee@djh-wl.de	☏ (2338) 434 ✆ (2338) 3674	124	15.01–15.12	۱۰۱ Ⓟ
▲ **Gommern** Manheimerstr 12, 39245 Gommern. ⊖ jh-gommern@djh-sachsen-anhalt.de	☏ (39200) 40080 ✆ (39200) 40082	100	01.01–23.12; 28–31.12	۱۰۱ Ⓟ ⬚

Location/Address	Telephone No. Fax No.	Beds	Opening Dates	Facilities
▲ **Göppingen** - JH Hohenstaufen Schottengasse 45, 73037 Göppingen.	☎ (7165) 438 ❻ (7165) 1418	128	03.01–27.11	⑩ P
▲ **Gorenzen** Hagen 2-4, 06343 Gorenzen. ⓔ jh-gorenzen@djh-sachsen-anhalt.de	☎ (34782) 20384; (34782) 21356 ❻ (34782) 21357	125	01.01–23.12; 28–31.12	♦♦♦ ⑩ & P
▲ **Görlitz** - "Friedensgrenze" Goethestr 17, 02826 Görlitz.	☎ (3581) 406510 ❻ (3581) 406510	90	📅	♦♦♦ ⑩ 1 S P
▲ **Goslar** Rammelsberger Str 25, 38644 Goslar.	☎ (5321) 22240 ❻ (5321) 41376	168	27.12.00– 23.12.01	♦♦♦ ⑩ & P
▲ **Gößweinstein** Etzdorferstr 6, 91327 Gößweinstein (Bavaria).	☎ (9242) 259 ❻ (9242) 7135	129	16.01–30.11	♦♦♦ ⑩
▲ **Göttingen** Habichtsweg 2, 37075 Göttingen. ⓔ jh-goettingen@djh-hannover.de	☎ (551) 57622 ❻ (551) 43887	161	27.12.00– 23.12.01	♦♦♦ ⑩ & P
▲ **Gotha** Mozartstr. 1, Postfach 100246, 99852 Gotha.	☎ (3621) 854008 ❻ (3621) 854008	120	28.12.00– 23.12.01	♦♦♦ ⑩ Ⓡ P
▲ **Graal-Müritz** An der Jugendherberge 32, 18181 Seeheilbad Graal-Müritz. ⓔ jh-graal-mueritz@t-online.de	☎ (38206) 77520 ❻ (38206) 77204	80	01.04–31.10	♦♦♦ ⑩ Ⓡ P
▲ **Grabow** Jugendherberge 01, 19300 Grabow.	☎ (38756) 27954; (38756) 27954; 01723896097 ❻ (38756) 27954	48	30.12.00– 19.12.01	♦♦♦ ⑩ Ⓡ
▲ **Gräfenroda** - "Olga Benario" Waldstr 134, 99330 Gräfenroda.	☎ (36205) 76290 ❻ (36205) 76421	60	27.12.00– 23.12.01	♦♦♦ ⑩ Ⓡ P
▲ **Grävenwiesbach** - Richard-Schirrmann-JH Hasselborner Str. 20, 61279 Grävenwiesbach. ⓔ graevenwiesbach@djh-hessen.de	☎ (6086) 520 ❻ (6086) 970352	150	27.12.00– 23.12.01	♦♦♦ ⑩ 2.5 NE P
▲ **Greifswald** Pestalozzistr. 11/12, D-17489 Greifswald. ⓔ jh-greifswald@t-online.de		132	30.12.00– 21.12.01	♦♦♦ ⑩ Ⓡ 1 SE & P ☕
▲ **Greiz** - "Juri Gagarin" Amselstieg 12, 07973 Greiz.	☎ (3661) 2176 ❻ (3661) 687808	92	28.12.00– 23.12.01	♦♦♦ ⑩ Ⓡ P 🗄 ☕
▲ **Grethen** Naturfreundehaus "Leipziger Haus" Herbergsweg 5, 04668 Parthenstein.	☎ (3437) 763449 ❻ (3437) 763449	107	📅	♦♦♦ ⑩ & P
▲ **Groß Reken** Coesfelder Str 18, 48734 Reken. ⓔ jh-gross.reken@djh-wl.de	☎ (2864) 1023 ❻ (2864) 2044	126	27.12.00– 23.12.01	♦♦♦ ⑩ P
▲ **Grumbach** - "Raummühle" Jöhstädter Str 19, 09477 Jöhstadt.	☎ (37343) 2288 ❻ (37343) 88003	62	📅	♦♦♦ ⑩ 2 NW P 🗄
▲ **Günzburg** Schillerstr 12, 89312 Günzburg (Bavaria).	☎ (8221) 34487 ❻ (8221) 31390	34	16.01–14.11	♦♦♦ ⑩
▲ **Güstrow-Schabernack** Heidberg 33, 18273 Güstrow. ⓔ jh-guestrow@t-online.de	☎ (3843) 840044 ❻ (3843) 840045	110	18.01–20.12	♦♦♦ ⑩ Ⓡ 6 SE P 🗄 ☕

Location/Address	Telephone No. Fax No.	Beds	Opening Dates	Facilities
▲ **Gunzenhausen** Spitalstr. 3, 91710 Gunzenhausen (Bavaria).	☎ (9831) 67020 🖷 (9831) 670211	132	🔟	⫯⫯ ¶⚬¶ ℝ 0.5 N 🚹 ☞ P 🅾
▲ **Gütersloh** "Haus der Jugend und des Sports", Wiesenstr 40, 33330 Gütersloh. ✉ jghgt@t-online.de	☎ (5241) 822181 🖷 (5241) 822184	67	08.01–13.07; 13.08–14.12	⫯⫯ ¶⚬¶ 🚹 P
▲ **Hagen** Eppenhauser Str 65a, 58093 Hagen. ✉ jh-hagen@djh-wl.de	☎ (2331) 50254 🖷 (2331) 588576	133	27.12.00– 23.12.01	⫯⫯ ¶⚬¶ P
▲ **Hahnenklee** Hahnenkleer Str 11, 38644 Goslar - OT Hahnenklee- Bockswiese.	☎ (5325) 2256 🖷 (5325) 3524	122	27.12.00– 23.12.01	⫯⫯ ¶⚬¶ P
▲ **Haidmühle** - JH Frauenberg Frauenberg 45, 94145 Haidmühle (Bavaria).	☎ (8556) 467 🖷 (8556) 1021	157	01.01–14.11; 27–31.12	⫯⫯ ¶⚬¶ 🅾
▲ **Haldensleben** Bornsche Str 94, 39340 Haldensleben.	☎ (3904) 40386 🖷 (3904) 40386	40	01.01–23.12; 28–31.12	⫯⫯ ¶⚬¶ ☞ P 🅾
▲ **Halle** **August-Bebel-Str 48a, 06108 Halle.** ✉ jh-halle@djh-sachsen-anhalt.de	☎ (345) 2024716 🖷 (345) 2025172	72	01.01–23.12; 28–31.12	⫯⫯ ¶⚬¶ P 🅾
Hallwangen ☞Dornstetten				
▲ **Haltern** Stockwieser Damm 255, 45721 Haltern/Stausee. ✉ jh-haltern@djh-wl.de	☎ (2364) 2258 🖷 (2364) 169604	138	27.12.00– 23.12.01	⫯⫯ ¶⚬¶ P
▲ **Hamburg** - Auf dem Stintfang (IBN) **Alfred-Wegener-Weg 5, 20459 Hamburg.** ✉ jh-stintfang@t-online.de	☎ (40) 313488; ⫯⫯ ℝ (40) 3191037 🖷 (40) 315407	332	05.02–23.12; 27–31.12	⫯⫯ ¶⚬¶ ℝ 2SW 🚹 ☞ 🅾 🚲
▲ **Hamburg** (IBN) JGH "Horner-Rennbahn", Rennbahnstr 100, 22111 Hamburg. ✉ jgh-hamburg@t-online.de	☎ (40) 6511671 🖷 (40) 6556516	265	01.01–04.02; 05.03–22.12	⫯⫯ ¶⚬¶ 5E 🚹 ☞ P 🚲
▲ **Hameln** Fischbecker Str 33, 31785 Hameln.	☎ (5151) 3425 🖷 (5151) 42316	106	27.12.00– 23.12.01	⫯⫯ ¶⚬¶ 🚹 P
▲ **Hamm** Jugendgästehaus "Sylverberg", Ostenallee 101, 59071 Hamm.	☎ (2381) 83837 🖷 (2381) 83844	60	27.12.00– 23.12.01	¶⚬¶ P
▲ **Hankensbüttel** Helmrichsweg 24, 29386 Hankensbüttel.	☎ (5832) 2500 🖷 (5832) 6596	142	27.12.00– 23.12.01	⫯⫯ ¶⚬¶ 🚹 P
▲ **Hannover** **Ferdinand-Wilhelm-Fricke-Weg 1, 30169 Hannover.** ✉ jh-hannover@djh-hannover.de	☎ (511) 1317674 🖷 (511) 18555	317	27.12.00– 23.12.01	⫯⫯ ¶⚬¶ 2S 🚹 P ☞
▲ **Hann.Münden** Prof-Oelkers-Str 10, 34346 Hann.Münden.	☎ (5541) 8853 🖷 (5541) 73439	135	27.12.00– 23.12.01	⫯⫯ ¶⚬¶ P
Hardter Wald ☞**Mönchengladbach**				

Location/Address	Telephone No. Fax No.	Beds	Opening Dates	Facilities
▲ Haren/EMS "St Nikolaus- JH", Nikolausweg 17, 49733 Haren (EMS).	☎ (5932) 2726	85	01.03–31.10	ᵻᵻᵻ ⵑⓄⵑ ℙ
▲ Hartenstein Salzlecke 10, 91235 Hartenstein (Bavaria).	☎ (9152) 1296 ⒻⒶⓍ (9152) 1328	68	16.01–30.11	ⵑⓄⵑ
▲ Hattingen Jugendbildungsstätte Welper, Falken-Freizeitwerk, Hüttenbauvereinigung Welper eV, Rathenaustrasse 59a, 45527 Hattingen-Welper.	☎ (2324) 94640 ⒻⒶⓍ (2324) 946494	104	27.12.00– 23.12.01	ⵑⓄⵑ ℙ
▲ Heide Poststr 4, 25746 Heide. ℮ jhheide@djh-nordmark.de	☎ (481) 71575 ⒻⒶⓍ (481) 72901	82	01.02–22.12	ᵻᵻᵻ ⵑⓄⵑ ⅃ ℙ ⤿
▲ Heidelberg Tiergartenstr 5, 69120 Heidelberg. ℮ jh-heidelberg@t-online.de	☎ (6221) 412066 ⒻⒶⓍ (6221) 402559	440	01.01–23.12; 27–31.12	ᵻᵻᵻ ⵑⓄⵑ Ⓡ 4NW ℙ ⊡
▲ Heidenheim Liststr 15, 89518 Heidenheim.	☎ (7321) 42045 ⒻⒶⓍ (7321) 949045	128	03.01–19.11	ᵻᵻᵻ ⵑⓄⵑ ⅃ ℙ
▲ Heilbronn - JH Rheinhardt Schirrmannstr 9, 74074 Heilbronn.	☎ (7131) 172961 ⒻⒶⓍ (7131) 164345	130	10.01–11.12	ⵑⓄⵑ ℙ ⊡
▲ Heldrungen - "Wasserburg" Schloßstr. 13, 06577 Heldrungen. ℮ jh-heldrungen@gmx.de	☎ (34673) 91224 ⒻⒶⓍ (34673) 98136	52	28.12.00– 23.12.01	ᵻᵻᵻ ⵑⓄⵑ Ⓡ ℙ
▲ Helgoland "Haus der Jugend", Postfach 580, 27487 Helgoland. ℮ haus-der-jugend-helgoland@t-online.de	☎ (4725) 341 ⒻⒶⓍ (4725) 7467	146	01.04–31.10	ᵻᵻᵻ ⵑⓄⵑ
▲ Hellenthal Platis 3, 53940 Hellenthal. ℮ jh-hellenthal@djh-rheinland.de	☎ (2482) 2238 ⒻⒶⓍ (2482) 2557	161	02.01–22.12	ᵻᵻᵻ ⵑⓄⵑ ⅃ ☞ ℙ ⊡
▲ Helmarshausen Gottsbürener Str. 15, 34385 Bad Karlshafen-Helmarshausen. ℮ helmarshausen@djh-hessen.de	☎ (5672) 1027 ⒻⒶⓍ (5672) 2976	178	27.12.00– 23.12.01	ᵻᵻᵻ ⵑⓄⵑ 1 SE ℙ
▲ Heppenheim JH "Starkenburg", 64646 Heppenheim. ℮ starkenburg@djh-hessen.de	☎ (6252) 77323 ⒻⒶⓍ (6252) 78185	121	25.12.00– 21.12.01	ᵻᵻᵻ ⵑⓄⵑ Ⓡ 1.5 NE ℙ
▲ Heringsdorf Puschkinstr 7/9, 17424 Seebad Heringsdorf. ℮ info@jh_heringsdorf@t-online.de	☎ (38378) 22325 ⒻⒶⓍ (38378) 32301	167	01.02–30.11	ᵻᵻᵻ ⵑⓄⵑ Ⓡ ⅃ ℙ
▲ Hermeskeil Adolf-Kolping-Str 4, 54411 Hermeskeil. ℮ jh-hermeskeil@djh-info.de	☎ (6503) 3097 ⒻⒶⓍ (6503) 6146	111	01.01–23.12; 27–31.12	ᵻᵻᵻ ⵑⓄⵑ ⒺⒸⒸ ℙ
Herrenwies ☞Forbach				
▲ Hessenstein, Burg 34516 Vöhl Ederbringhausen. ℮ burghessenstein@djh-hessen.de	☎ (6455) 300 ⒻⒶⓍ (6455) 8771	126	27.12.00– 23.12.01	ᵻᵻᵻ ⵑⓄⵑ 12S ℙ

Location/Address	Telephone No. Fax No.	Beds	Opening Dates	Facilities
▲ **Hilchenbach** Wilhelm-Münker-Str 9, 57271 Hilchenbach. ⊕ jh-hilchenbach@djh-wl.de	☎ (2733) 4396 ✆ (2733) 8085	86	01.02–23.12	⑪ P
▲ **Hilders** Jugendherberge, 36115 Hilders. ⊕ hilders@djh-hessen.de	☎ (6681) 365 ✆ (6681) 8429	144	27.12.00– 23.12.01	⑪⑪ ⑪ 1.5E P
▲ **Hildesheim** Schirrmannweg 4, 31139 Hildesheim.	☎ (5121) 42717 ✆ (5121) 47847	104	27.12.00– 23.12.01	⑪⑪ ⑪ ♿ P
▲ **Hitzacker** Wolfsschlucht 2 (An der Elbuferstrasse), 29456 Hitzacker.	☎ (5862) 244 ✆ (5862) 7767	165	27.12.00– 23.12.01	⑪⑪ ⑪ ♿ P ▣
▲ **Hochspeyer** - Naturpark-und Waldjugendherberge Trippstadter Strasse 150, 67691 Hochspeyer. ⊕ jh-hochspeyer@djh-info.de	☎ (6305) 336 ✆ (6305) 5152	149	01.01–23.12; 27–31.12	⑪⑪ ⑪ CC P ☕
▲ **Hof** Beethovenstr 44, 95032 Hof (Bavaria).	☎ (9281) 93277 ✆ (9281) 92016	91	01.01–30.11; 29–31.12	⑪⑪ ⑪ ▣
▲ **Hohe Fahrt** Am Edersee, 34516 Vöhl. ⊕ hohefahrt@djh-hessen.de	☎ (5635) 251 ✆ (5635) 8142	230	27.12.00– 23.12.01	⑪⑪ ⑪ R 4SW P
▲ **Hohenberg** Auf der Burg, 95691 Hohenberg (Bavaria). ⊕ sswhohenberg@t-online.de	☎ (9233) 77260 ✆ (9233) 772611	130	01.01–20.12; 27–31.12	⑪⑪ ⑪ ▣
Hohenstaufen ☞Göppingen				
▲ **Hoherodskopf** Jugendherberge, 63679 Schotten. ⊕ hoherodskopf@djh-hessen.de	☎ (6044) 2760 ✆ (6044) 784	112	27.12.00– 23.12.01	⑪⑪ 8NE P
▲ **Hohnstein** - Naturfreundehause "Burg Hohnstein" Am Markt 1, 01848 Hohnstein.	☎ (35975) 81202 ✆ (35975) 81203	250	▣	⑪⑪ ⑪
▲ **Holzminden** Am Steinhof, 37603 Holzminden.	☎ (5531) 4411 ✆ (5531) 120630	123	27.12.00– 23.12.01	⑪⑪ ⑪ P
▲ **Homburg** Sickinger Str 12, 66424 Homburg. ⊕ jh-homburg@djh-info.de	☎ (6841) 3679 ✆ (6841) 120220	71	01.01–23.12; 27–31.12	⑪ CC P
▲ **Hormersdorf** Am Greifenbachstauweiher, 09468 Geyer. ⊕ jhhormersdorf@djh-sachsen.de	☎ (37346) 1396 ✆ (37346) 1645	205	▣	⑪⑪ ⑪ R 4SW ♿ P ☕
▲ **Horn-Bad Meinberg** Jahnstr 36, 32805 Horn-Bad Meinberg. ⊕ jh-horn.bad.meinburg@djh-wl.de	☎ (5234) 2534 ✆ (5234) 69199	122	20.01–23.12	⑪ P
▲ **Hörnum** Friesenplatz 2, 25997 Hörnum/Sylt. ⊕ jhhoernum@djh-nordmark.de	☎ (4651) 880294 ✆ (4651) 881392	170	16.01–30.11	⑪⑪ ⑪ P
▲ **Höxter** "EURO-Umweltstudienplatz", An der Wilhelmshöhe 59, 37671 Höxter. ⊕ jh-hoexter@djh-wl.de	☎ (5271) 2233 ✆ (5271) 1237	132	06.01–22.12	⑪ P

Location/Address	Telephone No. Fax No.	Beds	Opening Dates	Facilities
▲ **Hude** Linteler Str 3, 27798 Hude. ✉ jh.hude.engstfeld@t-online.de	☎ (4408) 414 🖷 (4408) 970322	90	01.03–31.10	⑩ 🅿
▲ **Hürth** "Villehaus" Adolf- Dasbach-Weg 5, 50354 Hürth.	☎ (2233) 42463 🖷 (2233) 16351	72	01.01–23.12; 27–31.12	⑯ ⑩ 🅿
▲ **Husum** Schobüller Str 34, 25813 Husum. ✉ jhhusum@djh-nordmark.de	☎ (4841) 2714 🖷 (4841) 81568	181	01.02–22.12	⑯ ⑩ ♿ ✇ 🅿 ◨ ☎
▲ **Idar-Oberstein** Alte Treibe 23, 55743 Idar-Oberstein. ✉ jh-idar-oberstein@djh-info.de	☎ (6781) 24366 🖷 (6781) 26712	128	01.01–23.12; 27–31.12	⑯ ⑩ ♿ CC 🅿 ☎
▲ **Igersheim** Erlenbachtalstr 44, 97999 Igershcim.	☎ (7931) 6373 🖷 (7931) 52795	162	10.01–11.12	⑯ ⑩ 🅿
▲ **Ihrlerstein** - JH Kelheim Kornblumenweg 1, 93346 Ihrlerstein (Bavaria).	☎ (9441) 3309 🖷 (9441) 21792	122	01.01–14.12	⑯ ⑩ ◨
▲ **Ilmenau** Am Stollen 49, 98693 Ilmenau. ✉ jh-ilmenau@t-online.de	☎ (3677) 884681 🖷 (3677) 884682	130	29.12.00– 22.12.01	⑯ ⑩ Ⓡ ♿ 🅿
▲ **Ingolstadt** Friedhofstr 4 1/2, 85049 Ingolstadt (Bavaria).	☎ (841) 34177 🖷 (841) 910178	84	01.02–14.12	⑯ ⑩ ♿
▲ **Inselsberg** - "Großer Inselsberg" 98599 Brotterode.	☎ (36259) 62329 🖷 (36259) 30821	63	28.12.00– 22.12.01	⑩ Ⓡ
▲ **Inzmühlen** Wehlener Weg 10, 21256 Handeloh. ✉ jhinzmuehlen@djh-nordmark.de	☎ (4188) 342 🖷 (4188) 7858	164	01.02–22.12	⑯ ⑩ ♿ 🅿 🚲
▲ **Isny** - Georg-Sulzberger-JH Dekan-Marquardt-Str 18, 88316 Isny.	☎ (7562) 2550 🖷 (7562) 55547	131	10.01–27.11	⑩ 🅿
▲ **Itzehoe** Juliengardeweg 13, 25524 Itzehoe. ✉ djh@iz-web.de	☎ (4821) 62270 🖷 (4821) 5710	75	16.01–14.12	⑯ ⑩ 🅿 🚲
▲ **Jena** - Internationales Jugendgästehaus des Ib Am Herrenberge 3, 07745 Jena. ✉ jugendgaestehaus.jena@ internationaler-bund.de	☎ (3641) 687230 🖷 (3641) 687202	140	06.01–19.12	⑯ ⑩ Ⓡ 3.5 W CC 🅿
▲ **Jever** Mooshütter Weg 12,26441 Jever. ✉ jugendherberge-jever@t-online.de	☎ (4461) 3590 🖷 (4461) 3565	50	01.04–31.10	⑯ ⑩
▲ **Johanngeorgenstadt** Hospitalstr 5, 08349 Johanngeorgenstadt. ✉ jhjohanngeorgenstadt@djh-sachsen.de	☎ (3773) 882194 🖷 (3773) 889150	60	🗓	⑯ ⑩ 1 S 🅿 ◨
▲ **Jonsdorf** - "Dreiländereck" Hainstr 14, 02796 Jonsdorf. ✉ jhjonsdorf@djh-sachsen.de	☎ (35844) 72130 🖷 (35844) 72131	72	🗓	⑯ ⑩ 🅿

Josefsthal ☞**Schliersee**

Location/Address	Telephone No. Fax No.	Beds	Opening Dates	Facilities
▲ **Juist** Loogster Pad 20, 26571 Juist, (North Sea). ⊖ djh-juist@web.de	☏ (4935) 92910 ✆ (4935) 8294	294	01.01–31.10	ⅲ �ⓞ ⒭ 1.5W
▲ **Kandern** - Platzhof Auf der Scheideck, 79400 Kandern.	☏ (7626) 484 ✆ (7626) 6809	69	01.03–31.10	ⅲ ⓞ ℗
▲ **Kappeln** Eckernförder Str 2, 24376 Kappeln. ⊖ jhkappeln@djh-nordmark.de	☏ (4642) 8550 ✆ (4642) 81086	170	06.01–22.12	ⅲ ⓞ ♿ ℗ ⓐ ⏍
▲ **Karlsruhe** Moltkestr 24, 76133 Karlsruhe.	☏ (721) 28248 ✆ (721) 27647	167	27.12.00– 22.12.01	ⅲ ⓞ 4NW ℗
▲ **Kassel** Schenkendorfstr 18, 34119 Kassel. ⊖ kassel@djh-hessen.de	☏ (561) 776455; (561) 776933 ✆ (561) 776832	209	02.01–23.12; 27–30.12	ⅲ ⓞ ⒭ 1.5NW ♿ ☕
▲ **Katzhütte** Bahnhofstr 82, 98746 Katzhütte. ⊖ jhkatzhuette@t-online.de	☏ (36781) 37785 ✆ (36781) 33806	70	28.12.00– 22.12.01	ⓞ ⒭
▲ **Kehl** Altrheinweg 11, 77694 Kehl.	☏ (7851) 2330 ✆ (7851) 76608	122	27.12.00– 22.12.01	ⅲ ⓞ 1SW ℗
Kelheim ☞**Ihrlerstein**				
▲ **Kempten** Saarlandstr 1, 87437 Kempten (Bavaria).	☏ (831) 73663 ✆ (831) 770381	82	01.01–31.10; 28–31.12	ⓞ
▲ **Kevelaer** Am Michelsweg 11, 47626 Kevelaer. ⊖ jh-kevelaer@djh-rheinland.de	☏ (2832) 8267 ✆ (2832) 899432	130	01.01–23.12; 27–31.12	ⅲ ⓞ ⚲ ℗
▲ **Kiel** (IBN) Johannesstr 1, 24143 Kiel. ⊖ jhkiel@djh-nordmark.de	☏ (431) 731488 ✆ (431) 735723	265	27.12.00– 23.12.01	ⅲ ⓞ 2SE ♿ ℗
▲ **Kirchberg** Gaggstatter Str 35, 74592 Kirchberg.	☏ (7954) 230 ✆ (7954) 1319	90	24.01–23.12	ⓞ ℗
▲ **Kleve** St Annaberg 2, 47533 Kleve Materborn. ⊖ jh-kleve@djh-rheinland.de	☏ (2821) 23671 ✆ (2821) 24778	106	01.01–23.12; 27–31.12	ⅲ ⓞ ℗
▲ **Klingenthal** - "Aschberg" Grenzweg 22, 08248 Klingenthal. ⊖ jhklingenthal@djh-sachsen.de	☏ (37467) 22094 ✆ (37467) 22099	122	⏍12	ⅲ ⓞ ⒭ 3N ℗
▲ **Koblenz** Festung Ehrenbreitstein, 56077 Koblenz. ⊖ jh-koblenz@djh-info.de	☏ (261) 97287-0 ✆ (261) 97287-30	183	01.01–23.12; 27–31.12	ⅲ ⓞ 6NE ♿ ⊏CC⊐ ℗ ⏍
▲ **Kochel** Badstr 2, 82431 Kochel (Bavaria).	☏ (8851) 5296 ✆ (8851) 7019	31	01.01–14.11; 27–31.12	ⓞ
▲ **Köln** - Deutz (IBN) **Siegesstr 5a, 50679 Köln.** ⊖ jh-koeln-deutz@djh-rheinland.de	☏ (221) 814711 ✆ (221) 884425	320	01.01–23.12; 27–31.12	ⅲ ⓞ 3E ♿ ℗ ⓐ
▲ **Köln** - Riehl **An der Schanz 14, 50735 Köln.** ⊖ jh-koeln-riehl@djh-rheinland.de	☏ (221) 767081 ✆ (221) 761555	366	01.01–23.12; 27–31.12	ⅲ ⓞ 6NE ♿ ℗ ⓐ ⏍

Location/Address	Telephone No. Fax No.	Beds	Opening Dates	Facilities
▲ **Königsberg** Schlossberg 10, 97486 Königsberg (Bavaria).	☎ (9525) 237 ❺ (9525) 8114	89	08.01–14.12	ⅲ ⦿
▲ **Königsbronn** Weilerweg 12, 89551 Königsbronn-Ochsenberg.	☎ (7328) 6600 ❺ (7328) 7451	116	01.02–23.12	ⅲ ⦿ ⅋ ▣
▲ **Konstanz** - Otto-Möricke-Turm Zur Allmannshöhe 18, 78464 Konstanz.	☎ (7531) 32260 ❺ (7531) 31163	160	🚏	ⅲ ⦿ 5NE ▣
▲ **Korbach** Enser Str 9, 34497 Korbach. ℮ korbach@djh-hessen.de	☎ (5631) 8360 ❺ (5631) 4835	98	27.12.00– 23.12.01	ⅲ ⦿ 0.5W ⅋
▲ **Köriser See** Am See 5, 15746 Groß Köris. ℮ jh-koeriser-see@jugendherberge.de	☎ (33766) 62730 ❺ (33766) 62734	78	🚏(Ⓡ 01.11.00– 28.02.01)	ⅲ ⦿ Ⓡ
▲ **Köthener See** Dorfstr 20, 15748 Märkisch-Bucholz. ℮ jh-koethener-see@jugendherberge.de	☎ (33765) 80555 ❺ (33765) 84870	110	🚏(Ⓡ 01.11.00– 28.02.01)	ⅲ ⦿ Ⓡ ⧉
▲ **Kretzschau** 06712 Kretzschau. ℮ jh-kretzschau@djh-sachsen-anhalt.de	☎ (3441) 212678; (3441) 210173 ❺ (3441) 210174	204	01.01–23.12; 28–31.12	ⅲ ⦿ ⅋ ▣
▲ **Kreuth** - JH Kreuth am Tegernsee Nördliche Hauptstr 91, 83708 Kreuth (Bavaria).	☎ (8029) 99560 ❺ (8029) 995629	103	01.01–31.10; 27–31.12	ⅲ ⦿ Ⓡ ⧉
▲ **Kronach** Festung 1, 96317 Kronach (Bavaria).	☎ (9261) 94412 ❺ (9261) 629109	106	01.02–14.12 (28.12–01.01 ⅲ only)	⦿ ⧉
▲ **Kühlungsborn** Dünenstr 4, 18225 Ostseebad Kühlungsborn. ℮ jugendherberge-kuehlungsborn@t-online.de	☎ (38293) 17270 ❺ (38293) 17279	124	01.04–31.10	ⅲ ⦿ Ⓡ ⅋ ▣
▲ **Lam** Jugendherbergsweg 1, 93462 Lam (Bavaria).	☎ (9943) 1068 ❺ (9943) 2936	130	01.01–31.10; 27–31.12	ⅲ ⦿
▲ **Landshut** Richard-Schirrmann-Weg 6, 84028 Landshut (Bavaria). ℮ stadt.landshut.jh@landshut.org	☎ (871) 23449 ❺ (871) 274947	100	08.01–22.12	ⅲ ⦿ ⅋ ✒
▲ **Langenwetzendorf** Greizerstr. (Am Schwimmbad), 07957 Langenwetzendorf.	☎ (36625) 20305 ❺ (36625) 52023	72	28.12.00– 22.12.01	⦿ Ⓡ ▣
▲ **Langeoog** Domäne Melkhörn, 26465 Langeoog, (North Sea).	☎ (4972) 276 ❺ (4972) 6694	126	01.04–31.10	⦿ Ⓡ 5E
▲ **Laubach** Felix-Klipstein-Weg 35, 35321 Laubach. ℮ laubach@djh-hessen.de	☎ (6405) 1376 ❺ (6405) 7046	122	Closed in 2001 for renovation	⦿ 2N ▣
▲ **Lauenburg** Am Sportplatz 7, 21481 Lauenburg. ℮ jhlauenburg@djh-nordmark.de	☎ (4153) 2598 ❺ (4153) 2310	130	06.01–22.12	ⅲ ⦿ ▣ ♿

Location/Address	Telephone No. Fax No.	Beds	Opening Dates	Facilities
▲ **Lauterbach** Fritz-Ebel-Allee 50, 36341 Lauterbach. e lauterbach@djh-hessen.de	☎ (6641) 2181 f (6641) 61200	172	27.12.00– 23.12.01	♐ †◯† ⦿ 4NE P
▲ **Leer** Süderkreuzstr 7, 26789 Leer.	☎ (491) 2126 f (491) 61576	94	01.03–31.10	†◯† ⦿
▲ **Leinburg** - JH Weissenbrunn Badstr 15, 91227 Leinburg (Bavaria).	☎ (9187) 1529 f (9187) 5920	60	16.01–30.11	⦿
▲ **Leipzig** - Leipzig-Centrum Volksgartenstrasse 24, 04347 Leipzig. e jhleipzig@djh-sachsen.de	☎ (341) 245700 f (341) 2457012	176	01.01–22.12; 28–31.12	†◯† ⦿ R 4NE P
▲ **Lenggries** Jugendherbergsstr 10, 83661 Lenggries (Bavaria).	☎ (8042) 2424 f (8042) 4532	93	01.01–30.11; 27–31.12	⦿ P
▲ **Lichtenfels** Alte Coburger Str 43, 96215 Lichtenfels (Bavaria).	☎ (9571) 71039 f (9571) 71877	87	01.02–14.12	†◯† ⦿ P
▲ **Lichtenstein** An der Jugendherberge 3, 09350 Lichtenstein. e jhlichtenstein@djh-sachsen.de	☎ (37204) 2718 f (37204) 87387	80	12	†◯† ⦿ 1SE P
▲ **Liepnitzsee** Wandlitzer Str 6, 16359 Lanke/Ützdorf. e jh-liepnitzsee@jugendherberge.de	☎ (33397) 21659 f (33397) 62750	39	12 (R 01.11.00– 28.02.01)	†◯† ⦿ R
▲ **Limburg** Auf dem Guckucksberg, 65549 Limburg. e limburg@djh-hessen.de	☎ (6431) 41493 f (6431) 43873	162	27.12.00– 23.12.01	†◯† ⦿ 1.5S P
▲ **Lindau** Herbergsweg 11, 88131 Lindau (Bavaria). e jhlindau@djh-bayern.de	☎ (8382) 96710 f (8382) 967150	240	12	†◯† ⦿ 5NW ♿ P ⌨ ☕
▲ **Lindlar** Umweltstudienplatz, Jugendherberge 30, 51789 Lindlar. e jh-lindlar@djh-rheinland.de	☎ (2266) 5264 f (2266) 45517	170	01.03–23.12; 27–31.12	†◯† ⦿ P
▲ **Lingen** Lengericher Str 62, 49811 Lingen. e jhlingen@aol.com	☎ (591) 973060 f (591) 76954	152	01.01–14.12	†◯† ⦿ ♿ P
▲ **Linsengericht** Geislitz, 63589 Linsengericht. e linsengericht@djh-hessen.de	☎ (6051) 72029 f (6051) 75694	124	27.12.00– 23.12.01	†◯† ⦿ 6S P
▲ **List** JH Mövenberg, 25992 List/Sylt. e jhlist@djh-nordmark.de	☎ (4651) 870397 f (4651) 871039	333	27.12.00- 04.11.01	†◯† ⦿ P ⌨ 🚲
▲ **Löhne-Gohfeld** TV Die Naturfreunde e.V., In den Tannen 63, 32584 Löhne.	☎ (5731) 81012 f (5731) 81031	84	27.12.00– 23.12.01	†◯† ⦿ ♿ P
▲ **Lohr** Brunnenwiesenweg 13, 97816 Lohr (Bavaria).	☎ (9352) 2444 f (9352) 70873	94	01.02–14.12	†◯† ⦿
▲ **Lörrach** Steinenweg 40, 79540 Lörrach.	☎ (7621) 47040 f (7621) 18156	168	27.12.00– 22.12.01	†◯† ⦿ 3SE ♿ P

Location/Address	Telephone No. Fax No.	Beds	Opening Dates	Facilities
▲ Lübben Zum Wendenfürsten 8, 15907 Lübben. ⓔ jh-luebben@jugendherberge.de	❶ (3546) 3046 ❻ (3546) 182597	127	🏠(Ⓡ) 01.11.00– 28.02.01)	♙♙ ⦿ Ⓡ 2.5SE 🅶
▲ Lübeck IBN Am Gertrudenkirchhof 4, 23568 Lübeck. ⓔ jhluebeck@djh-nordmark.de	❶ (451) 33433 ❻ (451) 34540	217	01.01–23.12; 27–31.12	♙♙ ⦿ 2NE ♿ 🅿 🅶
▲ Lübeck - JGH Mengstr 33, 23552 Lübeck. ⓔ jghluebeck@djh-nordmark.de	❶ (451) 7020399 ❻ (451) 77012	73	06.01–22.12	♙♙ ⦿ 1W
▲ Ludwigsburg JH + YGH Gemsenbergstr 21, 71640 Ludwigsburg.	❶ (7141) 51564 ❻ (7141) 59440	121	10.01–17.12	♙♙ ⦿ 🅿
▲ Ludwigstein "Jugendburg", 37214 Witzenhausen.	❶ (5542) 501710 ❻ (5542) 501712	170	🏠	♙♙ ⦿ Ⓡ 🅿
▲ Lüneburg Soltauer Str 133, 21335 Lüneburg.	❶ (4131) 41864 ❻ (4131) 45747	105	27.12.00– 23.12.01	♙♙ ⦿ 🅿
▲ Maasholm 24404 Maasholm. ⓔ jhkappeln@djh-nordmark.de	❶ (4642) 8550 ❻ (4642) 81086	32	13.04–31.10	♙♙ ⦿ Ⓡ ♂ 🅿
▲ Magdeburg, Magdeburger Hof Leiterstrasse 10, 39104 Magdeburg. ⓔ jh-magdeburg@djh-sachsen-anhalt.de	❶ (391) 5321010 ❻ (391) 5321020	250	01.01–23.12; 28–31.12	♙♙ ⦿ Ⓡ ♿ ECC ☕
Maibrunn ☞St Englmar				
▲ Mainz - Rhein-Main-Jugendherberge, Jugendgästehaus Mainz Otto-Brunfels-Schneise 4, 55130 Mainz. ⓔ jh-mainz@djh-info.de	❶ (6131) 85332 ❻ (6131) 82422	166	01.01–23.12; 27–31.12	♙♙ ⦿ Ⓡ 5SE ♿ ECC 🅿 ☕
▲ Malente Kellerseestr 48, 23714 Bad Malente-Gremsm. ⓔ jhmalente@djh-nordmark.de	❶ (4523) 1723 ❻ (4523) 2539	206	06.01–04.12	♙♙ ⦿ ♿ 🅿 ☁
▲ Malchow Platz der Freiheit 3, 17213 Malchow.	❶ (39932) 14590 ❻ (39932) 14579	131	01.02–31.10	♙♙ 🅿
▲ Manderscheid - Vulkaneifel-Jugendherberge,Jugendgästehaus Mosenbergstr 17, 54531 Manderscheid. ⓔ jh-manderscheid@djh-info.de	❶ (6572) 557 ❻ (6572) 4759	105	01.01–23.12; 27–31.12	♙♙ ⦿ ♿ ECC 🅿 ☕ 🚲
▲ Mannheim - Lindenhof Rheinpromenade 21, 68163 Mannheim.	❶ (621) 822718 ❻ (621) 824073	106	27.12.00– 22.12.01	♙♙ ⦿ 2W 🅿
▲ Marburg Jahnstr 1, 35037 Marburg. ⓔ marburg@djh-hessen.de	❶ (6421) 23461 ❻ (6421) 12191	164	27.12.00– 23.12.01	♙♙ ⦿ Ⓡ 0.5SE ♿
▲ Mardorf Warteweg 2, 31535 Neustadt-Mardorf. ⓔ jh-mardorf@djh-hannover.de	❶ (5036) 457 ❻ (5036) 1554	164	27.12.00– 23.12.01	♙♙ ⦿ ♿ 🅿
▲ Marktredwitz Wunsiedlerstr 29, 95615 Marktredwitz (Bavaria).	❶ (9231) 81082 ❻ (9231) 87346	40	🏠	⦿

Location/Address	Telephone No. Fax No.	Beds	Opening Dates	Facilities
▲ **Martinfeld** Bernteröderstr. 141, 37308 Schimberg/ OT Martinfeld. ✉ jh-martinfeld@t-online.de	☎ (36082) 89339 🖷 (36082) 90296	100	28.12.00– 23.12.01	††† ⦿ 🅿
▲ **Mauth** Jugendherbergsstr 11, 94151 Mauth (Bavaria).	☎ (8557) 289 🖷 (8557) 1581	96	01.01–31.10; 27–31.12	††† ⦿ ⬛
▲ **Mayen** Am Knüppchen 5, 56727 Mayen. ✉ jh-mayen@djh-info.de	☎ (2651) 2355 🖷 (2651) 78378	130	01.01–23.12; 27–31.12	⦿ ᴇᴄᴄ 🅿 ☕
▲ **Meinerzhagen** Bergstr. 1, 58540 Meinerzhagen. ✉ jh-meinerzhagen@djh-wl.de	☎ (2354) 2280 🖷 (2354) 14341	150	02.01–01.11; 01–23.12	⦿ ♿ 🅿
▲ **Meisdorf** Falkensteiner Weg 2B, 06463 Meisdorf. ✉ jh-meisdorf@djh-sachsen-anhalt.de	☎ (34743) 8257 🖷 (34743) 92540	101	01.01–23.12; 28–31.12	††† ⦿ ♿ 🅿 ⬛
▲ **Melle** Fr-Ludwig-Jahn-Str 1, 49324 Melle. ✉ djh-melle@t-online.de	☎ (5422) 2434 🖷 (5422) 3988	67	🔲	††† ⦿ 🅿
▲ **Melsungen** Lindenbergstr 23, 34212 Melsungen. ✉ melsungen@djh-hessen.de	☎ (5661) 2650 🖷 (5661) 51928	132	27.12.00– 23.12.01	††† ⦿ 1W ♿
▲ **Memmingen** Kempterstr 42, 87700 Memmingen (Bavaria).	☎ (8331) 494087 🖷 (8331) 494087	60	01.03–30.11	††† ⦿
▲ **Menzenschwand** OT Menzenschwand, Vorderdorfstr 10, 79837 St Blasien.	☎ (7675) 326 🖷 (7675) 1435	102	27.12.00– 22.12.01	††† ⦿ 🅿
▲ **Meppen** - Jugend-und Kulturgästehaus "Koppelschleuse Meppen" Halter Damm 1, 49716 Meppen. ✉ koppelschleuse-meppen@djh-unterweser.de	☎ (05931) 4099770 🖷 (05931) 4099773	120	01.04–31.12	††† ⦿ ♿ ᴇᴄᴄ 🅿 ⬛ ☕ 🚲
▲ **Merzalben** Tannenstr 20, 66978 Merzalben. ✉ jh-merzalben@djh-info.de	☎ (6395) 6271 🖷 (6395) 7089	103	01.01–23.12; 27–31.12	⦿ ᴇᴄᴄ
▲ **Meschede** "Haus Dortmund", Warsteiner Straße, 59872 Meschede.	☎ (291) 6666 🖷 (291) 1589	100	27.12.00– 23.12.01	††† ⦿ 🅿
▲ **Milow** Friedensstr 21, 14715 Milow. ✉ jh-milow@jugendherberge.de	☎ (3386) 280361 🖷 (3386) 280369	96	🔲(Ⓡ ††† 15.12.00– 15.02.01)	††† ⦿ Ⓡ
▲ **Mirow 21** Retzower Str, 17252 Mirow. ✉ mirow21@djh.org	☎ (39833) 20726 🖷 (39833) 22057	80	30.12.00– 19.12.01	††† ⦿ Ⓡ ♿ 🅿
▲ **Mittenwald** Buckelwiesen 7, 82481 Mittenwald (Bavaria).	☎ (8823) 1701 🖷 (8823) 2907	111	01.01–14.11; 28–31.12	††† ⦿
▲ **Möhnesee** Südufer 20, 59519 Möhnesee-Körbecke. ✉ jh-moehnesee@djh-wl.de	☎ (2924) 305 🖷 (2924) 2788	203	27.12.00– 23.12.01	††† ⦿ 🅿

Location/Address	Telephone No. Fax No.	Beds	Opening Dates	Facilities
▲ **Mölln** Am Ziegelsee 2, 23879 Mölln. ⊜ jhmoelln@djh-nordmark.de	✆ (4542) 2601 ⊕ (4542) 86718	162	28.01–14.12	ᵗᵗ ᵗᵒᵢ ℗ 🏍
▲ **Mönchengladbach** - JH "Hardter Wald" Umweltstudienplatz, Brahmsstr 156, 41169 Mönchengladbach. ⊜ jh-hardter-wald@djh-rheinland.de	✆ (2161) 560900 ⊕ (2161) 556464	131	01.01–23.12; 27–31.12	ᵗᵒᵢ Ⓡ
▲ **Monschau** - JH Burg-Monschau Auf dem Schloss 4, 52156 Monschau. ⊜ jh-monschau-burg@djh-rheinland.de	✆ (2472) 2314 ⊕ (2472) 4391	96	29.01–23.12; 27–31.12	ᵗᵒᵢ
▲ **Monschau** - JH Monschau-Hagard Hargardsgasse 5, 52156 Monschau. ⊜ jh-monschau-hargard@djh-rheinland.de	✆ (2472) 2180 ⊕ (2472) 4527	148	02.01–03.12	ᵗᵒᵢ ℗
▲ **Montabaur** Richard-Schirrmann-Str, 56410 Montabaur. ⊜ jh-montabaur@djh-info.de	✆ (2602) 5121 ⊕ (2602) 180176	136	01.01–23.12; 27–31.12	ᵗᵗ ᵗᵒᵢ ♿ ᴄᴄ ℗ ☕
▲ **Morbach** Jugendherberge und Kreisjugendzentrum Bischofsdron, Jugendherbergsstr 16, 54497 Morbach. ⊜ jh-morbach@djh-info.de	✆ (6533) 3389 ⊕ (6533) 2787	137	01.01–23.12; 27–31.12	ᵗᵒᵢ ᴄᴄ ℗
▲ **Morsbach** Obere Kirchstr 21, 51597 Morsbach. ⊜ jh-morsbach@djh-rheinland.de	✆ (2294) 8662 ⊕ (2294) 7807	166	01.01–23.12; 27–31.12	ᵗᵗ ᵗᵒᵢ ℗
▲ **Mosbach** - Mutschlers Mühle Beim Elzstadion (OT Neckarelz), 74821 Mosbach.	✆ (6261) 7191 ⊕ (6261) 61812	140	27.12.00– 22.12.01	ᵗᵗ ᵗᵒᵢ 3SW ℗ ⊡
▲ **Mosenberg** Jugendherberge, 34590 Wabern. ⊜ mosenberg@djh-hessen.de	✆ (5681) 2691 ⊕ (5681) 60208	130	27.12.00– 23.12.01	ᵗᵗ ᵗᵒᵢ 7S ℗
▲ **Müden** Wiesenweg 32, 29328 Müden.	✆ (5053) 225 ⊕ (5053) 1021	156	27.12.00– 23.12.01	ᵗᵗ ᵗᵒᵢ ♿ ℗ ⊡
▲ **Mühldorf** Friedr.-Ludwig-Jahn-Str 19, 84453 Mühldorf (Bavaria).	✆ (8631) 7370 ⊕ (8631) 7437	52	🛏	ᵗᵒᵢ ⛄
▲ **Mühlhausen** Auf dem Tonberg 1, 99974 Mühlhausen. ⊜ jh-muehlhausen@gmx.de	✆ (3601) 813318 ⊕ (3601) 813320	78	28.12.00– 21.12.01	ᵗᵗ ᵗᵒᵢ Ⓡ ♿ ℗
▲ **Mülheim** - "JH Kahlenberg" Mendener Str 3, 45470 Mülheim. ⊜ jugendherberge@stadt-mh.de	✆ (208) 382191 ⊕ (208) 382196	70	03.01–20.12 every second weekend in the month	ᵗᵗ ᵗᵒᵢ ℗
▲ **Münchehofe** Strasse der Jugend 2, 15374 Münchehofe.	✆ (33432) 8734/ 44 ⊕ (33432) 73154	96	🛏	ᵗᵗ ᵗᵒᵢ
▲ **München** - Neuhausen ⒤ᴮᴺ **Wendl-Dietrich Str 20,** **80634 München (Bavaria).** ⊜ jhmuenchen@djh-bayern.de	✆ (89) 131156 ⊕ (89) 1678745	385	01.01–30.11	ᵗᵒᵢ Ⓡ ᴄᴄ ⊡ ☕

Location/Address	Telephone No. Fax No.	Beds	Opening Dates	Facilities
▲ **München** - JGH Thalkirchen IBN **Miesingstr 4, 81379 München (Bavaria).** e jghmuenchen@djh-bayern.de	t (89) 7236550; (89) 7236560 f (89) 7242567	352	12	R CC P
▲ **Münster** - Aasee IBN **"JGH", Bismarckallee 31, 48151 Münster.** e jgh-muenster@djh-wl.de	t (0251) 5302810 f (0251) 5302850	208	01.01–23.12; 27–31.12	R 2W P
▲ **Murchin** Jugendherberge Nr 1, 17390 Murchin.	t (3971) 210732 f (3971) 210732	48	30.12.00–21.12.01	R P
▲ **Murrhardt** - Eugen-Nägele-JH Karnsberger Str 1, 71540 Murrhardt.	t (7192) 7501 f (7192) 29058	142	12	P
▲ **Mylau** - "Walderholung" 08468 Schneidenbach.	t (3765) 34584 f (3765) 64455	43	12	
▲ **Naumburg** Am Tennisplatz 9, 06618 Naumburg. e jh-naumburg@djh-sachsen-anhalt.de	t (3445) 703422 f (3445) 703422	204	01.01–23.12; 28–31.12	R P
▲ **Nebra** Altenburgstrasse 29, 06642 Nebra. e jh-nebra@djh-sachsen-anhalt.de	t (34461) 25454 f (34461) 25456	140	01.01–23.12; 28–31.12	P
▲ **Neckargemünd-Dilsberg** - JH Dilsberg OT Dilsberg, Untere Str 1, 69151 Neckargemünd.	t (6223) 2133 f (6223) 74871	77	12	P
▲ **Neidenberga** - "Schloss" Ortsstr 1, 07338 Neidenberga.	t (36737) 22262 f (36737) 32503	80	28.12.00–22.12.01	R P
▲ **Neschwitz** - Schloß Kastanienallee 1, 02699 Neschwitz.	t (35933) 30040 f (35933) 38611	61	12	P
▲ **Nettetal-Hinsbeck** - JH Hinsbeck Heide 1, 41334 Nettetal. e jh-hinsbeck@djh-rheinland.de	t (2153) 6492 f (2153) 89598	161	01.01–23.12	P
▲ **Neudorf** - "Am Fichtelberg" Vierenstr 26, 09465 Sehmatal-Neudorf. e jhneudorf@djh-sachsen.de	t (37342) 8282 f (37342) 8220	128	12	3S P
▲ **Neuhaus am Rennweg** - "Am Rennweg" Apelsbergstr 54, 98724 Neuhaus.	t (3679) 722862 f (3679) 700384	80	29.12.00–20.12.01	R P
▲ **Neuhausen** - Jugendbaude Bergstr 12, 09544 Neuhausen.	t (37361) 45634 f (37361) 45626	68	12	1.5E
▲ **Neukirch** - Naturfreundehaus "Valtenberghaus" Karl-Berger-Str. 16, 01904 Neukirch/Lausitz.	t (35951) 31484 f (35951) 37108	122	12	
▲ **Neumünster** Gartenstr. 32, 24534 Neumünster. e info@kiek-in-nms.de	t (4321) 419960 f (4321) 4199699	208	01.01–23.12; 28–31.12	P
▲ **Neureichenau** - JH Rosenbergergut Ortsteil Lackenhäuser 146, 94089 Neureichenau (Bavaria).	t (8583) 1239 f (8583) 1566	109	01.01–14.12; 27–31.12	
▲ **Neuschönau** - JH Waldhäuser Herbergsweg 2, 94556 Neuschönau (Bavaria).	t (8553) 6000 f (8553) 829	117	01.01–14.11; 27–31.12	

Location/Address	Telephone No. Fax No.	Beds	Opening Dates	Facilities
▲ Neuss-Uedesheim Macherscheiderstr 113, 41468 Neuss-Uedesheim. ❷ jh-neuss@djh-rheinland.de	❶ (02131) 718750 ❸ (02131) 7187510	131	01.01–23.12; 27–31.12	♦♦♦ ⑩ Ⓡ 8S Ⓟ ☞ ♻
▲ Neustadt/Weinstr. - Pfalz-Jugendherberge,Jugendgästehaus Hans-Geiger-Str. 27, 67434 Neustadt/Weinstr. ❷ jh-neustadt@djh-info.de	❶ (6321) 2289 ❸ (6321) 82947	122	01.01–23.12; 27–31.12	♦♦♦ ⑩ ♿ Ⓒ︎Ⓒ︎ Ⓟ ☞
Neustadt/Schw ☞Titisee-Neustadt				
▲ Nideggen Rather Str 27, 52385 Nideggen. ❷ jh-nideggen@djh-rheinland.de	❶ (2427) 1226 ❸ (2427) 8453	122	01.01–23.12; 27–31.12	⑩ Ⓟ
▲ Niebüll Deezbülldeich 2, 25899 Niebüll-Deezbüll.	❶ (4661) 8762 ❸ (4661) 20457	37	13.04–31.10	♦♦♦ ⑩ Ⓡ Ⓟ
▲ Norddeich Strandstr 1, 26506 Norden.	❶ (4931) 8064 ❸ (4931) 81828	96	🔲₁₂	⑩ Ⓟ
▲ Nordenham Strandallee 12, 26954 Nordenham. ❷ djhnham@aol.com	❶ (4731) 88262 ❸ (4731) 88034	158	🔲₁₂	♦♦♦ ⑩ ♿ Ⓟ
▲ Norderney - Südstr Südstr 1, 26535 Norderney, (North Sea).	❶ (4932) 2451 ❸ (4921) 83600	121	01.02–31.10	♦♦♦ ⑩ Ⓡ 1E
▲ Norderney - Dünensender Am Dünensender 3, 26548 Norderney, (North Sea). ❷ jh-norderney-duenensender@ djh-unterweser-ems.de	❶ (4932) 2574 ❸ (4921) 83266	144	01.03–31.10	⑩ Ⓡ 4E
▲ Nördlingen Kaiserwiese 1, 86720 Nördlingen (Bavaria).	❶ (9081) 271816 ❸ (9081) 271816	104	01.03–31.10	♦♦♦ ⑩
▲ Nordhausen - JGH "Rothleimmühle" Parkallee 2, 99734 Nordhausen. ❷ rothleimmuehle@t-online.de	❶ (3631) 902391 ❸ (3631) 902393	128	01.12.00– 30.01.01	♦♦♦ ⑩ Ⓡ Ⓟ
▲ Northeim "Adolf-Galland-Jugendheim", Brauereistr 1, 37154 Northeim.	❶ (5551) 8672 ❸ (5551) 911108	103	27.12.00– 23.12.01	♦♦♦ ⑩ ♿ Ⓟ
▲ Nottuln St Amand-Montrond-Str 6, 48301 Nottuln. ❷ jh-nottuln@djh-wl.de	❶ (2502) 7878 ❸ (2502) 9619	132	08.01–20.12	♦♦♦ ⑩ Ⓟ
▲ **Nürnberg** - JGH (IBN) **Burg 2, 90403 Nürnberg (Bavaria).**	❶ (911) 2309360 ❸ (911) 23093611	320	01.01–23.12; 27–31.12	♦♦♦ ⑩ Ⓡ ♿ Ⓒ︎Ⓒ︎
▲ Oberammergau Malensteinweg 10, 82487 Oberammergau (Bavaria).	❶ (8822) 4114 ❸ (8822) 1695	130	01.01–14.11; 27–31.12	♦♦♦ ⑩
▲ Oberbernhards Hauptstr 5, 36115 Hilders-Oberbernhards. ❷ oberbernhards@djh-hessen.de	❶ (6657) 240 ❸ (6657) 8896	257	27.12.00– 23.12.01	♦♦♦ ⑩ 8NW Ⓟ
▲ Oberhundem Wilhelm-Münker-Weg 1, 57399 Kirchhundem. ❷ jh-oberhundem@djh-wl.de	❶ (2723) 72640 ❸ (2723) 73597	106	16.01–14.12	⑩ Ⓟ

Location/Address	Telephone No. Fax No.	Beds	Opening Dates	Facilities
▲ **Oberoderwitz** Zur Lindenallee 5, 02791 Oderwitz.	☏ (35842) 26544 ❺ (35842) 27726	138	ⓓ12	ⅲ ⑩ 2E ℗
▲ **Oberreifenberg** Limesstr 14, 61389 Schmitten. ⓔ oberreifenberg@djh-hessen.de	☏ (6082) 2440 ❺ (6082) 3305	226	27.12.00– 23.12.01	⑩ 3SW ℗
▲ **Oberstdorf-Kornau** Kornau 8, 87561 Oberstdorf-Kornau (Bavaria).	☏ (8322) 2225; (8322) 2510 ❺ (8322) 80446	188	01.01–14.11; 28–31.12	ⅲ ⑩ ℗ ⊡
▲ **Oberwesel** - Jugendgästehaus Auf dem Schönberg, 55430 Oberwesel. ⓔ jh-oberwesel@djh-info.de	☏ (6744) 93330 ❺ (6744) 7446	179	01.01–23.12; 27–31.12	ⅲ ⑩ ♿ ⒸⒸ ℗ ☞
▲ **Ochsenfurt** Hauptstr 1, 97199 Ochsenfurt (Bavaria).	☏ (9331) 2666 ❺ (9331) 2696	30	01.04–31.10	ⅲ ⑩
Oelsnitz ☞**Taltitz**				
▲ **Oerlinghausen** Auf dem Berge 11, 33813 Oerlinghausen. ⓔ jh-oerlinghausen@djh-wl.de	☏ (5202) 2053 ❺ (5202) 15456	127	04.01–21.12	ⅲ ⑩ ℗
▲ **Ohorn** Schleißbergstr 39, 01896 Ohorn.	☏ (35955) 72762 ❺ (35955) 72762	46	ⓓ12	ⅲ ⑩ 2NE ℗
▲ **Oldenburg/Holstein** Göhlerstr 58a, 23758 Oldenburg. ⓔ jholdenburg@djh-nordmark.de	☏ (4361) 7670 ❺ (4361) 60731	80	06.01–22.12	ⅲ ⑩ ℗ ⊡
▲ **Oldenburg/Oldenburg** Alexander Str 65, 26121 Oldenburg. ⓔ jh-oldenburg@djh-unterweser-ems.de	☏ (441) 87135 ❺ (441) 8852493	104	ⓓ12	ⅲ ⑩ 1NE ℗
▲ **Ortenberg** - Schloss Ortenberg Burgweg 21/Schloss, 77799 Ortenberg.	☏ (781) 31749 ❺ (781) 9481031	146	27.12.00– 22.12.01	ⅲ ⑩ ℗
▲ **Osnabrück** YGH, Iburger Str 183A, 49082 Osnabrück. ⓔ jh-osnabrueck@djh-unterweser-ems.de	☏ (541) 54284 ❺ (541) 54294	145	ⓓ12	ⅲ ⑩ 2S ♿ ℗
▲ **Ossa** Dorfstr 69, 04643 Ossa.	☏ (34346) 60587 ❺ (34346) 60587	52	ⓓ12	ⅲ ⑩ ℗
▲ **Otterndorf** Schleusenstr 147, 21762 Otterndorf. ⓔ jhotterndorf@djh-nordmark.de	☏ (4751) 3165 ❺ (4751) 4577	212	06.01–22.12	ⅲ ⑩ ♿ ℗ ⊡ ⮂
▲ **Ottobeuren** Kaltenbrunnweg 11, 87724 Ottobeuren (Bavaria).	☏ (8332) 368 ❺ (8332) 7219	102	01.03–31.10	⑩
▲ **Paderborn** Meinwerkstr 16, 33098 Paderborn. ⓔ jh-paderborn@djh-wl.de	☏ (5251) 22055 ❺ (5251) 280017	108	03.01–03.12	ⅲ ⑩ ℗
▲ **Panschwitz-Kuckau** Cisinskistr 1, 01920 Panschwitz-Kuckau.	☏ (35796) 96963 ❺ (35796) 96964	60	ⓓ12	ⅲ ⑩ ℗ ⊡
▲ **Papenburg** Kirchstr 38-40, 26871 Papenburg.	☏ (4961) 2793 ❺ (4961) 916554	75	01.03–31.10	ⅲ ⑩ ℗
▲ **Passau** Veste Oberhaus 125, 94034 Passau (Bavaria).	☏ (851) 493780 ❺ (851) 4937820	82	ⓓ12	ⅲ ⑩ ℗

Location/Address	Telephone No. Fax No.	Beds	Opening Dates	Facilities
▲ **Pforzheim** - Burg Rabeneck OT Dillweissenstein, Kräheneckstr 4, 75180 Pforzheim.	☏ (7231) 972660 ♟ (7231) 972661	96	27.12.00– 22.12.01	♦♦ �🍽 3SW P
▲ **Pirna-Copitz** - "Tor zur sächsischen Schweiz" Birkwitzer Str 51, 01796 Pirna-Copitz.	☏ (3501) 445601 ♟ (3501) 445602	166	01.01–31.10	♦♦ �🍽 R 3NE P
▲ **Plau am See** Meyenburger Chaussee 1a, 19395 Plau am See.	☏ (38735) 44345 ♟ (38735) 44345	124	01.04–31.10	♦♦ �🍽 R P
▲ **Plauen** - "Reusaer Waldhaus" Reusaer Waldhaus 1, 08529 Plauen.	☏ (3741) 472811 ♟ (3741) 472812	74	🗓	♦♦ �🍽 4SE P
▲ **Plön** Ascheberger Str 67, 24306 Plön. ✉ jhploen@djh-nordmark.de	☏ (4522) 2576 ♟ (4522) 2166	221	06.01– 14.12.01; 31.12.01– 14.12.02	♦♦ �🍽 P ⚓
▲ **Plothen** - "Am Hausteich" 07907 Plothen.	☏ (36648) 22329 ♟ (36648) 26013	167	28.12.00– 22.12.01	♦♦ �🍽 R ♿ P
▲ **Porta Westfalica** Kirchsiek 30, 32457 Porta Westfalica-Hausberge. ✉ jh-porta.westfalica@djh-wl.de	☏ (571) 70250 ♟ (571) 7100047	95	27.12.00– 23.12.01	�🍽 P
▲ **Pottenstein** Jugendherbergsstr 20, 91278 Pottenstein (Bavaria).	☏ (9243) 92910 ♟ (9243) 929111	163	🗓	♦♦ �🍽 ♿
▲ **Prebelow** Prebelow 02, 16831 Zechlinerhütte. ✉ jh-prebelow@jugendherberge.de	☏ (33921) 70222 ♟ (33921) 70362	98	🗓 (R 01.11.00– 28.02.01)	♦♦ �🍽 R
▲ **Prien** Carl-Braun-Str. 66, 83209 Prien (Bavaria).	☏ (8051) 68770 ♟ (8051) 687715	109	16.01–30.11	♦♦ �🍽
▲ **Prüm** Pferdemarkt, 54595 Prüm.	☏ (6551) 2500 ♟ (6551) 70030	74	Closed for 2001	♦♦ �🍽
▲ **Pullach** - JH "Burg Schwaneck" Burgweg 4-6, 82049 Pullach (Bavaria).	☏ (89) 74486672 ♟ (89) 74486680	138	02.01–19.12	�🍽
▲ **Quedlinburg** Neuendorf 28, 06484 Quedlinburg. ✉ jh-quedlinburg@djh-sachsen-anhalt.de	☏ (3946) 811703 ♟ (3946) 811705	54	01.01–23.12; 27–31.12	♦♦ ⌷ P 🍴
Radebeul ☞Dresden				
▲ **Radevormwald** Telegrafenstr 50, 42477 Radevormwald. ✉ jh-radevormwald@djh-rheinland.de	☏ (2195) 1063 ♟ (2195) 6323	97	Closed 2001. Re–opening Summer 2002	♦♦ ⌷ P
▲ **Radis** Bahnhofstr 18, 06773 Radis. ✉ jh-radis@djh-sachsen-anhalt.de	☏ (34953) 39288 ♟ (34953) 21429	121	01.01–23.12; 28–31.12	♦♦ ⌷ P ▣
▲ **Ratingen** Götschenbeck 8, 40882 Ratingen. ✉ jh-ratingen@djh-rheinland.de	☏ (2102) 20400 ♟ (2102) 204010	160	01.01–23.12; 27–31.12	♦♦ ⌷ ♿ P

Location/Address	Telephone No. Fax No.	Beds	Opening Dates	Facilities
▲ **Ratzeburg** Fischerstr 20, 23909 Ratzeburg. ✉ jhratzeburg@djh-nordmark.de	☎ (4541) 3707 ✆ (4541) 84780	135	06.01–22.12	ᵻᵻᵻ ᵒᴵ P ⬚ ♿
▲ **Ravensburg** - Veitsburg Veitsburgstr 1, 88212 Ravensburg.	☎ (751) 25363 ✆ (751) 13769	110	24.01–18.12; 27–31.12	ᵻᵻᵻ ᵒᴵ ♿ P ⬚
▲ **Rechenberg** - Schloss Zum Schloß 7, 74597 Stimpfach.	☎ (7967) 372 ✆ (7967) 8985	100	17.01–11.12	ᵻᵻᵻ ᵒᴵ P
▲ **Regensburg** (IBN) Wöhrdstr 60, 93059 Regensburg (Bavaria).	☎ (941) 57402 ✆ (941) 52411	170	⌷₁₂	ᵻᵻᵻ ᵒᴵ Ⓡ ⬚
▲ **Rendsburg** Rotenhöfer Weg 48, 24768 Rendsburg. ✉ jhrendsburg@djh-nordmark.de	☎ (4331) 71205 ✆ (4331) 75521	138	01.02–22.12	ᵻᵻᵻ ᵒᴵ ♿ P ⬚ ♿
▲ **Rheine** Mühlenstr 75, 48431 Rheine. ✉ jh-rheine@djh-wl.de	☎ (5971) 2407 ✆ (5971) 13526	53	27.12.00– 23.12.01	ᵒᴵ ♿ P
▲ **Ribnitz Damgarten** Am Wasserwerk, 18311 Ribnitz-Damgarten. ✉ jugendherberge.tanzhaus@t-online.de	☎ (3821) 812311 ✆ (3821) 812311	24	30.12.00– 21.12.01	ᵻᵻᵻ ᵒᴵ
▲ **Rinteln** Am Bären 1, 31737 Rinteln. ✉ jh-rinteln@djh-hannover.de	☎ (5751) 2405 ✆ (5751) 44630	96	27.12.00– 23.12.01	ᵻᵻᵻ ᵒᴵ ♿ P
▲ **Rittersgrün** Zur Jugendherberge 2, 08355 Rittersgrün.	☎ (37757) 7260 ✆ (37757) 7260	52	⌷₁₂	ᵒᴵ P ⬚
▲ **Rochlitz** - "Schweizerhaus" Zaßnitzer Str 1, 09306 Rochlitz.	☎ (3737) 42131 ✆ (3737) 149053	49	⌷₁₂	ᵻᵻᵻ ᵒᴵ 3E P ⬚
▲ **Rödinghausen** Jugendheim des Kreises Herford, Zum Nonnenstein 21, 32289 Rödinghausen.	☎ (5746) 8173 ✆ (5746) 920425	80	27.12.00– 20.12.01	ᵻᵻᵻ ᵒᴵ P
Rosenbergergut ☞Neureichenau				
▲ **Rostock** JGS 'Traditionsschiff', PF 48, 18106 Rostock, Schmarl-Dorf.	☎ (381) 716224 ✆ (381) 714014	50	30.12.00– 21.12.01	ᵻᵻᵻ ᵒᴵ Ⓡ P
▲ **Rostock-Warnemünde** Parkstraße 46, 18119 Rostock OT. Warnemünde. ✉ jh.warne@t-online.de	☎ (381) 548170 ✆ (381) 5481723	191	Closed. Reopening in December 2001	ᵻᵻᵻ ᵒᴵ Ⓡ P
▲ **Rotenburg/Fulda** Obertor 17, 36199 Rotenburg. ✉ rotenburg@djh-hessen.de	☎ (6623) 2792 ✆ (6623) 43177	125	27.12.00– 23.12.01	ᵻᵻᵻ ᵒᴵ 0.5N
▲ **Rotenburg/Wümme** Verdener Str 104, 27356 Rotenburg. ✉ jh-rotenburg@djh-unterweser-ems.de	☎ (4261) 83041 ✆ (4261) 84233	224	⌷₁₂	ᵻᵻᵻ ᵒᴵ Ⓡ 1SW P ⬚
▲ **Rothenburg-Tauber** (IBN) Mühlacker 1, 91541 Rothenburg (Bavaria). ✉ jhrothen@aol.com	☎ (9861) 94160 ✆ (9861) 941620	184	⌷₁₂	ᵻᵻᵻ ᵒᴵ P ⬚
▲ **Rothenfels** 97851 Rothenfels (Bavaria).	☎ (9393) 99999 ✆ (9393) 99997	168	06.01–05.04; 17.04–14.12	ᵒᴵ

Location/Address	Telephone No. Fax No.	Beds	Opening Dates	Facilities
Rudenberg ☞**Titisee-Neustadt**				
▲ **Rüdesheim** Am Kreuzberg, 65385 Rüdesheim. ℮ ruedesheim@djh-hessen.de	✆ (6722) 2711 🖷 (6722) 48284	155	27.12.00– 23.12.01	♦♦♦ ⑩ [1.5E] 🄿
▲ **Rurberg** 52152 Simmerath-Rurberg. ℮ jh-rurberg@djh-rheinland.de	✆ (2473) 2200 🖷 (2473) 4911	174	01.02–02.12; 27–31.12	♦♦♦ ⑩ ☞ 🄿 ⬤
▲ **Rüthen** Am Rabenknapp 4, 59602 Rüthen. ℮ jh-ruethen@djh-wl.de	✆ (2952) 483 🖷 (2952) 2717	121	15.01–14.12	⑩ 🄿
▲ **Ruttelerfeld** Zollweg 27, 26340 Zetel.	✆ (4452) 416 🖷 (4452) 8230	111	🗓	♦♦♦ ⑩ 🄿
▲ **Saarbrücken** - Europa-Jugendherberge, Jugendgästehaus Meerwiesertalweg 31, 66123 Saarbrücken. ℮ jh-saarbruecken@djh-info.de	✆ (681) 33040 🖷 (681) 374911	192	01.01–23.12; 27–31.12	♦♦♦ ⑩ [4NE] ⓓ 🄒🄲🄲 🄿 ⬤
▲ **Saarburg** Bottelter 8, 54439 Saarburg. ℮ jh-saarburg@djh-info.de	✆ (6581) 2555 🖷 (6581) 1082	102	01.01–23.12; 27–31.12	⑩ 🄒🄲🄲 🄿
▲ **Saldenburg** Ritter-Tuschl-Str 20, 94163 Saldenburg (Bavaria).	✆ (8504) 1655 🖷 (8504) 4449	140	01–09.01; 01.02–30.11; 27–31.12	♦♦♦ ⑩
▲ **Sandhatten** Wöschenweg 28, 26209 Hatten.	✆ (4482) 330 🖷 (4482) 8498	122	🗓	♦♦♦ ⑩ [1.5 NW] 🄿
▲ **Sargenroth** - Waldjugendherberge Kirchweg 1, 55471 Sargenroth. ℮ jh-sargenroth@djh-info.de	✆ (6761) 2500 🖷 (6761) 6378	134	01.01–23.12; 27–31.12	♦♦♦ ⑩ ⓓ 🄒🄲🄲
▲ **Sayda** Mortelgrund 8, 09619 Sayda. ℮ jhsayda@djh-sachsen.de	✆ (37365) 1277 🖷 (37365) 1337	140	🗓	♦♦♦ ⑩ [3 SW] 🄿 ▣ ⬤
▲ **Scharbeutz-Klingberg** Uhlenflucht 30, 23684 Scharbeutz. ℮ jhklingberg@djh-nordmark.de	✆ (4524) 428 🖷 (4524) 1637	262	21.01–14.12	♦♦♦ ⑩ 🄿 🚲
▲ **Schellerhau** - "Rotwasserhütte" Hauptstr 115, 01776 Schellerhau.	✆ (35052) 64227 🖷 (35052) 64227	46	🗓	♦♦♦ ⑩ 🄿
▲ **Schierke** - JGH Brockenstrasse 48, 38879 Schierke. ℮ jh-schierke@djh-sachsen-anhalt.de	✆ (39455) 51066 🖷 (39455) 51067	272	01.01–23.12; 28–31.12	♦♦♦ ⑩ ⓓ 🄿 ▣
▲ **Schillighörn** Inselstr 6, 26434 Wangerland.	✆ (4426) 371 🖷 (4426) 506	132	01–31.01; 01.03–31.12	⑩ [0.5N] 🄿
▲ **Schleiden-Gemünd** - JH Gemünd Im Wingertchen 9, 53937 Schleiden-Gemünd. ℮ jh-gemuend@djh-rheinland.de	✆ (2444) 2241 🖷 (2444) 3386	163	01.01–23.12; 27–31.12	♦♦♦ ⑩ ☞ 🄿
▲ **Schleswig** Spielkoppel 1, 24837 Schleswig. ℮ jhschleswig@djh-nordmark.de	✆ (4621) 23893 🖷 (4621) 20796	120	16.01–14.12	♦♦♦ ⑩ 🄿 🚲

Location/Address	Telephone No. Fax No.	Beds	Opening Dates	Facilities
▲ **Schliersee** - JH Josefsthal Josefsthaler Str. 19, 83727 Schliersee (Bavaria). ⓔ jhjosefsthal@djh-bayern.de	☎ (8026) 97380 ✆ (8026) 71610	93	01.01–31.10; 27–31.12	♦♦ ⑩ ⓢ
▲ **Schluchsee** - Seebrugg Haus 9, 79859 Schluchsee, (OT Seebrugg).	☎ (7656) 494 ✆ (7656) 1889	134	27.12.00– 22.12.01	♦♦ ⑩ ③SW ℗
▲ **Schluchsee** - Wolfsgrund Im Wolfsgrund 28, 79859 Schluchsee.	☎ (7656) 329 ✆ (7656) 9237	133	27.12.00– 22.12.01	♦♦ ⑩ ①NE ℗ ⓢ
▲ **Schmallenberg** Im Lenninghof 20, 57392 Schmallenberg. ⓔ jh-schmallenberg@djh-wl.de	☎ (2972) 6098 ✆ (2972) 4918	134	02.01–30.11	♦♦ ⑩ ℗
▲ **Schnett** "Auf dem Simmersberg", Kirchberg 25, 98666 Schnett. ⓔ jh-schnett@t-online.de	☎ (36874) 39532 ✆ (36874) 39532	61	28.12.00– 22.12.01	♦♦ ⑩ ⓡ ℗
▲ **Schöna** - Naturfreundehaus "Am Zirkelstein" Am Zirkelstein 109 b, 01814 Schöna.	☎ (35028) 80425 ✆ (35028) 81424	152	⑫	
▲ **Schönberg** Stakendorfer Weg 1, 24217 Schönberg. ⓔ jhschoenberg@djh-nordmark.de	☎ (4344) 2974 ✆ (4344) 4484	233	06.01–22.12	♦♦ ⑩ ♿ ℗ ⓢ 🚲
▲ **Schönbrunn/Ebersdorf** Nr 102 (Bellevue), 07368 Ebersdorf, OT Schönbrunn.	☎ (36651) 87064 ✆ (36651) 55413	72	28.12.00– 21.12.01	⑩ ⓡ ℗ ⓦ
▲ **Schöneck** Am Stadtpark 52, 08261 Schöneck.	☎ (37464) 8106 ✆ (37464) 8107	63	⑫	♦♦ ⑩ ①E ℗ ⓢ
▲ **Schöningen am Elm** Richard-Schirrmann-Str 6a, 38364 Schöningen am Elm.	☎ (5352) 3898 ✆ (5352) 3752	92	27.12.00– 23.12.01	♦♦ ⑩ ℗
▲ **Schönwalde** Am Ruhsal 1, 23744 Schönwalde am Bungsberg.	☎ (4528) 206 ✆ (4528) 9732	60	13.04–31.10	♦♦ ⑩
▲ **Schwäbisch Hall** Langenfelderweg 5, 74523 Schwäbisch Hall.	☎ (791) 41050 ✆ (791) 47998	143	03–16.01; 07.02–11.12	♦♦ ⑩ ℗ ⓢ
▲ **Schwarzburg** "Hans Breuer" Am Buschbach 2, 07427 Schwarzburg. ⓔ jugendherberge_hans_breuer_@t-online.de	☎ (36730) 22223 ✆ (36730) 33555	163	28.12.00– 22.12.01	♦♦ ⑩ ⓡ ℗
▲ **Schweinfurt** Niederwerrnerstr 17 1/2, 97421 Schweinfurt (Bavaria). ⓔ jugendherberge@schweinfurt.de	☎ (9721) 21404 ✆ (9721) 23581	110	09.01–21.12	♦♦ ⑩
▲ **Schwerin** Waldschulweg 3, 19061 Schwerin. ⓔ jh-schwerin@t-online.de	☎ (385) 3260006 ✆ (385) 3260303	91	30.12.00– 15.12.01	♦♦ ⑩ ℗
Seebrugg ☞**Schluchsee**				
▲ **Sigmaringen** - Hohenzollern-JH Hohenzollernstr 31, 72488 Sigmaringen.	☎ (7571) 13277 ✆ (7571) 61159	121	03–27.01; 07.02–11.12	♦♦ ⑩ ℗

Location/Address	Telephone No. Fax No.	Beds	Opening Dates	Facilities
▲ **Silberborn** Schießhäuser Str 4, 37603 Silberborn.	✆ (5536) 568 ❺ (5536) 1533	161	27.12.00– 23.12.01	♦♦♦ ⍾⊙⍾ 🅿
▲ **Singen** Friedingerstr 28, 78224 Singen.	✆ (7731) 42590 ❺ (7731) 48842	105	⬚	♦♦♦ ⍾⊙⍾ ⬚1 NE 🅿
▲ **Soest** Kaiser-Friedrich-Platz 2, 59494 Soest. ⅇ jh-soest@djh-wl.de	✆ (2921) 16283 ❺ (2921) 14623	104	Reopening April 2001	♦♦♦ ⍾⊙⍾ 🅿
▲ **Solingen-Gräfrath** Flockertsholzerweg 10, 42653 Solingen. ⅇ jh-solingen@djh-rheinland.de	✆ (212) 591198 ❺ (212) 594179	120	01.01–23.12; 27–31.12	⍾⊙⍾ 🅿
Sonnenbühl ☞**Erpfingen**				
▲ **Sondershausen** - JH "Juventas" Güntherstr 26/27 99706 Sondershausen.	✆ (3632) 601193 ❺ (3632) 782259	50	⬚	⍾⊙⍾ 🅿 ⬚
▲ **Sorpesee** Am Sorpesee 7, 59846 Sundern-Langscheid. ⅇ jh-sorpesee@djh-wl.de	✆ (2935) 1776 ❺ (2935) 7254	166	19.01–20.12	♦♦♦ ⍾⊙⍾ 🅿
▲ **Sosa** - "Skihütte" Am Frölichwald 9, 08326 Sosa.	✆ (37752) 8268 ❺ (37752) 8268	28	⬚	♦♦♦ ⍾⊙⍾ ⬚1 W 🅿
▲ **Sosa** - Naturfreundehaus "Rote Grube" Rote Grube 1, 08326 Sosa.	✆ (3773) 58019 ❺ (3773) 882540	60	⬚	♦♦♦ ⍾⊙⍾ ⬚3.5 E 🅿
▲ **Spalt** - JH Wernfels Burgweg 7-9, 91174 Spalt (Bavaria). ⅇ info@cvjm-bayern.de	✆ (9873) 515 ❺ (9873) 244	167	01.01–19.12; 28–31.12	♦♦♦ ⍾⊙⍾ ⛵ ⬚
▲ **Speyer** - Kurpfalz-Jugendherberge, Jugendgästehaus Geibstr 5, 67346 Speyer. ⅇ jh-speyer@djh-info.de	✆ (6232) 61597 ❺ (6232) 61596	160	01.01–23.12; 27–31.12	⍾⊙⍾ ♿ ⟨ECC⟩ 🅿 🍵
▲ **Spiekeroog** Bid' Utkiek 1, 26474 Spiekeroog, (North Sea).	✆ (4976) 329	54	15.03–30.10	♦♦♦ ⓡ
▲ **Springe** In der Worth 25, 31832 Springe.	✆ (5041) 1455 ❺ (5041) 2963	92	27.12.00– 23.12.01	⍾⊙⍾ 🅿
St Blasien ☞**Menzenschwand**				
▲ **St Englmar** - JH Maibrunn Haus Nr 5, 94379 St Englmar (Bavaria).	✆ (9965) 271 ❺ (9965) 1342	59	01.01–31.10; 16–31.12	⍾⊙⍾
▲ **St Goar** Bismarckweg 17, 56329 St Goar. ⅇ jh-st-goar@djh-info.de	✆ (6741) 388 ❺ (6741) 2869	130	01.01–23.12; 27–31.12	⍾⊙⍾ ⟨ECC⟩
▲ **St Michaelisdonn** Am Sportplatz 1, 25693 St Michaelisdonn.	✆ (4853) 923 ❺ (4853) 8576	70	16.01–09.12	♦♦♦ ⍾⊙⍾ ♿ ⬚ 🚲
▲ **Stade** Kehdinger Mühren 11, 21682 Stade. ⅇ jhstade@djh-nordmark.de	✆ (4141) 46368 ❺ (4141) 2817	139	06.01–22.12	♦♦♦ ⍾⊙⍾ ♿ 🚲
▲ **Steinbach/Donnersberg** Brühlstraße 41, 67808 Steinbach. ⅇ jh-steinbach@djh-info.de	✆ (6357) 360 ❺ (6357) 1583	104	01.01–23.12; 27–31.12	♦♦♦ ⍾⊙⍾ ⟨ECC⟩ 🅿 🍵
Steinebach ☞**Wörthsee**				

Location/Address	Telephone No. Fax No.	Beds	Opening Dates	Facilities
▲ **Stralsund** Am Kütertor 1, 18439 Stralsund. ⊖ jh-stralsund@t-online.de	☎ (3831) 292160 ✆ (3831) 297676	164	29.12.00– 31.10.01	♦♦♦ ❘⊙❘ Ⓡ
▲ **Stralsund-Devin** Strandstr 21, 18439 Stralsund OT. Devin. ⊖ jh-devin@t-online.de	☎ (3831) 490289 ✆ (3831) 490291	161	01.03–31.12	♦♦♦ ❘⊙❘ Ⓡ ⅗ Ⓟ
▲ **Straubing** Friedhofstr 12, 94315 Straubing (Bavaria).	☎ (9421) 80436 ✆ (9421) 12094	57	01.04–31.10	❘⊙❘
▲ **Strehla** Torgauer Str 33, 01616 Strehla. ⊖ jhstrehla@djh-sachsen.de	☎ (35264) 92030 ✆ (35264) 92031	72	🕮	♦♦♦ ❘⊙❘ 2W Ⓟ
Streitberg ☞**Wiesenttal**				
▲ **Strub** - JH Berchtesgaden Gebirgsjägerstr 52, 83489 Strub (Bavaria).	☎ (8652) 94370 ✆ (8652) 943737	360	01.01–14.11; 27–31.12	♦♦♦ ❘⊙❘ ⚹ 🗖
▲ **Stuttgart** **Haußmannstr 27, 70188 Stuttgart** **(enter via Werastr, corner Kernerstr).** ⊖ jh-stuttgart@t-online.de	☎ (711) 241583 ✆ (711) 2361041	285	🕮	♦♦♦ ❘⊙❘ 1 SE
Sudelfeld ☞**Bayrischzell**				
▲ **Syke** - "Oscar-Heidrich-JH" Nordwohlder Str 59, 28857 Syke.	☎ (4242) 50314 ✆ (4242) 66346	128	🕮	♦♦♦ ❘⊙❘ 3W ⅗ Ⓟ
▲ **Taltitz** - "Talsperre Pirk" Dobenecker Weg 27, 08606 Oelsnitz, OT Taltitz. ⊖ jhtaltitz@djh-sachsen.de	☎ (37421) 23019 ✆ (37421) 20202	82	🕮	♦♦♦ ❘⊙❘ 3W Ⓟ
▲ **Tambach-Dietharz** Oberhoferstr 3, 99897 Tambach-Dietharz.	☎ (36252) 36149 ✆ (36252) 36564	120	28.12.00– 22.12.01	♦♦♦ ❘⊙❘ Ⓡ ⅗ Ⓟ ☕
Tannenlohe ☞**Windischeschenbach**				
▲ **Tauberbischofsheim** Schirrmannweg 2, 97941 Tauberbischofsheim.	☎ (9341) 3152 ✆ (9341) 95052	100	27.12.00– 22.12.01	♦♦♦ ❘⊙❘ 2NW Ⓟ
▲ **Tecklenburg** Am Herrengarten 5, 49545 Tecklenburg. ⊖ jh-tecklenburg@djh-wl.de	☎ (5482) 360 ✆ (5482) 7937	128	27.12.00– 23.12.01	♦♦♦ ❘⊙❘ Ⓟ
▲ **Teterow** Am Seebahnhof 7, 17166 Teterow.	☎ (3996) 172668 ✆ (3996) 172668	80	01.05–30.09	♦♦♦ ❘⊙❘ Ⓡ Ⓟ
▲ **Thale** Waldkater-Bodetal 1, 06502 Thale. ⊖ jh-thale@djh-sachsen-anhalt.de	☎ (3947) 2881 ✆ (3947) 91653	204	01.01–23.12; 28–31.12	♦♦♦ ❘⊙❘ Ⓟ 🗖 ☕
▲ **Thallichtenberg** Burg Lichtenberg, 66871 Thallichtenberg. ⊖ jh-thallichtenberg@djh-info.de	☎ (6381) 2632 ✆ (6381) 80933	106	01.01–23.12; 27–31.12	♦♦♦ ❘⊙❘ ⅗ ⅭⅭ Ⓟ ☕
▲ **Tharandt** - "Am Tharandter Wald" Pienner Str 55, 01737 Tharandt.	☎ (35203) 37272 ✆ (35203) 37738	69	🕮	♦♦♦ ❘⊙❘ 3SW Ⓟ 🗖
▲ **Tholey** - Schaumberg-Jugendherberge,Jugendgästehaus Am Schaumberg 2, 66636 Tholey. ⊖ jh-tholey@djh-info.de	☎ (6853) 2271 ✆ (6853) 5534	116	01.01–23.12; 27–31.12	♦♦♦ ❘⊙❘ ⅭⅭ Ⓟ ☕

Location/Address	Telephone No. Fax No.	Beds	Opening Dates	Facilities
▲ **Thülsfelder Talsperre** Am Campingplatz 7, 49681 Garrel-Petersfeld. ℮ jh-thuelsfelde@djh-unterwesser-ems.de	☎ (4495) 475 ✆ (4495) 365	160	🔲	⦿ ⃦ 🅿
▲ **Titisee-Neustadt** - JH Rudenberg Ortsteil Neustadt, Rudenberg 6, 79822 Titisee-Neustadt.	☎ (7651) 7360 ✆ (7651) 4299	146	27.12.00– 22.12.01	⫯⫯⫯ ⦿ 2NE 🅿
▲ **Titisee-Neustadt** - JH Veltishof Ortsteil Titisee, Bruderhalde 27, 79822 Titisee-Neustadt.	☎ (7652) 238 ✆ (7652) 756	128	27.12.00– 22.12.01	⫯⫯⫯ ⦿ 2NW 🅿
▲ **Todtnauberg** - Fleinerhaus OT Todtnauberg, Radschertstr 12, 79674 Todtnau.	☎ (7671) 275 ✆ (7671) 721	148	27.12.00– 22.12.01	⫯⫯⫯ ⦿ 1N 🅿
▲ **Tönning** Badallee 28, 25832 Tönning. ℮ jhtoenning@djh-nordmark.de	☎ (4861) 1280 ✆ (4861) 5956	209	06.01–14.12	⫯⫯⫯ ⦿ ⃦ 🅿 🔲 ⧓
▲ **Torfhaus** Nr 3, 38667 Torfhaus.	☎ (5320) 242 ✆ (5320) 254	174	27.12.00– 23.12.01	⫯⫯⫯ ⦿ ⃦ 🅿
▲ **Tossens** Meldgrodenweg 1, 26969 Butjadingen.	☎ (4736) 716 ✆ (4736) 817	123	01.04–31.10	⦿ Ⓡ 🅿
▲ **Traben-Trarbach** Hirtenpfad 6, 56841 Traben-Trarbach. ℮ jh-traben-trarbach@djh-info.de	☎ (6541) 9278 ✆ (6541) 3759	176	01.01–23.12; 27–31.12	⫯⫯⫯ ⦿ ECC 🅿 ⧓
▲ **Traunstein** Traunerstr 22, 83278 Traunstein (Bavaria).	☎ (861) 4742 ✆ (861) 12382	57	16.01–30.11	⦿
▲ **Trausnitz** Burggasse 2, 92555 Trausnitz (Bavaria).	☎ (9655) 9215-0 ✆ (9655) 921531	131	🔲	⫯⫯⫯ ⦿ 🅿
▲ **Travemünde** "Jugendfreizeitstätte Priwall", Mecklenburger Landstr 69, 23570 Travemünde ℮ info@jfs-priwall.de	☎ (4502) 2576 ✆ (4502) 4620	80	01.04–14.10	⫯⫯⫯ ⦿ 🅿 ⧓
▲ **Triberg/Schw** Rohrbacher Str 35, 78098 Triberg.	☎ (7722) 4110 ✆ (7722) 6662	125	27.12.00– 22.12.01	⫯⫯⫯ ⦿ 2SE 🅿 ⧓
▲ **Trier** - Jugendgästehaus An der Jugendherberge 4, 54292 Trier. ℮ jh-trier@djh-info-de	☎ (651) 146620 ✆ (651) 1466230	248	01.01–23.12; 27–31.12	⫯⫯⫯ ⦿ 3SW ECC ⧓ ⦿ ⧓
▲ **Tübingen** Gartenstr 22/2, 72074 Tübingen.	☎ (7071) 23002 ✆ (7071) 25061	161	🔲	⫯⫯⫯ ⦿ 🅿
▲ **Überlingen** - Martin-Buber-Jugendbegegnungsstätte Alte Nussdorfer Str 26, 88662 Überlingen.	☎ (7551) 4204 ✆ (7551) 1277	259	27.12.00– 22.12.01	⫯⫯⫯ ⦿ 2SE 🅿 ⧓
▲ **Ueckermünde-Bellin** Dorfstraße, 17373 Ueckermünde. ℮ jh-ueckermuende@t-online.de	☎ (39771) 22411 ✆ (39771) 22554	80	01.02–30.11	⫯⫯⫯ ⦿ Ⓡ 7W ⃦ 🅿
▲ **Uelsen/ Grafschaft Bentheim** Linnenbachweg 12, 49843 Uelsen. ℮ jugendherberge@uelsen.de	☎ (5942) 718 ✆ (5942) 922935	104	01.03–31.10	⦿ 2S

Location/Address	Telephone No. Fax No.	Beds	Opening Dates	Facilities
▲ **Uelzen** Fischerhof 1, 29525 Uelzen.	☎ (581) 5312 ✆ (581) 14210	166	27.12.00– 23.12.01	ⅲ ⅲⓄ Ⓟ ⌾
▲ **Ulm** - Geschwister-Scholl-JH Grimmelfinger Weg 45, 89077 Ulm.	☎ (731) 384455 ✆ (731) 384511	147	10.01–11.12	ⅲⓄ Ⓟ ⌾
Urach ☞**Bad Urach**				
Urfeld ☞**Walchensee**				
▲ **Uslar** Kupferhammer 13, 37170 Uslar.	☎ (5571) 2298 ✆ (5571) 1288	104	27.12.00– 23.12.01	ⅲ ⅲⓄ ♿ Ⓟ
▲ **Velbert** Am Buschberg 17, 42549 Velbert (YH + YGH).	☎ (2051) 84317 ✆ (2051) 81202	120	29.01–30.11	ⅲ ⅲⓄ ♿ Ⓟ
▲ **Verden** Saumurplatz 1, 27283 Verden. ✉ jh-verden@djh-unterweser-ems.de	☎ (4231) 61163 ✆ (4231) 68121	124	🏠12	ⅲ ⅲⓄ ♿ Ⓟ
▲ **Villingen** OT Villingen, St-Georgener-Str 36, 78048 Villingen-Schwenningen.	☎ (7721) 54149 ✆ (7721) 52616	134	🏠12	ⅲ ⅲⓄ 2NW Ⓟ ⌾
▲ **Vlotho** Oeynhauser Str 15, 32602 Vlotho. ✉ jh-vlotho@djh-wl.de	☎ (5733) 4063 ✆ (5733) 18139	108	27.12.00– 23.12.01	ⅲ ⅲⓄ Ⓟ
Vöhl ☞**Hessenstein und Hohe Fahrt**				
Wabern ☞**Mosenberg**				
▲ **Walchensee** - JH Urfeld Mittenwalder Str 17, 82432 Walchensee (Bavaria).	☎ (8851) 230 ✆ (8851) 1022	97	01.01–14.11; 27–31.12	ⅲ ⅲⓄ
▲ **Waldeck** Klippenberg 3, 34513 Waldeck. ✉ waldeck@djh-hessen.de	☎ (5623) 5313 ✆ (5623) 6254	161	27.12.00– 23.12.01	ⅲ ⅲⓄ 2.5NW Ⓟ
▲ **Waldheim** - Naturfreundehaus "Am Breitenberg" Breitenbergstr. 21, 04736 Waldheim.	☎ (34327) 92116 ✆ (018050) 5254021430	39	🏠12	ⅲ ⅲⓄ
Waldhäuser ☞**Neuschönau**				
▲ **Waldmünchen** Schlosshof 1, 93449 Waldmünchen (Bavaria). ✉ office@jugendbildungsstaette.org	☎ (9972) 94140 ✆ (9972) 941433	120	🏠12	ⅲ ⅲⓄ Ⓡ ♿ Ⓟ ⌾
▲ **Walldürn** Auf der Heide 37, 74731 Walldürn.	☎ (6282) 283 ✆ (6282) 40194	102	27.12.00– 22.12.01	ⅲ ⅲⓄ 3N Ⓟ
▲ **Waltersdorf** - "Gut Drauf-JH" Am Jägerwäldchen 2, 02763 Bertsdorf-Hörnitz. ✉ jhwaltersdorf@djh-sachsen.de	☎ (35841) 35099 ✆ (35841) 37773	166	🏠12	ⅲ ⅲⓄ ♿ Ⓟ
▲ **Wandlitz** Prenzlauer Chaussee 146, 16348 Wandlitz. ✉ jh-wandlitz@jugendherberge.de	☎ (33397) 22109 ✆ (33397) 62735	148	08.01–30.06	ⅲ ⅲⓄ
▲ **Wangerooge** "Westturm", 26486 Wangerooge, (North Sea).	☎ (4469) 439 ✆ (4469) 8578	136	01.05–30.09	ⅲⓄ Ⓡ 4W
▲ **Waren** Auf dem Nesselberg 2, 17192 Waren.	☎ (3991) 667606 ✆ (3991) 667606	58	01.04–31.10	ⅲ ⅲⓄ Ⓡ ⚲ Ⓟ

Location/Address	Telephone No. Fax No.	Beds	Opening Dates	Facilities
▲ **Warmbad** 09429 Wolkenstein, OT Warmbad.	☎ (37369) 9437 ❻ (37369) 5665	62	01.01–23.12; 27–31.12	♂♀ ¶⊙¶ 3NW ☐
▲ **Weikersheim** - YGH Haus der Musik Im Heiligen Wöhr 1, 97990 Weikersheim.	☎ (7934) 7025; (7934) 7026 ❻ (7934) 7709	143	01.01–19.11; 27–31.12	♂♀ ¶⊙¶ ⅊ ☐ ⊡
▲ **Weilburg** Am Steinbühl, 35781 Weilburg-Odersbach. ✉ weilburg@djh-hessen.de	☎ (6471) 7116 ❻ (6471) 1542	135	27.12.00– 23.12.01	♂♀ ¶⊙¶ 2E ☐
▲ **Weimar** - JGH "Maxim Gorki" **Zum Wilden Graben 12, 99425 Weimar.** ✉ jgh-weimar@gmx.de	☎ (3643) 850750 ❻ (3643) 850749	60	28.12.00– 20.12.01	♂♀ ¶⊙¶ ⓡ ⊏CC⊐ ☐ ⊒
▲ **Weimar** - "Germania" Carl-August Allee 13, 99423 Weimar. ✉ jh-germania@t-online.de	☎ (3643) 850490 ❻ (3643) 850491	120	28.12.00– 22.12.01	♂♀ ¶⊙¶ ⓡ ⊏CC⊐ ⊒
▲ **Weimar** - "Am Poseckschen Garten" Humboldstr 17, 99423 Weimar. ✉ jh-posgarten@gmx.de	☎ (3643) 850792 ❻ (3643) 850793	104	28.12.00– 20.12.01	♂♀ ¶⊙¶ ⊏CC⊐ ⊒
▲ **Weimar** - JGH "Am Ettersberg" Ettersberg-Siedlung, 99427 Weimar. ✉ jgh-weimar@lycosmail.com	☎ (3643) 421111 ❻ (3643) 421112	66	🗓	♂♀ ¶⊙¶ ⓡ ☐ ⊡
▲ **Weinheim/Bgstr** Breslauer Str 46, 69469 Weinheim.	☎ (6201) 68484 ❻ (6201) 182730	129	27.12.00– 22.12.01	♂♀ ¶⊙¶ 2W ☐ ⊡ ☄
▲ **Weiskirchen** Jugendherbergsstr 12, 66709 Weiskirchen. ✉ jh-weiskirchen@djh-info.de	☎ (6876) 231 ❻ (6876) 1444	126	01.01–23.12; 27–31.12	♂♀ ¶⊙¶ ⅊ ⊏CC⊐ ☐ ⊒
Weißenbrunn ☞**Leinburg**				
▲ **Werdau** Jugendheimweg 1, 08412 Werdau.	☎ (3761) 3514 ❻ (3761) 3514	40	🗓	♂♀ ¶⊙¶ ☐ ⊡
Wernfels ☞**Spalt**				
▲ **Wernigerode** Am Eichberg 5, 38855 Wernigerode. ✉ jh-wernigerode@djh-sachsen-anhalt.de	☎ (3943) 606176 ❻ (3943) 606177	205	01.01–23.12; 28–31.12	♂♀ ¶⊙¶ 1.5NW ☐ ⊒
▲ **Wertheim** - Frankenland Alte-Steige 16, 97877 Wertheim.	☎ (9342) 6451 ❻ (9342) 7354	99	27.12.00– 22.12.01	♂♀ ¶⊙¶ 2W ☐
▲ **Westensee** Am See 24, 24259 Westensee. ✉ jhwestensee@djh-nordmark.de	☎ (4305) 542 ❻ (4305) 1360	138	06.01–22.12	♂♀ ¶⊙¶ ⅊ ☐ ⊡ ☄
▲ **Westerstede** "Hössensportanlage", Jahnallee 1, 26655 Westerstede; Postfach 1129, 26641 Westerstede. ✉ hoessen-sportzentrum@t-online.de	☎ (4488) 84690 ❻ (4488) 78317	68	03.01–21.12	♂♀ ¶⊙¶ 2SW ⅊ ☐
▲ **Wetzlar** Richard-Schirrmann-Str 3, 35578 Wetzlar. ✉ wetzlar@djh-hessen.de	☎ (6441) 71068 ❻ (6441) 75826	190	27.12.00– 23.12.01	♂♀ ¶⊙¶ 2SW ⅊

Location/Address	Telephone No. Fax No.	Beds	Opening Dates	Facilities
▲ **Wewelsburg** Burgwall 17, 33142 Büren-Wewelsburg. e jh-wewelsburg@djh-wl.de	☎ (2955) 6155 ✆ (2955) 6946	210	27.12–09.01; 11.02–23.12	ⅲ ⑩ P
▲ **Wieden** - JH Belchen Oberwieden 16, 79695 Wieden.	☎ (7673) 538 ✆ (7673) 504	154	27.12.00– 22.12.01	ⅲ ⑩ 2W P
▲ **Wiehl** An der Krähenhardt 6, 51674 Wiehl. e jh-wiehl@djh-rheinland.de	☎ (2262) 93410 ✆ (2262) 91598	175	01.06–23.12; 27–31.12	ⅲ ⑩ P
▲ **Wiesbaden** Blücherstr 66, 65195 Wiesbaden. e wiesbaden@djh-hessen.de	☎ (611) 48657; (611) 449081 ✆ (611) 441119	220	02.01–23.12	ⅲ ⑩ 2W P
▲ **Wiesenttal-Streitberg** - JH Streitberg Am Gailing 6, 91346 Wiesenttal-Streitberg (Bavaria).	☎ (9196) 288 ✆ (9196) 1543	122	🔒12	ⅲ ⑩ 🔒
▲ **Wildenstein, Burg** 88637 Leibertingen.	☎ (7466) 411 ✆ (7466) 417	164	01.01–26.11; 27–31.12	ⅲ ⑩ P 🔒
▲ **Willingen** Am Lukasheim 9-12, 34508 Willingen. e willingen@djh-hessen.de	☎ (5632) 6347 ✆ (5632) 4343	124	27.12.00– 23.12.01	ⅲ ⑩ 4NE P
▲ **Windeck-Rosbach** - "Waldjugendherberge" Herbergsstr 19, 51570 Windeck-Rosbach. e jh.windeck@djh-rheinland.de	☎ (2292) 5042 ✆ (2292) 6569	142	01.01–23.12; 27–31.12	ⅲ ⑩ ♿ 🐕 P
▲ **Windischeschenbach** - JH Tannenlohe Haus 1, 92670 Windischeschenbach (Bavaria).	☎ (9637) 267 ✆ (9637) 276	162	16.01–14.12	ⅲ ⑩ ♿ 🔒
▲ **Windischleuba** - JH Schloß Windischleuba Pestalozziplatz 1, 04603 Windischleuba. e jugendherberge-windischleuba@t-online.de	☎ (3447) 834471 ✆ (3447) 832702	149	🔒12	ⅲ ⑩ P
▲ **Wingst** Molkereistr 11, 21789 Wingst. e jhwingst@djh-nordmark.de	☎ (4778) 262 ✆ (4778) 7594	201	06–31.01; 01.03–22.12	ⅲ ⑩ ♿ P 🔒 🚲
▲ **Winterberg** Astenberg 1, 59955 Winterberg. e jh-winterberg@djh-wl.de	☎ (2981) 2289 ✆ (2981) 569	170	27.12–31.10; 01.12–23.12	⑩ P
▲ **Wipperfürth** Ostlandstr 34, 51688 Wipperfürth. e jh-wipperfuerth@djh-rheinland.de	☎ (2267) 1228 ✆ (2267) 80977	144	01.01–23.12; 27–31.12	⑩ ♿ P
▲ **Wismar** Juri-Gagarin-Str. 30a, D-23966 Wismar. e jh-wismar@t-online.de	☎ (3841) 32680 ✆ (3841) 326868	78	21.12.00– 19.12.01	ⅲ ⑩ ⓡ 2W ♿ P
▲ **Wittdün** Mittelstr 1, 25946 Wittdün/Amrum. e jhwittduen@djh-nordmark.de	☎ (4682) 2010 ✆ (4682) 1747	218	01.02–30.11	ⅲ ⑩ ♿ 🔒 🚲
▲ **Wittenberg-Lutherstadt** Schloss, 06886 Lutherstadt-Wittenberg. e jugendherberge@wittenberg.de	☎ (3491) 403255 ✆ (3491) 409422	104	01.01–23.12; 28–31.12	⑩ P 🔒
▲ **Wolfsburg** Lessingstr 60, 38440 Wolfsburg.	☎ (5361) 13337 ✆ (5361) 16630	68	27.12.00– 23.12.01	ⅲ ⑩ ♿ P

Location/Address	Telephone No. Fax No.	Beds	Opening Dates	Facilities
▲ **Wolfstein** Rötherweg 24, 67752 Wolfstein. ⊖ jh-wolfstein@djh-info.de	☎ (6304) 1408 ⊕ (6304) 683	160	01.01–23.12; 27–31.12	♦♦♦ �Ⓞ & ⒸⒸ P ⓞ
▲ **Worms** - Jugendgästehaus Dechaneigasse 1, 67547 Worms. ⊖ jh-worms@djh-info.de	☎ (6241) 25780 ⊕ (6241) 27394	114	01.01–23.12; 27–31.12	♦♦♦ Ⓞ ⒸⒸ ☕
▲ **Worpswede** Hammeweg 2, 27726 Worpswede. ⊖ jh-worpswede@djh-unterweser-ems.de	☎ (4792) 1360 ⊕ (4792) 4381	164	ⓡ₁₂	♦♦♦ Ⓞ & P
▲ **Wörthsee** - JH Steinebach Herbergsstr 10, 82237 Wörthsee (Bavaria).	☎ (8153) 7206 ⊕ (8153) 89214	30	16.01–30.11	Ⓞ
▲ **Wunsiedel** Am Katharinenberg 4, 95632 Wunsiedel (Bavaria).	☎ (9232) 1851 ⊕ (9232) 70629	112	11.01–30.11	♦♦♦ Ⓞ Ⓡ & ♂ ⓞ
▲ **Wuppertal-Barmen** Obere Lichtenplatzerstr 70, 42287 Wuppertal. ⊖ jh-wuppertal@djh-rheinland.de	☎ (202) 552372 ⊕ (202) 557354	140	01.01–24.12; 27–31.12	Ⓞ ♂
▲ **Würzburg** - JGH ⒾⒷⓃ Burkarderstr 44, 97082 Würzburg (Bavaria).	☎ (931) 42590; (931) 42595 ⊕ (931) 416862	254	ⓡ₁₂	♦♦♦ Ⓞ &
▲ **Wüstewohlde** Wüstewohlde Nr 20, 27624 Ringstedt.	☎ (4708) 234 ⊕ (4708) 234	74	ⓡ₁₂	Ⓞ P
▲ **Wyk auf Föhr** Fehrstieg 41, 25938 Wyk auf Föhr. ⊖ jhwyk@djh-nordmark.de	☎ (4681) 2355 ⊕ (4681) 5527	168	01.02–22.12	♦♦♦ Ⓞ P ⓞ
▲ **Zeven-Bademühlen** Haus Nr 1, 27404 Zeven.	☎ (4281) 2550 ⊕ (4281) 80293	130	ⓡ₁₂	♦♦♦ Ⓞ 4W & P
▲ **Zielow** 17207 Ludorf, OT. Zielow. ⊖ jh-zielow@t-online.de	☎ (39923) 2547 ⊕ (39923) 28096	98	30.12.00– 19.12.01	♦♦♦ Ⓞ Ⓡ P
▲ **Zingst** Glebbe 14, 18374 Ostseebad Zingst. ⊖ jh-zingst@t-online.de	☎ (38232) 15465 ⊕ (38232) 12285	160	01.02–02.01	♦♦♦ Ⓞ Ⓡ P
▲ **Zinnwald** - "Jägerhütte" Bergmannsweg 8, 01773 Altenberg. ⊖ jhzinnwald@djh-sachsen.de	☎ (35056) 32361 ⊕ (35056) 32317	70	ⓡ₁₂	♦♦♦ Ⓞ 3SE P
▲ **Zinnwald** - "Klügelhütte" Hochmoorweg 12, 01773 Altenberg.	☎ (35056) 35882 ⊕ (35056) 32458	47	ⓡ₁₂	♦♦♦ Ⓞ 3S ⓞ
▲ **Zöblitz** Freiberger Str. 37, 09517 Zöblitz.	☎ (37363) 14871 ⊕ (37363) 14871	55	ⓡ₁₂	♦♦♦ Ⓞ
▲ **Zuflucht** Schwarzwaldhochstrasse, 72250 Zuflucht.	☎ (7804) 611 ⊕ (7804) 1323	228	01.01–10.11; 27–31.12	♦♦♦ Ⓞ P ⓞ
▲ **Zwiesel** Hindenburgstr 26, 94227 Zwiesel (Bavaria).	☎ (9922) 1061 ⊕ (9922) 60191	53	01.01–14.11; 27–31.12	♦♦♦ Ⓞ P
▲ **Zwingenberg** Die Lange Schneise 11, 64673 Zwingenberg. ⊖ zwingenberg@djh-hessen.de	☎ (6251) 75938 ⊕ (6251) 788113	125	27.12.00– 23.12.01	Ⓞ 1NE

Greece

GRECE

GRIECHENLAND

GRECIA

IYHF Athens International Hostel,
16 Victor Hugo Street,
Athens, Greece.

☎ (30) (1) 5234170
📠 (30) (1) 5234015

Capital:	Athens	**Population:**	10,257,000
Language:	Greek (Hellenic)	**Size:**	131,044 sq km
Currency:	GDR (drachma)	**Telephone Country Code:**	30

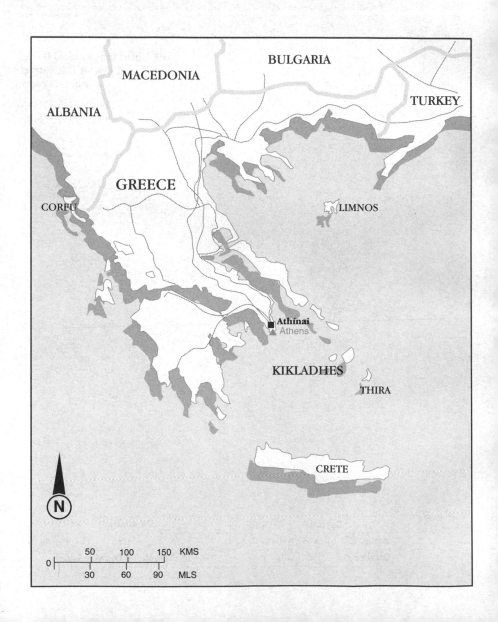

ALBANIA

MACEDONIA

BULGARIA

TURKEY

GREECE

CORFU

LIMNOS

Athínai
Athens

KIKLADHES

THIRA

CRETE

N

| 0 | 50 | 100 | 150 | KMS |
| | 30 | 60 | 90 | MLS |

English

Reconfirm transportation schedules - these are prone to change at short notice. Hostels are located in cities.

Price range

Price range GDR 2,300-2,850. € 6.74-8.35. ⃞BB inc ⃞.

Rooms and Reservations

Ⓡ ⃞₁₂ (All Rooms). Reservations via (IBN) or Hostel by ❶ ❶. All hostels are non-smoking.

Guests

The maximum stay is 6 days. Age limits may apply for children - check with hostel. ⁂ welcome. Group bookings via Hostel by ❶.

Open times

Main hostels: open ⃞₁₂, ⃝. Reception open: ⃝.

Meals

⃝ BLD Ⓡ For individuals & for ⁂. ⛝ Not all utensils provided - check with hostel. Charges may apply.

Travelling around

For ease of travel use 🚂 ⛴ 🚌 Self-Drive. Drive on the right. There is no rail network in Western Greece

Travel/Activity Packages

Tours/sightseeing and accommodation/transport packages available. Package bookings via Hostel by ❶.

Passports and Visas

Passport, Photo ID and Visa required.

Health

Emergency medical treatment is free. Medical insurance is recommended. EU Nationals require Form E111 to obtain treatment within EU countries.

Français

Veuillez reconfirmer vos horaires de transport - ceux-ci ont tendance à varier au dernier moment. Les auberges sont situées dans les villes.

Tarifs des nuitées

Tarifs des nuitées 2,300-2,850 GDR. € 6.74-8.35. ⃞BB inc ⃞.

Chambres et réservations

Ⓡ ⃞₁₂ (Toutes chambres). Réservations via (IBN) ou l'auberge par ❶ ❶. Toutes les auberges sont non-fumeurs.

Usagers

La durée maximale du séjour est de 6 jours. Il est possible que des limites d'âge soient en vigueur pour les enfants - vérifiez auprès de l'auberge. Accueil des ⁂. Réservations pour groupes via l'auberge par ❶.

Horaires d'ouverture

Grandes auberges: ouvertes ⃞₁₂, ⃝. Accueil ouvert ⃝.

Repas

⃝ BLD Ⓡ Pour individuels & pour ⁂. ⛝ Pas tous les ustensils sont fournis - à vérifier auprès de l'auberge. Une contribution pourra vous être demandée.

Déplacements

Modes de transport recommandés 🚂 ⛴ 🚌 Voiture. La conduite est à droite. Il n'existe pas de réseau ferroviaire dans l'ouest de la Grèce.

Forfaits Voyages/Activités

Forfaits circuits touristiques et hébergement/transport disponibles. Réservations des forfaits via l'auberge par ❸.

Passeports et visas

Passeport, pièce d'identité avec photo et visa obligatoires.

Santé

Soins d'urgence gratuits. Une assurance médicale de voyage est conseillée. Les ressortissants de l'Union Européenne doivent se munir du formulaire E111 pour bénéficier de soins médicaux dans les états de l'UE.

Deutsch

Fahrpläne von Verkehrsmitteln erneut bestätigen lassen - diese können sich leicht kurzfristig ändern. Herbergen befinden sich in Städten.

Preisspanne

Preisspanne 2,300-2,850 GDR. € 6.74-8.35. BB inc 🍴.

Zimmer und Reservierungen

❿ 🖼 (Alle Zimmer). Reservierungen über IBN oder die Herberge per ❸ ❸. Rauchen ist in allen Herbergen NICHT gestattet.

Gäste

Der maximale Aufenthalt beträgt 6 Tage. Altersbegrenzungen für Kinder möglich - in der Herberge nachfragen. ♦♦♦ willkommen. Gruppenbuchungen über Herberge per ❸.

Öffnungszeiten

Hauptherbergen: Zugang 🖼, ⌚. Rezeption ⌚.

Mahlzeiten

🍽 BLD ❿ Für Einzelreisende & für ♦♦♦. ♂ Nicht alle Utensilien werden bereitgestellt - in der Herberge nachfragen. Kosten können anfallen.

Reisen im Land

Reisen ist einfach mit 🚂 ⛴ 🚌 Selbstfahrer. Rechts fahren. Es besteht kein Eisenbahnnetz in West-griechenland.

Reise-/Aktivitäten-Packages

Touren/sightseeing und Unterkunft/Transport-Packages erhältlich. Package-Buchungen über Herberge per ❸.

Reisepässe und Visa

Reisepass, Personalausweis und Einreisevisum erforderlich.

Gesundheit

Nur im Notfall sind medizinische Behandlungen kostenlos. Unfall-/Krankenversicherung wird empfohlen. EU Staatsangehörige benötigen Formular E111 für ärztliche Behandlungen innerhalb der EU Länder.

Español

Es aconsejable comprobar los horarios de los transportes, ya que suelen cambiar con frecuencia. Los albergues están situados en las ciudades.

Tarifas mínima y máxima

Tarifas mínima y máxima 2,300-2,850 GDR. € 6.74-8.35. BB inc 🍴.

Habitaciones y Reservas

❿ 🖼 (Todas las habitaciones). Reservas por IBN o a través del albergue por ❸ ❸. Está prohibido fumar en todos los albergues.

Huéspedes

La estancia máxima es de 6 días. Es posible que exista un límite de edad para los niños - consulte con el albergue. Se admiten ♦♦♦. Reservas de grupo a través del albergue por ❶.

Horarios y fechas de apertura

Albergues principales - abiertos 🗓, 🕐. Horario de recepción: 🕐.

Comidas

🍽 BLD ⓡ Para individuales y para ♦♦♦. ☞ La cocina no dispone de todos los utensilios - consulte con el albergue. Es posible que se aplique un suplemento por el uso de la misma.

Desplazamientos

Transportes recomendados: 🚃 ⛴ 🚌 Automóvil. Se circula por la derecha. No hay una red ferroviaria en el oeste de Grecia.

Viajes Combinados con Actividades

Viajes combinados con visitas turísticas y alojamiento/transporte. Reserva de viajes combinados a través del albergue por ❶.

Pasaportes y Visados

Pasaporte o carnet de identidad y visado obligatorios.

Información Sanitaria

Asistencia médica de urgencia gratuita. Seguro médico recomendado. Los ciudadanos procedentes de países pertenecientes a la UE necesitan el impreso E111 para obtener asistencia médica en dichos países.

Athens - IYHF Athens International Hostel "Victor Hugo"

16 Victor Hugo St, 10438 Athens.
❶ (1) 5234170
❶ (1) 5234015
📧 athenshostel@interland.gr

Open Dates:	🗓
Open Hours:	🕐
Reservations:	ⓡ ⒾⒷⓃ
Price Range:	GDR 2,300-2,850 € 6.74-8.35 BBinc 🗨
Beds:	140 - 11x^{2}🛏 29x^{4}🛏
Facilities:	♦♦♦ 4x ♦♦♦ 🍽 (BL) ☞ 🍵 🏨 🧺 🔲 🖼 ⑧ 🔁 Ⓘ 🛒

Directions:	1.2NW from city centre
✈	Helliniko 15km
A🚌	#E91 Omonia Bus Stop 600m
⛴	Piraeus 8km
🚃	Central 500m
🚌	A7, B7 400m ap Kanigos Square
🚋	#1, #12 300m ap Agiou Konstantinou str
Ⓤ	Line 2, Metaxourhio, 150m; Omonia Sq. 500m

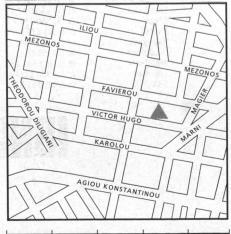

HOSTELLING
INTERNATIONAL

Make your credit card bookings at these centres
Réservez par cartes de crédit aux centres suivants
Reservieren Sie per Kreditkarte bei diesen Zentren
Reserve con tarjeta de crédito en los siguientes centros

English

Australia	☎ (2) 9261 1111
Canada	☎ (800) 663 5777
England & Wales	☎ (1629) 581 418
France	☎ (1) 44 89 87 27
Northern Ireland	☎ (28) 9032 4733
Republic of Ireland	☎ (1) 830 1766
New Zealand	☎ (3) 379 9808
Scotland	☎ (8701) 553 255
Switzerland	☎ (1) 360 1414
USA	☎ (202) 783 6161

Français

Angleterre & Pays de Galles	☎ (1692) 581 418
Australie	☎ (2) 9261 1111
Canada	☎ (800) 663 5777
Écosse	☎ (8701) 553 255
États-Unis	☎ (202) 783 6161
France	☎ (1) 44 89 87 27
Irlande du Nord	☎ (28) 9032 4733
Nouvelle-Zélande	☎ (3) 379 9808
République d'Irlande	☎ (1) 830 1766
Suisse	☎ (1) 360 1414

Deutsch

Australien	☎ (2) 9261 1111
England & Wales	☎ (1629) 581 418
Frankreich	☎ (1) 44 89 87 27
Irland	☎ (1) 830 1766
Kanada	☎ (800) 663 5777
Neuseeland	☎ (3) 379 9808
Nordirland	☎ (28) 9032 4733
Schottland	☎ (8701) 553 255
Schweiz	☎ (1) 360 1414
USA	☎ (202) 783 6161

Español

Australia	☎ (2) 9261 1111
Canadá	☎ (800) 663 5777
Escocia	☎ (8701) 553 255
Estados Unidos	☎ (202) 783 6161
Francia	☎ (1) 44 89 87 27
Inglaterra y Gales	☎ (1629) 581 418
Irlanda del Norte	☎ (28) 9032 4733
Nueva Zelanda	☎ (3) 379 9808
República de Irlanda	☎ (1) 830 1766
Suiza	☎ (1) 360 1414

IBN INTERNATIONAL BOOKING NETWORK

Hungary

HONGRIE

UNGARN

HUNGRIA

Magyarországi Ifjusági Szállások Szövetsége
H-1077 Budapest VII., Almàssy tèr 6. IV/404, Hungary

Postal Address: H-1410 Budapest, PO Box 119, Hungary

☎ (36) (1) 3435167
🖷 (36) (1) 3435167

Travel Section: Mellow Mood Ltd.
1134 Budapest
Dózsa Gy. út 152

☎ (36) (1) 3298644, 3408585
🖷 (36) (1) 3208425
✉ travel@hostels.hu
🖳 www.hostels.hu

A copy of the Hostel Directory for this Country can be obtained from:
Tourinform Offices
eg Keleti Rail Station, Budapest,
All Hostels
The National Office

Capital:	Budapest	**Population:**	10,750,000
Language:	Hungarian	**Size:**	93,030 sq km
Currency:	Ft (forints)	**Telephone Country Code:**	36

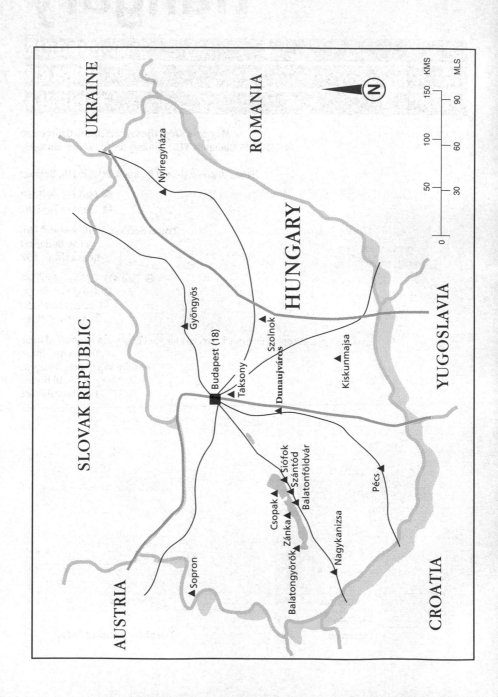

English

Hostels are located in cities, in the countryside and on hills/mountains.

Price range

Price range HUF 1500-3500. € 6-15. 🔲.

Rooms and Reservations

R during Jun-Sep. (¹🛏 ²🛏 ³🛏).
Reservations via National Booking Centre or Hostel by ❶ ❷ ❸. Smoking is limited - please check.

Guests

Membership Card and Passport/Photo ID are required. Pets are allowed - check with hostel. ††† welcome. Group bookings via National Booking Centre or Hostel by ❶ ❷ ❸.

Open times

Main hostels: open 🗓, 🕐. Reception open: 🕐. **Other hostels** open 🗓, 🕐. Reception open: 🕐. **Seasonal hostels** are generally open Jun-Aug.

Meals

🍽 B **R** For individuals & for †††. 🍴.

Travelling around

For ease of travel use 🚂 🚌 Self-Drive. Drinking alcohol and driving is strictly forbidden.

Travel/Activity Packages

Tours/sightseeing, cycling/mountain biking and accommodation/transport packages available. Package bookings via 🚐 National Booking Centre or Hostel by ❶ ❷ ❸.

Passports and Visas

Passport required.

Health

Medical insurance is recommended.

Français

Les auberges sont situées dans les villes, à la campagne et à la montagne.

Tarifs des nuitées

Tarifs des nuitées 1500-3500 HUF. € 6-15. 🔲.

Chambres et réservations

R juin-sep. (¹🛏 ²🛏 ³🛏). Réservations via le Centre National de Réservation ou l'auberge par ❶ ❷ ❸. Il est permis de fumer dans certaines chambres - veuillez vérifier.

Usagers

La carte d'adhérent ainsi que le passeport/pièce d'identité avec photo sont à présenter. Les animaux domestiques sont autorisés mais vérifiez lesquels auprès de l'auberge. Accueil des †††. Réservations pour groupes via le Centre National de Réservation ou l'auberge par ❶ ❷ ❸.

Horaires d'ouverture

Grandes auberges: ouvertes 🗓, 🕐. Accueil ouvert 🕐. **Autres auberges:** ouvertes 🗓, 🕐. Accueil ouvert 🕐. **Auberges saisonnières** ouvertes généralement juin-août.

Repas

🍽 B **R** Pour individuels & pour †††. 🍴.

Déplacements

Modes de transport recommandés 🚂 🚌 Voiture. Il est strictement interdit de conduire sous l'influence de l'alcool.

Forfaits Voyages/Activités

Forfaits circuits touristiques, cyclotourisme/VTT et hébergement/transport disponibles.

Réservations des forfaits via 🖂 le Centre National de Réservation ou l'auberge par ❶ ❻ ❸.

Passeports et visas

Passeport obligatoire.

Santé

Une assurance médicale de voyage est conseillée.

Deutsch

Herbergen befinden sich in Städten, auf dem Land und in Bergen/Gebirgen.

Preisspanne

Preisspanne 1500-3500 HUF. € 6-15. 🗐.

Zimmer und Reservierungen

❿ während Jun-Sept. (¹🛏 ²🛏 ³🛏). Reservierungen über Nationales Buchungszentrum oder Herberge per ❶ ❻ ❸. Rauchen ist begrenzt - bitte checken.

Gäste

Mitgliedsausweis und Reisepass/Personalausweis sind erforderlich. Haustiere sind erlaubt - in der Herberge nachfragen. ⋔ willkommen. Gruppenbuchungen über Nationales Buchungszentrum oder Herberge per ❶ ❻ ❸.

Öffnungszeiten

Hauptherbergen: Zugang 🗃, 🕔. Rezeption 🕔. **Andere Herbergen:** Zugang 🗃, 🕔. Rezeption 🕔. **Saison-Herbergen** sind normalerweise Jun-Aug geöffnet.

Mahlzeiten

🍽 B ❿ Für Einzelreisende & für ⋔. 🍴.

Reisen im Land

Reisen ist einfach mit 🚕 🚌 Selbstfahrer. Alkohol am Steuer ist streng verboten.

Reise-/Aktivitäten-Packages

Touren/sightseeing, Fahrrad/Mountainbiking und Unterkunft/Transport-Packages erhältlich. Package-Buchungen über 🖂 Nationales Buchungszentrum oder Herberge per ❶ ❻ ❸.

Reisepässe und Visa

Reisepass erforderlich.

Gesundheit

Unfall-/Krankenversicherung wird empfohlen.

Español

Los albergues están situados en las ciudades, el campo y la montaña.

Tarifas mínima y máxima

Tarifas mínima y máxima 1500-3500 HUF. € 6-15. 🗐.

Habitaciones y Reservas

❿ en jun-sep. (¹🛏 ²🛏 ³🛏). Reservas a través de la Central Nacional de Reservas o el albergue por ❶ ❻ ❸. Está permitido fumar sólo en algunas salas/habitaciones - infórmese.

Huéspedes

Los huéspedes deben presentar su Carnet de Alberguista y su pasaporte o carnet de identidad. Se admiten animales - consulte con el albergue. Se admiten ⋔. Reservas de grupo a través de la Central Nacional de Reservas o el albergue por ❶ ❻ ❸.

Horarios y fechas de apertura

Albergues principales - abiertos 🗃, 🕔. Horario de recepción: 🕔. **Otros albergues -**

abiertos 📧, 🕔. Horario de recepción: 🕔.
Albergues de temporada suelen abrir:
jun-ago.

Comidas

🍽 B (R) Para individuales y para 👪. 🔒.

Desplazamientos

Transportes recomendados: 🚲 🚌
Automóvil. Esta estrictamente prohibido
conducir bajo la influencia del alcohol.

Viajes Combinados con Actividades

Viajes combinados con visitas turísticas,
cicloturismo/bicicleta de montaña y
alojamiento/transporte. Reserva de viajes
combinados por 🖥 o a través de la Central
Nacional de Reservas o el albergue por 📞 📠
✉.

Pasaportes y Visados

Pasaporte obligatorio.

Información Sanitaria

Seguro médico recomendado.

"A person travels the world over in search of what he needs and returns home to find it."

"L'on parcourt le monde à la recherche de ce dont on a besoin et l'on revient chez soi pour le trouver."

„Der Mensch bereist die ganze Welt auf der Suche nach dem, was er braucht und kehrt heim, um es dort zu finden."

"Recorremos el mundo en busca de lo que necesitamos para al final encontrarlo en casa a nustro regreso"

George Moore

Balaton - Zánka

Zánkai Gyermek és Ifjúsági Centrum,
8250 Zánka/Balaton Nord.
☎ (87) 568500
🖷 (87) 568588
✉ zankaedu@mail.matav.hu

Open Dates: 🗓

Open Hours: 🕒

Reservations: **Ⓡ**

Price Range: US$5.00-21.00 € 6.00-21.00 🛏

Beds: 2600 - 5x^1🛏 222x^2🛏 82x^3🛏
60x^4🛏 146x^6🛏 85x^{6+}🛏

Facilities: ♿ 👫 300x 👫 🍽 🍴 ☕ 🛏
📺 🎱5 x🍽 🔲 📷 🏧 🔒 ⬆
🅿 ℹ 🧺 ♻ ⚠ 🌀 💱 🔍 🏛
🏡

Directions:
🚢   Zánka
🚂   Zánkafürdö
🚌   Zánka

Attractions: 🏌 ⛰ 🔍 100m 🚴 🏃 ∪3km 🎣
🏊

Budapest - Csillebérci Szabadidö és Ifjúsági Központ

Konkoly Thege Miklós u. 21,
1121 Budapest XII.
☎ (1) 2754033 or (1) 3956537
🖷 (1) 3957327
✉ csill@mail.datanet.hu

Open Dates: 🗓

Open Hours: 🕒

Reservations: **Ⓡ** **⊂CC⊃**

Price Range: US$6.00-22.00 🛏

Beds: 200 - 30x^2🛏 40x^3🛏 5x^4🛏

Facilities: ♿ 👫 4x 👫 🍽 🍴 ☕ 🛏 📺
🎱5 x🍽 🔲 📷 🏧 🔒 🅿 ℹ 🧺
♻ ⚠ 🌀 💱 🔍 🏛 🏡

Directions:
✈   Ferihegy 2 35km
🚂   Déli 5km
🚌   No. 90
Ⓤ   U2 Déli 5km

Attractions: 🏌 ⛰ 🔍 🚴 🏃 ∪10km 🎣 🏊

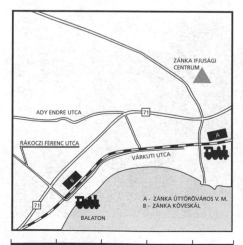

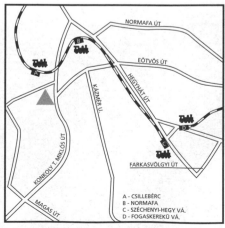

Budapest -
Hostel Fortuna

Gyáli Út 3/B,
1097 Budapest IX.
☎ (1) 2150660
📠 (1) 3208425
✉ info@reservation.hu

Open Dates: 🗓

Open Hours: ☺

Reservations: ® ⊢CC⊣

Price Range: 3800-5500 HUF ᴿᴿ ⁱⁿᶜ 🛏

Beds: 81 - 2x¹🛏 14x²🛏 5x³🛏 9x⁴🛏

Facilities: ♦♦♦ ♦♦ 🍽 ♂ 🍺 🚲 🛏 🖥 ▢
          📷 🅿 ⓘ 🛏 🏠

Directions: 2SW from city centre

✈ Ferihegy 2 15km

A🚐 Airport minibus 15km

🚢 Nemzetközi hajóállomás 4km

🚂 Keleti pályaudvar 3km

🚋 24 ap Nagyvárad tér

Ⓤ M3 Nagyvárad tér

Attractions: 🚴 🏊

Location/Address	Telephone No. Fax No.	Beds	Opening Dates	Facilities
△ *Balaton Csopak* - *Ifjúsági Üdülő* Sport u 9, 8229 Csopak.	☎ *(87) 446505* 🖷 *(87) 446515*	*292*	*01.05–30.09*	[icons]
△ *Balatongyörök* - *Ifjùsàgi Üdülö* Szépkilàtò, 8313 Balatongyörök.	☎ *(83) 346018* 🖷 *(92) 312770*	*264*	*15.05–15.09*	[icons]
▲ Balaton Siófok - Benjamin Panzió Siófoki út 9, 8600 Balatonszéplak-Felsö.	☎ (84) 350704	29		[icons]
▲ Balaton Szántód - Hotel Rév Szt. István u. 162, 8622 Szántód. ℮ revhotel@elender.hu	☎ (84) 348245 🖷 (84) 348245	124	01.04–31.10	[icons]
▲ Balaton - Zánka **Zánkai Gyermek és Ifjúsági Centrum, 8250 Zánka/Balaton Nord.** ℮ zankaedu@mail.matav.hu	☎ (87) 568500 🖷 (87) 568588	2600		[icons]
▲ Budapest - Csillebérci Szabadidö és Ifjúsági Központ **Konkoly Thege Miklós u. 21, 1121 Budapest XII.** ℮ csill@mail.datanet.hu	☎ (1) 2754033 or (1) 3956537 🖷 (1) 3957327	200		[icons]
▲ Budapest - Travellers' Hostel Diáksport Dózsa György út 152, 1134 Budapest XIII. ℮ info@hostels.hu	☎ (1) 3298644, 3408585 🖷 (1) 3208425	135		[icons]
▲ Budapest - Hostel Fortuna **Gyáli Út 3/B, 1097 Budapest IX.** ℮ info@reservation.hu	☎ (1) 2150660 🖷 (1) 3208425	81		[icons]
▲ Budapest - Hotel Góliat Kerekes u. 12-20, 1135 Budapest XIII. ℮ goliat@eravishotels.hu	☎ (1) 3501456 🖷 (1) 3494985	375		[icons]
▲ Budapest - Hotel Griff Junior Bartók B út 152, 1113 Budapest XI. ℮ junior@eravishotels.hu	☎ (1) 2032398 🖷 (1) 2031255	625		[icons]
△ *Budapest* - *Hostel Landler* Bartók B út 17, 1114 Budapest XI, Universum. ℮ universumhostels@mail.matav.hu	☎ *(1) 4633621,* 4633622 🖷 *(1) 2757046*	*250*	*01.07–05.09*	[icons]
▲ Budapest - Hotel Rila Fehér Holló Utca 2, 1097 Budapest IX. ℮ universumhostels@mail.matar.hu	☎ (1) 2161621 🖷 (1) 2155184	74		[icons]
△ *Budapest* - *Hostel Rózsa* Bercsényi u 28, 1117 Budapest XI, Universum. ℮ universumhostels@mail.matav.hu	☎ *(1) 4634250* 🖷 *(1) 2757046*	*200*	*01.07–05.09*	[icons]
△ *Budapest* - *Travellers' Hostel Schönherz* Irinyi J. u. 42, 1114 Budapest XI. ℮ travellers@hostels.hu	☎ *(1) 3408585* 🖷 *(1) 3208425*	*600*	*01.07–31.08*	[icons]
▲ Budapest - Hotel Stadion Ifjúság Útja 1-3, 1148 Budapest. ℮ hstadion@matavnet.hu	☎ (1) 2512222 🖷 (1) 2512062	80		[icons]

Location/Address	Telephone No. Fax No.	Beds	Opening Dates	Facilities
▲ Budapest - Hotel Touring Pünkösdfürdő u 38, 1039 Budapest III. ℮ touring@touring.hu	☎ (1) 2503184 ✆ (1) 2431595	365		
△ *Budapest - Hostel Vásárhelyi Kruspér u 2-4, 1111 Budapest XI, Universum.* ℮ *universumhostels@mail.matav.hu*	☎ *(1) 4634326, (1) 4634356* ✆ *(1) 2757046*	*500*	*01.07–05.09*	
△ *Budapest - Travellers' Hostel Bánki Podmaniczky u 8, 1067 Budapest VI.* ℮ *travellers@hostels.hu*	☎ *(1) 3408585* ✆ *(1) 3208425*	*80*	*01.07–31.08*	1 N
△ *Budapest - Best Hostel Podmaniczky u. 27, I/13., 1067 Budapest VI.* ℮ *bestyh@mail.datanet.hu*	☎ *(1) 3324934* ✆ *(1) 2692926*	*30*		1 N
△ *Budapest - Central Park Hostel Ajtósi Dürer sor 23, 1146 Budapest XIV.*	☎ *(1) 3431416* ✆ *(1) 3517393*	*210*	*05.07–31.08*	1.5 SW
▲ Budapest - Travellers' Hostel Hill Ménesi ut 5., 1118 Budapest XI. ℮ info@hostels.hu	☎ (1) 3408585 ✆ (1) 3208425	120	01.07–05.09	0.5 E
△ *Budapest - Travellers HostelUniversitas Irinyi u. 9-11, 1111 Budapest XI.* ℮ *info@hostels.hu*	☎ *(1) 3408585* ✆ *(1) 3208425*	*600*	*01.07–31.08*	1 W
▲ Dunaujváros - Kerpely Antal Kollégium Dózsa Gy. ut 33-37, 2400 Dunaujváros. ℮ kerpely@makacs.poliod.hu	☎ (25) 551120 ✆ (25) 410434	110		
△ *Gyöngyös - Energia Szálló Róbert Károly út 19, 3200 Gyöngyös.*	☎ *(37) 311363* ✆ *(37) 328027*	*220*		
▲ Kiskunmajsa - Jonathermál Rt. Motel, Kemping Kökút 26, 6133 Kiskunmajsa. ℮ jonathermal@mail.datanet.hu	☎ (77) 481855 ✆ (77) 481013	100		
△ *Nyiregyháza - Paradise Hotel and Youth Center Sóstófürdő, Sóstói u 76, 4431 Nyiregyháza.*	☎ *(42) 402011, 402038* ✆ *(42) 402011, 402038*	*269*		
▲ Pécs - Hotel Laterum Hajnóczy J.u. 37-39., 7633 Pécs.	☎ (72) 252108, (72) 252113 ✆ (72) 252131	416		
△ *Pécs - JPTE Kollégium Szántó Kovács János u. 1, 7633 Pécs.* ℮ *sebestye@btkstud.jpte.hu*	☎ *(72) 251203* ✆ *(72) 251203*	*255*		
▲ Siófok - Hotel Ezüstpart Liszt Ferenc sétány 2-4, 8609 Siófok, Balatonszéplak Felsö. ℮ reserve@balaton.hunguest.hu	☎ (84) 350622 ✆ (84) 351095	1608		
△ *Sopron - Ciklámen Bungalows Brennbergi-völgy, 9400 Sopron.* ℮ *pannonia_med_hotel@sopron.hu*	☎ *(99) 312180* ✆ *(99) 340766*	*52*	*01.05–31.10*	

Location/Address	Telephone No. Fax No.	Beds	Opening Dates	Facilities
▲ **Szolnok** - Turisztikai És Szabadidöközpont PF. 178, 5001 Szolnok-Tiszaliget. ❺ turisztikaikozpont@szolnex.hu	☎ (56) 424705 📠 (56) 424335	320	🛏	👫 🍽 1.5E ♿ 👞 P 🔒 🍺 🛵
△ *Taksony - Sziget Panzió Sziget sétány, Pf.9., 2335 Taksony.* ❺ *sziget@mail.interware.hu*	☎ *(24) 477477* 📠 *(24) 477774*	64	🛏	👫 🍽 R ⊂CC⊃ 👞 P 🍺

YOUTH HOSTEL ACCOMMODATION
OUTSIDE THE ASSURED STANDARDS SCHEME

Location/Address	Telephone No. Fax No.	Beds	Opening Dates	Facilities
Budapest - Hostel Apáczai Papnövelde u 4-6, 1053 Budapest V. Universum. ❺ universumhostels@mail.matav.hu	☎ (1) 2670311 📠 (1) 2757046	180	25.06–25.08	👫 🍽 R 👞 P 🔒
Budapest - Caterina Hostel Andrássy ut 47. III/18, 1061 Budapest VI. ❺ caterina@mail.inext.hu	☎ (1) 3420804, 2919538 📠 (1)3526147	20	🛏	👫 👞 P 🔒
Budapest - Station Guesthouse Mexikói ut 36/B, 1145 Budapest XIV. ❺ station@mail.matav.hu	☎ (1) 2218864 📠 (1) 3834034	45	🛏	R 3.5NE 👞 P 🔒 🍺

"Travelling is like gambling: it is always connected with winning and losing, and generally where it is least expected we receive more or less what we hoped for."

"Le voyage est pareil au jeu: il est toujours question de gagner et de perdre, et en général l'on reçoit plus ou moins ce que l'on espérait, alors que l'on s'y attend le moins."

„Reisen kommt dem Glücksspiel gleich: es ist immer mit Gewinn und Verlust verbunden, und wir bekommen allgemein dort, wo wir es am wenigsten erwarten, mehr oder weniger das, was wir erhofft hatten."

"El viajar es como un juego de azar: tiene que ver siempre con ganar y perder y, generalmente, en el momento menos pensado recibimos más o menos lo que esperábamos."

Johann Wolfgang Von Goethe

Iceland

ISLANDE
ISLAND
ISLANDIA

Bandalag Íslenskra Farfugla,
(Icelandic Youth Hostel Association)
Sundlaugavegur 34,
105 Reykjavík, Iceland.

☎ (354) 553 8110
📠 (354) 588 9201
✉ info@hostel.is
🖥 www.hostel.is

Office Hours: Monday-Friday, 09.00-17.00hrs

A copy of the Hostel Directory for this Country can be obtained from:
The National Office

Capital:	Reykjavík		**Population:**	265,000
Language:	Icelandic		**Size:**	103,000 sq km
Currency:	Kr (kronúr)		**Telephone Country Code:**	354

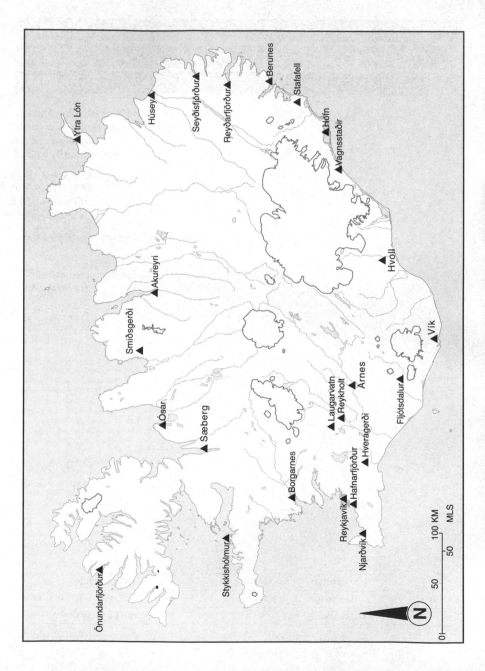

English

HI Iceland also runs a travel section which offers professional assistance while planning or arranging your travels in Iceland. For further information take a look at our homepage www.hostel.is. Hostels are located in cities, in the countryside and on the coast.

Price range

Price range IKR 1250-1500. 📖.

Rooms and Reservations

R during May-Sep. (¹🛏 ²🛏 ³🛏 ⁴🛏 👪). Reservations via National Booking Centre, Hostel or National Office by ❶ ❷. Smoking is limited - please check.

Guests

Membership Card is required. 👪 welcome. Group bookings via National Booking Centre, Hostel or National Office by ❶ ❷.

Open times

Main hostels: open 📖, 08:00-24:00hrs. Reception open: 08:00-24:00hrs. Resident manager.

Meals

🍴 B **R** For individuals & for 👪. 🔥.

Travelling around

For ease of travel use 🚐 Self-Drive.

Travel/Activity Packages

Tours/sightseeing, walking/trekking and accommodation/transport packages available. Package bookings via National Booking Centre or National Office by ❶ ❷.

Health

Medical insurance is recommended. EU Nationals require Form E111 to obtain treatment within EU countries.

Français

HI Iceland gère également un bureau de voyage qui propose un service professionnel pour la préparation de vos voyages en Islande. Pour un complément d'informations, jetez un coup d'oeil sur notre site Web à www.hostel.is. Les auberges sont situées dans les villes, à la campagne et sur le littoral.

Tarifs des nuitées

Tarifs des nuitées 1250-1500 IKR. 📖.

Chambres et réservations

R mai-sep. (¹🛏 ²🛏 ³🛏 ⁴🛏 👪). Réservations via le Centre National de Réservation, l'auberge ou le Bureau National par ❶ ❷. Il est permis de fumer dans certaines chambres - veuillez vérifier.

Usagers

La carte d'adhérent est à présenter. Accueil des 👪. Réservations pour groupes via le Centre National de Réservation, l'auberge ou le Bureau National par ❶ ❷.

Horaires d'ouverture

Grandes auberges: ouvertes 📖, entre 8h-24h. Accueil ouvert entre 8h-24h. Gérant réside sur place.

Repas

🍴 B **R** Pour individuels & pour 👪. 🔥.

Déplacements

Modes de transport recommandés 🚐 Voiture.

Forfaits Voyages/Activités

Forfaits circuits touristiques, randonnées pédestres et hébergement/transport disponibles. Réservations des forfaits via le Centre National de Réservation ou le Bureau National par ❶ ❷.

Santé

Une assurance médicale de voyage est conseillée. Les ressortissants de l'Union Européenne doivent se munir du formulaire E111 pour bénéficier de soins médicaux dans les états de l'UE.

Deutsch

HI Island betreibt auch eine Reiseabteilung, die fachliche Hilfe beim Planen und Arrangieren Ihrer Reisen innerhalb Islands bietet. Weitere Informationen finden Sie auf unserer Webseite www.hostel.is. Herbergen befinden sich in Städten, auf dem Land und an der Küste.

Preisspanne

Preisspanne 1250-1500 IKR. 🈺.

Zimmer und Reservierungen

R während Mai-Sept. (¹🐾 ²🐾 ³🐾 ⁴🐾 👬).
Reservierungen über Nationales Buchungszentrum, Herberge oder Landesverband per ❶ ❷. Rauchen ist begrenzt - bitte checken.

Gäste

Mitgliedsausweis ist erforderlich.
👬 willkommen. Gruppenbuchungen über Nationales Buchungszentrum, Herberge oder Landesverband per ❶ ❷.

Öffnungszeiten

Hauptherbergen: Zugang 🖥, 08:00-24:00Uhr. Rezeption zwischen 08:00-24:00Uhr. Herbergsmanager wohnt im Haus.

Mahlzeiten

🍽 B **R** Für Einzelreisende & für 👬. 👞.

Reisen im Land

Reisen ist einfach mit 🚐 Selbstfahrer.

Reise-/Aktivitäten-Packages

Touren/sightseeing, wandern/trekking und Unterkunft/Transport-Packages erhältlich. Package-Buchungen über Nationales Buchungszentrum oder Landesverband per ❶ ❷.

Gesundheit

Unfall-/Krankenversicherung wird empfohlen. EU Staatsangehörige benötigen Formular E111 für ärztliche Behandlungen innerhalb der EU Länder.

Español

Hostelling International Islandia también tiene una seccion de viajes que ofrece un servicio profesional para ayudarle a planear y organizar sus viajes por el pais. Para más información, consulte nuestra página de Internet www.hostel.is. Los albergues están situados en las ciudades, el campo y la costa.

Tarifas mínima y máxima

Tarifas mínima y máxima 1250-1500 IKR. 🈺.

Habitaciones y Reservas

R en may-sep. (¹🐾 ²🐾 ³🐾 ⁴🐾 👬).
Reservas a través de la Central Nacional de Reservas, el albergue o la Asociación Nacional por ❶ ❷. Está permitido fumar sólo en algunas salas/habitaciones - infórmese.

Huéspedes

Los huéspedes deben presentar su Carnet de Alberguista. Se admiten 👬. Reservas de grupo a través de la Central Nacional de Reservas, el albergue o la Asociación Nacional por ❶ ❷.

Horarios y fechas de apertura

Albergues principales - abiertos ▣, 08:00-24:00h. Horario de recepción: 08:00-24:00h. Gerente residente.

Comidas

¶⊙| B Ⓡ Para individuales y para ♦♦♦. ☞.

Desplazamientos

Transportes recomendados: 🚐 Automóvil.

Viajes Combinados con Actividades

Viajes combinados con visitas turísticas, senderismo y alojamiento/transporte. Reserva de viajes combinados a través de la Central Nacional de Reservas o la Asociación Nacional por ❶ ❷.

Información Sanitaria

Seguro médico recomendado. Los ciudadanos procedentes de países pertenecientes a la UE necesitan el impreso E111 para obtener asistencia médica en dichos países.

"They change their climate, not their soul, who rush across the sea."

"Ils changent de climat, pas d'âme, ceux qui se précipitent pour traverser les océans."

„Die, die über das Meer eilen, wechseln zwar das Klima, jedoch nicht ihre Seele."

"Cambian de clima, no de alma, quienes veloces atraviesan mares."

Horace

Location/Address	Telephone No. Fax No.	Beds	Opening Dates	Facilities
▲ **Akureyri** Stórholt 1, 600 Akureyri. ℮ storholt@nett.is	☏ 4623657, 8944299 ℻ 4612549	56	10.01–15.12	� ⌂ ㏄ ⚿ Ⓟ
▲ **Árnes** Gnúpverjahreppur, 801 Selfoss. ℮ bergleif@centrum.is	☏ 4866048/ 8612645 ℻ 4866091	32	⑫	♟ ⑂ Ⓡ ㏄ ⚿ Ⓟ
▲ **Berunes** Berufjörd, 765 Djúpivogur. ℮ berunes@simnet.is	☏ 4788988/ 8550026 ℻ 4788988	34	01.05–01.10	♟ ⑂ ㏄ ⚿ Ⓟ ⮭
△ *Fljótsdalur* *Fljótshlíð, 861 Hvolsvollur.*	☏ *4878498,* *4878497*	*15*	*15.04–15.10*	*⚿ Ⓟ*
▲ **Hafnarfjörður** - Arahús Strandgata 21, 220 Hafnarfjörður. ℮ arah@mmedia.is	☏ 5550795 ℻ 5553658	34	15.05–31.08	♟ ⚿ Ⓟ
▲ **Hafnarfjörður** - Hraunbyrgi Hjallabraut 51, Box 190, 220 Hafnarfjörður. ℮ hostel@hraunbuar	☏ 5650900 ℻ 5551211	50	⑫	♟ ⑂ ㏄ ⚿ Ⓟ ⌂
▲ **Hamar** Golfskálinn Hamri, 310 Borgarnes. ℮ gb@aknet.is	☏ 4371663 ℻ 4372063	14	15.05–15.09	♟ ⑂ ⚿ Ⓟ
▲ **Höfn** - Nýibær Hafnarbraut 8, 780 Höfn. ℮ nyibaer@simnet.is	☏ 4781736/ 8642159 ℻ 4781965	33	01.03–31.12	♟ ⑂ ㏄ ⚿ Ⓟ ⌂
▲ **Húsey** Tungnahreppur, 701 Egilsstadir.	☏ 4713010 ℻ 4713009	21	20.05–30.09	♟ ⚿ Ⓟ ⌂
▲ **Hveragerði** Ból, Hveramörk 14, 810 Hveragerði.	☏ 4834198, 4834588 ℻ 4834088	33	01.05–15.09	♟ ⑂ ㏄ ⚿ Ⓟ
▲ **Hvoll** Skaftárhreppur, 880 Klaustur. ℮ nupsstadarskogur@isholf.is	☏ 4874785/ 4874784 ℻ 4874890	37	01.04–01.10	♟ ⑂ Ⓡ ⚿ Ⓟ ⌂ ⮭
▲ **Laugarvatn** - Dalsel 840 Laugarvatn.	☏ 4861215, 8995409 ℻ 4861215	21	⑫	♟ ⑂ ㏄ ⚿ Ⓟ ⌂
▲ **Njarðvík** - Strönd Njarðvíkurbraut 52-54, 260 Innri Njarðvík. ℮ strond@centrum.is	☏ 4216211 ℻ 4216211	50	⑫	♟ ⑂ ㏄ ⚿ Ⓟ ⌂
▲ **Önundarfjördur** Korpudalur Kirkjubol, 425 Flateyri. ℮ korpudalur@centrum.is	☏ 4567808/ 8922030 ℻ 4567808	24	01.06–01.09	♟ ⑂ ⚿ Ⓟ ⌂
▲ **Ósar** Pverárhreppi, V-Hún, 531 Hvammstangi. ℮ osar@isholf.is	☏ 8622778 ℻ 4512678	20	01.05–01.10	♟ ㏄ ⚿ Ⓟ ⌂ ⮭
▲ **Reydarfjördur** - Tærgesenshùsinu Búdargata 4, 730 Reydarfjördur. ℮ gistirey@mmedia	☏ 4741447/ 8922207 ℻ 4741547	22	⑫	♟ ⑂ ㏄ ⚿ Ⓟ ⌂

Location/Address	Telephone No. Fax No.	Beds	Opening Dates	Facilities
▲ **Reykholt** Biskupstungum, 801 Selfoss.	t 4868830, 4868810 f 4868709	70	10.06–20.08	CC P
▲ **Reykjavík** Sundlaugavegur 34, 105 Reykjavík. e info@hostel.is	t 5538110 f 5889201	170	05.01–20.12	3W CC P
▲ **Seyðisfjörður** - Hafaldan Ránargata 9, 710 Seyðisfjörður. e thorag@simnet.is	t 4721410/ 8917010 f 4721610	28	15.04–15.10	CC P
▲ **Sæberg** Reykir, Hrútafjörður, 500 Brú. e saeberg@isholf.is	t 4510015 f 4510034	32	12	P
▲ **Smiðsgerði** Hólahreppur, 550 Sauðárkrókur. e jaf@ismennt.is	t 8634992/ 4537483/ 4311050 f 4537483	11	15.06–20.08	P
▲ **Stafafell** Lóni, 781 Höfn. e stafafel@eldhorn.is	t 4781717 f 4781785	56	01.04–01.10	P
▲ **Stykkishólmur** Höfðagata 1, 340 Stykkishólmur.	t 4381095/ 8612517 f 4381417	50	01.05–30.09	P
▲ **Vagnsstadir** Sudursveit, A-Skaftafellssysla, 781 Höfn. e glacierjeeps@simnet.is	t 4781048, 4781567 f 4782167	28	15.06–10.09	CC P
▲ **Vík** - Norður - Vík Suðurvíkurvegur 5, 870 Vík. e nordur-vik@simnet.is	t 4871106/ 8672389/ 8611779 f 4871303	18	15.05–15.09	R P
▲ **Ytra Lón** Langanes, 681 Þórshöfn. e ytralon@mmedia.is	t 4681242, 8543797 f 4681242	8	12	P

"The tourist who moves about to see and hear and open himself to all the influences of the places which condense centuries of human greatness is only a man in search of excellence."

"Le touriste qui voyage pour voir et entendre et s'ouvrir à toutes les influences des lieux qui condensent des siècles de grandeur humaine est tout simplement un homme à la recherche de l'excellence."

„Der Tourist, der unterwegs ist, um zu schauen und zu hören und sich den Einflüssen der Orte zu eröffnen, die Jahrhunderte menschlicher Größe zusammenfassen, ist einfach ein Mensch auf der Suche nach Großartigem."

"El turista que se desplaza para ver y oír y abrirse a todas las influencias de los lugares en que se condensan siglos de grandeza humana es simplemente un hombre en busca de excelencia."

Max Lerner

Ireland (Northern)

IRLANDE DU NORD
NORDIRLAND
IRLANDA DEL NORTE

Hostelling International - Northern Ireland,
22 Donegall Road, Belfast,
BT12 5JN, Northern Ireland.

t (44) (28) 90324733
f (44) (28) 90439699
e info@hini.org.uk
w www.hini.org.uk

Office Hours: Monday-Friday, 09.00-17.00hrs

A copy of the Hostel Directory for this Country can be obtained from:
The National Office

Capital:	Belfast	**Population:**	1,578,100
Language:	English	**Size:**	14,120 sq km
Currency:	£ (Sterling)	**Telephone Country Code:**	44

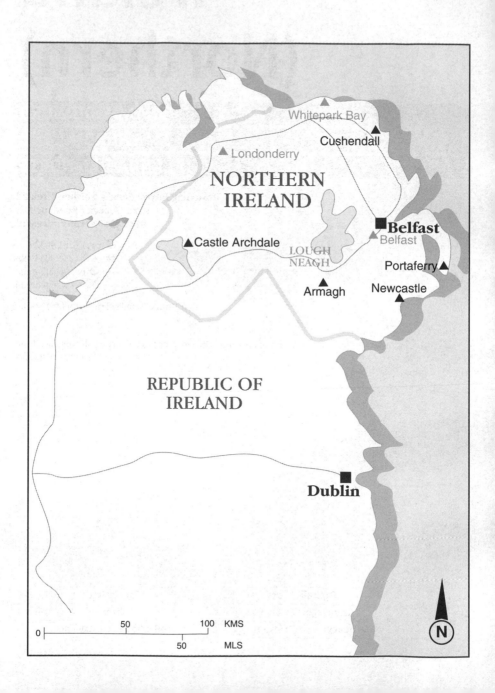

NORTHERN
IRELAND

Whitepark Bay

Cushendall

▲ Londonderry

■ **Belfast**
Belfast

▲Castle Archdale

LOUGH
NEAGH

Portaferry ▲

Armagh

Newcastle

REPUBLIC OF
IRELAND

■ **Dublin**

50   100   KMS

0

50   MLS

N

English

Northern Ireland is small - one can travel east to west or north to south of the province and return in one day. For specific details check with head office or individual hostels. Hostels are located in cities, in the countryside and on the coast.

Price range

Price range £8.00-12.50. € 12.80-20.00.

Rooms and Reservations

R during Jun-Sep. (All Rooms). Reservations via **IBN** Hostel or National Office by **t** **f** **e**. Smoking is limited - please check.

Guests

Membership Card and Passport/Photo ID are required. Age limits may apply for children - check with hostel. **iii** welcome. Group bookings via **IBN** Hostel or National Office by **t** **f** **e**.

Open times

Main hostels: open 🗓, ⊕. Reception open: ⊕. Resident manager. **Other hostels:** open Mar-Dec, 07:30-11:00hrs, 17:00-23:00hrs. Reception open: 07:30-11:00hrs, 17:00-23:00hrs. Resident manager. **Seasonal hostels** are generally open Mar-Oct.

Meals

🍽 BD **R** For individuals & for **iii**. ♂.

Discounts

HI Member Discounts available - see discounts section and www.iyhf.org.

Travelling around

For ease of travel use 🚄 🚌 Self-Drive. Bus services are more extensive April - Sept.

Travel/Activity Packages

Tours/sightseeing packages available.

Health

Medical insurance is recommended. EU Nationals require Form E111 to obtain treatment within EU countries.

Français

L'Irlande du Nord est un petit territoire que l'on peut franchir d'est en ouest ou du nord au sud - et revenir à son point de depart - en un seul jour. Pour plus de renseignements, veuillez contacter le bureau national ou chaque auberge. Les auberges sont situées dans les villes, à la campagne et sur le littoral.

Tarifs des nuitées

Tarifs des nuitées 8.00-12.50£. € 12.80-20.00.

Chambres et réservations

R juin-sep. (Toutes chambres). Réservations via **IBN** l'auberge et le Bureau National par **t** **f** **e**. Il est permis de fumer dans certaines chambres - veuillez vérifier.

Usagers

La carte d'adhérent ainsi que le passeport/pièce d'identité avec photo sont à présenter. Il est possible que des limites d'âge soient en vigueur pour les enfants - vérifiez auprès de l'auberge. Accueil des **iii**. Réservations pour groupes via **IBN** l'auberge et le Bureau National par **t** **f** **e**.

Horaires d'ouverture

Grandes auberges: ouvertes 🗓, ⊕. Accueil ouvert ⊕. Gérant réside sur place. **Autres auberges:** ouvertes mar-déc, entre 7h30-11h, 17h-23h. Accueil ouvert entre 7h30-11h,

17h-23h. Gérant réside sur place. **Auberges saisonnières** ouvertes généralement mar-oct.

Repas

🍽 BD **R** Pour individuels & pour 👪. 🐾.

Remises

Remises pour les adhérents HI - voir la section "Remises" et notre site: www.iyhf.org.

Déplacements

Modes de transport recommandés � 🚐 Voiture. Les services de bus sont plus nombreux entre avril et septembre.

Forfaits Voyages/Activités

Forfaits circuits touristiques disponibles.

Santé

Une assurance médicale de voyage est conseillée. Les ressortissants de l'Union Européenne doivent se munir du formulaire E111 pour bénéficier de soins médicaux dans les états de l'UE.

Deutsch

Nordirland ist klein - man kann an einem Tag von Osten nach Westen oder von Norden nach Süden und zurück reisen. Besondere Einzelheiten erhalten Sie von der Hauptgeschäftsstelle oder einzelnen Jugendherbergen. Herbergen befinden sich in Städten, auf dem Land und an der Küste.

Preisspanne

Preisspanne 8.00-12.50 £. € 12.80-20.00.

Zimmer und Reservierungen

R während Jun-Sept. (Alle Zimmer). Reservierungen über **IBN** Herberge oder Landesverband per ❶ ❷ ❸. Rauchen ist begrenzt - bitte checken.

Gäste

Mitgliedsausweis und Reisepass/ Personalausweis sind erforderlich. Altersbegrenzungen für Kinder möglich - in der Herberge nachfragen. 👪 willkommen. Gruppenbuchungen über **IBN** Herberge oder Landesverband per ❶ ❷ ❸.

Öffnungszeiten

Hauptherbergen: Zugang 🖥, 🕒. Rezeption 🕒. Herbergsmanager wohnt im Haus. **Andere Herbergen:** Zugang zwischen Mär-Dez, 07:30-11:00Uhr, 17:00-23:00Uhr. Rezeption zwischen 07:30-11:00Uhr, 17:00-23:00Uhr. Herbergsmanager wohnt im Haus. **Saison-Herbergen** sind normalerweise Mär-Okt geöffnet.

Mahlzeiten

🍽 BD **R** Für Einzelreisende & für 👪. 🐾.

Ermäßigungen

HI-Mitgliedsrabatt ist erhältlich – siehe Teil für Rabatte und Ermäßigungen und www.iyhf.org.

Reisen im Land

Reisen ist einfach mit � 🚐 Selbstfahrer. April - Sept sind die Busdienste umfangreicher.

Reise-/Aktivitäten-Packages

Touren/sightseeing-Packages erhältlich.

Gesundheit

Unfall-/Krankenversicherung wird empfohlen. EU Staatsangehörige benötigen Formular E111 für ärztliche Behandlungen innerhalb der EU Länder.

Español

Irlanda del Norte es pequeña; se puede atravesar del este al oeste o del norte al sur y volver en una sola día. Para mas informacion contacte con la Asociacion Nacional o directamente con los albergues. Los albergues están situados en las ciudades, el campo y la costa.

Tarifas mínima y máxima

Tarifas mínima y máxima 8.00-12.50£. € 12.80-20.00.

Habitaciones y Reservas

R en jun-sep. (Todas las habitaciones). Reservas por **IBN** o a través del albergue o la Asociación Nacional por **t** **f** **e**. Está permitido fumar sólo en algunas salas/ habitaciones - infórmese.

Huéspedes

Los huéspedes deben presentar su Carnet de Alberguista y su pasaporte o carnet de identidad. Es posible que exista un límite de edad para los niños - consulte con el albergue. Se admiten **iii**. Reservas de grupo por **IBN** o a través del albergue o la Asociación Nacional por **t** **f** **e**.

Horarios y fechas de apertura

Albergues principales - abiertos 🕒, 🕑. Horario de recepción: 🕑. Gerente residente.

Otros albergues - abiertos mar-dic, 07:30-11:00h, 17:00-23:00h. Horario de recepción: 07:30-11:00h, 17:00-23:00h. Gerente residente. **Albergues de temporada** suelen abrir: mar-oct.

Comidas

🍴 BD **R** Para individuales y para **iii**. ☕.

Descuentos

Se conceden descuentos a los miembros de Hostelling International – véase la sección sobre descuentos y nuestra página Internet en www.iyhf.org.

Desplazamientos

Transportes recomendados: �# 🚌 Automóvil. Las companias de autobuses amplian sus servicios de abril a septiembre.

Viajes Combinados con Actividades

Viajes combinados con visitas turísticas.

Información Sanitaria

Seguro médico recomendado. Los ciudadanos procedentes de países pertenecientes a la UE necesitan el impreso E111 para obtener asistencia médica en dichos países.

"Own only what you can carry with you; know language, know countries, know people. Let your memory be your travel bag."

"Ne possède que ce que tu peux emporter avec toi; connais les langues, connais les pays, connais les gens. Que ta mémoire te serve de sac de voyage."

„Besitze nur, was du mitnehmen kannst; lerne Sprache, Länder, Leute kennen. Lass deine Erinnerung deine Reisetasche sein."

"Posee solamente lo que puedas llevar contigo; conoce los idiomas, conoce los países, conoce a la gente. Deja que tu memoria sea tu bolso de viaje."

Alexander Solzhenitsyn

Belfast -
International YH

22 Donegall Rd,
Belfast BT12 5JN.
t (28) 90315435
f (28) 90439699
e info@hini.org.uk

Open Dates: 🗓

Open Hours: 🕐

Reservations: **R** (IBN) -CC-

Price Range: £12.00-13.00 🛏

Beds: 120

Facilities: ♿ 👪 👨‍👦 🍳 🍷 🛄 📺 🎒 ▯
▭ 🚿 🔘 🔾 🅿 ℹ 🧺 🏔

Directions: 1 SW from city centre

✈ Belfast International 30.6km

⛴ Larne 35.7km, Donegall Quay
3.2km

🚎 Central 5km

🚌 89, 90 from City centre ap YH

Attractions: 🚵

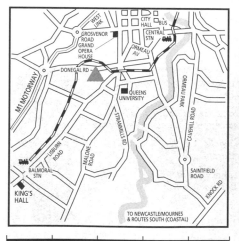

WEST LINK
CITY HALL
BUS
GROSVENOR ROAD
GRAND OPERA HOUSE
CENTRAL STN
ORMEAU AV
DONEGAL RD
M1 MOTORWAY
QUEENS UNIVERSITY
ORMEAU PARK
STRANMILLS RD
LISBURN ROAD
MALONE ROAD
CAVEHILL ROAD
BALMORAL STN
SAINTFIELD ROAD
KING'S HALL
KNOCK RD
TO NEWCASTLE/MOURNES & ROUTES SOUTH (COASTAL)

0 6km

Location/Address	Telephone No. Fax No.	Beds	Opening Dates	Facilities
▲ **Armagh City** 39 Abbey St, Armagh, BT61 7EB. ⓔ info@hini.org.uk	ⓣ (28) 37511800 ⓕ (28) 37511801	62	🔟	⁙ ⑩ 0.2SW ⑤ ⒸⒸ ☞ Ⓟ ⑥ ☕
▲ **Belfast** - International YH (IBN) **22 Donegall Rd, Belfast BT12 5JN.** ⓔ info@hini.org.uk	ⓣ (28) 90315435 ⓕ (28) 90439699	120	🔟	⁙ ⑩ Ⓡ 1SW ⑤ ⒸⒸ Ⓟ ⑥ ☕
△ *Castle Archdale* *Irvinestown, Co Fermanagh BT94 1PP.* ⓔ *info@hini.org.uk*	ⓣ *(28) 68628118* ⓕ *(28) 68628118*	*52*	*01.03–31.10*	⁙ ⑩ Ⓡ ⒸⒸ ☞ Ⓟ ⑥
▲ **Cushendall** Layde Rd, Cushendall, Co Antrim BT44 0NQ. ⓔ info@hini.org.uk	ⓣ (28) 21771344 ⓕ (28) 21772042	54	01.03–23.12	⁙ ⑩ Ⓡ ⒸⒸ ☞ Ⓟ
▲ **Londonderry** (IBN) Derry City Youth Hostel, 4-6 Magazine St, Londonderry BT48 6HJ.	ⓣ (28) 71284100 ⓕ (28) 71284101	120	🔟	⁙ ⑩ Ⓡ ⑤ ⒸⒸ ☞ ⑥ ☕
△ *Newcastle* *30 Downs Rd, Newcastle,* *Co Down BT33 0AG.* ⓔ *info@hini.org.uk*	ⓣ *(28) 43722133* ⓕ *(28) 43722133*	*40*	*01.03–23.12*	⁙ ⑩ ⒸⒸ ☞ ⑥
▲ **Portaferry** Barholm, 11 The Strand, Portaferry, Co Down BT22 1PS. ⓔ info@hini.org.uk	ⓣ (28) 42729784 ⓕ (28) 42729598	42	🔟	⁙ ⑩ Ⓡ 9W ⑤ Ⓟ ⑥
▲ **Whitepark Bay** (IBN) 157 Whitepark Bay Rd, Ballintoy, Ballycastle, Co Antrim BT54 6NH. ⓔ info@hini.org.uk	ⓣ (28) 20731745 ⓕ (28) 20732034	54	🔟	⁙ ⑩ Ⓡ 9W ⑤ ⒸⒸ ☞ Ⓟ ⑥

"Travel only with thy equals or thy betters; if there are none, travel alone."

"Ne voyage qu'avec tes égaux ou tes supérieurs; si tu n'en as pas, voyage tout seul."

„Reise nur mit deinesgleichen oder Höherstehenden; wenn es keine gibt, reise allein."

"Viaja solamente con tus iguales o con tus superiores; si no tienes ninguno, viaja solo."

The Dhammapada

International Booking Network

The advantages are cle[ar]

Ireland (Republic of)

IRLANDE (REPUBLIQUE D')
IRLAND
IRLANDA (REPUBLICA DE)

**An Óige, Irish Youth Hostel Association,
61 Mountjoy Street, Dublin 7, Republic of Ireland**

☎ (353) (1) 8304555
✆ (353) (1) 8305808
✉ mailbox@anoige.ie
🖳 www.irelandyha.org

Office Hours: Monday-Friday, 09.00-17.30hrs.

A copy of the Hostel Directory for this Country can be obtained from:
The National Office, or the Irish Tourist Board (office in most countries)

Capital:	Dublin	**Population:**	3,626,087
Language:	English/Irish	**Size:**	70,283 sq km
Currency:	IR£ (Irish punt)	**Telephone Country Code:**	353

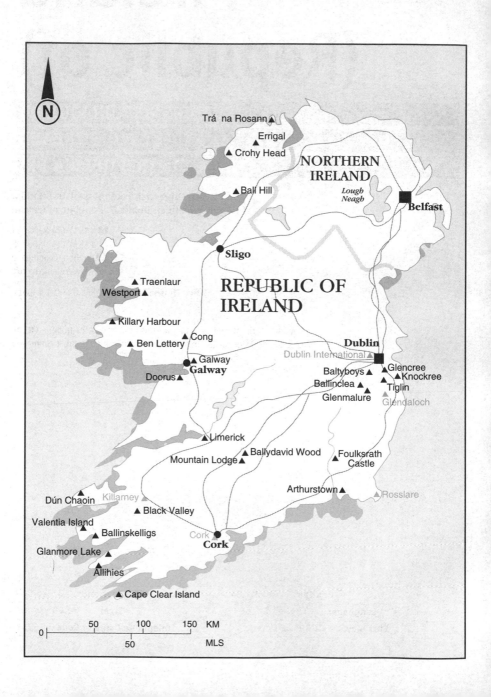

N

Trá na Rosann▲
Errigal
▲
▲ Crohy Head

NORTHERN
IRELAND

▲Ball Hill

Lough
Neagh

■
Belfast

●**Sligo**

▲Traenlaur
Westport▲

REPUBLIC OF
IRELAND

▲Killary Harbour

▲ Ben Lettery

▲Cong

●▲Galway
Galway

Doorus▲

Dublin
Dublin International▲■

Baltyboys ▲   ▲Glencree
                   ▲Knockree
Ballinclea ▲   Tiglin
Glenmalure   ▲
                   Glendaloch

▲Limerick

Mountain Lodge▲   ▲Ballydavid Wood   ▲Foulksrath
                                          Castle

Dún Chaoin▲   Killarney   Arthurstown ▲   Rosslare

Valentia Island▲ ▲ Black Valley

▲ Ballinskelligs

Glanmore Lake ▲   Cork
Allihies▲   ●
                  Cork

▲Cape Clear Island

0   50   100   150   KM
|————|————|————|
        50   MLS

English

Ensure that you have reserved your first night's accommodation. During high season, pre-book accommodation in Dublin, Cork, Limerick, Killarney and Glendaloch hostels. Hostels are located in cities, in the countryside, on the coast and on hills/mountains.

Price range

Price range IRP 5.00-8.50. € 6.35-10.80. 🏷 Sheet sleeping bag required.

Rooms and Reservations

🅡 during Mar, Apr, Jul-Sep. (²🚪 🚪). Reservations via (IBN) 🖱 National Booking Centre, Hostel or National Office by ❶ ❶ ❸. Smoking is limited - please check.

Guests

Membership Card is required. ♦♦♦ welcome. Group bookings via 🖱 National Booking Centre, Hostel or National Office by ❶ ❶ ❸.

Open times

Main hostels: open 🗓. Reception open: 07:00-22:00hrs. Resident manager. **Other hostels:** open Apr-Oct, 07:30-10:00hrs, 17:00-22:00hrs. Reception open: 07:30-10:00hrs, 17:00-22:00hrs. Resident manager. **Seasonal hostels** are generally open Jul, Aug.

Meals

🍴 BLD 🅡 For ♦♦♦. 🔥.

Discounts

HI Member Discounts available - see discounts section and www.iyhf.org.

Travelling around

For ease of travel use 🚎 🚌 Self-Drive. Car rental companies may require drivers to be over 23 years of age.

Travel/Activity Packages

Cycling/mountain biking, walking/trekking and accommodation/transport packages available. Package bookings via 🖱 National Booking Centre or National Office by ❶ ❶ ❸.

Passports and Visas

Passport and Visa required.

Health

Medical insurance is recommended. EU Nationals require Form E111 to obtain treatment within EU countries.

Français

Il est fortement conseillé de réserver ses premières nuitées. En pleine saison, réservez à l'avance vos séjours dans les auberges de Dublin, Cork, Limerick, Killarney et Glendaloch. Les auberges sont situées dans les villes, à la campagne, sur le littoral et à la montagne.

Tarifs des nuitées

Tarifs des nuitées 5.00-8.50 IRP. € 6.35-10.80. 🏷 Sac-drap obligatoire.

Chambres et réservations

🅡 mar, avril, juil-sep. (²🚪 🚪). Réservations via (IBN) 🖱 le Centre National de Réservation, l'auberge ou le Bureau National par ❶ ❶ ❸. Il est permis de fumer dans certaines chambres - veuillez vérifier.

Usagers

La carte d'adhérent est à présenter. Accueil des ♦♦♦. Réservations pour groupes via 🖱 le Centre National de Réservation, l'auberge ou le Bureau National par ❶ ❶ ❸.

Horaires d'ouverture

Grandes auberges: ouvertes 🗓. Accueil ouvert entre 7h-22h. Gérant réside sur place.

Autres auberges: ouvertes avril-oct, entre 7h30-10h, 17h-22h. Accueil ouvert entre 7h30-10h, 17h-22h. Gérant réside sur place. **Auberges saisonnières** ouvertes généralement juil, août.

Repas

⍥ BLD ⓡ Pour ♔. ♂.

Remises

Remises pour les adhérents HI - voir la section "Remises" et notre site: www.iyhf.org.

Déplacements

Modes de transport recommandés 🚐 🚍 Voiture. Les sociétés de location de véhicules exigent que les conducteurs soient âgés d'au moins 23 ans.

Forfaits Voyages/Activités

Forfaits cyclotourisme/VTT, randonnées pédestres et hébergement/transport disponibles. Réservations des forfaits via 🖰 le Centre National de Réservation ou le Bureau National par ❶ ❷ ❸.

Passeports et visas

Passeport et visa obligatoires.

Santé

Une assurance médicale de voyage est conseillée. Les ressortissants de l'Union Européenne doivent se munir du formulaire E111 pour bénéficier de soins médicaux dans les états de l'UE.

Deutsch

Versichern Sie, dass Sie Ihre Unterkunft für die ersten Nächte reserviert haben. In der Hochsaison Unterkunft in Herbergen in Dublin, Cork, Limerick, Killarney und Glendaloch im Voraus buchen. Herbergen befinden sich in Städten, auf dem Land, an der Küste und in Bergen/Gebirgen.

Preisspanne

Preisspanne 5.00-8.50 IRP. € 6.35-10.80. ⍥ Leinenschlafsack erforderlich.

Zimmer und Reservierungen

ⓡ während Mär, Apr, Jul-Sept. (²🐖 ⁴🐖). Reservierungen über ⓘⒷⓃ 🖰 Nationales Buchungszentrum, Herberge oder Landesverband per ❶ ❷ ❸. Rauchen ist begrenzt - bitte checken.

Gäste

Mitgliedsausweis ist erforderlich. ♔ willkommen. Gruppenbuchungen über 🖰 Nationales Buchungszentrum, Herberge oder Landesverband per ❶ ❷ ❸.

Öffnungszeiten

Hauptherbergen: Zugang 🔲. Rezeption zwischen 07:00-22:00Uhr. Herbergsmanager wohnt im Haus. **Andere Herbergen:** Zugang zwischen Apr-Okt, 07:30-10:00Uhr, 17:00-22:00Uhr. Rezeption zwischen 07:30-10:00Uhr, 17:00-22:00Uhr. Herbergsmanager wohnt im Haus. **Saison-Herbergen** sind normalerweise Jul, Aug geöffnet.

Mahlzeiten

⍥ BLD ⓡ Für ♔. ♂.

Ermäßigungen

HI-Mitgliedsrabatt ist erhältlich – siehe Teil für Rabatte und Ermäßigungen und www.iyhf.org.

Reisen im Land

Reisen ist einfach mit 🚐 🚍 Selbstfahrer. Mietwagenfirmen erlauben u. U. nur Fahrer von über 23 Jahren.

Reise-/Aktivitäten-Packages

Fahrrad/Mountainbiking, wandern/trekking und Unterkunft/Transport-Packages erhältlich.
Package-Buchungen über ☏ Nationales Buchungszentrum oder Landesverband per ❶ ❷ ❸.

Reisepässe und Visa

Reisepass/Einreisevisum erforderlich.

Gesundheit

Unfall-/Krankenversicherung wird empfohlen. EU Staatsangehörige benötigen Formular E111 für ärztliche Behandlungen innerhalb der EU Länder.

Español

Es importante reservar la primera noche de su estancia. Durante la temporada alta es necesario reservar con antelación en los albergues de Dublín, Cork, Limerick, Killarney y Glendaloch. Los albergues están situados en las ciudades, el campo, la costa y la montaña.

Tarifas mínima y máxima

Tarifas mínima y máxima 5.00-8.50 IRP. € 6.35-10.80. 🛏 Saco sábana imprescindible.

Habitaciones y Reservas

🆁 en mar, abr, jul-sep. (↗ ↖). Reservas por ⒾⒷⓃ ☏ o a través de la Central Nacional de Reservas, el albergue o la Asociación Nacional por ❶ ❷ ❸. Está permitido fumar sólo en algunas salas/habitaciones - infórmese.

Huéspedes

Los huéspedes deben presentar su Carnet de Alberguista. Se admiten ♦♦♦. Reservas de grupo por ☏ o a través de la Central Nacional de Reservas, el albergue o la Asociación Nacional por ❶ ❷ ❸.

Horarios y fechas de apertura

Albergues principales - abiertos 🗓. Horario de recepción: 07:00-22:00h. Gerente residente. **Otros albergues** - abiertos abr-oct, 07:30-10:00h, 17:00-22:00h. Horario de recepción: 07:30-10:00h, 17:00-22:00h. Gerente residente. **Albergues de temporada** suelen abrir: jul, ago.

Comidas

🍽 BLD 🆁 Para ♦♦♦. 👞.

Descuentos

Se conceden descuentos a los miembros de Hostelling International – véase la sección sobre descuentos y nuestra página Internet en www.iyhf.org.

Desplazamientos

Transportes recomendados: 🚌 🚍 Automóvil. Es posible que las compañías de alquiler de automoviles exijan a los conductores que sean mayores de 23 anos.

Viajes Combinados con Actividades

Viajes combinados con cicloturismo/bicicleta de montaña, senderismo y alojamiento/ transporte. Reserva de viajes combinados por ☏ o a través de la Central Nacional de Reservas o la Asociación Nacional por ❶ ❷ ❸.

Pasaportes y Visados

Pasaporte y visado obligatorios.

Información Sanitaria

Seguro médico recomendado. Los ciudadanos procedentes de países pertenecientes a la UE necesitan el impreso E111 para obtener asistencia médica en dichos países.

Cork -
International Youth Hostel

1-2 Redclyffe,
Western Rd,
Cork.
❶ (21) 4543289
❶ (21) 4343715
❷ mailbox@anoige.ie

Open Dates:	🗓
Open Hours:	🕘
Reservations:	(IBN) ⌐CC⌐
Price Range:	IRP 7.50-14.50 € 9.53-18.42 🗊
Beds:	102 - 3x² 5x⁴ 11x⁶ 1x⁶
Facilities:	♿ 👫 18x 👬 ⛴ ☕ 🔥 🏨 📺 ♨ 🅿 ⓘ 🚿 ✂
Directions:	2W from city centre
✈	Cork 5km
A🚌	Airport bus to Central Bus Station 1km
⛴	Cork (Seasonal) 16km
🚂	Cork 2km
🚌	No 8 from City 1km ap Outside Hostel
Attractions:	⚲ 🏊

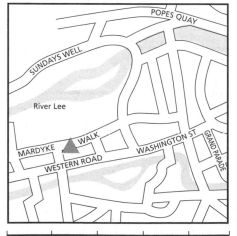

Dublin -
International Youth Hostel

61 Mountjoy St.,
Dublin 7.
❶ (1) 8301766
❶ (1) 8301600
❷ dublininternational@anoige.ie

Open Dates:	🗓
Open Hours:	🕘
Reservations:	ⓡ (IBN) ⌐CC⌐
Price Range:	IRP 10.00-17.00 € 12.70-21.59 BBinc 🗊
Beds:	350 - 3x² 3x³ 3x⁴ 12x⁶ 26x⁶
Facilities:	👫 14x 👬 ⛴ ☕ 🚲 🔥 🏨 📺 🏕1 x🍴 🖫 🖼 ♨ ⑧ 🅿 ⓘ 🚿 ✂
Directions:	1NW from city centre
✈	Dublin 16km
A🚌	41/41a/41b/41c 500m
⛴	Dublin 4km; Dun Laoghaire 10km
🚂	Connolly 2km; Heuston 3km
🚌	10/16/19/120 ap Outside Hostel
Ⓤ	Connolly 2km
Attractions:	⚲ 🏊 1.5km

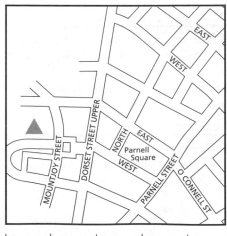

Glendaloch - International Youth Hostel

The Lodge,
Glendalough,
Co Wicklow.
(t) (404) 45342
(f) (404) 45690
(e) mailbox@anoige.ie

Open Dates:	12
Open Hours:	
Reservations:	R IBN CC
Price Range:	IRP 8.50-15.00 € 13.34-19.05
Beds:	120 - 2x2 6x4 10x6 4x6+
Facilities:	18x 2 x
Directions:	
(airport)	Dublin 60km
(ferry)	Dublin 50km; Dun Laoghaire 40km
(train)	Rathdrum 13km
(bus)	St Kevins bus from Dublin City 50km ap Glendalough
Attractions:	

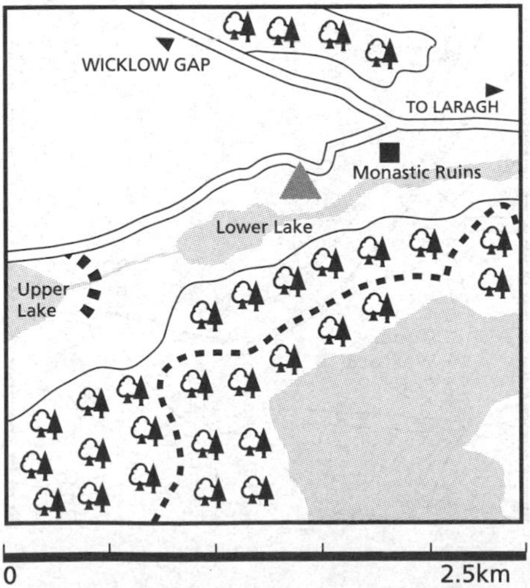

Killarney - International Youth Hostel

Aghadoe House,
Killarney,
Co Kerry.
(t) (64) 31240
(f) (64) 34300
(e) anoige@killarney.iol.ie

Open Dates:	12
Open Hours:	
Reservations:	R IBN CC
Price Range:	IRP 8.00-15.00 € 10.16-19.05
Beds:	190 - 5x2 20x4 6x6 6x6+
Facilities:	26x 1 x
Directions:	4W from city centre
(airport)	Kerry International 10km; Cork 92km; Shannon 120km
(ferry)	Cork (Seasonal) 92km
(train)	Killarney 5km
(bus)	Free transfer from station ap At Hostel
Attractions:	5km 5km

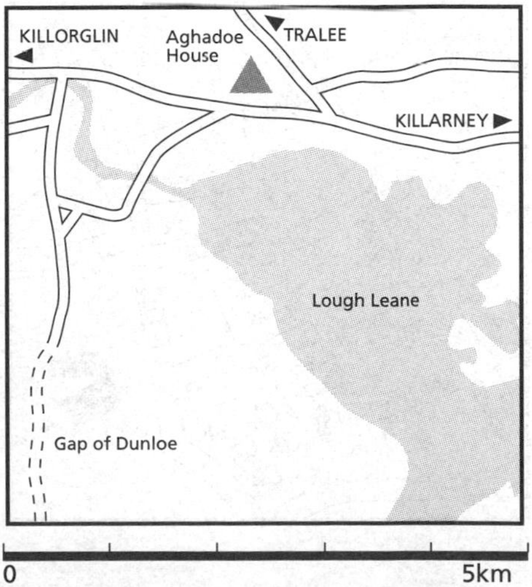

Limerick - City

1 Pery Square,
Limerick.
☎ (61) 314672
🖷 (61) 314672
✉ mailbox@anoige.ie

Open Dates: 🗓

Reservations: **R** **CC**

Price Range: IRP 6.50-9.50 € 8.26-12.07

Beds: 68 - 2x² 4x⁶

Facilities: 4x 4x 🍽 🛏 🚿 ✿ 🛋 📺 📖 🗑 1 x 🍸 📷 🛒 P ℹ 🔌 ⚓ 🎏

Directions:

✈ Shannon 24km

A🚌 to Limerick City Centre 500m

🚂 Limerick 500m

🚌 Limerick 500m

Attractions: 🚴

Rosslare Harbour

Goulding St,
Rosslare Harbour,
Co Wexford.
☎ (53) 33399
🖷 (53) 33624
✉ rosslareyh@oceanfree.net

Open Dates: 🗓

Reservations: **IBN** **CC**

Price Range: IRP 7.00-10.00 € 8.89-12.70 🗄

Beds: 68 - 1x² 6x⁴ 7x⁶

Facilities: 13x 🍽 🛏 ✿ 🛋 📺 🗑 🏠 P ℹ

Directions:

✈ Waterford 82km, Dublin 163km, Cork 208km

🚢 Rosslare Harbour 500m

🚂 Rosslare Harbour 500m

🚌 Dublin to Rosslare Harbour YH 500m

Attractions: 🔍 🏃 🏊 500m

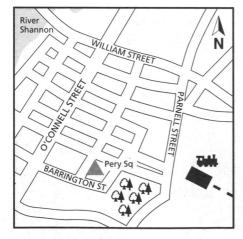

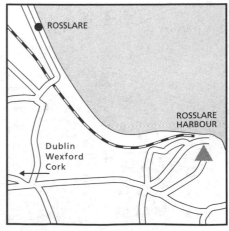

Location/Address	Telephone No. Fax No.	Beds	Opening Dates	Facilities
△ **Allihies** *Cabermeelabo, Near Allihies, Beara, Co Cork.* ℮ mailbox@anoige.ie	☎ (27) 73014	34	01.06–30.09	� ⛟ 🅿 ⊡ ✿
△ **Arthurstown** *Coastguard Station, Arthurstown,* *Co Wexford.* ℮ mailbox@anoige.ie	☎ (51) 389411	30	01.06–30.09	� ⛟ 🅿 ✿
△ **Ball Hill** *Near Donegal Town, Donegal.* ℮ mailbox@anoige.ie	☎ (73) 21174 ℻ (73) 22604	66	11.04–30.09	� ⛟ 🅿 ✿
△ **Ballinclea** *Near Donard, Co Wicklow.* ℮ mailbox@anoige.ie	☎ (45) 404657 ℻ (45) 404657	40	* 01.03–30.11	� ⓡ ⛟ 🅿 ✿
△ **Ballinskelligs** *Prior House, Ballinskelligs, Co Kerry.* ℮ mailbox@anoige.ie	☎ (66) 9479229	22	11.04–30.09	� ⛟ 🅿 ✿
△ **Ballydavid Wood House** *Glen of Aberlow, Near Bansha, Co Tipperary.* ℮ mailbox@anoige.ie	☎ (62) 54148	40	* 01.03–30.11	� ⛟ 🅿 ✿
△ **Baltyboys** *Near Blessington, Co Wicklow.* ℮ mailbox@anoige.ie	☎ (45) 867266 ℻ (45) 867032	36	* 01.03–30.11	ⓡ ⛟ 🅿 ✿
△ **Ben Lettery** *Near Recess, Co Galway.* ℮ mailbox@anoige.ie	☎ (95) 51136 ℻ (95) 51136	50	11.04–30.09	� ⛟ 🅿 ✿
△ **Black Valley** *Near Beaufort, Gap of Dunloe, Co Kerry.* ℮ mailbox@anoige.ie	☎ (64) 34712	46	01.03–30.11	� ⛟ 🅿 ✿
△ **Cape Clear Island** *South Harbour, Cape Clear Island,* *Skibbereen, Co Cork.* ℮ lasmuigh@tinet.ie	☎ (28) 39198 ℻ (28) 39144	32	01.03–30.11	� ⓡ ⛟ ✿
▲ **Cong** *Lisloughrey, Quay Rd, Cong, Co Mayo.* ℮ quiet.man.cong@iol.ie	☎ (92) 46089 ℻ (92) 46448	80	🗓12	� ⟨CC⟩ ⛟ 🅿 ⊡ ✿
▲ **Cork** - International Youth Hostel ⒾⒷⓃ **1-2 Redclyffe, Western Rd, Cork.** ℮ mailbox@anoige.ie	☎ (21) 4543289 ℻ (21) 4343715	102	🗓12	� 🍽 2W ♿ ⟨CC⟩ ⛟ 🅿 ✿
△ **Crohy Head** *Near Dungloe, Co Donegal.* ℮ mailbox@anoige.ie	☎ (75) 21950	38	11.04–30.09	� ⛟ 🅿 ✿
△ **Doorus House** *Near Kinvara, Co Galway.* ℮ mailbox@anoige.ie	☎ (91) 637512 ℻ (91) 637512	56	🗓12	⛟ 🅿 ✿
▲ **Dublin** - International Youth Hostel ⒾⒷⓃ **61 Mountjoy St., Dublin 7.** ℮ dublininternational@anoige.ie	☎ (1) 8301766 ℻ (1) 8301600	350	🗓12	� 🍽 ⓡ 1NW ⟨CC⟩ ⛟ 🅿 ⊡ ♿ ✿

Location/Address	Telephone No. Fax No.	Beds	Opening Dates	Facilities
▲ **Dún Chaoin** Near Ballyferriter, Co Kerry. e mailbox@anoige.ie	☎ (66) 9156121 🖷 (66) 9156355	52	🗓12	♦♦♦ �🍽 ☞ P ☀
△ *Errigal* Dunlewy, Co Donegal. e errigalhostel@eircom.net	☎ (75) 31180	46	🗓12	♦♦♦ �🍽 ☞ P ☀
△ *Foulksrath Castle* Near Jenkinstown, Co Kilkenny. e mailbox@anoige.ie	☎ (56) 67674 🖷 (56) 67144	52	🗓12	☞ P ☀
△ *Galway* St Mary's College, St Mary's Rd, Galway. e mailbox@anoige.ie	☎ (91) 527411 🖷 (91) 528710	120	01.07–25.08	♦♦♦ �🍽 R 1W ECC ☞ P ☀
△ *Glanmore Lake* Near Lauragh, Killarney, Co Kerry. e mailbox@anoige.ie	☎ (64) 83181	36	11.04–30.09	☞ P ☀
△ *Glencree* Stone House, Glencree, Near Enniskerry, Co Wicklow. e mailbox@anoige.ie	☎ (1) 2864037 🖷 (1) 2766142	40	🗓12	♦♦♦ R ☞ ☀
▲ **Glendaloch -** International Youth Hostel **IBN** **The Lodge, Glendalough, Co Wicklow.** e mailbox@anoige.ie	☎ (404) 45342 🖷 (404) 45690	120	🗓12	♦♦♦ �🍽 R ♿ ECC ☞ P ⬜ ☀
△ *Glenmalure* Near Greenane, Co Wicklow. e mailbox@anoige.ie		16	* 01.07–31.08	R ☞ P ☀
▲ **Killarney -** International Youth Hostel **IBN** **Aghadoe House, Killarney, Co Kerry.** e anoige@killarney.iol.ie	☎ (64) 31240 🖷 (64) 34300	190	🗓12	♦♦♦ ⛑ R 4W ♿ ECC ☞ P ⬜ 🚲 ☀
△ *Killary Harbour* Near Rosroe, Renvyle, Co Galway. e mailbox@anoige.ie	☎ (95) 43417	44	01.03–30.09	♦♦♦ ☞ P ☀
△ *Knockree* Lacken House, Knockree, Near Enniskerry, Co Wicklow. e mailbox@anoige.ie	☎ (1) 2864036	58	🗓12	R ☞ P ☀
▲ **Limerick -** City **1 Pery Square, Limerick.** e mailbox@anoige.ie	☎ (61) 314672 🖷 (61) 314672	68	🗓12	♦♦♦ ⛑ R ECC ☞ P 🚲 ☀
△ *Mountain Lodge* Near Burncourt, Co Tipperary. e mailbox@anoige.ie	☎ (52) 67277	30	01.03–30.09	♦♦♦ ☞ P ☀
△ *Rosslare Harbour* **IBN** *Goulding St, Rosslare Harbour, Co Wexford.* e rosslareyh@oceanfree.net	☎ (53) 33399 🖷 (53) 33624	68	🗓12	♦♦♦ ⛑ ECC ☞ P ☀

Location/Address	Telephone No. Fax No.	Beds	Opening Dates	Facilities
△ ***Tiglin*** *Near Ashford, Co Wicklow.* e *mailbox@anoige.ie*	t *(404) 49049* f *(404) 49049*	*52*	12	R P
△ ***Trá na Rosann*** *Near Downings, Co Donegal.* e *mailbox@anoige.ie*	t *(74) 55374*	*34*	*11.04–30.09*	P
△ ***Traenlaur Lodge*** *Lough Feeagh, Near Newport, Co Mayo.* e *mailbox@anoige.ie*	t *(98) 41358*	*32*	*11.04–30.09*	P
△ ***Valentia Island*** *Knightstown, Valentia Island, Co Kerry.* e *mailbox@anoige.ie*	t *(66) 9476154*	*40*	*01.06–30.09*	P
▲ **Westport** Club Atlantic Hostel, Altamont St, Westport, Co Mayo. e mailbox@anoige.ie	t (98) 26644 f (98) 26241	140	01.03–31.10	P

"To travel hopefully is a better thing than to arrive."

"Voyager avec espoir est mieux que d'arriver."

„Mit Hoffnung zu reisen ist besser, als sein Ziel zu erreichen."

"Viajar con esperanza es mejor que llegar."

Robert Louis Stevenson

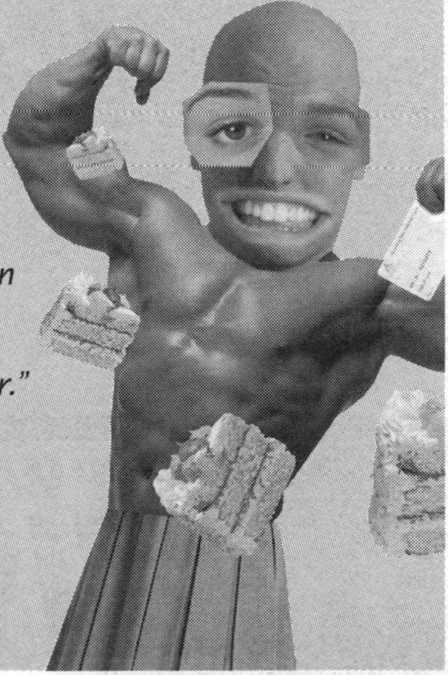

HOSTELLING
INTERNATIONAL

Take the HI way!

For HI quality accommodation at the best prices.

Visit one of our 4200 hostels in over 60 countries.

www.iyhf.org

Israel

ISRAEL

ISRAEL

ISRAEL

Israel Youth Hostels Association,
Binyanei Hauma, 1 Shazar Street, PO Box 6001
Jerusalem 91060, Israel.

☏ (972) (2) 655 8400
✆ (972) (2) 655 8430
(972) (2) 655 8432 (Travel)
✉ iyha@iyha.org.il
🖳 www.youth-hostels.org.il

Office Hours: Sunday-Thursday, 08.00-16.00hrs

A copy of the Hostel Directory for this Country can be obtained from:
All I.Y.H.A. Hostels

Capital:	Jerusalem	**Population:**	6,000,000
Language:	Hebrew/Arabic	**Size:**	20,770 sq km
Currency:	New shequel	**Telephone Country Code:**	972

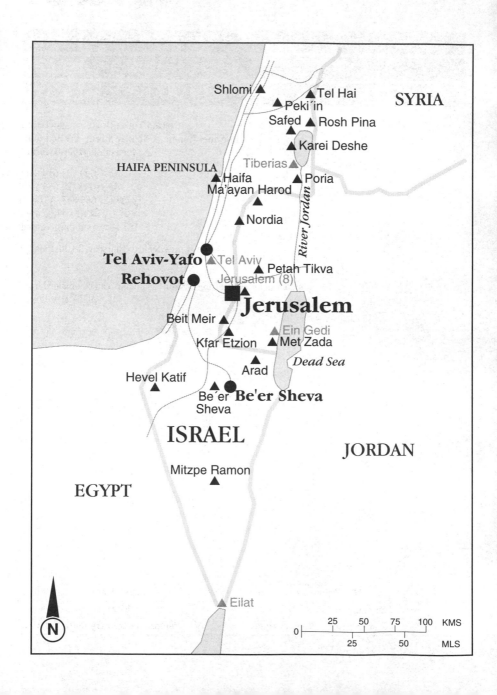

Shlomi ▲

▲ Tel Hai

▲ Peki'in

SYRIA

Safed ▲ ▲ Rosh Pina

▲ Karei Deshe

HAIFA PENINSULA

Tiberias ▲

▲ Haifa

▲ Poria

Ma'ayan Harod

▲

River Jordan

▲ Nordia

Tel Aviv-Yafo ● ▲ Tel Aviv

Rehovot ● ▲ Petah Tikva

Jerusalem (8)

■ **Jerusalem**

Beit Meir ▲

▲ Ein Gedi

▲

Kfar Etzion ▲ Met Zada

▲

Arad

Dead Sea

Hevel Katif

▲ ● **Be'er Sheva**

Be'er

Sheva

ISRAEL

JORDAN

Mitzpe Ramon

▲

EGYPT

▲ Eilat

N

	25	50	75	100	KMS
0					
		25		50	MLS

English

Hostels are located in cities, in the countryside, on the coast and on hills/mountains.

Price range

Price range $17.50-28.00. € 18.16-29.05. BB|inc 🗩.

Rooms and Reservations

R 🖳 (All Rooms). Reservations via (IBN) 🐾 National Booking Centre or Hostel by ❶ ❶ ❷. Hostels are single sex only. All hostels are non-smoking.

Guests

Membership Card and Passport/Photo ID are required. The maximum stay is 21 days. Age limits may apply for children - check with hostel. ♦♦♦ welcome. Group bookings via (IBN) 🐾 National Booking Centre or Hostel by ❶ ❶ ❷ (Reservation charges may apply).

Open times

Main hostels: open 🖳, 🕐. Reception open: 14:00-24.00hrs. **Other hostels:** open 🖳, 08:00-23:00hrs. Reception open: 14:00-23:00hrs. Resident manager.

Meals

🍴 BD **R** For individuals & for ♦♦♦.

Discounts

HI Member Discounts available - see discounts section and www.iyhf.org.

Travelling around

For ease of travel use 🚌 🚗 Self-Drive.

Travel/Activity Packages

Tours/sightseeing, walking/trekking and accommodation/transport packages available. Package bookings via 🐾 National Booking Centre, Hostel or National Office by ❶ ❶ ❷.

Passports and Visas

Passport required.

Health

Medical insurance is recommended.

Français

Les auberges sont situées dans les villes, à la campagne, sur le littoral et à la montagne.

Tarifs des nuitées

Tarifs des nuitées 17.50-28.00$. € 18.16-29.5. BB|inc 🗩.

Chambres et réservations

R 🖳 (Toutes chambres). Réservations via (IBN) 🐾 le Centre National de Réservation ou l'auberge par ❶ ❶ ❷. Les auberges sont uniquement non-mixtes. Toutes les auberges sont non-fumeurs.

Usagers

La carte d'adhérent ainsi que le passeport/pièce d'identité avec photo sont à présenter. La durée maximale du séjour est de 21 jours. Il est possible que des limites d'âge soient en vigueur pour les enfants - vérifiez auprès de l'auberge. Accueil des ♦♦♦. Réservations pour groupes via (IBN) 🐾 le Centre National de Réservation ou l'auberge par ❶ ❶ ❷ (Des frais de réservation pourront vous être facturés).

Horaires d'ouverture

Grandes auberges: ouvertes 🖳, 🕐. Accueil ouvert entre 14h-24.00h. **Autres auberges:** ouvertes 🖳, entre 8h-23h. Accueil ouvert entre 14h-23h. Gérant réside sur place.

Repas

🍴 BD **R** Pour individuels & pour ♦♦♦.

Remises

Remises pour les adhérents HI - voir la section "Remises" et notre site: www.iyhf.org.

Déplacements

Modes de transport recommandés 🚍 🚐 Voiture.

Forfaits Voyages/Activités

Forfaits circuits touristiques, randonnées pédestres et hébergement/transport disponibles. Réservations des forfaits via 🖥 le Centre National de Réservation, l'auberge ou le Bureau National par ❶ ❷ ❸.

Passeports et visas

Passeport obligatoire.

Santé

Une assurance médicale de voyage est conseillée.

Deutsch

Herbergen befinden sich in Städten, auf dem Land, an der Küste und in Bergen/Gebirgen.

Preisspanne

Preisspanne 17.50-28.00 $. € 18.16-29.05. BB inc 🍴.

Zimmer und Reservierungen

❿ 🛏 (Alle Zimmer). Reservierungen über IBN 🖥 Nationales Buchungszentrum oder Herberge per ❶ ❷ ❸. Herbergen sind nur Single Sex. Rauchen ist in allen Herbergen NICHT gestattet.

Gäste

Mitgliedsausweis und Reisepass/Personalausweis sind erforderlich. Der maximale Aufenthalt beträgt 21 Tage. Altersbegrenzungen für Kinder möglich - in der

Herberge nachfragen. 👪 willkommen. Gruppenbuchungen über IBN 🖥 Nationales Buchungszentrum oder Herberge per ❶ ❷ ❸ (Reservierungskosten könnten anfallen).

Öffnungszeiten

Hauptherbergen: Zugang 🛏, 🕐. Rezeption zwischen 14:00-24.00Uhr. **Andere Herbergen:** Zugang 🛏, 08:00-23:00Uhr. Rezeption zwischen 14:00-23:00Uhr. Herbergsmanager wohnt im Haus.

Mahlzeiten

🍽 BD ❿ Für Einzelreisende & für 👪.

Ermäßigungen

HI-Mitgliedsrabatt ist erhältlich – siehe Teil für Rabatte und Ermäßigungen und www.iyhf.org.

Reisen im Land

Reisen ist einfach mit 🚍 🚐 Selbstfahrer.

Reise-/Aktivitäten-Packages

Touren/sightseeing, wandern/trekking und Unterkunft/Transport-Packages erhältlich. Package-Buchungen über 🖥 Nationales Buchungszentrum, Herberge oder Landesverband per ❶ ❷ ❸.

Reisepässe und Visa

Reisepass erforderlich.

Gesundheit

Unfall-/Krankenversicherung wird empfohlen.

Español

Los albergues están situados en las ciudades, el campo, la costa y la montaña.

Tarifas mínima y máxima

Tarifas mínima y máxima 17.50-28.00$. € 18.16-29.05. BB inc 🍴.

Habitaciones y Reservas

R 🔲 (Todas las habitaciones). Reservas por **(IBN)** 🖥 o a través de la Central Nacional de Reservas o el albergue por **①** **⑥** **⑧**. Los albergues son sólo para hombres o mujeres. Está prohibido fumar en todos los albergues.

Huéspedes

Los huéspedes deben presentar su Carnet de Alberguista y su pasaporte o carnet de identidad. La estancia máxima es de 21 días. Es posible que exista un límite de edad para los niños - consulte con el albergue. Se admiten ✦✦✦. Reservas de grupo por **(IBN)** 🖥 o a través de la Central Nacional de Reservas o el albergue por **①** **⑥** **⑧** (Es posible que se aplique un suplemento en concepto de gastos de reserva).

Horarios y fechas de apertura

Albergues principales - abiertos 🔲, ⏱. Horario de recepción: 14:00-24.00h. **Otros albergues** - abiertos 🔲, 08:00-23:00h. Horario de recepción: 14:00h-23:00h. Gerente residente.

Comidas

🍴 BD **R** Para individuales y para ✦✦✦.

Descuentos

Se conceden descuentos a los miembros de Hostelling International – véase la sección sobre descuentos y nuestra página Internet en www.iyhf.org.

Desplazamientos

Transportes recomendados: 🚂 🚌 Automóvil.

Viajes Combinados con Actividades

Viajes combinados con visitas turísticas, senderismo y alojamiento/transporte. Reserva de viajes combinados por 🖥 o a través de la Central Nacional de Reservas, el albergue o la Asociación Nacional por **①** **⑥** **⑧**.

Pasaportes y Visados

Pasaporte obligatorio.

Información Sanitaria

Seguro médico recomendado.

"Though we travel the world over to find the beautiful, we must carry it with us or we find it not."

"Bien que nous parcourons le monde pour trouver ce qui est beau, nous devons le porter en nous ou nous ne le trouvons pas."

„Obwohl wir die ganze Welt bereisen, um das Schöne zu finden, müssen wir es in uns selber tragen, sonst werden wir es nicht finden."

"Aunque demos la vuelta al mundo buscando la belleza, tenemos que llevarla dentro de nosotros mismos o no la encontraremos"

Ralph Waldo Emerson

Eilat -
Eilat Youth Hostel (IYHA)

Arava Rd,
Eilat.
☎ (7) 6370088
📠 (7) 6375835
✉ eilat@iyha.org.il

Open Dates:	🗓
Open Hours:	🕐
Reservations:	**IBN** **CC**
Price Range:	$17.50-28.00 € 18.16-29.05 **BB** inc 🍴
Beds:	487 - 13x^2🛏 28x^4🛏 17x^5🛏 44x^6🛏
Facilities:	♿ 👫 102x 👫 🍽 🍺 🏨 📺 🧺1 x🍴 ♨ 🔢 ⊜ 🔲 🅿 ℹ 🧺 ✤ ◉
Directions:	2S from city centre
✈	Ben Gurion 354km
A🚌	475 354km
⛴	Eilat 1km
🚌	394 from Tel Aviv Central Bus Station to Eilat
Attractions:	⛰ 🔍 🏃

Ein Gedi - Beit Sarah

Ein Gedi,
Mobile Post,
Dead Sea 86980.
☎ (7) 6584165
📠 (7) 6584445
✉ eingedi@iyha.org.il

Open Dates:	🗓
Open Hours:	07.00-21.00hrs (Sun-Fri); 07.00-11.00hrs; 16.00-19.00hrs (Sat)
Reservations:	**IBN** **CC**
Price Range:	$17.50-28.00 € 18.16-29.05 **BB** inc 🍴
Beds:	254 - 1x^2🛏 24x^4🛏 26x^6🛏
Facilities:	👫 52x 👫 🍽 🍺 📺 🧺2 x🍴 🔳 🔢 ⊜ 🅿 ℹ ✤
Directions:	
✈	Ben Gurion 175km
🚌	475/421 from Tel Aviv Bus Station, 486/487 from Jerusalem
Attractions:	⛰ 🔍100m 🏃 🏊

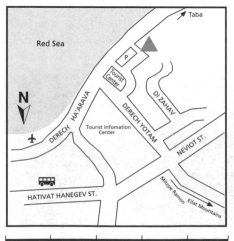

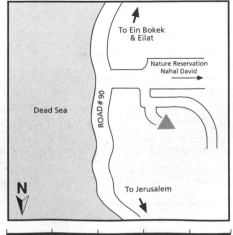

Jerusalem -
Hadavidka

67 Ha Nevi'im St,
Jerusalem.
☎ (2) 5384555
✆ (2) 5388790
✉ davidka@iyha.org.il

Open Dates:	🗓
Open Hours:	🕐
Reservations:	IBN CC
Price Range:	$17.50-28.00 € 18.16-29.05 BB inc 🗒
Beds:	333 - 1x🛏 5x🛏 58x🛏 16x🛏
Facilities:	⁂ 64x ⁂ 🍴 ☕ 🛏 📺 🖥 4 x🍸 📷 ♿ 🔢 ⊜ 💲 🅿 ℹ
Directions:	0.5 W from city centre
✈	Ben Gurion 65km
A🚌	Jerusalem Central Bus Station
🚌	13, 18, 20, 21, 23, 35, 36, 27 ap Davidka

Jerusalem -
Yitzhak Rabin

1 Nahman Avigad St,
PO Box 39100,
Jerusalem 91390.
☎ (2) 6780101
✆ (2) 6796566
✉ rabin@iyha.org.il

Open Dates:	🗓
Open Hours:	🕐
Reservations:	CC
Price Range:	$17.50-28.00 € 18.16-29.05 BB inc 🗒
Beds:	308
Facilities:	♿ ⁂ 77x ⁂ 🍴 ☕ 🛏 📺 🖥 9 x🍸 ♿ ⊜ 💲 🅿 ℹ 🎮
Directions:	4 SE from city centre
✈	Ben Gurion 65km
A🚌	Jerusalem Central Bus Station
🚌	17, 28, 9 from Central Bus Station

Attractions:

There are 8 hostels in Jerusalem. See following pages.

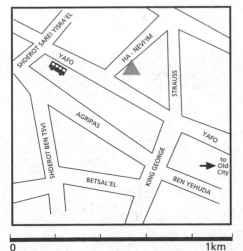

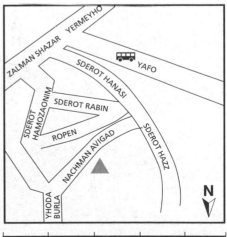

Karei Deshe - Yoram Walter Katz

Yoram,
Karei Deshe,
Mobile Post,
Korazim 12365.
☏ (6) 6720601
✆ (6) 6724818
✉ karidesh@kinneret.co.il

Open Dates:	🗓️
Open Hours:	🕐
Reservations:	⊂CC⊃
Price Range:	$17.50-28.00 € 18.16-29.05 BB inc 🍴
Beds:	288 - 10x² 28x⁴ 26x⁶
Facilities:	♿ 👫 64x 👫 🍴 ☕ 🧳 📺 7 x🍷 🖼️ 🎱 ⊜ 🅿️ ⓘ ♻️ ⛺

Directions:

✈️	Ben Gurion 150km
A🚌	830/835 from Tel Aviv Bus Station - Tiberias 140km
🚌	459, 841 from Tiberias Central Bus Station. Tiberias 10km

Attractions: 🏞️ ⛰️ 🔍100m 🚶 🏊

Metzada - Massada

Isaac H Taylor Hostel,
Metzada,
Mobile Post,
Dead Sea 86935.
☏ (7) 6584349
✆ (7) 6584650
✉ massada@iyha.org.il

Open Dates:	🗓️
Open Hours:	(Sun-Fri) 08.00-13.00hrs; 15.00-19.00hrs; (Sat) 09.30-11.00hrs; 16.00-19.00hrs
Reservations:	⊂CC⊃
Price Range:	$17.50-28.00 € 18.16-29.05 BB inc 🍴
Beds:	140 - 3x³ 3x⁴ 13x⁶ 7x⁶
Facilities:	♿ 👫 23x 👫 🍴 📺 1 x🍷 🖼️ 🎱 ⊜ ⓘ ♻️

Directions:

✈️	Ben Gurion 140km
🚌	421 (1 morning only) Tel Aviv Central Bus Station; from Jerusalem 444, 486; from Be'er Sheva 384, 385. ap Massada YH

Attractions: ⛰️ 🔍 🚶 ⚓2km 🏊5km

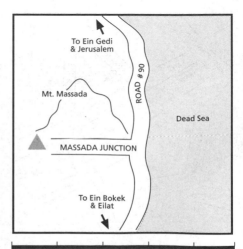

Mitzpe Ramon -
Beit Noam

PO Box 2,
Mitzpe Ramon 80600.
📞 (7) 6588443, (7) 6595187
📠 (7) 6588074
📧 mitzpe@iyha.org.il

Open Dates:	📅
Open Hours:	07.00-23.00hrs (Fri); 07.00-10.00hrs; 16.00-23.00hrs (Sat)
Reservations:	CC
Price Range:	$17.50-28.00 € 18.16-29.05 BB inc 🍽
Beds:	242 - 4x² 6x³ 3x⁴ 34x⁶
Facilities:	♿ 👫 37x 👫 🍽 🏨 📺 3 x 🍴 📷 ♨ 8 ☺ P 🅿 ♻ ⚙
Directions:	0.1E from city centre
✈	Ben Gurion 250km
A🚌	Tel Aviv Central Bus Station 370 113km
🚌	060 from Beersheba Central Bus Station ap Mitzpe Ramon YH
Attractions:	⛰ 🚶

Tel Aviv

36 Bnei Dan St,
Tel Aviv 62260.
📞 (3) 5441748, (3) 5460719
📠 (3) 5441030
📧 telaviv@iyha.org.il

Open Dates:	📅
Open Hours:	🕐
Reservations:	IBN CC
Price Range:	$17.50-28.00 € 18.16-29.05 BB inc 🍽
Beds:	305 - 3x² 50x⁴ 24x⁵
Facilities:	♿ 👫 77x 👫 🍽 🏨 📺 🖥 10 x 🍴 📷 ♨ 8 ☺ 🚻 ♻
Directions:	3N from city centre
✈	Ben Gurion 20km
A🚌	222
🚆	Northern Railway 3km
🚌	5, 24, 25 from Tel Aviv Central Bus Station 3km ap Yehuda Macabi St
Attractions:	🔍 ⛵ 2km

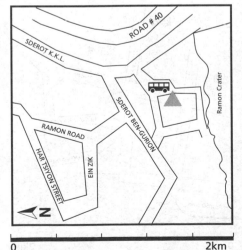

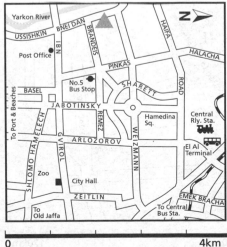

Tel Hai -
Posluns Family

Mobile Post,
Upper Galilee 12100.
☎ (6) 6940043
🖷 (6) 6941743
✉ telhai@iyha.org.il

Open Dates:	🗓
Open Hours:	🕐
Reservations:	⊏CC⊐
Price Range:	$17.50-28.00 € 18.16-29.05 BBinc 🗏
Beds:	280 - 49x 4🛏 14x 6🛏
Facilities:	🚻 63x 🚻 🍴 🍺 🛌 📺 5 x 🍽 🎞 🎱 ⊜ 🅿 ℹ ⚘ 🀄
Directions:	③N from city centre
✈	Ben Gurion 200km
🚌	842/845 from Tel Aviv Central Bus Station 19.4km ap 20, 23 Kiriat Shmone to Tel Hai 3km
Attractions:	🏕 ⛰ 🏊 🎿 ∪40km ⚓ 🚣10km

Tiberias -
Yosef Meyouhas

2 Jordan St,
PO Box 81,
Tiberias 14100.
☎ (6) 6721775, (6) 6790350
🖷 (6) 6720372
✉ tiberias@iyha.org.il

Open Dates:	🗓
Open Hours:	🕐
Reservations:	⊏IBN⊐ ⊏CC⊐
Price Range:	$17.50-28.00 € 18.16-29.05 BBinc 🗏
Beds:	248 - 8x 2🛏 3x 3🛏 25x 4🛏 7x 5🛏 13x 6🛏
Facilities:	🚻 56x 🚻 🍴 🛌 📺 1 x 🍽 🎞 🎱 ⊜ ℹ 🂠 ⚘ 🔍 🎴
Directions:	0.1NW from city centre
✈	Ben Gurion 132km
🚌	830/835 Tel Aviv Bus Station - Tiberas Central Bus Station
Attractions:	🏕 ⛰ 🔍1km 🎿 🚣

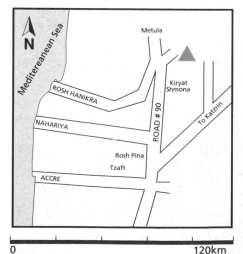

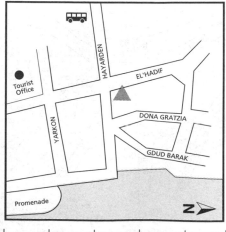

Location/Address	Telephone No. Fax No.	Beds	Opening Dates	Facilities
▲ **Arad** - Blau-Weiss Blau-Weiss Hostel, 4 Ha'atad St, Arad. ✉ arad@iyha.org.il	☎ (7) 9957150 📠 (7) 9955078	203	🔟	♦♦ 🍴 ♿ ᴇᴄᴄ 🅿
▲ **Beersheba/Be'er Sheva** - Beit Yatziv Beit Yatziv, PO Box 7, 79 Rehov Ha' Atzmaut, Beersheba.	☎ (7) 6277444, (7) 6271490 📠 (7) 6275735	220	🔟	♦♦ 🍴 1N ♿ ᴇᴄᴄ 🅿
▲ **Beit Meir** - Ramot Shapita Ramot Shapira, Beit Meir, PO Box 7216, Jerusalem. (20km W Jerusalem).	☎ (2) 5342691, (2) 5343793 📠 (2) 5342098	300	🔟	♦♦ 🍴 ᴇᴄᴄ 🅿
▲ **Eilat** - Eilat Youth Hostel (IYHA) ᴵᴮᴺ **Arava Rd, Eilat.** ✉ eilat@iyha.org.il	☎ (7) 6370088 📠 (7) 6375835	487	🔟	♦♦ 🍴 2S ♿ ᴇᴄᴄ 🅿 ☕
▲ **Ein Gedi** - Beit Sarah ᴵᴮᴺ **Ein Gedi, Mobile Post, Dead Sea 86980.** ✉ eingedi@iyha.org.il	☎ (7) 6584165 📠 (7) 6584445	254	🔟	♦♦ 🍴 ᴇᴄᴄ 🅿 ☕
△ *Gush Katif* *Hadarom, Hevel Katif, Hof Gaza,* *Mobile Post 79779.*	☎ *(7) 6847596* 📠 *(7) 6847680*	*220*	🔟	♦♦ 🍴 ℝ
▲ **Haifa** 'Carmel', Haifa, 18 Zvie Ytzhak St, Kffat Zait-Haifa.	☎ (4) 8531944 📠 (4) 8532516	188	🔟	♦♦ 🍴 8S ᴇᴄᴄ 🅿
▲ **Jerusalem** - Waterman Wise 8 Hapisga St, PO Box 16350, Jerusalem, Bayit Vegan. ✉ 02#6Y20990@doat.net	☎ (2) 6420990, (2) 6423366 📠 (2) 6423362	300	🔟	♦♦ 🍴 3SW ᴇᴄᴄ
△ *Jerusalem* - *Ein Karem* *PO Box 16091, Jerusalem.*	☎ *(2) 6416282*	*32*	🔟	🍴 6SW ᴇᴄᴄ
△ *Jerusalem* - *Beit-Bernstein* *Town Centre, 1 Keren Hayessod St,* *Jerusalem.*	☎ *(2) 6258286* 📠 *(2) 6245875*	*55*	🔟	♦♦ 🍴 1W ᴇᴄᴄ
▲ **Jerusalem** - Forest PO Box 3353, Jerusalem 91032.	☎ (2) 6752911 📠 (2) 6413522	140	🔟	♦♦ 🍴 6SW ᴇᴄᴄ 🅿
△ *Jerusalem* - *Old City* *PO Box 7880, 2 Rehov Ararat,* *Jewish Quarter, Old City, Jerusalem.*	☎ *(2) 6288611* 📠 *(2) 6288611*	*66*	🔟	♦♦ 🍴 2E ᴇᴄᴄ
▲ **Jerusalem** - Beit Shmuel 13 King David St, Jerusalem. ✉ btshmel@netvision.net.il	☎ (2) 6203491 📠 (2) 6203467	240	🔟	♦♦ 🍴 1E ᴇᴄᴄ
▲ **Jerusalem** - Hadavidka ᴵᴮᴺ **67 Ha Nevi'im St, Jerusalem.** ✉ davidka@iyha.org.il	☎ (2) 5384555 📠 (2) 5388790	333	🔟	♦♦ 🍴 0.5W ᴇᴄᴄ 🅿 ☕
▲ **Jerusalem** - Yitzhak Rabin 1 Nahman Avigad St, PO Box 39100, **Jerusalem 91390.** ✉ rabin@iyha.org.il	☎ (2) 6780101 📠 (2) 6796566	308	🔟	♦♦ 🍴 4SE ♿ ᴇᴄᴄ 🅿 ☕

Location/Address	Telephone No. Fax No.	Beds	Opening Dates	Facilities
▲ Karei Deshe - Yoram Walter Katz **Yoram, Karei Deshe, Mobile Post, Korazim 12365.** ⓔ karidesh@kinneret.co.il	☎ (6) 6720601 ✆ (6) 6724818	288	▥12	⁜ ◎ ♿ ⅽⅽ P ☕
△ *Kfar Etzion* *Doar Na Mount Hebron.*	☎ (2) 9935133, (2) 9935233 ✆ (2) 9932433	225	▥12	⁜ ◎ ⅽⅽ ☞
▲ Ma'ayan Harod Hankin, Maayan Harod, PO Box 2291 Afula. ⓔ mayan@iyha.org.il	☎ (6) 6531669 ✆ (6) 6531660	140	▥12	⁜ ◎ ⅽⅽ P ☕
▲ Metzada - Massada **Isaac H Taylor Hostel, Metzada, Mobile Post, Dead Sea 86935.** ⓔ massada@iyha.org.il	☎ (7) 6584349 ✆ (7) 6584650	140	▥12	⁜ ◎ ♿ ⅽⅽ
▲ Mitzpe Ramon - Beit Noam **PO Box 2, Mitzpe Ramon 80600.** ⓔ mitzpe@iyha.org.il	☎ (7) 6588443, (7) 6595187 ✆ (7) 6588074	242	▥12	⁜ ◎ 0.1E ♿ ⅽⅽ P
▲ Nordia PO Box 90, Moshau Nordia. ⓔ nordia@iyha.org.il	☎ (9) 8620089 ✆ (9) 8610130	208	▥12	⁜ ◎ ⅽⅽ P
▲ Peki'in PO Box 910, Peki'in 24914. ⓔ pekiin@iyha.org.il	☎ (4) 9574111 ✆ (4) 9574116	250	▥12	⁜ ◎ ♿ ⅽⅽ P ☕
▲ Petah Tikva Yad Labanim, Petah Tiqva 49404, Yahalom St. ⓔ petachtikva@iyha.org.il	☎ (3) 9226666 ✆ (3) 9226666	204	▥12	⁜ ◎ ⅽⅽ
▲ Poria Taiber, Poria, PO Box 232, Tiberias 14104. ⓔ poria@iyha.org.il	☎ (6) 6750050 ✆ (6) 6751628	180	▥12	⁜ ◎ ⅽⅽ P
▲ Rosh Pina Nature Friends, Rehov HaHalutzim, Rosh Pina 1200.	☎ (6) 6937086 ✆ (6) 6934312	100	▥12	⁜ ◎ ⅽⅽ P
▲ Safed Beit Binyamin, PO Box 1139, Zfat 13401. ⓔ tzfat@iyha.org.il	☎ (6) 6921086 ✆ (6) 6973514	120	▥12	⁜ ◎ ♿ ⅽⅽ P
▲ Shlomi PO Box 2120, Shlomi. (5km E of Rosh Haniqra). ⓔ shlomi@iyha.org.il	☎ (4) 9808975 ✆ (4) 9809163	400	▥12	⁜ ◎ ♿ ⅽⅽ P ☕
▲ Tel Aviv IBN **36 Bnei Dan St, Tel Aviv 62260.** ⓔ telaviv@iyha.org.il	☎ (3) 5441748, (3) 5460719 ✆ (3) 5441030	305	▥12	⁜ ◎ 3N ♿ ⅽⅽ ☕
▲ Tel Hai - Posluns Family **Mobile Post, Upper Galilee 12100.** ⓔ telhai@iyha.org.il	☎ (6) 6940043 ✆ (6) 6941743	280	▥12	⁜ ◎ 3N ⅽⅽ P ☕
▲ Tiberias - Yosef Meyouhas IBN **2 Jordan St, PO Box 81, Tiberias 14100.** ⓔ tiberias@iyha.org.il	☎ (6) 6721775, (6) 6790350 ✆ (6) 6720372	248	▥12	⁜ ◎ 0.1 NW ⅽⅽ

Italy

ITALIE
ITALIEN
ITALIA

**Associazione Italiana Alberghi per la Gioventù,
Via Cavour 44, 00184 Roma, Italy.**

☎ (39) (06) 4871152
✆ (39) (06) 4880492
📧 aig@uni.net
🖥 www.hostels-aig.org

Office Hours: Monday-Thursday, 07.30-17.00hrs, Friday 07.30-15.00hrs

A copy of the Hostel Directory for this Country can be obtained from:
The National Office

Capital:	Roma	**Population:**	57,000,000
Language:	Italian	**Size:**	301,225 sq km
Currency:	L (lire)	**Telephone Country Code:**	39

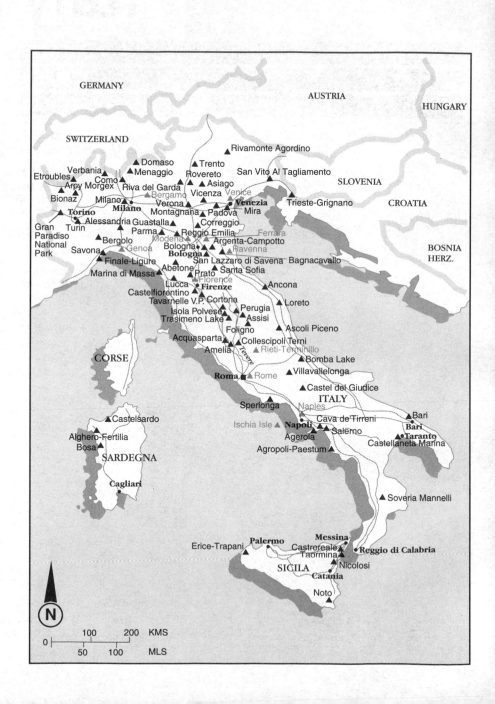

GERMANY

AUSTRIA

HUNGARY

SWITZERLAND

▲ Rivamonte Agordino

▲ Domaso
Verbania▲ ▲ Menaggio ▲ Trento
Etroubles▲ Como Rovereto San Vito Al Tagliamento
Arpy Morgex Riva del Garda ▲ Asiago SLOVENIA
Bionaz▲ Milano▲● Bergamo Vicenza Venice
▲Torino **Milano** Verona▲ ▲Venezia CROATIA
Gran Montagnana Padova Mira Trieste-Grignano
Paradiso Turin ▲ Alessandria Guastalla▲ ▲Correggio
National Parma▲ ▲Reggio Emilia Ferrara
Park Bergolo ▲Modena ▲Argenta-Campotto BOSNIA
Savona▲ Genoa **Bologna**▲ ▲Ravenna HERZ.
Finale-Ligure ▲ San Lazzaro di Savena Bagnacavallo
Marina di Massa▲ Abetone▲ Santa Sofia
Lucca▲ Prato ▲Ancona
Castelfiorentino ▲**Firenze**
Tavarnelle V.P. Cortona Florence
Isola Polvese Perugia▲ ▲Loreto
Trasimeno Lake ▲Assisi
Foligno▲ ▲Ascoli Piceno
Acquasparta▲ Collescipoli Terni
Amelia ▲Rieti-Terminillo
Tevere
CORSE ▲Bomba Lake
Roma▲ Rome ▲Villavallelonga
▲Castel del Giudice
Sperlonga ITALY
▲Castelsardo Ischia Isle ▲ **Napoli** Cava de'Tirreni ▲Bari
Alghero-Fertilia Agerola▲● Salerno **Bari**
Bosa▲ Agropoli-Paestum ▲ **Taranto**
SARDEGNA Castellaneta Marina

Cagliari
▲Soveria Mannelli

Palermo **Messina**
Erice-Trapani▲ Castroreale ●**Reggio di Calabria**
Taormina
SICILA ▲Nicolosi
Catania
Noto▲

N

0 ‖ 100 200 KMS
50 100 MLS

English

Hostels are located in cities, in the countryside, on the coast and on hills/mountains.

Price range

Price range ITL 13.000-35.000. € 6.71-18.08. BB inc 🛏.

Rooms and Reservations

R during Jun-Sep. (All Rooms). Reservations via IBN 🖥 National Booking Centre or Hostel by ❶ ❷. (Reservation charges may apply). Smoking is limited - please check.

Guests

Membership Card and Passport/Photo ID are required. ⅲ welcome. Group bookings via IBN 🖥 National Booking Centre or Hostel by ❶ ❷.

Open times

Main hostels: open 🗓, 14:00-24:00hrs. Reception open: 07:00-24:00hrs. Resident manager. **Other hostels:** open 🗓, 15:30-23:30hrs. Reception open: 15:30-22:00hrs. Resident manager.

Meals

🍽 BD **R** For individuals & for ⅲ.

Discounts

HI Member Discounts available - see discounts section and www.iyhf.org.

Travelling around

For ease of travel use 🚐 Self-Drive.

Travel/Activity Packages

Tours/sightseeing, winter sports, waters sports, cycling/mountain biking, walking/trekking and accommodation/transport packages available.

Package bookings via National Booking Centre by ❶ ❷.

Passports and Visas

Passport and Visa required.

Health

Emergency medical treatment is free. Medical insurance is recommended. EU Nationals require Form E111 to obtain treatment within EU countries.

Français

Les auberges sont situées dans les villes, à la campagne, sur le littoral et à la montagne.

Tarifs des nuitées

Tarifs des nuitées 13.000-35.000 ITL. € 6.71-18.8. BB inc 🛏.

Chambres et réservations

R juin-sep. (Toutes chambres). Réservations via IBN 🖥 le Centre National de Réservation ou l'auberge par ❶ ❷. (Des frais de réservation pourront vous être facturés). Il est permis de fumer dans certaines chambres - veuillez vérifier.

Usagers

La carte d'adhérent ainsi que le passeport/pièce d'identité avec photo sont à présenter. Accueil des ⅲ. Réservations pour groupes via IBN 🖥 le Centre National de Réservation ou l'auberge par ❶ ❷.

Horaires d'ouverture

Grandes auberges: ouvertes 🗓, entre 14h-24h. Accueil ouvert entre 7h-24h. Gérant réside sur place. **Autres auberges:** ouvertes 🗓, entre 15h30-23h30. Accueil ouvert entre 15h30-22h. Gérant réside sur place.

Repas

🍽 BD **R** Pour individuels & pour ♦♦♦.

Remises

Remises pour les adhérents HI - voir la section "Remises" et notre site: www.iyhf.org.

Déplacements

Modes de transport recommandés 🚅 Voiture.

Forfaits Voyages/Activités

Forfaits circuits touristiques, sports d'hiver, sports aquatiques, cyclotourisme/VTT, randonnées pédestres et hébergement/transport disponibles. Réservations des forfaits via le Centre National de Réservation par ❶ ❷.

Passeports et visas

Passeport et visa obligatoires.

Santé

Soins d'urgence gratuits. Une assurance médicale de voyage est conseillée. Les ressortissants de l'Union Européenne doivent se munir du formulaire E111 pour bénéficier de soins médicaux dans les états de l'UE.

Deutsch

Herbergen befinden sich in Städten, auf dem Land, an der Küste und in Bergen/Gebirgen.

Preisspanne

Preisspanne 13.000-35.000 ITL. € 6.71-18.08. BB inc 🍴.

Zimmer und Reservierungen

R während Jun-Sept. (Alle Zimmer). Reservierungen über (IBN) 🖥 Nationales Buchungszentrum oder Herberge per ❶ ❷. (Reservierungskosten könnten anfallen). Rauchen ist begrenzt - bitte checken.

Gäste

Mitgliedsausweis und Reisepass/Personalausweis sind erforderlich. ♦♦♦ willkommen. Gruppenbuchungen über (IBN) 🖥 Nationales Buchungszentrum oder Herberge per ❶ ❷.

Öffnungszeiten

Hauptherbergen: Zugang 🔲, 14:00-24:00Uhr. Rezeption zwischen 07:00-24:00Uhr. Herbergsmanager wohnt im Haus. **Andere Herbergen:** Zugang 🔲, 15:30-23:30Uhr. Rezeption zwischen 15:30-22:00Uhr. Herbergsmanager wohnt im Haus.

Mahlzeiten

🍽 BD **R** Für Einzelreisende & für ♦♦♦.

Ermäßigungen

HI-Mitgliedsrabatt ist erhältlich – siehe Teil für Rabatte und Ermäßigungen und www.iyhf.org.

Reisen im Land

Reisen ist einfach mit 🚅 Selbstfahrer.

Reise-/Aktivitäten-Packages

Touren/sightseeing, Wintersport, Wassersport, Fahrrad/Mountainbiking, wandern/trekking und Unterkunft/Transport-Packages erhältlich. Package-Buchungen über Nationales Buchungszentrum per ❶ ❷.

Reisepässe und Visa

Reisepass/Einreisevisum erforderlich.

Gesundheit

Nur im Notfall sind medizinische Behandlungen kostenlos. Unfall-/Krankenversicherung wird empfohlen. EU Staatsangehörige benötigen Formular E111 für ärztliche Behandlungen innerhalb der EU Länder.

Español

Los albergues están situados en las ciudades, el campo, la costa y la montaña.

Tarifas mínima y máxima

Tarifas mínima y máxima 13.000-35.000 ITL. € 6.71-18.08. BB inc 🛏.

Habitaciones y Reservas

R en jun-sep. (Todas las habitaciones). Reservas por (IBN) 📠 o a través de la Central Nacional de Reservas o el albergue por ❶ ❷. (Es posible que se aplique un suplemento en concepto de gastos de reserva). Está permitido fumar sólo en algunas salas/habitaciones - infórmese.

Huéspedes

Los huéspedes deben presentar su Carnet de Alberguista y su pasaporte o carnet de identidad. Se admiten ⅲ. Reservas de grupo por (IBN) 📠 o a través de la Central Nacional de Reservas o el albergue por ❶ ❷.

Horarios y fechas de apertura

Albergues principales - abiertos 🖿, 14:00-24:00h. Horario de recepción: 07:00-24:00h. Gerente residente. **Otros albergues** - abiertos 🖿, 15:30-23:30h. Horario de recepción: 15:30-22:00h. Gerente residente.

Comidas

🍴 BD **R** Para individuales y para ⅲ.

Descuentos

Se conceden descuentos a los miembros de Hostelling International – véase la sección sobre descuentos y nuestra página Internet en www.iyhf.org.

Desplazamientos

Transportes recomendados: 🚍 Automóvil.

Viajes Combinados con Actividades

Viajes combinados con visitas turísticas, deportes de invierno, deportes náuticos, cicloturismo/bicicleta de montaña, senderismo y alojamiento/transporte. Reserva de viajes combinados a través de la Central Nacional de Reservas por ❶ ❷.

Pasaportes y Visados

Pasaporte y visado obligatorios.

Información Sanitaria

Asistencia médica de urgencia gratuita. Seguro médico recomendado. Los ciudadanos procedentes de países pertenecientes a la UE necesitan el impreso E111 para obtener asistencia médica en dichos países.

"Certainly, travel is more than the seeing of sights; it is a change that goes on, deep and permanent, in the ideas of living."

"Il est certain que le voyage, c'est plus que la simple visite des sites touristiques; c'est un changement en continu, profond et permanent, sur l'idée que nous nous faisons de la vie."

„Gewiss ist Reisen mehr als Sehenswürdigkeiten anschauen; es findet eine tiefe und bleibende Veränderung der Lebensansichten statt."

"No cabe duda que viajar es más que hacer turismo; es un cambio continuo, profundo y permanente, en el concepto que tenemos de la vida"

Miriam Beard

Ancona -
Ostello Ancona

Via Lamaticci 7,
60126 Ancona AN.
📞 (071) 42257
📠 (071) 42257

Open Dates:	🗓
Open Hours:	07.00-12.00hrs; 15.30-24.00hrs
Reservations:	IBN
Price Range:	23000 Lire (overnight only) (👪 25000 Lire) € 11.88 (👪 12.91) 🍽
Beds:	56 - 4x² 3x⁴ 6x⁶
Facilities:	♿ 👪 🛏 🏨 📺 🧺 🅿
Directions:	2SE from city centre
✈	Raffaello Sanzio 15km
🚂	Ancona Centrale 200m
🚌	200m ap Piazza Rosselli

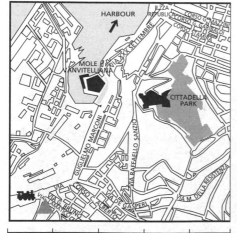

Assisi -
Ostello della Pace

Via Di Valecchie 177,
06081 Assisi PG.
📞 (075) 816767
📠 (075) 816767

Open Dates:	01-09.01; 01.03-31.12
Open Hours:	07.00-10.00hrs; 15.30-23.30hrs
Reservations:	R CC
Price Range:	25000 Lire (👪 30000 Lire) € 12.91 (👪 15.49) BB inc 🍽
Beds:	64 - 2x² 2x⁴ 6x⁶ 2x⁶ᵗ
Facilities:	👪 3x 👪 🍽 🍷 ⚙ 🏨 📁 📀 🖼 🅿 ℹ 🧺 ♻ 🏠 🏡
Directions:	0.8S from city centre
✈	Sant'egidio-Francesco D'Assisi 11km
🚂	Assisi 1.7km
🚌	S.ta Maria Degli Angeli-Assisi 800m ap Porta San Pietro 800m
Attractions:	⛲ ⛰ 🚴 🚶 ∪3km 🎿2.5km ⛵2.5km

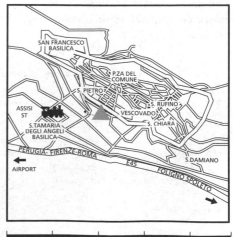

Bergamo -
Nuovo Ostello di Bergamo

Via Galileo Ferraris 1,
24123 Bergamo BG.
❶ (035) 361724; (035) 343038
❶ (035) 361724
❷ hostelbg@spm.it

Open Dates:	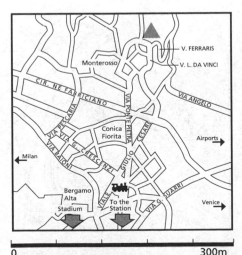 🗓
Open Hours:	07.00-24.00hrs
Reservations:	**Ⓡ** **(IBN)** **-CC-**
Price Range:	26000 Lire (**♦♦♦** 30000-35000 Lire) €13.43 (**♦♦♦** 15.49-18.08) BBinc 🍽
Beds:	84 - 2x^1🛏 11x^2🛏 4x^4🛏 8x^6🛏
Facilities:	♿ **♦♦♦** 9x **♦♦♦** 🍽 ♨ 📺 📼 1 x🍴 🔲 🎒 🚻 💱 🅿 ℹ ♫ 🏠
Directions:	2S from city centre
✈	Orio al Serio 7km
🚂	Bergamo 2km
🚌	14 100m ap Via Quintino Basso
Attractions:	🏞 ⛰ 🚴 🚶 ⚲2km ≈4km

Bologna -
Due Torri-San Sisto 2

Via Viadagola 5,
40127 Bologna BO.
❶ (051) 501810
❶ (051) 501810

Open Dates:	20.01-19.12
Open Hours:	07.00-12.00hrs; 15.30-24.00hrs
Price Range:	23000 Lire (**♦♦♦** 25000-27000 Lire) €11.88 (**♦♦♦** 12.91-13.94) BBinc 🍽
Beds:	75 - 7x^2🛏 2x^3🛏 12x^4🛏 2x^5🛏
Facilities:	♿ **♦♦♦** 3x **♦♦♦** 🍽 ☕ ♨ 🚻 📺 1 x🍴 🔲 🎒 🅿 ℹ 💱 ♫ 🏕 🛖 🏠
Directions:	6NE from city centre
✈	Marconi 10km
🚂	Centrale 5km
🚌	93-301 100m ap San Sisto 100m
Attractions:	🏞 ⛰ 🚴 ⚲5km ⚲2km ≈2km

There are 2 hostels in Bologna. See following
pages.

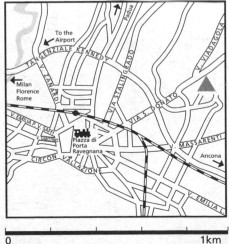

Florence -
Villa Camerata

Viale Augusto Righi 2-4,
50137 Firenze FI.
ⓣ (055) 601451
ⓕ (055) 610300

Open Dates:	🗓12
Open Hours:	07.00-24.00hrs (Rooms open from 14.00hrs)
Reservations:	Ⓡ (IBN)
Price Range:	28000 Lire (👫 30000-35000 Lire) € 14.46 (👫 15.49-18.08) BB inc 🍴
Beds:	322 - 6x³🛏 34x⁴🛏 9x⁵🛏 3x⁶🛏 12x⁶⁺🛏
Facilities:	♿ 👫 7x 👫 🍽 (BD) 👕 ⚙ 🛄 📺 🛍 1 x 🍸 🚰 ♨ Ⓟ ⓘ 👕 ❄ 🎒
Directions:	3NE from city centre
✈	Vespucci 10km
⛴	Livorno 99km
🚍	Santa Maria Novella 5km
🚌	17 400m ap Salviatino 400m
Attractions:	⛰ 🚶

There are 2 hostels in Florence. See following pages.

Foligno -
Ostello Pierantoni

Via Pierantoni 23,
06034 Foligno PG.
ⓣ (0742) 342566
ⓕ (0742) 343559
ⓔ falcinelli@edisons.it OR
folhostel@tiscalinet.it

Open Dates:	🗓12
Open Hours:	07.00-24.00hrs (Rooms from 14.00hrs)
Reservations:	Ⓡ (CC)
Price Range:	25000 Lire (👫 30000 Lire) € 12.91 (👫 15.49) BB inc 🍴
Beds:	203 - 13x²🛏 4x³🛏 19x⁴🛏 12x⁶🛏 2x⁶⁺🛏
Facilities:	♿ 👫 👫 🍽 👕 🚲 🛄 📺 🛍 1 x 🍸 🚰 🖥 🎱 ⬆ Ⓟ ⓘ 👕 ❄ 🎒
Directions:	04E from city centre
✈	Sant'Egidio-Francesco D'assisi. 26km
🚍	Foligno 500m
🚌	Navetta B 100m
Attractions:	🌲 ⛰ 🚴 🚶 🎣2.5km ⛵1km

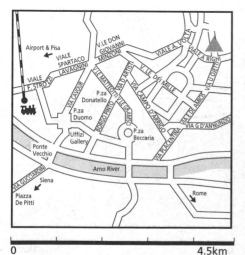

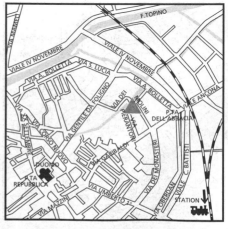

Genoa -
Genova

Via Costanzi 120N,
16135 Genova GE.
📞 (010) 2422457
📠 (010) 2422457
📧 hostelge@iol.it

Open Dates:	01.02-19.12
Open Hours:	07.00-11.30hrs; 15.30-24.00hrs
Reservations:	**R** **IBN**
Price Range:	25000 Lire (**†††** 28000-35000 Lire) € 12.91 (**†††** 14.46-18.08) BB^{inc} 🍽
Beds:	213 - 13x⁴🛏 19x⁶🛏
Facilities:	♿ **†††** 9x **†††** 🍴 (BD) 🍷 ✿ 🛏 📺 🧺 1 x🍷 🔲 💼 ⊞ 🔢 💱 🅿 ℹ 🛴
Directions:	3N from city centre
✈	Cristoforo Colombo 10km
⛴	Genova 3km
🚂	Principe 3km
🚌	40 50m ap Via Costanzi

Ischia Isle -
Il Gabbiano

SS. Forio-Panza N.162,
80075 Forio D'Ischia NA.
📞 (081) 909422
📠 (081) 909422

Open Dates:	01.04-30.09
Reservations:	**R** **IBN**
Price Range:	30000 Lire (including breakfast) € 15.49
Beds:	100
Facilities:	♿ **†††** ✿ 🛏 📺 ⚓
Directions:	
✈	Napoli Capodichino (by boat)
⛴	Forio D'Ischia 1.5km
🚌	To/from harbour 50m
Attractions:	🔍 🏊

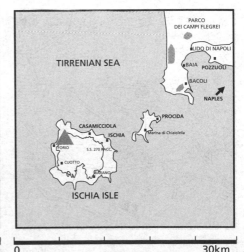

Loreto - Loreto

Via Aldo Moro 46,
60025 Loreto AN.
☎ (071) 7501026
✆ (071) 7501026

Open Dates:	🗓
Open Hours:	07.00-01.00hrs
Reservations:	**R** IBN
Price Range:	26000 Lire (👪 28000-35000 Lire) (overnight only) € 13.43 (👪 14.46-18.08) 📖
Beds:	230 - 5x¹🛏 10x²🛏 11x³🛏 11x⁴🛏 16x⁵🛏 8x⁶🛏
Facilities:	♿ 👪 👪 🍽 🍷 🛋 📺 🎮 3 x🍴 🗄 🖼 🔢 ♿ 🅿 ℹ 🐾 🌸 🏠 🌳

Directions:

✈	Ancona-Falconara 30km
⛴	Ancona 25km
🚊	Loreto 2km
🚌	Bus (Line) 50m ap Via Marconi

Attractions: 🔺 🏃 ∪4km 🏊400m ⚓400m

Marina di Massa e Carrara-Partaccia - Ostello Apuano

Viale delle Pinete 237,
54037 Marina di Massa e Carrara Partaccia MS.
☎ (0585) 780034
✆ (0585) 774266; (0585) 74858
✉ ostelloapuano@hotmail.com

Open Dates:	16.03-30.09
Open Hours:	07.00-23.30hrs
Reservations:	**R** CC
Price Range:	15000-16000 Lire (overnight only) € 7.75-8.26 📖
Beds:	200 - 1x²🛏 2x⁴🛏 21x⁶🛏
Facilities:	👪 2 (except July & August)x 👪 🍽 🍷 🛋 📺 📋 🗄 🅿 ℹ 🐾 🌸 🔍 🖥

Directions:

✈	Galilei 60km
⛴	Livorno 70km
🚊	Carrara 4km
🚌	N. Via Avenza Mare ap Viale Delle Pinete 500m

Attractions: 🔺 📷10m 🚴 🏃 ∪30km 🏊1km ⚓10m

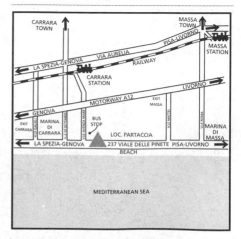

Naples - Mergellina

Salita della Grotta a Piedigrotta 23,
80122 Napoli NA.
❶ (081) 7612346; (081) 7611215
❶ (081) 7612391

Open Dates: 🗓️

Open Hours: 06.30-00.30hrs

Reservations: **R** **IBN**

Price Range: 25000 Lire (🚻 30000 Lire)
€ 12.91 (🚻 15.49) BB|inc 🛍️

Beds: 200 - 36x²🛏️ 16x⁴🛏️ 11x⁶🛏️

Facilities: 🚻 16x 🚻 🍴 (BD) ☕ ⚙️ 🏨
📺 🔘 🧳 🔢 🔌 P ℹ️ 🎿 ✂️
🌲

Directions: 1N from city centre

✈️ Capodichino 8km

⛴️ Napoli 2km

🚂 Mergellina 300m

🚌 150-152 400m ap Via G. Bruno
400m

U Mergellina 300m

Attractions: ⛰️ 📷 🏊5km

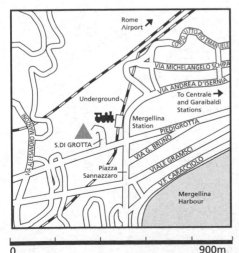

Ravenna - Dante

Via Aurelio Nicolodi 12 (quartiere
Trieste),
48100 Ravenna RA.
❶ (0544) 421164
❶ (0544) 421164
❷ hostelravenna@hotmail.com

Open Dates: 🗓️

Open Hours: 07.00-10.00hrs; 15.30-23.30hrs

Reservations: **R** **IBN** **CC**

Price Range: 24000 Lire (🚻 27000 Lire) €
12.39 (🚻 13.94) BB|inc 🛍️

Beds: 140 - 4x¹🛏️ 2x²🛏️ 12x⁴🛏️ 8x⁶🛏️

Facilities: ♿ 🚻 21x 🚻 🍴 ☕ 🏨 📺 📋
🛏️1 x🍴 🧳 🔢 🔌 P ✂️ 🌲

Directions:

✈️ Bologna "Marconi" 85km

🚂 Ravenna 800m

🚌 1, 11, 70 100m

Attractions: 🎿 ⛰️ ∪1.2km 🎣1km 🏊2km

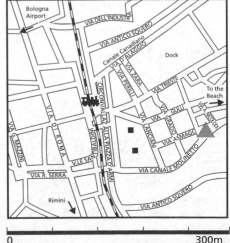

Rome - Foro Italico - A F Pessina YH

Viale delle Olimpiadi 61,
00194 Roma RM.
☎ (06) 3236267
✆ (06) 3242613

Open Dates:	🗓
Open Hours:	07.00-24.00hrs (Rooms open from 14.00hrs)
Reservations:	**R** **IBN**
Price Range:	28000-30000 Lire € 14.46-15.49 BB inc 🍽
Beds:	334 - 14x⁶⚿ 35x⁶⚿
Facilities:	♿ 👬 🍴 🍺 ☼ 👥 📺 1 x 🍸 💼 🧺 🔒 ⬆ 🅿 ℹ 🧴 ❀ 🏠 🎴
Directions:	5NW from city centre
✈	Fiumicino 28km
🚂	Termini 6km
🚌	32, 280, 628 ap Lungotevere Maresciallo Cadorna
Ⓤ	Line A Ottaviano 2km
Attractions:	🚴

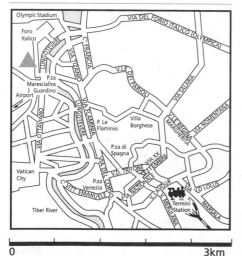

Turin - Torino

Via Alby 1,
10131 Torino TO.
☎ (011) 6602939
✆ (011) 6604445
✉ hostelto@tin.it

Open Dates:	01.02-20.12
Open Hours:	07.00-10.00hrs; 15.30-23.30hrs
Reservations:	**R**
Price Range:	20000-22000 Lire (👫 22000-24000 Lire) € 10.33-11.36 (👫 11.36-12.39) BB inc 🍽
Beds:	76 - 1x¹⚿ 2x²⚿ 2x³⚿ 10x⁴⚿ 4x⁶⚿
Facilities:	4x 👬 🍴 (BD) ☼ 📺 🅾 🖼 🔒 🅿 ❀ 🔍 🎴
Directions:	2E from city centre
✈	Caselle 16km
🚂	Porta Nuova 1.8km
🚌	52 (64 on Sunday) 200m
Attractions:	∪6km ⚲500m 🏊2km

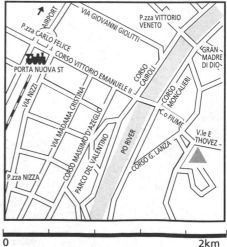

Venice - Venezia

Fondamenta Zitelle 86,
Isola della Giudecca,
30123 Venezia VE.
☎ (041) 5238211
☎ (041) 5235689
e vehostel@tin.it

Open Dates:	01.01-11.12; 28-31.12
Open Hours:	07.00-24.00hrs (Rooms open from 14.00hrs)
Reservations:	**R** (IBN) **CC**
Price Range:	30000 Lire € 15.49 BBinc 🛏
Beds:	260 - 20x 🛏
Facilities:	👥 🍽 🍷 🛏 📷 8 7 🏠 🏢
Directions:	1S from city centre
✈	Marco Polo 10km
🚅	Santa Lucia 2km
🚌	42 Boat, 82 200m ap Zitelle

Vicenza - Olimpico

Viale Giuriolo 9,
36100,
Vicenza VI.
☎ (0444) 540222
☎ (0444) 547762

Open Dates:	🗓
Open Hours:	07.30-09.30hrs; 15.30-23.30hrs
Price Range:	26000 Lire (👥 28000-31000 Lire) € 13.43 (👥 14.46-16.01) 🛏
Beds:	85
Facilities:	♿ 👥 🍷 🛏 📺 🏢
Directions:	
✈	"Marco Polo" Venezia 75km
🚅	1.5km
🚌	1, 2, 4, 5, 7 50m

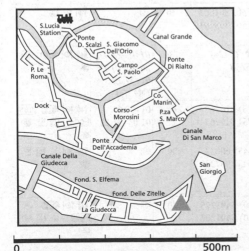

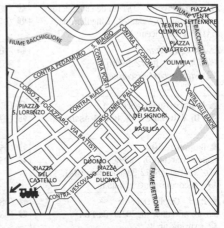

Location/Address	Telephone No. Fax No.	Beds	Opening Dates	Facilities
▲ **Abetone** - Renzo Bizzarri Strada Statale dell'Abetone, 51021 Abetone PT. 🄴 baicchienrico@freedomland.it	🅣 (0573) 60117 🄵 (0573) 606656	64	01.01–30.04; 15.06–30.09; 01–31.12 (🄵₁₂ 🆁 ⅲ)	ⅲ 🍽 🆁 🅿 🄾 🍵
▲ **Acquasparta** - San Francesco Via San Francesco 1, 05021 Acquasparta, TR.	🅣 (0744) 943167 🄵 (0744) 944168	120	🄵₁₂	ⅲ 🍽 🆁 ⛦ 🅿
△ *Agerola-San Lazzaro* - *'Beata Solitudo'* *Piazza Generale Avitabile,* *80051 Agerola-San Lazzaro NA.* 🄴 *paolog@ptn.pandora.it*	🅣 *(081) 8025048* 🄵 *(081) 8025048*	*16*	*01.01–14.09;* *01.10–31.12*	🖝 🅿 🄾 ✿
▲ **Agropoli-Paestum** - La Lanterna Via Lanterna 8, Loc.tà San Marco, 84043 Agropoli SA. 🄴 lanterna@cilento.it	🅣 (0974) 838364 🄵 (0974) 838364	56	15.03–30.10	ⅲ 🍽 ⛦ 🅿 🍵 ✿
△ *Alghero-Fertilia* - *'Ostello dei Giuliani'* *Via Zara 1, 07040 Alghero-Fertilia SS.* 🄴 *ostellodeigiuliani@tiscalinet.it*	🅣 *(079) 930353;* *(079) 930015* 🄵 *(079) 930353*	*50*	🄵₁₂	🍽 🅿
△ *Alessandria* - *Santa Maria Di Castello* *Piazza Santa Maria Di Castello 14,* *15100 Alessandria.*	🅣 *(0131) 304400;* *(0131) 304401*	*70*	🄵₁₂	ⅲ ⛦
▲ **Amelia** - Giustiniani Piazza Matteotti, 05022 Amelia (TR).	🅣 (0744) 981453 🄵 (0744) 982237	60	01.03–31.12	ⅲ 🍽 🆁 ⛦ 🍵 🚲
▲ **Ancona** - Ostello Ancona 🄸🄱🄽 **Via Lamaticci 7, 60126 Ancona AN.**	🅣 (071) 42257 🄵 (071) 42257	56	🄵₁₂	ⅲ 2SE ⛦ 🖝 🅿
▲ **Argenta** - Campotto Via Cardinala 27, 44010 Campotto di Argenta FE.	🅣 (0532) 808035 🄵 (0532) 808035	52	01.03; 31.10 (ⅲ 🄵₁₂)	ⅲ ⛦ 🅿 🄾
△ *Arpy Morgex* - *'Valdigne. M. Blanc'* *Loc.Arpy, 11017 Morgex AO.* 🄴 *yh.arpy@tin.it*	🅣 *(0165) 841684;* *(010) 2471826* 🄵 *(0165) 841684;* *(010) 2471828*	*130*	*01.01–08.04;* *17.06–02.09;* *07–31.12 (ⅲ* *07.12–31.12)*	ⅲ 🍽 ⛦ 🄲🄲 🅿 🄾 🍵 🚲
▲ **Ascoli Piceno** - 'Ostello de Longobardi' Via Soderini 26, Palazzetto Longobardo, 63100 Ascoli Piceno AP.	🅣 (0736) 261862 🄵 (0736) 259191	30	🄵₁₂	🍽 🖝 🅿
△ *Asiago* - *Ekar* *Via Ekar 2-5, 36012 Asiago VI.* 🄴 *ostelloechar@tiscalinet.it*	🅣 / 🄵: *(0424)* *455138*	*130*	*01.01–28.02;* *20.05–10.09;* *01–31.12* (ⅲ 🄵₁₂)	ⅲ 🍽 🆁 🅿 🍵
▲ **Assisi** - Ostello della Pace **Via Di Valecchie 177, 06081 Assisi PG.**	🅣 (075) 816767 🄵 (075) 816767	64	01–09.01; 01.03–31.12	ⅲ 🍽 🆁 0.8S 🄲🄲 🅿 🄾 🍵 ✿
▲ **Bagnacavallo** - Antico Convento Di SanFrancesco Via Cadorna, 48012 Bagnacavallo (RA). 🄴 anticoconvento@infinito.it	🅣 (0545) 60622 🄵 (0545) 937228	90	🄵₁₂	ⅲ 🍽 ⛦ 🅿 🄾 🍵
▲ **Bari** - Ostello Del Sole S.S. 16 Adriatica 78, 70126 Bari BA. 🄴 sworld@tin.it	🅣 (080) 5491175 🄵 (080) 5491202	30	🄵₁₂	ⅲ 🍽 🆁 ⛦ 🄲🄲 🖝 🅿 🍵 ✿

Location/Address	Telephone No. Fax No.	Beds	Opening Dates	Facilities
▲ **Bergamo** - Nuovo Ostello di Bergamo IBN **Via Galileo Ferraris 1, 24123 Bergamo BG.** e hostelbg@spm.it	t (035) 361724; (035) 343038 f (035) 361724	84	12	R 2S CC P
△ ***Bergolo*** - *Le Langhe* *Via Roma 22, 12070 Bergolo CN.*	t *(0173) 87222* f *(0173) 87222*	*34*	*01.03–31.10* *(12)*	CC P
▲ **Bionaz** - La Batise Plan de Veyne - 11010 Bionaz (AO).	t (0165) 730105 f (0165) 730214	38	12	R P
▲ **Bologna** - Due Torri-San Sisto 2 **Via Viadagola 5, 40127 Bologna BO.**	t (051) 501810 f (051) 501810	75	20.01–19.12	6NE P
▲ **Bologna** - San Sisto Via Viadagola 14, 40127 Bologna.	t (051) 501810 f (051) 501810	35	12	R 6NE P
▲ **Bomba Lake** - Isola Verde Via Lago, 66042 Bomba CH. e isolverd@tin.it	t (0872) 860475; (0872) 860568 f (0872) 860450	28	12	CC P
△ ***Bosa*** - *Malaspina* *Via Sardegna 1-08013, Bosa Marina NU.*	t *(0785) 375009* f *(0785) 375009*	*48*	12	P
▲ **Castelfiorentino** Viale Roosevelt 26, 50051 Castelfiorentino (FI).	t (0571) 64002 f (0571) 64002	84	12	0.5NE P
△ ***Castellaneta Marina*** - *Villini Paradiso* *Via Zond 2, 74010 Castellaneta Marina (TA).*	t *(099) 8433200* f *(099) 8430046*	*20*	12	R CC P
▲ **Castelsardo** - Golfo Dell' Asinara Via Sardegna 1, Loc-Ta' Lu Bagnu (SS). e ostello.asinara@tiscalinet.it	t (079) 474031; (079) 587008 f (079) 587142	110	01.04–30.09	2E CC P
▲ **Castel del Giudice** - "La Castellana" Via Fontana Vecchia 1, 86080 Castel del Giudice IS.	t (0865) 946222 f (0865) 946222	60	12	R P
△ ***Castroreale*** - *'Ostello Delle Aquile'* *Salita Federico II d'Aragona,* *98053 Castroreale Centro ME.*	t *(090) 9746398* f *(090) 9746446*	*24*	*01.04–31.10*	
▲ **Cava De' Tirreni** - Borgo Scacciaventi Piazza San Francesco 1, 84013 Cava De' Tirreni (SA).	t (089) 466631 f (089) 466631	140	01.04–30.09	P
▲ **Collescipoli-Terni** - Garibaldini YH Corso Dei Garibaldini 61, 05033 Collescipoli TR.	t (0744) 800467 f (0744) 800467	37	During 2001	
▲ **Como** - 'Villa Olmo' Via Bellinzona 2, 22100 Como CO. e ostellocomo@tin.it	t (031) 573800 f (031) 573800	76	01.03–30.11	R P
▲ **Correggio** - La Rocchetta Corso Cavour 19, 42015 Correggio (RE). e ostello-correggio@hotmail.com	t (0522) 632361 f (0522) 632361	25	01.04–31.10	R CC P
▲ **Cortona** - 'San Marco' Via Maffei 57, 52044 Cortona AR.	t (0575) 601392; (0575) 601765 f (0575) 601392	80	15.03–15.10 (12)	CC P

Location/Address	Telephone No. Fax No.	Beds	Opening Dates	Facilities
▲ **Domaso** - La Vespa Via Case Sparse 12, 22013 Domaso (CO). 📧 ostellolavespa@tiscalinet.it	☎ (0344) 97449 📠 (0344) 97575	25	01.04–31.10	††† ⑩ ំ ᴄᴄ 🅿 ⑥ ☕
▲ **Erice-Trapani** - G.Amodeo Strada Provinciale Trapani-Erice, Km 2⁰, 91100 Raganzili Erice TP.	☎ (0923) 552964 📠 (0923) 552964	52	01.01–03.11; 04–31.12	⑩ ᴄᴄ 🅿 ☕ ❂
▲ **Etroubles** - Dortoir Echevennoz Frazione Echevennoz, 11014 Etroubles (AO).	☎ Info: (06) 4871152 📠 Info: (06) 4880492	11	⒃	††† ᴦ ᴄᴄ ❦ 🅿
▲ **Ferrara** - Estense (IBN) Corso Biagio Rossetti 24, 44100 Ferrara. 📧 hostelferrara@hotmail.com	☎ (0532) 204227 📠 (0532) 204227	72	⒃	††† Ⓡ 0.5N ᴦ 🅿 ☕
▲ **Finale-Ligure** - 'Vuillermin Castle' Via Generale Caviglia 46, 17024 Finale-Ligure SV. 📧 hostelfinaleligure@libero.it	☎ (019) 690515; (0347) 2414683 📠 (019) 690515	69	15.03–15.10	††† ⑩ Ⓡ ᴦ ᴄᴄ ⑥ ☕ ❂
▲ **Florence** - Villa Camerata (IBN) **Viale Augusto Righi 2-4,** **50137 Firenze FI.**	☎ (055) 601451 📠 (055) 610300	322	⒃	††† ⑩ Ⓡ 3NE ᴦ 🅿 ⑥ ☕ ❂
▲ **Florence** - Carmine YH Via Del Leone 35, 50124 Firenze FI.	☎ (055) 291974 📠 Info: (055) 610300	84	15.03–31.10	0.5SW ᴦ
▲ **Foligno** - Ostello Pierantoni **Via Pierantoni 23, 06034 Foligno PG.** 📧 falcinelli@edisons.it OR folhostel@tiscalinet.it	☎ (0742) 342566 📠 (0742) 343559	203	⒃	††† ⑩ Ⓡ 0.4E ᴦ ᴄᴄ 🅿 ⑥ ☕ ☟
▲ **Genoa** - Genova (IBN) **Via Costanzi 120N, 16135 Genova GE.** 📧 hostelge@iol.it	☎ (010) 2422457 📠 (010) 2422457	213	01.02–19.12	††† ⑩ Ⓡ 3N ᴦ 🅿 ⑥ ☕ ❂
▲ **Gran Paradiso National Park-Noasca** - "Parco Nazionale" Frazione Gere Sopra, 10080 Noasca TO.	☎ (0124) 901107 📠 (0124) 901107	68	01.03–15.10 (††† Ⓡ) 01.01–10.01; 01.03–31.12)	††† ⑩ ᴦ 🅿 ☕
△ *Guastalla* - 'Quadrio Michelotti" *Via Lido Po 11-13, 42016 Guastalla, RE.* 📧 *lunetia@tin.it*	☎ *(0522) 219287* 📠 *(0522) 839228*	*25*	*01.04–15.10*	††† ᴦ ❦ 🅿 ☕
▲ **Ischia Isle** - Il Gabbiano (IBN) **SS. Forio-Panza N.162,** **80075 Forio D'Ischia NA.**	☎ (081) 909422 📠 (081) 909422	100	01.04–30.09	††† Ⓡ ᴦ ❂
▲ **Isola Polvese-Trasimeno Lake** - Il Poggio Isola Polvese, 06060 San Feliciano, PG.	☎ (075) 9659550 📠 (075) 9659551	76	01.03–31.10 (⒃ †††)	††† ⑩ 2NE ᴦ ⑥ ☕
▲ **Loreto** - Loreto (IBN) **Via Aldo Moro 46, 60025 Loreto AN.**	☎ (071) 7501026 📠 (071) 7501026	230	⒃	††† ⑩ Ⓡ ᴦ 🅿 ⑥ ☕

Location/Address	Telephone No. Fax No.	Beds	Opening Dates	Facilities
▲ **Lucca** - 'Il Serchio' Via della Cavallerizza, 55100 Lucca LU.	❶ Info: (0583) 341811; Info: (0586) 862517 ❶ Info: (0583) 341811	90	🗓12	♦♦ 🍽 P 🍺
▲ **Marina di Massa e Carrara-Partaccia** - Ostello Apuano **Viale delle Pinete 237, 54037 Marina di** **Massa e Carrara Partaccia MS.** ⓔ ostelloapuano@hotmail.com	❶ (0585) 780034 ❶ (0585) 774266; (0585) 74858	200	16.03–30.09	♦♦ 🍽 ⓡ ⒸⒸ ♂ P 🔒 🍺
▲ **Menaggio** - La Primula Via Quattro Novembre 86, 22017 Menaggio CO. ⓔ menaggiohostel@mclink.it	❶ (0344) 32356 ❶ (0344) 31677	50	15.03–05.11	♦♦ 🍽 ⓡ ♂ P 🔒 🍺 ✿
▲ **Milano** - "Piero Rotta" Via Martino Bassi 2 (access from via Salmoirag hi 1) (QT8-San Siro), 20148 Milano MI.	❶ (02) 39267095 ❶ (02) 33000191	380	13.01–23.12	♦♦ 3NW ♿ P 🔒 🍺 ✿
▲ **Mira** - Ostello Di Mira Via Giare 169, 30030 Mira-Giare (VE). ⓔ ostellomiravenezia@tin.it	❶ (041) 5679203 ❶ (041) 5676457	56	01.03–30.09	♦♦ 🍽 ♿ ⒸⒸ ♂ P
▲ **Modena** - San Filippo Neri Ⓘ🅱Ⓝ Via Santa Orsola 48/52, 41100 Modena. ⓔ hostelmodena@hotmail.com	❶ (059) 234598 ❶ (059) 234598	80	🗓12	♦♦ ⓡ ♿ ⒸⒸ ✿
▲ **Montagnana** - 'Rocca degli Alberi' Castello degli Alberi (Porta Legnago), 35044 Montagnana PD.	❶ (0429) 81076; (049) 8070266 ❶ (0429) 81076; (049) 8070266	48	01.04–15.10	♦♦ ⓡ P
▲ **Naples** - Mergellina Ⓘ🅱Ⓝ **Salita della Grotta a Piedigrotta 23,** **80122 Napoli NA.**	❶ (081) 7612346; (081) 7611215 ❶ (081) 7612391	200	🗓12	♦♦ 🍽 ⓡ 1N P 🔒 🍺 ✿
▲ **Nicolosi** - Etna Via della Quercia 7, 95030 Nicolosi CT. ⓔ etnahostel@hotmail.com	❶ (095) 7914686 ❶ (095) 7914701	70	🗓12	♦♦ 🍽 🔒 🍺
▲ **Noto** - Il Castello Via Fratelli Bandiera, 96017 Noto (SR).	❶ (0931) 571534 ❶ (0931) 571534	68	🗓12	♦♦ 🍽 ⓡ ♿ ⒸⒸ ♂ P 🍺 ✿
▲ **Padova** - Centro Ospitalita' Città di Padova, Via A. Aleardi 30, 35122 Padova PD. ⓔ pdyhtl@tin.it	❶ (049) 8752219 ❶ (049) 654210	112	07.01–24.12	♦♦ 🍽 ♿ ⒸⒸ P 🔒 🍺
△ *Parma* - *'Cittadella'* *Parco Cittadella 5, 43100 Parma PR.*	❶ *(0521) 961434*	*50*	*01.04–31.10*	P
▲ **Perugia** - Baldelli Mombelli Via Maniconi, 06077 Perugia-Ponte Felcino. ⓔ perugiahostel@pg.technet.it	❶ (075) 5011366 ❶ (075) 5026805	90	Opening during 2001	♦♦ 🍽 ⓡ 8SW ♿ ⒸⒸ P 🔒 🍺 ✿
▲ **Perugia** - Mario Spagnoli Via Cortonese 4, 06127 Perugia-Pian Di Massiano. ⓔ perugiahostel@pg.technet.it	❶ (075) 5011366 ❶ (075) 5026805	186	🗓12	♦♦ 🍽 ⓡ ♿ ⒸⒸ P 🔒 🍺 🚲 ✿

Location/Address	Telephone No. Fax No.	Beds	Opening Dates	Facilities
▲ **Prato** - Villa Fiorelli Parco Di Galceti, Via Di Galceti 64, 59100 Prato.	❶ (0574) 697611 ❺ (0574) 6976256	52	🛏12	♯♯♯ ⑩ ® ③N Ġ ◱ ☕
▲ **Ravenna** - Dante (IBN) **Via Aurelio Nicolodi 12** **(quartiere Trieste), 48100 Ravenna RA.** 🅴 hostelravenna@hotmail.com	❶ (0544) 421164 ❺ (0544) 421164	140	🛏12	♯♯♯ ⑩ ® Ġ ⊟CC⊟ P ☕ ☕
▲ **Reggio Emilia** - Basilica Della Ghiara Via Guasco, 42100 Reggio Emilia.	❶ Info: (0522) 454795 ❺ Info: (051) 224913	100	🛏12	♯♯♯ ⑩ ® Ġ P
△ *Reggio Emilia* - *Reggio Emilia* *Via dell 'Abbadessa 8,* *42100 Reggio Emilia RE.*	❶ *(0522) 454795*	*36*	*03.01–31.03;* *07.04–22.12* *(♯♯♯ 🛏12)*	⑩ ✶ P
▲ **Rieti-Terminillo** - 'Ostello della Neve' (IBN) Anello Panoramico (Campoforogna), 02017 Rieti-Terminillo RI.	❶ (0746) 261169 ❺ (0746) 261169	120	01.01–15.05; 15.06–31.08; 01–31.12	♯♯♯ ⑩ ® P ☕
▲ **Riva del Garda** - 'Benacus' Piazza Cavour 10, 38066 Riva del Garda TN. 🅴 ostelloriva@anthesi.com	❶ (0464) 554911 ❺ (0464) 559966	100	01.04–31.10	⑩ ® P
△ *Rivamonte Agordino* - *Imperina* *Localita le Miniere,* *32020 Rivamonte Agordino BL.*	❶ *(0437) 62099*	*44*	*01.04–30.09* *(♯♯♯ 🛏12)*	P ☕
▲ **Rome** - Foro Italico - A F Pessina YH (IBN) **Viale delle Olimpiadi 61,** **00194 Roma RM.**	❶ (06) 3236267 ❺ (06) 3242613	334	🛏12	⑩ ® ⑤NW Ġ P ☕ ✿
▲ **Rovereto** - Città di Rovereto Via delle Scuole 16/18, 38068 Rovereto TN.	❶ (0464) 433707 ❺ (0464) 424137	90	01.01–02.02; 25.02–31.12	♯♯♯ ⑩ Ġ ⊟CC⊟ P ◱ ☕ ✿
▲ **Salerno** - Ave Gratia Plena Via Dei Canali, 84100 Salerno SA.	❶ Info: (089) 790251 ❺ Info: (089) 405792	150	🛏12	♯♯♯ ⑩ Ġ ◱ ☕ 🚲 ✿
▲ **San Lazzaro di Savena** - Village Centro Europa Uno Localita' Cicogna, Via Emilia 297, 40068 San Lazzaro di Savena - BO.	❶ (051) 6258352; (051) 6255239 ❺ (051) 6258352	42	🛏12	♯♯♯ ⑩ ® Ġ ✶ P ◱ ☕
▲ **Santa Sofia** Piazza Matteotti, 47018 Santa Sofia FO.	❶ (0543) 970014	26	🛏12	♯♯♯ Ġ P ☕
▲ **San Vito Al Tagliamento** - Europa Via Amalteo 39, 33078 San Vito Al Tagliamento (PN). 🅴 wwwbat@tin.it	❶ (0434) 876898 ❺ (0434) 877156	35	🛏12	♯♯♯ ® Ġ ⊟CC⊟ P ◱ 🚲
▲ **Savona** - 'Villa De Franceschini' Via alla Stra 29 (Conca Verde), 17100 Savona SV. 🅴 concaverdehostel@iol.it	❶ (019) 263222 ❺ (019) 263222	244	15.03–15.10	♯♯♯ ⑩ Ġ P ☕ ✿

Location/Address	Telephone No. Fax No.	Beds	Opening Dates	Facilities
▲ **Savona** - "Priamar Fortress" Corso Giuseppe Mazzini, Fortezza Priamar, 17100 Savona SV. ℮ priamarhostel@iol.it	☎ (019) 812653 ❺ (019) 812653	60	01.01–15.10; 16–31.12	♯♯ ⑩ ® ⊂CC⊐ P ▣ ● ☼
▲ **Soveria Mannelli** - 'La Pineta' Localita' Bivio Bonacci, 88049 Soveria Mannelli-CZ.	☎ (0968) 666079; (0968) 662115 ❺ (0968) 666079	52	⓬	⑩ ® ⊂CC⊐ P ☕
▲ **Sperlonga** - Marina Degli Ulivi Contrada Fiorelle, 04029 Sperlonga (LT).	☎ Info: (0771) 549296 ❺ Info: (0771) 549296	60	Opening during 2001	♯♯ ♿ P
▲ **Taormina** - Ulisse Vico San Francesco Di Paola 9, 98039 Taormina (ME).	☎ (0942) 23193 ❻❻ (0942) 23211	28	10.02–30.10; 08.12–31.12	⑩ ⚐ ● ♻
▲ **Tavarnelle Val Di Pesa** - Ostello Del Chianti Via Roma 137, 50028 Tavarnelle V.P. (FI).	☎ (055) 8050265 ❺ (055) 8050265	82	15.03–31.10	♯♯ ⑩ ♿ P
▲ **Trasimeno Lake** - Torricella Via Del Lavoro 10, 06060 Torricella di San Feliciano PG.	☎ (075) 843508 ❺ (075) 843508	88	01.03–31.10	♯♯ ⑩ P ▣ ☕
▲ **Trento** - Giovane Europa Via Manzoni 17, 38100 Trento TN. ℮ ostellotrento@interfree.it	☎ (0461) 234567 ❺ (0461) 268434	68	01–06.01; 01.02–31.12	♯♯ ⑩ ⊂CC⊐ ☕ ☼
▲ **Trieste-Grignano** - Tergeste Viale Miramare 331, 34014 Trieste-Grignano, TS.	☎ (040) 224102 ❺ (040) 224102	74	⓬	⑩ ® 8NW P ●
▲ **Turin** - Torino **Via Alby 1, 10131 Torino TO.** ℮ hostelto@tin.it	☎ (011) 6602939 ❺ (011) 6604445	76	01.02–20.12	♯♯ ⑩ ® 2E P ▣ ☼
▲ **Venice** - Venezia ⟨IBN⟩ **Fondamenta Zitelle 86, Isola della Giudecca, 30123 Venezia VE.** ℮ vehostel@tin.it	☎ (041) 5238211 ❺ (041) 5235689	260	01.01–11.12; 28–31.12	⑩ ® 1S ⊂CC⊐ ●
▲ **Verbania** - Verbania Via Alle Rose 7 - 28048 Verbania VB.	☎ (0323) 501648 ❺ (0323) 507877	72	01.01–06.01; 01.03–31.10; 05.12–31.12 (♯♯ ® 06–29.02)	♯♯ ⑩ ♿ P ▣ ●
▲ **Verona** - 'Villa Francescatti' Salita Fontana del Ferro 15 (Veronetta), 37129 Verona VR.	☎ (045) 590360 ❺ (045) 8009127	120	⓬	♯♯ ⑩ 3NW ▣ ☼
▲ **Vicenza** - Olimpico **Viale Giuriolo 9, 36100, Vicenza VI.**	☎ (0444) 540222 ❺ (0444) 547762	85	⓬	♯♯ ♿ ♻
▲ **Villavallelonga** - Tre Confini Via Aia Canale, 67050 Villavallelonga (AQ). ℮ treconfini@hotmail.com	☎ (0863) 949406 ❺ (0963) 949406	48	01.04–30.09; 01.12–28.02	♯♯ ⑩ ♿ P ▣ ☕

Luxembourg

Centrale des Auberges de Jeunesse Luxembourgeoises,
24-26 Place de la Gare, L-1616,
Luxembourg

☎ (352) 26293-500
🖷 (352) 26293-503
✉ information@youthhostels.lu
🖳 www.youthhostels.lu

Office Hours: Monday-Friday, 10.00-18.00hrs

A copy of the Hostel Directory for this Country can be obtained from:
The National Office

Capital:	Luxembourg
Language:	Lëtzebuergesch
Currency:	LUF (franc) and BEF

Population:	400,000
Size:	2,586 sq km
Telephone Country Code:	352

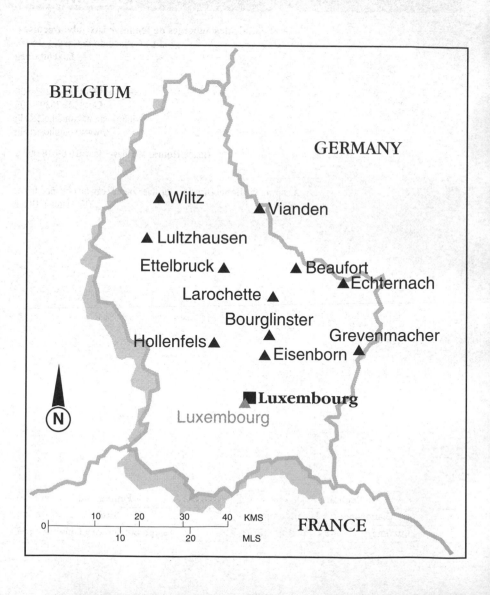

BELGIUM

GERMANY

▲ Wiltz

▲ Vianden

▲ Lultzhausen

Ettelbruck ▲

▲ Beaufort

▲ Echternach

Larochette ▲

Bourglinster
▲

Grevenmacher

Hollenfels ▲

▲ Eisenborn

▲

■ **Luxembourg**

Luxembourg

N

10 20 30 40 KMS

0

10 20 MLS

FRANCE

English

Hostels are located in cities and in the countryside.

Price range

Price range LUF 375-670. € 9.30-16.61. BB|inc
📱.

Rooms and Reservations

R 📱 (All Rooms). Reservations via Hostel or National Office by ☎ ❶ ✉. Smoking is limited - please check.

Guests

Membership Card and Passport/Photo ID are required. ⅲ welcome. Group bookings via Hostel or National Office by ☎ ❶ ✉.

Open times

Main hostels: open 📱, 07:30-02:00hrs. Resident manager. **Other hostels:** open 07:30-22:00hrs. Reception open: 17:00-21:00hrs. Resident manager.

Meals

🍽 BLD For individuals & for ⅲ. ☞.

Discounts

III Member Discounts available - see discounts section and www.iyhf.org.

Travelling around

For ease of travel use 🚆 🚌 Self-Drive.

Travel/Activity Packages

Tours/sightseeing, water sports, cycling/ mountain biking, walking/trekking and accommodation/transport packages available. Package bookings via 📠 or National Office by ☎ ❶ ✉.

Passports and Visas

Photo ID required.

Health

Medical insurance is recommended. EU Nationals require Form E111 to obtain treatment within EU countries.

Français

Les auberges sont situées dans les villes et à la campagne.

Tarifs des nuitées

Tarifs des nuitées 375 670 LUF. € 9.30-16.61. BB|inc 📱.

Chambres et réservations

R 📱 (Toutes chambres). Réservations via l'auberge ou le Bureau National par ☎ ❶ ✉. Il est permis de fumer dans certaines chambres - veuillez vérifier.

Usagers

La carte d'adhérent ainsi que le passeport/pièce d'identité avec photo sont à présenter. Accueil des ⅲ. Réservations pour groupes via l'auberge ou le Bureau National par ☎ ❶ ✉.

Horaires d'ouverture

Grandes auberges: ouvertes 📱, entre 7h30-2h. Gérant réside sur place. **Autres auberges:** ouvertes entre 7h30-22h. Accueil ouvert entre 17h-21h. Gérant réside sur place.

Repas

🍽 BLD Pour individuels & pour ⅲ. ☞.

Remises

Remises pour les adhérents HI - voir la section "Remises" et notre site: www.iyhf.org.

Déplacements

Modes de transport recommandés 🚆 🚌 Voiture.

Forfaits Voyages/Activités

Forfaits circuits touristiques, sports aquatiques, cyclotourisme/VTT, randonnées pédestres et hébergement/transport disponibles. Réservations des forfaits via 🖰 ou le Bureau National par ❶ ❶ ❷.

Passeports et visas

Pièce d'identité avec photo obligatoire.

Santé

Une assurance médicale de voyage est conseillée. Les ressortissants de l'Union Européenne doivent se munir du formulaire E111 pour bénéficier de soins médicaux dans les états de l'UE.

Deutsch

Herbergen befinden sich in Städten und auf dem Land.

Preisspanne

Preisspanne 375-670 LUF. € 9.30-16.61. [BB]inc 🔟.

Zimmer und Reservierungen

❿ 🔟 (Alle Zimmer). Reservierungen über Herberge oder Landesverband per ❶ ❶ ❷. Rauchen ist begrenzt - bitte checken.

Gäste

Mitgliedsausweis und Reisepass/ Personalausweis sind erforderlich. ⅲ willkommen. Gruppenbuchungen über Herberge oder Landesverband per ❶ ❶ ❷.

Öffnungszeiten

Hauptherbergen: Zugang 🔟, 07:30-02:00Uhr. Herbergsmanager wohnt im Haus. **Andere Herbergen:** Zugang zwischen 07:30-22:00Uhr. Rezeption zwischen

17:00-21:00Uhr. Herbergsmanager wohnt im Haus.

Mahlzeiten

⅋ BLD Für Einzelreisende & für ⅲ. ⚓.

Ermäßigungen

HI-Mitgliedsrabatt ist erhältlich – siehe Teil für Rabatte und Ermäßigungen und www.iyhf.org.

Reisen im Land

Reisen ist einfach mit 🚌 🚐 Selbstfahrer.

Reise-/Aktivitäten-Packages

Touren/sightseeing, Wassersport, Fahrrad/ Mountainbiking, wandern/trekking und Unterkunft/Transport-Packages erhältlich. Package-Buchungen über 🖰 oder die Landesverband per ❶ ❶ ❷.

Reisepässe und Visa

Personalausweis erforderlich.

Gesundheit

Unfall-/Krankenversicherung wird empfohlen. EU Staatsangehörige benötigen Formular E111 für ärztliche Behandlungen innerhalb der EU Länder.

Español

Los albergues están situados en las ciudades y el campo.

Tarifas mínima y máxima

Tarifas mínima y máxima 375-670 LUF. € 9.30-16.61. [BB]inc 🔟.

Habitaciones y Reservas

❿ 🔟 (Todas las habitaciones). Reservas a través del albergue o la Asociación Nacional por ❶ ❶ ❷. Está permitido fumar sólo en algunas salas/habitaciones - infórmese.

Huéspedes

Los huéspedes deben presentar su Carnet de Alberguista y su pasaporte o carnet de identidad. Se admiten ⋔. Reservas de grupo a través del albergue o la Asociación Nacional por ❶ ❹ ❺.

Horarios y fechas de apertura

Albergues principales - abiertos 🗓, 07:30-02:00h. Gerente residente. **Otros albergues** - abiertos 07:30-22:00h. Horario de recepción: 17:00-21:00h. Gerente residente.

Comidas

🍽 BLD Para individuales y para ⋔. ♂.

Descuentos

Se conceden descuentos a los miembros de Hostelling International – véase la sección sobre descuentos y nuestra página Internet en www.iyhf.org.

Desplazamientos

Transportes recomendados: 🚃 🚐 Automóvil.

Viajes Combinados con Actividades

Viajes combinados con visitas turísticas, deportes náuticos, cicloturismo/bicicleta de montaña, senderismo y alojamiento/transporte. Reserva de viajes combinados por 🖰 o a través de la Asociación Nacional por ❶ ❹ ❺.

Pasaportes y Visados

Carnet de identidad obligatorio.

Información Sanitaria

Seguro médico recomendado. Los ciudadanos procedentes de países pertenecientes a la UE necesitan el impreso E111 para obtener asistencia médica en dichos países.

"Certainly, travel is more than the seeing of sights; it is a change that goes on, deep and permanent, in the ideas of living."

"Il est certain que le voyage, c'est plus que la simple visite des sites touristiques; c'est un changement en continu, profond et permanent, sur l'idée que nous nous faisons de la vie."

„Gewiss ist Reisen mehr als Sehenswürdigkeiten anschauen; es findet eine tiefe und bleibende Veränderung der Lebensansichten statt."

"No cabe duda que viajar es más que hacer turismo; es un cambio continuo, profundo y permanente, en el concepto que tenemos de la vida"

Miriam Beard

Larochette -
Centre Osterbour

45 Osterbour,
L-7622 Larochette.
☏ (352) 837081, (352) 878324
fax (352) 878326

Open Dates:	🗓12
Open Hours:	07.30-10.00hrs; 17.00-22.00hrs
Price Range:	LUF 475-655 € 11.77-16.24 BBinc 🛏
Beds:	75 - 2x¹🛏 14x²🛏 7x⁵🛏 1x⁶🛏
Facilities:	⛹ 7x ⛹ 🍽 🛏 📺 1 x 🍷 🔄 🅿 ℹ 🚻 ♿ 🏛 🏘
Directions:	1N from city centre
🚌	300m
Attractions:	🌳 ⛰ 🎿 🏊 2km

Luxembourg City -
Mansfeld

2 rue du Fort Olisy (Pfaffenthal),
L-2261 Luxembourg.
☏ (352) 226889, (352) 221920
fax (352) 223360
e luxembourg@youthhostels.lu

Open Dates:	🗓12
Open Hours:	🕐
Reservations:	IBN CC
Price Range:	LUF 435-670 € 10.78-16.61 BBinc 🛏
Beds:	274 - 15x²🛏 8x⁴🛏 18x⁶🛏 6x⁶⁺🛏
Facilities:	⛹ 8x ⛹ 🍽 🔄 🛏 📺 🔄 📷 🅿 ♿ 🏛 🔍
Directions:	1NE from city centre
✈	Findel 5km
A🚌	#9 300m
🚂	Luxembourg 2km
🚌	#9 300m
Attractions:	🚴 🎿

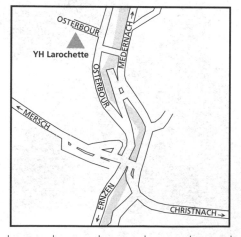

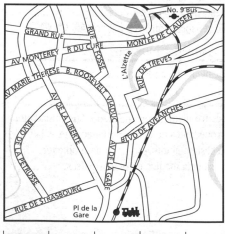

Location/Address	Telephone No. Fax No.	Beds	Opening Dates	Facilities
▲ **Beaufort** 6 rue de l'Auberge, L-6315 Beaufort. @ beaufort@youthhostels.lu	☏ (352) 836075 ⊕ (352) 869467	88	16.03–15.11; 16.12–31.12	⦿ 1SW ☞ P
▲ **Bourglinster** 2 Rue De Gonderange, L-6161 Bourglinster. @ bourglinster@youthhostels.lu		54	01.02–31.12	††† ⦿ P ⬳
▲ **Echternach** 9 rue A Duchscher, L-6434 Echternach. @ echternach@youthhostels.lu	☏ (352) 720158 ⊕ (352) 728735	130	01.01–15.01; 16.02–15.11	††† ⦿ 0.2W ☞ P
▲ **Eisenborn** Centre de Formation et de Rencontre, 5 ruc de la Forêt, L-6196 Eisenborn. @ eisenborn@youthhostels.lu	☏ (352) 780355 ⊕ (352) 788459	52	🔒12	††† ⦿ Ⓡ 0.5E ♿ P
▲ **Ettelbrück** - Carlo Hemmer Rue G D Joséphine Charlotte, BP 17, L-9013 Ettelbrück. @ ettelbruck@youthhostels.lu	☏ (352) 812269 ⊕ (352) 816935	72	01–15.01; 16.03–15.11; 16–31.12	††† ⦿ 1SW ☞ P
▲ **Grevenmacher** 15 Gruewereck, L-6734 Grevenmacher.	☏ (352) 750222 ⊕ (352) 759146	54	15.03–15.11	††† ⦿ 1N P
▲ **Hollenfels** 2 rue du Château, L-7435 Hollenfels.	☏ (352) 307037 ⊕ (352) 305783	103	🔒12	††† ⦿ 0.1W ☞ P
▲ **Larochette** - Centre Osterbour 45 Osterbour, L-7622 Larochette.	☏ (352) 837081, (352) 878324 ⊕ (352) 878326	75	🔒12	††† ⦿ 1N P 🖸
▲ **Lultzhausen** rue du Village, L-9666 Lultzhausen.	☏ (352) 839424 ⊕ (352) 899245	98	01.06–31.12	††† ⦿ ☞ P
▲ **Luxembourg City** - Mansfeld (IBN) 2 rue du Fort Olisy (Pfaffenthal), L-2261 Luxembourg. @ luxembourg@youthhostels.lu	☏ (352) 226889, (352) 221920 ⊕ (352) 223360	274	🔒12	††† ⦿ 1NE ⊂CC⊃ ☞ P 🖸
▲ **Vianden** 3 Montée du Château, L-9408 Vianden. @ vianden@youthhostels.lu	☏ (352) 834177 ⊕ (352) 849427	90	16.03–15.11; 16.12–31.12	⦿ 1N ☞
▲ **Wiltz** 6 rue de la Montagne, L-9538 Wiltz.	☏ (352) 958039 ⊕ (352) 959440	72	🔒12	††† ⦿ 0.5S ☞ P 🖸

HOSTELLING
INTERNATIONAL

Make your credit card bookings at these centres
Réservez par cartes de crédit aux centres suivants
Reservieren Sie per Kreditkarte bei diesen Zentren
Reserve con tarjeta de crédito en los siguientes centros

English

Australia	☎ (2) 9261 1111
Canada	☎ (800) 663 5777
England & Wales	☎ (1629) 581 418
France	☎ (1) 44 89 87 27
Northern Ireland	☎ (28) 9032 4733
Republic of Ireland	☎ (1) 830 1766
New Zealand	☎ (3) 379 9808
Scotland	☎ (8701) 553 255
Switzerland	☎ (1) 360 1414
USA	☎ (202) 783 6161

Français

Angleterre & Pays de Galles	☎ (1692) 581 418
Australie	☎ (2) 9261 1111
Canada	☎ (800) 663 5777
Écosse	☎ (8701) 553 255
États-Unis	☎ (202) 783 6161
France	☎ (1) 44 89 87 27
Irlande du Nord	☎ (28) 9032 4733
Nouvelle-Zélande	☎ (3) 379 9808
République d'Irlande	☎ (1) 830 1766
Suisse	☎ (1) 360 1414

Deutsch

Australien	☎ (2) 9261 1111
England & Wales	☎ (1629) 581 418
Frankreich	☎ (1) 44 89 87 27
Irland	☎ (1) 830 1766
Kanada	☎ (800) 663 5777
Neuseeland	☎ (3) 379 9808
Nordirland	☎ (28) 9032 4733
Schottland	☎ (8701) 553 255
Schweiz	☎ (1) 360 1414
USA	☎ (202) 783 6161

Español

Australia	☎ (2) 9261 1111
Canadá	☎ (800) 663 5777
Escocia	☎ (8701) 553 255
Estados Unidos	☎ (202) 783 6161
Francia	☎ (1) 44 89 87 27
Inglaterra y Gales	☎ (1629) 581 418
Irlanda del Norte	☎ (28) 9032 4733
Nueva Zelanda	☎ (3) 379 9808
República de Irlanda	☎ (1) 830 1766
Suiza	☎ (1) 360 1414

INTERNATIONAL
BOOKING
NETWORK

Malta

MALTE

MALTA

MALTA

**NSTS Hostelling International,
220 St. Paul St, Valletta VLT 07, Malta.**

☏ (356) 244983
✆ (356) 230330
✉ nsts@nsts.org
🖳 www.nsts.org

A copy of the Hostel Directory for this Country can be obtained from:
The National Office

Capital:	Valletta	Population:	379,750
Language:	Maltese, English	Size:	356 sq km
Currency:	Malta Lira (MLT)	Telephone Country Code:	356

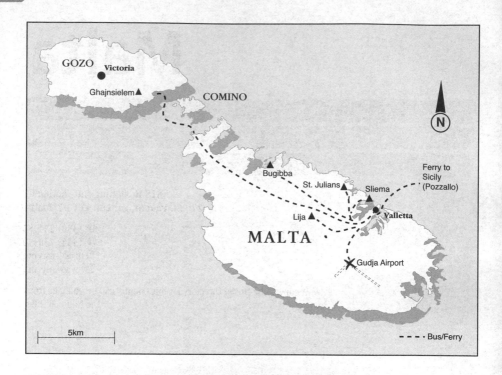

MALTA

GOZO

Victoria

Ghajnsielem▲

COMINO

Bugibba▲

St. Julians▲

Sliema▲

Ferry to Sicily (Pozzallo)

Valletta

Lija▲

MALTA

✕ Gudja Airport

5km

- - - - Bus/Ferry

N

English

Hostels are located in cities and on the coast.

Price range

Price range MLT 4-6. € 9.80-14.70. [BB] inc 🛏️.

Rooms and Reservations

ℝ during Apr-Sep. (All Rooms). Reservations via National Office by ☎ 🖷 📧. All hostels are non-smoking.

Guests

Membership Card and Passport/Photo ID are required. 👪 welcome. Group bookings via National Office.

Open times

Main hostels: open 🗓️, 🕐. Reception open: 🕐. Resident manager. **Other hostels:** open 🕐. Reception open: 09:00-17:00hrs. Resident

manager. **Seasonal hostels** are generally open Apr-Oct.

Meals

🍽️ B 🍴.

Travelling around

For ease of travel use ✈️.

Travel/Activity Packages

Tours/sightseeing, water sports and accommodation/transport packages available. Package bookings via National Office by ☎ 🖷 📧.

Passports and Visas

Passport required.

Health

Medical insurance is recommended.

Français

Les auberges sont situées dans les villes ou sur le littoral.

Tarifs des nuitées

Tarifs des nuitées 4-6 MLT. € 9.80-14.70. BB^inc 🔲.

Chambres et réservations

R avril-sep. (Toutes chambres). Réservations via le Bureau National par ❶ ❻ ❸. Toutes les auberges sont non-fumeurs.

Usagers

La carte d'adhérent ainsi que le passeport/pièce d'identité avec photo sont à présenter. Accueil des ♦♦♦. Réservations pour groupes via le Bureau National.

Horaires d'ouverture

Grandes auberges: ouvertes ▣, ◔. Accueil ouvert ◔. Gérant réside sur place. **Autres auberges:** ouvertes ◔. Accueil ouvert entre 9h-17h. Gérant réside sur place. **Auberges saisonnières** ouvertes généralement avril-oct.

Repas

⚍ B ✎.

Déplacements

Modes de transport recommandés ✈.

Forfaits Voyages/Activités

Forfaits circuits touristiques, sports aquatiques et hébergement/transport disponibles. Réservations des forfaits via le Bureau National par ❶ ❻ ❸.

Passeports et visas

Passeport obligatoire.

Santé

Une assurance médicale de voyage est conseillée.

Deutsch

Herbergen befinden sich in Städten und an der Küste.

Preisspanne

Preisspanne 4-6 MLT. € 9.80-14.70. BB^inc 🔲.

Zimmer und Reservierungen

R während Apr-Sept. (Alle Zimmer). Reservierungen über Landesverband per ❶ ❻ ❸. Rauchen ist in allen Herbergen NICHT gestattet.

Gäste

Mitgliedsausweis und Reisepass/ Personalausweis sind erforderlich. ♦♦♦ willkommen. Gruppenbuchungen über Landesverband.

Öffnungszeiten

Hauptherbergen: Zugang ▣, ◔. Rezeption ◔. Herbergsmanager wohnt im Haus. **Andere Herbergen:** Zugang ◔. Rezeption zwischen 09:00-17:00Uhr. Herbergsmanager wohnt im Haus. **Saison-Herbergen** sind normalerweise Apr-Okt geöffnet.

Mahlzeiten

⚍ B ✎.

Reisen im Land

Reisen ist einfach mit ✈.

Reise-/Aktivitäten-Packages

Touren/sightseeing, Wassersport und Unterkunft/Transport-Packages erhältlich. Package-Buchungen über Landesverband per ❶ ❻ ❸.

Reisepässe und Visa

Reisepass erforderlich.

Gesundheit

Unfall-/Krankenversicherung wird empfohlen.

Español

Los albergues están situados en las ciudades y la costa.

Tarifas mínima y máxima

Tarifas mínima y máxima 4-6 MLT. € 9.80-14.70. BB inc 🍴.

Habitaciones y Reservas

R en abr-sep. (Todas las habitaciones). Reservas a través de la Asociación Nacional por por ❶ ❷ ❸. Está prohibido fumar en todos los albergues.

Huéspedes

Los huéspedes deben presentar su Carnet de Alberguista y su pasaporte o carnet de identidad. Se admiten 👫. Reservas de grupo a través de la Asociación Nacional.

Horarios y fechas de apertura

Albergues principales - abiertos 📅, ⏰. Horario de recepción: ⏰. Gerente residente. **Otros albergues** - abiertos ⏰. Horario de recepción: 09:00-17:00h. Gerente residente. **Albergues de temporada** suelen abrir: abr-oct.

Comidas

🍴 B ☕.

Desplazamientos

Transportes recomendados: ✈.

Viajes Combinados con Actividades

Viajes combinados con visitas turísticas, deportes náuticos y alojamiento/transporte. Reserva de viajes combinados a través de la Asociación Nacional por ❶ ❷ ❸.

Pasaportes y Visados

Pasaporte obligatorio.

Información Sanitaria

Seguro médico recomendado.

Location/Address	Telephone No. Fax No.	Beds	Opening Dates	Facilities		
▲ **Bugibba** - Crystal Hotel Triq Il-Halel.	❶ (356) 573022 ❷ (356) 571975	30	01.04–31.10	👫 🍴 **R** 0.1 S	P 🍴	☕
▲ **Gozo** - St. Joseph Home Hostel Mgarr Rd, Ghajnsielem, Gozo.	❶ (356) 556439 ❷ (356) 556439	50	📅	👫 **R**	0.2 SW	
▲ **Lija** - University Residence Robert Mifsud Bonnici St, Lija.	❶ (356) 436168 ❷ (356) 434963	250	📅	👫 🍴 **R** 0.1 E ♿ ☕ P 🍴		☕
▲ **Sliema** - Hibernia House Gateway Hostel Depiro St, Sliema.	❶ (356) 333859 ❷ (356) 230330	130	📅	👫 🍴 **R** 0.3 W ☕ P 🍴		☕
▲ **St Julian's** - Pinto Guest House Sacred Heart Ave, St Julians.	❶ (356) 313897 ❷ (356) 319852	30	01.04–31.10	👫 🍴 **R** 0.5 SW	P 🍴	☕

Netherlands

PAYS-BAS
NIEDERLANDE
PAISES BAJOS

**Stichting Nederlandse Jeugdherberg Centrale,
Postbus 9191, 1006 AD Amsterdam, Netherlands.**

📞 (31) (10) 2646064 (information),
(31) (20) 6392929(👫)
🛈 (31) (10) 2646061
🖳 www.njhc.org

Office Hours: Monday-Friday 09.00-17.00hrs

A copy of the Hostel Directory for this Country can be obtained from:
The National Office

Capital:	Amsterdam	**Population:**	15,423,000
Language:	Dutch	**Size:**	40,844 sq km
Currency:	Fl (guilders)	**Telephone Country Code:**	31

English

If the two popular hostels in Amsterdam are fully booked try the hostel in Soest or Bunnik. Hostels are located in cities, in the countryside and on the coast.

Price range

Price range Hfl 27,25-33,25. € 12,36-15,09. BB inc 🔲.

Rooms and Reservations

R during May-Sep. (🏸 🏸 🏸). Reservations via IBN Hostel or National Office by ❶ ❻ ❸. (Reservation charges may apply).

Guests

Membership Card is required. ♦♦♦ welcome. Group bookings via IBN National Booking Centre or Hostel by ❶ ❻ ❸ (Reservation charges may apply).

Open times

Main hostels: open 🔲, 07:00-24:00hrs. Reception open: 09:00-17:00hrs. Resident manager.

Meals

🍽 BLD R For individuals & for ♦♦♦.

Discounts

HI Member Discounts available - see discounts section and www.iyhf.org.

Travelling around

For ease of travel use 🚐 🚌.

Travel/Activity Packages

Winter sports, water sports, cycling/mountain biking and walking/trekking packages available. Package bookings via National Booking Centre or Hostel by ❶ ❻ ❸.

Passports and Visas

Passport required.

Health

Medical insurance is recommended. EU Nationals require Form E111 to obtain treatment within EU countries.

Français

Si les deux auberges d'Amsterdam - qui sont d'ordinaire très demandées - affichent complet, essayez l'auberge de Soest ou de Bunnik. Les auberges sont situées dans les villes, à la campagne et sur le littoral.

Tarifs des nuitées

Tarifs des nuitées 27,25-33,25 Hfl. € 12,36-15,9. BB inc 🔲.

Chambres et réservations

R mai-sep. (🏸 🏸 🏸). Réservations via IBN l'auberge et le Bureau National par ❶ ❻ ❸. (Des frais de réservation pourront vous être facturés).

Usagers

La carte d'adhérent est à présenter. Accueil des ♦♦♦. Réservations pour groupes via IBN le Centre National de Réservation ou l'auberge par ❶ ❻ ❸ (Des frais de réservation pourront vous être facturés).

Horaires d'ouverture

Grandes auberges: ouvertes 🔲, entre 7h-24h. Accueil ouvert entre 9h-17h. Gérant réside sur place.

Repas

🍽 BLD R Pour individuels & pour ♦♦♦.

Remises

Remises pour les adhérents HI - voir la section "Remises" et notre site: www.iyhf.org.

Déplacements

Modes de transport recommandés 🚆 🚌.

Forfaits Voyages/Activités

Forfaits sports d'hiver, sports aquatiques, cyclotourisme/VTT et randonnées pédestres disponibles. Réservations des forfaits via le Centre National de Réservation ou l'auberge par ❶ ❷ ❸.

Passeports et visas

Passeport obligatoire.

Santé

Une assurance médicale de voyage est conseillée. Les ressortissants de l'Union Européenne doivent se munir du formulaire E111 pour bénéficier de soins médicaux dans les états de l'UE.

Deutsch

Falls die beiden beliebten Herbergen in Amsterdam ausgebucht sind, versuchen Sie die Herberge in Soest oder Bunnik. Herbergen befinden sich in Städten, auf dem Land und an der Küste.

Preisspanne

Preisspanne 27,25-33,25 Hfl. € 12,36-15,09. BB inc 🍴.

Zimmer und Reservierungen

R während Mai-Sept. (²🚲 ³🚲 ⁴🚲). Reservierungen über IBN Herberge oder Landesverband per ❶ ❷ ❸. (Reservierungskosten könnten anfallen).

Gäste

Mitgliedsausweis ist erforderlich. 👪 willkommen. Gruppenbuchungen über IBN Nationales Buchungszentrum oder Herberge per ❶ ❷ ❸ (Reservierungskosten könnten anfallen).

Öffnungszeiten

Hauptherbergen: Zugang 🔓, 07:00-24:00Uhr. Rezeption zwischen 09:00-17:00Uhr. Herbergsmanager wohnt im Haus.

Mahlzeiten

🍽 BLD R Für Einzelreisende & für 👪.

Ermäßigungen

HI-Mitgliedsrabatt ist erhältlich – siehe Teil für Rabatte und Ermäßigungen und www.iyhf.org.

Reisen im Land

Reisen ist einfach mit 🚆 🚌.

Reise-/Aktivitäten-Packages

Wintersport, Wassersport, Fahrrad/ Mountainbiking und wandern/trekking -Packages erhältlich. Package-Buchungen über Nationales Buchungszentrum oder Herberge per ❶ ❷ ❸.

Reisepässe und Visa

Reisepass erforderlich.

Gesundheit

Unfall-/Krankenversicherung wird empfohlen. EU Staatsangehörige benötigen Formular E111 für ärztliche Behandlungen innerhalb der EU Länder.

Español

Si los dos albergues más frecuentados de Amsterdam están completos, pruebe en el albergue de Soest o en el de Bunnik. Los albergues están situados en las ciudades, el campo y la costa.

Tarifas mínima y máxima

Tarifas mínima y máxima 27,25-33,25 Hfl. € 12,36-15,09. BB inc ⊠.

Habitaciones y Reservas

R en may-sep. (☂ ☂ ☂). Reservas por IBN o a través del albergue o la Asociación Nacional por ❶ ❷ ❸. (Es posible que se aplique un suplemento en concepto de gastos de reserva).

Huéspedes

Los huéspedes deben presentar su Carnet de Alberguista. Se admiten ⅲ. Reservas de grupo por IBN o a través de la Central Nacional de Reservas o el albergue por ❶ ❷ ❸ (Es posible que se aplique un suplemento en concepto de gastos de reserva).

Horarios y fechas de apertura

Albergues principales - abiertos 🗓, 07:00-24:00h. Horario de recepción: 09:00-17:00h. Gerente residente.

Comidas

⦿ BLD **R** Para individuales y para ⅲ.

Descuentos

Se conceden descuentos a los miembros de Hostelling International – véase la sección sobre descuentos y nuestra página Internet en www.iyhf.org.

Desplazamientos

Transportes recomendados: 🚌 🚐.

Viajes Combinados con Actividades

Viajes combinados con deportes de invierno, deportes náuticos, cicloturismo/bicicleta de montaña y senderismo. Reserva de viajes combinados a través de la Central Nacional de Reservas o el albergue por ❶ ❷ ❸.

Pasaportes y Visados

Pasaporte obligatorio.

Información Sanitaria

Seguro médico recomendado. Los ciudadanos procedentes de países pertenecientes a la UE necesitan el impreso E111 para obtener asistencia médica en dichos países.

"The true traveler is he who goes on foot, and even then, he sits down a lot of the time."

"Le vrai voyageur est celui qui va à pied, et encore, il s'assoit une grande partie du temps."

„Der wahre Reisende ist derjenige, der zu Fuß geht, und selbst dann setzt er sich sehr häufig nieder."

"El verdadero viajero es el que va a pie, y aun así pasa mucho tiempo sentado."

Colette

Amsterdam -
Vondelpark

Zandpad 5,
1054 GA Amsterdam.
☎ (20) 5898996
🖷 (20) 5898955

Open Dates:	🗓
Open Hours:	🕐
Reservations:	**R** IBN CC
Price Range:	Hfl 39.75-49.00 BBinc 🍽
Beds:	475 - 6x¹ 17x² 34x⁴ 1x⁵ 35x⁶ 8x⁶
Facilities:	👥 75x 👥 🍽 🍷 🛏 🖥5 x 🍴 💼 🔒 ⬆ ℹ ♿ ♻ ⛲

Directions:

✈	Schiphol 10km
A🚌	NZH 197, 370, Interliner ap Leidseplein
🚆	Amsterdam CS 3km
🚋	1, 2, 5 ap Leidseplein
Attractions:	🚲

Amsterdam -
Stadsdoelen

Kloveniersburgwal 97,
1011 KB Amsterdam.
☎ (20) 6246832
🖷 (20) 6391035

Open Dates:	01.03-31.12
Open Hours:	🕐
Reservations:	**R** IBN CC
Price Range:	Hfl 35.25-42.75 BBinc 🍽
Beds:	184 - 9x⁶
Facilities:	🍽 🍷 🍷 🛏 📺 🔒 🖼 🔒 ℹ ♿ 🔍

Directions:

✈	Schiphol 10km
🚆	Amsterdam CS 1.5km
🚋	9, 16, 24, 25 500m ap Munt
U	Nieuwmarkt 500m

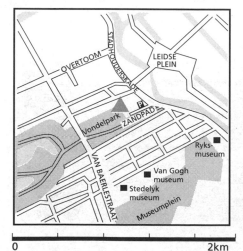

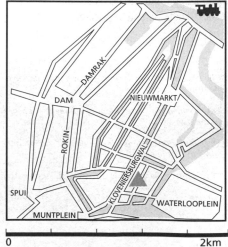

Apeldoorn

Asselsestraat 330,
7312 TS Apeldoorn.
t (55) 3553118
f (55) 3553811

Open Dates:	🗓
Open Hours:	07.00-24.00 hrs
Reservations:	**R** **CC**
Price Range:	Hfl 37.50-46.00 BB inc 🍽
Beds:	117 - 3x² 1x³ 16x⁴ 6x⁶ 1x⁶
Facilities:	16x 🍽 3 x 8 P

Directions:

✈	Schiphol 95km
🚆	Apeldoorn 3km
🚌	4, 7 ap Chamavenlaan

Attractions: 🏞 🚲 ⚓ 1.5km

Arnhem - Alteveer

Diepenbrocklaan 27,
6815 AH Arnhem.
t (26) 4420114
f (26) 3514892

Open Dates:	🗓
Open Hours:	07.00-24.00 hrs
Reservations:	**IBN** **CC**
Price Range:	Hfl 37.50-46.00 BB inc 🍽
Beds:	200 - 4x² 1x³ 12x⁴ 3x⁶ 15x⁶
Facilities:	15x 🍽 📺 4 x 8 P

Directions:	4NW from city centre
✈	Schiphol 110km
🚆	Arnhem 2.5km
🚌	3 ap Ziekenhuis Rijnstaete

Attractions: 🏞 🚲 ↺1km ⚲1km ⚓1.5km

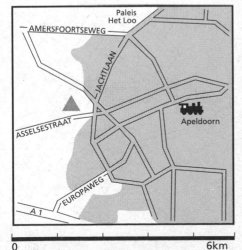

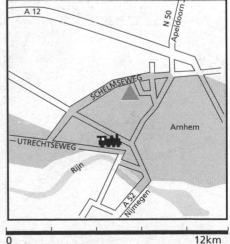

Bunnik

Rhijnauwenselaan 14,
3981 HH Bunnik.
☏ (30) 6561277
✆ (30) 6571065

Open Dates:	🗓12
Open Hours:	07.00-00.30 hrs
Reservations:	CC
Price Range:	Hfl 37.50-46.00 BB inc
Beds:	137 - 1x² 1x³ 6x⁴ 1x⁵ 10x⁶ 4x⁶
Facilities:	††† 6x ††† 🍽 🍷 🚪 📺 3 x 🍴 🔒 🅿 ℹ 🧳 ♣ ⛰ 🔍 🏫 🏡 🏛

Directions:

✈	Schiphol 55km
🚂	Utrecht CS 5Km; Bunnik 3km
🚌	From Utrecht CS 40, 41, 43 500m ap Rhijnauwen YH

Attractions: ⛲ 🏞 3km

Den Haag

Scheepmakersstraat 27,
2515 VA Den Haag.
☏ (70) 3157888
✆ (70) 3157877

Open Dates:	🗓12
Open Hours:	🕐
Reservations:	IBN CC
Price Range:	Hfl 39.75-49.00 BB inc
Beds:	220 - 12x² 24x⁴ 6x⁶ 8x⁶
Facilities:	††† 24x ††† 🍽 🍷 🚪 📺 🧳 🌾 3 x 🍴 🔒 🖼 8 🔼 🅿 ℹ 🧳 🏛

Directions:

✈	Schiphol 46km
⛴	Hoek van Holland (Ferries to Great Britain) 25km
🚂	Den Haag Hollands Spoor 400m; Den Haag Centraal 1km
🚊	1,9,12,16 ap Rijswijkse Plein

Attractions: 🔍3km 🚴

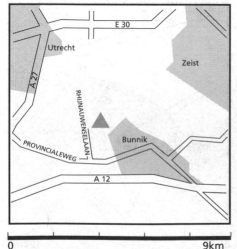

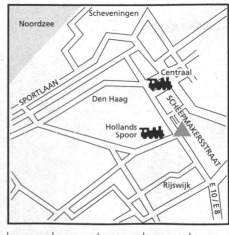

Domburg

Duinvlietweg 8,
4356 ND Domburg.
☎ (118) 581254
✆ (118) 583342

Open Dates: 🗓️

Reservations: **R** **CC**

Price Range: Hfl 37.50-46.00 BB inc

Beds: 112

Facilities: 👬 🍴 ☕ 🅿️

Directions:

✈	Schiphol 190km
🚂	Middelburg 13km
🚌	ZWN 53 200m ap Westhove YH

Haarlem

Jan Gijzenpad 3,
2024 CL Haarlem.
☎ (23) 5373793
✆ (23) 5371176

Open Dates: 🗓️

Open Hours: 07.00-24.00hrs

Reservations: **R** **CC**

Price Range: Hfl 37.50-46.00 BB inc 🏧

Beds: 140 3x² 19x⁴ 7x⁶ 2x⁶

Facilities: ♿ 👬 🍴 ☕ 👥 📺 1 x 📞 ⭕
📷 🔢 🅿️ 📋 💱 🐾 🛏️

Directions:

✈	Schiphol 15km
🚂	Santpoort-Zuid 500m, Haarlem 3km
🚌	2 ap Haarlem Youth Hostel

Attractions: 🔍7km 🔍5km 🏊500m

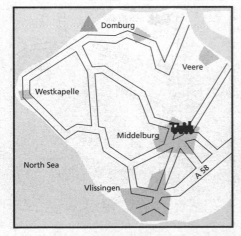

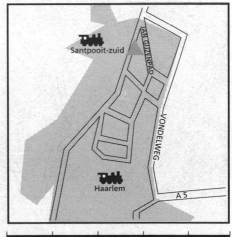

Heemskerk

Tolweg 9,
1967 NG Heemskerk.
☎ (251) 232288
🖶 (251) 251024

Open Dates:	20.03-30.10 (⌦ 👬)
Open Hours:	07.00-24.00 hrs
Price Range:	Hfl 37.50-46.00 BB inc ⌦
Beds:	203 - 1x¹ 9x² 1x³ 5x⁴ 1x⁶ 12x⁶
Facilities:	👬 5x 👬 ⍩ ☕ 📺 3 x ♨ 🖼 8 P ℹ ✿ ⚙ ⚘ ▦ ⌗

Directions:

✈	Schiphol 25km
🚌	Beverwijk 2km
🚌	74 300m ap Jan van Kuikweg
Attractions:	⛳ 🎯 5km 🚴 ∪500m ⚒500m 🏊 1km

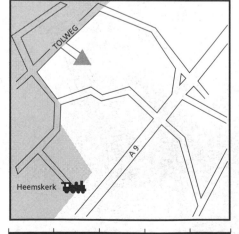

Rotterdam

Rochussenstraat 107-109,
3015 EH Rotterdam.
☎ (10) 4365763
🖶 (10) 4365569

Open Dates:	⌦
Open Hours:	07.00-01.00hrs (01.11-29.02. 08.00-24.00hrs)
Reservations:	IBN CC
Price Range:	Hfl 37.50-46.00 BB inc ⌦
Beds:	152 - 2x² 1x³ 8x⁴ 1x⁵ 6x⁶ 6x⁶
Facilities:	👬 6x 👬 ⍩ ☕ 👥 📺 ♨ ⍩ 🖼 8 ℹ ⚙ ✿

Directions:	2SW from city centre
✈	Schiphol 95Km; Rotterdam 10km
A 🚌	Bus 33 2km
🚢	Europort 20km
🚌	Rotterdam CS 2km
🚋	4 ap Saftlevenstraat 100m
U	Metro Dijkzigt 100m

Soest

Bosstraat 16,
3766 AG Soest.
❶ (35) 6012296
❺ (35) 6028921

Open Dates: 🗓

Reservations: CC

Price Range: Hfl 37.50-46.00 BB inc

Beds: 140

Facilities: ♦♦♦ 🍴 🍺 ⬜ P

Directions:

✈ | Schiphol 50km
🚂 | Soest-Zuid 500m
🚌 | 70, 72

Terschelling

Burg Van Heusdenweg 39,
8881 EE West-Terschelling.
❶ (562) 442338
❺ (562) 443312

Open Dates: 🗓

Reservations: R CC

Price Range: Hfl 37.50-46.00 BB inc

Beds: 148

Facilities: ♿ ♦♦♦ 🍴 🍺 ⬜ P

Directions:

✈ | Schiphol 130km
🚢 | Harlingen-Terschelling. Normal ferry 2hrs; Fast ferry 45mins
🚂 | Harlingen - Haven
🚌 | any from 🚢 ap YH

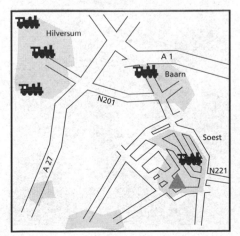

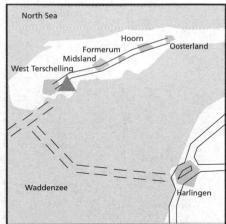

Texel - Panorama

Schansweg 7,
1791 LK Den Burg,
Texel.
☎ (222) 315441
✆ (222) 313889

Open Dates: 🗓12

Open Hours: 07.30-00.30hrs; 00.30-07.30hrs
key service

Reservations: **Ⓡ** **⌐CC⌐**

Price Range: Hfl 37.50-46.00 [BB]inc 🍴

Beds: 139 - 1x³🛏 9x⁴🛏 1x⁵🛏 12x⁶🛏
3x⁶🛏

Facilities: 🚻 10x 🚻 🍽 🛎 📺 1 x 🍷 8
🅿 ℹ ♿ ⚠ ⚲ 🖥 🛐

Directions:

✈ Schiphol 95km

⛴ 't Horntje 6km

🚂 Den Helder 10km

🚌 29 ap De Keet

Attractions: 🏛5km 🚴 ∪6km ⚲8km ⚓6km

There are 2 hostels in Texel. See following pages.

"Sloth makes all things difficult, but industry, all things easy. He that rises late must trot all day, and shall scarce overtake his business at night, while laziness travels so slowly that poverty soon overtakes him."

"La paresse rend tout difficile alors que l'industrie tout facile. Celui qui se lève tard doit courir partout, et aura du mal à dépasser son travail en fin de journée, tandis que la paresse voyage si lentement que la pauvreté aura tôt fait de le dépasser."

„Trägheit macht alle Dinge schwierig, aber Fleiß alle Dinge einfach. Derjenige, der spät aufsteht, muss den ganzen Tag traben und wird selten seine Aufgaben bis zum Abend erledigt haben, wobei Faulheit sich so langsam bewegt, dass Armut ihn bald überholt."

"La indolencia lo hace todo difícil, mientras que la industria, todo fácil. El que se levanta tarde tiene que pasarse todo el día corriendo, y apenas si ha logrado adelantar su trabajo por la noche, en tanto que la pereza viaja tan lentamente que la pobreza tarda poco en adelantarle."

Benjamin Franklin

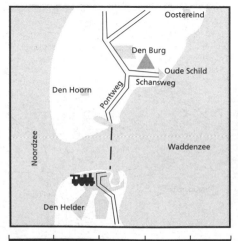

Location/Address	Telephone No. Fax No.	Beds	Opening Dates	Facilities
▲ **Ameland** Oranjeweg 59, 9161 CB Hollum Ameland.	☎ (519) 555353 🖷 (519) 555355	144		
▲ **Amsterdam** - Vondelpark (IBN) **Zandpad 5, 1054 GA Amsterdam.**	☎ (20) 5898996 🖷 (20) 5898955	475		
▲ **Amsterdam** - Stadsdoelen (IBN) **Kloveniersburgwal 97,** **1011 KB Amsterdam.**	☎ (20) 6246832 🖷 (20) 6391035	184	01.03–31.12	
▲ **Apeldoorn** **Asselsestraat 330, 7312 TS Apeldoorn.**	☎ (55) 3553118 🖷 (55) 3553811	117		
▲ **Arnhem** - Alteveer (IBN) **Diepenbrocklaan 27, 6815 AH Arnhem.**	☎ (26) 4420114 🖷 (26) 3514892	200		4NW
▲ **Bakkum** Heereweg 84, 1901 ME Bakkum.	☎ (251) 652226 🖷 (251) 670027	152	01.03–01.11	
▲ **Bergen op Zoom** Boslustweg 1, 4624 RB Bergen op Zoom.	☎ (164) 233261 🖷 (164) 239133	176	20.03–30.10	
▲ **Bunnik** **Rhijnauwenselaan 14, 3981 HH Bunnik.**	☎ (30) 6561277 🖷 (30) 6571065	137		
▲ **Chaam** Putvenweg 1, 4861 RB Chaam.	☎ (161) 491323 🖷 (161) 491756	133	20.03–30.10 01.04–01.11)	
▲ **Den Haag** (IBN) **Scheepmakersstraat 27,** **2515 VA Den Haag.**	☎ (70) 3157888 🖷 (70) 3157877	220		
▲ **Domburg** **Duinvlietweg 8, 4356 ND Domburg.**	☎ (118) 581254 🖷 (118) 583342	112		
▲ **Doorwerth** Kerklaan 50, 6865 GZ Doorwerth.	☎ (26) 3334300 🖷 (26) 3337060	104	01.05–31.08	
▲ **Dordrecht** Baanhoekweg 25, 3313 LA Dordrecht.	☎ (78) 6212167 🖷 (78) 6212163	120		
▲ **Egmond** Herenweg 118, 1935 AJ Egmond.	☎ (72) 5062269 🖷 (72) 5067034	132	01.01–01.11	
▲ **Elst** Veenendaalsestraatweg 65, 3921 EB Elst.	☎ (318) 471219 🖷 (318) 472460	200	15.06–15.08	
▲ **Gorssel** Dortherweg 34, 7216 PT Gorssel.	☎ (573) 431615 🖷 (573) 431832	90	26.02–01.11	
▲ **Grou** Raadhuisstraat 18, 9001 AG Grou.	☎ (566) 621528 🖷 (566) 621005	210	(except Christmas & New Years Eve)	
▲ **Haarlem** **Jan Gijzenpad 3, 2024 CL Haarlem.**	☎ (23) 5373793 🖷 (23) 5371176	140		
The Hague ☞ Den Haag				
▲ **Heeg** 't Eilân 65, 8621 CT Heeg.	☎ (515) 442258 🖷 (515) 442550	160	01.04–18.10	
▲ **Heemskerk** **Tolweg 9, 1967 NG Heemskerk.**	☎ (251) 232288 🖷 (251) 251024	203	20.03–30.10	

Location/Address	Telephone No. Fax No.	Beds	Opening Dates	Facilities
△ **Hoorn** *Schellinkhouterdijk 1a, 1621 MJ Hoorn.*	☎ (229) 214256	50	01.07–01.09	⑩ P ☕
▲ **Maastricht** Dousbergweg 4, 6216 GC Maastricht.	☎ (43) 3466777 📠 (43) 3466755	220	⑫	⋔ ⑩ ⅛ P ⑥ ☕
▲ **Meppel** Leonard Springerlaan 14, 7941 GW Meppel.	☎ (522) 251706 📠 (522) 262287	72	01.05–01.10 (⋔ on request)	⋔ ⑩ ⅜ P ⑥ ☕
▲ **Nijverdal** Duivenbreeweg 43, 7441 EA Nijverdal.	☎ (548) 612252 📠 (548) 615372	96	20.03–01.11 (⑫ ⋔)	⋔ ⑩ ⅭⅭ P ☕
▲ **Noordwijk** Langevelderlaan 45, 2204 BC Noordwijk.	☎ (252) 372920 📠 (252) 377061	130	20.03–01.11 (⑫ ⋔)	⋔ ⑩ Ⓡ ⅭⅭ P ☕
▲ **Orvelte** Zuideresweg 10, 9441 TZ Orvelte.	☎ 593 322263 📠 593 322344	39	08.07–20.08	⋔ ⑩ 1S ⑥ ☕
▲ **Rotterdam** (IBN) **Rochussenstraat 107-109, 3015 EH Rotterdam.**	☎ (10) 4365763 📠 (10) 4365569	152	⑫	⋔ ⑩ 2SW ⅭⅭ ⅜ ⑥ ☕
▲ **Sneek** Oude Oppenhuizerweg 20, 8606 JC Sneek.	☎ (515) 412132 📠 (515) 412188	116	20.03–30.10 (⑫ ⋔)	⋔ ⑩ P ⑥ ☕
▲ **Soest** **Bosstraat 16, 3766 AG Soest.**	☎ (35) 6012296 📠 (35) 6028921	140	⑫	⋔ ⑩ ⅭⅭ P ⑥ ☕
▲ **Terschelling** **Burg Van Heusdenweg 39, 8881 EE West-Terschelling.**	☎ (562) 442338 📠 (562) 443312	148	⑫	⋔ ⑩ Ⓡ ⅛ ⅭⅭ P ⑥ ☕
△ *Texel - De Eyercoogh* *For information and reservation please contact 'Panorama', Schansweg 7, 1791 LK Den Burg, Texel.*	☎ (222) 315441 📠 (222) 313889	102	01.07–31.08 (⋔ 01.04–15.10)	⑩ P ☕
▲ **Texel - Panorama** **Schansweg 7, 1791 LK Den Burg, Texel.**	☎ (222) 315441 📠 (222) 313889	139	⑫	⋔ ⑩ Ⓡ ⅭⅭ P
▲ **Valkenswaard** Past Heerkensdreef 20, 5552 BG Valkenswaard.	☎ (40) 2015334 📠 (40) 2047932	136	20.03–30.10 (⑫ ⋔)	⋔ ⑩ Ⓡ P ⑥ ☕

"A wise traveller never despises his own country."

"Le voyageur sage ne méprise jamais son propre pays."

„Ein weiser Reisender verachtet nie das eigene Land."

"El viajero sabio nunca desprecia su propio país."

Carlo Goldoni

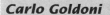

Norway

NORVEGE
NORWEGEN
NORUEGA

**Norske Vandrerhjem,
Dronningensgate 26, N-0154 Oslo, Norway.**

☎ (47) 23139300
fax (47) 23139350
e hostels@online.no
www www.vandrerhjem.no

Office Hours: Monday-Friday 08.30-16.00hrs

A copy of the Hostel Directory for this Country can be obtained from:
The National Office

Capital:	Oslo		**Population:**	4,300,000
Language:	Norwegian		**Size:**	324,219 sq km
Currency:	NOK (krone)		**Telephone Country Code:**	47

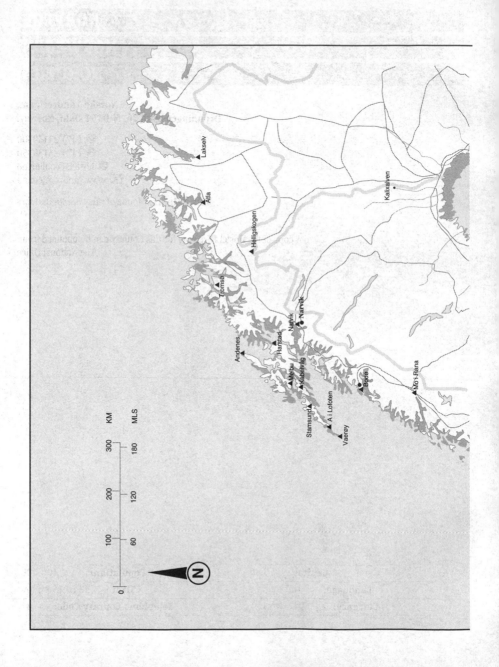

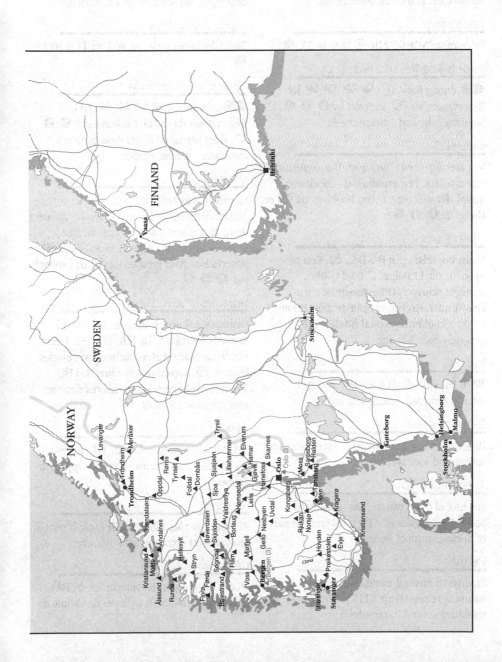

English

Hostels are located in cities, in the countryside, on the coast and on hills/mountains.

Price range

Price range NOK 95-210. € 11,9-26,25. 🏨.

Rooms and Reservations

R during Jun-Aug. (¹🛏 ²🛏 ³🛏 ⁴🛏 👫). Reservations via 🖥 or Hostel by ❶ ❷ ❸. Smoking is limited - please check.

Guests

Membership Card is required. The maximum stay is 6 days. Pets are allowed - check with hostel. 👫 welcome. Group bookings via 🖥 or Hostel by ❶ ❷ ❸.

Open times

Main hostels: open Feb-Dec, 🕐. Reception open: 07:00-11:00hrs, 17:00-23:00hrs. Resident manager. **Other hostels:** open Feb-Nov, 🕐. Reception open: 07:00-11:00hrs, 17:00-23:00hrs. **Seasonal hostels** are generally open Jun-Aug.

Meals

🍽 B For individuals & for 👫. 🍴 Not all utensils provided - check with hostel.

Discounts

HI Member Discounts available - see discounts section and www.iyhf.org.

Travelling around

For ease of travel use ✈ 🚆 ⛴ 🚌 Self-Drive. No railway in the northernmost part of Norway, north of Bodø.

Health

Emergency medical treatment is free. EU Nationals require Form E111 to obtain treatment within EU countries.

Français

Les auberges sont situées dans les villes, à la campagne, sur le littoral et à la montagne.

Tarifs des nuitées

Tarifs des nuitées 95-210 NOK. € 11,9-26,25. 🏨.

Chambres et réservations

R juin-août. (¹🛏 ²🛏 ³🛏 ⁴🛏 👫). Réservations via 🖥 ou l'auberge par ❶ ❷ ❸. Il est permis de fumer dans certaines chambres - veuillez vérifier.

Usagers

La carte d'adhérent est à présenter. La durée maximale du séjour est de 6 jours. Les animaux domestiques sont autorisés mais vérifiez lesquels auprès de l'auberge. Accueil des 👫. Réservations pour groupes via 🖥 ou l'auberge par ❶ ❷ ❸.

Horaires d'ouverture

Grandes auberges: ouvertes fév-déc, 🕐. Accueil ouvert entre 7h-11h, 17h-23h. Gérant réside sur place. **Autres auberges:** ouvertes fév-nov, 🕐. Accueil ouvert entre 7h-11h, 17h-23h. **Auberges saisonnières** ouvertes généralement juin-août.

Repas

🍽 B Pour individuels & pour 👫. 🍴 Pas tous les ustensils sont fournis - à vérifier auprès de l'auberge.

Remises

Remises pour les adhérents HI - voir la section "Remises" et notre site: www.iyhf.org.

Déplacements

Modes de transport recommandés ✈ 🚆 ⛴ 🚌 Voiture. Il n'y a pas de chemin de fer dans l'extrême nord de la Norvège, au nord de Bodø.

Santé

Soins d'urgence gratuits. Les ressortissants de l'Union Européenne doivent se munir du formulaire E111 pour bénéficier de soins médicaux dans les états de l'UE.

Deutsch

Herbergen befinden sich in Städten, auf dem Land, an der Küste und in Bergen/Gebirgen.

Preisspanne

Preisspanne 95-210 NOK. € 11,9-26,25. 🏧.

Zimmer und Reservierungen

R während Jun-Aug. (^{1}➦ ^{2}➦ ^{3}➦ ^{4}➦ ♦♦♦). Reservierungen über 🖱 oder die Herberge per ❶ ❷ ❸. Rauchen ist begrenzt - bitte checken.

Gäste

Mitgliedsausweis ist erforderlich. Der maximale Aufenthalt beträgt 6 Tage. Haustiere sind erlaubt - in der Herberge nachfragen. ♦♦♦ willkommen. Gruppenbuchungen über 🖱 oder die Herberge per ❶ ❷ ❸.

Öffnungszeiten

Hauptherbergen: Zugang zwischen Feb-Dez, ☻. Rezeption zwischen 07:00-11:00Uhr, 17:00-23:00Uhr. Herbergsmanager wohnt im Haus. **Andere Herbergen:** Zugang zwischen Feb-Nov, ☻. Rezeption zwischen 07:00-11:00Uhr, 17:00-23:00Uhr. **Saison-Herbergen** sind normalerweise Jun-Aug geöffnet.

Mahlzeiten

🍽 B Für Einzelreisende & für ♦♦♦. ☞ Nicht alle Utensilien werden bereitgestellt - in der Herberge nachfragen.

Ermäßigungen

HI-Mitgliedsrabatt ist erhältlich – siehe Teil für Rabatte und Ermäßigungen und www.iyhf.org.

Reisen im Land

Reisen ist einfach mit ✈ 🚌 ⛴ 🚐 Selbstfahrer. Keine Eisenbahn im nördlichsten Teil von Norwegen, nördlich von Bodø.

Gesundheit

Nur im Notfall sind medizinische Behandlungen kostenlos. EU Staatsangehörige benötigen Formular E111 für ärztliche Behandlungen innerhalb der EU Länder.

Español

Los albergues están situados en las ciudades, el campo, la costa y la montaña.

Tarifas mínima y máxima

Tarifas mínima y máxima 95-210 NOK. € 11,9-26,25. 🏧.

Habitaciones y Reservas

R en jun-ago. (^{1}➦ ^{2}➦ ^{3}➦ ^{4}➦ ♦♦♦). Reservas por 🖱 o a través del albergue por ❶ ❷ ❸. Está permitido fumar sólo en algunas salas/habitaciones - infórmese.

Huéspedes

Los huéspedes deben presentar su Carnet de Alberguista. La estancia máxima es de 6 días. Se admiten animales - consulte con el albergue. Se admiten ♦♦♦. Reservas de grupo por 🖱 o a través del albergue por ❶ ❷ ❸.

Horarios y fechas de apertura

Albergues principales - abiertos feb-dic, ⊕.
Horario de recepción: 07:00-11:00h,
17:00-23:00h. Gerente residente. **Otros
albergues** - abiertos feb-nov, ⊕. Horario de
recepción: 07:00-11:00h, 17:00-23:00h.
Albergues de temporada suelen abrir:
jun-ago.

Comidas

🍽 B Para individuales y para ††† . ☞ La cocina
no dispone de todos los utensilios - consulte
con el albergue.

Descuentos

Se conceden descuentos a los miembros de
Hostelling International – véase la sección
sobre descuentos y nuestra página Internet en
www.iyhf.org.

Desplazamientos

Transportes recomendados: ✈ 🚆 ⛴
🚌 Automóvil. La parte más septentrional de
Noruega, más al norte de Bodø, no tiene red
ferroviaria.

Información Sanitaria

Asistencia médica de urgencia gratuita. Los
ciudadanos procedentes de países
pertenecientes a la UE necesitan el impreso
E111 para obtener asistencia médica en dichos
países.

Bergen - Montana

Johan Blyttsvei 30,
5096 Bergen,
Hordaland.
☎ 55208070
📠 55208075
✉ montvh@online.no

Open Dates:	03.01-20.12 (††† 23.12-20.12)
Open Hours:	⊕
Reservations:	**R** **IBN** **CC**
Price Range:	NOK 120-275 € 15.00-34.40 BB inc 🍽
Beds:	266 - 28x² 40x⁴ 10x⁵ 1x⁶
Facilities:	♿ ††† ††† 🍽 (B) ☞ 👥 📺 ◻ 🔥 1 x ▼ ▦ 🖼 👕 P 🏔 🔍 ▦
Directions:	6 SE from city centre
✈	Bergen 20km
⛴	Strandkaiterminalen 5.5km
🚆	5km
🚌	Bus #31 200m
Attractions:	🎣 ⛰ 🚴

There are 3 hostels in Bergen. See following
pages.

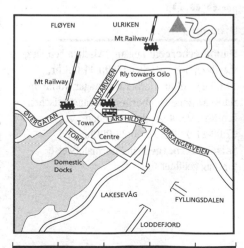

Kongsberg YH

Vinjesgt 1,
3616 Kongsberg,
Buskerud.
t 32732024
f 32720534
e vh.bergm@online.no

Open Dates:	01.01-23.12; 26-31.12
Open Hours:	07.00-23.00hrs
Reservations:	**R** **CC**
Price Range:	NOK 195-395 BB inc H
Beds:	99 - 2x² 5x³ 15x⁴ 4x⁵
Facilities:	& ††† 24x ††† ⦿ ☞ ⚙ ⚙ ☷ TV ☳5 x ☂ ⬚ ▣ ⊞ P 🛈 ⬚ ⚓
Directions:	0.2W from city centre
✈	Torp 100km
🚂	300m
🚌	100m
Attractions:	⌂ ⛰ ≋ 2,5Km ⚓ ⚡ ∪ ⚲ ≈ 1km

Kristiansand -
Tangen

Skansen 8,
4610 Kristiansand,
Vest-Agder.
t 38028310
f 38027505
e hostlkrs@online.no

Open Dates:	15.01-15.12
Open Hours:	07.00-23.00hrs
Reservations:	**R** **CC**
Price Range:	NOK 180-415 € 22.50-51.90 BB inc H
Beds:	179 - 15x² 31x⁴ 5x⁵
Facilities:	& ††† 36x ††† ⦿ (B) ☞ ☷ TV ⬚ ▣ P 🛈 ⬚ ⚓
Directions:	0.8E from city centre
✈	20km
⛴	Vestrehavn 1.2km
🚂	1.4km
🚌	400m
Attractions:	⚲ 80m ≈ 50m

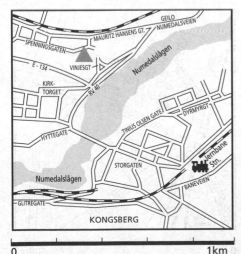

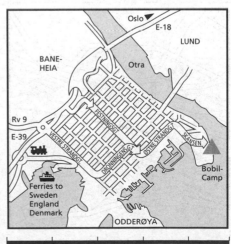

Lillehammer -
Skysstasjonen

Jernbanetorget 2,
2609 Lillehammer,
Oppland.
☎ 61248700
📠 61262577
✉ lillehammervandrerhjem@c2i.net

Open Dates:	15.01-30.11 (👪 📅12)
Open Hours:	08.00-12.00hrs; 17.00-22.00hrs
Reservations:	CC
Price Range:	NOK 175-350 € 21.09-43.75 BB inc
Beds:	84 - 12x² 15x⁴
Facilities:	♿ 👪 👪 🍴 🍳 ✿ 🛏 📺 1 x 🍸 🔲 ♨ ⬆ 🅿 ℹ ⛰
Directions:	0.2S from city centre
✈	Oslo International Airport Gardermoen 140km
⛴	1km
🚂	5m
🚌	5m

Attractions: 🎿 🚶 🚶

Oslo -
Haraldsheim

Haraldsheimvn 4,
0409 Oslo.
☎ 22222965, 22155043
📠 22221025
✉ post@haraldsheim.oslo.no

Open Dates:	02.01-22.12
Open Hours:	🕐
Reservations:	R IBN CC
Price Range:	NOK 160-350 € 20.00-43.08 BB inc 🏠
Beds:	270 - 8x² 63x⁴
Facilities:	👪 63x 👪 🍴 🍳 🛏 📺 🖼 3 x 🍸 🔲 🖼 8 🅿 🛄 ✿ ⛰ 🔍 ♨
Directions:	5NE from city centre
✈	Gardermoen 45km
🚂	Oslo S.
🚌	Ekspress 100m
🚎	Kjelsås 1km

Attractions: 🏌 🚶 ⛏1km ⛵2.5km

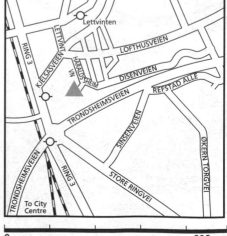

Sarpsborg -
Tuneheimen

Tuneveien 44,
1710 Sarpsborg,
Østfold.
☎ 69145001
📠 69142291
✉ tuneheim@online.no

Open Dates:	02.01-22.12
Reservations:	[CC]
Price Range:	NOK 195-330 € 24.40-41.25 [BB]inc 🍴
Beds:	91 - 3x¹🛏 3x²🛏 1x³🛏 16x⁴🛏 3x⁵🛏
Facilities:	♦♦♦ ♦♦ 🍴 ☞ TV 3 x 🍽 🔲 P 🚼

Directions:

🚃	2km
🚌	Ekspress 100m

Attractions: 🔍300m ⚓2km ⛵500m

Trondheim -
Rosenborg

Weidemannsvei 41,
7043 Trondheim,
Sør-Trøndelag.
☎ 73874450
📠 73874455
✉ tr-vanas@online.no

Open Dates:	03.01-18.12
Open Hours:	07.00-00.00hrs
Reservations:	R [CC]
Price Range:	NOK 175-390 € 22.00-48.75 [BB]inc 🍴
Beds:	212 - 2x¹🛏 8x²🛏 35x⁴🛏 9x⁶🛏
Facilities:	♦♦♦ 50x ♦♦♦ 🍴 (BD) ☞ 🚊 TV 2 x 🍽 🔲 🖼 🏧 P ⓘ 🚼 ♺ ⚠ 🔭

Directions:

✈	35km
A🚌	600m
⛴	2km
🚃	2km
🚌	Ekspress 300m

Attractions: 🔱 ⛰ 🔍 🚴 🎿 18Km 🚶 🏃 ↻6km ⚓3km ⛵2km

0   5km

Location/Address	Telephone No. Fax No.	Beds	Opening Dates	Facilities
▲ Å - Lofoten 8392 Sørvågen, Nordland.	☏ 76091121, 76091162 🖷 76091282	70	🔲	♟ ⑩ ⊞ ♂ 🅿 ⬚
▲ Ålesund YH Parkgaten 14, 6003 Ålesund. 🅴 eaaa@online.no	☏ 70115830 🖷 70115859	48	01.05–30.09	♟ ⊞ ♂ ⬚
▲ Åndalsnes - Setnes 6300 Åndalsnes, Møre og Romsdal. 🅴 andalsnes.vandrerhjem@c2i.net	☏ 71221382 🖷 71226835	89	20.05–10.09	♟ ♿ ⊞ ♂ 🅿 ⬚
▲ Alta YH Midtbakkvn 52, 9511 Alta, Finnmark. 🅴 vandrehjem@trollnet.no	☏ 78434409 🖷 78434409	59	20.06–20.08	♟ 0.8N ⊞ ♂ 🅿 ⬚
△ *Andenes - Lankanholmen* *Sjøbus,Tusenhjemmet,* *8480 Andenes.*	☏ *76142850;* *76141222* 🖷 *76142855*	*10*	*01.06–01.09*	♟ Ⓡ ⊞ ♂ 🅿 ⬚ 🚵
▲ Balestrand YH - Kringsjå 6899 Balestrand, Sogn og Fjordane. 🅴 vandrerhjem@kringsja.no	☏ 57691303 🖷 57691670	64	26.06–18.08	♟ ⑩ ⊞ ♂ 🅿 ⬚
▲ Bergen - Montana **IBN** **Johan Blyttsvei 30, 5096 Bergen,** **Hordaland.** 🅴 montvh@online.no	☏ 55208070 🖷 55208075	266	03.01–20.12 (♟ 23.12–20.12)	♟ Ⓡ 6SE ♿ ⊞ ♂ 🅿 ⬚
▲ Bergen - Nord Hylkjeneset 108, 5109 Hylkje. 🅴 aasane@online.no	☏ 55395151 🖷 55395199	110	20.06–20.08	♟ ⑩ 15N ♿ ⊞ ♂ 🅿 ⬚ 🚵
△ *Bergen - YMCA* *Nedre Korskirkealm 4, 5017 Bergen.* 🅴 *ymca@online.no*	☏ *55606055* 🖷 *55606051*	*175*	*01.05–17.09*	♟ ⊞ ♂ 🅿 ⬚ ☕
△ *Bodø* *Sjøgt 55, PB 218, 8001 Bodø.*	☏ *75521122* 🖷 *75521122*	*58*	*04.01–20.12* *(Closed Easter)*	♟ ♂ 🅿 ⬚
▲ Borlaug YH 6888 Steinklepp, Sogn og Fjordane.	☏ 57668780, 91109946 🖷 57668744	50	05.01–20.12	♟ ⑩ ⊞ ♂ 🅿
▲ Bøverdalen YH 2687 Bøverdalen, Oppland.	☏ 61212064 🖷 61212064	34	01.06–01.10	♟ ⑩ ♂ 🅿 ⬚
▲ Dombås - Trolltun 2660 Dombås, Oppland. 🅴 vandrerhjem@trolltun.no	☏ 61241500 🖷 61241330	78	01.01–23.12; 27.12–31.12	♟ ⑩ 2NE ♿ ☕ ⊞ ♂ 🅿 ⬚ 🍺
▲ Elverum YH - Elverum Hostel & Apartments Meierigt. 28, Box 1311, 2405 Elverum, Hedmark. 🅴 elverum.vandrerhjem@c2i.net	☏ 62415567 🖷 62415600	48	15.06–14.08	♟ ⑩ ♿ ⊞ ♂ 🅿 ⬚ 🚵
▲ Evje - Setesdal Rafting andAktivitetssenter, 4735 Evje. 🅴 troll.mountain@online.no	☏ 37931177; 91616969 🖷 37931334	40	01.06–01.10	♟ ⑩ Ⓡ ♿ ⊞ ♂ 🅿 ⬚ 🍺 🚵 ✿
△ *Flåm YH* *5742 Flåm.* 🅴 *hostel@flaam-camping.no*	☏ *57632121* 🖷 *57632380*	*31*	*01.05–30.09*	♟ ♂ 🅿 ⬚

Location/Address	Telephone No. Fax No.	Beds	Opening Dates	Facilities
▲ **Florø YH Åsgården** Havrenesveien 32 B, 6900 Florø. ℮ asgarden@online.no	☎ 57752300 ✇ 57752301	12	15.06–15.08	¶O⟨ 1.5SW⟩ CC ⌂ P ⬚
▲ **Folldal** - Sletten Fjellgard 2584 Dalholen, Hedmark. ℮ sletten@fjellgard.no	☎ 62493108 ✇ 62493108	47	10.06–31.08 (††† 🛏12 R)	††† ¶O⟨ 16 W⟩ ⌂ P ⬚
▲ **Førde YH** Box 557, 6801 Førde, Sogn & Fjordane. ℮ foerde.camping@c2i.net	☎ 57826500 ✇ 57826555	32	15.06–1.09 (††† 🛏12)	♿ CC ⌂ P ⬚
▲ **Geilo** - Hostel & Sportell Gjeilegutuvn. 1, PB 130, 3581 Geilo, Buskerud. ℮ geilo.vandrerhjem@bu.telia.no	☎ 32090300 ✇ 32091896	140	01.01–30.04; 01.06–30.09; 01.11–22.12; 27-31.12	††† ¶O⟨ R ⟨0.2E⟩ CC ⌂ P ⬚
▲ **Gjøvik YH** - Hovdetun Parkveien, 2819 Gjøvik. ℮ hovdetun@ol.telia.no	☎ 61171011 ✇ 61172602	152	02.01–23.12 (Closed Easter)	††† ¶O⟨ R ⟩ CC ⌂ P ⬚
▲ **Halden YH** Box 2110, Brødløs, 1760 Halden.	☎ 69216968 ✇ 69216603	35	25.06–08.08	††† ♿ ⌂ P ⬚
▲ **Hamar YH** - Vikingskipet Motell & Hostel Åkersvikavn. 10, 2321 Hamar. ℮ firmavmv@online.no	☎ 62526060 ✇ 62532460	138	🛏12	††† ¶O⟨ 2E⟩ ♿ CC ⌂ P ⬚
▲ **Harstad YH** Trondenesvn 110, Boks 626, 9486 Harstad, Troms.	☎ 77072800 ✇ 77072666	101	01.06–20.08	††† ¶O⟨ 3N⟩ CC ⌂ P ⬚
▲ **Hellesylt YH** 6218 Hellesylt, Møre og Romsdal.	☎ 70265128; 70263657 ✇ 70263657; 70265128	54	01.06–01.09	††† ¶O⟨0.5NW⟩ ⌂ P ⬚ 🚲
△ *Helligskogen YH* - *Fjellstue* *Write to: John Bertiniussen Uranusun. 36,* *9024 Tomasjord, Located Skibotndalen (E8),* *Troms.*	☎ 77715460 (Off season 77633891) ✇ 77715460	40	20.06–20.08	††† ¶O⟨ ⌂ P
▲ **Hemsedal YH** - Fossheim 3560 Hemsedal, Buskerud. ℮ aashild@hemsedal.online.no	☎ 32060315 ✇ 32060745	80	01.06–15.09 (††† 01.05–15.11)	††† ¶O⟨ R ⟩ CC ⌂ P
▲ **Hønefoss YH** Box 347, 3502 Hønefoss.	☎ 32122903, 93080899 ✇ 32123614	60	01.07–25.08 (††† 01.06–31.08)	††† ¶O⟨ 2N⟩ CC ⌂ P ⬚
▲ **Hovden** - Fjellstoge & Vandrerhjem Lundane, 4755 Hovden. ℮ fjellsto@online.no	☎ 37939543 ✇ 37939818	32	15.01–01.05; 15.06–15.09	††† ¶O⟨ 3N⟩ CC ⌂ P ⬚
▲ **Kabelvåg YH** - Lofoten Folkehøgskole 8310 Kabelvåg. ℮ post@lofoten.fhs.no	☎ 76069898 ✇ 76069881	103	01.06–15.08	††† ¶O⟨ ⌂ P ⬚
▲ **Kongsberg YH** **Vinjesgt 1, 3616 Kongsberg, Buskerud.** ℮ vh.bergm@online.no	☎ 32732024 ✇ 32720534	99	01.01–23.12; 26–31.12	††† ¶O⟨ R ⟨0.2W⟩ ♿ CC ⌂ P ⬚ 🚲 ❀

Location/Address	Telephone No. Fax No.	Beds	Opening Dates	Facilities
▲ **Kragerø YH** Lovisenbergvn 20, 3770 Kragerø, Telemark.	☎ 35985700 ✆ 35985701	100	18.06–22.08	ᵻᵻᵻ ⱺ 1S ᵹ ᴇᴄᴄ ☞ P ⓞ
▲ **Kristiansand** - Tangen **Skansen 8, 4610 Kristiansand, Vest-Agder.** ✉ hostlkrs@online.no	☎ 38028310 ✆ 38027505	179	15.01–15.12	ᵻᵻᵻ ⓡ 0.8E ᵹ ᴇᴄᴄ ☞ P ⓞ
▲ **Kristiansund** - Atlanten Dalav 22, 6511 Kristiansund N, Møre og Romsdal. ✉ resepsjonen@atlanten.no	☎ 71671104 ✆ 71672405	30	01.06–30.09	ᵻᵻᵻ ⱺ ᵹ ᴇᴄᴄ ☞ P ⓞ
▲ **Lakselv** - Karalaks Box 74, 9700 Lakselv.	☎ 78461476 ✆ 78461996	50	01.06–01.09	ᵻᵻᵻ ⱺ 8S ᵹ ☞ P ⓞ
▲ **Leira YH** - Valdres Folkehøgskule P.B. 101, 2907 Leira.	☎ 61359500 ✆ 61359501	74	28.05–10.08	ᵻᵻᵻ ⱺ ☞ P ⓞ
△ *Levanger YH - Moan* *7600 Levanger, Nord-Trøndelag.*	☎ *74081638* ✆ *74081638*	*45*	*01.05–31.08* (🔒 ⓡ)	ᵻᵻᵻ ⱺ ᵹ ☞ P ⓞ
▲ **Lillehammer** - Skysstasjonen **Jernbanetorget 2, 2609 Lillehammer, Oppland.** ✉ lillehammervandrerhjem@c2i.net	☎ 61248700 ✆ 61262577	84	15.01–30.11 (ᵻᵻᵻ 🔒)	ᵻᵻᵻ ⱺ 0.2S ᵹ ᴇᴄᴄ ☞ P ⓞ ❄
▲ **Melbu YH** P A Kvaalsgt 5, Box 121, 8459 Melbu, Nordland.	☎ 76157106, 76159130 ✆ 76158382	100	🔒	ᵻᵻᵻ ⱺ ᴇᴄᴄ ☞ P ⓞ
▲ **Meråker YH** - Brenna Camping 7530 Meråker.	☎ 74810234 ✆ 74810234	30	15.06–15.08	ᵻᵻᵻ ⱺ 2E ᴇᴄᴄ ☞ P ⓞ
▲ **Mjølfjell YH** 5700 Voss, Hordaland. ✉ muhas@online.no	☎ 56523150 ✆ 56523151	40	01.03–30.04; 15.06–01.10 (rest of year ⓡ)	ᵻᵻᵻ ⱺ ⓡ ᵹ ᴇᴄᴄ ☞ P ⓞ
▲ **Mo i Rana** - Fageråsen Box 1227, 8602 Mo, Nordland. ✉ mo.vandrerhjem@c2i.net	☎ 75150963, 90162135 ✆ 75151530	59	01.06–31.08	ᵻᵻᵻ ᴇᴄᴄ ☞ P ⓞ
▲ **Molde** - Gjestestova Romsdalsgt. 5, 6413 Molde, Møre Og Romsdal. ✉ gjestestova@online.no	☎ 71216180 ✆ 71242309	60	15.06–15.08	ᵻᵻᵻ ⱺ ᴇᴄᴄ ☞ P ⓞ
▲ **Moss** - Vansjøheimen Nesparken, 1530 Moss, Østfold. ✉ speide-h@frisurf.no	☎ 69255334 ✆ 69250166	68	01.06–01.09 (02.09–31.05 ⓡ)	ᵻᵻᵻ ⱺ ᴇᴄᴄ ☞ P ⓞ ❄
▲ **Narvik** - SSIN Tiurveien 22, 8516 Narvik, Nordland. ✉ ssin@ssin.no	☎ 76962200 ✆ 76962025	120	23.06–14.08	ᵻᵻᵻ ᵹ ᴇᴄᴄ ☞ P ⓞ
▲ **Nesbyen YH** Sutøya Feriepark, 3540 Nesbyen. ✉ sutferie@online.no	☎ 32071397 ✆ 32070111	40	01.05–15.09	ᵻᵻᵻ ⱺ ᴇᴄᴄ ☞ P ⓞ
▲ **Norsjø** 3812 Akkerhaugen, Telemark. ✉ norsjou@start.no	☎ 35958277 ✆ 35958283	48	🔒	ᵻᵻᵻ ᵹ ☞ P ⓞ ⛍

Location/Address	Telephone No. Fax No.	Beds	Opening Dates	Facilities
▲ **Oppdal YH** Sletvold Park Apartments, Gamle Kongevei, 7340 Oppdal.	☎ 72404090 ❺ 72404101	64	01.05–30.11	ﬁﬁﬁ ⦿l ɕɕɟ ♂ P ⬚
▲ **Oslo** - Ekeberg Kongsvn.82, PB.23 Bekkelagshøgda, N-1109 Oslo.	☎ 22741890 (Off season: 22152185) ❺ 22747505 (Off season: 22713497)	55	01.06–14.08	ﬁﬁﬁ ⓡ 5 SE ⛃ ɕɕɟ ♂ P ⬚
▲ **Oslo** - Haraldsheim (IBN) **Haraldsheimvn 4, 0409 Oslo.** ⊖ post@haraldsheim.oslo.no	☎ 22222965, 22155043 ❺ 22221025	270	02.01–22.12	ﬁﬁﬁ ⦿l ⓡ 5 NE ɕɕɟ ♂ P ⬚
▲ **Oslo** - Holtekilen Michelets vei 55, 1368 Stabekk. ⊖ holtekil@alfanett.no	☎ 67518040 (Off season: 22152185) ❺ 67591230 (Off season: 22713497)	199	25.05–20.08	ﬁﬁﬁ ⦿l ⓡ 9 W ɕɕɟ ♂ P ⬚
△ *Preikestolen - Jørpeland* *4100 Jørpeland. Write to: PB 239,* *4001 Stavanger.*	☎ *97165551* *(02.09-01.06);* *51840200* ❺ *51749111*	*42*	*01.06–02.09*	ﬁﬁﬁ ⦿l ⓡ ɕɕɟ ♂ P
▲ **Rjukan YH** Birkelandsgt 2, 3660 Rjukan, Telemark.	☎ 35090527 ❺ 35090996	78	⬚12	ﬁﬁﬁ ⦿l ⛃ ♂ P
▲ **Røros YH** - Idrettsparken Hotel & Hostel Øra 25, 7374 Røros, Sør-Trøndelag.	☎ 72411089 ❺ 72412377	34	⬚12	ﬁﬁﬁ ⦿l ɕɕɟ ♂ P ⬚
△ *Runde YH* *6096 Runde.* ⊖ *runde@runde.no*	☎ *70085916* ❺ *70085870*	*65*	⬚12	ﬁﬁﬁ ɕɕɟ ♂ P ⬚ ✿
▲ **Sarpsborg** - Tuneheimen **Tuneveien 44, 1710 Sarpsborg, Østfold.** ⊖ tuneheim@online.no	☎ 69145001 ❺ 69142291	91	02.01–22.12	ﬁﬁﬁ ⦿l ɕɕɟ ♂ P ⬚
▲ **Sjoa YH** 2670 Sjoa, Oppland. ⊖ sjoa-vh@online.no	☎ 61236200 ❺ 61236014	83	01.05–01.10	ﬁﬁﬁ ⦿l ⛃ ɕɕɟ ♂ P ⬚
▲ **Sjusjøen YH** - Fjellheimen 2612 Sjusjøen. ⊖ lars.hostmelingen@sjusjoen-hoyfjell.no	☎ 62363409 ❺ 62363404	89	⬚12	ﬁﬁﬁ ⦿l ɕɕɟ P
▲ **Skarnes** - Solbakken 2100 Skarnes. ⊖ solbakk@east.no	☎ 62961233 ❺ 62961233	46	01.06–15.08	ﬁﬁﬁ ⛃ ♂ P ⬚ ⬚
▲ **Skien YH** Moflatvn 65, 3733 Skien, Telemark.	☎ 35504870 ❺ 35504879	82	⬚12	ﬁﬁﬁ ⦿l ⛃ ɕɕɟ ♂ P ⬚
△ *Skjolden YH* *6876 Skjolden, Sogn og Fjordane.* ⊖ *kaare.bauge@c2i.net*	☎ *57686615 Shut:* *57686676* ❺ *57681214*	*35*	*15.06–31.08*	ﬁﬁﬁ ⦿l ɕɕɟ ♂ P ⬚

Location/Address	Telephone No. Fax No.	Beds	Opening Dates	Facilities
△ **Sogndal YH** *P.b. 174, 6856 Sogndal, Sogn og Fjordane.* ❷ *sogndal.folkehogskule@vestdata.no*	☎ 57672033 ✇ 57673145	83	*14.06–13.08*	ᵻᵻᵻ ❢❶❷ ☛ 🅿 ⊡
△ **Stamsund YH** - *Justad Rorbuer & Hostel* *P.b.110, 8378 Stamsund, Lofoten, Nordland.*	☎ 76089334 ✇ 76089739	60	*01.01–15.10;* *15.12–31.12*	ᵻᵻᵻ ♿ ☛ 🅿 ⊡
▲ **Stavanger YH** - Mosvangen Henrik Ibsensgt. 21, 4021 Stavanger, Rogaland. ❷ mosvangen@c2i.net	☎ 51872900 ✇ 51870630	44	20.05–15.09 (🔲₁₂ ᵻᵻᵻ)	ᵻᵻᵻ ❢❶❷ ⓡ ☛ 🅿
▲ **Stryn YH** 6783 Stryn, Sogn og Fjordane. ❷ jonnbein@online.no	☎ 57871106, 57871336 ✇ 57871106	76	01.06–31.08	ᵻᵻᵻ ❢❶❷ 1N ⟨CC⟩ ☛ 🅿 ⊡
▲ **Sunndalsøra YH** Trædal, 6600 Sunndalsøra, Møre og Romsdal. ❷ jtredal@eunet.no	☎ 71691301 ✇ 71690555	55	01.01–20.12	ᵻᵻᵻ ❢❶❷ ♿ ⟨CC⟩ ☛ 🅿 ⊡
▲ **Tønsberg YH** Dr Blancas gt 22, 3111 Tønsberg, Vestfold. ❷ tonsvand@online.no	☎ 33312175 ✇ 33312176	102	05.01–20.12	ᵻᵻᵻ ❢❶❷ ⓡ 0.4NW ⟨CC⟩ ☛ 🅿 ⊡ 🚲
▲ **Tromsø YH** Elverhøy, Gitta Jønsonsv 4, 9012 Tromsø, Troms. ❷ hostels@online.no	☎ 77685319 (Shut 23139300) ✇ 77685319 (Shut 23139350)	50	20.06–18.08	ᵻᵻᵻ 2N 🅿
▲ **Trondheim** - Rosenborg **Weidemannsvei 41, 7043 Trondheim, Sør-Trøndelag.** ❷ tr-vanas@online.no	☎ 73874450 ✇ 73874455	212	03.01–18.12	ᵻᵻᵻ ❢❶❷ ⓡ ⟨CC⟩ ☛ 🅿 ⊡
▲ **Trysil YH** - Kjølen Hotell 2423 Østby. ❷ post@kjolen-hotell.no	☎ 62455100 ✇ 62455102	56	🔲₁₂	ᵻᵻᵻ ❢❶❷ ⟨CC⟩ ☛ 🅿 ⊡ ☕ 🚲
▲ **Tynset** - Tynset Hotel, Motel & Hostel Brugata 6, 2500 Tynset, Hedmark. ❷ kaare.fiskvik@tynset-hotel.com	☎ 62480600 ✇ 62480497	36	🔲₁₂ (Christmas, Easter, Whitsun ⓡ)	ᵻᵻᵻ ❢❶❷ ⓡ ⟨CC⟩ ☛ 🅿 ⊡
▲ **Uvdal YH** 3632 Uvdal, Buskerud.	☎ 32743020, 94218071 ✇ 32743020	46	01.06–01.09 (01.09–01.06 ⓡ)	ᵻᵻᵻ ❢❶❷ ⓡ ⟨CC⟩ ☛ 🅿 ⊡ 🚲
△ **Værøy YH** - *Langodden Rorbu Camping* *8063 Værøy, Nordland.*	☎ 76095352, 92618477 ✇ 76095701	58	*01.06–25.08*	ᵻᵻᵻ ☛ 🅿 ⊡
▲ **Valdresflya YH** 2953 Beitostoelen, Oppland.	☎ 94107021 (Shut 22152185)	46	01.06–01.09	ᵻᵻᵻ ❢❶❷ ⓡ ♿ 🅿 ☕
▲ **Voss** Evangerveien 68, 5700 Voss, Hordaland. ❷ voss-hostel@voss.online.no	☎ 56512017 ✇ 56510837	180	01.02–15.11	ᵻᵻᵻ ❢❶❷ ⓡ 0.4W ♿ ⟨CC⟩ ☛ 🅿 ⊡ ☕ 🚲 ⚙

Poland

POLOGNE

POLEN

POLONIA

**Polskie Towarzystwo Schronisk Młodzieżowych,
00-791 Warszawa, ul Chocimska 28,
Poland.**

❶ (48) (22) 8498128
❶ (48) (22) 8498354
e hostellingpol.ptsm@pro.onet.pl

Office Hours: Monday-Friday 08.00-16.00hrs

Travel Section: "Junior" Travel and "Hostelling Polska" Travel
ul. Chocimska 28, 00-791 Warszawa

❶ (48) (22) 8498128
❶ (48) (220 8498354

A copy of the Hostel Directory for this Country can be obtained from:
The National Office

Capital:	Warsaw	**Population:**	38,581,000
Language:	Polish	**Size:**	312,677 sq km
Currency:	Zł (złoty)	**Telephone Country Code:**	48

POLAND

GERMANY

CZECH REPUBLIC

SLOVAK REPUBLIC

Smołdzino ▲ ▲ Łeba
Ustka ▲ ▲ Gdynia
Słupsk ▲ Gdańsk ●
Chmielno ▲ Malbork ▲ ▲ Frombork
Koszalin ▲
Świnoujście ▲ ▲ Pobierowo ▲ Elbląg
Wapnica ▲ ▲ Wolin
Szczecin ▲
Sępólno Krajeńskie ▲ ▲ Grudziądz
Wałcz ▲
Piła ▲ ▲ Bydgoszcz
Chodzież ▲ Toruń ▲
Inowrocław ▲
Gorzòw Wlkp ▲ ▲ Włocławek
Trzemeszno ▲
Kobylnica ▲ Strzelno
Szamotuły ▲ ▲ Gniezno ▲
Poznań ▲
Mosina ▲ Żerków ▲
Nowy Jaromierz ▲ Osieczna ▲ Konin ▲
Przytok ▲ Zaniemyśl ▲ Kalisz ▲ Łódź ▲
Zielona Góra ▲ Śmigiel ▲ Ludwikòw ▲
Lubsko ▲ Żagań ▲
Łagòw k. Zgorzelca ▲ Legnica ▲ Zduńska Wola ▲
Przemkòw ▲
Kamień ▲ Złotoryja ▲ Wrocław
Myślibórz ▲ ● Wrocław Radomsko ▲
Michałowice ▲ Jelenia Góra ▲ Kuraszków ▲
Karpniki ▲ Oława ▲
Szklarska Poręba ▲ ▲ Bukowiec ▲ Świdnica Częstochowa ▲
Karpacz ▲ Wałbrzych ▲ Zagórze Śl
Lężyce ▲ Nysa ▲
Gołaczów ▲ Kłodzko ▲ Kamień ▲ Opole ▲
Głuchołazy ▲
Zieleniec ▲ Paczków ▲ Góra Św. Anny ▲
Rybnica Leśna ▲ Polanica Zdrój ▲
Lądek ▲ Kletno ▲ Gliwice ▲
Bielsko-Biała ▲
Ustroń ▲
Szczyrk ▲ ▲ Istebna Zaolzie

N

0 50 100 150 KMS

50 MLS

RUSSIAN
FEDERATION

LITHUANIA

Gdynia▲
▲▲Gdansk
Malbork▲
▲Frombork
▲Elbląg

▲Lidzbark Warmiński
▲Kłębowo
Olsztyn▲   Mrągowo▲
Iława▲   Ostróda
▲Szczytno
Narty▲

▲Ełk

▲Pisz
Mońki
▲Białystok

POLAND

Białowieża▲

▲Włocławek
▲Ciechanów
▲Płońsk

BELORUSSIA

Warszawa▲ ■ Warszawa
Nieborów▲   ▲Radziejowice
▲Łódź   ▲Dęblin

Inowłódz▲   ▲Radom
Piotrków   Szydłowiec▲   ▲Puławy
Trybunalski▲
Radomsko▲   Święta Katarzyna
Mąchocice▲   ▲ ▲Nowa Słupia
Częstochowa▲   Kielce▲   ▲Łagów k. Kielc
▲Stalowa Wola
▲Pawełki   Nagłowice

▲Chełm

Sławków-Niwa
Gliwice▲   Łazy   Tarnów   ▲Łańcut
Bielsko-Biała▲   Kraków▲   Myślenice   ▲ ▲Rzeszów
Cieszyn▲Ozna▲   ▲Ciężkowice▲   Rozdziele
Ustroń   ▲Zawoja   ▲Lanckorona   ▲Jasło
Szczyrk▲   Żywiec   Biecz   Przemyśl▲
Istebna Zaolzie   Bóbrka k/Krosna
▲Nowy Sącz   Sanok▲   ▲Górzanka
Wetlina▲   ▲Bóbrka k/Soliny
Zakopane   Jabłonki▲   Myczków

UKRAINE

SLOVAK REPUBLIC

English

Hostels are located in cities, in the countryside, on the coast and on hills/mountains.

Price range

Price range PLN 35-90. € 8-21. ⒝inc 🖳.

Rooms and Reservations

🆁 during May-Sep. (¹🐄 ²🐄 ³🐄 ⁴🐄). Reservations via Hostel by ❶ ❷. (Reservation charges may apply). Smoking is limited - please check.

Guests

Membership Card and Passport/Photo ID are required. Pets are allowed - check with hostel. ⴕ welcome. Group bookings via Hostel or National Office by ❶ ❷ (Reservation charges may apply).

Open times

Main hostels: open 🖻, 07:00-10:00hrs, 16:00-20:00hrs. Reception open: ☺. **Other hostels:** open 🖻, 08:00-10:00hrs, 17:00-19:00hrs. Reception open: 17:00-20:00hrs. **Seasonal hostels** are generally open Jul, Aug.

Meals

🍽 BLD For individuals & for ⴕ. ♂.

Travelling around

For ease of travel use 🚌 🚐.

Travel/Activity Packages

Tours/sightseeing and accommodation/ transport packages available. Package bookings via Hostel or National Office by ❶ ❷.

Passports and Visas

Passport required.

Health

Medical insurance is recommended.

Français

Les auberges sont situées dans les villes, à la campagne, sur le littoral et à la montagne.

Tarifs des nuitées

Tarifs des nuitées 35-90 PLN. € 8-21. ⒝inc 🖳.

Chambres et réservations

🆁 mai-sep. (¹🐄 ²🐄 ³🐄 ⁴🐄). Réservations via l'auberge par ❶ ❷. (Des frais de réservation pourront vous être facturés). Il est permis de fumer dans certaines chambres - veuillez vérifier.

Usagers

La carte d'adhérent ainsi que le passeport/pièce d'identité avec photo sont à présenter. Les animaux domestiques sont autorisés mais vérifiez lesquels auprès de l'auberge. Accueil des ⴕ. Réservations pour groupes via l'auberge et le Bureau National par ❶ ❷ (Des frais de réservation pourront vous être facturés).

Horaires d'ouverture

Grandes auberges: ouvertes 🖻, entre 7h-10h, 16h-20h. Accueil ouvert ☺. **Autres auberges:** ouvertes 🖻, entre 8h-10h, 17h-19h. Accueil ouvert entre 17h-20h. **Auberges saisonnières** ouvertes généralement juil, août.

Repas

🍽 BLD Pour individuels & pour ⴕ. ♂.

Déplacements

Modes de transport recommandés 🚌 🚐.

Forfaits Voyages/Activités

Forfaits circuits touristiques et hébergement/ transport disponibles. Réservations des forfaits via l'auberge et le Bureau National par ❶ ❷.

Passeports et visas

Passeport obligatoire.

Santé

Une assurance médicale de voyage est conseillée.

Deutsch

Herbergen befinden sich in Städten, auf dem Land, an der Küste und in Bergen/Gebirgen.

Preisspanne

Preisspanne 35-90 PLN. € 8-21. BB|inc 🍽.

Zimmer und Reservierungen

ℝ während Mai-Sept. (¹🛏 ²🛏 ³🛏 ⁴🛏). Reservierungen über die Herberge per ❶ ❷. (Reservierungskosten könnten anfallen). Rauchen ist begrenzt - bitte checken.

Gäste

Mitgliedsausweis und Reisepass/ Personalausweis sind erforderlich. Haustiere sind erlaubt - in der Herberge nachfragen. ♦♦♦ willkommen. Gruppenbuchungen über Herberge oder Landesverband per ❶ ❷ (Reservierungskosten könnten anfallen).

Öffnungszeiten

Hauptherbergen: Zugang 🔑, 07:00-10:00Uhr, 16:00-20:00Uhr. Rezeption ℚ. **Andere Herbergen:** Zugang 🔑, 08:00-10:00Uhr, 17:00-19:00Uhr. Rezeption zwischen 17:00-20:00Uhr. **Saison-Herbergen** sind normalerweise Jul, Aug geöffnet.

Mahlzeiten

🍽 BLD Für Einzelreisende & für ♦♦♦. 💨.

Reisen im Land

Reisen ist einfach mit 🚌 🚃.

Reise-/Aktivitäten-Packages

Touren/sightseeing und Unterkunft/Transport-Packages erhältlich. Package-Buchungen über Herberge oder Landesverband per ❶ ❷.

Reisepässe und Visa

Reisepass erforderlich.

Gesundheit

Unfall-/Krankenversicherung wird empfohlen.

Español

Los albergues están situados en las ciudades, el campo, la costa y la montaña.

Tarifas mínima y máxima

Tarifas mínima y máxima 35-90 PLN. € 8-21. BB|inc 🍽.

Habitaciones y Reservas

ℝ en may-sep. (¹🛏 ²🛏 ³🛏 ⁴🛏). Reservas a través del albergue por ❶ ❷. (Es posible que se aplique un suplemento en concepto de gastos de reserva). Está permitido fumar sólo en algunas salas/habitaciones - infórmese.

Huéspedes

Los huéspedes deben presentar su Carnet de Alberguista y su pasaporte o carnet de identidad. Se admiten animales - consulte con el albergue. Se admiten ♦♦♦. Reservas de grupo a través del albergue o la Asociación Nacional por ❶ ❷ (Es posible que se aplique un suplemento en concepto de gastos de reserva).

Horarios y fechas de apertura

Albergues principales - abiertos 🗓, 07:00-10:00h, 16:00-20:00h. Horario de recepción: 🕐. **Otros albergues** - abiertos 🗓, 08:00-10:00h, 17:00-19:00h. Horario de recepción: 17:00-20:00h. **Albergues de temporada** suelen abrir: jul, ago.

Comidas

🍽 BLD Para individuales y para 👥. 🔔.

Desplazamientos

Transportes recomendados: 🚂 🚌.

Viajes Combinados con Actividades

Viajes combinados con visitas turísticas y alojamiento/transporte. Reserva de viajes combinados a través del albergue o la Asociación Nacional por ❶ ❷.

Pasaportes y Visados

Pasaporte obligatorio.

Información Sanitaria

Seguro médico recomendado.

"A person travels the world over in search of what he needs and returns home to find it."

"L'on parcourt le monde à la recherche de ce dont on a besoin et l'on revient chez soi pour le trouver."

„Der Mensch bereist die ganze Welt auf der Suche nach dem, was er braucht und kehrt heim, um es dort zu finden."

"Recorremos el mundo en busca de lo que necesitamos para al final encontrarlo en casa a nustro regreso"

George Moore

Kłębowo - "Świteź"

**11-100 Lidzbarka Warmiński,
Kłębowo 50.**
☏ (89) 7662382, (89) 7662360
✆ (89) 7662381

Open Dates: 🗓

Open Hours: 06.00-23.00hrs

Reservations: **R**

Price Range: USD 4.00-8.00 BB|inc ◫

Beds: 180 - 1x¹⚤ 3x²⚤ 8x³⚤ 12x⁴⚤ 20x⁵⚤

Facilities: 👫 24x 👬 🍽 ☕ ⛉ 📺 🛏1 x🍴 📷 👝 🅿 ℹ 🎱 ✂ 🏔 ❸ ⚲ 🔍 ⛏ 🏠

Directions:

✈	Gdańsk 120km
⛴	Gdańsk; Gdynia 120km
🚆	Olsztyn 50km
🚌	PKS from Lidzbark Warmiński 8km

Attractions: ⚲ 🚲 🎣 ⊍12km ⚓100m

Ustroń-Jaszowiec - "Wiecha"

**ul.Stroma 5,
43-450 Ustroń-Jaszowiec.**
☏ (33) 8543501, (33) 8542741
✆ (33) 8543501

Open Dates: 🗓

Open Hours: 06.00-23.00hrs

Reservations: **R**

Price Range: USD 6.00-10.00 BB|inc ◫

Beds: 170 - 3x¹⚤ 10x²⚤ 10x³⚤ 10x⁴⚤ 11x⁶⚤ 1x⁶⚤

Facilities: 👫 33x 👬 🍽 ☕ ⛉ 📺3 x🍴 📷 👝 🅿 ℹ 🎱 ✂ ❸ 🏠

Directions:

✈	Katowice - Pyrzowice 90km
🚆	Ustroń - Polana 3km
🚌	PKS Ustroń - Polana 3km

Attractions: ⚲ ⛰ 🎿 1200m 🎣 🎿 ⊍15km ⚲800m ⚓500m

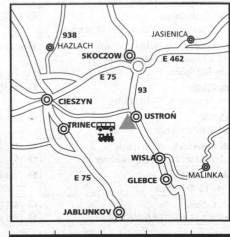

Location/Address	Telephone No. Fax No.	Beds	Opening Dates	Facilities
△ *Białowieża - "Paprotka"* *ul. Gen. Waszkiewicza 4, 17-230 Białowieża.*	☏ *(85) 6812560* ✆ *(85) 6812560*	*48*		♟ Ⓡ ☞ Ⓟ
▲ Białystok ul. Piłsudskiego 7b, 15-443 Białystok.	☏ (85) 6524250	50		♟ Ⓡ ☞ Ⓟ
△ *Białystok - "Trzy Sosny"* *ul. Leśna 20, 16-001 Białystok-Kleosin.*	☏ *(85) 6631311* ✆ *(85) 6631311*	*120*		♟ ⦿ Ⓡ ☞ Ⓟ ⊙ ☕
▲ Biecz ul. Parkowa 1, 38-250 Biecz.	☏ (13) 4471829	60		♟ Ⓡ ☞ Ⓟ
△ *Bielsko-Biała - "Bolek i Lolek"* *ul. Komorowicka 25, 43-300 Bielsko-Biała.*	☏ *(33) 8167466* ✆ *(33) 8167466*	*92*		♟ Ⓡ ☞
▲ Bóbrkak/Krosna 38-458 Chorkówka.	☏ (13) 4313097	30	01.05–31.10	♟ Ⓡ ☞
△ *Bóbrka k/Soliny* *Bóbrka k/Soliny, 38-612 Solina.*	☏ *(13) 4691861*	*45*	*01.07–31.08*	☞ Ⓟ
▲ Bukowiec - "Skalnik" ul. Szkolna 2, 58-532 Kostrzyca.	☏ (75) 7182628 ✆ (75) 7182628	47		♟ Ⓡ ☞ Ⓟ
▲ Bydgoszcz ul. Sowińskiego 5, 85-083 Bydgoszcz.	☏ (52) 3227570 ✆ (52) 3287769	100		♟ Ⓡ ☞ Ⓟ
▲ Chełm ul. Czarnieckiego 8, 22-100 Chełm.	☏ (82) 5640022	49		Ⓡ ☞ Ⓟ
▲ Chmielno - "Checz Dlo Wanogów" ul.Gryfa Pomorskiego 33, 83-333 Chmielno.	☏ (58) 6842322 ✆ (58) 6842205	50		♟ Ⓡ ☞ Ⓟ
△ *Chodziez - "Gotyniec"* *ul. Kochanowkiego 1, 64-800 Chodzież.*	☏ *(67) 2829060*	*56*		♟ ⦿ Ⓡ ☞ Ⓟ ☕
▲ Ciechanów ul. 17 Stycznia 66, 06-400 Ciechanów.	☏ (23) 6722404, (23) 6724832	35		Ⓡ ☞ Ⓟ ☕
▲ Ciężkowice ul. Św Andrzeja 6, 33-190 Ciężkowice.	☏ (14) 6510119	40		Ⓡ ☞ Ⓟ
△ *Cieszyn* *ul. Błogocka 24, 43-300 Cieszyn.*	☏ *(33) 8521629*	*65*		♟ ⦿ Ⓡ ☞ Ⓟ ⊙ ☕
▲ Częstochowa ul. Jasnogórska 84/90, 42-200 Częstochowa.	☏ (34) 3243121	90	01.07–31.08	♟ ☞ Ⓟ
△ *Dęblin - "Lotnikòw Polskich"* *ul. 15 Putku Piechoty "Wilków" 5, 08-520 Dęblin.*	☏ *(81) 8830354*	*52*	*01.07–25.08*	☞ Ⓟ
▲ Elbląg ul. Browarna 1, 82-300 Elbląg.	☏ (55) 2325670	120	01.07–25.08	♟ ☞ Ⓟ
△ *Ełk* *ul. Sikorskiego 7a, 19-300 Ełk.*	☏ *(87) 6102514*	*45*	*01.07–31.08*	♟ ☞ Ⓟ
▲ Frombork - "Copernicus" ul. Elbląska 11, 14-530 Frombork.	☏ (55) 2437453 ✆ (55) 2437453	120		♟ Ⓡ ☞ Ⓟ
▲ Gòrzanka 38-613 Wołkowyja.	☏ (13) 4692577	50		♟ ⦿ Ⓡ ☞ Ⓟ ☕
△ *Gdynia* *ul. Morska 108C, 81-216 Gdynia.*	☏ *(58) 6270005* ✆ *(58) 6270005*	*100*		♟ Ⓡ ☞ Ⓟ

Location/Address	Telephone No. Fax No.	Beds	Opening Dates	Facilities
▲ Gliwice ul. Żwirki i Wigury 85, 44-100 Gliwice.	☎ (32) 2302525, (32) 2302882	80	🄵12	♟♟ ¶0¶ Ⓡ ♂ 🅿
△ Głuchołazy Powstańców Śląskich 33, 48-340 Głuchołazy.	☎ (77) 4391756, (77) 4391547	50	🄵12	♟♟ ¶0¶ ♂ 🅿
▲ Głuchołazy ul. M. Sktodowskicj 9, 48-340 Głuchołazy.	☎ (77) 4391340	100	01.07–25.08	♟♟ ♂ 🅿
▲ Góra Św. Anny ul. Szkolna 1, 47-154 Góra Św. Anny.	☎ (77) 4615473	50	🄵12	♟♟ Ⓡ ♂ 🅿
▲ Gorzòw Wielkopolski ul.St.Wyszyńskiego 8, 66-400 Gorzòw Wlkp.	☎ (95) 7227470 ☎ (95) 7227470	70	🄵12	♟♟ Ⓡ ♂ 🅿
▲ Gołaczów ul.Górska 1, Gołaczów k/Kudowy, 57-343 Lewin Kłodzki.	☎ (74) 8662813 ☎ (74) 8661629	47	🄵12	♟♟ Ⓡ ♂ 🅿
△ Grudziądz ul. Gen. Hallera 37, 86-300 Grudziądz.	☎ (56) 6435540	156	🄵12	♟♟ Ⓡ ♂ 🅿
▲ Iława ul. Mierosławskiego 6, 14-200 Iława.	☎ (89) 6486464	80	🄵12	♟♟ ¶0¶ Ⓡ 🅿
△ Inowrocław ul.Poznańska 345a, 88-100 Inowrocław.	☎ (52) 3537222	70	28.06–28.08	♟♟ ♂ 🅿
▲ Inowłódz ul. Spalska 5, 97-215 Inowłódz.	☎ (44) 7101122	32	01.07–31.08	♟♟ ♂ 🅿
△ Jabłonki - "Pod Jelonkiem" 38-606 Baligród.	☎ (13) 4684026, (13) 4684296	45	🄵12	♟♟ Ⓡ ♂ 🅿
▲ Jasło ul. Czackiego 4, 38-200 Jasło.	☎ (13) 4463464	25	01.07–31.08	♟♟ ♂ 🅿
△ Jedlina Zdròj - "Ad-ew-ka" ul. Kłodzka 81, 58-330 Jedlina Zdròj.	☎ (74) 8455235, (74) 8455507	35	🄵12	♟♟ ¶0¶ Ⓡ ♂ 🅿 ☕
△ Jelenia Góra - "Bartek" ul. Bartka Zwycięzcy 10, 58-500 Jelenia Góra.	☎ (75) 7525746 ☎ 7525746	56	🄵12	♟♟ Ⓡ ♂ 🅿
▲ Kalisz ul. Wał Piastowski 3, 62-800 Kalisz.	☎ (62) 7572404	52	🄵12	♟♟ Ⓡ ♂ 🅿
△ Kamień - "Halny" Kamień k/ Świeradowa, 59-870 Mirsk.	☎ (75) 7834336	60	🄵12	♟♟ ¶0¶ Ⓡ ♂ 🅿
△ Kielce - "Wędrownik" ul. Szymanowskiego 5, 25-361 Kielce.	☎ (41) 3423735 ☎ (41) 3423735	70	🄵12	♟♟ ¶0¶ Ⓡ ♂ 🅿
▲ Kłębowo - "Świteź" 11-100 Lidzbarka Warmiński, Kłębowo 50.	☎ (89) 7662382, (89) 7662360 ☎ (89) 7662381	180	🄵12	♟♟ ¶0¶ Ⓡ ♂ 🅿
▲ Kletno Kletno 8, 57-550 Stronie Śl.	☎ (74) 8141358	40	🄵12	Ⓡ ♂ 🅿
△ Kłodzko ul. Nadrzeczna 5, 57-300 Kłodzko.	☎ (74) 8672524	50	🄵12	♟♟ Ⓡ ♂ 🅿
▲ Kobylnica - "Sarenka" ul. Poznańska 50, 62-006 Kobylnica.	☎ (61) 8150103	45	🄵12	♟♟ Ⓡ ♂ 🅿 ☕

Location/Address	Telephone No. Fax No.	Beds	Opening Dates	Facilities
△ *Konin-Gosławice* *ul. Leopolda Staffa 5,* *62-505 Konin Gosławice.*	☎ *(63) 2427235* 🖷 *(63) 2455126*	*60*	🔲	� Ⓡ ☞ Ⓟ
▲ Koszalin - "Gościniec" ul. Gnieźnieńska 3, 75-735 Koszalin.	☎ (94) 3426068	80	🔲	♦╫ Ⓡ ☞ Ⓟ
▲ Kraków ul. Grochowa 21, 30-731 Kraków.	☎ (12) 6532691, (12) 4271351	110	🔲	Ⓡ ☞ Ⓟ
△ *Kraków* *ul. Szablowskiego 1C, 30-127 Kraków.*	☎ *(12) 6372441*	*150*	*01.07–25.08*	♦╫ 🍴 Ⓡ ☞ Ⓟ ☕
▲ Kuraszków Kuraszków 50, 55-035 Oborniki Śląskie.	☎ (71) 3102571	50	🔲	Ⓡ ☞ Ⓟ
△ *Lądek Zdrój - "Skalniak"* *Stójków 36, 57-540 Lądek Zdrój.*	☎ *(74) 8146645*	*30*	🔲	♦╫ Ⓡ ☞ Ⓟ
▲ Łagów - "Łuzyce" ul. Leśna 4, 59-910 Łagów.	☎ (75) 7715908	40	🔲	♦╫ Ⓡ ☞ Ⓟ ☕
△ *Łagów k/Kielc* *ul. Szkolna 1a, 27-430 Łagów.*	☎ *(41) 3074104*	*48*	🔲	♦╫ Ⓡ ☞ Ⓟ
▲ Lanckorona ul.Kazimierza Wielkiego 1, 34-143 Lanckorona.	☎ (33) 8763589	80	🔲	♦╫ 🍴 Ⓡ ☞ Ⓟ
△ *Łańcut* *ul. Mickiewicza 3, 37-100 Łańcut.*	☎ *(17) 2252961*	*22*	*01.07–25.08*	♦╫ ☞ Ⓟ
▲ Łeba - "Chaber" Łeba, ul.Turystyczna 1, 84-360 Łeba.	☎ (59) 8661435 🖷 (59) 8662435	120	🔲	♦╫ Ⓡ Ⓟ
△ *Legnica* *ul. Jordana 17, 59-220 Legnica.*	☎ *(76) 8625412*	*60*	🔲	♦╫ 🍴 Ⓡ ☞ Ⓟ
▲ Łęzyce - "U Anny" Łęzyce 41, 57-340 Duszniki-Zdrój.	☎ (74) 8669301, (74) 8660202	100	🔲	♦╫ 🍴 Ⓡ ♿ ☞ Ⓟ ☕
▲ Lidzbark Warmiński ul. Szkolna 3, 11-100 Lidzbark Warmiński.	☎ (89) 7672444	60	01.07–31.08	♦╫ ☞ Ⓟ
△ *Łódź* *ul. Legionów 27, 91-069 Łódź.*	☎ *(42) 6302377* 🖷 *(42) 6306683*	*83*	🔲	♦╫ Ⓡ ☞ Ⓟ ⬚
▲ Lubsko ul.Dąbrowskiego 6, 68-300 Lubsko.	☎ (68) 3720398 🖷 (68) 3721167	45	🔲	♦╫ Ⓡ ☞
△ *Ludwików* *63-422 Antonin Ludwików.*	☎ *(62) 7348178*	*30*	*01.07–25.08*	Ⓡ ☞ Ⓟ
▲ Mąchocice Mąchocice-Scholasteria, 26-001 Masłów.	☎ (41) 3112165	46	🔲	♦╫ Ⓡ ☞ Ⓟ
△ *Malbork* *ul. Żeromskiego 45, 82-200 Malbork.*	☎ *(55) 2722408*	*56*	🔲	♦╫ 🍴 Ⓡ ☞ Ⓟ
▲ Milicz-Sławoszowice ul. Kolejowa 28, 56-300 Milicz-Sławoszowice.	☎ (71) 3840299 🖷 (71) 3841767	70	🔲	♦╫ 🍴 Ⓡ ♿ ☞ Ⓟ ☕
△ *Mońki* *ul. Ełcka 36, 19-100 Mońki.*	☎ *(85) 7162638,* *(85) 7162595* 🖷 *7162638,* *7162595*	*40*	🔲	♦╫ 🍴 Ⓡ ☞ Ⓟ ☕

Location/Address	Telephone No. Fax No.	Beds	Opening Dates	Facilities
▲ Mosina ul. Topolowa 2, 62-050 Mosina.	☏ (61) 8132734	25	01.07–31.08	††† ⛍ 🅿
▲ Mrągowo ul.Wojska Polskiego 2, 11-700 Mrągowo.	☏ (89) 7412712	60	01.07–31.08	††† ⛍ 🅿
△ Myczków Myczków, 38-610 Polańczyk.	☏ (13) 4692005	30	01.07–31.08	⛍ 🅿
▲ Myślenice ul. Zdrojowa 16, 32-400 Myślenice.	☏ (12) 2721163	100	🔲	††† 🍽 Ⓡ ⛍ 🅿 ☕
△ Myślibórz Myślibórz, 59-422 Piotrowice.	☏ (76) 8708886	46	🔲	††† Ⓡ ⛍ 🅿
▲ Nagłowice 28-362 Nagłowice.	☏ (41) 3814518, (41) 3814382	60	🔲	††† 🍽 Ⓡ ♿ ⛍ 🅿 ☕
△ Nieborów AL. Legionòw Polskich 92, 96-416 Nieborów.	☏ (46) 8385694 🖷 8385694	25	01.07–25.08	⛍ 🅿
▲ Nowa Słupia - "Pod Pielgrzymem" ul. Świętokrzyska 64, 26-006 Nowa Słupia.	☏ (41) 3177016	60	🔲	††† Ⓡ ⛍ 🅿
△ Nowy Jaromierz Nowy Jaromierz, 64-220 Kargowa.	☏ (68) 3525027, (68) 3525142	35	🔲	Ⓡ ⛍ 🅿
△ Nysa - "Pod Ziębickim Lwem" ul. Moniuszki 9/10, 48-300 Nysa.	☏ (77) 4333731	48	🔲	††† Ⓡ ⛍ 🅿
▲ Olsztyn ul. Kopernika 45, 10-512 Olsztyn.	☏ (89) 5276650 🖷 (89) 5276650	80	🔲	††† Ⓡ ⛍ 🅿
▲ Opole ul. Torawa 7, 45-587 Opole.	☏ (77) 4542855	50	🔲	††† ⛍ 🅿
△ Osieczna - "Morena" ul. Kopernika 4, 64-113 Osieczna.	☏ (65) 5350134	60	🔲	††† 🍽 Ⓡ ⛍ 🅿
▲ Ostróda ul.Kościuszki 5, 13-100 Ostróda.	☏ (89) 6465563	80	01.07–25.08	⛍ 🅿
▲ Paczków - "Pod Basztą" ul. Kołłątaja 9, 48-370 Paczków.	☏ (77) 4316441	50	🔲	††† Ⓡ ⛍
▲ Pawełki ul. Głòwna 14, 42-718 Kochcice.	☏ (34) 3533716	40	🔲	††† Ⓡ ⛍ 🅿
△ Piła - "Staszicówka" AL. WP 45, 64-920 Piła.	☏ (67) 2132583	40	🔲	††† Ⓡ ⛍ 🅿
▲ Piotrków Trybunalski ul. Broniewskiego 16, 97-300 Piotrków Trybunalski.	☏ (44) 6470905	47	🔲	††† Ⓡ ⛍ 🅿
△ Pisz ul. Gizewiusza 10, 12-200 Pisz.	☏ (87) 5232027	24	01.07–31.08	Ⓡ ⛍ 🅿
▲ Płońsk ul. Sienkiewicza 8, 09-100 Płońsk.	☏ (23) 6622844	49	🔲	††† Ⓡ ⛍ 🅿 ☕
△ Polanica Zdrój ul. Chopina 4, 57-320 Polanica-Zdrój.	☏ (74) 8681503, (74) 8681344	45	🔲	††† 🍽 Ⓡ ⛍ 🅿 ☕
△ Poznań ul. Drzymały 3, 60-613 Poznań.	☏ (61) 8485836 🖷 (61) 8485836	80	🔲	††† 🍽 Ⓡ ⛍ 🅿 ☕

Location/Address	Telephone No. Fax No.	Beds	Opening Dates	Facilities
△ *Poznań* ul. *Berwińskiego 2/3, 60-765 Poznań.*	(61) 8664040 (61) 8664040	52		
▲ Poznań - "Hanka" ul. Biskupińska 27, 60-463 Poznań.	(61) 8221063 (61) 8221063	65		
△ *Poznań - im PE Strzeleckiego* ul. *Głuszyna 127, 61-329 Poznań.*	(61) 8788461 (61) 8788461	65		
▲ Przytok 66-003 Zabór.	(68) 3274315, (68) 3274410	42		
△ *Puławy* ul. *Włostowicka 27, 24-100 Puławy.*	(81) 8883656, (81) 8863367 (81) 8883656	110		
▲ Radom ul. Miła 18, 26-600 Radom.	(48) 40560 (48) 40560	40		
▲ Radomsko ul.Piastowska 21, 97-500 Radomsko.	(44) 6834495	50	01.07–31.08	
△ *Rozdziele* 32-731 Żegocina.	(14) 6133087	54		
▲ Rybnica Leśna Rybnica Leśna 54, 58-352 Unisław Śląski.	(74) 8451591	44		
△ *Rzeszòw* Rynek 25, 35-064 Rzeszòw.	(17) 8534430	100		
▲ Sanok ul. Konarskiego 10, 38-500 Sanok.	(13) 4630925	66	01.07–31.08	
△ *Sępòlno Krajeńskie* ul. *Hallera 29, 89-400 Sępòlno Krajeńskie.*	(52) 3882686, (52) 3882051	30	01.07–25.08	
▲ Sławkòw Niwa ul. Niwa 45, 42-533 Sławkòw.	(32) 2931100	60		
△ *Słupsk* ul. *Deotymy 15a, 76-200 Słupsk.*	(59) 8424631	88	01.07–25.08	
▲ Śmigiel ul. M. Konopnickiej 5, 64-030 Śmigiel.	(65) 5180279	46		
▲ Smołdzino 76-214 Smołdzino.	(59) 8117321	40	01.07–25.08	
▲ Stalowa Wola ul. Podleśna 15, 37-450 Stalowa Wola.	(15) 8421772	40	01.07–25.08	
△ *Strzelno* ul. *Parkowa 10, 88-320 Strzelno.*	(52) 3189568	35	01.07–25.08	
▲ Strużnica - "Sokolik" 58-515 Karpniki.	(75) 7137224	40		
▲ Świdnica ul. Kanonierska 3, 58-100 Świdnica.	(74) 8522645	44		
△ *Święta Katarzyna* ul. *Kielecka 45, 26-013 Święta Katarzyna.*	(41) 3112206	45		
▲ Świnoujście ul.Gdyńska 26, 72-600 Świnoujście.	(91) 3270613	120		

Location/Address	Telephone No. Fax No.	Beds	Opening Dates	Facilities
△ *Szamotuły* ul.Obornicka 12, 64-500 Szamotuły.	☎ *(61) 2921165* 🖷 *(61) 2921165*	*44*	🔲	♯ Ⓡ ✧ Ⓟ
▲ Szczecin - "Elka-Sen" ul.3 Maja 1a, 70-214 Szczecin.	☎ (91) 4335604 🖷 (91) 4335604	44	🔲	♯ Ⓡ ✧ Ⓟ ☕
△ *Szczecin* ul. Monte Cassino 19a, 70-467 Szczecin.	☎ *(91) 4224761* 🖷 *(91) 4235696*	*130*	🔲	♯ Ⓡ 2NW ⊂CC⊃ ✧ Ⓟ
▲ Szczyrk - "Hondrasik" ul. Sportowa 2, 43-370 Szczyrk.	☎ (33) 8178933	68	🔲	♯ Ⓡ ✧ Ⓟ
▲ Szczytno - "Pod Kasztanem" ul. Pasymska 7, 12-100 Szczytno.	☎ (89) 6243992	50	🔲	♯ Ⓡ ✧ Ⓟ
△ *Szklarska Poręba - "Wojtek"* ul. Piastowska 1, 58-585 Szklarska Poręba.	☎ *(75) 7172141* 🖷 *(75) 7172141*	*73*	🔲	♯ Ⓡ ✧ Ⓟ
▲ Szydłowiec ul. Kolejowa 16, 26-500 Szydłowiec.	☎ (48) 6170137	30	🔲	♯ Ⓡ ✧ Ⓟ
▲ Tarnòw ul. Konarskiego 17, 33-100 Tarnòw.	☎ (14) 6216916	44	🔲	Ⓡ ✧ Ⓟ
△ *Toruń* ul. Św. Józefa 26, 87-100 Toruń.	☎ *(56) 6544107,* *(56) 6544580*	*30*	🔲	♯ Ⓡ ✧ Ⓟ
△ *Trzemeszno* ul. Wyszyńskiego 3, 88-340 Trzemeszno.	☎ *(52) 3154067*	50	01.06–30.09	♯ ✧ Ⓟ
▲ Ustka ul.Jagiellońska 1, 76-270 Ustka.	☎ (59) 8145317, (59) 8145081	42	🔲	♯ Ⓡ ✧ Ⓟ
▲ Ustroń-Jaszowiec - "Wiecha" **ul.Stroma 5, 43-450 Ustroń-Jaszowiec.**	☎ (33) 8543501, (33) 8542741 🖷 (33) 8543501	170	🔲	♯ 🍽 Ⓡ ✧ Ⓟ
△ *Wałbrzych - "Daisy"* ul. Markoniego 1, 58-302 Wałbrzych.	☎ *(74) 8477942*	*60*	🔲	♯ Ⓡ ✧ Ⓟ
▲ Wałcz Al.Zdobywcòw Wału Pomorskiego 76, 78-600 Wałcz.	☎ (67) 2582749	31	01.07–25.08	♯ ✧ Ⓟ
△ *Wapnica* ul. Jodłowa 3, 72-517 Wapnica.	☎ *(91) 3284106*	70	01.07–25.08	✧ Ⓟ
▲ Warszawa ul. Karolkowa 53a, 01-197 Warszawa.	☎ (22) 6328829 🖷 (22) 6329746	140	🔲	♯ 🍽 Ⓡ ✧ Ⓟ
△ *Warszawa* ul. Smolna 30, 00-375 Warszawa.	☎ *(22) 8278952* 🖷 *(22) 8278952*	*120*	🔲	♯ Ⓡ ✧ Ⓟ
▲ Wetlina 38-608 Wetlina.	☎ 090302748	56	🔲	♯ 🍽 Ⓡ ✧ Ⓟ ☕
△ *Włocławek - "Kujawiak"* ul. Mechaników 1, 87-800 Włocławek.	☎ *(54) 2362410*	*48*	🔲	♯ 🍽 Ⓡ ✧ Ⓟ
▲ Wolin ul. Spokojna 1, 72-500 Wolin.	☎ (91) 3261790	50	01.07–25.08	✧ Ⓟ
▲ Wrocław ul. Kiełczowska 43, 51-315 Wrocław.	☎ (71) 3457396, (71) 3457399 🖷 (71) 3457399	100	🔲	♯ 🍽 Ⓡ ✧ Ⓟ

Location/Address	Telephone No. Fax No.	Beds	Opening Dates	Facilities
△ **Wrocław** ul.Kołłątaja 20, 50-007 Wrocław.	☏ (71) 3438856 ☏ (71) 3438856	47	🏠	ⅲ ⓡ ⚲ 🅿
▲ **Zagórze Śląskie** - "Gwarek" ul. Główna 17, 58-321 Jugowice.	☏ (74) 8453383	60	🏠	ⅲ 🍴 ⓡ ⚲ 🅿 ☕
△ **Zakopane** - Szarotka ul. Nowotarska 45, 34-500 Zakopane.	☏ (18) 2013618, 2066203 ☏ (18) 2066203	270	🏠	ⅲ 🍴 ⓡ 🅿
▲ **Zaniemyśl** ul. Poznańska 28, 63-020 Zaniemyśl.	☏ (61) 2857289	45	🏠	ⅲ ⓡ ⚲ 🅿
△ **Zawoja** 34-223, Zawoja-Wilczna.	☏ (33) 8775106	40	🏠	ⅲ ⓡ ⚲ 🅿
▲ **Zduńska Wola** - "Czekay" ul.Dolna 41, 98-220 Zduńska Wola.	☏ (43) 8232440, 8232374	86	🏠	ⅲ ⓡ ⚲ 🅿 ☕
△ **Zieleniec** - "Adamski" Zieleniec 68, 57-350 Duszniki Zdrój.	☏ (74) 8660435 ☏ (74) 8660425	32	🏠	ⅲ ⓡ ⚲ 🅿
△ **Zielona Góra** ul. Wyspiańskiego 58, 65-036 Zielona Góra.	☏ (68) 3270840 ☏ (68) 3270840	129	🏠	ⅲ ⓡ ⚲ 🅿
▲ **Zielona Góra** ul. Długa 13, 65-401 Zielona Góra.	☏ (68) 3202237 ☏ (68) 3202571	49		ⅲ 🍴 ⓡ ⚲ 🅿 ☕
△ **Złotoryja** ul. Kolejowa 2, 59-500 Złotoryja.	☏ (76) 8783674	56	🏠	ⅲ ⓡ ⚲ 🅿
▲ **Żagań** ul.X Lecia Pl 19/21, 68-100 Żagań.	☏ (68) 3773235 ☏ (68) 3772456	40	🏠	ⅲ ⓡ ⚲ 🅿
▲ **Żerków** ul. Cmentarna 8, 63-210 Żerków.	☏ (62) 7403015	37	🏠	ⅲ ⓡ ⚲ 🅿
△ **Żywiec** - "Pod Grojcem" ul Słonki 4, 34-300 Żywiec.	☏ (33) 8612639	73	🏠	ⅲ ⓡ ⚲ 🅿

YOUTH HOSTEL ACCOMMODATION
OUTSIDE THE ASSURED STANDARDS SCHEME

Location/Address	Telephone No. Fax No.	Beds	Opening Dates	Facilities
Gdańsk ul.Wałowa 21, 80-858 Gdańsk.	☏ (58) 3012313 ☏ (58) 3012313	100	🏠	ⅲ 🍴 ⓡ ⚲ 🅿 ☕
Gdańsk ul. Grunwaldzka 244, 80-226 Gdańsk-Wrzeszcz.	☏ (58) 3411660	208	🏠	ⅲ ⓡ ♿ ⚲ 🅿 ☕
Gdańsk ul. Kartuska 245, 80-125 Gdańsk.	☏ (58) 3024187 ☏ (58) 3024187	152	🏠	ⅲ 🍴 ⓡ ⚲ 🅿 ☕
Gniezno ul. Pocztowa 11, 62-200 Gniezno.	☏ (61) 4262780 ☏ (61) 4262780	75	🏠	ⅲ ⓡ ⚲ 🅿
Istebna Zaolzie - "Zaolzianka" 43-470 Istebna 563.	☏ (33) 8556049	100	🏠	ⅲ ⓡ ⚲ 🅿
Karpacz - "Liczyrzepa" ul. Gimnazjalna 9, 58-540 Karpacz.	☏ (75) 7619290 ☏ 7619290	66	🏠	ⅲ 🍴 ⓡ ⚲ 🅿
Kraków - "Oleandry" ul. Oleandry 4, 30-060 Kraków.	☏ (12) 6338822, 6338920 ☏ (12) 6338920	350	🏠	ⅲ 🍴 ⓡ ⚲ ☕

Location/Address	Telephone No. Fax No.	Beds	Opening Dates	Facilities
Łazy Łazy, 32-048 Jerzmanowice.	☎ (12) 3895208	61		
Michałowice - "Złoty Widok" ul.Kolonijna 14, 58-572 Michałowice.	☎ (75) 7553344 🖷 (75) 7553344	46		
Nowy Sącz Al.Batorego 72, 33-300 Nowy Sącz.	☎ (18) 4423897	50		
Pobierowo ul. Mickiewicza 19, 72-404 Pobierowo.	☎ (91) 3864243 🖷 (91) 3864243	60		
Przemków ul. Głogowska 27, 59-325 Przemków.	☎ (76) 8319465	60		
Przemyśl - "Matecznik" ul.Lelewela 6, 37-700 Przemyśl	☎ (16) 6706145	54		

"Travelling is like gambling: it is always connected with winning and losing, and generally where it is least expected we receive more or less what we hoped for."

"Le voyage est pareil au jeu: il est toujours question de gagner et de perdre, et en général l'on reçoit plus ou moins ce que l'on espérait, alors que l'on s'y attend le moins."

„Reisen kommt dem Glücksspiel gleich: es ist immer mit Gewinn und Verlust verbunden, und wir bekommen allgemein dort, wo wir es am wenigsten erwarten, mehr oder weniger das, was wir erhofft hatten."

"El viajar es como un juego de azar: tiene que ver siempre con ganar y perder y, generalmente, en el momento menos pensado recibimos más o menos lo que esperábamos."

Johann Wolfgang Von Goethe

Welcome to the HI world!

HOSTELLING INTERNATIONAL

The HI world offers you

4200 hostels.

Internet booking

Thousands of discounts.

Quality accommodation.

www.iyhf.org

Portugal

PORTUGAL

PORTUGAL

PORTUGAL

**MOVIJOVEM - Agência de Turismo Jovem
Cooperativa de Interesse Público e Resposabilidade Lda,
Av Duque d'Ávila 137, 1069-017 Lisbon, Portugal.**

❶ (351) (21) 359 60 00
❶ (351) (21) 353 59 82 (Board)
(351) (21) 359 60 01 (Reservations)
(351) (21) 359 60 02 (General)
❷ movijovem@movijovem.pt (General)
informacoes@movijovem.pt (Information)
reservas@movijovem.pt (Reservations)

🖳 http://www.cartaojovem.pt
http://www.pousadasdejuventude.pt

Opening Hours: Monday-Friday, 09.00-13.00hrs
14.00-18.00hrs

A copy of the Hostel Directory for this Country can be obtained from:
The National Office

Capital:	Lisboa	**Population:**	10,500,000
Language:	Portuguese	**Size:**	92,082 sq km
Currency:	PTE (Portuguese Escudos)	**Telephone Country Code:**	351

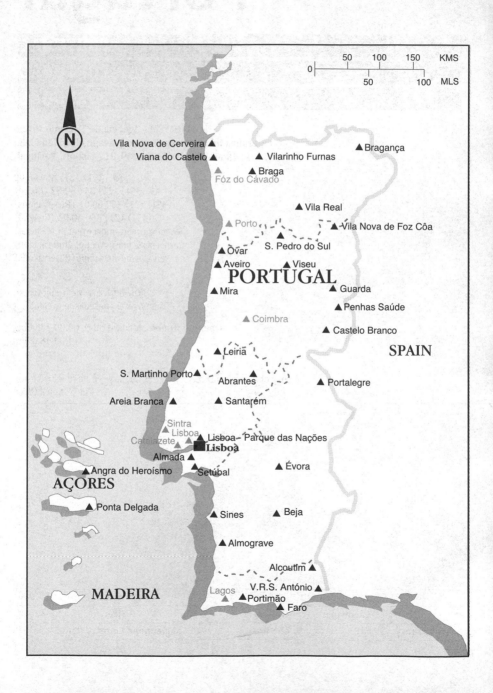

0   50   100   150   KMS

50   100   MLS

N

Vila Nova de Cerveira ▲
Viana do Castelo ▲   ▲ Vilarinho Furnas   ▲ Bragança
▲ ▲ Braga
Fóz do Cávado

▲ Vila Real

▲ Porto   ▲ Vila Nova de Foz Côa
▲ Ovar   S. Pedro do Sul
▲ Aveiro   ▲ Viseu
PORTUGAL
▲ Mira   ▲ Guarda
▲ Penhas Saúde
▲ Coimbra
▲ Castelo Branco
SPAIN
▲ Leiria
S. Martinho Porto ▲
▲ Abrantes ▲   ▲ Portalegre
Areia Branca ▲   ▲ Santarém
Sintra
▲ Lisboa
Carnazete   ▲ Lisboa – Parque das Nações
■ **Lisboa**
Almada ▲
▲ Angra do Heroísmo   Setúbal   ▲ Évora
AÇORES
▲ Ponta Delgada
▲ Sines   ▲ Beja
▲ Almograve
Alcoutim ▲
V.R.S. António ▲
MADEIRA   Lagos
▲ Portimão
▲ Faro

English

Hostels are located in cities, in the countryside, on the coast and on hills/mountains.

Price range

Price range PTE 1,400-2,900. € 6,98-14,47. BB inc 🍴.

Rooms and Reservations

R 🛏 (All Rooms). Reservations via IBN 🖥 National Booking Centre, Hostel or National Office by ☎ ✉ @. Smoking rooms are available.

Guests

Membership Card and Passport/Photo ID are required. ♦♦♦ welcome. Group bookings via IBN 🖥 National Booking Centre, Hostel or National Office by ☎ ✉ @ (Reservation charges may apply).

Open times

Main hostels: open 🛏, ⊙. Reception open: 08:00-24:00hrs. Resident manager. **Other hostels:** open 🛏, 18:00-12:00hrs. Reception open: 08:00-12:00hrs, 18:00-24:00hrs.

Meals

🍽 BLD R For individuals & for ♦♦♦. ☜.

Travelling around

For ease of travel use 🚃 🚌 Self-Drive.

Travel/Activity Packages

Water sports, cycling/mountain biking, walking/trekking and accommodation/transport packages available. Package bookings via National Booking Centre, Hostel or National Office by ☎ ✉.

Passports and Visas

Passport, Photo ID and Visa required.

Health

Medical insurance is recommended. EU Nationals require Form E111 to obtain treatment within EU countries.

Français

Les auberges sont situées dans les villes, à la campagne, sur le littoral et à la montagne.

Tarifs des nuitées

Tarifs des nuitées 1,400-2,900 PTE. € 6,98-14,47. BB inc 🍴.

Chambres et réservations

R 🛏 (Toutes chambres). Réservations via IBN 🖥 le Centre National de Réservation, l'auberge ou le Bureau National par ☎ ✉ @. Des chambres pour fumeurs sont disponibles.

Usagers

La carte d'adhérent ainsi que le passeport/pièce d'identité avec photo sont à présenter. Accueil des ♦♦♦. Réservations pour groupes via IBN 🖥 le Centre National de Réservation, l'auberge ou le Bureau National par ☎ ✉ @ (Des frais de réservation pourront vous être facturés).

Horaires d'ouverture

Grandes auberges: ouvertes 🛏, ⊙. Accueil ouvert entre 8h-24h. Gérant réside sur place. **Autres auberges:** ouvertes 🛏, entre 18h-12h. Accueil ouvert entre 8h-12h, 18h-24h.

Repas

🍽 BLD R Pour individuels & pour ♦♦♦. ☜.

Déplacements

Modes de transport recommandés 🚃 🚌 Voiture.

Forfaits Voyages/Activités

Forfaits sports aquatiques, cyclotourisme/VTT, randonnées pédestres et hébergement/transport disponibles. Réservations des forfaits via le Centre National de Réservation, l'auberge ou le Bureau National par ❶ ❻.

Passeports et visas

Passeport, pièce d'identité avec photo et visa obligatoires.

Santé

Une assurance médicale de voyage est conseillée. Les ressortissants de l'Union Européenne doivent se munir du formulaire E111 pour bénéficier de soins médicaux dans les états de l'UE.

Deutsch

Herbergen befinden sich in Städten, auf dem Land, an der Küste und in Bergen/Gebirgen.

Preisspanne

Preisspanne 1,400-2,900 PTE. € 6,98-14,47. BB^inc 🗊.

Zimmer und Reservierungen

❿ 🖳 (Alle Zimmer). Reservierungen über (IBN) 🖳 Nationales Buchungszentrum, Herberge oder Landesverband per ❶ ❻ ❸. Es gibt Zimmer für Raucher.

Gäste

Mitgliedsausweis und Reisepass/ Personalausweis sind erforderlich. ♦♦♦ willkommen. Gruppenbuchungen über (IBN) 🖳 Nationales Buchungszentrum, Herberge oder Landesverband per ❶ ❻ ❸ (Reservierungskosten könnten anfallen).

Öffnungszeiten

Hauptherbergen: Zugang 🖳, ◷. Rezeption zwischen 08:00-24:00Uhr. Herbergsmanager wohnt im Haus. **Andere Herbergen:** Zugang 🖳, 18:00-12:00Uhr. Rezeption zwischen 08:00-12:00Uhr, 18:00-24:00Uhr.

Mahlzeiten

🍴 BLD ❿ Für Einzelreisende & für ♦♦♦. ♂.

Reisen im Land

Reisen ist einfach mit 🚐 🚌 Selbstfahrer.

Reise-/Aktivitäten-Packages

Wassersport, Fahrrad/Mountainbiking, Wandern/Trekking und Unterkunft/Transport-Packages erhältlich. Package-Buchungen über Nationales Buchungszentrum, Herberge oder Landesverband per ❶ ❻.

Reisepässe und Visa

Reisepass, Personalausweis und Einreisevisum erforderlich.

Gesundheit

Unfall-/Krankenversicherung wird empfohlen. EU Staatsangehörige benötigen Formular E111 für ärztliche Behandlungen innerhalb der EU Länder.

Español

Los albergues están situados en las ciudades, el campo, la costa y la montaña.

Tarifas mínima y máxima

Tarifas mínima y máxima 1,400-2,900 PTE. € 6,98-14,47. BB^inc 🗊.

Habitaciones y Reservas

❿ 🖳 (Todas las habitaciones). Reservas por (IBN) 🖳 o a través de la Central Nacional de Reservas, el albergue o la Asociación Nacional por ❶ ❷ ❸. Los albergues disponen de habitaciones para fumadores.

Huéspedes

Los huéspedes deben presentar su Carnet de Alberguista y su pasaporte o carnet de identidad. Se admiten ♦♦♦. Reservas de grupo por ⟨IBN⟩ ↩ o a través de la Central Nacional de Reservas, el albergue o la Asociación Nacional por ❶ ❷ ❸ (Es posible que se aplique un suplemento en concepto de gastos de reserva).

Horarios y fechas de apertura

Albergues principales - abiertos 🗓, ☺. Horario de recepción: 08:00-24:00h. Gerente residente. **Otros albergues** - abiertos 🗓, 18:00-12:00h. Horario de recepción: 08:00-12:00h, 18:00-24:00h.

Comidas

🍴 BLD ⟨R⟩ Para individuales y para ♦♦♦. ♂.

Desplazamientos

Transportes recomendados: 🚋 🚌 Automóvil.

Viajes Combinados con Actividades

Viajes combinados con deportes náuticos, cicloturismo/bicicleta de montaña, senderismo y alojamiento/transporte. Reserva de viajes combinados a través de la Central Nacional de Reservas, el albergue o la Asociación Nacional por ❶ ❷.

Pasaportes y Visados

Pasaporte o carnet de identidad y visado obligatorios.

Información Sanitaria

Seguro médico recomendado. Los ciudadanos procedentes de países pertenecientes a la UE necesitan el impreso E111 para obtener asistencia médica en dichos países.

Almada

Quinta do Bucelinho-Pragal-Almada, 2800 Almada.
❶ (21) 2943491/ 2943492
❷ (21) 2943497
❸ almada@movijovem.pt

Open Dates: 🗓

Open Hours: ☺

Reservations: ⟨R⟩ ⟨CC⟩

Price Range: PTE 2000-2.500 € 9.98-12.47
⟨BB⟩inc

Beds: 120 - 13x³🛏 22x⁴🛏 1x⁶🛏

Facilities: ♿ ♦♦♦ ♦♦♦ 🍴 ▦ 🛏 📺 ↩3 x
🍳 ▣ ☺ ⬍ Ⓟ Ⓘ ⚡ ⚲

Directions: ⟨2E⟩ from city centre

✈ Portela de Sacavém 20km

⛴ Cacilhas 1km

🚆 Pragal 1km

🚌 53 1km ap Centro Sul 1km

Attractions: ⚲5km 🚶

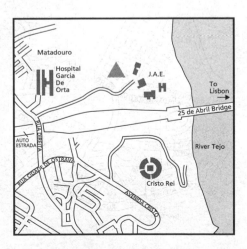

Porto

Rua Paulo da Gama 551,
4169-006 Porto.
- **❶** (22) 6177257
- **❶** (22) 6177247
- **❷** porto@movijovem.pt

Open Dates:	🗓
Open Hours:	🕐
Reservations:	**R** **IBN** **-CC-**
Price Range:	PTE 2000-2.500 € 9.98-12.47 BB inc 💬
Beds:	164 - 24x² 29x⁴
Facilities:	♿ ♦♦♦ ♦♦♦ ℗ ✎ 🍵 ≜ 📺 📟 1 x 🍷 ▣ 8 ▤ 🅿 ℹ ✿
Directions:	7 SE from city centre
✈	SÁ Carneiro 20km
A 🚌	36, 56 20km
🚐	São Bento 8km
🚌	35 100m ap Paulo da Gama 100m
Attractions:	🎭 2km 🚶 ⚓ 500m

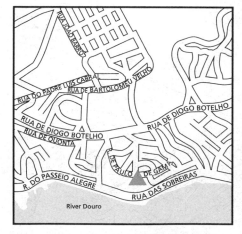

River Douro

Viana Do Castelo

Rua da Argaçosa (Zona da Azenha
D.Prior),
4900-394 Viana do Castelo.
- **❶** (258) 820870
- **❶** (258) 820871
- **❷** vianacastelo@movijovem.pt

Open Dates:	🗓
Open Hours:	🕐
Reservations:	**R**
Price Range:	PTE 2000-2.500 € 9.98-12.47 BB inc 💬
Beds:	82 - 9x² 16x⁴
Facilities:	♿ ♦♦♦ ♦♦♦ ℗ ✎ 🍵 ≜ 📺 📟 1 x 🍷 ▣ 8 ⊜ ▤ 🅿 ℹ ✿ 🔍
Directions:	0.7 W from city centre
✈	Sá Carneiro 60km
⛴	Viana Do Castelo 100m
🚌	100m ap Azenhas Prior
Attractions:	🎭 100m 🚶 ⚲ 100m ⚓ 800m

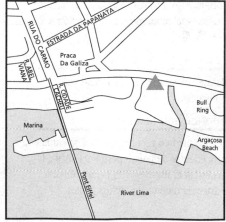

River Lima

Location/Address	Telephone No. Fax No.	Beds	Opening Dates	Facilities
▲ **Abrantes** Av. Eng. Adelino Amaro Da Costa, 2200 Abrantes. e abrantes@movijovem.pt	❶ (241) 379210 ❶ (241) 379211	80	🕭12	iłi 🍴 🆁 1N 🚹 ⋲CC⋺ ☞ 🅿 🔘 🍺 🏍
▲ **Alcoutim** 8970 Alcoutim. e alcoutim@movijovem.pt	❶ (281) 546004 ❶ (281) 546004	70	🕭12	iłi 🍴 🆁 0.5N 🚹 ⋲CC⋺ ☞ 🅿 🔘 🍺
▲ **Almada** **Quinta do Bucelinho-Pragal-Almada,** **2800 Almada.** e almada@movijovem.pt	❶ (21) 2943491/ 2943492 ❶ (21) 2943497	120	🕭12	iłi 🍴 🆁 2E 🚹 ⋲CC⋺ 🅿 🔘 🍺
▲ **Almograve** Almograve - 7630 Odemira. e almograve@movijovem.pt	❶ (283) 640000 ❶ (283) 647035	100	🕭12	iłi 🍴 🆁 01F 🚹 ⋲CC⋺ ☞ 🅿 🔘 🍺
▲ **Angra Do Heroísmo** Negrito, S.Mateus, 9700 Angra Do Heroísmo, Ilha Terceira-Açores. e angraheroismo@movijovem.pt	❶ (295) 642095 ❶ (295) 642095	62	🕭12	iłi 🆁 1SW 🚹 🅿 🏍
△ *Areia Branca* *Praia da Areia Branca, 2530 Lourinhã.* e *areiabranca@movijovem.pt*	❶ *(261) 422127* ❶ *(261) 422127*	*116*	🕭12	iłi 🍴 🆁 01SW ⋲CC⋺ ☞ 🅿
△ *Aveiro* *Rua das Pombas, Apartado 182,* *3810-150 Aveiro.* e *aveiro@movijovem.pt*	❶ *(234) 420536* ❶ *(234) 382395*	*52*	🕭12	🆁 2NW 🚹 ⋲CC⋺ 🅿
▲ **Beja** Rua Prof. Janeiro Acabado, 7800-506 Beja. e beja@movijovem.pt	❶ (284) 325458 ❶ (284) 325468	50	🕭12	iłi 🆁 1NE 🚹 ⋲CC⋺ ☞ 🅿 🔘 🏍
△ *Braga* *Rua de Santa Margarida 6, 4710-306 Braga.* e *braga@movijovem.pt*	❶ *(253) 616163* ❶ *(253) 616163*	*62*	🕭12	iłi 🆁 2NE ☞ 🅿 🍺
▲ **Bragança** - Bragança Forte de S.João (near Câmara Municipal) 5300-262 Bragança. e braganca@movijovem.pt	❶ (273) 304600 ❶ (273) 304601	96	🕭12	iłi 🍴 🆁 1SE 🚹 ⋲CC⋺ ☞ 🅿 🔘 🍺
△ *Castelo Branco* *Rua Dr. Francisco José Palmeiro,* *6000-230 Castelo Branco.* e *castelobranco@movijovem.pt*	❶ *(272) 323838* ❶ *(272) 323838*	*64*	🕭12	iłi 🆁 2E ⋲CC⋺ 🅿
▲ **Coimbra** [IBN] Rua Henriques Seco 14, 3000-145 Coimbra. e coimbra@movijovem.pt	❶ (239) 822955 ❶ (239) 821730	70	🕭12	iłi 🆁 3NW ⋲CC⋺ ☞ 🅿 🍺
▲ **Évora** Rua Miguel Bombarda 40, 7000-919 Évora. e evora@movijovem.pt	❶ (266) 744848 ❶ (266) 744843	90	🕭12	iłi 🍴 🆁 0.1W 🚹 ⋲CC⋺ 🅿 🍺
△ *Faro* *Rua da PSP, 8000-408 Faro.* e *faro@movijovem.pt*	❶ *(289) 826521* ❶ *(289) 826521*	*56*	🕭12	iłi 🆁 1.5SW 🚹 ⋲CC⋺ ☞ 🅿

Location/Address	Telephone No. Fax No.	Beds	Opening Dates	Facilities
▲ **Foz do Cávado** (IBN) Alameda Bom Jesus - Fão, 4740-322 Fão. e fozcavado@movijovem.pt	☏ (253) 981790 ✆ (253) 981790	84	⌷12	⁂ ⌷◯ R 0.1 NE ♿ ⸗CC⸗ ⬚ P ☕
△ *Guarda* *Av. Alexandre Herculano, 6300-659 Guarda.* e *guarda@movijovem.pt*	☏ *(271) 224482* ✆ *(271) 224482*	*56*	⌷12	⁂ R 1 N ♿ ⸗CC⸗ P
▲ **Lagos** (IBN) Rua Lançarote de Freitas 50, 8600-605 Lagos. e lagos@movijovem.pt	☏ (282) 761970 ✆ (282) 769684	62	⌷12	⁂ R 0.5N ♿ ⸗CC⸗ ⬚ ☕
▲ **Leiria** Largo Cândido dos Reis 9, 2400-112 Leiria. e leiria@movijovem.pt	☏ (244) 831868 ✆ (244) 831868	52	⌷12	⁂ R ♿ ⸗CC⸗ ⬚ ☕
▲ **Lisbon** - Parque Das Nações Via De Moscavide, Lote 47101, 1998 Lisboa-Expo. e lisboaparque@movijovem.pt	☏ (21) 8920890 ✆ (21) 8920891	92	⌷12	⌷◯ R 10NE ♿ ⬚ P ⊡ ☕
▲ **Lisbon** (IBN) Pousada de Juventude de Lisboa, Rua Andrade Corvo 46, 1050-009 Lisboa. e lisboa@movijovem.pt	☏ (21) 3532696 ✆ (21) 3537541	168	⌷12	⁂ ⌷◯ R 6N ♿ ⸗CC⸗ ☕
▲ **Lisbon** - Catalazete - Catalazete (IBN) Estrada Marginal (near Inatel), Catalazete, 2780 Oeiras. e catalazete@movijovem.pt	☏ (21) 4430638 ✆ (21) 4419267	94	⌷12	⁂ ⌷◯ R ♿ ⸗CC⸗ ⬚ P ⊡ ☕
Lisboa ☞**Lisbon**				
▲ **Mira** - PJ de Mira Pousada de Juventude de Mira, Parque de Campismo de Jovens, 3070 Praia de Mira. e mira@movijovem.pt	☏ (231) 471199 ✆ (231) 471275	58	⌷12	⁂ R 7E ⸗CC⸗ ⬚ P ☕
△ *Mira* - *Mira Youth Camping Park* *Parque de Campismo de Jovens,* *3070 Praia de Mira.*	☏ *(231) 471275* ✆ *(231) 471275*	*500*	*15.06–15.09*	⌷◯ R 7E ⬚ P ☕ 🏍
Oporto ☞**Porto**				
▲ **Ovar** Av D Manuel I (Est Nac 327) 3880 Ovar. e ovar@movijovem.pt	☏ (256) 591832 ✆ (256) 591832	84	⌷12	⁂ ⌷◯ R 7NW ♿ ⸗CC⸗ P ☕ 🏍
▲ **Penhas da Saúde** Serra da Estrela-Penhas da Sáude, 6200 Covilhã. e penhas@movijovem.pt	☏ (275) 335375 ✆ (275) 335109	108	⌷12	⁂ ⌷◯ R ♿ ⸗CC⸗ ⬚ P ☕
▲ **Ponta Delgada** Rua S.Francisco Xavier, 9500-243 Ponta Delgada, Ilha S.Miguel-Açores. e pontadelgada@movijovem.pt	☏ (296) 629431 ✆ (296) 629672	92	⌷12	⁂ R 0.2E P

Location/Address	Telephone No. / Fax No.	Beds	Opening Dates	Facilities
△ **Portalegre** *Estrada do Bonfim, Apartado 2,* *7300 Portalegre.* e portalegre@movijovem.pt	☎ (245) 330971 🖷 (245) 202665	52	🛏12	ⅢⅢ R 1.5E P
△ **Portimão** *Lugar do Coca Maravilhas,* *8500-320 Portimão.* e portimao@movijovem.pt	☎ (282) 491804 🖷 (282) 491804	180	🛏12	ⅢⅢ 🍴 R 4N CC ☞ P ☕
▲ **Porto** (IBN) **Rua Paulo da Gama 551, 4169-006 Porto.** e porto@movijovem.pt	☎ (22) 6177257 🖷 (22) 6177247	164	🛏12	ⅢⅢ 🍴 R 7SE ♿ CC ☞ P ☕
△ **Santarém** *Av. Grupo Forcados Amadores de Santarém,* *1, 2000-181 Santarém.* e santarem@movijovem.pt	☎ (243) 391914 🖷 (243) 391914	36	🛏12	ⅢⅢ R 1N ♿ CC P
△ **Setúbal** *Largo José Afonso, 2900-429 Setúbal.* e setubal@movijovem.pt	☎ (265) 534431 🖷 (265) 532965	64	🛏12	ⅢⅢ R 1E CC P
△ **São Martinho-Alfeizerão** *Estrada Nacional 8, 2460 Alfeizerão.* e smartinho@movijovem.pt	☎ (262) 999506 🖷 (262) 999506	60	🛏12	ⅢⅢ 🍴 R 2NE CC ☞ P ☕
▲ **Sines** Estrada da Floresta - Edificio E, 7520-137 Sines. e sines@movijovem.pt	☎ (269) 635361 🖷 (269) 635361	104	🛏12	ⅢⅢ 🍴 R 1NE ♿ CC P ☕
▲ **Sintra** (IBN) Stª Eufémia, S. Pedro de Sintra, 2710 Sintra. e sintra@movijovem.pt	☎ (21) 9241210 🖷 (21) 9233176	58	🛏12	ⅢⅢ 🍴 R 4S ♿ CC P
▲ **S.Pedro Do Sul** Termas De S.Pedro Do Sul, 3660 S.Pedro Do Sul. e spedrosul@movijovem.pt	☎ (232) 724543/4 🖷 (232) 724541	134	🛏12	ⅢⅢ 🍴 R 0.2W ♿ CC P ☕
▲ **Viana Do Castelo** **Rua da Argaçosa (Zona da Azenha** **D.Prior), 4900-394 Viana do Castelo.** e vianacastelo@movijovem.pt	☎ (258) 820870 🖷 (258) 820871	82	🛏12	ⅢⅢ 🍴 R 0.7W ♿ ☞ P ⬜ ☕
△ **Vila Nova de Cerveira** *Largo 16 de Fevereiro 21,* *4920 Vila Nova de Cerveira.* e cerveira@movijovem.pt	☎ (251) 796113 🖷 (251) 796113	56	🛏12	ⅢⅢ R 0.3NE CC ☞ P
▲ **Vila Nova De Foz Côa** Caminho Vicinal, Currauteles, No 5, 5150 Vila Nova De Foz Côa. e fozcoa@movijovem.pt	☎ (279) 768190 🖷 (279) 768191	84	🛏12	ⅢⅢ 🍴 R ♿ CC ☞ P ⬜ ☕
△ **Vila Real** *Rua Dr Manuel Cardona, 5000-558 Vila Real.* e vilareal@movijovem.pt	☎ (259) 373193 🖷 (259) 373193	64	🛏12	ⅢⅢ R 1.5W ♿ CC P ☕

Location/Address	Telephone No. Fax No.	Beds	Opening Dates	Facilities
△ *Viseu* *Portal do Fontelo, Carreira dos Carvalhos,* *3500 Viseu.* ℯ *viseu@movijovem.pt*	☏ *(232) 420620* ✆ *(232) 435445*	*70*	🗓12	♟ **R** 2NW ♿ ECC⊐ P
△ *Vila Real de Santo António* *Rua Dr. Sousa Martins, 40,* *8900 Vila Real de Santo António.* ℯ *vrsantonio@movijovem.pt*	☏ *(281) 544565* ✆ *(281) 544565*	*56*	🗓12	♟ **R** ECC⊐ 🛏 P ☕ 🛵
△ *Vilarinho das Furnas* *Campo do Gerês, 4840-030 Campo do Gerês.* ℯ *vilarinho@movijovem.pt*	☏ *(253) 351339* ✆ *(253) 352864*	*173*	🗓12	♟ 🍽 **R** ECC⊐ P ☕

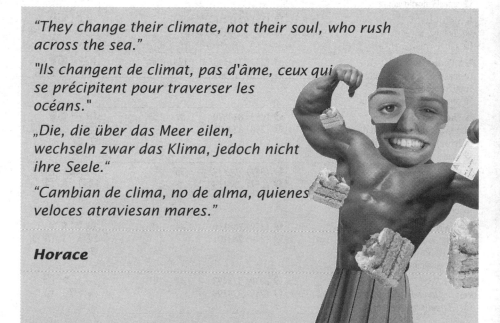

"They change their climate, not their soul, who rush
across the sea."

"Ils changent de climat, pas d'âme, ceux qui
se précipitent pour traverser les
océans."

„Die, die über das Meer eilen,
wechseln zwar das Klima, jedoch nicht
ihre Seele."

"Cambian de clima, no de alma, quienes
veloces atraviesan mares."

Horace

Scotland

ECOSSE

SCHOTTLAND

ESCOCIA

Scottish Youth Hostels Association,
7 Glebe Cresent, Stirling,
FK8 2JA, Scotland.

Central Reservation Service

☎ (44) (8701) 553255
🖷 (44) (1786) 891350
🄴 reservations@syha.org.uk
groups@syha.org.uk
🖳 www.syha.org.uk
www.rentahostel.com

Office Hours: CRS Hours, 08.00-20.00hrs

The National Office

☎ (44) (1786) 891400
🖷 (44) (1786) 891333
🄴 info@syha.org.uk
🖳 www.syha.org.uk

Office Hours: Monday-Friday, 08.45-17.00hrs

Travel Section: c/o Scottish Youth Hostels Association
7 Glebe Cresent, Stirling,
FK8 2JA, Scotland.

☎ (44) (8701) 553255

A copy of the Hostel Directory for this Country can be obtained from:
The National Office

Capital:	Edinburgh	Population:	5,112,100
Language:	English	Size:	78,781 sq km
Currency:	£ (Sterling)	Telephone Country Code:	44

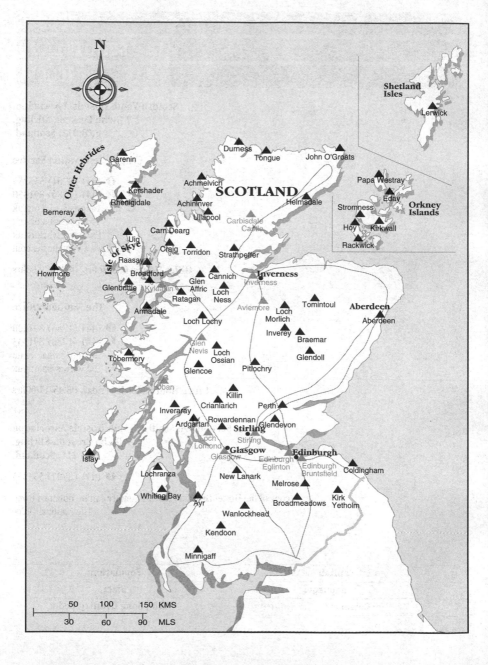

Scotland

SCOTLAND

Shetland Isles
Lerwick

Garenin
Durness
Tongue
John O'Groats

Outer Hebrides

Achmelvich
Kershader
Achininver
Helmsdale

Papa Westray
Eday
Stromness
Orkney Islands

Rhenigidale
Berneray
Ullapool
Carbisdale Castle

Hoy   Kirkwall
Rackwick

Carn Dearg
Uig
Craig   Torridon   Strathpeffer

Isle of Skye
Raasay
Broadford
Cannich   **Inverness**
Inverness

Howmore
Glenbrittle   Kyleakin
Glen Affric
Loch Ness
Ratagan

Aviemore
Loch Morlich
Tomintoul
Aberdeen
Aberdeen

Armadale
Loch Lochy
Inverey
Braemar

Glen Nevis
Loch Ossian
Glendoll

Tobermory
Glencoe
Pitlochry

Oban

Killin
Inveraray
Crianlarich
Perth

Ardgartan
Rowardennan
Glendevon

Loch Lomond
Stirling
Stirling

Islay
Glasgow
•**Glasgow**
Edinburgh   **Edinburgh**
Eglinton   Edinburgh Bruntsfield
Coldingham

Lochranza
New Lanark
Melrose

Whiting Bay
Ayr
Broadmeadows
Kirk Yetholm

Wanlockhead

Kendoon

Minnigaff

50   100   150 KMS
30   60   90   MLS

English

Check for specific information at National Office as hostels vary greatly in terms of location and/or facilities. Hostels are located in cities, in the countryside, on the coast and on hills/mountains.

Price range

Price range £6.00-13.75 (Edinburgh Central YH in August - £16.50). 🔲.

Rooms and Reservations

R 🔲 (All Rooms). Reservations via **IBN** 🔲 National Booking Centre or National Office by **t f e**. Smoking is limited - please check.

Guests

Membership Card and Passport/Photo ID are required. Age limits may apply for children - check with hostel. ♦♦♦ welcome. Group bookings via 🔲 National Booking Centre or National Office by **f e**.

Open times

Main hostels: open 🔲, 07:00-01:45hrs. Reception open: 14:00-01:45hrs. Resident manager. **Other hostels:** open 17:00-23:45hrs. Reception open: 17:00hrs.

Meals

♂.

Discounts

HI Member Discounts available - see discounts section and www.iyhf.org.

Travelling around

For ease of travel use 🚃 ⛴ 🚌 Self-Drive. Drive on the left.

Travel/Activity Packages

Winter sports, cycling/mountain biking and walking/trekking packages available. Package bookings via 🔲 National Booking Centre or National Office by **t f e**.

Passports and Visas

Passport required.

Health

EU Nationals require Form E111 to obtain treatment within EU countries.

Français

Pour tout renseignement spécifique, adressez-vous au bureau national de l'association car la situation géographique des auberges et les prestations qu'elles proposent varient énormément. Les auberges sont situées dans les villes, à la campagne, sur le littoral et à la montagne.

Tarifs des nuitées

Tarifs des nuitées 6.00-13.75£ (tarif de l'AJ Edinburgh Central en août: 16.50£). 🔲.

Chambres et réservations

R 🔲 (Toutes chambres). Réservations via **IBN** 🔲 le Centre National de Réservation ou le Bureau National par **t f e**. Il est permis de fumer dans certaines chambres - veuillez vérifier.

Usagers

La carte d'adhérent ainsi que le passeport/pièce d'identité avec photo sont à présenter. Il est possible que des limites d'âge soient en vigueur pour les enfants - vérifiez auprès de l'auberge. Accueil des ♦♦♦. Réservations pour groupes via 🔲 le Centre National de Réservation ou le Bureau National par **f e**.

Horaires d'ouverture

Grandes auberges: ouvertes , entre 7h-1h45. Accueil ouvert entre 14h-1h45. Gérant réside sur place. **Autres auberges:** ouvertes entre 17h-23h45. Accueil ouvert à partir de 17h.

Repas

☞.

Remises

Remises pour les adhérents HI - voir la section "Remises" et notre site: www.iyhf.org.

Déplacements

Modes de transport recommandés 🚂 ⛴ 🚌 Voiture. Conduite à gauche.

Forfaits Voyages/Activités

Forfaits sports d'hiver, cyclotourisme/VTT, randonnées pédestres disponibles. Réservations des forfaits via 💻 le Centre National de Réservation ou le Bureau National par ❶ ❻ ℮.

Passeports et visas

Passeport obligatoire.

Santé

Les ressortissants de l'Union Européenne doivent se munir du formulaire E111 pour bénéficier de soins médicaux dans les états de l'UE.

Deutsch

Spezielle Informationen bei der Nationalen Geschäftsstelle einholen, da die Herbergen hinsichlich Ort und/oder Einrichtungen sehr stark variieren. Herbergen befinden sich in Städten, auf dem Land, an der Küste und in Bergen/Gebirgen.

Preisspanne

Preisspanne 6.00-13.75 £ (Jugendherberge Edinburgh Central im August - 16.50 £). 🛏.

Zimmer und Reservierungen

R 🛏 (Alle Zimmer). Reservierungen über **IBN** 💻 Nationales Buchungszentrum oder Landesverband per ❶ ❻ ℮. Rauchen ist begrenzt - bitte checken.

Gäste

Mitgliedsausweis und Reisepass/ Personalausweis sind erforderlich. Altersbegrenzungen für Kinder möglich - in der Herberge nachfragen. ♔♔♔ willkommen. Gruppenbuchungen über 💻 Nationales Buchungszentrum oder Landesverband per ❻ ℮.

Öffnungszeiten

Hauptherbergen: Zugang 🛏, 07:00-01:45Uhr. Rezeption zwischen 14:00-01:45Uhr. Herbergsmanager wohnt im Haus. **Andere Herbergen:** Zugang zwischen 17:00-23:45Uhr. Rezeption ab 17:00Uhr geöffnet.

Mahlzeiten

☞.

Ermäßigungen

HI-Mitgliedsrabatt ist erhältlich – siehe Teil für Rabatte und Ermäßigungen und www.iyhf.org.

Reisen im Land

Reisen ist einfach mit 🚂 ⛴ 🚌 Selbstfahrer. Links fahren.

Reise-/Aktivitäten-Packages

Wintersport, Fahrrad/Mountainbiking und wandern/trekking-Packages erhältlich. Package-Buchungen über 💻 Nationales Buchungszentrum oder Landesverband per ❶ ❻ ℮.

Reisepässe und Visa

Reisepass erforderlich.

Gesundheit

EU Staatsangehörige benötigen Formular E111
für ärztliche Behandlungen innerhalb der EU
Länder.

Español

Infórmese en la Asociacion nacional ya que los
albergues varían mucho en cuanto a ubicación
y/o prestaciones. Los albergues están situados
en las ciudades, el campo, la costa y la
montaña.

Tarifas mínima y máxima

Tarifas mínima y máxima 6.00-13.75£ (tarifa
del albergue Edinburgh Central en agosto:
16.50£). ⟱.

Habitaciones y Reservas

R 🔲 (Todas las habitaciones). Reservas
por ⟨IBN⟩ ⟱ o a través de la Central Nacional
de Reservas o la Asociación Nacional por **t**
f **e**. Está permitido fumar sólo en algunas
salas/habitaciones - infórmese.

Huéspedes

Los huéspedes deben presentar su Carnet de
Alberguista y su pasaporte o carnet de
identidad. Es posible que exista un límite de
edad para los niños - consulte con el albergue.
Se admiten ⁂. Reservas de grupo por ⟱ o a
través de la Central Nacional de Reservas o de la
Asociación Nacional por **f** **e**.

Horarios y fechas de apertura

Albergues principales - abiertos 🔲,
07:00-01:45h. Horario de recepción:
14:00-01:45h. Gerente residente. **Otros**

albergues - abiertos: 17:00-23:45h.
Recepción abierta a partir de las 17:00h.

Comidas

✆.

Descuentos

Se conceden descuentos a los miembros de
Hostelling International – véase la sección
sobre descuentos y nuestra página Internet en
www.iyhf.org.

Desplazamientos

Transportes recomendados: 🚐 ⛴ 🚌
Automóvil. Se circula por la izquierda.

Viajes Combinados con Actividades

Viajes combinados con deportes de invierno,
cicloturismo/bicicleta de montaña y
senderismo. Reserva de viajes combinados por
⟱ o a través de la Central Nacional de
Reservas o la Asociación Nacional por **t** **f**
e.

Pasaportes y Visados

Pasaporte obligatorio.

Información Sanitaria

Los ciudadanos procedentes de países
pertenecientes a la UE necesitan el impreso
E111 para obtener asistencia médica en dichos
países.

Aberdeen -
The King George VI Memorial Hostel

**8 Queen's Rd,
Aberdeen AB15 4ZT.**
☎ **(1224) 646988**

Open Dates:	🗓
Open Hours:	14.00-02.00hrs
Reservations:	R CC
Price Range:	£10.75-13.25 BB inc 🛏
Beds:	116 - 2x² 13x⁴ 1x⁵ 4x⁶ 3x⁶
Facilities:	⋔⋔⋔ 14x ⋔⋔⋔ ☞ 🍴 TV 🔒 📷 8 P ℹ ⏳ ♻ 🏕
Directions:	2W from city centre
✈	Aberdeen 10km
A🚌	Outside hostel
⛴	Aberdeen 2km
🚂	Aberdeen 2km
🚌	14, 15 2km ap Outside hostel
Attractions:	🔍 ≋ 1000m ⛹ ∪2km ✎1km ⚓1km

Aviemore

**25 Grampian Rd,
Aviemore,
Inverness-shire,
PH22 1PR.**
☎ **(1479) 810345**

Open Dates:	🗓
Open Hours:	14.00-02.00hrs
Reservations:	R IBN CC
Price Range:	£10.75-13.25 BB inc 🛏
Beds:	114 - 2x³ 13x⁴ 7x⁶ 2x⁶
Facilities:	⋔⋔⋔ 24x ⋔⋔⋔ ☞ 🍴 TV 🔒 📷 8 P ℹ ⏳ ♻ 🏕
Directions:	
✈	Inverness 70km
🚂	Aviemore 400m
🚌	Aviemore 400m ap Train Station
Attractions:	🐾 ⛰ ≋ 1300m ⛹ ✳ ∪ ✎800m ⚓400m

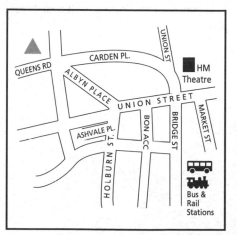

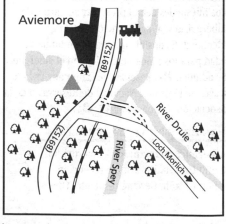

Ayr

5 Craigweil Rd,
Ayr KA7 2XJ.
☎ (1292) 262322

Open Dates:	30.03-28.10
Open Hours:	17.00-23.45hrs
Reservations:	**R** **CC**
Price Range:	£8.00-9.25 🗒
Beds:	60 - 2x⁴🚂 2x⁶🚂 5x⁶🚂
Facilities:	🚻 2x 🚻 🍽 (BD) ⛄ 🛋 📺 🔘
	📷 🔠 🅿 ℹ 🧺 ♻ 🏠 🎣

Directions:

✈	Prestwick International 15km
A🚌	Ayr Bus Station 1.5km
⛴	Ardrossan 28.5km; Stranraer 80km
🚂	Ayr 1.5km
Attractions:	🔍 ∪6.5km ⚲1.5km ⚓1.5km

Carbisdale Castle

Carbisdale,
Culrain,
Ardgay,
Ross-shire IV24 3DP.
☎ (1549) 421232

Open Dates:	02.03-28.10
Open Hours:	14.00-23.45hrs
Reservations:	**IBN** **CC**
Price Range:	£11.25-13.75 **BB**ⁱⁿᶜ 🗒
Beds:	200 - 1x⁴🚂 2x⁵🚂 5x⁶🚂 14x⁶🚂
Facilities:	🚻 3x 🚻 🍽 (BD) ⛄ 🛋 📺
	1 x🍴 🔘 📷 🏛 🔠 🅿 ℹ ♻ 🔍
	🏠 🎣

Directions:

✈	Inverness 90km
🚂	Culrain 500m
🚌	Ardgay 7km ap YH
Attractions:	⛳ ⛺ 🚶 ∪15km ⚲15km ⚓15km

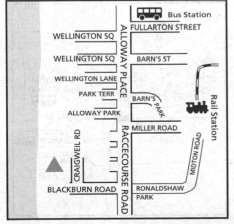

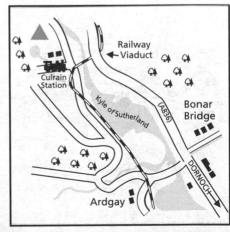

Edinburgh - Eglinton

18 Eglinton Crescent,
Edinburgh EH12 5DD.
☎ (131) 3371120

Open Dates:	🗓️
Open Hours:	14.00-02.00hrs
Reservations:	**R** **IBN** **CC**
Price Range:	£11.25-13.75 BB inc 🍽️
Beds:	160 - 2x² 9x⁴ 10x⁶ 7x⁶
Facilities:	🚻 3x 🚻 🍽️ (BD) 👕 🏘️ 📺 1 x 🍷 ▣ 🖼️ 🔒 ℹ️ 🎱
Directions:	2W from city centre
✈	Edinburgh International 11km
A 🚌	To Haymarket 500m
⛴️	Newcastle 400km
🚂	Haymarket 500m
🚌	3, 4, 12, 13, 22, 26, 28, Palmerston 400m ap Haymarket; Palmerston Place

Glasgow

7/8 Park Terrace,
Glasgow G3 6BY.
☎ (141) 3323004

Open Dates:	🗓️
Open Hours:	14.00-02.00hrs
Reservations:	**R** **IBN** **CC**
Price Range:	£11.25-13.75 BB inc 🍽️
Beds:	138 - 1x² 12x⁴ 4x⁵ 10x⁶ 3x⁶
Facilities:	🚻 12x 🚻 🍽️ (BD) 👕 🏘️ 📺 ▣1 x 🍷 ▣ 🖼️ ♿ 🔒 💲 🅿️ ℹ️ 🎱 ⚫ 🏠
Directions:	2W from city centre
✈	Glasgow International 25km
A 🚌	Buchanan Street 2km
🚂	Central 2km
🚌	11, 59 1km ap Woodlands Rd
U	Kelvinbridge 2km

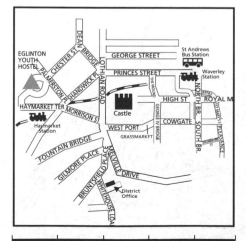

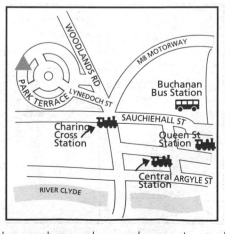

Inverness -
Millburn

Victoria Dr,
Inverness IV2 3QB.
☎ **(1463) 231771**

Open Dates:	🗓
Open Hours:	14.00-02.00hrs
Reservations:	Ⓡ IBN CC
Price Range:	£11.25-13.75 BB inc 🍴
Beds:	166 - 4x² 4x³ 3x⁴ 24x⁶
Facilities:	♦♦♦ 10x ♦♦ ⑩ (BD) ☞ 🛏 📺 1 x 🍷 ⑩ 📷 ⑧ 🅿 ⓘ 🐾 ❀ 🏠
Directions:	1S from city centre
✈	Inverness 8km
🚂	Inverness 1km
🚌	Inverness 1km ap Bus Station
Attractions:	⛵ ⚲3km 🚣3km

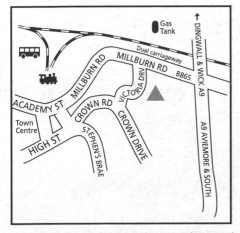

Loch Lomond -
Loch Lomond Arden

Alexandria,
Dumbartonshire G83 8RB.
☎ **(1389) 850226**

Open Dates:	🗓
Open Hours:	14.00-02.00hrs
Reservations:	Ⓡ IBN CC
Price Range:	£10.75-13.25 BB inc 🍴
Beds:	160 - 2x² 3x⁴ 1x⁵ 6x⁶ 10x⁶
Facilities:	♦♦♦ 4x ♦♦ ⑩ (BD) ☞ 🛏 📺 2 x 🍷 ⑩ 📷 ♿ ⑧ 🅿 ⓘ ❀ 🔍 🏠 🏕
Directions:	
✈	Glasgow 24km
🚂	Balloch 3.2km
🚌	ap At driveway
Attractions:	⛵ ⛰ 🚶 ∪ 🚣3km

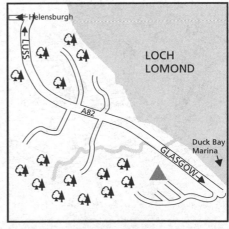

Melrose -
Priorwood

Melrose,
Roxburghshire TD6 9EF.
☎ (1896) 822521

Open Dates:	🗓12
Open Hours:	14.00-23.45hrs
Reservations:	CC
Price Range:	£10.00-11.25 BB inc 🍴
Beds:	86 - 9x⁴🛏 3x⁶🛏 3x⁶⁺🛏
Facilities:	👪 9x 👪 🍴 (BD) ✑ 🛋 📺 ▢
	🖼 8 P ℹ 🧺 ❄ 🏠

Directions:

✈	Edinburgh 75km
⛴	Hull 320km
🚂	Edinburgh 75km

Attractions: ⚘ ▲ 🚶 ∪8km ⚲1km ⚓6km

New Lanark -
Wee Row

Rosedale St,
New Lanark ML11 9DJ.
☎ (1555) 666710

Open Dates:	02.03-28.10
Open Hours:	17.00-23.45hrs
Reservations:	R CC
Price Range:	£10.00-11.25 BB inc 🍴
Beds:	66 - 2x²🛏 14x⁴🛏 2x⁵🛏
Facilities:	👪 16x 👪 🍴 (BD) ✑ 🛋 📺
	🍴1 x🍴 ▢ 🖼 🏛 8 P ℹ 🧺
	🏠 🏤

Directions:

✈	Glasgow 59km; Edinburgh 54km
🚂	Lanark 2.5km
🚌	Local Bus 100m

Attractions: ⚘ 🚶 ∪ ⚓

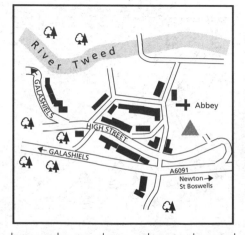

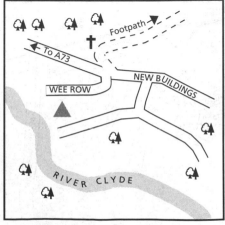

Oban - Esplanade

Oban,
Argyll PA34 5AF.
☎ (1631) 562025

Open Dates:	📅
Open Hours:	17.00-02.00hrs
Reservations:	Ⓡ ⒾⒷⓃ ⒸⒸ
Price Range:	£10.75-14.25 BBinc 🍽
Beds:	154 - 11x🛏 6x🛏 6x🛏
Facilities:	👪 4x 👪 ☂ 🏠 📺 ⊙ 🧺 🔢
	🅿 ⓘ 🚰 🏡

Directions:

✈	Glasgow 150km
⛴	Oban 1.5km
🚂	Oban 1.5km
🚌	Oban 1.5km

Attractions: 🏌 ⛰ 📷 🏊1.5km

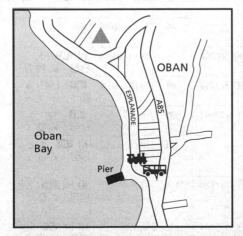

Stirling - St John St

Stirling FK8 1EA.
☎ (1786) 473442

Open Dates:	📅
Open Hours:	14.00-02.00hrs
Reservations:	Ⓡ ⒾⒷⓃ ⒸⒸ
Price Range:	£11.25-13.75 BBinc 🍽
Beds:	126 - 7x²🛏 9x⁴🛏 12x⁵🛏 3x⁶🛏
Facilities:	♿ 👪 24x 👪 🍽 (BD) ☂ 🛏
	📺 1 x🍴 ⊙ 🧺 ⊞ 🔢 🅿 ⓘ 🚰
	🌸 🏡 🎋

Directions:

✈	Glasgow 50km; Edinburgh 50km
🚂	Stirling 1km
🚌	Stirling 1km

Attractions: 🏌 ⛰ 🏃 ⌒ ⚲ 🏊

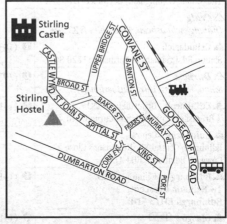

Location/Address	Telephone No. Fax No.	Beds	Opening Dates	Facilities
▲ **Aberdeen** - The King George VI Memorial Hostel **8 Queen's Rd, Aberdeen AB15 4ZT.**	☎ (1224) 646988	116	🛏️	♂♀ R 2W CC ☞ P 🔒
△ *Achininver* *Achiltibuie, Ullapool, Ross-shire IV26 2YL.*	☎ *(1854) 622254*	*20*	*11.05–30.09*	CC ☞
△ *Achmelvich* *Recharn, Lairg, Sutherland IV27 4JB.*	☎ *(1571) 844480*	*36*	*30.03–30.09*	♂♀ R CC ☞ P
▲ **Armadale** Ardvasar, Sleat, Isle of Skye IV45 8RS.	☎ (1471) 844260	42	30.03–30.09	R CC ☞ P
▲ **Aviemore** (IBN) **25 Grampian Rd, Aviemore, Inverness-shire, PH22 1PR.**	☎ (1479) 810345	114	🛏️	R CC ☞ P 🔒
▲ **Ayr** **5 Craigweil Rd, Ayr KA7 2XJ.**	☎ (1292) 262322	60	30.03–28.10	♂♀ 🍽️ R CC ☞ P 🔒
▲ **Braemar** Corrie Feragie, Glenshee Rd, Braemar, Aberdeenshire AB35 5YQ.	☎ (1339) 741659	59	21.12.00–28.10.01	CC ☞ P 🔒
▲ **Broadford** Isle of Skye IV49 9AA.	☎ (1471) 822442	66	02.03–28.10	♂♀ R CC ☞ P 🔒
△ *Broadmeadows* *Old Broadmeadows, Yarrowford, Selkirk TD7 5LZ.*	☎ *(1750) 76262*	*28*	*30.03–30.09*	CC ☞ P
▲ **Cannich** Beauly, Inverness-shire IV4 7LT.	☎ (1456) 415244	54	30.03–28.10	♂♀ ♿ CC ☞ P
▲ **Carbisdale Castle** (IBN) **Carbisdale, Culrain, Ardgay, Ross-shire IV24 3DP.**	☎ (1549) 421232	200	02.03–28.10	♂♀ 🍽️ CC ☞ P 🔒
▲ **Carn Dearg** Gairloch, Ross-shire IV21 2DJ.	☎ (1445) 712219	44	11.05–30.09	R CC ☞ P
▲ **Coldingham** The Mount, Coldingham, Berwicks TD14 5PA.	☎ (1890) 771298	46	30.03–30.09	♂♀ CC ☞ P
△ *Craig* *Diabaig, Achnasheen, Ross-shire IV22 2HE.*		*16*	*11.05–30.09*	☞
▲ **Crianlarich** Station Rd, Crianlarich, Perthshire FK20 8QN.	☎ (1838) 300260	75	28.01–03.01	♂♀ R ♿ CC ☞ P 🔒
△ *Durness* *Smoo, Durness, Lairg, Sutherland IV27 4QA.*	☎ *(1971) 511244*	*40*	*30.03–30.09*	R CC ☞ P
▲ **Edinburgh** - Bruntsfield (IBN) 7 Bruntsfield Crescent, Edinburgh EH10 4EZ.	☎ (131) 4472994	130	🛏️	R 4W CC ☞ 🔒
▲ **Edinburgh** - Central Edinburgh Central YH, Robertsons Close, Cowgate, Edinburgh EH1 1LY.		121	30.06–27.08	♂♀ R 0.1W CC ☞ 🔒
▲ **Edinburgh** - Eglinton (IBN) **18 Eglinton Crescent, Edinburgh EH12 5DD.**	☎ (131) 3371120	160	🛏️	♂♀ 🍽️ R 2W CC ☞ 🔒
▲ **Glasgow** (IBN) **7/8 Park Terrace, Glasgow G3 6BY.**	☎ (141) 3323004	138	🛏️	♂♀ 🍽️ R 2W CC ☞ P 🔒

Location/Address	Telephone No. Fax No.	Beds	Opening Dates	Facilities
△ *Glen Affric* *Allt Beithe, Glen Affric, Cannich, by Beauly,* *Inverness-shire IV47 7ND.*		26	30.03–28.10	**R** ♂
▲ **Glenbrittle** Isle of Skye IV47 8TA.	✆ (1478) 640278	39	30.03–30.09	⌐CC⌐ ♂ **P**
▲ **Glencoe** Ballachulish, Argyll PA39 4HX.	✆ (1855) 811219	60	🔲	♥♥ **R** ⌐CC⌐ ♂ **P** 🔲
△ *Glendevon* *Dollar, Clackmannanshire FK14 7JY.*	✆ *(1259) 781206*	36	30.03–30.09	⌐CC⌐ ♂
▲ **Glendoll** Clova, Kirriemuir, Angus DD8 4RD.	✆ (1575) 550236	45	30.03–30.09	♥♥ ⌐CC⌐ ♂ **P**
▲ **Glen Nevis** [IBN] Fort William, Inverness-shire PH33 6ST.	✆ (1397) 702336	109	🔲	♥♥ **R** ⌐CC⌐ ♂ **P** 🔲
△ *Helmsdale* *Sutherland KW8 6JR.*	✆ *(1431) 821577*	38	*11.05–30.09*	♂
▲ **Inveraray** Argyllshire PA32 8XD.	✆ (1499) 302454	38	30.03–30.09	♥♥ ⌐CC⌐ ♂ **P**
△ *Inverey* *by Braemar, Aberdeenshire AB35 5YB.*	✆ *(1339) 741969*	17	*11.05–30.09*	**R** ♂ **P**
▲ **Inverness** - Millburn [IBN] **Victoria Dr, Inverness IV2 3QB.**	✆ (1463) 231771	166	🔲	♥♥ ¶◯¶ **R** 1S ⌐CC⌐ ♂ **P** 🔲
▲ **Islay** Port Charlotte, Isle of Islay PA48 7TX.	✆ (1496) 850385	42	30.03–30.09	♥♥ **R** ♂ **P** 🔲
▲ **John o' Groats** Canisbay, Wick, Caithness KW1 4YH.	✆ (1955) 611424	40	30.03–30.09	⌐CC⌐ ♂ **P**
△ *Kendoon* *Dalry, Castle Douglas,* *Kircudbrightshire DG7 3UD.*	✆ *(1644) 460680*	36	*30.03–30.09*	♂
▲ **Killin** Killin, Perthshire FK21 8TN.	✆ (1567) 820546	42	02.03–28.10	⌐CC⌐ ♂ **P**
▲ **Kirkwall** Old Scapa Rd, Kirkwall, Orkney KW15 1BB.	✆ (1856) 872243	90	30.03–30.09	♥♥ **R** ♿ ⌐CC⌐ ♂ **P** 🔲
▲ **Kirk Yetholm** Kirk Yetholm, Kelso, Roxburghshire TD5 8PG.	✆ (1573) 420631	27	30.03–30.09	♥♥ **R** ⌐CC⌐ ♂ **P**
▲ **Kyleakin** [IBN] Kyleakin, Isle of Skye IV41 8PL.	✆ (1599) 534585	125	🔲	♥♥ ¶◯¶ **R** ⌐CC⌐ ♂ **P** 🔲
▲ **Lerwick** Islesburgh House, King Harald St, Lerwick, Shetland ZE1 0EQ.	✆ (1595) 692114	64	30.03–30.09	♥♥ **R** ♿ ♂ **P** 🔲
▲ **Loch Lochy** South Laggan, Loch Lochy, Spean Bridge, Inverness-shire PH34 4EA.	✆ (1809) 501239	60	30.03–28.10	⌐CC⌐ ♂ **P**
▲ **Loch Long (Ardgartan)** Arrochar, Dumbartonshire G83 7AR.	✆ (1301) 702362	60	30.03–25.11	♥♥ ¶◯¶ **R** ⌐CC⌐ ♂ **P** 🔲

Location/Address	Telephone No. Fax No.	Beds	Opening Dates	Facilities
▲ **Loch Lomond** - Loch Lomond Arden (IBN) **Alexandria, Dumbartonshire G83 8RB.**	☎ (1389) 850226	160	🗓	††† ⦿ R CC ♂ P 🔲
▲ **Loch Morlich** Glenmore, Aviemore, Inverness-shire PH22 1QY.	☎ (1479) 861238	82	🗓	††† ⦿ R CC ♂ P 🔲
▲ **Loch Ness** Glenmoriston, Inverness-shire IV3 6YD.	☎ (1320) 351274	54	30.03–28.10	††† CC ♂ P
△ *Loch Ossian* *Corrour, Inverness-shire PH30 4AA.*	☎ *(1397) 732207*	*20*	*30.03–28.10*	CC ♂
▲ **Lochranza** Lochranza, Isle of Arran KA27 8HL.	☎ (1770) 830631	68	02.03–28.10	††† R CC ♂ P 🔲
▲ **Melrose** - Priorwood **Melrose, Roxburghshire TD6 9EF.**	☎ (1896) 822521	86	🗓	††† ⦿ CC ♂ P 🔲
▲ **Minnigaff** Newton Stewart, Wigtownshire DG8 6PL.	☎ (1671) 402211	36	30.03–30.09	CC ♂ P
▲ **New Lanark** - Wee Row **Rosedale St, New Lanark ML11 9DJ.**	☎ (1555) 666710	66	02.03–28.10	††† ⦿ R CC ♂ P 🔲
▲ **Oban** - Esplanade (IBN) **Oban, Argyll PA34 5AF.**	☎ (1631) 562025	154	🗓	††† R CC ♂ P 🔲
▲ **Perth** 107 Glasgow Rd, Perth PH2 0NS.	☎ (1738) 623658	62	02.03–28.10	††† R 2W CC ♂ P 🔲
▲ **Pitlochry** Braeknowe, Knockard Rd, Pitlochry PH16 5HJ.	☎ (1796) 472308	75	🗓	††† ⦿ R CC ♂ P 🔲
△ *Raasay* *Creachan Cottage, Raasay, Kyle, Ross-shire IV40 8NT.*	☎ *(1478) 660240*	*30*	*11.05–30.09*	R ♂ P
▲ **Ratagan** Glenshiel, Kyle, Ross-shire IV40 8HP.	☎ (1599) 511243	44	02.03–28.10	♿ CC ♂ P 🔲
▲ **Rowardennan** Rowardennan by Drymen, Glasgow G63 0AR.	☎ (1360) 870259	80	02.03–28.10	††† ⦿ R CC ♂ P 🔲
▲ **Stirling** - St John St (IBN) **Stirling FK8 1EA.**	☎ (1786) 473442	126	🗓	††† ⦿ R ♿ CC ♂ P 🔲
▲ **Strathpeffer** Strathpeffer, Ross-shire IV14 9BT.	☎ (1997) 421532	54	11.05–30.09	CC ♂ P
▲ **Stromness** Hellihole Rd, Stromness, Orkney KW16 3DE.	☎ (1856) 850589	38	11.05–30.09	CC ♂
▲ **Tobermory** Isle of Mull, Argyll PA75 6NU.	☎ (1688) 302481	40	02.03–28.10	R CC ♂
△ *Tomintoul* *Main St, Tomintoul, Ballindalloch, Banffshire AB37 9HA.*	☎ *(1807) 580282*	*38*	*11.05–30.09*	R ♂ P
▲ **Tongue** Lairg, Sutherland IV27 4XH.	☎ (1847) 611301	40	30.03–30.09	CC ♂ P
▲ **Torridon** Achnasheen, Ross-shire IV22 2EZ.	☎ (1445) 791284	60	02.03–28.10	††† CC ♂ P 🔲

Location/Address	Telephone No. Fax No.	Beds	Opening Dates	Facilities
▲ Uig Uig, Isle of Skye IV51 9YD.	☎ (1470) 542211	62	30.03–28.10	♦♦♦ ⊂CC⊃ ☞ 🅿
▲ Ullapool Shore St, Ullapool, Ross-shire IV26 2UJ.	☎ (1854) 612254	62	28.01–04.01	Ⓡ ⊂CC⊃ ☞ 🄪
▲ Wanlockhead Lotus Lodge, Wanlockhead, Biggar, Lanarkshire ML12 6UT.	☎ (1659) 74252	28	30.03–30.09	⊂CC⊃ ☞ 🅿
▲ Whiting Bay Shore Rd, Whiting Bay, Isle of Arran KA27 8QW.	☎ (1770) 700339	48	30.03–28.10	♦♦♦ Ⓡ ⊂CC⊃ ☞ 🅿

YOUTH HOSTEL ACCOMMODATION
OUTSIDE THE ASSURED STANDARDS SCHEME

Location/Address	Telephone No.	Beds	Opening Dates	Facilities
Berneray Isle of Berneray, North Uist, HS6 5BQ.		16	🔒	☞
Eday London Bay, Eday, Orkney KW17 2AB.	☎ (01857) 622206	24	30.03–28.10	Ⓡ ☞
Garenin Carloway, Isle of Lewis, HS2 9AL.		14	🔒	☞
Howmore South Uist, HS8 5SH.		17	🔒	☞
Hoy Stromness, Orkney KW16 3NJ.	☎ (1856) 873535	26	01.05–11.09	Ⓡ ☞
Kershader Ravenspoint, Kershader, South Lochs, Isle of Lewis, HS2 9QA.	☎ (1851) 880236	14	🔒	☞ 🄪
Papa Westray Beltane House, Papa Westray, Orkney KW17 2BU.	☎ (1857) 644267	16	🔒	Ⓡ ☞
Rackwick Rackwick Outdoor Centre, Hoy, Stromness, Orkney, KW16 3NJ.	☎ (1856) 873535 Ext 2404	8	13.03–11.09	Ⓡ ☞
Rhenigidale Isle of Harris, HS3 3BD.		11	🔒	☞

International Booking Network

The advantages are cle

Slovenia

SLOVENIE
SLOWENIEN
ESLOVENIA

**PZS-Hostelling International Slovenia,
Gosposvetska 84, 2000 MARIBOR, Slovenija.**

☎ (386) (2) 2342137
📠 (386) (2) 2342136
✉ pzs@psdsi.com
🖥 www.psdsi.com/pzs/

A copy of the Hostel Directory for this Country can be obtained from:
The National Office

Capital:	Ljubljana	**Population:**	1,965,986
Language:	Slovene	**Size:**	20,254 sq km
Currency:	Slovene Tolar (SIT)	**Telephone Country Code:**	386

English

Hostels are located in cities, in the countryside, on the coast and on hills/mountains.

Price range

Price range max SIT 2,700. € 13,50. BB inc 🛏.

Rooms and Reservations

R during Jun-Aug, Dec. (All Rooms). Reservations via Hostel or National Office by **t** **f** **e**. (Reservation charges may apply). All hostels are non-smoking.

Guests

Membership Card and Passport/Photo ID are required. Pets are allowed - check with hostel. 👪 welcome. Group bookings via Hostel or National Office by **t** **f** **e**.

Open times

Main hostels: open 🗓, 07:00-22:00hrs. Reception open: 07:00-22:00hrs. Resident manager. **Other hostels:** open 🗓. **Seasonal hostels** are generally open Jul, Aug.

Meals

🍽 BLD **R** For individuals & for 👪. 🍴.

Travelling around

For ease of travel use ✈ 🚂 🚌 Self-Drive.

Passports and Visas

Passport/Photo ID required.

Health

Emergency medical treatment is free. Medical insurance is recommended.

Français

Les auberges sont situées dans les villes, à la campagne, sur le littoral et à la montagne.

Tarifs des nuitées

Tarifs des nuitées 2,700 SIT max. € 13,50. BB inc 🍴.

Chambres et réservations

ℝ juin-août, déc. (Toutes chambres). Réservations via l'auberge et le Bureau National par 🄣 🄕 🄔. (Des frais de réservation pourront vous être facturés). Toutes les auberges sont non-fumeurs.

Usagers

La carte d'adhérent ainsi que le passeport/pièce d'identité avec photo sont à présenter. Les animaux domestiques sont autorisés mais vérifiez lesquels auprès de l'auberge. Accueil des ♦♦♦. Réservations pour groupes via l'auberge et le Bureau National par 🄣 🄕 🄔.

Horaires d'ouverture

Grandes auberges: ouvertes 🕗, entre 7h-22h. Accueil ouvert entre 7h-22h. Gérant réside sur place. **Autres auberges:** ouvertes 🕗. **Auberges saisonnières** ouvertes généralement juil, août.

Repas

🍽 BLD ℝ Pour individuels & pour ♦♦♦. ♂.

Déplacements

Modes de transport recommandés ✈ 🚂 🚌 Voiture.

Passeports et visas

Passeport/pièce d'identité avec photo obligatoires.

Santé

Soins d'urgence gratuits. Une assurance médicale de voyage est conseillée.

Deutsch

Herbergen befinden sich in Städten, auf dem Land, an der Küste und in Bergen/Gebirgen.

Preisspanne

Preisspanne 2,700 SIT max. € 13,50. BB inc 🍴.

Zimmer und Reservierungen

ℝ während Jun-Aug, Dez. (Alle Zimmer). Reservierungen über Herberge oder Landesverband per 🄣 🄕 🄔. (Reservierungskosten könnten anfallen). Rauchen ist in allen Herbergen NICHT gestattet.

Gäste

Mitgliedsausweis und Reisepass/ Personalausweis sind erforderlich. Haustiere sind erlaubt - in der Herberge nachfragen. ♦♦♦ willkommen. Gruppenbuchungen über Herberge oder Landesverband per 🄣 🄕 🄔.

Öffnungszeiten

Hauptherbergen: Zugang 🕗, 07:00-22:00Uhr. Rezeption zwischen 07:00-22:00Uhr. Herbergsmanager wohnt im Haus. **Andere Herbergen:** Zugang 🕗. **Saison-Herbergen** sind normalerweise Jul, Aug geöffnet.

Mahlzeiten

🍽 BLD **R** Für Einzelreisende & für **ŧŧŧ**. 🐾.

Reisen im Land

Reisen ist einfach mit ✈ 🚌 🚐 Selbstfahrer.

Reisepässe und Visa

Reisepass/Personalausweis erforderlich.

Gesundheit

Nur im Notfall sind medizinische Behandlungen kostenlos. Unfall-/Krankenversicherung wird empfohlen.

Español

Los albergues están situados en las ciudades, el campo, la costa y la montaña.

Tarifas mínima y máxima

Tarifas mínima y máxima 2,700 SIT max. € 13,50. BB inc 🍽.

Habitaciones y Reservas

R en jun-ago, dic. (Todas las habitaciones). Reservas a través del albergue o la Asociación Nacional por **❶** **❻** **❸**. (Es posible que se aplique un suplemento en concepto de gastos de reserva). Está prohibido fumar en todos los albergues.

Huéspedes

Los huéspedes deben presentar su Carnet de Alberguista y su pasaporte o carnet de identidad. Se admiten animales - consulte con el albergue. Se admiten **ŧŧŧ**. Reservas de grupo a través del albergue o la Asociación Nacional por **❶** **❻** **❸**.

Horarios y fechas de apertura

Albergues principales - abiertos 🗓, 07:00-22:00h. Horario de recepción: 07:00-22:00h. Gerente residente. **Otros albergues** - abiertos 🗓. **Albergues de temporada** suelen abrir: jul, ago.

Comidas

🍽 BLD **R** Para individuales y para **ŧŧŧ**. 🐾.

Desplazamientos

Transportes recomendados: ✈ 🚌 🚐 Automóvil.

Pasaportes y Visados

Pasaporte o carnet de identidad obligatorio.

Información Sanitaria

Asistencia médica de urgencia gratuita. Seguro médico recomendado.

"The tourist who moves about to see and hear and open himself to all the influences of the places which condense centuries of human greatness is only a man in search of excellence."

"Le touriste qui voyage pour voir et entendre et s'ouvrir à toutes les influences des lieux qui condensent des siècles de grandeur humaine est tout simplement un homme à la recherche de l'excellence."

„Der Tourist, der unterwegs ist, um zu schauen und zu hören und sich den Einflüssen der Orte zu eröffnen, die Jahrhunderte menschlicher Größe zusammenfassen, ist einfach ein Mensch auf der Suche nach Großartigem."

"El turista que se desplaza para ver y oír y abrirse a todas las influencias de los lugares en que se condensan siglos de grandeza humana es simplemente un hombre en busca de excelencia."

Max Lerner

Bled - Bledec

Grajska 17,
4260 Bled.
❶ (4) 5745250
❶ (4) 5745251

Open Dates: 🗓

Open Hours: 07.00-22.00hrs

Reservations: **R**

Price Range: 2600 SIT € 13.00 🗐

Beds: 56 - 1x² 2x³ 6x⁴ 2x⁵ 1x⁶ 1x⁶

Facilities: 👫 👫 🍴 🍽 📺 1 x 🍸 🔒 ☺ 🅿 ℹ️ ♿

Directions: 0.5 NE from city centre

✈ Brnik 32km

🚂 Bled 2km

🚌 ap Bled Autobusna Postaja 200m

Attractions: ⛳ ⛰ 🏊 🚶 ⚲ 🚣

Location/Address	Telephone No. Fax No.	Beds	Opening Dates	Facilities
▲ **Bled** - Bledec **Grajska 17, 4260 Bled.**	✆ (4) 5745250 🖷 (4) 5745251	56	🗓12	👪 🍽 Ⓡ 0.5 NE 🅿 ⑥ 🍷
▲ **Koper** Dijaški dom Koper, Cankarjeva 5, 6000 Koper.	✆ (5) 6273250 🖷 (5) 6273182	30	01.01–30.06; 01.09–31.12 (3 beds); 01.07–25.08 (30 beds)	🍽 Ⓡ 🅿 ⑥
▲ **Lendava** - Petišovci Terme Lendava, Tomšičeva 29, 9220 Lendava.	✆ (2) 5751004 🖷 (2) 5751723	20	🗓12	👪 🍽 Ⓡ 4 SW ♿ ⒸⒸ 🚺 🅿 🍷 🚲
▲ **Ljubljana** - Tabor Vidovdanska 7, 1000 Ljubljana. ℯ andrej.cepin@guest.arnes.si	✆ (1) 2321067, (1) 2321060 🖷 (1) 2321060	50	25.06–25.08	👪 🍽 Ⓡ 🅿
▲ **Maribor** Dijaški dom 26 Junij Maribor, Železnikova 12, 2000 Maribor. ℯ vojteh.stefanciosa@guest.arnes.si	✆ (2) 4711800 🖷 (2) 4711800	50	01.07–20.08	👪 🍽 Ⓡ 🅿
▲ **Piran** - Val Penzion Val, Gregorčičeva 38a, 6300 Piran. ℯ penzion.val@siol.net	✆ (5) 673255 🖷 (5) 6732556	54	🗓12	👪 🍽 Ⓡ ⒸⒸ ⑥ 🍷 🚲 ⚙
▲ **Rogla** - Jelka Annexe Hotel Planja, Rogla, Cesta Na Roglo 15, 3214 Zreče. ℯ rogla@turizem.si	✆ (3) 7577100 🖷 (3) 5766010	50	01.04–25.11	👪 🍽 Ⓡ ⒸⒸ 🅿 🍷

"Travel is ninety percent anticipation and ten
percent recollection"

"Le voyage c'est 90% de l'anticipation et 10%
de souvenir"

„Reisen ist neunzig Prozent Erwartung und zehn
Prozent Erinnerung."

"Viajar es un 90% de expectativa y un 10%
de recuerdos."

Edward Street

Spain

ESPAGNE

SPANIEN

ESPAÑA

Red Española de Albergues Juveniles,
c/ José Ortega y Gasset 71,
Madrid 28006, Spain.

☎ (34) 913477700
🖷 (34) 914018160
🖳 www.mtas.es/injuve/intercambios/albergues/reaj.html

Office Hours: Monday-Friday, 09.00-14.00hrs

A copy of the Hostel Directory for this Country can be obtained from:
The National Office

Capital:	Madrid		**Population:**	39,433,942
Language:	Spanish		**Size:**	504,782 sq km
Currency:	Ptas (pesetas)		**Telephone Country Code:**	34

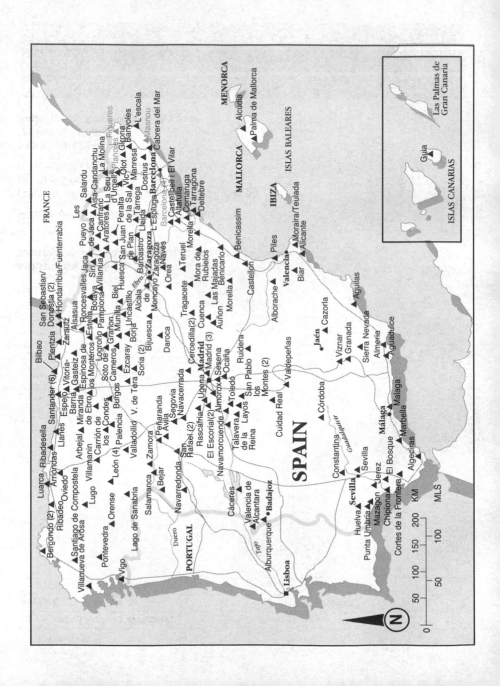

English

Hostels are located in cities, in the countryside, on the coast and on hills/mountains.

Price range

BB inc 🛏 🍴.

Rooms and Reservations

R 🛏 (All Rooms). Reservations via IBN Hostel or Regional Association by ❶ ❷ ❸. (Reservation charges may apply). Smoking is limited - please check.

Guests

Membership Card and Passport/Photo ID are required. ♦♦♦ welcome. Group bookings via IBN or Regional Association by ❶ ❷ ❸.

Open times

Main hostels: open 🛏, 08:00-22:30hrs in winter; 08:00-23:30hrs in summer. Reception open: 09:30-19:00hrs. Resident manager. **Other hostels:** open 🛏, 08:00-22:30hrs in winter; 08:00-23:30hrs in summer. Reception open: 09:30-19:00hrs. Resident manager. **Seasonal hostels** are generally open Jun-Aug.

Meals

🍽 BLD For individuals & for ♦♦♦. ♂.

Travelling around

For ease of travel use ✈ 🚂 🚌 Self-Drive.

Travel/Activity Packages

Winter sports, water sports, cycling/mountain biking and walking/trekking packages available.

Passports and Visas

Passport required.

Health

Emergency medical treatment is free. EU Nationals require Form E111 to obtain treatment within EU countries.

Français

Les auberges sont situées dans les villes, à la campagne, sur le littoral et à la montagne.

Tarifs des nuitées

BB inc 🛏 🍴.

Chambres et réservations

R 🛏 (Toutes chambres). Réservations via IBN l'auberge ou l'Association Régionale par ❶ ❷ ❸. (Des frais de réservation pourront vous être facturés). Il est permis de fumer dans certaines chambres - veuillez vérifier.

Usagers

La carte d'adhérent ainsi que le passeport/pièce d'identité avec photo sont à présenter. Accueil des ♦♦♦. Réservations pour groupes via IBN ou l'Association Régionale par ❶ ❷ ❸.

Horaires d'ouverture

Grandes auberges: ouvertes 🛏, entre 8h-22h30 en hiver; 8h-23h30 en été. Accueil ouvert entre 9h30-19h. Gérant réside sur place. **Autres auberges:** ouvertes 🛏, entre 8h-22h30 en hiver; 8h-23h30 en été. Accueil ouvert entre 9h30-19h. Gérant réside sur place. **Auberges saisonnières** ouvertes généralement juin-août.

Repas

🍽 BLD Pour individuels & pour ♦♦♦. ♂.

Déplacements

Modes de transport recommandés ✈ 🚂 🚌 Voiture.

Forfaits Voyages/Activités

Forfaits sports d'hiver, sports aquatiques, cyclotourisme/VTT et randonnées pédestres disponibles.

Passeports et visas

Passeport obligatoire.

Santé

Soins d'urgence gratuits. Les ressortissants de l'Union Européenne doivent se munir du formulaire E111 pour bénéficier de soins médicaux dans les états de l'UE.

Deutsch

Herbergen befinden sich in Städten, auf dem Land, an der Küste und in Bergen/Gebirgen.

Preisspanne

BB inc SH .

Zimmer und Reservierungen

R (Alle Zimmer). Reservierungen über IBN Herberge oder Regionale Verbände per t f e. (Reservierungskosten könnten anfallen). Rauchen ist begrenzt - bitte checken.

Gäste

Mitgliedsausweis und Reisepass/ Personalausweis sind erforderlich.
willkommen. Gruppenbuchungen über IBN oder Regionale Verbände per t f e.

Öffnungszeiten

Hauptherbergen: Zugang 12, 08:00-22:30Uhr im Winter; 08:00-23:30Uhr im Sommer. Rezeption zwischen 09:30-19:00Uhr. Herbergsmanager wohnt im Haus. **Andere Herbergen:** Zugang 12, 08:00-22:30Uhr im Winter; 08:00-23:30Uhr im Sommer. Rezeption zwischen 09:30-19:00Uhr. Herbergsmanager wohnt im Haus. **Saison-Herbergen** sind normalerweise Jun-Aug geöffnet.

Mahlzeiten

BLD Für Einzelreisende & für .

Reisen im Land

Reisen ist einfach mit Selbstfahrer.

Reise-/Aktivitäten-Packages

Wintersport, Wassersport, Fahrrad/ Mountainbiking und wandern/trekking -Packages erhältlich.

Reisepässe und Visa

Reisepass erforderlich.

Gesundheit

Nur im Notfall sind medizinische Behandlungen kostenlos. EU Staatsangehörige benötigen Formular E111 für ärztliche Behandlungen innerhalb der EU Länder.

Español

Los albergues están situados en las ciudades, el campo, la costa y la montaña.

Tarifas mínima y máxima

BB inc SH .

Habitaciones y Reservas

R 12 (Todas las habitaciones). Reservas por IBN, a través del albergue o a través de la Asociación Regional por t f e. (Es posible que se aplique un suplemento en concepto de gastos de reserva). Está permitido fumar sólo en algunas salas/habitaciones - infórmese.

Huéspedes

Los huéspedes deben presentar su Carnet de Alberguista y su pasaporte o carnet de identidad. Se admiten **♀♀♀**. Reservas de grupo por (IBN) o a través de la Asociación Regional por **❶ ❷ ❸**.

Horarios y fechas de apertura

Albergues principales - abiertos 🗓, 08:00-22:30h en invierno; 08:00-23:30h en verano. Horario de recepción: 09:30-19:00h. Gerente residente. **Otros albergues** - abiertos 🗓, 08:00-22:30h en invierno; 08:00-23:30h en verano. Horario de recepción: 09:30-19:00h. Gerente residente. **Albergues de temporada** suelen abrir: jun-ago.

Comidas

🍽 BLD Para individuales y para **♀♀♀**. ✂.

Desplazamientos

Transportes recomendados: ✈ 🚃 🚌 Automóvil.

Viajes Combinados con Actividades

Viajes combinados con deportes de invierno, deportes náuticos, cicloturismo/bicicleta de montaña y senderismo.

Pasaportes y Visados

Pasaporte obligatorio.

Información Sanitaria

Asistencia médica de urgencia gratuita. Los ciudadanos procedentes de países pertenecientes a la UE necesitan el impreso E111 para obtener asistencia médica en dichos países.

"Of journeying the benefits are many: the freshness it bringeth to the heart, the seeing and hearing of marvelous things, the delight of beholding new cities, the meeting of unknown friends, and the learning of high manners."

Le voyage apporte bien des bienfaits: la fraîcheur qu'il donne au coeur, l'occasion de voir et d'entendre bien des merveilles, le délice de découvrir de nouvelles cités, la rencontre d'amis inconnus et l'apprentissage de belles mannières."

„Wer reist, gewinnt viel: die Frische, die es dem Herzen bringt, das Sehen und Hören wunderbarer Dinge, die Freude, neue Städte zu betrachten, unbekannte Freunde zu treffen und edle Sitten zu erlernen."

"Muchas son las ventajas que deparan los viajes: el frescor que aportan al corazón, la oportunidad de ver y oír cosas maravillosas, el placer de descubrir nuevas ciudades, los encuentros con amigos desconocidos y el aprendizaje de buenos modales."

Sadi, Gulistan

Alburquerque -
Castillo de Luna

c/ Castillo,
s/n 06510 Alburquerque (Badajoz).
📞 924 400041
📠 924 401523

Open Dates:	01.06-31.08 (Fri-Sun 01.09-31.05)
Price Range:	900-1340 ptas € 5.41-8.05
Beds:	8 - 4x^2
Facilities:	🚻 🍽️
Directions:	
🚂	3.7km

Alcúdia - La Victòria

Ctra. Cap Pinar Km. 4,
07400 Alcúdia (Mallorca).
📞 902 111188
📠 971 176096
📧 xib@bitel.es

Open Dates:	01.03-31.10
Open Hours:	08.00-12.00hrs
Reservations:	**R**
Price Range:	1800 ptas € 10.81
Beds:	120 - 20x^6
Facilities:	♿ 🚻 🍽️ 🛏️ ☕ 🏨 📺 🔘 🖼️ 🔒 🅿️ ℹ️ ⚡ ♻️ ⚠️ 🌐 🔍 ⌨️ 👥

Directions:	
✈️	Son San Juan, Palma de Mallorca 46km
A 🚐	Alcúdia - Aeropuerto
🚂	Inca 16km
🚐	From Palma - Alcúdia
Attractions:	🏞️ ⛰️ 🔍300m 🚴 🏃 ⛵

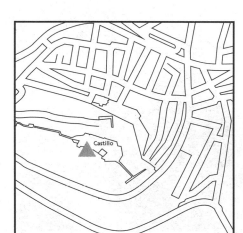

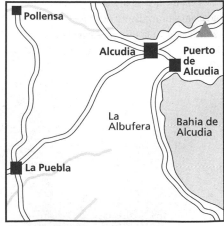

Barcelona - Mare de Déu de Montserrat

Passeig Mare de Déu del Coll 41-51, 08023 Barcelona.
☎ 932 105151
🖷 932 100798
✉ alberg_barcelona@tujuca.com

Open Dates:	01.01-23.12; 26-31.12
Open Hours:	07.00-00.00hrs
Reservations:	**R** **IBN** **CC**
Price Range:	1960 2575 ptas € 11.78-15.42 BBinc 🍴
Beds:	223 - 5x²🛏 2x⁴🛏 25x⁶🛏 6x⁶🛏
Facilities:	♿ ♦♦♦ 🍴 ♨ 📺 🎮1 x 🍷 🖻 🖼 8 P ⓘ 🛏 🦂 ⚠ 🔍

Directions:

✈	"El Prat" Barcelona 20km
A🚌	#28 Pza Cataluña
⛴	Barcelona 2km
🚆	Sants-Station (Barcelona 4km)
🚌	25 10m, 28 2m ap Norte and San
U	Linea 3 - Green "Valcarca" 500m

Attractions: 🔍 🚴 U5km ⚲1km 🏊1km

Benicasim - Argentina

Avda Ferrandiz Salvador 40, 12560 Benicàssim (Castelló).
☎ 964 300949; 964 302709
🖷 964 300473
✉ rosario.espinosa@ivaj.m400.gva.es

Open Dates:	22.02-22.12
Open Hours:	07.00-00.00hrs
Reservations:	**R**
Price Range:	900-1400 ptas € 4.62-8.41 BBinc 🍴
Beds:	140 - 28x²🛏 22x³🛏 3x⁴🛏 1x⁶🛏
Facilities:	♿ ♦♦♦8x ♦♦♦ 🍴 ♨ 📺 🎮3 x 🍷 🖻 🖼 P ⓘ 🦂 🔍 🏓

Directions:

✈	Manises, Valencia 70km
🚆	Benicàsim 1.5km
🚌	from Castellón 100m

Attractions: 🔍 🚶 ⚲ 🏊

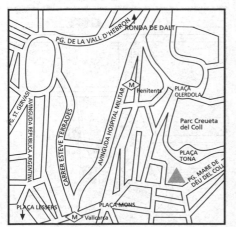

0   920m

Bilbao -
Bilbao-Aterpetxea

**Carretera Basurto-Kastrexana 70,
48002 Bilbao.**
📞 944 270054
📠 944 275479
✉ aterpe@albergue.bilbao.net

Open Dates: 🗓

Reservations: Ⓡ ⌐CC⌐

Price Range: 2300-2500 ptas € 13.83-15.03
BB inc 🗐

Beds: 142 - 2x¹🛏 24x²🛏 4x³🛏 14x⁴🛏
4x⁶🛏

Facilities: ♿ 🚹 🚹 🍴 📺 🗐 🐕 🗷 🖼
🔢 ⬆ Ⓟ ✂ 🔍

Directions:

🚌 58

Attractions: 🚴 🏃

Córdoba

**Plaza Judá Leví S/N.,
14003 Córdoba.**
📞 957 290166
📠 957 290500
✉ informacion@inturjoven.
junta.andalucia.es

Open Dates: 🗓

Reservations: Ⓡ ⌐CC⌐

Price Range: 1700-2300 ptas € 7.22-13.83 🗐

Beds: 170 - 32x²🛏 26x³🛏 7x⁴🛏

Facilities: ♿ 🍴 🔌 🗷 🛏 📺 1 x🍽 ⊜ ⬆
🏠

Directions:

🚂 Cordoba 1.5km

🚌 3, 12, 50m

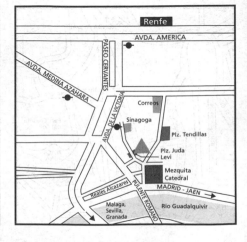

Donostia-San Sebastián - La Sirena

Paseo de Igeldo 25,
2008 Donostia-San Sebastián.
📞 943 310268; 943 311293
📠 943 214090
📧 udala.youthostel@donostia.org

Open Dates:	🗓️
Open Hours:	08.00-11.00hrs; 15.00-00.00hrs
Reservations:	**R** **CC**
Price Range:	2000-2250 ptas € 12.03-13.53 BBinc
Beds:	96 - 1x² 4x⁴ 4x⁶ 5x⁶
Facilities:	♿ 🍴 🛏️ 📺 🖥️ 📷 💱 ℹ️ 🧺 ♿ 🎪
Directions:	2SW from city centre
✈	Hondarribia 20km
A🚐	From City Center of San Sebastian
🚢	Santurtzi 120km
🚂	North Station - San Sebastian 3km
🚐	5, 6, 15, 16, 24, 25, 27 ap Ventaberri or Igeldo
Attractions:	🏌️ ⛰️ 🚴 ⚲ 🏃 ∪ ⚲

Granada - Albergue Juvenil Granada

Avda Ramon y Cajal 2,
18003 Granada.
📞 958 002900
📠 958 002908
📧 informacion@inturjoven.junta-andalucia.es

Open Dates:	🗓️
Open Hours:	🕐
Reservations:	**R**
Price Range:	1200-2300 ptas € 7.22-13.83
Beds:	229 - 44x² 46x³
Facilities:	♿ 👥 🍴 🛏️ 📺 🧺 📷 💱 P 🧺 🎪
Directions:	
✈	Santa Fé 20km
A🚐	From City Center of Granada
🚂	Granada - "Avda de los Andaluces" 1.5km
🚐	11 ap YH
Attractions:	⛰️ 🏊 ⚲1km 🚣1km

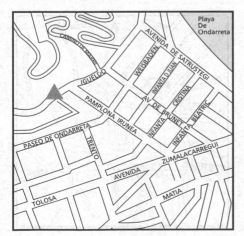

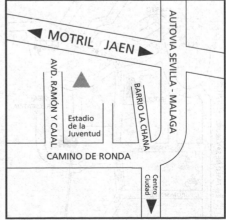

Llanes - Juventudes

c/ Celso Amieva 7,
33500 Llanes (Asturias).
☎ 98 5400770
✆ 98 5400770

Open Dates: 🗓

Open Hours: 09.00-13.30hrs; 18.00-20.00hrs

Price Range: 941-1326 ptas € 5.66-7.97
BB inc 🍴

Beds: 16 - 8x²

Facilities: ♿ 👥 🍽 🛏 📺 📖 8 ⬍ ℹ
🍴 🔥 ⛺ 🏕

Directions:

✈	Ranón (Avilés) 150km
A🚌	(Alsa) Llanes - Oviedo - Avilés
🚂	F.E.V.E. Oviedo - Llanes 300m
🚌	Oviedo - Llanes (Alsa)

Attractions: 🏕 ⛰ 📷 🎿 ∪ ♒ ⛵ 1km

Madrid - Sta Cruz de Marcenado

Calle Sta Cruz de Marcenado No 28,
28015 Madrid.
☎ 915 474532
✆ 915 481196

Open Dates: 🗓

Open Hours: 09.00-20.00hrs

Reservations: Ⓡ

Price Range: 1200-1820 ptas € 7.22-10.94
BB inc 🍴

Beds: 72 - 2x² 6x⁴ 2x⁶ 4x⁶

Facilities: ♿ 🍽 (B) 🛏 📺 🔲 🖼 ⬍ ℹ
🍴

Directions:

✈	Barajas 12km
A🚌	Colón - Aeropuerto
🚂	Chamartin 8km
🚌	"C" 1, 2, 44, 133, 21 500m
Ⓤ	Linea 4 - Argüelles 500m

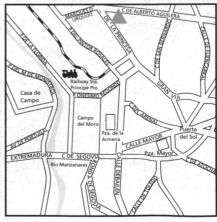

Miranda de Ebro - Fernán Gonzalez

c/ Anduva 82,
09200 Miranda de Ebro (Burgos).
🕿 947 320932
📠 947 320334

Open Dates: 🗓
Reservations: **R**
Price Range: 1100-1600 ptas € 6.61-9.61 🍴
Beds: 110 - 13x¹ 👤 12x² 👤 24x³ 👤
Facilities: 👫 🍴 ☕ 📺 📗 🔲 ⑧ ⊖ 🅿 ⊞

Directions:

🚌   Miranda de Ebro 1.5km

Attractions: ⚲ ⚘

Navarredonda de Gredos - Albergue Juvenil "Navarredonda de Gredos"

Crta. Comarcal C-500 Km 41.5,
05635 Navarredonda de Gredos (Avila).
🕿 920 348005
📠 920 348005
📧 albmgredos@durnet.es

Open Dates: 🗓
Open Hours: 08.00-00.00hrs
Reservations: **R** **CC**
Price Range: 1100-1600 ptas BB^inc 🍴
Beds: 63 - 3x¹ 👤 20x² 👤 5x⁴ 👤
Facilities: 👫5x 👫 🍴 ☕ 🛏 📺 📗1 x 🍸
🔲 🅿 ℹ ♿ ⌂ ⚲ ⊞

Directions:

✈   Barajas 179km

🚌   Avila 64km

🚐   Avila 64km ap YH

Attractions: 🌲 ⛰ 🚶 ∪1.5km ⚲ ⚘

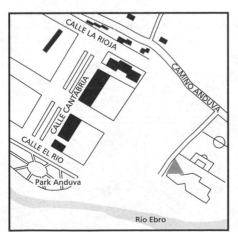

Salamanca - Albergue Juvenil "Salamanca"

C/ Escoto 13-15,
37008 Salamanca.
☎ 923 269141
✆ 923 269141; 923 214227
@ esterra@mmteam.disgumad.es

Open Dates: 🗓

Reservations: **R**

Price Range: 1870 ptas € 9.01-10.81 [BB]inc

Beds: 44 - 1x⁶💤 2x⁶💤

Facilities: ♿ ♗ 🍴 🍽 ▣ ⚒ **P**

Directions:

✈   Barajas (Madrid) 200km

🚌   Salamanca 1km

🚍   1,4, 250m ap Gran Vía & Plaza Mayor

Attractions: 🚲

Santiago de Compostela - Monte do Gozo

Carretera de Santiago-Aeropuerto KM 3,
15820 Santiago de Compostela (A Coruña).
☎ 981 558942
✆ 981 562892

Open Dates: 🗓

Open Hours: 🕐

Price Range: 970-1425 ptas € 5.83-8.57
[BB]inc 🍴

Beds: 300 - 38x⁶💤

Facilities: ♿ ♗ 🍴 🍷 🏨 📺 ▤ 🍽1 x
🍷 ▣ 🖼 ⚒ 🔟 **P** ℹ 💤 ⚘
⛰ ⊙ ⚲ 👥

Directions:

✈   "Lavacolla", Santiago 8km

🚌   Santiago 2km

🚃   1.5km

Attractions: 🏞 ⛰ 🚲 🏃 ⋃ 🏊

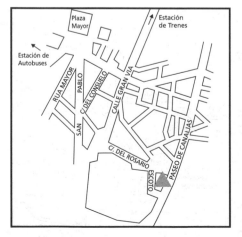

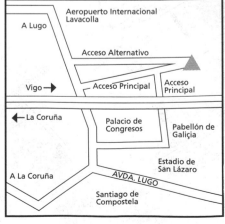

Sevilla

Isaac Peral 2,
41012 Sevilla.
☎ 955 056500
🖷 955 056508
✉ informacion@inturjoven.
junta-andalucia.es

Open Dates: 🗓	
Open Hours: 🕐	
Reservations: **R**	
Price Range:	1200-2300 ptas € 7.22-13.83
Beds:	277 - 65x² 47x³
Facilities:	♿ 👫 🍴 🛏 📺 200 x🍽 🧳 ♨ ⊜ ⬆ 🔌 ✿

Directions:

✈	San Pablo 10km
A🚌	From City Center
🚂	"Sta Justa" 2km
🚌	6, 34

Zaragoza -
Baltasar Gracián

c/ Franco y López 4,
50005 Zaragoza.
☎ 976 551387; 974 378016
🖷 976 553432; 976 714049
✉ mtmosquera@aragob.es

Open Dates: 🗓	
Reservations: **R**	
Price Range:	1350-1750 ptas € 8.12-10.52 📖
Beds:	50 - 5x² 8x⁴ 1x⁶
Facilities:	♿ 👫 🍴 (B) ☂ 🛏 📺 🔘 🅿 ✿ 🔍 ▦

Directions:

✈	Zaragoza
🚂	Zaragoza, El Portillo
🚌	Zaragoza

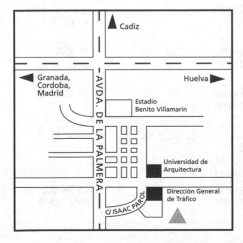

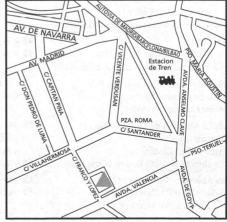

Location/Address	Telephone No. Fax No.	Beds	Opening Dates	Facilities
▲ **Aguadulce** Campillo del Moro S/N, 04720 Aguadulce (Almeria). ℮ reservas@inturjoven.junta-andalucia.es	☎ 950 340346 ✆ 950 345855	218	🔲	♨ 🍽 Ⓡ ♿ ⌘ ☞ 🅿
▲ **Aguilas** - Calarreona Ctra. de Vera Km4, 30880 Aguilas (Murcia).	☎ 968 413029 ✆ 968 413029	82	🔲	🍽 Ⓡ
▲ **Albarracín** - Rosa Bríos c/ Santa María, 5, Albarracín 44100 (Teruel).	☎ 978 710005 (Ⓡ 976 714797) ✆ 978 641033; 978 710005	70	🔲	♨ 🍽 Ⓡ ♿ ☞ 🖻
▲ **Alacant** - "La Florida" Avda Orihuela 59, 03007 Alicante.	☎ 965 113044 (Ⓡ 963 985900) ✆ 965 282754	184	01.01–30.06	🍽 Ⓡ 🖻 ☕
▲ **Alborache** - Torre D'Alborache Ctra de Macastre, s/n 46369 Alborache (Valencia).	☎ 962 508123, 962 508124 (Ⓡ 963 985900) ✆ 962 508020	140	01.02–17.12	🍽 Ⓡ ♿ 🅿 🖻
▲ **Alburquerque** - Castillo de Luna **c/ Castillo,** **s/n 06510 Alburquerque (Badajoz).**	☎ 924 400041 ✆ 924 401523	8	01.06–31.08 (Fri–Sun 01.09–31.05)	♨ 🍽
▲ **Alcalá de Moncayo** c/ Puerta del Lugar s/n, 50591 Alcalá de Moncayo (Zaragoza).	☎ 976 646459; 608 970981 ✆ 976 646459	86	🔲	♨ 🍽 Ⓡ 🅿 ☕
▲ **Alcúdia** - La Victòria **Ctra. Cap Pinar Km. 4,** **07400 Alcúdia (Mallorca).** ℮ xib@bitel.es	☎ 902 111188 ✆ 971 176096	120	01.03–31.10	🍽 Ⓡ ♿ ☞ 🅿 🖻 ☕
△ *Alfaro* *Plaza Araña, 26540 Alfaro (La Rioja).*	☎ 941 29100 Ext 6202; 941 291229	*40*	🔲 ♨	♨ 🍽 Ⓡ
▲ **Algeciras** Barriada El Pelayo, Ctra. N-340, km 95,600, 11390 Algeciras (Cádiz). ℮ reservas@inturjoven.junta-andalucia.es	☎ 956 679060 ✆ 956 679017	100	🔲	♨ 🍽 Ⓡ 8SE ♿ ⌘ ☞ 🅿 🖻
▲ **Almería** c/ Isla de Fuerteventura S/N, 04007 Almería. ℮ reservas@inturjoven.junta-andalucia.es	☎ 950 269788 ✆ 950 271744	164	🔲	🍽 Ⓡ ♿ ⌘ ☞ 🅿
▲ **Almorox** - "Ecogranja San Pol" Camino Cadalso-Pinar, 45900 Almorox (Toledo).	☎ 918 623265, 914 730020	58	🔲	🍽 Ⓡ 🅿
▲ **La Almunia de Doña Godina** - Ramón yCajal" Avda Laviaga Castillo, La Almunia de Doña Godina (Zaragoza).	☎ 976 600833 (Ⓡ 976 714797) ✆ 976 600833	72	🔲	🍽 ☞ 🅿 🖻
▲ **Alsasua** - "Sto Cristo de Otadia" Zelai 91, 31800 Alsasua (Navarra). ℮ aalsasua@cfnavarra.es	☎ 948 564814 ✆ 948 564973	88	🔲	♨ 🍽 Ⓡ ♿ ⌘ 🅿 🖻

Location/Address	Telephone No. Fax No.	Beds	Opening Dates	Facilities
▲ Altafulla - "Casa Gran" Placeta 12, 43893 Altafulla (Tarragona). ℮ alberg_altafulla@tujuca.com	☎ 977 650779 (ℝ 934 838363) 🖷 977 650588	65	11.01–22.12	⋔ ⦿ ℝ 🖷
△ *Aratores* - *"Sta. M- De Aratores" Molino De Aratores, s/n 22860 Aratores (Huesca).* ℮ *ep.ara1@escolapios.es*	☎ *974 348051* 🖷 *976 423019*	*60*	🔟 ⋔ *only*	ℝ 👤 ⸨CC⸩ P 🖷
▲ Arbejal Carretera Arbejal, 34843 Arbejal (Palencia).	☎ 979 870174	80	🔟	⋔ ⦿ ℝ 2NW P
▲ Arriondas c/del Barco, 12. 33540 Arriondas (Asturias).	☎ 985 840334 🖷 985 841282	12	🔟	⦿ ℝ P
▲ Auñón - "Entrepeñas" Poblado de Entrepeñas, 19130 Auñón (Guadalajara).	☎ 949 358415 🖷 949 222062	64	01.01–30.10; 10–31.12	⦿ ℝ 👤
▲ Avila - "Profesor Arturo Duperier" Av de Juventud s/n, 05003 Avila.	☎ 920 221716 🖷 920 221716	90	01.07–15.08	⦿ ℝ P 🖷
▲ Baños de Montemayor - Residencia Juvenil "Joaquin Sama" c/ Calvo Sotelo, s/n, 10750 Baños de Montemayor (Cáceres).	☎ 923 428003	10	01.06–31.08 (Thurs–Sun 01.09–31.05)	⋔ ⦿ ℝ
▲ Banyoles - "Alberg Banyoles" Calle Migdia, 10, 17829 Banyoles (Girona).	☎ 972 475454 🖷 972 576747	100	🔟	⦿ ℝ 👤 ⸨CC⸩
▲ Barbastro - "Joaquin Costa" Av. Monseñor Escrivá s/n, 22300 Barbastro (Huesca).	☎ 974 311834 🖷 974 313527	120	🔟	⦿ ℝ
▲ Barcelona - Mare de Déu de Montserrat ⸨IBN⸩ **Passeig Mare de Déu del Coll 41-51, 08023 Barcelona.** ℮ alberg_barcelona@tujuca.com	☎ 932 105151 🖷 932 100798	223	01.01–23.12; 26–31.12	⦿ ℝ 👤 ⸨CC⸩ P 🖷
▲ Barcelona - Hostal de Joves Passeig Pujades 29, 08018 Barcelona.	☎ 933 003104	68	🔟	ℝ 👔 🖷 ☕
▲ Barcelona - Pere Tarrés Numancia 149-151, 08029 Barcelona. ℮ alberg@perelarres.org	☎ 934 102309 🖷 934 196268	90	03.01–24.12	⋔ ⦿ ℝ 👔 P 🖷
▲ Barcelona - Studio Duquesa de Orleans, 56 Bis, 08034-Barcelona.	☎ 932 050961	40	01.07–30.09	⋔ ⦿ ℝ 🖷 ☕
▲ Barría - Monasterio-Albergue de Barría 01208 Barría (Araba).	☎ 945 317132; 945 181988 🖷 945 317168	200	🔟	⋔ ⦿ ℝ 👤 👔 🖷
▲ Béjar - "Llano Alto" El Castañal, 37715 Béjar (Salamanca).	☎ 923 404052 🖷 923 400702	160	🔟	⋔ ⦿ ℝ P
▲ Benicarló - "Sant Crist del Mar R.J" Avda de Yecla 29, 12580 Benicarló (Castelló).	☎ 964 470500 (ℝ 963 985900) 🖷 964 460225	80	01.01–30.06, 01.07–15.08, 01.10–31.12 (Closed weekends)	⋔ ⦿ ℝ

Location/Address	Telephone No. Fax No.	Beds	Opening Dates	Facilities
▲ **Benicasim** - Argentina **Avda Ferrandiz Salvador 40,** **12560 Benicàssim (Castelló).** ⓔ rosario.espinosa@ivaj.m400.gva.es	☎ 964 300949; 964 302709 🖷 964 300473	140	22.02–22.12	♟♑ ⓡ 👪 🅿 🔲
▲ **Bergondo** - "Albergue Juvenil Gandarío" 15167 Bergondo (A Coruña). ⓔ gandario@teleline.es	☎ 981 791005 🖷 (81) 794217	300	🗓	♑ 👪 🅿 ☕
▲ **Bergondo** - "Marina Española" 15167 Bergondo (A Coruña).	☎ 981 620118	110	🗓	♑ 🅿
▲ **Biar** Les Llomes de la Mare de Deu, 6 03410 Biar (Alicante). ⓔ albergbiar@ctv.es	☎ 965 810875 🖷 965 810875	68	🗓	♑ ⓡ 👪 🅿 🔲
▲ **Bijuesca** c/Virgen III, 12, 50316 Bijuesca (Zaragoza). ⓔ ib3100717@ibercaja.públic.es	☎ 976 847292	50	🗓	♑ ⓡ 🔲
▲ **Bilbao** - Bilbao-Aterpetxea **Carretera Basurto-Kastrexana 70,** **48002 Bilbao.** ⓔ aterpe@albergue.bilbao.net	☎ 944 270054 🖷 944 275479	142	🗓	♟♑ ⓡ 👪 ⟨CC⟩ 🅿 🔲
▲ **Boñar** - Pardomino Avda de Asturias No. 13, 24850 Boñar (León).	☎ 987 741581; 987 735510 🖷 987 741581	200	🗓	♟♑ ⓡ 1N 🅿 🔲 ☕
▲ **Borja** - "Santuario de la Misericordia" Santuario de la Misericordia, 50540 Borja (Zaragoza). ⓔ jjmarti@aragob.es	☎ 976 867844; 976 714797 🖷 976 714049	52	01.01–30.09 (♟ only)	ⓡ 🔲
▲ **El Bosque** c/Molino de Enmedio S/N, 11670-El Bosque (Cádiz). ⓔ reservas@inturjoven.junta-andalucia.es	☎ 956 716212 🖷 956 716258	79	🗓	♑ ⓡ 👪 ⟨CC⟩
△ *Botaya* - *Casa del Herrero* *c/Unica, s/n 22711 Botaya (Huesca).*	☎ *974 359853;* *976 215325* 🖷 *976 274414*	*46*	🗓 *♟ only*	♟♑ ⓡ 🅿
▲ **Brañavieja** - "Estación de Invierno Alto Campoo" Brañavieja (Santander).	☎ 908 309133	42	01.01–31.08; 01.10–31.12	♑ ⓡ 👪 ♂ 🅿 🔲 ☕
▲ **Burgos** - "Gil de Siloe R.J." Avda General Vigón s/n, 09006 Burgos.	☎ 947 220362 🖷 947 220362	108	01.07–15.08	♟♑ ⓡ 👪 🅿 🔲 ☕
▲ **Cabrera de Mar** - "Torre Ametller" Veinat de Sta Elena d'Agell, Cabrera de Mar, 08349 Barcelona. ⓔ albergecabrera@tujuca.com	☎ 937 594448 (ⓡ 934 838363) 🖷 937 500495	150	12.02–24.12; 27–31.12	♟♑ ⓡ 👪 🅿 🔲
△ *Candanchu* - *"Albergue Aysa Candanchu"* *Puerto de Somport-* *Candanchu-22889 Huesca.*	☎ *974 378016* (ⓡ *976 714797*) 🖷 *974 714049*	*40*	*01.01–30.05;* *01.07–15.10;* *01–31.12*	♟♑ ⟨CC⟩ 🅿 ☕

Location/Address	Telephone No. Fax No.	Beds	Opening Dates	Facilities
△ *Canfranc* *Plaza del Pilar 2-3,* *22880 Canfranc-Estación (Huesca).*	☎ *974 378016* (ℝ *976 714797)* 🖶 *974 293040;* *976 714049*	*36*	*01.01–31.05;* *01.07–31.12* *(👪 only)*	ℝ ⌐CC⌐ ♂ 🖭
▲ Canyamars - Mas Silvestre Veinat Rimblas, 14, 08319 Canyamars (Barcelona). ✉ alberg_canyamars@tujuca.com	☎ 937 955014 (ℝ 934 838363) 🖶 937 955199	160	01.01–06.01; 27.02–08.12; 26.12–31.12	⏧ ℝ P
▲ Caracenilla - Peñarrubias c/ Consuelo, 4, 16540. Caracenilla (Cuenca).	☎ 969 272711; 969 272652	30	🗓	👪 ⏧ ℝ P 🖭
▲ Carrión de los Condes - Rio Carrion Pl. Martin Campagnat, 1, 34120 Carrion de los Condes (Palencia).	☎ 979 881063 🖶 979 881063	170	🗓	👪 ⏧ ℝ ⌐CC⌐ ♂ P 🖭 ☕
▲ Castelló de la Plana - El Maestrat Avda. Germans Bou, 26, 12003 Castelló de la Plana.	☎ 964 220457; 964 2235403 (ℝ 963 985900) 🖶 964 237600	84	01.01–30.07	👪 ⏧ ℝ ♂
▲ Castelló de la Plana - Mare de Deu del Lledó c/ Orfebres Santalínea 2, 12005 Castelló de la Plana.	☎ 964 254096; 964 254392 (ℝ 963 985900) 🖶 964 216677	90	CLOSED FOR REPAIRS	⏧ ℝ
▲ Castellbell i El Vilar (Barcelona) - "Viladomsde Baix" Carretera de la Bauma a Vacarisses, K 5, 150-08296 Castellbell i El Vilar (Barcelona).	☎ 938 282236 🖶 937 805299		🗓	⏧ ℝ ♿ ⌐CC⌐ P
▲ Cazorla Pza Mauricio Martínez 6, 23470 Cazorla (Jaén). ✉ reservas@inturjoven.junta-andalucia.es	☎ 953 720329 🖶 953 720203	120	🗓	⏧ ℝ ♿ ⌐CC⌐ 🖭
▲ Cercedilla - Alvaro Iglesias Puerto de Navacerrada, Cercedilla 28470 Madrid.	☎ 918 523887 🖶 918 523891	92	02.01–15.08; 16.09–30.12	⏧ ℝ P
▲ Cercedilla - Villa Castora Cta de las Dehesas s/n, Cercedilla, 28470 Madrid.	☎ 918 520334 🖶 918 522411	80	02.01–15.08; 01.10–30.12	👪 ⏧ ℝ
▲ Cercedilla - Las Dehesas Crta de las Dehesas s/n, Cercedilla, 28470 Madrid.	☎ 918 520135 🖶 918 521836	72	02.01–15.08; 01.10–30.12	⏧ ℝ ♿ P
▲ Chipiona Pinar de la Villa s/n, 11550 Chipiona (Cádiz). ✉ reservas@inturjoven.junta-andalucia.es	☎ 956 371480 🖶 965 371480	216	Easter & Summer (🗓 👪)	👪 ⏧ ℝ
▲ Ciudad Real - Albergue Juvenil Orea Ctra Toledo s/n, 13080 Cíudad Real.	☎ 926 690241 🖶 949 836435	120	🗓	👪 ⏧ ♿ P 🖭
▲ Constantina c/ Cuesta Blanca S/N, 41450 Constantina (Sevilla). ✉ reservas@inturjoven.junta-andalucia.es	☎ 955 881589 🖶 955 881619	93	🗓	⏧ ℝ ♿ P

Location/Address	Telephone No. Fax No.	Beds	Opening Dates	Facilities
▲ **Comaruga** - Sta Maria del Mar Av Palfuriana 80, 43880 Comaruga (Tarragona). e alberg_comaruga@tujuca.com	☏ 977 680008 (Ⓡ 934 838363) ❶ 977 682959	180	01.02–30.11	
▲ **Córdoba** **Plaza Judá Leví S/N., 14003 Córdoba.** e informacion@inturjoven.junta.andalucia.es	☏ 957 290166 ❶ 957 290500	170		
▲ **Cortes de la Frontera** Crta A373, Villamartín - Puerta del Espino Km, 51 600 Cortes de la Frontera (Málaga). e reservas@inturjoven.junta-andalucia.es	☏ 954 277087 ❶ 954 277462	146	01.07–31.12 (only weekends)	
△ *Daroca - Albergue Juvenil Daroca* *c/ Cortes de Aragón, 13,* *50360 Daroca (Zaragoza).*	☏ *976 800129;* *976 801268* ❶ *976 800362*	*60*		
▲ **Deltebre** - Mn. Antoni Batlle Avda de les Goles de L'Ebre, s/n, 43580 Deltebre (Tarragona). e alberg_deltebre@tujuca.com	☏ 977 480136 ❶ 977 481284	120		
▲ **Donostia-San Sebastian** - La Sirena **Paseo de Igeldo 25,** **2008 Donostia-San Sebastian.** e udala.youthostel@donostia.org	☏ 943 310268; 943 311293 ❶ 943 214090	96		2SW
▲ **Donostia-San Sebastian** - Ulia-Mendi Parque de Ulia, Paseo de Ulia 299, 20013 Donostia-San Sebastian. e udalayouthostel@donostia.org	☏ 943 310268 ❶ 943 214090	60	01.01–31.08; 01.10–31.12 (♦♦♦ only)	5NE
▲ **Empúries** - L'Escala Les Coves, 41, 17130 L'Escala (Girona). e alberg_empuries@tujuca.com	☏ 972 771200 (Ⓡ 934 838363) ❶ 972 771572	68	02.01–31.09; 16.10–20.12	
▲ **Espejo** Ctra. de Barrio, 1, 01423 Espejo (Araba).	☏ 947 351150; 945 181988 ❶ 945 181988	116		
▲ **L'Espluga de Francolí** - Jaume I Les Masies s/n, 43440 L'Espluga de Francolí (Tarragona). e alberg_espluga@tujuca.com	☏ 977 870356 (Ⓡ 934 838363) ❶ 977 870414	160		
▲ **Espinosa** - Espinosa de los Monteros Carretera de Baranda S/N, 09560 Espinosa de los Monteros (Burgos).	☏ 947 143660; 947 120449 ❶ 947 120449	75		0.6N
▲ **Estella** - Oncineda Monasterio de Irache S/N, 31200 Estella (Navarra). e oncineda@accesocero.es	☏ 948 555022 ❶ 948 551745	125		
△ *Ezcaray - Molino Viejo* *Camino de los Molinos s/n,* *26280 Ezcaray (La Rioja).*	☏ *941 354197*	*49*		
▲ **Figueres** - "Tramuntana" Ⓘ Ⓑ Ⓝ Anicet de Pagès, 2 17600 Figueres (Girona). e alberg_figueres@tujuca.com	☏ 972 501213 ❶ 972 673808	50	Closed for repairs	

Location/Address	Telephone No. Fax No.	Beds	Opening Dates	Facilities
Fuenterrabia ☞Hondarribia				
▲ **Girona** - Cerveri de Girona Dels Ciutadans, 9, 17004 Girona. @ alberg_giroua@tujuca.com	☎ 972 218003 (ℝ 934 838363) 🖷 972 212023	100	🖅	ⅱ ⑪ ℝ ㋹ 🔟
▲ **Granada** - Albergue Juvenil Granada **Avda Ramon y Cajal 2, 18003 Granada.** @ informacion@inturjoven.junta-andalucia.es	☎ 958 002900 🖷 958 002908	229	🖅	⑪ ℝ ㋹ ℗
△ *Grañón* - *Ermita el Carrasquedo Crta Cordorales, s/n 26259 Grañón (La Rioja).*	☎ 941 746000	40	01.01–15.09; 01.10–31.12	ⅱ ℝ
△ *Guía* - *Albergue Juvenil San Fernando Av Juventud s/n, Sta Maria de Guía, Gran Canaria.*	☎ 928 550827 🖷 928 882728	87	🖅	ⅱ ⑪ ℝ ℗ 🔟
▲ **Hondarribia-Fuenterrabia** - "Juan Sebastian Elkano" Carretera del Faro, s/n 20280 Hondarribia, Gipuzkoa. @ juv.hondarribia@gazteria.gipuzkoa.met	☎ 943 641550 (ℝ ⅱ only) 🖷 943 640028	200	02.01–23.12; 26–30.12	ⅱ ⑪ ㋹ ℗
▲ **Huelva** Avenida Marchena Colombo 14, 21004 Huelva. @ reservas@inturjoven.junta-andalucia.es	☎ 959 253793 🖷 959 253499	128	🖅	⑪ ℝ ㋹
△ *Jaca* - *Escuelas Pías Avda Perimetral s/n, 22700 Jaca (Huesca).*	☎ 974 360536 🖷 974 362559	150	🖅	⑪ ℝ ㋹ ☞ ℗ 🔟 🍷
▲ **Jerez de la Frontera** Avda Carrero Blanco 30, 11408 -Jérez de la Frontera (Cádiz). @ reservas@inturjoven.junta-andalucia.es	☎ 956 143901 🖷 956 143263	120	🖅	⑪ ℝ ㋹ ℗
▲ **Layos** - El Castillo de Layos c/ Conde de Mora 14, Layos (Toledo). @ layoscam@cempr	☎ 925 376585 🖷 913 572564	120	🖅	⑪ ℝ ℗
▲ **Lekároz** - "Valle De Baztan" 31795 Lekároz (Navarra). @ aubaztan@cfnavarra.es	☎ 948 581804 🖷 948 581838	90	🖅	ⅱ ⑪ ℝ ㋹ ㏄ ℗ 🔟 🍷
▲ **León** - Albergue Municipal de León C/ Campos Góticos, s/n 24005 León.	☎ 987 259508; 987 255805 🖷 987 272765	96	🖅	ℝ ☞ 🔟
▲ **León** - Infanta Doña Sancha C/ Corredera 4, 24004 León.	☎ 987 203009; 987 203459 🖷 987 251525	124	01.07–15.08	⑪ ℝ ㋹ ☞ 🔟
▲ **León** - Consejo de Europa Paseo del Parque 2, 24005 León.	☎ 987 200206; 987 202969 🖷 987 251453	94	01.07–15.08	⑪ ℝ 🔟 🍷
▲ **León** - Miguel de Unamuno San Pelayo 15, 24003 León.	☎ 987 233010; 987 233203 🖷 987 233010	60	01.07–30.09	ⅱ ⑪ ℝ ℗ 🔟 🍷
▲ **Lés** - "Matacabos" Sant Jaume s/n, 25540 Lés, Val D'Aran (Lleida).	☎ 973 648048 (ℝ 934 838363) 🖷 973 648352	46	🖅	ⅱ ⑪ ℝ

Location/Address	Telephone No. Fax No.	Beds	Opening Dates	Facilities
▲ Llanes - Juventudes c/ Celso Amieva 7, 33500 Llanes (Asturias).	☎ 98 5400770 ❻ 98 5400770	16	⌷₁₂	⑂ ⓵
Lleida ☞La Seu d'Urgell				
▲ Lleida - Sant Anastasi Rambla d'Aragó 11, 25003 Lleida. 🅴 alberg_lleida@tujuca.com	☎ 973 266099 (🆁 934 838363) ❻ 973 261865	120	⌷₁₂	⑂ ⑂ 🆁 🗇
▲ Logroño - Residencia Universitaria c/ Caballero de la Rosa 38, 26004 Logroño.	☎ 941 291145	92	01.07–30.09	⑂ 🆁 🗇
▲ Loredo Bajada Playa de Loredo s/n, 39140 Loredo (Cantabria).	☎ 942 504160; 919 464221	48	01.01–31.08; 01.10–31.12	🗇
▲ Luarca - Fernán Coronas El Villar S/N, 33700 Luarca (Asturias).	☎ 98 5640676 ❻ 98 5640557	18	⌷₁₂	⑂ 🆁 🅿
▲ Lugo - Eijo Garay c/ Pintor Corredoira 4, 27002 Lugo.	☎ 982 220450 ❻ 982 230524	100	01.07–30.09	⑂ 🆁 🅿 🗇
▲ Lugo - Hermanos Pedrosa R.J. Pintor Corredoira 2, 27002 Lugo.	☎ 982 221090	100	01.07–30.09	⑂ 🅿
▲ Madrid - "San Fermín" Auda. De Los Fueros, 36, 28041 Madrid. 🅴 albergue@retemail.es	☎ 917 920897 ❻ 917 924724	60	⌷₁₂	⑂ ⓵ ⌗ 🅿 🗇 ☕
▲ Madrid - Richard Schirrman Casa de Campo, 28011 Madrid.	☎ 914 635699 ❻ 914 644685	132	⌷₁₂	⑂ 🆁 ⓵ 🅿 🗇 ☕
▲ Madrid - Sta Cruz de Marcenado Calle Sta Cruz de Marcenado No 28, 28015 Madrid.	☎ 915 474532 ❻ 915 481196	72		🆁 ⓵ 🗇
▲ Las Majadas - Los Callejones Plaza Mayor s/n, 16142 Las Majadas (Cuenca).	☎ 969 283050 ❻ 969 283121	60	⌷₁₂	⑂ 🆁 🔄CC
▲ Málaga Plaza Pio XII 6, 29007 Málaga. 🅴 reservas@inturjoven.junta-andalucia.es	☎ 952 308500 ❻ 952 308504	110	⌷₁₂	⑂ 🆁 ⓵ 🔄CC
▲ Manresa - Del Carme Pl del Milcentenari de Manresa, s/n 08240 Manresa (Barcelona). 🅴 alberg_olot@tujuca.com	☎ 938 750396 (🆁 934 838363) ❻ 938 726838	71	06.01–07.08; 29.08–21.12	⑂ ⑂ 🆁 ⓵ ⌗ 🅿
▲ Marbella Calle Trapiche 2, 29600 Marbella (Málaga). 🅴 reservas@inturjoven.junta-andalucia.es	☎ 952 771491 ❻ 952 863227	141	⌷₁₂	⑂ 🆁 ⓵ 🅿
▲ El Masnou - Josep Ma Batista i Roca ⌷IBN⌷ Av dels Srs Cusí i Furtunet 52, 08320 El Masnou (Barcelona). 🅴 albergelmasnou@tujuca.com	☎ 935 555600 ❻ 935 400552	84	11.01–07.12	⑂ 🆁 ⓵ 🅿
▲ Mazagón Cuesta de la Barca S/N, 21130 Mazagón (Huelva). 🅴 reservas@inturjoven.junta-andalucia.es	☎ 959 536262 ❻ 959 536201	132	⌷₁₂ (⑂ Only except Easter & Summer)	⑂ 🆁 ⓵ 🅿

Location/Address	Telephone No. Fax No.	Beds	Opening Dates	Facilities
▲ **Miranda de Ebro** - Fernán Gonzalez c/ Anduva 82, **09200 Miranda de Ebro (Burgos).**	☏ 947 320932 📠 947 320334	110	🗓	♯♯ ⵟⵔ ℝ ⛵ 🅿 ⛃
▲ **La Molina** - Mare de Déu de les Neus Ctra de Font Canaleta, 17537 La Molina (Girona). ✉ alberg_lamolina@tujuca.com	☏ 72 892012 (ℝ 934 838363) 📠 72 892050	148	01.01–23.12; 26–31.12	♯♯ ⵟⵔ ℝ 🅿 ⛃
▲ **Moraira-Teulada** - La Marina Cami Del Campament, 31, 03724 Moraira-Teulada (Alicante).	☏ 966 492030; 966 492044 📠 966 491051	130	🗓	♯♯ ⵟⵔ ℝ ♿ ⛵ 🅿 ⛃ ☕
▲ **Morella** - Francesc de Vinatea Crta. Morella Forcall, km. 4,5 12300 Morella (Castelló).	☏ 964 160100 (ℝ 963 985900) 📠 963 985900	60	🗓	♯♯ ⵟⵔ ℝ ♿ 🅿 ⛽
△ *Munilla* - *Hayedo de Santiago c/ Cipriano Martinez 29, 26586 Munilla (La Rioja).*	☏ *941 394213*	*50*	🗓	ⵟⵔ ℝ
▲ **Navamorcuende** - El Chortalillo Camino de la Tablada s/n, 45630 Navamorcuende, (Toledo.).	☏ 925 811186	136	🗓	ⵟⵔ ℝ 🅿 ⛃
▲ **Navarredonda de Gredos** - Albergue Juvenil "Navarredonda de Gredos" **Crta. Comarcal C-500 Km 41.5, 05635 Navarredonda de Gredos (Avila).** ✉ albmgredos@durnet.es	☏ 920 348005 📠 920 348005	63	🗓	♯♯ ⵟⵔ ℝ ⊟CC⊟ 🅿 ⛃ ⛽
▲ **Naves (Lleida)** - "Alberg Rectoria de la Selva" c/ La Selva, 25286 Naves (Lleida).	☏ 972 264200 📠 972 271896	111	🗓	♯♯ ⵟⵔ ℝ ♿ ⊟CC⊟ 🅿
▲ **Nogueira de Ramuin** - A Penalba Nogueira de Ramuin, 32004 Orense.	☏ 988 201127	30	01.01–30.06; 01.10–31.12	ⵟⵔ ⛃
▲ **Nogueira de Ramuin** - Monasterio de San Estevo de Rivas do Sil Nogueira de Ramuin, 32004 Orense.	☏ 988 201127	32	01.01–30.06; 01.10–31.12	⛃
▲ **Olot** - Torre Malagrida Passeig de Barcelona 15, 17800 Olot (Girona). ✉ alber_alot@tujuca.com	☏ 972 264200 (ℝ 934 838363) 📠 972 271896	76	🗓	♯♯ ⵟⵔ ℝ ♿ ⊟CC⊟ ⛃
▲ **Orea** - Albergue el Autillo Llano Hoz Seca, 19311 Orea (Guadalajara).	☏ 949 836470 📠 948 836470	70	🗓	ⵟⵔ 🅿 ⛃
▲ **Ourense** - Florentino López Cuevillas Arturo Perez Serantes 2, 32005 Ourense.	☏ 988 252412; 988 252451	60	01.07–30.09	♿ 🅿
▲ **Oviedo** - Ramon Mendéndez Pidal Avda Julian Clavería 14, 33006 Oviedo.	☏ 985 232054 📠 985 233393	6	01.01–30.06; 01.10–31.12; 01.07–30.09	ⵟⵔ 🅿
▲ **Palencia** - Escuela Castilla R.J. Avenida de San Telmo S/N, 34004 Palencia.	☏ 979 721475; 979 721650	65	Closed for repairs	♯♯ ⵟⵔ ⛵ 🅿 ⛃ ⛽
▲ **Palencia** - Residencia Victorio Macho Doctor Fleming S/N, 34004 Palencia.	☏ 979 711676	42	01.07–15.08	♯♯ ⵟⵔ ℝ ⛃

Las Palmas ☞ **Guía**

Location/Address	Telephone No. Fax No.	Beds	Opening Dates	Facilities
▲ **Palma de Mallorca** - "Platja de Palma" Calle Costa Brava, 13, 07610 Palma de Mallorca. e albergue.platja.de.palma@bitel.es	☎ 902 111188 🖷 971 176096	94	🗓	ⅲ ⅰⓄⅼ ⲉⲥⲥ ☞ ☕
▲ **Pamplona** - Fuerte del Principe Goroabe 36; 31002 Pamplona-Iruña (Navarra). e residencia.fuerte.principe@cfnavarra.es	☎ 948 291206 🖷 948 290540	25	🗓	ⅰⓄⅼ Ⓡ 0.5 SE ♿ Ⓟ 🗐
▲ **Peñaranda de Bracamonte** - Resid. "Diego de Torres y Villarroel" c/ Severo Ochoa 4, 37300 Peñaranda de Bracamonte (Salamanca).	☎ 923 540988; 923 296000 🖷 923 540988	50	🗓	ⅲ ⅰⓄⅼ Ⓡ 🗐
▲ **Peralta de la Sal** - Escuelas Pias Plaza Escuelas Pias No 1. 22513 Peralta de la Sal (Huesca).	☎ 974 411031 🖷 974 411203	80	🗓	ⅲ ⅰⓄⅼ Ⓡ ☞ Ⓟ 🗐 ☕
▲ **Pesquera** - Fernandez de Los Rios 39491 Pesquera (Cantabria).	☎ 942 778614	42	🗓	🗐
▲ **Piles** - Mar i Vent Doctor Fleming s/n, 46712 Platja De Piles (Valencia).	☎ 962 831625 (Ⓡ 963 985900) 🖷 962 831121	89	01.02–15.12	ⅲ ⅰⓄⅼ Ⓡ ♿ ☞ 🗐
▲ **Planoles** - Pere Figuera (IBN) Ctra de Neva Prat Cap Riu S/N, 17535 Planoles, Girona. e alberg_planoles@tujuca	☎ 972 736177 🖷 972 736431	170	🗓	ⅲ ⅰⓄⅼ Ⓡ ♿ Ⓟ
▲ **Plentzia** - A.J. Plentzia Ibitoki, 1, 48620 Plentzia (Bizkaia).	☎ 946 771866; 944 208746 (Ⓡ ⅲ only) 🖷 946 773041	12	08.01–21.12	ⅲ ⅰⓄⅼ Ⓡ ♿ Ⓟ
▲ **Poble Nou Del Delta** - L'Encanyissada Poble Nou Del Delta, 43549 Amposta (Tarragona). e alberg_poblenou@tujuca.com	☎ 977 742203 🖷 977 742709	50	07.01–01.04; 14.09–25.12	ⅲ ⅰⓄⅼ Ⓡ
▲ **Poo de Llanes** - Fonte del Cai Carretera General, 33500 Poo de Llanes (Asturias).	☎ 985 400205 🖷 985 401019	10	🗓	ⅰⓄⅼ Ⓡ ☞
▲ **Pueyo De Jaca** - "A.J. Quinta Vista Alegre" c/ Afueras, 1, 22662 El Pueyo de Jaca (Huesca).	☎ 974 487045 🖷 974 487045	84	🗓	ⅰⓄⅼ ☕
▲ **Punta Umbría** Avenida Océano 13, 2110 Punta Umbria (Huelva). e reservas@inturjoven.junta-andalucia.es	☎ 959 311650 🖷 959 314229	102	Christmas, Easter and Summer	ⅰⓄⅼ Ⓡ ♿
▲ **Queralbs** - Pic de Áliga c/ Núria, 17534 s/n Queralbs (Girona). e alberg_tarrega@tujuca.com	☎ 972 732048 🖷 972 732048	138	🗓	ⅲ ⅰⓄⅼ Ⓡ
▲ **Rascafria** - Los Batanes Rascafria, 28740 Madrid.	☎ 918 691511 🖷 918 690125	122	02.01–15.08; 01.10–30.12	ⅲ ⅰⓄⅼ Ⓡ ♿ Ⓟ
▲ **Ribadeo** - A Devesa 27700 Ribadeo, Lugo.	☎ 982 123300	75	15.06–30.08	ⅲ Ⓡ Ⓟ 🗐

Location/Address	Telephone No. Fax No.	Beds	Opening Dates	Facilities
▲ **Ribadesella** - "Roberto Frassinelli" c/ Ricardo Cangas, s/n 33560-Ribadesella (Asturias).	☎ 985 861380	6	Easter, Summer & Christmas	⋔ Ⓡ ☞
▲ **Roncesvalles** - Roncesvalles Orreaga Real Colegiata, Roncesvalles (Navarra). ✉ aronces@cfnavarra.es	☎ 948 760307; 948 760302 ✆ 948 760362	80	01.01–31.10; 01–31.12	ⓣⓞⓛ Ⓡ ♿ ⒸⒸ Ⓟ 🗑
▲ **Ruidera** - Alonso Quijano CRTA. de las Lagunas, s/n. 13249 Ossa de Montiel (Albacete).	☎ 926 528053	80	🔟	⋔ ⓣⓞⓛ
▲ **Ruiloba** - "Gargantia" B-° La Iglesia, s/n 39527 Ruiloba (Cantabria).	☎ 942 720172; 908 285167	40	🔟	Ⓟ 🌢
▲ **San Martin de Castañeda** Ctra. Lago Sanabria, San Martin de Castañeda, 49361 Zamora.	☎ 980 622053; 980 521700 ✆ 980 622053	70	🔟	ⓣⓞⓛ Ⓡ Ⓟ 🗑
▲ **Salamanca** - Albergue Juvenil "Salamanca" **C/ Escoto 13-15, 37008 Salamanca.** ✉ esterra@mmteam.disgumad.es	☎ 923 269141 ✆ 923 269141; 923 214227	44	🔟	⋔ ⓣⓞⓛ Ⓡ ♿ Ⓟ 🗑
▲ **Salardú** - Era Garona CRTA. de Viella, 25598 Salardú, Lleida.	☎ 973 645271 ✆ 973 644136	180	🔟	⋔ Ⓡ ♿ ⒸⒸ Ⓟ 🗑
△ *San Juan de Plan* - *El Molin* *c/ Las Callerizas,* *s/n 22367 San Juan de Plan, Huesca.*	☎ *974 506208;* *974 506097* ✆ *974 506208*	*22*	🔟	Ⓡ Ⓟ 🌢
▲ **San Lorenzo del Escorial** - Sta Maria Buen Aire Finca de la Herreria s/n, San Lorenzo de el Escorial, 28200 Madrid.	☎ 918 903640 ✆ 918 903792	88	02.01–15.08; 01.10–30.12	ⓣⓞⓛ Ⓡ Ⓟ
▲ **San Lorenzo del Escorial** - El Escorial c/ Residencia 14, San Lorenzo de El Escorial, 28200 Madrid.	☎ 918 905924 ✆ 918 900620	85	02.01–15.08; 01.10–30.12	⋔ ⓣⓞⓛ Ⓡ ♿ 🗑 🌢
▲ **San Pablo de los Montes** - Baños del Sagrario c/ Peña del Soto, 36, 45120 San Pablo de los Montes (Toledo).	☎ 608 913968	300	🔟	ⓣⓞⓛ Ⓡ ☞ Ⓟ 🗑
▲ **San Rafael** Paseo de San Juan, s/n 40410 San Rafael (Segovia).	☎ 921 171457; 921 417384	50	🔟	ⓣⓞⓛ Ⓡ
▲ **San Rafael** - El Recreo c/ Pinar No. 1, 40410 San Rafael (Segovia).	☎ 921 171900 ✆ 921 171900	80	🔟	⋔ ⓣⓞⓛ Ⓡ ♿ ⒸⒸ Ⓟ
San Sebastian 🕮Donostia				
▲ **San Vicente del Monte** 39592 San Vicente del Monte (Cantabria).	☎ 919 464193	50	🔟	🗑
▲ **Santiago de Compostela** - Monte do Gozo **Carretera de Santiago-Aeropuerto KM 3, 15820 Santiago de Compostela (A Coruña).**	☎ 981 558942 ✆ 981 562892	300	🔟	ⓣⓞⓛ ♿ Ⓟ 🗑 🌢
▲ **Segovia** - Emperador Teodosio Avda Conde de Sepúlveda s/n, 40002 Segovia.	☎ 921 441111; 921 441047	118	01.07–15.08	⋔ ⓣⓞⓛ Ⓡ ♿ 🗑

Location/Address	Telephone No. Fax No.	Beds	Opening Dates	Facilities
▲ **Seseña** - Sta Maria del Sagrario Ctra de Andalucía Km 36, 200, 45224 Seseña Nuevo (Toledo).	☎ 918 936152 📠 918 936152	55	01.01–14.09; 21.10–31.12	⍾ P
▲ **La Seu d'Urgell** - La Valira Joaquin Viola 57, 25700 La Seu d'Urgell (Lleida). ✉ alberg_laseu@tujuca.com	☎ 973 353897 (ℝ 934 838363) 📠 973 353874	100	🗐 (except 24–25.12)	⍾ ℝ ♿ P 🗐
▲ **Sevilla** **Isaac Peral 2, 41012 Sevilla.** ✉ informacion@inturjoven.junta-andalucia.es	☎ 955 056500 📠 955 056508	277	🗐	⍾ ℝ ♿
▲ **Sierra Nevada** C/ Peñones, 22. 18196 Sierra Nevada (Granada). ✉ reservas@inturjoven.junta-andalucia.es	☎ 958 480305 📠 958 481377	214	🗐	⍾ ℝ ♿ CC P
△ *Sin - Tella Sin Calle Unica, s/n 22366 SIN (Huesca).*	☎ *974 506212*	*49*	🗐	⍾ ℝ CC P
▲ **Siresa** - "Albergue Juvenil del Nucleo de las Escuelas de Siresa" c/Reclusa, s/n, Siresa-22790 (Huesca).	☎ 976 615283; 619 561004 📠 976 615283	53	🗐	⍾ ✄ 🗐
▲ **Solorzano** - Albergue Juvenil Gerardo Diego B-º Quintana, s/n 39739 Solorzano (Cantabria).	☎ 942 676342; 919 464220	60	01.01–31.08; 01.10–31.12	✄ 🗐
▲ **Soncillo** Avda Alejandro Rodriguez Valcarcel s/n 09572 Soncillo (Burgos).	☎ 947 7153024; 947 153080	60	🗐 ⍾⍾⍾ only	⍾⍾⍾ ⍾ ℝ
▲ **Soria** - Antonio Machado R.J. Plaza José Antonio 1, 42004 Soria.	☎ 975 220089	80	01.07–15.08	⍾⍾⍾ ⍾
▲ **Soria** - Juan A. Gaya Nuño Paseo de San Francisco 1, 42003 Soria.	☎ 975 221466 📠 975 225621	105	01.07–15.08	⍾ ℝ ♿ ✄ 🗐
△ *Soto de Cameros - Hospital San Jose c/ San Jose s/n, 26132 Soto de Cameros (La Rioja).*	☎ *941 291100* 📠 *941 256120*	*46*	🗐	⍾
▲ **Talavera de la Reina** - Albergue Juv. Talavera Carretera de Cervera km 3,5, 45600 Talavera de la Reina (Toledo).	☎ 925 709482; 925 709588; 925 810409 📠 925 709588	100	🗐	⍾⍾⍾ ⍾ 35S P
▲ **Tàrrega** - Residencia Ca N'Aleix Plaça Del Carme, 5, Tarrega (Lleida).	☎ 973 313053 📠 973 500037	110	07.01–01.08; 26.08–23.12	⍾⍾⍾ ⍾ ℝ
▲ **Teruel** - Luis Buñuel Ciudad Escolar s/n, 44003 Teruel.	☎ 978 601712; 978 602223 (ℝ 976 714797) 📠 978 605351; 976 714049	160	01–31.07; 01–30.09	⍾⍾⍾ ⍾ ℝ P
▲ **El Toboso** - El Quijote Avda. Castilla-La Mancha, 12, 45820. El Toboso (Toledo).	☎ 925 197398	50	🗐	⍾⍾⍾ ⍾ CC

Location/Address	Telephone No. Fax No.	Beds	Opening Dates	Facilities
▲ **Toledo** Castillo de San Servando, Toledo.	☎ 925 224554	46	01.01–15.08; 15.09–31.12 (Closed Easter & Christmas)	☞ 🅿 ⬚
▲ **Tragacete** - San Blas 16150 Tragacete (Cuenca).	☎ 969 289131 ✆ 969 178866	64	🗓 (👫 Only)	⑩ Ⓡ
▲ **Ugena** - La Chopera Camino de Yuncos S/N. 45217 Ugena (Toledo).	☎ 925 592741; 916 414422	200	🗓	👫 ☞ 🅿
▲ **Uña** - La Cañadilla c/ Egido 23, 16152 Uña (Cuenca).	☎ 969 281332; 969 281464 ✆ 969 281332	30	🗓	⑩ Ⓡ ₵₵₵ 🅿
▲ **Uncastillo** - Ayllon c/ Mediavilla 30, 50678 Uncastillo (Zaragoza).	☎ 976 679400 ✆ 976 679497	50	🗓	⑩ Ⓡ ☞ ⬚
△ *Undués de Lerda* *c/ Herrería,* *50689 Undués de Lerda (Zaragoza).*	☎ *948 88105;* *689 488745* ✆ *948 888105*	56	*01.03–30.01*	👫 ⑩ ☞ 🅿 ⬚ ☕
▲ **Valdeavellano de Tera** C/Soledad S/N 42165 Valdeavellano de Tera (Soria).	☎ 975 233042	70	🗓	⑩ Ⓡ
▲ **Valdepeñas** - El Cañaveral Crta Comarcal de Valdepeñas/ San Carlos del Valle, s/n 13300 Valdepeñas (Ciudad Real).	☎ 926 338255; 926 322804; 926 322516 ✆ 926 322808	48	🗓	☞
▲ **Valencia de Alcántara** - Sta Mª de Guadalupe Puerto Roque, 10500 Valencia de Alcántara (Cáceres).	☎ 927 584059	10	01.06–31.08 (Thurs–Sun)	👫 ⑩ Ⓡ ♿ 🅿
▲ **Valladolid** - Rio Esgueva c/ Paseo Cementerio, 2, 47011 Valladolid.	☎ 983 251550	80	🗓	👫 ⑩ Ⓡ ☞ ⬚ ☕
▲ **La Vecilla** - "Sta. Catalina" Finca Santa Catalina, 24840 La Vecilla (León).	☎ 987 741212 ✆ 987 741212	70	🗓	👫 ⑩ Ⓡ ♿ ☞ 🅿 ⬚ ☕
▲ **Vic** - Canonge Collel Avgd D'Olimpia S/N, 08500 Vic (Barcelona). ✉ alberg_vic@tujuca.com	☎ 938 894938 (Ⓡ 934 838363)	156	06.01–21.12	👫 ⑩ Ⓡ ₵₵₵ 🅿 ⬚
Vitoria 🖙Gasteiz				
▲ **Vigo** - Altamar c/ Cesáreo González 4, 36210 Vigo (Pontevedra).	☎ 986 290808 ✆ 986 211595	80	01.07–30.09	👫 ⑩ ♿ ⬚ ☕
▲ **Villalba de la Sierra** - Casa Flores c/ Constitucion, 44, 16140 Villalba de la Sierra (Cuenca).	☎ 969 281250	20	🗓	⑩ ₵₵₵ ☞ ☕
▲ **Villamanín** Plaza del Ayuntamiento S/N 24680 Villamanín (León).	☎ 987 598243; 987 240002 ✆ 987 240002	54	🗓	👫 ⑩ Ⓡ 🅿
▲ **Villanúa** - "Sta. Mª del Pilar" Camino de la Selva S/N, 22870 Villanúa (Huesca).	☎ 974 378016 ✆ 976 293040; 976 714049	100	🗓	👫 ⑩ Ⓡ ♿ 🅿

Location/Address	Telephone No. Fax No.	Beds	Opening Dates	Facilities
▲ **Vitoria-Gasteiz** - Carlos Abaitua Escultor Isaac Diez, S/N 01007 Vitoria-Gasteiz (Araba). ⓔ abaitua@clienteeuskaltel.es	ⓣ 945 148100; 945 181988 ⓕ 945 148100	20	01.01–30.06; 01.07–30.09; 01.10–31.12	⑩ Ⓡ ♿ Ⓟ
▲ **Viveiro (Lugo)** - Area Playa de Area - Viveiro, 27837 Vivero (Lugo).	ⓣ 982 560851	120	01.07–30.08	⋔ Ⓡ
▲ **Viznar** Camino de Fuente Grande S/N, 18179 Viznar (Granada). ⓔ reservas@inturjoven.junta-andalucia.es	ⓣ 958 543307 ⓕ 958 543448	108	⒓	⑩ Ⓡ ♿ ᚛CC᚜ ☛ Ⓟ
▲ **Yeste** - Arroyo de la Sierra Valle del Tus, 02480 Yeste (Albacete).	ⓣ 967 574127	45	⒓	⋔ ⑩ Ⓡ ♿ ᚛CC᚜ ☛ Ⓟ ⚑
▲ **Zamora** - Doña Urraca c/ Villalpando No. 7, 49002 Zamora.	ⓣ 980 512671 ⓕ 980 512659	115	01.07–15.08	⋔ ⑩ Ⓡ 〔0.4NW〕♿ Ⓟ ⓸
▲ **Zaragoza** - Baltasar Gracián **c/ Franco y López 4, 50005 Zaragoza.** ⓔ mtmosquera@aragob.es	ⓣ 976 551387; 974 378016 ⓕ 976 553432; 976 714049	50	⒓	⋔ ⑩ Ⓡ ♿ ☛ Ⓟ ⓸
▲ **Zarautz** - Monte Albertia San Inazio 25, 20800 Zarautz, Gipuzkoa. ⓔ juv.zarautz@gazteria.gipuzkoa.met	ⓣ 943 132910 ⓕ 943 130006	182	01.01–31.08; 01.10–31.12	⋔ ⑩ ♿ Ⓟ

YOUTH HOSTEL ACCOMMODATION
OUTSIDE THE ASSURED STANDARDS SCHEME

Biel Avda. de la Mina, s/n. Biel, 50619 (Zaragoza).	ⓣ 976 669001 ⓕ 976 669001	26	⒓	Ⓡ ⓸
Mora de Rubielos c/Pedro Esteban, 28 44400 Mora De Rubielos (Teruel).	ⓣ 978 800000 ⓕ 978 806050	59	⒓	⑩ Ⓡ ☛ Ⓟ ⓸

"Own only what you can carry with you; know language, know countries, know people. Let your memory be your travel bag."

"Ne possède que ce que tu peux emporter avec toi; connais les langues, connais les pays, connais les gens. Que ta mémoire te serve de sac de voyage."

„Besitze nur, was du mitnehmen kannst; lerne Sprache, Länder, Leute kennen. Lass deine Erinnerung deine Reisetasche sein."

"Posee solamente lo que puedas llevar contigo; conoce los idiomas, conoce los países, conoce a la gente. Deja que tu memoria sea tu bolso de viaje."

Alexander Solzhenitsyn

Sweden

SUEDE

SCHWEDEN

SUECIA

Svenska Turistföreningen (STF),
Amiralitetshuset, Skeppsholmen,
PO Box 25,
101 20 Stockholm, Sweden.

☎ (46) (8) 4632100
📠 (46) (8) 6781958
✉ info@stfturist.se
🖥 www.stfturist.se

Office Hours: Monday-Friday, 09.00-17.00hrs

A copy of the Hostel Directory for this Country can be obtained from:
The National Office

Capital:	Stockholm
Language:	Swedish
Currency:	SEK (1Krona/*crown* = 100 öre)

Population:	8.8 million
Size:	449,964 sq km
Telephone Country Code:	46

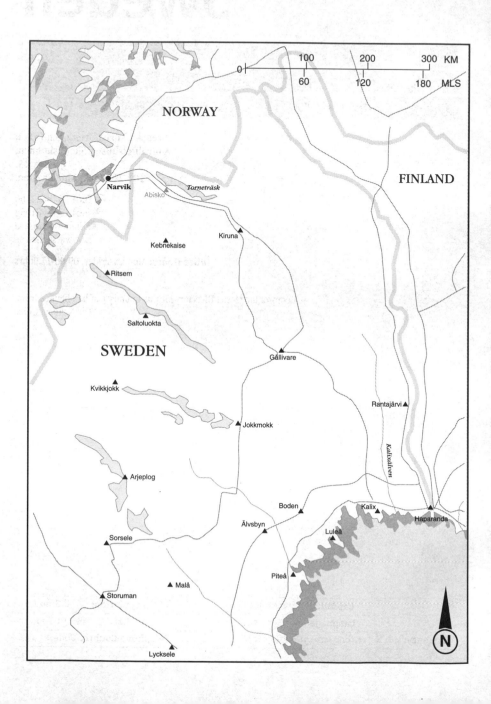

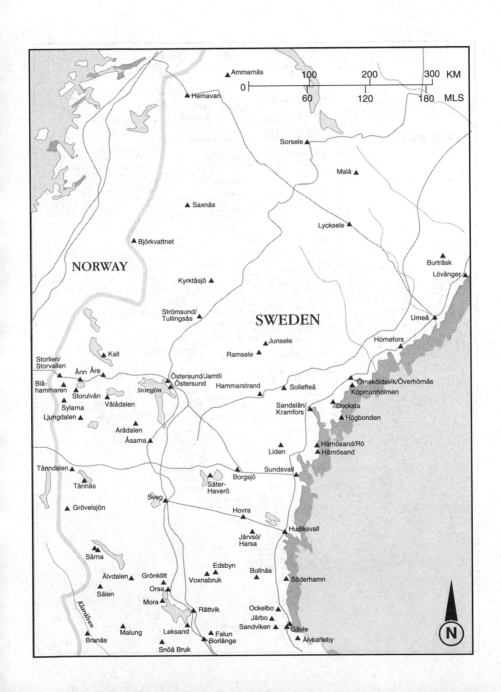

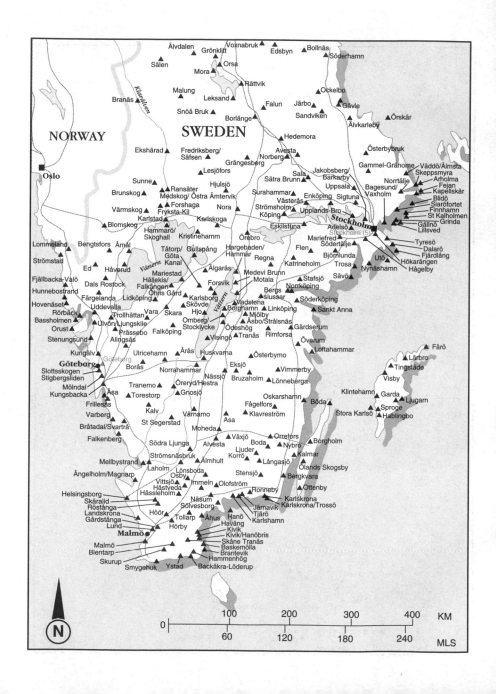

Älvdalen Grönklitt Voxnabruk Edsbyn Bollnäs Söderhamn
Sålen Mora Orsa
Malung Rättvik
Branäs Leksand Ockelbo
Snöå Bruk Falun Järbo Gävle
Borlänge Sandviken Örskär
NORWAY SWEDEN Hedemora Älvkarleby
Ekshärad Fredriksberg/ Avesta Österbybruk
Säfsen Norberg
Grängesberg Gammel-Gränome Väddö/Älmsta
Lesjöfors Sala Jakobsberg/ Skeppsmyra
Oslo Sunne Hjulsjö Sätra Brunn Barkarby Norrtälje Arholma
Ransäter Uppsala Bagesund/ Fejan
Brunskog Medskog/ Östra Ämtervik Surahammar Enköping Sigtuna Vaxholm Kapellskär
Forshaga Västerås Blidö
Värmskog Fryksta-Kil Nora Strömsholm Upplands-Bro Siaröfortet
Karlstad Karlskoga Köping Finnhamn
Blomskog Eskilstuna Stockholm St Kalholmen
Hammarö/ Adelsö Gällnö Grinda
Skoghall Kristinehamn Örebro Mariefred Lillsved
Lommeland Bengtsfors Åmål Tåtorp/ Gullspång Flen Södertälje Tyresö
Göta Hargebaden/ Björnlunda Dalarö
Strömstad Kanal Hammar Regna Katrineholm Utö Fjärdlång
Ed Håverud Mariestad Älgarås Medevi Brunn Trosa Hökarängen
Fjällbacka-Valö Dals Rostock Hällekis/ Motala Nynäshamn Hågelby
Hunnebostrand Falkängen Forsvik Stafsjö Sävö
Hovenäset Färgelanda Lidköping Öhns Gård Karlsborg Bergs Norrköping
Rörbäck Uddevalla Skövde slussar Söderköping
Bassholmen Trollhättan Vara Skara Hjo Vadstena Sankt Anna
Orust Ulvön/Ljungskile Omberg/ Borghamn Linköping
Stenungsund Prässebo Falköping Stocklycke Ödeshög Åsbo/Strålsnäs Gärdserum
Alingsås Visingö Tranås Rimforsa Överum
Kungälv Ulricehamn Årås Huskvarna Österbymo Loftahammar Fårö
Göteborg Borås Eksjö Lärbro
Slottsskogen Norrahammar Nässjö Vimmerby Tingstäde
Stigbergsliden Tranemo Öreryd/Hestra Bruzaholm Lönneberga Visby
Mölndal Åsa Torestorp Gnosjö Klintehamn Garda
Kungsbacka Oskarshamn Böda Ljugarn
Frillesås Kalv Fågelfors Stora Karlsö Sproge
Varberg Värnamo Klavreström Hablingbo
Bråtadal/Svartrå St Segerstad Åsa
Falkenberg Moheda Växjö Orrefors Borgholm
Södra Ljunga Alvesta Boda Nybro
Ljuder Kalmar
Mellbystrand Strömsnäsbruk Älmhult Korrö Långasjö Ölands Skogsby
Ängelholm/Magnarp Laholm Lönsboda Stensjö Bergkvara
Vittsjö/ Osby Immeln Olofström Ottenby
Helsingborg Hästveda Näsum Ronneby
Skäralid Hässleholm Sölvesborg Karlskrona
Röstånga Hanö Järnavik Karlskrona/Trossö
Landskrona Höör Tollarp Åhus Tjärö
Gårdstånga Hörby Haväng Karlshamn
Lund Malmö Kivik
Kivik/Hanöbris
Malmö Skåne Tranås
Blentarp Baskemölla
Skurup Brantevik
Smygehuk Ystad Backåkra-Löderup Hammenhög

KM
0 100 200 300 400
60 120 180 240
N MLS

English

Hostels are located in cities, in the countryside, on the coast and on hills/mountains.

Price range

Price range SEK 90-190. € 10-22. ▦ Sheet sleeping bag required.

Rooms and Reservations

R during Jun-Aug. (All Rooms). Reservations via (IBN) 🖳 or Hostel by ☉ ❶ ⓔ. All hostels are non-smoking.

Guests

Membership Card is required. ♦♦♦ welcome. Group bookings via 🖳 or Hostel by ☉ ❶ ⓔ (Reservation charges may apply).

Open times

Main hostels: open ▦, ⏰. Reception open: ⏰. **Other hostels:** open ▦, 08:00-10:00hrs, 17:00-20:00hrs. Reception open: 08:00-10:00hrs, 17:00-20:00hrs. **Seasonal hostels** are generally open Jun-Aug.

Meals

⊙ B **R** For ♦♦♦. 👞.

Travelling around

For ease of travel use 🚌 🚐 Self-Drive.

Travel/Activity Packages

Walking/trekking packages available.

Passports and Visas

Passport required.

Health

Medical insurance is recommended. EU Nationals require Form E111 to obtain treatment within EU countries.

Français

Les auberges sont situées dans les villes, à la campagne, sur le littoral et à la montagne.

Tarifs des nuitées

Tarifs des nuitées 90-190 SEK. € 10-22. ▦ Sac-drap obligatoire.

Chambres et réservations

R juin-août. (Toutes chambres). Réservations via (IBN) 🖳 ou l'auberge par ☉ ❶ ⓔ. Toutes les auberges sont non-fumeurs.

Usagers

La carte d'adhérent est à présenter. Accueil des ♦♦♦. Réservations pour groupes via 🖳 ou l'auberge par ☉ ❶ ⓔ (Des frais de réservation pourront vous être facturés).

Horaires d'ouverture

Grandes auberges: ouvertes ▦, ⏰. Accueil ouvert ⏰. **Autres auberges:** ouvertes ▦, entre 8h-10h, 17h-20h. Accueil ouvert entre 8h-10h, 17h-20h. **Auberges saisonnières** ouvertes généralement juin-août.

Repas

⊙ B **R** Pour ♦♦♦. 👞.

Déplacements

Modes de transport recommandés 🚌 🚐 Voiture.

Forfaits Voyages/Activités

Forfaits randonnées pédestres disponibles.

Passeports et visas

Passeport obligatoire.

Santé

Une assurance médicale de voyage est conseillée. Les ressortissants de l'Union Européenne doivent se munir du formulaire

E111 pour bénéficier de soins médicaux dans les états de l'UE.

Deutsch

Herbergen befinden sich in Städten, auf dem Land, an der Küste und in Bergen/Gebirgen.

Preisspanne

Preisspanne 90-190 SEK. € 10-22. 🗒 Leinenschlafsack erforderlich.

Zimmer und Reservierungen

🆁 während Jun-Aug. (Alle Zimmer). Reservierungen über (IBN) ⌨ oder die Herberge per ☎ 🖷 ✉. Rauchen ist in allen Herbergen NICHT gestattet.

Gäste

Mitgliedsausweis ist erforderlich. ♦♦♦ willkommen. Gruppenbuchungen über ⌨ oder die Herberge per ☎ 🖷 ✉ (Reservierungskosten könnten anfallen).

Öffnungszeiten

Hauptherbergen: Zugang 🗒, 🕐. Rezeption 🕐. **Andere Herbergen:** Zugang 🗒, 08:00-10:00Uhr, 17:00-20:00Uhr. Rezeption zwischen 08:00-10:00Uhr, 17:00-20:00Uhr. **Saison-Herbergen** sind normalerweise Jun-Aug geöffnet.

Mahlzeiten.

🍽 B 🆁 Für ♦♦♦. 🍴.

Reisen im Land

Reisen ist einfach mit 🚂 🚌 Selbstfahrer.

Reise-/Aktivitäten-Packages

Wandern/Trekking-Packages erhältlich.

Reisepässe und Visa

Reisepass erforderlich.

Gesundheit

Unfall-/Krankenversicherung wird empfohlen. EU Staatsangehörige benötigen Formular E111 für ärztliche Behandlungen innerhalb der EU Länder.

Español

Los albergues están situados en las ciudades, el campo, la costa y la montaña.

Tarifas mínima y máxima

Tarifas mínima y máxima 90-190 SEK. € 10-22. 🗒 Saco sábana imprescindible.

Habitaciones y Reservas

🆁 en jun-ago. (Todas las habitaciones). Reservas por (IBN) ⌨ o a través del albergue por ☎ 🖷 ✉. Está prohibido fumar en todos los albergues.

Huéspedes

Los huéspedes deben presentar su Carnet de Alberguista. Se admiten ♦♦♦. Reservas de grupo por ⌨ o a través del albergue por ☎ 🖷 ✉ (Es posible que se aplique un suplemento en concepto de gastos de reserva).

Horarios y fechas de apertura

Albergues principales - abiertos 🗒, 🕐. Horario de recepción: 🕐. **Otros albergues** - abiertos 🗒, 08:00-10:00h, 17:00-20:00h. Horario de recepción: 08:00-10:00h, 17:00-20:00h. **Albergues de temporada** suelen abrir: jun-ago.

Comidas

🍽 B 🆁 Para ♦♦♦. 🍴.

Desplazamientos

Transportes recomendados: 🚂 🚌 Automóvil.

Viajes Combinados con Actividades

Viajes combinados con senderismo.

Pasaportes y Visados

Pasaporte obligatorio.

Información Sanitaria

Seguro médico recomendado. Los ciudadanos procedentes de países pertenecientes a la UE necesitan el impreso E111 para obtener asistencia médica en dichos países.

"In former days, women were unwelcome in Kyokans (Japanese-style inns) when they travelled alone. I learned from a newspaper article that such would never happen in youth hostels, and that stimulated me to stay at hostels. I was amazed to know that so many different people from all walks of life stayed together in one room, knowing each other, becoming friends and making pleasant company among themselves."

"Dans le temps, les femmes n'étaient pas les bienvenues dans les Kyokans (auberges japonaises), lorsqu'elles voyageaient seules. Lorsque j'ai lu dans un article de journal que cela n'arriverait jamais dans les Auberges de Jeunesse, j'ai eu envie d'y faire un séjour. J'ai été vraiment fascinée de voir que tant de gens d'horizons différents partageaient la même chambrée, apprenaient à se connaître, devenaient amis et passaient du bon temps tous ensemble."

"Früher waren Frauen in "Kyokans" (japanischen Gästehäusern) nicht willkommen wenn sie allein reisten. In einem Zeitungsartikel las ich, dass so etwas in Jugendherbergen niemals geschehen könnte, was mich dazu anregte, in Jugendherbergen zu übernachten. Ich war erstaunt, wieviele Menschen aus allen Berufen und Gesellschaftsschichten hier zusammenkommen, Zimmer miteinander teilen, neue Freundschaften schließen und gemeinsam viel Vergnügen haben."

"Antiguamente, las mujeres que viajaban solas no eran bienvenidas en los Kyokans (hostales japoneses). Cuando leí un día en el periódico que ésto no podría nunca suceder en un albergue juvenil, me entraron ganas de alojarme en uno de ellos. Quedé maravillada al comprobar que tantas personas diferentes, de todas las profesiones y condiciones sociales, compartían una misma habitación, se conocían, hacían amistad y lo pasaban bien juntas."

Sugako Hashida

Göteborg -
Slottsskogen

Slottsskogen,
Vegagatan 21,
41311 Göteborg.
t (31) 426520
f (31) 142102
e mail@slottsskogenvh.se

Open Dates:	🗓
Open Hours:	08.00-12.00hrs; 15.00-22.00hrs
Reservations:	**R** **CC**
Price Range:	SEK 100-140 🏨
Beds:	140 - 16x² 2x³ 16x⁴ 2x⁵ 2x⁶
Facilities:	♦♦♦ 20x ♦♦♦ ℅ (B) 🖊 ⚄ 📺 ✒ 1 x 🍽 ⬛ 🖼 ♿ 🅿 Ⓘ 🏊

Directions:

✈	Landvetter 25km
⛴	Stena Line & Seacat 800m
🚆	Central Station 2km
🚌	50, 51, 87, 210, 703, 705 200m ap Olivedalsgatan/Linnéplatsen 200m
🚊	1, 2 200m ap Olivedalsgatan 200m

Attractions: 🚴

Göteborg -
Stigbergsliden

Stigbergsliden 10,
41463 Göteborg.
t (31) 241620
f (31) 246520
e vandrarhem.stigbergsliden@swipnet.se

Open Dates:	🗓
Open Hours:	08.00-10.00hrs; 16.00-22.00hrs
Reservations:	**CC**
Price Range:	SEK 110-150 🏨
Beds:	90 - 1x¹ 10x² 1x³ 14x⁴ 1x⁵ 1x⁶
Facilities:	♿ ♦♦♦ 16x ♦♦♦ ℅ 🖊 📺 ⬛ ♿ 🈸 🅿 ✂ 🔍 🏠

Directions:

✈	Landvetter 25km
A🚌	Central Station 3km
⛴	Stena/Seacat 300m, Skandiahamnen 3km
🚆	Central Station 3km
🚊	Brunnsparken 3, 9, 4 300m ap Stigbergstorget 50m

Attractions: 🚴

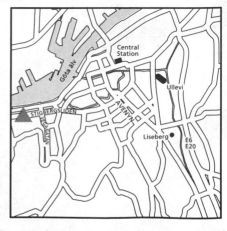

Göteborg - Torrekulla

**STF Vandrarhem Mölndal,
Torrekulla Turiststation,
42835 Kållered.**
☏ (31) 7951495
✆ (31) 7955140
📧 info@torrekulla.stfturist.se

Open Dates:	📅
Open Hours:	Sept-Apr 08.00-10.00hrs; 16.00-18.30hrs, May-Aug 08.00-10.00hrs; 16.00-22.00hrs
Reservations:	ⓡ (IBN) ꜀CC꜀
Price Range:	SEK 110-150 🏷
Beds:	140 - 3x¹ 4x² 8x³ 11x⁴ 3x⁵ 3x⁶
Facilities:	♿ 🛏 🛏 🍽 (B) 🚻 🧺 📺 🅿 ⚠ 🏧 🏠

Directions:

✈	Landvetter 35km
⛴	Stena Line 14km
🚆	Fast train from Centralstation. No. 4 from Brunnsparken.
🚌	760 at Mölndal Broplatsen terminus ap Torrekulla

Attractions: 🎿 🚲 🚶 ⚓ 800m

Stockholm - af Chapman/Skeppsholmen

**Flaggmansvägen 8,
11149 Stockholm.**
☏ (8) 4632266
✆ (8) 6117155
📧 info@chapman.stfturist.se

Open Dates:	📅
Open Hours:	🕐
Reservations:	ⓡ (IBN) ꜀CC꜀
Price Range:	SEK 115-175 🏷
Beds:	290 - 20x² 13x³ 22x⁴ 1x⁵ 8x⁶ 8x⁶
Facilities:	♿ 🛏 36x 🛏 🍽 🚻 🧺 📺 🅾 🖼 🏧 ⑧ ▣ 🅿 🏤

Directions:

✈	Arlanda 40km
A🚌	City Terminal 2km
🚆	Central Station 2km
🚌	#65 100m ap af Chapman
Ⓤ	Kungsträdgården 500m

Stockholm - Långholmen

Kronohäktet,
Box 9116,
10272 Stockholm.
t (8) 6680510
f (8) 7208575
e vandrarhem@langholmen.com

Open Dates:	🗓12
Open Hours:	🕐
Reservations:	**R** ⊂CC⊐
Price Range:	SEK 160-180 🏧
Beds:	254 - 71x² 11x³ 13x⁴
Facilities:	♿ 👥 30x 👥 🍴 📷 🛏 📺 5x🍽 🗄 🖼 🔋 ⬆ 🅿 📋 🔌 ⚡ 🏠 🎣

Directions:

✈	Arlanda 40km
A🚌	City Terminal 3km
🚕	Central Station 3.5km
🚌	#4, ap Långholmsg 700m
Ⓤ	Hornstull 700m

Attractions: 🔍

There are 3 hostels in Stockholm. See following pages.

Stockholm - Zinkensdamm

SFT Vandrarhem Zinkensdamm,
Zinkens väg 20,
11741 Stockholm.
t (8) 6168100
f (8) 6168120
e zinkensdamm@telia.com

Open Dates:	🗓12
Open Hours:	🕐
Reservations:	**R** ⊂CC⊐
Price Range:	SEK 145-185 (Extra charge for 1 & 2 bedded rooms) 🏧
Beds:	510 - 26x² 8x³ 107x⁴ 1x⁶
Facilities:	♿ 👥 👥 🍴 (B) 📷 💬 🛏 📺 2x🍽 🗄 🖼 🔋 ⬆ 🅿 📋 🔌 ⚡ 🖃 🏠

Directions:

✈	Arlanda 40km
A🚌	City Terminal 3km
🚕	Central Station 3km
Ⓤ	Zinkensdamm 500m

Attractions: 🔍 🚲

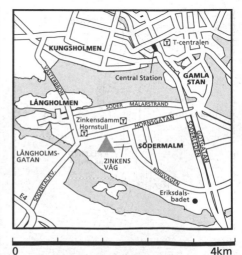

Location/Address	Telephone No. Fax No.	Beds	Opening Dates	Facilities
▲ Åhus STF Vandrarhem Åhus, Stavgatan 3, 29631 Åhus.	☎ (44) 248535 🖷 (44) 247718	32	🔟	⍟ Ⓡ ⅊ ⚲ 🅿 🍺 ✿
▲ Älgarås STF Vandrarhem Älgarås, Box 102, 54502 Älgarås.	☎ (506) 40450 🖷 (506) 40237	26	01.02–01.11	⍟ 🍽 Ⓡ ⚲ 🅿
▲ Alingsås STF Vandrarhem Alingsås, Villa Plantaget, 44134 Alingsås.	☎ (322) 636987 🖷 (322) 633229	42	🔟	⍟ 🍽 ⋶CC⋸ ⚲ 🅿
▲ Älmhult SFT Vandrarhem Älmhult, Sjöstugan, 34394 Älmhult.	☎ (476) 71600 🖷 (476) 12632	24	01.05–01.09	⍟ 🍽 ⚲ 🅿 🗍
▲ Älvdalen STF Vandrarhem Älvdalen, Tre Björnar, Dalgatan 31, 79631 Älvdalen. 📧 trebjornar@telia.com	☎ (251) 10482 🖷 (251) 10482	34	🔟	⍟ 🍽 Ⓡ ⚲ 🅿 🗍 🚲
▲ Alvesta STF Vandrarhem Alvesta, Hamrarnavägen 3, 34232 Alvesta. 📧 eksalen@hotmail.com	☎ (472) 12700 🖷 (472) 12701	50	08.01–15.12	⍟ 2S ⅊ ⋶CC⋸ ⚲ 🅿 🗍
▲ Älvkarleby STF Vandrarhem Älvkarleby, Laxön, 81494 Älvkarleby.	☎ (26) 82122 🖷 (26) 72861	66	01.01–20.12	⍟ ⚲ 🅿
▲ Älvsbyn STF Vandrarhem Älvsbyn, Nyfors 1, 94236 Älvsbyn.	☎ (929) 55630 🖷 (929) 10527	56	🔟	⍟ 🍽 ⚲ 🅿 🗍
▲ Åmål STF Vandrarhem Åmål, Gerdinsgatan 7, 66237 Åmål. 📧 lokrantz@home.se	☎ (532) 10205 🖷 (532) 10205	48	🔟	⍟ 🍽 ⅊ ⚲ 🅿
▲ Ammarnäs STF Vandrarhem, Ammarnäs, Box 21, 92075 Ammarnäs.	☎ (952) 60045 🖷 (952) 60251	44	🔟	⍟ 🍽 Ⓡ ⚲ 🅿
▲ Ängelholm STF Vandrarhem Ängelholm, Magnarp 174, 26083 Vejbystrand.	☎ (431) 452364 🖷 (431) 452364	60	01.04–31.10	⍟ 🍽 Ⓡ ⚲ 🅿 🗍
▲ Ånn STF Vandrarhem Ånn, Ånn 2467, 83015 Duved.	☎ (647) 71070 🖷 (647) 71070	33	🔟	⍟ 🍽 ⚲ 🅿
▲ Arådalen STF Vandrarhem Arådalen, Västra Arådalen, 84031 Åsarna, Jämtland.	☎ (687) 14054	18	19.06–29.08	⍟ ⚲ 🅿 🍺
▲ Arjeplog STF Vandrarhem Arjeplog, Lyktan, Lugnetvägen 4, 93090 Arjeplog.	☎ (961) 61210 🖷 (961) 10150	30	01.05–30.11	🍽 ⚲ 🅿
▲ Årås STF Vandrarhem Årås, Kölingared, 56593 Mullsjö.	☎ (515) 91151	28	17.06–13.08	⍟ 🍽 Ⓡ ⋶CC⋸ ⚲ 🅿

Location/Address	Telephone No. Fax No.	Beds	Opening Dates	Facilities
▲ **Åre** STF Vandrarhem Åre, Brattlandsgården, 83010 Undersåker.	☎ (647) 30138, (10) 6905885 ☏ (647) 30138	66		♔♔ Ⓡ ☛ 🅿 ▣
▲ **Åsa** STF Vandrarhem Åsa, Kuggaviksgården, 43031 Åsa.	☎ (340) 651285 ☏ (340) 651242; Mobile (070) 6330256	31	15.05–15.08	♔♔ ⊙| ⊂CC⊃ ☛
▲ **Asa-Lammhult** STF Vandrarhem Asa, 36030 Lammhult.	☎ (472) 263110, (472) 263003	35		♔♔ Ⓡ & ☛ 🅿 ▣
▲ **Åsarna** STF Vandrarhem Åsarna, Box 245, 84031 Åsarna. ✉ info@asarnaskicenter.se	☎ (687) 30230 ☏ (687) 30360	85		♔♔ ⊙| ⊂CC⊃ ☛ 🅿 ▣
▲ **Åsbo/Strålsnäs** STF Vandrarhem Åsbo/Strålsnäs, 590 15 Boxholm.	☎ (142) 57090, (142) 57341 ☏ (142) 57090	22	01.06–31.07	☛ 🅿 ▣
▲ **Avesta** STF Vandrarhem Avesta, Älvbrovägen 33, 77435 Avesta.	☎ (226) 80623 ☏ (226) 80623	36		♔♔ ☛ 🅿 ▣
▲ **Backåkra** STF Vandrarhem Backåkra/Löderup, Kustvägen, 27645 Löderup, Skåne. ✉ backakra.vandrarhem@swipnet.se	☎ (411) 526080 ☏ (411) 526121	70	01.05–31.08	♔♔ ⊙| Ⓡ ☛ 🅿 ▣
▲ **Baskemölla** STF Vandrarhem Baskemölla, Simrishamn, Tjörnedalavägen 81, 27294 Simrishamn.	☎ (414) 26173 ☏ (414) 26054	56		♔♔ ⊙| & ☛ 🅿 ▣
▲ **Bassholmen** STF Vandrarhem Bassholmen, c/o Fritidskontoret, 45181 Uddevalla.	☎ (522) 651308 ☏ (522) 16080	38	14.06–06.08	♔♔ ⊙| Ⓡ ☛ 🅿
▲ **Bengtsfors** STF Vandrarhem Bengtsfors, Gammelgården, 66631 Bengtsfors.	☎ (531) 61075 ☏ (531) 61075	50	15.05–15.08	♔♔ ⊙| ☛ 🅿
▲ **Bergkvara** STF Vandrarhem Bergkvara, Storgatan 66, 38542 Bergkvara.	☎ (486) 26040 ☏ (486) 26004	60		♔♔ ⊙| ⊂CC⊃ ☛ 🅿 ▣
▲ **Bergs Slussar** STF Vandrarhem Bergs Slussar, S-59077 Vreta Kloster.	☎ 013 60330	26	30.04–02.09	♔♔ Ⓡ & ⊂CC⊃ ☛ 🅿 ▣ ⬮
▲ **Björkfors** STF Vandrarhem Björkfors, 590 41 Rimforsa. ✉ basunda@xpress.se	☎ (494) 60047	30		♔♔ Ⓡ & ☛ 🅿 ▣
▲ **Björkvattnet** STF Vandrarhem Björkvattnet, Björkvattnet 1425, 83090 Gäddede.	☎ (672) 23024 ☏ (672) 23024	38		♔♔ Ⓡ ☛ 🅿
▲ **Björnlunda** STF Vandrarhem Björnlunda, Box 81, 64050 Björnlunda.	☎ (158) 20014, (158) 20702 ☏ (158) 20702	13	01.06–26.08	♔♔ ☛ 🅿

Location/Address	Telephone No. Fax No.	Beds	Opening Dates	Facilities
▲ Blentarp STF Vandrarhem Blentarp, 270 35 Blentarp.	☎ (416) 24377 ✆ (416) 24485	50	01.05–30.09	ⅲ ℝ 0.2SE ⅁ ✆ ℙ ⓞ ☕
▲ Blomskog STF Vandrarhem Blomskog, 67292 Årjäng.	☎ (573) 31035	34	22.05–26.09	ⅲ ℽ ✆ ℙ ⓞ
▲ Böda STF Vandrarhem Böda, Mellböda, 38074 Löttorp.	☎ (485) 22038 ✆ (485) 22198	165	01.06–15.08	ⅲ ℽ ℝ ⊄⊂ ✆ ℙ ⓞ
▲ Boda STF Vandrarhem Boda, Bolet 5, 36065 Boda Glasbruk. 📧 anita.braneus@emmaboda.mail.telia.com	☎ (481) 24230 ✆ (481) 24006	45	01.05–31.10	ⅲ ⊄⊂ ✆ ℙ
▲ Boden STF Vandrarhem Boden, Fabriksgatan 6, 96131 Boden.	☎ (921) 13335 ✆ (921) 13335	33	▥	✆ ℙ ⓞ ☕
▲ Bogesund/Vaxholm STF Vandrarhem Bogesund/Vaxholm, 18593 Vaxholm.	☎ (8) 541 32240	60	▥	ⅲ ℽ ⅁ ⊄⊂ ✆ ℙ ⓞ ☕
▲ Bollnäs STF Vandrarhem Bollnäs, Lenninge 6003, 82191 Bollnäs.	☎ (278) 23092 ✆ (278) 23092	50	▥	ⅲ ℽ ✆ ℙ ⓞ
▲ Borås STF Vandrarhem Borås, Box 440 22 Sjöbo 4, 50004 Borås.	☎ (33) 353280 ✆ (33) 140582	44	▥	ⅲ ℽ ✆ ℙ ⓞ
▲ Borghamn STF Vandrarhem Borghamn, Borghamnsvägen 1, 592 93 Borghamn. 📧 info@borghamnsvandrarhem.se	☎ (143) 20368 ✆ (143) 20378	73	▥	ⅲ ℽ ℝ 15N ⅁ ⊄⊂ ✆ ℙ ⓞ ☕ ⊶
▲ Borgholm STF Vandrarhem Rosenfors, Södra vägen 7, 38736 Borgholm.	☎ (485) 10756 ✆ (485) 77878	103	30.04–15.09	ⅲ ℽ ℝ ✆ ℙ ☕
▲ Borgsjö STF Vandrarhem Borgsjö, Borgsjöbyn, 84197 Erikslund.	☎ (690) 20075	30	15.06–15.08	ⅲ ℽ ✆
▲ Borlänge STF Vandrarhem Borlänge, Kornstigen 23A, 78452 Borlänge. 📧 vandrarhem@borlange.se	☎ (243) 227615 ✆ (243) 16411	75	02.01–23.12; 27–30.12	ⅲ ℽ ⊄⊂ ✆ ℙ ⓞ
▲ Branäs STF Vandrarhem Branäs, Box 28, 68060 Sysslebäck. 📧 info@branas.se	☎ (564) 35200 ✆ (564) 43260	40	16.05–23.10	ⅲ ℝ ⅁ ⊄⊂ ✆ ℙ ⓞ
▲ Bråtadal/Svartrå STF Vandrarhem Bråtadal/Svartrå, 31060 Ullared.	☎ (346) 23343 ✆ (346) 33014	45	15.03–15.12	ⅲ ℽ ℝ ⅁ ✆ ℙ ⓞ
▲ Brantevik STF Vandrarhem Brantevik, Råkulle Gård, Gislövsvägen 12, 27238 Brantevik.	☎ (414) 20020	23	01.03–30.11	ⅲ ℝ ⅁ ✆ ℙ

Location/Address	Telephone No. Fax No.	Beds	Opening Dates	Facilities
▲ **Brunskog** STF Vandrarhem Brunskog, Bergamon, 67194 Edane.	☎ (570) 52141 ✆ (570) 52149	70	⓬	ᴬ ⊙ ⓡ ♂ P
▲ **Bruzaholm** STF Vandrarhem Bruzaholm, Wäduren AB, Eksjövägen 13, Box 25, 57034 Bruzaholm. ℮ nave@telia.com	☎ (381) 20200 ✆ (381) 20200	38	⓬	ᴬ ⊙ ♿ ⒸⒸ ♂ P ⊡
▲ **Burträsk** STF Vandrarhem Burträsk, Hembygdsgården, Box 72, 93721 Burträsk.	☎ (914) 55013, (914) 10287 ✆ (914) 55070	38	01.05–31.08	ᴬ ⓡ ♂ P
▲ **Dals Rostock** STF Vandrarhem, Dals Rostock, Kroppefjälls Fritidscenter, 46450 Dals Rostock.	☎ (530) 20360 ✆ (530) 20345	54	⓬	ᴬ ⊙ ⓡ ♂ P ⊡
▲ **Docksta** STF Vandrarhem Docksta, 87033 Docksta. ℮ kustladan@telia.com	☎ (613) 13064, (613) 40391 ✆ (613) 40391	80	⓬	ᴬ ⊙ ⓡ ⒸⒸ ♂ P ⊡
▲ **Ed** STF Vandrarhem Ed, Strömstadsvägen 18, 668 31 Ed.	☎ (534) 10191	54	15.05–31.08	ᴬ ♂ P ⊡
▲ **Edsbyn** STF Vandrarhem Edsbyn, Hogatan 15, 82894 Edsbyn. ℮ hogatan15@hotmail.com	☎ (271) 34462 ✆ (271) 34176	36	⓬	ᴬ ⓡ ♂ P
▲ **Ekshärad** STF Vandrarhem Ekshärad, Klarälvsvägen 35, Pilgrimen, Box 105, 68050 Ekshärad.	☎ (563) 40590 ✆ (563) 40590	22	⓬	ᴬ ⊙ ♂ P
▲ **Eksjö** STF Vandrarhem Eksjö, Österlånggatan 31, 57580 Eksjö. ℮ vandrarhem@eksjo.se	☎ (381) 36180 ✆ (381) 17755	57	⓬	ᴬ ⒸⒸ ♂ P
▲ **Enköping** STF Vandrarhem Enköping, Bredsand, 74591 Enköping.	☎ (171) 80066	48	⓬	ᴬ 6S ♿ ♂ P
▲ **Eskilstuna** STF Vandrarhem Eskilstuna, Vilsta Sporthotell, 63229 Eskilstuna. ℮ vilsta.sporthotell@swipnet.se	☎ (16) 513080 ✆ (16) 513086	40	⓬	ᴬ ♿ ⒸⒸ ♂ P ⊡
▲ **Fågelfors** STF Vandrarhem Fågelfors, Värdshuset Bruksgården, Bruksgatan 65, 570 75 Fågelfors. ℮ info@vardshusetbruksgarden.se	☎ (491) 51250 ✆ (491) 51255	36	18.06–10.08 (02.01–17.06; 11.08–22.12 ⓡ only)	ᴬ ⓡ ⒸⒸ ♂ P
▲ **Falköping** STF Vandrarhem Falköping, Lidgatan 4, 52132 Falköping.	☎ (515) 85020 ✆ (515) 10043	46	⓬	ᴬ ⊙ ⓡ ♂ P ⊡
▲ **Falun** STF Vandrarhem Falun, Vandrarvägen 3, 79143 Falun. ℮ stf.falun@falun.mail.telia.com	☎ (23) 10560 ✆ (23) 14102	140	08.01–21.12	ᴬ ⊙ ⓡ 4E ♂ P

Location/Address	Telephone No. Fax No.	Beds	Opening Dates	Facilities
▲ Fårö STF Vandrarhem Fårö, Fårögården, 62035 Fårösund.	☎ (498) 223639	46	20.05–31.08	♦♦♦ ⑩ Ⓡ ♂ Ⓟ
▲ Färgelanda STF Vandrarhem Färgelanda, Dagsholm, 45892 Färgelanda.	☎ (528) 19990 ⊕ (528) 19999	50	01.06–31.08	♦♦♦ ⑩ Ⓡ ⅀ 〔CC〕 ♂ Ⓟ ⬚
▲ Fjällbacka/Valö STF Vandrarhem Fjällbacka, Valö, 45071 Fjällbacka.	☎ (525) 31234	12	02.05–25.08	♦♦♦ Ⓡ ♂ ⬚
▲ Flen STF Vandrarhem Flen, Ansgarsgården, Finntorp, 642 91 Flen.	☎ (157) 51140 ⊕ (157) 14832	80	🗄	♦♦♦ ⑩ Ⓡ ⅀ ♂ Ⓟ ⬚ ☕
▲ Forshaga STF Vandrarhem Forshaga, Slottet, Folkets Hus, Slottsvägen 9, Box 76, 66722 Forshaga.	☎ (54) 873040, (54) 873051 ⊕ (54) 870780, (54) 873053	20	15.05–15.09	♦♦♦ ⑩ 〔CC〕 ♂ Ⓟ ☕
▲ Forsvik STF Vandrarhem Forsvik, Bruksvägen 11, 54673 Forsvik.	☎ (505) 41352, (505) 41137	49	01.06–31.08	♦♦♦ ♂ Ⓟ
▲ Fredriksberg-Säfsen STF Vandrarhem Fredriksberg, Ludvikav 13, 770 10 Fredriksberg. ⊜ vandrarhem.059120776@telia.com	☎ (591) 20565 ⊕ (591) 20776	40	🗄	♦♦♦ ⑩ Ⓡ ⅀ 〔CC〕 ♂ Ⓟ ⬚
▲ Frillesås STF Vandrarhem Frillesås, Vallersvik, Box 64, 43030 Frillesås.	☎ (340) 653000 ⊕ (340) 653551	42	29.05–27.08	♦♦♦ ⑩ 〔CC〕 ♂ Ⓟ ⬚
▲ Fryksta/Kil STF Vandrarhem Fryksta/Kil, Box 193, 66525 Kil.	☎ (554) 40850 ⊕ (554) 13772	40	🗄	♦♦♦ ⅀ ♂ ⬚
▲ Gällivare STF Vandrarhem Gällivare, Barnhemsv 2, Andra Sidan, 98239 Gällivare.	☎ (970) 14380 ⊕ (970) 16586	110	🗄	♦♦♦ ⑩ ♂ Ⓟ ⬚
▲ Gammel-Gränome STF Vandrarhem Gammel-Gränome, Stavby, 74794 Alunda.	☎ (174) 13108	27	🗄	♦♦♦ ♂ Ⓟ
▲ Garda STF Vandrarhem Garda, Kommunhuset, 62016 Ljugarn. ⊜ gardavh@sverige.nu	☎ (498) 491391 ⊕ (498) 491181	30	01.02–20.12	♦♦♦ Ⓡ ♂ Ⓟ ⬚
▲ Gärdserum STF Vandrarhem, Gärdserum, 59797 Åtvidaberg. ⊜ gardserumsvandrarhem@ebrevet.nu	☎ (120) 20134 ⊕ (120) 20261	20	01.05–01.09	♦♦♦ ♂ Ⓟ
▲ Gårdstånga STF Vandrarhem Gårdstånga, Flyingevägen Gårdstånga, 24032 Flyinge.	☎ (46) 52087 ⊕ (46) 2110873	36	01.01–24.12	♦♦♦ ⑩ Ⓡ ♂ Ⓟ ⬚

Location/Address	Telephone No. Fax No.	Beds	Opening Dates	Facilities
▲ Gävle - I STF Vandrarhem Gävle, Södra Rådmansgatan 1, 80251 Gävle. 🄴 stf.vandrarhem@telia.com	🕽 (26) 621745 🖷 (26) 615990	72	🏠12	👫 ♿ ⊡CC⊡ ✧ 🅿 🗗 ᭦
▲ Gävle - II STF Vandrarhem Gävle Engeltofta, Bönavägen 118, 80595 Gävle, Gästrikland.	🕽 (26) 96160, (26) 96063 🖷 (26) 96055	74	01.05–31.08	👫 🍴 7NE ♿ ✧ 🅿 🗗 ᭦
▲ Gnosjö STF Vandrarhem Gnosjö, Furuhall, 33580 Gnosjö.	🕽 (370) 331115, 0704899713 🖷 (370) 331110	33	🏠12	👫 ⓡ ✧ 🅿 🗗
▲ Göteborg STF Vandrarhem Kungälv, Färjevägen 2, 44231 Kungälv, Bohuslän. 🄴 johan.lenander@mailbox.hogia.net	🕽 (303) 18900 🖷 (303) 19295	50	15.04–15.09	👫 ⓡ 15N ♿ ✧ 🅿 🗗 ᭦
▲ Göteborg - Slottsskogen **Slottsskogen, Vegagatan 21, 41311 Göteborg.** 🄴 mail@slottsskogenvh.se	🕽 (31) 426520 🖷 (31) 142102	140	🏠12	👫 🍴 ⓡ ⊡CC⊡ ✧ 🅿 🗗
▲ Göteborg - Stigbergsliden **Stigbergsliden 10, 41463 Göteborg.** 🄴 vandrarhem.stigbergsliden@swipnet.se	🕽 (31) 241620 🖷 (31) 246520	90	🏠12	👫 🍴 ♿ ⊡CC⊡ ✧ 🅿 🗗
▲ Göteborg - Torrekulla IBN **STF Vandrarhem Mölndal, Torrekulla T uriststation, 42835 Kållered.** 🄴 info@torrekulla.stfturist.se Gothenburg ☞Göteborg	🕽 (31) 7951495 🖷 (31) 7955140	140	🏠12	👫 🍴 ⓡ ♿ ⊡CC⊡ ✧ 🅿
▲ Grängesberg - Bergsmansgården STF Vandrarhem Grängesberg, Bergsmansgården, Hårdtorpsvägen 15, 77240 Grängesberg.	🕽 (240) 21830 🖷 (240) 21830	45	10.06–29.08	👫 ✧ 🅿 🗗
▲ Grönklitt STF Vandrarhem Grönklitt, 79498 Orsa. 🄴 fritid@orsa-gronklitt.se	🕽 (250) 46200 🖷 (250) 46111	40	🏠12	👫 🍴 ⊡CC⊡ ✧ 🅿 🗗
▲ Gullspång STF Vandrarhem Gullspång, Alhöjden Box 6, 54721 Gullspång.	🕽 (551) 20786 🖷 (551) 20277	36	🏠12	👫 🍴 ⓡ ✧ 🅿 🗗
▲ Hablingbo STF Vandrarhem Hablingbo, Hablingbo, 62011 Havdhem.	🕽 (498) 487070 🖷 (498) 487095	32	01.05–30.09	👫 🍴 ⊡CC⊡ ✧ 🅿 🗗 ᭦
▲ Hågelby STF Vandrarhem Hågelby, Hågelbygård, 14743 Tumba. 🄴 hagelbyparken@hagelby.se	🕽 (8) 53062020 🖷 (8) 53062020	28	🏠12	👫 🍴 ⓡ ⊡CC⊡ ✧ 🅿 🗗
▲ Hällekis STF Vandrarhem Hällekis, Falkängen, Falkängsvägen, 53374 Hällekis.	🕽 (510) 540653 🖷 (510) 540085	100	🏠12	👫 🍴 ✧ 🅿

Location/Address	Telephone No. Fax No.	Beds	Opening Dates	Facilities
▲ **Hammarö** STF Vandrarhem Hammarö, Skoghall Djupsundsvägen 1, 66334 Skoghall.	☎ (54) 510440 🖶 (54) 518158	80	07.06–08.08	♔ ┠⊙┤ ⚲ ℙ ⊡
▲ **Hammenhög** STF Vandrarhem Hammenhög, Skolgatan 20, 27650 Hammenhög.	☎ (414) 440095 🖶 (414) 440041	72	15.05–15.09	♔ ┠⊙┤ ⟦CC⟧ ⚲ ℙ
▲ **Hammarstrand** STF Vandrarhem Hammarstrand, Hotell, 84070 Hammarstrand.	☎ (696) 10780 🖶 (696) 55790	34	01.06–31.08	♔ ┠⊙┤ ⚲ ℙ
▲ **Hanö** STF Vandrarhem, Hanö, 29407 Sölvesborg.	☎ (456) 53000	24	⟦⊡⟧	♔ ⟨R⟩ ⚲ ℙ
▲ **Hargebaden/Hammar** STF Vandrarhem Hargebaden/Hammar, Hargebaden, 69694 Hammar.	☎ (583) 770556	40	15.04–15.09	♔ ┠⊙┤ ⚲ ℙ
▲ **Härnösand** STF Vandrarhem Härnösand, Volontären 14, 87162 Härnösand.	☎ (611) 10446	70	11.06–06.08	♔ ┠⊙┤ ⚲ ℙ ⊡
▲ **Härnösand-Rö** STF Vandrarhem Härnösand-Rö, PL1672 Rö, 870 15 Utansjö.	☎ (611) 64011 🖶 (611) 64008	37	⟦⊡⟧	♔ ┠⊙┤ ⟨R⟩ ⚳ ⚲ ℙ ⟐
▲ **Haparanda** STF Vandrarhem Haparanda, Strandgatan 26, 95331 Haparanda.	☎ (922) 61171 🖶 (922) 61784	45	⟦⊡⟧	♔ ┠⊙┤ ⚳ ⟦CC⟧ ⚲ ⊡
▲ **Hässleholm** STF Vandrarhem Hässleholm, Hässleholmsgården 303, 28135 Hässleholm. @ hassleholmsgarden.hassleholm@swipnet.se	☎ (451) 268234 🖶 (451) 268232	35	⟦⊡⟧	♔ ⚲ ℙ ⊡
▲ **Hästveda** STF Vandrarhem Hästveda, Hembygdsparken, Box 97, 28023 Hästveda.	☎ (451) 30273 🖶 (451) 30864	35	01.04–31.10	♔ ⟨R⟩ ⚳ ⚲ ℙ ⊡
▲ **Haväng** STF Vandrarhem Haväng, Skepparpsgården, 27737 Kivik.	☎ (414) 74071 🖶 (414) 74073	50	01.05–15.09	♔ ⟨R⟩ ⚲ ℙ
▲ **Håverud** STF Vandrarhem Håverud, Museiv 3, 46472 Håverud.	☎ (530) 30275, (530) 30745	38	⟦⊡⟧	♔ ⟨R⟩ ⚲ ⊡
▲ **Hedemora** STF Vandrarhem Hedemora, Hälla, Hällavägen, 77630 Hedemora.	☎ (225) 711350 🖶 (225) 711350	40	⟦⊡⟧	♔ ┠⊙┤ ⚲ ℙ ⊡
▲ **Helsingborg** STF Vandrarhem Helsingborg, KFUM Nyckelbo Scoutstigen, 25284 Helsingborg.	☎ (42) 92005 🖶 (42) 91050	30	01.05–30.09	♔ ┠⊙┤ ⟨R⟩ ⚳ ⚲ ⊡
▲ **Hemavan** STF Vandrarhem Hemavan, FBU-gården, Box 163, 92066 Hemavan. @ info@fbu.to	☎ (954) 30002 🖶 (954) 30510	48	15.06–30.09	♔ ┠⊙┤ ⟦CC⟧ ⚲ ℙ ⊡

Location/Address	Telephone No. Fax No.	Beds	Opening Dates	Facilities
▲ **Hjo** STF Vandrarhem Hjo, Villa Eira, Stadsparken, 54433 Hjo.	☎ (503) 10085	47	01.05–31.08	♟♟♟ ✆ P 🅾
▲ **Hjulsjö** SFT Vandrarhem Hjulsjö, Mårtensbo Gård, 712 91 Hällefors. ✉ martensbo@stockholm.mail.telia.com	☎ (587) 62102 ✆ (587) 62102	33	12	♟♟♟ R 25 SE ✆ P 🅾 ☕
▲ **Högbonden** STF Vandrarhem Högbonden, Fyrvaktarbostaden, Sund 1688, 870 33 Docksta.	☎ (613) 23005 ✆ (613) 42119	30	01.06–30.09	♟♟♟ R ✆ P ☕
▲ **Hörby** STF Vandrarhem Hörby, Kursgården i Hörby, 24292 Hörby.	☎ (415) 14830 ✆ (415) 14328	40	07.06–15.08	♟♟♟ ⦿ ✆
▲ **Höör** STF Vandrarhem Höör, Backagården, Stenskogen, 24391 Höör.	☎ (413) 25510 ✆ (413) 25956	48	12	♟♟♟ ⦿ R CC ✆ P 🅾
▲ **Hörnefors** STF Vandrarhem Hörnefors, Sundelinsvägen 62, 91020 Hörnefors.	☎ (930) 20480	40	01.06–31.08	♟♟♟ ♿ ✆ P 🅾
▲ **Hovenäset** STF Vandrarhem Hovenäset, c/o Granander, Parkgatan 6, 45631 Kungshamn.	☎ (523) 37463	34	08.06–16.08	♟♟♟ R ♿ ✆ P 🅾
▲ **Hovra** STF Vandrarhem Hovra, 82042 Korskrogen.	☎ (651) 767093 ✆ (651) 767092	30	12	♟♟♟ ♿ ✆ P 🅾
▲ **Hudiksvall** STF Vandrarhem Hudiksvall, Malnbaden, Box 19, 82421 Hudiksvall.	☎ (650) 13260 ✆ (650) 13260	36	12	♟♟♟ CC ✆ P 🅾
▲ **Hunnebostrand** STF Vandrarhem Hunnebostrand, Gammelgården, 45046 Hunnebostrand.	☎ (523) 58730	82	01.05–30.09	♟♟♟ ⦿ R ✆ P ☕
▲ **Huskvarna** STF Vandrarhem Huskvarna, Odengatan 10, 56132 Huskvarna.	☎ (36) 148870 ✆ (36) 148840	98	12	♟♟♟ ⦿ ♿ CC ✆ ☕
▲ **Immeln** SFT Vandrarhem Immeln, Pl 2338, 28063 Sibbhult.	☎ (44) 96090 ✆ (44) 96090	30	12	♟♟♟ ♿ CC ✆ 🅾
▲ **Jakobsberg/Barkarby** STF Vandrarhem Jakobsberg/Barkarby, Kaptensvägen 7, 17738 Järfälla. ✉ vandrarhemmet.majorskan@swipnet.se	☎ (8) 4457270 ✆ (8) 4457273	60	12	♟♟♟ R 1 W CC ✆ P 🅾 ☕
▲ **Järbo** STF Vandrarhem Järbo, Britta Zachrisson, Vandrarhemsvägen 4, 81195 Järbo.	☎ (290) 70151	30	12	♟♟♟ R ✆ P 🅾
▲ **Järnavik** STF Vandrarhem Järnavik, Gula Huset, Box 19, 37010 Bräkne-Hoby.	☎ (457) 82200 ✆ (457) 82201	26	12	R ♿ ✆ P 🅾 ☕

Location/Address	Telephone No. Fax No.	Beds	Opening Dates	Facilities
▲ **Järvsö** STF Vandrarhem Järvsö, Harsagården, Harsa, 82040 Järvsö. @ info@harsa.se	☎ (651) 49511 🖷 (651) 49590	28	⓬	††† ▯⊙▯ 18NE ⊢CC⊣ ☞ P ◗
▲ **Jokkmokk** STF Vandrarhem Jokkmokk, Åsgård, Åsgatan 20, 96231 Jokkmokk. @ asgard@jokkmokkhostel.com	☎ (971) 55977 🖷 (971) 55977	50	⓬	††† ▯⊙▯ Ⓡ ⊢CC⊣ ☞ P ▯
▲ **Junsele** STF Vandrarhem Junsele, Kullberg 3031, 88037 Junsele.	☎ (621) 30000 🖷 (621) 30000	46	⓬	††† ▯⊙▯ 12N ☞ P ▯
▲ **Kalix** STF Vandrarhem Kalix, Grytnäs Herrgård, Box 148, 95222 Kalix.	☎ (923) 10733 🖷	37	15.06–20.08	††† ☞ P
▲ **Kalmar** STF Vandrarhem Kalmar, Rappeg 1, 39230 Kalmar. @ info@hotellsvanen.se	☎ (480) 12928 🖷 (480) 88293	69	⓬	††† ▯⊙▯ 1N ⊢CC⊣ ☞ P ▯ ◗
▲ **Kall** STF Vandrarhem Kall, Kallgården, Kall 2255, 830 05 Järpen. @ info@kallgarden.se	☎ (647) 41200 🖷 (647) 41004	72	⓬	††† ▯⊙▯ Ⓡ ⊢CC⊣ ☞ P ▯
▲ **Kalv** STF Vandrarhem, Kalv, Erikslund 2, 51261 Kalv.	☎ (325) 51000 🖷 (325) 51083	27	15.05–15.08	††† ☞ P
▲ **Karlsborg** STF Vandrarhem Karlsborg, Ankarvägen, 54630 Karlsborg.	☎ (505) 44600 🖷 (505) 44600	84	01.06–31.08	††† Ⓡ ☞ P
▲ **Karlshamn** STF Vandrarhem Karlshamn, Surbrunnsvägen IC, 374 39 Karlshamn. @ stfturistkhamn@hotmail.com	☎ (454) 14040 🖷 (454) 14040	72	⓬	††† Ⓡ 0.3NE ⊢CC⊣ ☞ P ▯
▲ **Karlskoga** STF Vandrarhem Karlskoga, Grönfeldtsudden, 69141 Karlskoga.	☎ (586) 56780	92	⓬	††† ▯⊙▯ ⅋ ☞ P ▯
▲ **Karlskrona/Trossö** STF Vandrarhem Karlskrona/Trossö, Drottninggatan 39, 37132 Karlskrona. @ trosso.vandrarhem@karlskrona.mail.telia.com	☎ (455) 10020 🖷 (455) 10020	45	⓬	††† ⅋ ☞ P
▲ **Karlskrona** STF Vandrarhem Karlskrona, Ruthensparre, Bredgatan 16, 37122 Karlskrona. @ trosso.vandrarhem@karlskrona.telia.com	☎ (455) 10020 🖷 (455) 10020	60	16.06–14.08	††† Ⓡ ☞ P ▯
▲ **Karlstad** STF Vandrarhem Karlstad, Ulleberg, 65342 Karlstad.	☎ (54) 566840 🖷 (54) 566042	102	10.01–15.12	††† ▯⊙▯ ⅋ ☞ P
▲ **Katrineholm** STF Vandrarhem Katrineholm, Stora Djulö, 64192 Katrineholm.	☎ (150) 10225 🖷 (150) 10225	43	23.05–25.08	††† ▯⊙▯ Ⓡ 3S ☞ P ▯

Location/Address	Telephone No. Fax No.	Beds	Opening Dates	Facilities
▲ **Kiruna** STF Vandrarhem Kiruna, Bergmästaregatan 7, 98133 Kiruna.	☎ (980) 17195 🖷 (980) 17195	88	🖀12	♔ ℹ️ ⓇＣＣ ♂ 🅿 ⊡
▲ **Kivik** STF Vandrarhem Kivik, Tittutvägen, 277 30 Kivik.	☎ (414) 71195 🖷 (414) 70050	35	🖀12	♔ ℹ️ Ⓡ ♂ 🅿
▲ **Kivik/Hanöbris** STF Vandrarhem Kivik Hanöbris, Eliselundsvägen 6, 27730 Kivik.	☎ (414) 70050 🖷 (414) 70050	40	15.06–15.08	♔ Ⓡ ♂ 🅿
▲ **Klavreström** STF Vandrarhem Klavreström, Malmvägen 1, 36072 Klavreström. ✉ stfvhem.klavrestroem@swipnet.se	☎ (474) 40944 🖷 (474) 40944	70	🖀12	♔ ℹ️ Ⓡ ♿ ♂ 🅿 ⊡
▲ **Klintehamn** STF Vandrarhem Klintehamn, Pensionat Warfsholm, Box 56, 62020 Klintehamn.	☎ (498) 240010, (708) 445302 🖷 (498) 241411	50	21.01–19.12	♔ Ⓡ ♂ 🅿
▲ **Köping** STF Vandrarhem Köping, Ågärdsg 2D, 73132 Köping.	☎ (221) 24495 🖷 (221) 24495	40	10.01–09.12	♔ Ⓡ ＣＣ ♂ 🅿 ⊡
▲ **Köpmanholmen** STF Vandrarhem Köpmanholmen, Köpmanholmsvägen 2, 89340 Köpmanholmen.	☎ (660) 223496	36	15.05–15.09	♔ Ⓡ ♂ 🅿 ⊡
▲ **Korrö** STF Vandrarhem Korrö, 36024 Linneryd (5km S Linneryd on route 122).	☎ (470) 34249 🖷 (470) 34556	87	01.04–30.09	♔ ℹ️ ♂ 🅿
▲ **Kristinehamn** STF Vandrarhem Kristinehamn, Kvarndammen, 68100 Kristinehamn.	☎ (550) 88195 🖷 (550) 12393	16	01.05–30.08	♔ ℹ️ ♂ 🅿 ⊡
▲ **Kungsbacka** STF Vandrarhem Kungsbacka, Klovsten, c/o Kungsbacka Turistbyrå, 434 32 Kungsbacka.	☎ (300) 34595	38	19.06–13.08	♔ ♿ ♂ 🅿 ⊡
▲ **Kvikkjokk** STF Vandrarhem Kvikkjokk, Kvikkjokk Fjällstation, 96202 Kvikkjokk. ✉ info@kvikkjokk.stfturist.se	☎ (971) 21022 🖷 (971) 21039	60	17.03–01.05; 16.06–12.09	♔ ℹ️ Ⓡ ＣＣ ♂ 🅿 ⊡ ☕
▲ **Kyrktåsjö** STF Vandrarhem Kyrktåsjö, Tåsjödalens Pl 1525, 83080 Hoting. ✉ vandrarhemkyrktasjo@telia.com	☎ (671) 713510	20	🖀12	♔ Ⓡ ♂
▲ **Laholm** STF Vandrarhem Laholm, Tivolivägen 4, 31230 Laholm. ✉ vandrarhem@laholm.se	☎ (430) 13318 🖷 (430) 15325	68	🖀12	♔ ℹ️ Ⓡ ＣＣ ♂ 🅿 ⊡
▲ **Landskrona** STF Vandrarhem Landskrona, St Olovsgatan 15, 26136 Landskrona.	☎ (418) 12063 🖷 (418) 13075	45	10.01–10.12	♔ ℹ️ ♂ 🅿
▲ **Långasjö** STF Vandrarhem Långasjö, Stallgatan, 36195 Långasjö.	☎ (471) 50310	43	🖀12	♔ Ⓡ ♿ ♂ 🅿

Location/Address	Telephone No. Fax No.	Beds	Opening Dates	Facilities
▲ Lärbro STF Vandrarhem Lärbro, Kappelshamnsvägen 10, 620 34 Lärbro. ✉ bokning@grannen.nu	☎ (498) 225033	120	15.05–31.08	ⅲ ⌐CC⌐ ⚲ P 🖸 🍵
▲ Leksand STF Vandrarhem Leksand, Källberget, Parkgården, Box 3051, 79335 Leksand.	☎ (247) 15250 🖷 (247) 10186	80	⌐₁₂	ⅲ 2.5S ⚲ P 🖸
▲ Lesjöfors STF Vandrarhem Lesjöfors, Esperanto Gården, Stiftelsevägen 1, 68096 Lesjöfors. ✉ egarden@esperanto.se	☎ (590) 30909 🖷 (590) 30359	58	⌐₁₂	ⅲ ⌐○⌐ ⌐ ⚲ P
▲ Liden STF Vandrarhem Liden, Larmvägen 2, 86041 Liden.	☎ (692) 10567	36	01.06–31.08	⚲ P 🖸
▲ Lidköping STF Vandrarhem Lidköping, Gamla Stadens Torg Nicolaigatan 2, 53132 Lidköping.	☎ (510) 66430	52	08.11–16.09	ⅲ ⌐○⌐ ⚲ P 🖸
▲ Linköping STF Vandrarhem Linköping, Klostergatan 52A, 58223 Linköping.	☎ (13) 149090 🖷 (13) 148300	84	08.01–21.12	ⅲ ⓡ ♿ ⚲ P
▲ Ljuder STF Vandrarhem Ljuder, Grimsnäs Herrgård, 36053 Skruv. ✉ ljudersvandrarhem@bizland.com	☎ (478) 20400 🖷 (478) 20400	70	01.04–30.09	ⅲ ⓡ ♿ ⌐CC⌐ ⚲ P 🖸
▲ Ljugarn STF Vandrarhem Ljugarn, Strandridaregården, 62016 Ljugarn. ✉ stf.ljugarn@gamma.telenordia.se	☎ (498) 493184 🖷 (498) 482424	31	15.05–31.08	ⅲ ⓡ ⚲ P
▲ Ljungdalen STF Vandrarhem Ljungdalen, Dunsjögården, Box 15, 84035 Ljungdalen.	☎ (687) 20285, (687) 20367 (15.10-23.06)	40	⌐₁₂	ⅲ ⚲ P 🖸
▲ Loftahammar STF Vandrarhem Loftahammar, Trillin, Trillinvägen 3, Box 57, 59095 Loftahammar.	☎ (493) 61110 🖷 (493) 61929	25	⌐₁₂	ⅲ ⌐○⌐ ♿ ⌐CC⌐ ⚲ P 🖸
▲ Lommeland STF Vandrarhem Lommeland, Råsshult, PI 3135 Röd Lommeland, 45293 Strömstad.	☎ (526) 42027 🖷 (526) 42020	57	20.05–01.09	ⅲ ⚲ P 🖸
▲ Lönneberga STF Vandrarhem Lönneberga, Lönneberga vägen, 57794 Silverdalen.	☎ (495) 40036, (070) 5745168 🖷 (070) 6192851	55	⌐₁₂	ⅲ ⓡ ⚲ P
▲ Lönsboda STF Vandrarhem Lönsboda, Tranebodavägen 12, 28070 Lönsboda.	☎ (479) 21525 🖷 (479) 21525	18	⌐₁₂	ⅲ ⌐○⌐ ⓡ ⚲ P
▲ Lövånger STF Vandrarhem Lövånger, Lövångers Kyrkstad, Box 13, 93010 Lövånger. ✉ info@lovangerskyrkstad.se	☎ (913) 10395 🖷 (913) 10759	80	⌐₁₂	ⅲ ⌐○⌐ ⌐CC⌐ ⚲ P

Location/Address	Telephone No. Fax No.	Beds	Opening Dates	Facilities
▲ Luleå STF Vandrarhem Luleå, N:a Gäddvik, Örnviksvägen 87, 97594 Luleå.	☎ (920) 252325 ✆ (920) 252419	68	🚋	⁙ ⁙⁙ 🍴 ᴄᴄ ✓ Ⓟ 🔄
▲ Lund STF Vandrarhem Lund, Tåget Vävaregatan 22, Bjeredsparken, 22237 Lund. ⓔ trainhostel@ebrevet.nu	☎ (46) 142820 ✆ (46) 320568	108	08.01–15.12	⁙⁙ 🍴 0.1 NW ✓ Ⓟ ☕
▲ Lycksele STF Vandrarhem Lycksele, Duvan i Lycksele AB, Storg 47, 92132 Lycksele.	☎ (950) 14670 ✆ (950) 10233	40	14.06–14.08	⁙⁙ 🍴 ᴄᴄ ✓ Ⓟ
▲ Malå STF Vandrarhem Malå, Hotellgatan 10, 93070 Malå.	☎ (953) 14291 ✆ (953) 14291	24	01.06–31.08	♿ ✓
▲ Malmö STF Vandrarhem Malmö, Backavägen 18, 21432 Malmö.	☎ (40) 82220 ✆ (40) 510659	157	11.01–17.12	⁙⁙ 🍴 Ⓡ ✓ Ⓟ 🔄
▲ Malung STF Vandrarhem Malung, Vallerås Turistgård, Mobyn PL 1448, 78233 Malung.	☎ (280) 14040 ✆ (280) 41057	46	🚋	⁙⁙ 🍴 ✓ Ⓟ
▲ Mariefred STF Vandrarhem Mariefred, Röda Korsets idé och utbildningscenter, 64781 Mariefred. ⓔ receptionen@gripsholm@redcross.se	☎ (159) 36100 ✆ (8) 4524600	70	15.06–15.08	⁙⁙ 🍴 1 W ᴄᴄ ✓ Ⓟ 🔄
▲ Mariestad STF Vandrarhem Mariestad, Hamngatan 20, 54230 Mariestad.	☎ (501) 10448	60	🚋	⁙⁙ Ⓡ ✓ Ⓟ
▲ Medevi Brunn STF Vandrarhem Medevi Brunn, Medevi Brunn, 59197 Motala.	☎ (141) 91100 ✆ (141) 91532	50	06.06–10.08	⁙⁙ 🍴 ᴄᴄ ✓ Ⓟ
▲ Mellbystrand STF Vandrarhem Mellbystrand, Kustvägen 152, 31261 Mellbystrand.	☎ (430) 25220 ✆ (430) 15325	37	01.06–31.08	⁙⁙ Ⓡ ✓ Ⓟ 🔄
▲ Mjölby STF Vandrarhem Mjölby, Hembygdsgården, Norrgårdsgatan 14, 59541 Mjölby.	☎ (142) 10016	60	07.01–21.12	⁙⁙ Ⓡ ✓ Ⓟ 🔄
Mölndal ☞ Göteborg				
▲ Moheda STF Vandrarhem Moheda, Kursgården Kronobergshed, 34036 Moheda.	☎ (472) 40052 ✆ (472) 40135	60	🚋	⁙⁙ 🍴 Ⓡ ✓ Ⓟ 🔄
▲ Mora STF Vandrarhem Mora, Målkull Ann's, Vasagatan 19, 79232 Mora. ⓔ ann@maalkullann.se	☎ (250) 38196 ✆ (250) 38195	62	🚋	⁙⁙ 🍴 ♿ ✓ Ⓟ
▲ Motala STF Vandrarhem Motala, Skogsborgsgatan 1, 59152 Motala, Östergötland. ⓔ skogsborg@mbox301.swipnet.se	☎ (141) 57436 ✆ (141) 57435	60	18.05–14.08	⁙⁙ 🍴 Ⓡ ♿ ✓ Ⓟ ☕

Location/Address	Telephone No. Fax No.	Beds	Opening Dates	Facilities
▲ **Nässjö** STF Vandrarhem Nässjö, Sörängens Folkhögskola, Rågången 4, 571 38 Nässjö.	☎ (380) 10645 ❻ (380) 19076	50	11.06–15.08	✝✝✝ 🍽 ✓ P 🔟
▲ **Nora** STF Vandrarhem Nora, Tåghem, Box 52, 71322 Nora.	☎ (587) 14676 ❻ (19) 312711	64	01.05–15.09	✝✝✝ 🍽 R ✓ P 🔟
▲ **Norberg** STF Vandrarhem Norberg, Gruvbyn Klackberg, 73891 Norberg.	☎ (223) 20247 ❻ (223) 23704	58	ⁱ²⁄	✝✝✝ 2NW ✓ P 🔟
▲ **Norrahammar** STF Vandrarhem Norrahammar, Spånhultsvägen 19, 56231 Norrahammar.	☎ (36) 61075 ❻ (36) 61078	35	ⁱ²⁄	✝✝✝ 🍽 R 9S ♿ ᶜᶜ⌐ ✓ 🛍
▲ **Norrköping** STF Vandrarhem Norrköping, Turistgården, Ingelstadsgatan 31, 60223 Norrköping.	☎ (11) 101160 ❻ (11) 186863	87	11.01–16.12	✝✝✝ 🍽 ♿ ᶜᶜ⌐ ✓
▲ **Norrköping** STF Vandrarhem Norrköping, Abborreberg, Lindö, Box 7100, 60007 Norrköping.	☎ (11) 319344 ❻ (11) 319146	60	01.05–15.09	✝✝✝ 🍽 5E ᶜᶜ⌐ ✓ P 🛍
▲ **Norrtälje** STF Vandrarhem Norrtälje, Brännäsgården, Bältartorpsgatan 6, Box 803, 76128 Norrtälje. @ brannasgarden@hotmail.com	☎ (176) 71569 ❻ (176) 71589	32	11.06–17.08	✝✝✝ 🍽 ✓
▲ **Nybro** STF Vandrarhem Nybro, Vasagatan 22, 38232 Nybro, Småland.	☎ (481) 10932 ❻ (481) 12117	100	01.03–31.10	✝✝✝ 🍽 ♿ ᶜᶜ⌐ ✓ P
▲ **Nynäshamn** STF Vandrarhem Nynäshamn, Nickstabadsvägen 15, 14943 Nynäshamn.	☎ (8) 52012780	42	ⁱ²⁄	✝✝✝ R ✓ P
▲ **Ockelbo** STF Vandrarhem Ockelbo, Perslundavägen 18, 81630 Ockelbo. @ obbk@ockelbo.se	☎ (297) 55691 ❻ (297) 55990	28	ⁱ²⁄	✝✝✝ R ♿ ✓ 🔟
▲ **Ödeshög** STF Vandrarhem Ödeshög, Hembygdsgården, Södra Vägen 63, 59931 Ödeshög.	☎ (144) 10700 ❻ (144) 10700	55	15.05–25.08	✝✝✝ 🍽 R ♿ ✓ P 🔟
▲ **Öhns Gård** STF Vandrarhem Öhns gård, Odensåker, 54015 Väring. @ info@ohnsgard.se	☎ (500) 441317 ❻ (500) 441210	50	ⁱ²⁄	✝✝✝ 🍽 ♿ ᶜᶜ⌐ ✓ P 🔟 🛍
▲ **Ölands Skogsby** STF Vandrarhem Ölands Skogsby, 38693 Färjestaden.	☎ (485) 38395 ❻ (485) 38324	70	28.04–31.08	✝✝✝ 🍽 ᶜᶜ⌐ ✓ 🔟
▲ **Olofström** STF Vandrarhem Olofström, Tåkasjövägen 36, 29337 Olofström.	☎ (454) 99499 ❻ (454) 99499	72	13.06–10.08	R 1N ✓ P 🔟

Location/Address	Telephone No. Fax No.	Beds	Opening Dates	Facilities
▲ **Omberg** STF Vandrarhem Omberg, Stocklycke, 59993 Ödeshög.	☎ (144) 33044	55	16.01–14.12	ⅲ ⁞⊙⁞ Ⓡ 🚻 ♿ 🏃 🅿
▲ **Örebro** STF Vandrarhem Örebro, Fanjunkarevägen 5, 70365 Örebro. ✉ vandrarhemmetorebro@usa.net	☎ (19) 310240 🖷 (19) 310256	112	01.01–20.12	ⅲ Ⓡ 1N ♿ ⧼CC⧽ 🏃 🅿 🚿
▲ **Öreryd Hestra** STF Vandrarhem Öreryd, 33027 Hestra.	☎ (370) 337035 🖷 (370) 337008	27	⌂2	ⅲ Ⓡ ♿ ⧼CC⧽ 🏃 🅿 🚿
▲ **Örnsköldsvik** STF Vandrarhem Örnsköldsvik, Pl 1980, 89440 Överhörnäs. ✉ sodersten@ebox.tninet.se	☎ (660) 70244	30	⌂2	ⅲ ⁞⊙⁞ Ⓡ 8W ⧼CC⧽ 🏃 🅿 🚿
▲ **Orrefors** STF Vandrarhem Orrefors, Box 28, Backabyggningen, Silversparregatan 14, 38040 Orrefors.	☎ (481) 30020 🖷 (481) 30020	64	01.05–01.09	ⅲ ⧼CC⧽ 🏃 🚿
▲ **Orsa** STF Vandrarhem Orsa, Box 95, 79422 Orsa. ✉ stfvandrarhem.orsa@telia.com	☎ (250) 42170 🖷 (250) 42365	68	⌂2	ⅲ 1E ♿ ⧼CC⧽ 🏃 🅿 🚿
▲ **Orust** STF Vandrarhem Orust, Tofta gård, Stocken, 47492 Ellös.	☎ (304) 50380	68	⌂2	ⅲ Ⓡ 🏃 🅿 🚿
▲ **Osby** STF Vandrarhem Osby, c/o Stora Hotellet, V Järnvägsgatan 17 28331 Osby. ✉ storahotellet@ebox.tninet.se	☎ (479) 31830 🖷 (479) 16222	30	22.06–10.08	ⅲ ⁞⊙⁞ ⧼CC⧽ 🏃 🅿
▲ **Oskarshamn** STF Vandrarhem Oskarshamn, Åsavägen 8, 57234 Oskarshamn.	☎ (491) 88198 🖷 (491) 81045	130	⌂2	ⅲ ⁞⊙⁞ 🏃 🅿 🚿
▲ **Österbybruk** STF Vandrarhem Österbybruk, Stråkvägen 3, Box 76, 74822 ðsterbybruk.	☎ (295) 21570 🖷 (295) 20050	36	⌂2	ⅲ ⁞⊙⁞ Ⓡ 🏃 🅿 🚿
▲ **Österbymo** STF Vandrarhem Österbymo, Ydregården, Box 37 57060 Österbymo. ✉ asiapacific25@hotmail.com	☎ (381) 60103 🖷 (381) 60999	20	01.05–30.09	ⅲ ⁞⊙⁞ 🏃 🅿 🍴
▲ **Östersund** STF Vandrarhem Östersund, Södra Gröngatan 36, 83135 Östersund.	☎ (63) 139100, (63) 34130	58	19.06–10.08	ⅲ Ⓡ 🏃 🅿
▲ **Östersund/Jamtli** STF Vandrarhem Östersund/Jamtli, Museiplan, Box 482, 83123 Östersund.	☎ (63) 105984	30	⌂2	ⅲ 1N 🏃 🅿 🚿
▲ **Östra Ämtervik** STF Vandrarhem Medskog/Östra Ämtervik, 686 96 Östra Ämtervik. ✉ medskog@delta.telenordia.se	☎ (565) 32123 🖷 (565) 32123	38	⌂2	ⅲ ⁞⊙⁞ ♿ 🏃 🅿 🚿 🍴 ♿

Location/Address	Telephone No. Fax No.	Beds	Opening Dates	Facilities
▲ **Ottenby** STF Vandrarhem Ottenby, Näsby, 38065 Degerhamn.	☏ (485) 662062 ✆ (485) 662161	146	🖷	♙♙ 🍴 ® ♿ 🍴 ℙ 🗗
▲ **Överum** STF Vandrarhem Överum, Källarbacken 2, Box 19, 59096 Överum.	☏ (493) 30302, (70) 6742621	26	🖷	♙♙ 🍴 ℙ
▲ **Persåsen** STF Vandrarhem Persåsen, Persåsen 3370, 83024 Oviken. ℯ info@persasen.com	☏ (643) 40180 ✆ (643) 40105	27	24.06–20.08	♙♙ 🍴 ® ♿ ⊂CC⊃ 🍴 ℙ 🗗
▲ **Piteå** STF Vandrarhem Piteå, Storgatan 3, 94131 Piteå.	☏ (911) 15880 ✆ (911) 15880	35	🖷	♙♙ ♿ 🍴 ℙ
▲ **Prässebo** STF Vandrarhem Prässebo, Pl 3606, 46012 Prässebo.	☏ (520) 667024	32	15.05–31.08	♙♙ ® ♿ 🍴 ℙ
▲ **Ramsele** STF Vandrarhem Ramsele, Prästbordet 1000, 88040 Ramsele.	☏ (623) 10167 ✆ (623) 10167	36	15.06–15.08	♙♙ 🍴 ® ♿ 🍴 ℙ 🗗
▲ **Ransäter** STF Vandrarhem Ransäter, Geijersvägen 1, 68493 Ransäter.	☏ (552) 30050	18	01.05–31.08	♙♙ 🍴 ℙ
▲ **Rättvik** STF Vandrarhem Rättvik, Centralgatan, 79530 Rättvik. ℯ rattviksparken@rattviksparken.fh.se	☏ (248) 10566 ✆ (248) 56113	104	🖷	♙♙ 🍴 ♿ ⊂CC⊃ 🍴 ℙ 🗗
▲ **Rantajärvi** STF Vandrarhem Rantajärvi, Rantajärvi 78, 957 94 Övertorneå. ℯ stfvandrarhen@camprautajarvi.se	☏ (927) 23000 ✆ (927) 23123	38	01.06–31.08	♙♙ 🍴 ♿ 🍴 ℙ 🗗
▲ **Regna** STF Vandrarhem Regna, Regnagården, 64010 Högsjö.	☏ (151) 70127 ✆ (151) 70127	40	🖷	♙♙ 🍴 ® 🍴 ℙ
▲ **Rimforsa** STF Vandrarhem Rimforsa, Kalvudden, 59041 Rimforsa. ℯ kalvudd@algonet.se	☏ (494) 20137	25	01.06–15.08	♙♙ 🍴 ® 🍴 ℙ
▲ **Romelestugan** STF Vandrarhem Romelestugan, Box 47, 24013 Genarp.	☏ (46) 55073, (46) 55138	26	🖷	♙♙ 🍴 ® 🍴 ℙ
▲ **Ronneby** STF Vandrarhem Ronneby, Övre Brunnsvägen 54, 37236 Ronneby.	☏ (457) 26300 ✆ (457) 26300	104	07.01–17.12	♙♙ 🍴 🍴 ℙ
▲ **Rörbäck** STF Vandrarhem Rörbäck, Bokenäs, v Rörbäck 29, 45196 Uddevalla. ℯ rorback@telia.com	☏ (522) 650190 ✆ (522) 650990	54	01.05–30.09	♙♙ ® 🍴 ℙ

Location/Address	Telephone No. Fax No.	Beds	Opening Dates	Facilities
▲ **Röstånga** STF Vandrarhem Röstånga, Röstånga Gästgivaregård, Marieholmsvägen 2, 26024 Röstånga. e info@rostongagastgivaregard.se	☏ (435) 29700 ⊕ (435) 29799	36	🄵	⫶⚑ 🅟 ⬤ 🅟 ⬤
▲ **Sala** STF Vandrarhem Sala, Sofielund, Mellandammen, 73336 Sala.	☏ (224) 12730	36	🄵	⫶⫶⫶ Ⓡ ♿ ⚑ 🅟
▲ **Sälen** STF Vandrarhem Sälen, Gräsheden, Box 58, 78067 Sälen.	☏ (280) 82040 ⊕ (280) 82045	62	🄵	⫶⫶⫶ ⫶⚑ Ⓡ ⚑ 🅟 ⊡
▲ **Sandslån/Kramfors** STF Vandrarhem Sandslån, Sandslån 3144, 87052 Nyland.	☏ (612) 50541 ⊕ (612) 50006	80	15.05–15.09	⫶⫶⫶ ⫶⚑ Ⓡ ⚑ 🅟
▲ **Sandviken** STF Vandrarhem Sandviken, Skogsfruvägen 22, 81141 Sandviken. e stf.vandrarhem@sandviken.se	☏ (26) 251915 ⊕ (26) 259865	69	02.01–20.12	⫶⫶⫶ ⫶⚑ ⚑ 🅟
▲ **Sankt Anna** STF Vandrarhem Sankt Anna, Gamla Färjeläget, 61498 St Anna. e yngve.andersson@mbox301.swipnet.se	☏ (121) 51312	32	01.06–31.08	⫶⫶⫶ ⫶⚑ ⚑ 🅟 ⊡ ⬤
▲ **Särna** STF Vandrarhem Särna, Björkhagen, Box 535, 79090 Särna.	☏ (253) 10308	25	🄵	⫶⫶⫶ ⫶⚑ Ⓡ ⚑ 🅟 ⊡
▲ **Särna** STF Vandrarhem Särna, Turistgården, Sjukstugev 4, 79090 Särna. e alpen.utreckling@swipnet.se	☏ (253) 10437 ⊕ (253) 10437	37	🄵	⫶⫶⫶ ⫶⚑ ⫶⚑ ⚑ 🅟 ⊡
▲ **Säter-Haverö** STF Vandrarhem Säter-Haverö, Haverö Hembygdsgård, Säter, 84193 Östavall.	☏ (690) 30137	14	05.06–15.08	⫶⫶⫶ ⚑ 🅟
▲ **Sätrabrunn** STF Vandrarhem Sätra Brunn 73326, Sala.	☏ (224) 54600 ⊕ (224) 54601	36	01.05–30.09	⫶⫶⫶ ⫶⚑ ⫶⚑ ⚑ 🅟
▲ **Saxnäs** STF Vandrarhem Saxnäs, Kultsjögården Box 6, 91088 Marsfjäll.	☏ (940) 70044 ⊕ (940) 70189	50	🄵	⫶⫶⫶ ⫶⚑ ⫶⚑ 🅟
▲ **Sigtuna** STF Vandrarhem Sigtuna, Ansgarsliden, Manfred Björkquists allè 12, Box 92, 19322 Sigtuna.	☏ (8) 59258478, (8) 5928200 ⊕ (8) 59258384	60	25.06–05.08	⫶⫶⫶ ⫶⚑ ⫶⚑ ⚑ 🅟
▲ **Skåne Tranås** STF Vandrarhem, Skåne Tranås, Helgonavägen, 27392 Tomelilla.	☏ (417) 20330 ⊕ (417) 20330	88	🄵	⫶⫶⫶ ⫶⚑ Ⓡ ⚑ 🅟 ⊡
▲ **Skara** STF Vandrarhem Skara, Vasaparken, 53232 Skara.	☏ (511) 12165, (511) 63619 ⊕ (511) 63656	65	🄵	⫶⫶⫶ ⫶⚑ ♿ ⫶⚑ ⚑ 🅟 ⊡

Location/Address	Telephone No. Fax No.	Beds	Opening Dates	Facilities
▲ Skäralid - Klippan STF Vandrarhem, Skäralid, PL 750, 26070 Ljungbyhed.	☏ (435) 442025 🖷 (435) 442383	29	🖼	♦♦♦ ⓡ ✆ ��
▲ Skövde STF Vandrarhem Skövde, Billingens Stugby & Camping, Alphyddevägen 54133 Skövde.	☏ (500) 471633 🖷 (500) 471044	18	🖼	♦♦♦ ✆ ⓟ ▣
▲ Skurup STF Vandrarhem Skurup, Bruksgatan 3, 27435 Skurup.	☏ (411) 536061 🖷 (411) 536061	32	11.06–12.08	♦♦♦ 🍴 ✆ ⓟ ▣
▲ Smygehuk STF Vandrarhem Smygehuk, Kustvägen, P1 314, 23178 Smygehuk. ✉ smygehuk.vh@telia.com	☏ (410) 24583 🖷 (410) 24509	43	🖼	♦♦♦ 🍴 ⓡ ✆ ⓟ
▲ Snöå Bruk STF Vandrarhem Snöå Bruk, 78051 Dala Järna. ✉ stf.vandrarhem@snoabruk.se	☏ (281) 24018 🖷 (281) 24045	91	🖼	♦♦♦ 🍴 ✆ ▣
▲ Söderhamn STF Vandrarhem Söderhamn, Mohedsvägen 59, 82692 Söderala.	☏ (270) 425233 🖷 (270) 425326	35	24.05–02.09	♦♦♦ 🍴 15W ㏄ ✆ ⓟ
▲ Söderköping STF Vandrarhem Söderköping, Mangelgården, Skönbergagatan 48, 61430 Söderköping. ✉ 012110213@telia.com	☏ (121) 10213	36	01.06–31.08	♦♦♦ ⓡ ♿ ✆ ⓟ
▲ Södertälje STF Vandrarhem Södertälje, Tvetagården, 15192 Södertälje.	☏ (8) 55098025 🖷 (8) 55098471	54	01.02–16.12	♦♦♦ 🍴 6SW ✆ ⓟ
▲ Södra Ljunga STF Vandrarhem Södra Ljunga, 34191 Ljungby. ✉ kenneth.037216160@telia.com	☏ (372) 16011 🖷 (372) 16160	50	🖼	♦♦♦ 🍴 ✆ ⓟ ▣
▲ Sollefteå STF Vandrarhem Sollefteå, Björklunden, Övergård 7006, 88193 Sollefteå. ✉ hotell@hotellbjorklunden.com	☏ (620) 15817 🖷 (620) 15917	26	🖼	♦♦♦ 3E ㏄ ✆ ⓟ
▲ Sölvesborg STF Vandrarhem Sölvesborg, Yndegården, Ynde Byvägen 22, 294 92 Sölvesborg. ✉ yndegarden@solvenet.se	☏ (456) 19811 🖷 (456) 19449	60	🖼	♦♦♦ 🍴 3NW ✆ ⓟ ▣
▲ Sorsele STF Vandrarhem Sorsele, Torggatan 1-2, 92070 Sorsele.	☏ (952) 10048 🖷 (952) 55281	24	10.06–31.08	♦♦♦ 🍴 ⓡ ✆ ⓟ ▣
▲ Stavsjö STF Vandrarhem Stavsjö, Störningsväg 8, 61895 Stafsjö.	☏ (11) 393384 🖷 (11) 393343	28	11.01–20.12	♦♦♦ 🍴 ♿ ㏄ ✆ ⓟ ▣
▲ Stenungsund STF Vandrarhem Stenungsund, Tollenäs, Pl 6109, 44491 Stenungsund.	☏ (303) 82120 🖷 (303) 770485	50	15.04–15.10	♦♦♦ 🍴 ⓡ ♿ ✆ ⓟ

Location/Address	Telephone No. Fax No.	Beds	Opening Dates	Facilities
▲ Stockholm - af Chapman/Skeppsholmen (IBN) Flaggmansvägen 8, 11149 Stockholm. ⊖ info@chapman.stfturist.se	☎ (8) 4632266 ❶ (8) 6117155	290	🔚	ⅲ ⦿ ⓡ ♿ ⋳cc⋲ ♂ 🅿 ⧈
▲ Stockholm STF Vandrarhem Backpackers Inn, Box 9116, 10272 Stockholm.	☎ (8) 6607515 ❶ (8) 6654039	300	27.06–10.08	ⅲ ⦿ 🅿
▲ Stockholm STF Vandrarhem Hökarängen, Martinskolan, Munstycksvägen 18, 12357 Farsta.	☎ (8) 941765 ❶ (8) 6041646	46	25.06–08.08	ⅲ ⦿ 3SW ♿ ♂ 🅿 ☕
▲ Stockholm - Långholmen Kronohäktet, Box 9116, 10272 Stockholm. ⊖ vandrarhem@langholmen.com	☎ (8) 6680510 ❶ (8) 7208575	254	🔚	ⅲ ⦿ ⓡ ♿ ⋳cc⋲ ♂ 🅿 ⧈
▲ Stockholm - Zinkensdamm SFT Vandrarhem Zinkensdamm, Zinkens väg 20, 11741 Stockholm. ⊖ zinkensdamm@telia.com	☎ (8) 6168100 ❶ (8) 6168120	510	🔚	ⅲ ⦿ ⓡ ♿ ⋳cc⋲ ♂ 🅿 ⧈ ☕

Hostels in the Archipelago/ AJ dans l'archipel/JH im Archipel/Albergues en el Archipiélago.

▲ Adelsö STF Vandrarhem Adelsö, 17892 Adelsö.	☎ (8) 56051450 ❶ (8) 56051400	30	15.06–31.08	ⅲ ⦿ ⓡ ♂ 🅿 ⧈
▲ Arholma STF Vandrarhem, Arholma 162, 76041 Arholma.	☎ (176) 56018	34	🔚	♂ 🅿
▲ Blidö STF Vandrarhem Blidö, Blidö Wärdshus AB, Stämmarsund 1429, 76017 BLIDÖ.	☎ (176) 82299 ❶ (176) 82232	60	🔚	ⅲ ⦿ ⓡ ♿ ⋳cc⋲ ♂ 🅿 ⧈ ☕
▲ Dalarö STF Vandrarhem Dalarö, Lotsen Tullbacken 4, 13054 Dalarö.	☎ (8) 50151636 ❶ (8) 50151636	8	🔚	50SE ♂ 🅿 ⧈
▲ Fejan STF Vandrarhem Fejan, 76015 Gräddö.	☎ (176) 43031 ❶ (176) 43205	53	01.05–30.09	⦿ ⋳cc⋲ ♂ 🅿
▲ Finnhamn STF Vandrarhem Finnhamn, Finnhamns Friluftsområde, Box 84, 13025 Ingmarsö.	☎ (8) 54246212 ❶ (8) 54246212	80	🔚	ⅲ ⓡ ⋳cc⋲ ♂
▲ Fjärdlång STF Vandrarhem, Fjärdlång, 13054 Dalarö.	☎ (8) 50156092	36	07.06–26.09	ⅲ ⓡ ♂ 🅿
▲ Gällnö STF Vandrarhem Gällnö, 130 33 Gällnö by.	☎ (8) 57166117 ❶ (8) 57166288	35	01.05–30.09	ⅲ ⓡ ♂
▲ Grinda STF Vandrarhem Grinda, Grinda Friluftsområde, Södra Bryggan, 10005 Stockholm 1.	☎ (8) 54249072 ❶ (8) 54249345	44	01.05–15.10	ⅲ ⓡ ♂

Location/Address	Telephone No. Fax No.	Beds	Opening Dates	Facilities
▲ **Kapellskär** STF Vandrarhem Kapellskär, Pl 985, Riddersholm, 76015 Gräddö.	☎ (176) 44169 ✆ (176) 239046	36	⬛ⁱ²	⁀⁀ ⓡ ♂ 🅿 ☙
▲ **Lillsved** STF Vandrarhem, Lillsved 13990, Värmdö.	☎ (8) 54138530 ✆ (8) 54138316	148	01.06–31.08	⁀⁀ 🍴 ♂ 🅿
▲ **Örskär** STF Vandrarhem Örskär, Örskärs Fyrplats, 74071 Öregrund. ⓔ orskars.vandrarhem@telia.com	☎ (173) 34021 ✆ (173) 34011	18	01.05–30.09	⁀⁀ ⓡ ♂ 🐾
▲ **Sävö** STF Vandrarhem Sävö, Lotsplatsen, Ekviken, 61075 Västerljung.	☎ (156) 40346 ✆ (156) 40346	32	⬛ⁱ²	⁀⁀ ♂ 🅿
▲ **Siaröfortet** STF Vandrarhem Siaröfortet, Kyrkogårdsön, 18495 Ljusterö.	☎ (8) 54242149 ✆ (8) 54242149	32	01.05–30.09	⁀⁀ ⓡ ⌐cc⌐ ♂
▲ **Skeppsmyra** STF Vandrarhem Skeppsmyra, Pensionat Lyckhem, 76042 Björkö. ⓔ lyckhem@algonet.se	☎ (176) 94027 ✆ (176) 94044	40	15.06–15.08	⁀⁀ ⓡ ⌐cc⌐ ♂ 🅿 🔲 🐾
▲ **Stora Kalholmen** STF Vandrarhem Stora Kalholmen, c/o Rubin, Sandhamnsvägen, 13469 Ingarö.	☎ (8) 54246023 ✆ (8) 57160125	22	10.06–20.08	⁀⁀ ⓡ ♂ 🅿
▲ **Tyresö** STF Vandrarhem Tyresö, Prinsvillan, Kyrkvägen 3, 13560 Tyresö.	☎ (8) 7700304 ✆ (8) 7700355	42	⬛ⁱ²	⁀⁀ ⓡ ♂ 🅿
▲ **Utö** STF Vandrarhem Utö, Gruvbyn, 13056 Utö.	☎ (8) 50157660 ✆ (8) 50157265	44	⬛ⁱ²	⁀⁀ 🍴 ⓡ ⌐cc⌐ ♂ 🅿 🔲
▲ **Väddö/Älmsta** STF Vandrarhem Väddö, Älmsta, Box 9, 76040 Väddö.	☎ (176) 50078	31	29.06–12.08	⁀⁀ ♂ 🅿
▲ **Stora Karlsö** STF Vandrarhem Stora Karlsö, 62020 Klintehamn.	☎ (498) 240500 ✆ (498) 240567	28	01.05–31.08	⁀⁀ 🍴 ⓡ ♂ 🅿
▲ **Stora Segerstad** STF Vandrarhem Stora Segerstad, 33021 Reftele. ⓔ segerstad.naturbruksgymnasium @educ.itjkpg.se	☎ (371) 23200, (371) 23209, (070) 5567551 ✆ (371) 23210	56	12.06–12.08	⁀⁀ 🍴 ♂ 🅿
▲ **Storvallen-Storlien** STF Vandrarhem Storvallen, Box 119, 83019 Storlien. ⓔ info@storvallen.km.scout.se	☎ (647) 70050 ✆ (647) 70050	44	⬛ⁱ²	⁀⁀ 🍴 ♿ ♂ 🅿 🔲
▲ **Strömsholm** STF Vandrarhem Strömsholm, Sofielundsvägen 33, 73040 Kolbäck.	☎ (220) 43774 ✆ (220) 24187	32	15.06–15.08	⁀⁀ ♿ ♂ 🅿 🔲

Location/Address	Telephone No. Fax No.	Beds	Opening Dates	Facilities
▲ **Strömsnäsbruk** STF Vandrarhem Strömsnäsbruk, Fågelvägen 2, 28733 Strömsnäsbruk. e hostel.g@swipnet.se	t (433) 20050 f (433) 20970	55	12	R CC P
▲ **Strömstad** STF Vandrarhem Strömstad, N Kyrkogatan 12, 45230 Strömstad.	t (526) 10193 f (70) 8410195	76	12.01–17.12	R P
▲ **Strömsund/Tullingsås** STF Vandrarhem Strömsund, Tullingsås, PL 6173, 83392 Strömsund.	t (670) 30088, (70) 2056173 f (670) 30088	70	12	R
▲ **Sundsvall** STF Vandrarhem Sundsvall, N Stadsberget, 85640 Sundsvall.	t (60) 612119 f (60) 617801	150	12	R
▲ **Sunne** STF Vandrarhem Sunne, Hembygdsvägen 7, 68631 Sunne.	t (565) 10788	71	12	P
▲ **Surahammar** STF Vandrarhem Surahammar, Stationsvägen 2, 73531 Surahammar.	t (220) 33008, (10) 6686474	68	01.04–30.09	R P
▲ **Sveg** STF Vandrarhem Sveg, Hotell Härjedalen, Vallarvägen 11, 84233 Sveg.	t (680) 10338	50	12	R P
▲ **Tännäs** STF Vandrarhem Tännäs, Tännäsgården, Bygatan 51, 84094 Tännäs. e kontakt@tannasgarden.nu	t (684) 24067 f (684) 24067	30	12	CC P
▲ **Tänndalen** STF Vandrarhem Tänndalen, Skarvruets fjällhotel, 84098 Tänndalen.	t (684) 22111 f (684) 22311	49	12	R CC P
▲ **Tåtorp** STF Vandrarhem Tåtorp/Göta Kanal, 549 93 Moholm. e jonas.fallstrom@c.lrf.se	t (506) 53086 f (506) 53086	28	15.05–15.10	R 20 SE P
▲ **Tingstäde** STF Vandrarhem Tingstäde, Box 73, 62033 Tingstäde. e tingstade@hotmail.com	t (498) 274333 f (498) 274830	26	01.05–31.08	P
▲ **Tjärö** STF Turiststation Tjärö, 37010 Bräkne Hoby. e info@tjaro.stfturist.se	t (454) 60063 f (454) 39063	100	01.05–12.09	R CC P
▲ **Tollarp** STF Vandrarhem Tollarp, Box 33, Lundgrensväg 2, 29010 Tollarp.	t (44) 310023	56	12	R P
▲ **Torestorp** STF Vandrarhem Torestorp, Solbergavägen 2, 51193 Torestorp.	t (320) 55141 f (320) 55143	37	01.05–15.09	R

Location/Address	Telephone No. Fax No.	Beds	Opening Dates	Facilities
▲ Tranås STF Vandrarhem Tranås, Hembygdsgården, 57339 Tranås.	☎ (140) 15166	35	15.01–15.12	††† ⓇⒸⒹ ♂ 🅿
▲ Tranemo STF Vandrarhem Tranemo, Tranan, Smedsgatan 2, 51431 Tranemo.	☎ (325) 76710, (70) 4690275 🖷 (325) 76710	42	☜12	††† Ⓡ ♿ ♂ 🅿 ⓞ
▲ Trollhättan STF Vandrarhem Trollhättan, Gula Villan, Tingvallavägen 12, 461 32 Trollhättan.	☎ (520) 12960 🖷 (520) 12960	70	☜12	††† ⑩ 3W ⒸⒸ ♂ 🅿
▲ Trosa STF Vandrarhem Trosa, Stensunds folkhögskola, 61991 Trosa.	☎ (156) 53200 🖷 (156) 53222	15	12.06–15.08	††† ⑩ ♂ 🅿 ⓞ
▲ Uddevalla STF Vandrarhem Uddevalla, Gustafsberg 124, 45191 Uddevalla.	☎ (522) 15200 🖷 (522) 511798	55	15.06–16.08	††† ⑩ 6SW ⒸⒸ ♂ ⓞ
▲ Ulricehamn STF Vandrarhem Ulricehamn, STF VH, 52390 Ulricehamn.	☎ (321) 10550 🖷 (321) 14802	40	☜12	††† ⑩ 2N ♂ 🅿
▲ Ulvön/Ljungskile STF Vandrarhem Ulvön/Ljungskile, Pl. 31482, 45993 Ljungskile.	☎ (522) 29184 🖷 (522) 20171	22	18.06–19.08	††† ♂ 🅿 ⓞ ☕
▲ Umeå STF Vandrarhem Umeå, Västra Esplanaden 10, 90326 Umeå. 📧 stfumea.vandrarhem@swipnet.se	☎ (90) 771650 🖷 (90) 771695	100	03.01–20.12	††† ⑩ ⒸⒸ ♂ ⓞ
▲ Upplands-Bro STF Vandrarhem Upplands-Bro, Säbyholm, Naturbruksgymnasiet, 19791 Bro.	☎ (8) 58242481 🖷 (8) 58242693	40	10.06–09.08	††† ♂ 🅿 ⓞ ☕
▲ Uppsala STF Vandrarhem Uppsala, Sunnersta Herrgård, Sunnerstavägen 24, 75651 Uppsala	☎ (18) 324220	84	☜12	††† ⑩ 6S ♂ 🅿
▲ Vadstena STF Vandrarhem Vadstena, Skänningegatan 20, Box 28, 59221 Vadstena.	☎ (143) 10302 🖷 (143) 10404	65	☜12	††† Ⓡ ⒸⒸ ♂ 🅿 ⓞ
▲ Vålådalen STF Vandrarhem Vålådalen, 83012 Vålådalen. 📧 info@valadalen.stfturist.se	☎ (647) 35300 🖷 (647) 35353	37	☜12	††† ⑩ ⒸⒸ ♂ 🅿
▲ Vara STF Vandrarhem Vara, Folkhögskolan, Badhusgatan, Box 145, 53481 Vara.	☎ (512) 10838	35	20.06–05.08	††† ⑩ Ⓡ ♿ ♂ 🅿 ⓞ
▲ Varberg STF Vandrarhem Varberg, Vare 325, 43291 Varberg.	☎ (340) 41173 🖷 (340) 41600	43	☜12	††† 7S ♂ 🅿
▲ Värmskog STF Vandrarhem Värmskog, 67195 Klässbol.	☎ (570) 461134	28	15.06–31.08	††† ⑩ ♂ 🅿 ⓞ

Location/Address	Telephone No. Fax No.	Beds	Opening Dates	Facilities
▲ **Värnamo** STF Vandrarhem Värnamo, Tättingvägen 1, 33142 Värnamo. ✉ smalandsagenturer@varnamo.mail.telia.com	☎ (370) 19898 📠 (370) 18235	89	17.01–22.12	👫 �🍴 ⓡ ♿ ⒸⒸ ☞ 🅿 ⬛
▲ **Västerås** STF Vandrarhem Västerås, Lövudden Hotell & Konferens, 72591 Västerås.	☎ (21) 185230 📠 (21) 123036	72	02.01–23.12	👫 🍴 5SW ⒸⒸ ☞ 🅿 ⬛
▲ **Växjö** STF Vandrarhem Växjö, Evedals Brunn, 35263 Växjö.	☎ (470) 63070 📠 (470) 63216	65	11.01–15.12	👫 🍴 ⓡ 6NE ☞ 🅿 ⬛
▲ **Vimmerby** STF Vandrarhem Vimmerby, Hörestadhult, 59800 Vimmerby.	☎ (492) 10225	27	01.06–31.08	👫 4E ☞
▲ **Visby** STF Vandrarhem Visby, Alléskolan, Gamla A7 Området, 62182 Visby.	☎ (498) 269842 📠 (498) 204290	99	12.06–11.08	👫 🍴 ♿ ☞ 🅿 ⬛
▲ **Visingsö** STF Vandrarhem Visingsö, Tunnerstad, 560 34 Visingsö.	☎ (390) 40191, Mobile (0707) 440191 📠 (390) 40191	29	🗓	👫 ⒸⒸ ☞ 🅿
▲ **Vittsjö** STF Vandrarhem Vittsjö, Lehultsväg 13, 28022 Vittsjö.	☎ (451) 22087 📠 (451) 22488	30	🗓	👫 🍴 ⓡ ⒸⒸ ☞ 🅿 ⬛
▲ **Voxnabruk** STF Vandrarhem Voxnabruk, Voxnadalens Kanot, Voxna 21, 82893 Voxnabruk.	☎ (271) 41150, (70) 5737871 📠 (271) 43080	28	🗓	👫 🍴 ⓡ ☞ 🅿 ⬛
▲ **Ystad** STF Vandrarhem Ystad, Kantarellen, Sandskog, Fritidsvägen, 27160 Ystad. ✉ ystad.kantarellen@home.se	☎ (411) 66566, (708) 577995 📠 (411) 10913	104	🗓	👫 🍴 ☞ 🅿 ⬛

MOUNTAIN CENTRES/
/ Centres de Montagne / Berggzentren / Centros de Montaña
(For further information, contact STF / *Pour de plus amples renseignements, s'adresser à la STF / Nach weiteren Angaben STF fragen / Para más información, diríjase a la STF*)

Location/Address	Telephone No. Fax No.	Beds	Opening Dates	Facilities
▲ **Dalarna** - Grövelsjön MC 79091 Idre. ✉ info@grovelsjon.stfturist.se	☎ (253) 596880 📠 (253) 23225	150	27.12–07.01; 10.02–22.04; 16.06–23.09	🍴 ☞ 🅿
▲ **Härjedalen** - Helags MC 84035 Ljungdalen.	☎ (687) 20150 📠 (687) 20150	72	28.12–07.01; 17.02–01.05; 21.06–16.09	☞
▲ **Jämtland** - Blåhammaren MC 83015 Duved. ✉ info@blahammaren.stfturist.se	☎ (647) 70120 📠 (647) 70637	52	03.03–01.05; 30.06–16.09	🍴 ☞
▲ **Jämtland** - Storulvån MC 83015 Duved. ✉ info@storulvan.stfturist.se	☎ (647) 72200 📠 (647) 74026	140	03.03–01.05; 30.06–16.09	🍴 ☞ 🅿

Location/Address	Telephone No. Fax No.	Beds	Opening Dates	Facilities
▲ Jämtland - Sylarna MC 83015 Duved. @ info@sylarna.stfturist.se	☎ (647) 75010 🖷 (647) 75012	100	03.03–01.05; 30.06–16.09	☞
▲ Jämtland - Vålådalen MC 83012 Vålådalen. @ info@valadalen.stfturist.se	☎ (647) 35300 🖷 (647) 35353	230	22.12–07.01; 10.02–16.04; 21.06–16.09	⑩ ☞ Ⓟ
▲ Lappland - Abisko MC 98107 Abisko. @ info@abisko.stfturist.se	☎ (980) 40200 🖷 (980) 40140	330	24.02–06.05; 09.06–23.09	⑩ ☞ Ⓟ
▲ Lappland - Kebnekaise MC 98129 Kiruna. @ info@kebnekaise.stfturist.se	☎ (980) 55000 🖷 (980) 55048	196	03.03–06.05; 17.06–17.09	⑩ ☞
▲ Lappland - Ritsem MC 98299 Gällivare. @ info@ritsem.stfturist.se	☎ (973) 42030 🖷 (973) 42050	40	02.03–14.05; 22.06–24.09	☞ Ⓟ
▲ Lappland - Saltoluokta MC 98299 Gällivare. @ info@saltoluokta.stfturist.se	☎ (973) 41010 🖷 (973) 41013	97	09.03–06.05; 16.06–16.09	⑩ ☞

"In former days, women were unwelcome in Kyokans (Japanese-style inns) when they travelled alone. I learned from a newspaper article that such would never happen in youth hostels, and that stimulated me to stay at hostels. I was amazed to know that so many different people from all walks of life stayed together in one room, knowing each other, becoming friends and making pleasant company among themselves."

"Dans le temps, les femmes n'étaient pas les bienvenues dans les Kyokans (auberges japonaises), lorsqu'elles voyageaient seules. Lorsque j'ai lu dans un article de journal que cela n'arriverait jamais dans les Auberges de Jeunesse, j'ai eu envie d'y faire un séjour. J'ai été vraiment fascinée de voir que tant de gens d'horizons différents partageaient la même chambrée, apprenaient à se connaître, devenaient amis et passaient du bon temps tous ensemble."

"Früher waren Frauen in "Kyokans" (japanischen Gästehäusern) nicht willkommen wenn sie allein reisten. In einem Zeitungsartikel las ich, dass so etwas in Jugendherbergen niemals geschehen könnte, was mich dazu anregte, in Jugendherbergen zu übernachten. Ich war erstaunt, wieviele Menschen aus allen Berufen und Gesellschaftsschichten hier zusammenkommen, Zimmer miteinander teilen, neue Freundschaften schließen und gemeinsam viel Vergnügen haben."

"Antiguamente, las mujeres que viajaban solas no eran bienvenidas en los Kyokans (hostales japoneses). Cuando leí un día en el periódico que ésto no podría nunca suceder en un albergue juvenil, me entraron ganas de alojarme en uno de ellos. Quedé maravillada al comprobar que tantas personas diferentes, de todas las profesiones y condiciones sociales, compartían una misma habitación, se conocían, hacían amistad y lo pasaban bien juntas."

Sugako Hashida

Mountain Huts/ *Cabanes de Montagne/*
Berghütten/ Cabañas de Montaña

(For further information, contact STF / *Pour de plus amples renseignements, s'adresser à la STF / Nach weiteren Angaben STF fragen / Para más información, diríjase a la STF*)
Most of these mountain huts are far from roads and railways and are situated near rough tracks; these tracks cover more than 4,700km, the best known being Kungsleden, in Lappland.
● 150-195 SEK.

La plupart de ces cabanes de montagne sont loin des routes et des chemins de fer et se trouvent près de sentiers primitifs; ces sentiers couvrent plus de 4700km - le mieux connu est Kungsleden, en Laponie. ● *150-195 SEK.*

Die meisten dieser Berghütten sind weit von einer Straße oder Bahnlinie abseits an Wanderwegen gelegen; diese erstrecken sich über mehr als 4700km - der bekannteste ist Kungsleden, in Lappland. ● 150-195 SEK.

La mayoría de las cabañas de montaña están alejados de las carreteras y de los ferrocarriles yse se encuentran cerca de senderos agrestes que cubren más de 4.700km - el más conocido es el Kungsleden, en Laponia. ● *150-195 SEK.*

Lappland		Tarrekaise	Stensdalen
Pältsa	Kaitumjaure	Njunjes	Gåsen
Kårsavagge	Teusajaure		
Abiskojaure	Vakkotavare		**Härjedalen**
Unna Allakas	Vaisaluokta	Aigert	
Alesjaure	Akka	Serve	Helags
Tjäktja	Kutjaure	Tärnasjöstugan	Fältjägarn
Vistas		Syterstugan	Skedbro
Nallo	Sitojaure	Viterskalet	Rogen
Sälka	Aktse	Bleriken	
Tarfala	Pårte		
Hukejaure	Pieskehaure	**Jämtland**	**Dalarna**
Sitasjaure	Vaimok	Anaris	Storrödtjärn
Singi	Såmmarlappa	Lunndörren	
		Vålåvalen	

Switzerland

SUISSE

SCHWEIZ

SUIZA

Schweizer Jugendherbergen,
Schaffhauserstrasse 14, Postfach 161,
CH 8042 Zürich, Switzerland.

☎ (41) (1) 3601414
📠 (41) (1) 3601460
e bookingoffice@youthhostel.ch
🖳 www.youthhostel.ch

Office Hours: Monday-Friday, 08.00-12.00hrs and 13.00-18.00hrs

A copy of the Hostel Directory for this Country can be obtained from:
The National Office

Capital:	Bern	**Population:**	7,123,500
Language: French/German/Italian/Romansh		**Size:**	41,284 sq km
Currency:	CHF	**Telephone Country Code:**	41

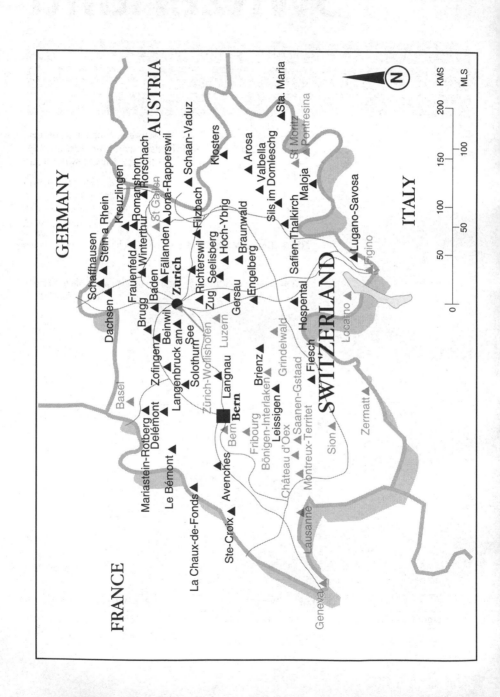

English

Hostels are located in cities, in the countryside and on hills/mountains.

Price range

Price range CHF 20.00-30.00. BB|inc 🛏.

Rooms and Reservations

R during Jan-Mar, Jun-Aug, Dec. (🛏 🛏 🛏 🛏 ♦♦♦). Reservations via **IBN** 🖥 or Hostel by ❶ ❷ ❸. (Reservation charges may apply). Smoking is limited - please check.

Guests

Membership Card and Passport/Photo ID are required. ♦♦♦ welcome. Group bookings via **IBN** 🖥 Hostel or National Office by ❶ ❷ ❸ (Reservation charges may apply).

Open times

Main hostels: open 📅, ⏰. Reception open: 07:00-10:00hrs, 16:00-23:00hrs. Resident manager. **Other hostels:** open Mar-Oct, ⏰. Reception open: 07:00-10:00hrs, 17:00-22:00hrs. Resident manager. **Seasonal hostels** are generally open Jan-Apr, Jun-Oct, Dec.

Meals

🍽 BLD **R** For individuals & for ♦♦♦.

Discounts

HI Member Discounts available - see discounts section and www.iyhf.org.

Travelling around

For ease of travel use 🚌 Foreign visitors are able to travel by rail in Switzerland at a favourable rate with a Swiss Pass. 🚐 Within towns. Self-Drive. Drive on right.

Travel/Activity Packages

Tours/sightseeing, winter sports and accommodation/transport packages available. Package bookings via 🖥 or Hostel by ❶ ❷ ❸.

Passports and Visas

Passport and Visa required.

Health

Medical insurance is recommended.

Français

Les auberges sont situées dans les villes, à la campagne et à la montagne.

Tarifs des nuitées

Tarifs des nuitées 20.00-30.00 CHF. BB|inc 🛏.

Chambres et réservations

R jan-mar, juin-août, déc. (🛏 🛏 🛏 🛏 ♦♦♦). Réservations via **IBN** 🖥 ou l'auberge par ❶ ❷ ❸. (Des frais de réservation pourront vous être facturés). Il est permis de fumer dans certaines chambres - veuillez vérifier.

Usagers

La carte d'adhérent ainsi que le passeport/pièce d'identité avec photo sont à présenter. Accueil des ♦♦♦. Réservations pour groupes via **IBN** 🖥 l'auberge et le Bureau National par ❶ ❷ ❸ (Des frais de réservation pourront vous être facturés).

Horaires d'ouverture

Grandes auberges: ouvertes 📅, ⏰. Accueil ouvert entre 7h-10h, 16h-23h. Gérant réside sur place. **Autres auberges:** ouvertes mar-oct, ⏰. Accueil ouvert entre 7h-10h, 17h-22h. Gérant réside sur place. **Auberges**

saisonnières ouvertes généralement jan-avril, juin, juil-oct, déc.

Repas

🍽️ BLD **R** Pour individuels & pour ⁛.

Remises

Remises pour les adhérents HI - voir la section "Remises" et notre site: www.iyhf.org.

Déplacements

Modes de transport recommandés 🚌 Grâce au Swiss Pass, les visiteurs étrangers peuvent voyager en Suisse en train à tarif réduit. 🚐 Services urbains. Voiture. Conduite à droite.

Forfaits Voyages/Activités

Forfaits circuits touristiques, sports d'hiver et hébergement/transport disponibles. Réservations des forfaits via 🖥️ ou l'auberge par ❶ ❷ ❸.

Passeports et visas

Passeport et visa obligatoires.

Santé

Une assurance médicale de voyage est conseillée.

Deutsch

Herbergen befinden sich in Städten, auf dem Land und in Bergen/Gebirgen.

Preisspanne

Preisspanne 20.00-30.00 CHF. ⓑⓑⁱⁿᶜ 🖥️.

Zimmer und Reservierungen

R während Jan-Mär, Jun-Aug, Dez. (1̇ 2̇ 3̇ 4̇ ⁛). Reservierungen über [IBN] 🖥️ oder Herberge per ❶ ❷ ❸. (Reservierungskosten könnten anfallen). Rauchen ist begrenzt - bitte checken.

Gäste

Mitgliedsausweis und Reisepass/ Personalausweis sind erforderlich. ⁛ willkommen. Gruppenbuchungen über [IBN] 🖥️ Herberge oder Landesverband per ❶ ❷ ❸ (Reservierungskosten könnten anfallen).

Öffnungszeiten

Hauptherbergen: Zugang 🖥️, 🕐. Rezeption zwischen 07:00-10:00Uhr, 16:00-23:00Uhr. Herbergsmanager wohnt im Haus. **Andere Herbergen:** Zugang zwischen Mär-Okt, 🕐. Rezeption zwischen 07:00-10:00Uhr, 17:00-22:00Uhr. Herbergsmanager wohnt im Haus. **Saison-Herbergen** sind normalerweise Jan-Apr, Jun-Okt, Dez geöffnet.

Mahlzeiten

🍽️ BLD **R** Für Einzelreisende & für ⁛.

Ermäßigungen

HI-Mitgliedsrabatt ist erhältlich – siehe Teil für Rabatte und Ermäßigungen und www.iyhf.org.

Reisen im Land

Reisen ist einfach mit 🚌 Mit dem Swiss Pass kann die Schweiz günstig bereist werden. (Nur für ausländische Gäste). 🚐 innerhalb der Städte. Selbstfahrer. Rechts fahren.

Reise-/Aktivitäten-Packages

Touren/sightseeing, Wintersport und Unterkunft/Transport-Packages erhältlich. Package-Buchungen über 🖥️ oder Herberge per ❶ ❷ ❸.

Reisepässe und Visa

Reisepass/Einreisevisum erforderlich.

Gesundheit

Unfall-/Krankenversicherung wird empfohlen.

Español

Los albergues están situados en las ciudades, el campo y la montaña.

Tarifas mínima y máxima

Tarifas mínima y máxima 20.00-30.00 CHF. BBinc.

Habitaciones y Reservas

R en ene-mar, jun-ago, dic. (1 2 3 4). Reservas por IBN o a través del albergue por t f e. (Es posible que se aplique un suplemento en concepto de gastos de reserva). Está permitido fumar sólo en algunas salas/habitaciones - infórmese.

Huéspedes

Los huéspedes deben presentar su Carnet de Alberguista y su pasaporte o carnet de identidad. Se admiten. Reservas de grupo por IBN o a través del albergue o la Asociación Nacional por t f e (Es posible que se aplique un suplemento en concepto de gastos de reserva).

Horarios y fechas de apertura

Albergues principales - abiertos 12, . Horario de recepción: 07:00-10:00h, 16:00-23:00h. Gerente residente. **Otros albergues** - abiertos mar-oct, . Horario de recepción: 07:00-10:00h, 17:00-22:00h. Gerente residente. **Albergues de temporada** suelen abrir: ene-abr, jun-oct, dic.

Comidas

BLD R Para individuales y para .

Descuentos

Se conceden descuentos a los miembros de Hostelling International – véase la sección sobre descuentos y nuestra página Internet en www.iyhf.org.

Desplazamientos

Transportes recomendados: La red ferrovial Suiza ofrece a los visitantes extranjeros la tarjeta de descuento Swiss Pass. Dentro de las ciudades. Automóvil. Se circula por la derecha.

Viajes Combinados con Actividades

Viajes combinados con visitas turísticas, deportes de invierno y alojamiento/transporte. Reserva de viajes combinados por o a través del albergue por t f e.

Pasaportes y Visados

Pasaporte y visado obligatorios.

Información Sanitaria

Seguro médico recomendado.

"Own only what you can carry with you; know language, know countries, know people. Let your memory be your travel bag."

"Ne possède que ce que tu peux emporter avec toi; connais les langues, connais les pays, connais les gens. Que ta mémoire te serve de sac de voyage."

„Besitze nur, was du mitnehmen kannst; lerne Sprache, Länder, Leute kennen. Lass deine Erinnerung deine Reisetasche sein."

"Posee solamente lo que puedas llevar contigo; conoce los idiomas, conoce los países, conoce a la gente. Deja que tu memoria sea tu bolso de viaje."

Alexander Solzhenitsyn

Basel

St. Alban-Kirchrain 10,
4052 Basel (Basel).
☎ (61) 2720572
✆ (61) 2720833
✉ basel@youthhostel.ch

Open Dates: 02.01-21.12

Open Hours: High Season. 07.00-10.00hrs;
14.00-24.00hrs. Low Season.
07.00-10.00hrs; 14.00-23.00hrs

Reservations: **R** (IBN) (CC)

Price Range: from CHF 29.00 BBinc 🍽

Beds: 194 - 8x¹🛏 10x²🛏 6x⁴🛏 5x⁶🛏
14x⁶⁺🛏

Facilities: ♿ ♜ 11x ♜ 🍴 ✿ 🛏 📺 📁
🛏1 x 🍷 🔲 🔒 ⬆ ✎ 🚲 🌳 🔍

Directions: [1 SE] from city centre

✈ Basel - Mulhouse 7km

🚅 Basel 1.5km

🚋 2 500m ap Kunstmuseum

Attractions: 🎿2km ⟿1.5km

Bönigen-Interlaken

Aareweg 21,
Am See,
3806 Bönigen (Bern).
☎ (33) 8224353
✆ (33) 8232058
✉ boenigen@youthhostel.ch

Open Dates: 01.01-07.01; 20.01-11.11;
15.12-31.12

Open Hours: High Season. 07.00-10.00hrs;
14.00-23.30hrs. Low Season.
07.00-10.00hrs; 16.00-23.00hrs

Reservations: **R** (IBN) (CC)

Price Range: from CHF 22.50 BBinc 🍽

Beds: 150 - 1x³🛏 6x⁴🛏 10x⁶🛏 3x⁶⁺🛏

Facilities: ♜ 6x ♜ 🍴 ♂ 🚲 ✿ 🛏 📺 📁
🛏2 x 🍷 🔲 🔒 🅿 ✎ 🚲 🌳 ⛰
🔍 🚊 ⛺

Directions: [2 E] from city centre

✈ Zürich 150km

🚅 Interlaken-East 1.8km

🚌 1+3 500m ap Lütschinenbrücke

Attractions: 🎠 ⛰ 🚴 🏊 2200m 🚶 🎿 ∪3km
🎿3km ⟿300m

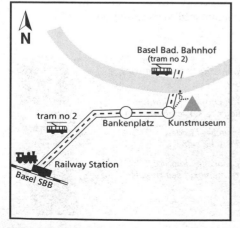

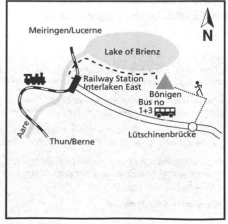

Grindelwald

Weid 12,
Terrassenweg,
3818 Grindelwald (Bern).
☏ (33) 8531009
🖷 (33) 8535029
✉ grindelwald@youthhostel.ch

Open Dates:	17.12-16.04; 23.05-28.10
Open Hours:	High Season. 06.30-10.00hrs; 15.00-24.00hrs. Low Season. 06.30-10.00hrs; 15.00-23.00hrs
Reservations:	**R** [IBN] -CC-
Price Range:	from CHF 26.00 BB inc 🛏
Beds:	125 - 4x² 15x⁴ 2x⁵ 6x⁶ 1x⁶
Facilities:	⋔ 15x ⋔ 🍽 🚲 ☼ 🏨 TV 📋 🧺 1x🍷 🔲 🔳 P 🛈 🐾 ♨ ⚠ 🐾 🏠
Directions:	1 NW from city centre
✈	Zürich 170km
🚂	Grindelwald 1km
🚌	4 100m ap Terrassenweg-Gaggi Säge
Attractions:	⛰ ⛰ 🔍 20km 🚵 ⛷ 2200m ⛸ 🏃 ∪ 20km 🎣 1km ⚓ 500m

Lausanne - Jeunotel

Ch.du Bois-de-Vaux 36,
1007 Lausanne (Vaud).
☏ (21) 6260222
🖷 (21) 6260226
✉ lausanne@youthhostel.ch

Open Dates:	🗓
Open Hours:	🕐
Reservations:	**R** [IBN] -CC-
Price Range:	from CHF 25.00 BB inc
Beds:	240 - 41x¹ 34x² 14x³ 17x⁴ 4x⁶
Facilities:	♿ ⋔ 17x ⋔ 🍽 🍷 ☼ 🏨 TV 1 x🍷 🔲 🔳 P 🛈 🐾 ⚠ 🐾 🏠
Directions:	1.5 SW from city centre
✈	Geneva 62km
🚂	Lausanne 1.5km
🚌	2 500m ap Bois-de-Vaux
🚇	Metro for Ouchy 1km ap Station
Attractions:	⛰ 🔍 400m 🚵 ⛷ 2800m ⛸ 🏃 ∪ 10km 🎣 400m ⚓ 200m

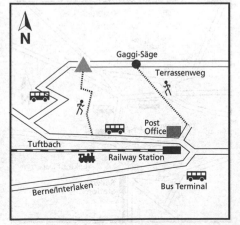

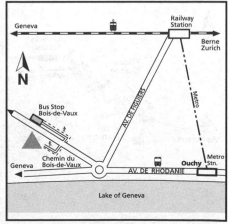

Locarno - Palagiovani

Via Varenna 18,
6600 Locarno (Ticino).
📞 (91) 7561500
📠 (91) 7561501
📧 locarno@youthhostel.ch

Open Dates:	🗓
Open Hours:	High Season. 08.00-10.00hrs; 15.00-23.30hrs. Low Season. 08.00-10.00hrs; 16.00-22.30hrs
Reservations:	**R** IBN CC
Price Range:	from CHF 28.50 BB inc 🛏
Beds:	188 - 54x² 14x⁴ 4x⁶
Facilities:	♿ 👬 14x 👬 🍽 ☼ 👥 📺 🧺 3 x 🍷 📋 🖼 🔒 ↕ ✏ 🚲 ⚽ 🔍
Directions:	1.5W from city centre
✈	Agno 35km
🚂	Locarno 1.5km
🚌	31, 36 50m ap Cinque Vie
🚃	Centovalli-Bahn 200m ap St. Antonio
Attractions:	⛲ ⛺ 🔍1.5km 🚴 🎿 ∪10km ⚓1.5km 🚤1.5km

Lucerne

am Rotsee,
Sedelstr 12,
6004 Lucerne (Lucerne).
📞 (41) 4208800
📠 (41) 4205616
📧 luzern@youthhostel.ch

Open Dates:	🗓
Open Hours:	High Season. 07.00-10.00hrs; 14.00-24.00hrs. Low Season. 07.30-10.00hrs; 16.00-24.00hrs
Reservations:	**R** IBN CC
Price Range:	from CHF 28.00 BB inc 🛏
Beds:	194 - 8x² 4x³ 18x⁴ 9x⁶ 2x⁶
Facilities:	👬 🍽 🚲 ☼ 👥 📺 📖 🧺 1 x 🍷 📋 🖼 🔒 🅿 ✏ 🚲 ⚽ 🔍 🌲
Directions:	2N from city centre
✈	Zürich 50km
🚂	Lucerne 2km
🚌	18 500m, 19 1km ap Jugendherberge/Rosenberg
Attractions:	⛲ ⛺ 🔍2km 🎿 ∪5km ⚓2km 🚤2km

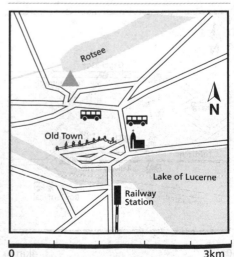

Montreux-Territet

Passage de l'Auberge 8,
1820 Montreux-Territet (Vaud).
☏ (21) 9634934
🖷 (21) 9632729
✉ montreux@youthhostel.ch

Open Dates:	01.02-30.11
Open Hours:	High Season. 07.00-10.00hrs; 16.00-23.00hrs. Low Season. 07.30-10.00hrs; 17.00-22.00hrs
Reservations:	R IBN CC
Price Range:	from CHF 27.00 BB inc 🖵
Beds:	112 - 5x² 6x⁴ 9x⁶ 3x⁶
Facilities:	♿ ♦♦♦ 6x ♦♦♦ ⃝ 🛵 ⚙ 🏠 📺 ♨2 x🍴 🗄 🖼 8 🅿 🛈 🐶 🎿 🍴
Directions:	2E from city centre
✈	Geneva 100km
⛴	Port de Territet 150m
🚂	Montreux 2km
🚌	1 100m ap Territet
Attractions:	🐟 ⛰ 🏛150m 🚶 ∪10km ∾500m ⛵1km

St. Gallen

Jüchstrasse 25,
9000 St. Gallen (St. Gallen).
☏ (71) 2454777
🖷 (71) 2454983
✉ st.gallen@youthhostel.ch

Open Dates:	03.03-03.12
Open Hours:	07.00-10.00hrs; 17.00-22.30hrs
Reservations:	R IBN CC
Price Range:	from CHF 21.50 RR inc 🖵
Beds:	88 - 6x² 4x⁴ 10x⁶
Facilities:	♿ ♦♦♦ 8x ♦♦♦ ⃝ 🏠 📺 ♨2 x🍴 🗄 8 🅿 🛈 🐶 🎿 🚲 🐶 🏠
Directions:	
✈	Zürich 80km
🚂	St. Gallen 1.5km
🚌	1 500m ap Singenberg
🚋	Trogenerbähnli 800m ap Schülerhaus
Attractions:	🐟 🚶 ∾8km ⛵2km

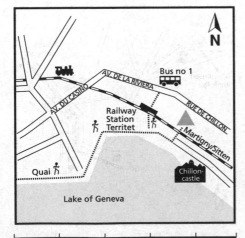

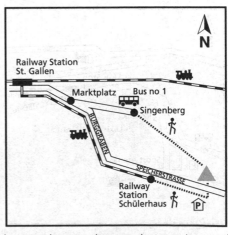

St. Moritz Bad

'Stille',
Via Surpunt 60,
7500 St. Moritz Bad (Graubünden).
☏ (81) 8333969
✆ (81) 8338046
✉ st.moritz@youthhostel.ch

Open Dates:	🗓
Open Hours:	Summer. 07.00-10.00hrs; 16.00-22.00hrs. Winter. 07.30-10.00hrs; 17.00-22.00hrs, 01-30.11. 07.30-09.00hrs; 17.00-19.30hrs.
Reservations:	**R** **IBN** **CC**
Price Range:	from CHF 40.50 inc. halfboard **BB** inc 🍽
Beds:	190 - 14x² 42x⁴
Facilities:	♦♦♦ 42x ♦♦♦ ⵓⵓ ⵓⵓ ⵓⵓ ⵓⵓ ⵓⵓ ⵓⵓ 3 x ⵓ ⵓ ⵓ ⵓ ⵓ ⵓ ⵓ ⵓ ⵓ
Directions:	**2S** from city centre
✈	Zürich 220km
🚂	St. Moritz 2km
🚌	Postauto 300m ap Hotel Sonne
Attractions:	ⵓ ⵓ ⵓ ⵓ 3300m ⵓ ⵓ ⵓ1km ⵓ1km ⵓ800m

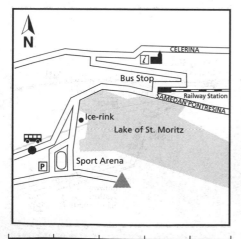

Schaffhausen

Belair,
Randenstr 65,
8200 Schaffhausen (Schaffhausen).
☏ (52) 6258800
✆ (52) 6245954
✉ schaffhausen@youthhostel.ch

Open Dates:	28.02-25.11
Open Hours:	08.00-10.00hrs; 17.30-22.00hrs
Reservations:	**R** **CC**
Price Range:	from CHF 20.00 **BB** inc 🍽
Beds:	88 - 1x¹ 2x² 1x³ 1x⁵ 2x⁶ 7x⁶
Facilities:	♦♦♦ ⵓ ⵓ ⵓ ⵓ ⵓ 1 x ⵓ ⵓ ⵓ ⵓ ⵓ ⵓ ⵓ ⵓ ⵓ ⵓ
Directions:	**1.5 NW** from city centre
✈	Zürich 40km
⛴	1.5km
🚂	Schaffhausen 1.5km
🚌	3 or 6 (direction Sommerwies) 100m ap Wiesli
Attractions:	ⵓ ⵓ ⵓ ⵓ ⵓ ⵓ

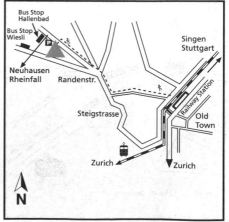

Zermatt

Winkelmatten,
3920 Zermatt (Wallis).
☎ (27) 9672320
🖷 (27) 9675306
📧 zermatt@youthhostel.ch

Open Dates:	01.01-19.04; 31.05-05.11; 02.12-31.12
Open Hours:	High Season. 06.30-10.00hrs; 16.00-23.00hrs. Low Season. 07.00-10.00hrs; 16.30-22.30hrs
Reservations:	Ⓡ ⒾⒷⓃ ⒸⒸ
Price Range:	from CHF 24.50 BBinc 🍴
Beds:	140 - 1x² 2x⁴ 1x⁶ 12x
Facilities:	♦♦♦ 🍽 🚲 ✿ 🛏 📁 3 x 🍷 🔲 🖼 8 𝒾 🎦 ❀ ♨ ⛷
Directions:	0.8 SE from city centre
✈	Geneva 235km
🚃	Zermatt 800m
🚌	Ortsbus 100m ap Luchre
Attractions:	⚲ ⛰ 🚴 ⛷ 3800m 🎿 🚶 ∪5km 🏊600m ⛴500m

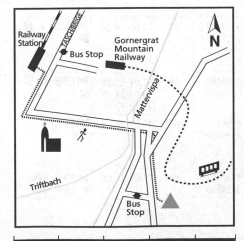

Zürich

Mutschellenstr 114,
8038 Zürich (Zürich).
☎ (1) 4823544
🖷 (1) 4801727
📧 zurich@youthhostel.ch

Open Dates:	🗓12
Open Hours:	🕐
Reservations:	Ⓡ ⒾⒷⓃ ⒸⒸ
Price Range:	from CHF 28.50 BBinc 🍴
Beds:	315 - 5x¹ 1x² 8x⁴ 46x⁶
Facilities:	♿ ♦♦♦ 4x ♦♦♦ 🍽 🚲 ✿ 🛏 📺 🎦2 x 🍷 🔲 🖼 8 ⏸ 𝐏 𝒾 🎦 ❀ ♨
Directions:	3 SW from city centre
✈	Zürich 8km
🚃	Zürich 4km
🚌	33 ap Jugendherberge
🚋	7 350m ap Morgental
Ⓤ	1/8 Zürich-Wollishofen 500m
Attractions:	⚲500m 🏊1km ⛴500m

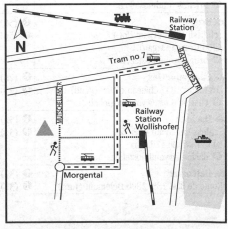

Location/Address	Telephone No. Fax No.	Beds	Opening Dates	Facilities
▲ **Arosa** Seewaldweg, 7050 Arosa (Graubünden). **e** arosa@youthhostel.ch	**t** (81) 3771397 **f** (81) 3771621	155	01.01-22.04; 16.06-21.10; 15.12-31.12	⦿ ☄
▲ **Avenches** rue du Lavoir 5, 1580 Avenches (Vaud).	**t** (26) 6752666 **f** (26) 6752717	76	11.04–19.10	♔ ⦿ ECC **P** 🗗
▲ **Baden** Kanalstr 7, 5400 Baden (Aargau). **e** baden@youthhostel.ch	**t** (56) 2216736 **f** (56) 2217660	83	13.04–24.12	⦿ ECC **P** 🗗
▲ **Basel** IBN **St. Alban-Kirchrain 10,** **4052 Basel (Basel).** **e** basel@youthhostel.ch	**t** (61) 2720572 **f** (61) 2720833	194	02.01-21.12	♔ ⦿ **R** 1 SE ♿ ECC 🗗 ✿
▲ **Beinwil am See** Seestrasse 71, 5712 Beinwil am See (Aargau). **e** beinwil@youthhostel.ch	**t** (62) 7711883 **f** (62) 7716123	98	03.03–11.12	♔ ⦿ ECC ☛ **P** 🗗 ✿
▲ **Le Bémont** 2877 Le Bémont (Jura). **e** bemont@youthhostel.ch	**t** (32) 9511707 **f** (32) 9512413	96	01.02–18.11	♔ ⦿ ECC ☛ **P** 🗗
▲ **Bern** IBN Weihergasse 4, 3005 Bern (Bern). **e** bern@youthhostel.ch	**t** (31) 3116316 **f** (31) 3125240	156	01.01-07.01; 21.01-31.12	⦿ ♿ ECC 🗗 ☄
▲ **Bönigen-Interlaken** IBN **Aareweg 21, Am See,** **3806 Bönigen (Bern).** **e** boenigen@youthhostel.ch	**t** (33) 8224353 **f** (33) 8232058	150	01.01-07.01; 20.01-11.11; 15.12-31.12	♔ ⦿ **R** 2E ECC ☛ **P** 🗗 ☄ ✿
▲ **Braunwald** 'Im Gyseneggli', 8784 Braunwald (Glarus). **e** braunwald@youthhostel.ch	**t** (55) 6431356 **f** (55) 6432435	82	01.01-16.04; 02.06-04.06; 16.06-21.10; 15.12-31.12	♔ ⦿ ECC ☛
▲ **Brienz** Strandweg 10, am See, 3855 Brienz (Bern). **e** brienz@youthhostel.ch	**t** (33) 9511152 **f** (33) 9512260	86	12.04–21.10	♔ ⦿ ECC ☛ **P** 🗗 ✿
▲ **Brugg** Schlössli Altenburg im Hof 11, 5200 Brugg (Aargau). **e** brugg@youthhostel.ch	**t** (56) 4411020 **f** (56) 4423820	52	01.03–31.10	⦿ ECC ☛ **P** 🗗
▲ **Château-d'Oex** Les Riaux, 1837 Château-d'Oex (Vaud). **e** chateau.d.oex@youthhostel.ch	**t** (26) 9246404 **f** (26) 9245843	50	01.01-19.03; 30.04-23.10; 14.12-31.12	⦿ ECC **P** 🗗 ☄
▲ **Dachsen** Schloss Laufen am Rheinfall, 8447 Dachsen (Zürich). **e** dachsen@youthhostel.ch	**t** (52) 6596152 **f** (52) 6596039	87	16.03-12.11	⦿ ECC ☛ **P** ☄
▲ **Delémont** Route de Bâle 185, 2800 Delémont (Jura).	**t** (32) 4222054 **f** (32) 4228830	80	01.04-21.10	♔ ⦿ ♿ ECC ☛ **P** 🗗 ☄

Location/Address	Telephone No. Fax No.	Beds	Opening Dates	Facilities
▲ **Engelberg** "Berghaus", Dorfstr 80, 6390 Engelberg (Obwalden). 🄴 engelberg@youthhostel.ch	🅃 (41) 6371292 🄵 (41) 6374988	106	01.01-16.04; 19.05-20.10; 24.11-31.12	ᵻᵻᵻ 🍽 🄿 🄾 🚲 🔆
△ *Fällanden* *'Im Rohrbuck', Maurstr 33,* *8117 Fällanden (Zürich).*	🅃 *(1) 8253144* 🄵 *(1) 8255480*	*46*	*24.02-10.12*	Ⓡ 🖑 🄿
▲ **Fiesch** Feriendorf Fiesch, 3984 Fiesch (Valais). 🄴 fiesch@youthhostel.ch	🅃 (27) 9701515 🄵 (27) 9701500	80	📠 from 01.12.00	ᵻᵻᵻ 🍽 Ⓡ ♿ 🅲🅲 🖑 🄿 🄾 🚲 🔆
▲ **Figino** ⒾⒷⓃ Via Casoro 2, 6918 Figino (Ticino). 🄴 figino@youthhostel.ch	🅃 (91) 9951151 🄵 (91) 9951070	160	03.03-27.10	ᵻᵻᵻ 🍽 🅲🅲 🖑 🄿 🄾 🚲 🔆
▲ **Filzbach** 'Lihn' Blaukreuz Kurs-und Ferienzentrum, 8757 Filzbach (Glarus). 🄴 filzbach@youthhostel.ch	🅃 (55) 6141342 🄵 (55) 6141707	50	01.01-16.12; 25.12-31.12	ᵻᵻᵻ 🍽 ♿ 🅲🅲 🄿 🄾
▲ **Frauenfeld** "Rüegerholz", Festhüttenstr 22, 8500 Frauenfeld (Thurgau).	🅃 (52) 7213680 🄵 (52) 7213680	38	01.01-16.01; 16.02-31.10; 01.12-31.12	🖑 🄿
▲ **Fribourg** ⒾⒷⓃ 2 rue de l'Hôpital, 1700 Fribourg (Fribourg). 🄴 fribourg@youthhostel.ch	🅃 (26) 3231916 🄵 (26) 3231940	70	09.02-26.11	🍽 ♿ 🅲🅲 🖑 🄾 🚲
▲ **Genève** ⒾⒷⓃ 30 rue Rothschild, 1202 Genève (Genève). 🄴 geneve@youthhostel.ch	🅃 (22) 7326260 🄵 (22) 7383987	340	📠	🍽 ♿ 🅲🅲 🖑 🄿 🄾 🚲
▲ **Gersau** Rotschuo, 6442 Gersau (Schwyz). 🄴 gersau@youthhostel.ch	🅃 (41) 8281277 🄵 (41) 8281263	96	01.03–30.11	ᵻᵻᵻ 🍽 🅲🅲 🖑 🄿 🄾 🔆
▲ **Grindelwald** ⒾⒷⓃ **Wcid 12, Terrassenweg,** **3818 Grindelwald (Bern).** 🄴 grindelwald@youthhostel.ch	🅃 (33) 8531009 🄵 (33) 8535029	125	17.12-16.04; 23.05-28.10	ᵻᵻᵻ 🍽 Ⓡ 1 NW 🅲🅲 🄿 🄾 🚲 🔆
Gstaad ☞Saanen-Gstaad				
▲ **Hoch-Ybrig** Fuederegg, 8842 Hoch-Ybrig (Schwyz). 🄴 hoch.ybrig@youthhostel.ch	🅃 (55) 4141766 🄵 (55) 4142065	86	01.01-16.04; 07.07-21.10; 01.12-31.12	ᵻᵻᵻ 🍽 🅲🅲 🖑 🚲 🔆
△ *Hospental* *Gotthardstrasse, 6493 Hospental (Uri).* 🄴 *hospental@youthhostel.ch*	🅃 *(41) 8870401* 🄵 *(41) 8870902*	*65*	*01.12–31.10*	🍽 🅲🅲 🖑 🄿 🄾 🚲 🔆
Interlaken ☞Bönigen				
▲ **Jona-Rapperswil** 'Busskirch', Hessenhofweg 10, 8645 Jona (St. Gallen). 🄴 jona@youthhostel.ch	🅃 (55) 2109927 🄵 (55) 2109928	74	02.02-29.10	ᵻᵻᵻ 🍽 ♿ 🅲🅲 🄿 🄾 🚲 🔆

Location/Address	Telephone No. Fax No.	Beds	Opening Dates	Facilities
▲ **Klosters** 'Soldanella', Talstr 73, 7250 Klosters (Graubünden). ⓔ klosters@youthhostel.ch	☏ (81) 4221316 ✆ (81) 4225209	84	01.01-23.04; 12.06-22.10; 15.12-31.12	ⅲ ⓨ ⒸⒸ Ⓟ 回 ✿
▲ **Kreuzlingen** 'Villa Hörnliberg', Promenadenstr 7, 8280 Kreuzlingen (Thurgau). ⓔ kreuzlingen@youthhostel.ch	☏ (71) 6882663 ✆ (71) 6884761	97	03.03-03.12	ⓨ ⒸⒸ
▲ **La Chaux-de-Fonds** Rue du Doubs 34, 2300 La Chaux-de-Fonds (Neuchâtel). ⓔ chaux.de.fonds@youthhostel.ch	☏ (32) 9684315 ✆ (32) 9682518	80	19.01-25.11	ⓨ ♿ ⒸⒸ ✇ Ⓟ 回 ⚙ ✿
△ *Langenbruck* *Haus Rosengarten, Bärenwilerstr. 10,* *4438 Langenbruck (Baselland).* ⓔ *bookingoffice@youthhostel.ch*	☏ *(1) 3601414* ✆ *(1) 3601460*	*49*	🄌 ⅲ *only*	Ⓡ ✇ Ⓟ
▲ **Langnau im Emmental** Mooseggstr 32, 3550 Langnau i.E. (Bern).	☏ (34) 4024526 ✆ (34) 4024526	50	01.01-24.02; 03.03-22.09; 14.10-31.12	✇ Ⓟ
▲ **Lausanne** - **Jeunotel** ⒾⒷⓃ **Ch.du Bois-de-Vaux 36,** **1007 Lausanne (Vaud).** ⓔ lausanne@youthhostel.ch	☏ (21) 6260222 ✆ (21) 6260226	240	🄌	ⅲ ⓨ Ⓡ 1.5 SW ♿ ⒸⒸ Ⓟ 回 ⬤ ✿
▲ **Leissigen** "La Nichée", Horbacher, 3706 Leissigen (Bern). ⓔ leissigen@youthhostel.ch	☏ (33) 8471214 ✆ (33) 8471497	43	09.04-15.10	ⅲ ⓨ ⒸⒸ Ⓟ ✿
Lenzerheide ☞**Valbella**				
Liechtenstein ☞**Schaan-Vaduz**				
▲ **Locarno** - **Palagiovani** ⒾⒷⓃ **Via Varenna 18, 6600 Locarno (Ticino).** ⓔ locarno@youthhostel.ch	☏ (91) 7561500 ✆ (91) 7561501	188	🄌	ⅲ ⓨ Ⓡ 1.5 W ♿ ⒸⒸ 回 ✿
▲ **Lugano** - **Savosa** Via Cantonale 13, 6942 Savosa (Ticino). ⓔ lugano@youthhostel.ch	☏ (91) 9662728 ✆ (91) 9682363	110	16.03–31.10	ⅲ ⓨ ♿ ⒸⒸ ✇ Ⓟ 回 ✿
▲ **Lucerne** ⒾⒷⓃ **am Rotsee, Sedelstr 12,** **6004 Lucerne (Lucerne).** ⓔ luzern@youthhostel.ch	☏ (41) 4208800 ✆ (41) 4205616	194	🄌	ⓨ Ⓡ 2N ⒸⒸ Ⓟ 回 ⚙ ✿
▲ **Maloja** Hauptstrasse, 7516 Maloja (Graubünden). ⓔ maloja@youthhostel.ch	☏ (81) 8333969 ✆ (81) 8338046	54	01.01-12.03; 22.06-14.10; 21.12-31.12	Ⓡ ⒸⒸ ✇ Ⓟ 回
▲ **Mariastein-Rotberg** Jugendburg, 4115 Mariastein (Solothurn). ⓔ mariastein@youthhostel.ch	☏ (61) 7311049 ✆ (61) 7312724	86	03.03-10.12	ⓨ ⒸⒸ ✇ Ⓟ

Location/Address	Telephone No. Fax No.	Beds	Opening Dates	Facilities
▲ **Montreux-Territet** (IBN) **Passage de l'Auberge 8,** **1820 Montreux-Territet (Vaud).** 📧 montreux@youthhostel.ch	☎ (21) 9634934 📠 (21) 9632729	112	01.02–30.11	👫 🍴 ® 2E 🚻 ⒸⒸ ℗ 🔌 🚲 ☼
▲ **Pontresina** - Tolais (IBN) Langlaufzentrum, 7504 Pontresina (Graubünden). 📧 pontresina@youthhostel.ch	☎ (81) 8427223 📠 (81) 8427031	130	01.01-15.04; 16.06-21.10; 08.12-31.12	👫 🍴 ⒸⒸ ℗ 🔌 🚲 ☼
Rapperswil-Jona ☞ **Jona-Rapperswil**				
Rheinfall ☞ **Dachsen & Schaffhausen**				
▲ **Richterswil** "Horn", Hornstr 5, 8805 Richterswil (Zürich). 📧 richterswil@youthhostel.ch	☎ (1) 7862188 📠 (1) 7862193	80	05.03-01.12	👫 🍴 🚻 ⒸⒸ ℗ 🔌 🚲
△ *Romanshorn* *Gottfried-Keller-Str 6,* *8590 Romanshorn (Thurgau).* 📧 *romanshorn@youthhostel.ch*	☎ *(71) 4631717* 📠 *(71) 4611990*	*114*	*01.03–31.10*	🍴 ℗ 🚲
△ *Rorschach* - *YH Rorschach Berg* *Im Ebnet, 9404 Rorschacherberg (St. Gallen).* *Postaddress: Seefeldstrasse 5, 9403 Goldach.*	☎ *(71) 8415411*	*20*	*01.04–31.10* *(👫 only)*	® 🔌 ℗
▲ **Rorschach** - YH Rorschach See Churerstrasse 4, 9400 Rorschach.	☎ (71) 8449712 📠 (71) 8449713	60	01.04–31.10	🍴 ⒸⒸ ℗ 🚲 ☼
▲ **Saanen-Gstaad** (IBN) Chalet Rüblihorn, 3792 Saanen (Bern). 📧 saanen@youthhostel.ch	☎ (33) 7441343 📠 (33) 7445542	78	01.01-19.03; 31.05-23.10; 13.12-31.12	👫 🍴 ⒸⒸ 🔌 ☼
▲ **St. Gallen** (IBN) **Jüchstrasse 25,** **9000 St. Gallen (St. Gallen).** 📧 st.gallen@youthhostel.ch	☎ (71) 2454777 📠 (71) 2454983	88	03.03-03.12	👫 🍴 ® 🚻 ⒸⒸ ℗ 🔌
△ *Sta Maria im Münstertal* *Chasa Plaz, 7536 Sta. Maria im Münstertal* *(Graubünden).*	☎ *(81) 8585052* 📠 *(81) 8585496*	*62*	*01.01-18.03;* *18.05-21.10,* *21.12-31.12*	🍴 ⒸⒸ 🔌 ℗ 🔌 🚲
▲ **Ste-Croix** 18 rue Centrale, 1450 Ste-Croix (Vaud). 📧 ste.croix@youthhostel.ch	☎ (24) 4541810 📠 (24) 4544522	58	12.05-22.10	👫 🍴 ⒸⒸ 🔌 🔌 🚲 ☼
▲ **St. Moritz Bad** (IBN) **Stille, Via Surpunt 60,** **7500 St. Moritz Bad (Graubünden).** 📧 st.moritz@youthhostel.ch	☎ (81) 8333969 📠 (81) 8338046	190	🔒	👫 🍴 ® 2S ⒸⒸ ℗ 🔌 🚲 ☼
△ *Safien-Thalkirch* *7109 Thalkirch (Graubünden).*	☎ *(81) 6471107* 📠 *(81) 6471107*	*30*	*01.12–31.10*	🔌 ℗
▲ **Schaan-Vaduz** Untere Rüttigasse 6, 9494 Schaan (Fürstentum Liechtenstein).	☎ (423) 2325022 📠 (423) 2325856	96	01.03–30.11	👫 🍴 🚻 ℗ 🔌
▲ **Schaffhausen** **Belair, Randenstr 65,** **8200 Schaffhausen (Schaffhausen).** 📧 schaffhausen@youthhostel.ch	☎ (52) 6258800 📠 (52) 6245954	88	28.02-25.11	🍴 ® 1.5NW ⒸⒸ 🔌 ℗ ☼

Location/Address	Telephone No. Fax No.	Beds	Opening Dates	Facilities
▲ Seelisberg Gadenhaus beim Rütli, 6377 Seelisberg (Uri).	☎ (41) 8201562 ✆ (41) 8201550	25	08.04-31.10	ℝ ✔ P ✿
△ *Sils im Domleschg* *Burg Ehrenfels,* *7411 Sils im Domleschg (Graubünden).*	☎ *(81) 6511518*	*40*	*01.04–31.10* ⅲ *only*	ℝ ✔
▲ Sion ⒤ⒷⓃ rue de l'Industrie 2, 1950 Sion (Valais). ℮ sion@youthhostel.ch	☎ (27) 3237470 ✆ (27) 3237438	80	02.02-26.11	⑩ ♿ ₵₵ ✔ ☐
▲ Solothurn "Am Land", Landhausquai 23, 4500 Solothurn (Solothurn). ℮ solothurn@youthhostel.ch	☎ (32) 6231706 ✆ (32) 6231639	92	14.01-18.11	⑩ ♿ ₵₵ ☐ ⚲ ✿
▲ Stein am Rhein Hemishoferstr 87, 8260 Stein am Rhein (Schaffhausen). ℮ stein@youthhostel.ch	☎ (52) 7411255 ✆ (52) 7415140	121	01.03-11.11	ⅲ ⑩ ₵₵ ✔ P
Vaduz ☞**Schaan**				
▲ Valbella-Lenzerheide Voa Sartons 41, 7077 Valbella (Graubünden). ℮ valbella@youthhostel.ch	☎ (81) 3841208 ✆ (81) 3844558	115	01.01-23.04; 28.06-29.10; 14.12-31.12	ⅲ ⑩ ₵₵ ✔ P ✿
△ *Winterthur* *Schloss Hegi, Hegifeldstr 125,* *8409 Winterthur (Zürich).* ℮ *winterthur@youthhostel.ch*	☎ *(52) 2423840* ✆ *(52) 2425830*	*48*	*01.03–31.10*	ℝ ✔
▲ Zermatt ⒤ⒷⓃ **Winkelmatten, 3920 Zermatt (Wallis).** ℮ zermatt@youthhostel.ch	☎ (27) 9672320 ✆ (27) 9675306	140	01.01-19.04; 31.05-05.11; 02.12-31.12	⑩ ℝ 0.8SE ₵₵ ☐ ⚲ ✿
▲ Zofingen General Guisan-Str 10, 4800 Zofingen (Aargau). ℮ zofingen@youthhostel.ch	☎ (62) 7522303 ✆ (62) 7522316	60	28.02-15.12	⑩ ₵₵ ✔ P ☐
▲ Zug Allmendstr 8, Sportstadion 'Herti', 6300 Zug (Zug). ℮ zug@youthhostel.ch	☎ (41) 7115354 ✆ (41) 7105121	92	01.01-03.01; 09.03-31.12	⑩ ♿ ₵₵ ✔ P ☐ ⚲
▲ Zürich ⒤ⒷⓃ **Mutschellenstr 114,** **8038 Zürich (Zürich).** ℮ zurich@youthhostel.ch	☎ (1) 4823544 ✆ (1) 4801727	315	🗓	ⅲ ⑩ ℝ 3SW ♿ ₵₵ P ☐ ⚲ ✿

Federal Republic of Yugoslavia

RÉPUBLIQUE FÉDÉRALE DE YUGOSLAVIE
BUNDESREPUBLIK JUGOSLAWIENS
REPUBLICA FEDERAL DE YUGOSLAVIA

**Ferijaini savez Jugoslavije,
11000 Beograd, Makedonska 22/2
Yugoslavia (Federal Republic of).**

☎ (381) (11) 622-956, 622-584
🖷 (381) (11) 322-07-62

Office Hours: Monday-Friday, 09.00-17.00hrs

Capital:	Belgrade	**Population:**	10,406,742
Language:	Serbian	**Size:**	107,173 sq km
Currency:	Din. (dinar)	**Telephone Country Code:**	381

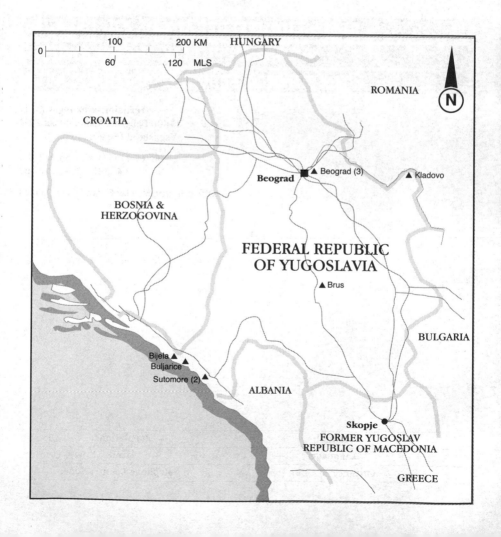

0   100   200 KM   HUNGARY

60   120   MLS

ROMANIA

N

CROATIA

▲ Beograd (3)   ▲ Kladovo

■ Beograd

BOSNIA &
HERZOGOVINA

**FEDERAL REPUBLIC
OF YUGOSLAVIA**

▲ Brus

BULGARIA

Bijela ▲
Buljarice ●
Sutomore (2) ▲

ALBANIA

Skopje ●

FORMER YUGOSLAV
REPUBLIC OF MACEDONIA

GREECE

English

Hostels are located in cities, in the countryside, on the coast and on hills/mountains.

Price range

Price range Dinar 125-500. € 5-20. [BB]inc 🗨.

Rooms and Reservations

R during Jan-Mar, Jul-Sep. (All Rooms). Reservations via Hostel by ❶ ❶. Smoking rooms are available.

Guests

Passport/Photo ID is required. ♦♦♦ welcome. Group bookings via Hostel by ❶ ❶.

Open times

Main hostels: open ▣, 🕓. Reception open: 🕓. Resident manager. **Other hostels:** open ▣, 🕓. Reception open: 07:00-23:00hrs. Resident manager. **Seasonal hostels** are generally open May-Sep.

Meals

♦️ BLD **R** For individuals & for ♦♦♦.

Travelling around

For ease of travel use ➤.

Travel/Activity Packages

Tours/sightseeing, winter sports, water sports, walking/trekking and accommodation/transport packages available. Package bookings via Hostel by ❶ ❶.

Passports and Visas

Passport and Visa required.

Health

Emergency medical treatment is free.

Français

Les auberges sont situées dans les villes, à la campagne, sur le littoral et à la montagne.

Tarifs des nuitées

Tarifs des nuitées 125-500 Dinar. € 5-20. [BB]inc 🗨.

Chambres et réservations

R jan- mar, juil-sep. (Toutes chambres). Réservations via l'auberge par ❶ ❶. Des chambres pour fumeurs sont disponibles.

Usagers

Le passeport/pièce d'identité avec photo est à présenter. Accueil des ♦♦♦. Réservations pour groupes via l'auberge par ❶ ❶.

Horaires d'ouverture

Grandes auberges: ouvertes ▣, 🕓. Accueil ouvert 🕓. Gérant réside sur place. **Autres auberges:** ouvertes ▣, 🕓. Accueil ouvert entre 7h-23h. Gérant réside sur place. **Auberges saisonnières** ouvertes généralement mai-sep.

Repas

♦️ BLD **R** Pour individuels & pour ♦♦♦.

Déplacements

Modes de transport recommandés ➤.

Forfaits Voyages/Activités

Forfaits circuits touristiques, sports d'hiver, sports aquatiques, randonnées pédestres et hébergement/transport disponibles. Réservations des forfaits via l'auberge par ❶ ❶.

Passeports et visas

Passeport et visa obligatoires.

Santé

Soins d'urgence gratuits.

Deutsch

Herbergen befinden sich in Städten, auf dem Land, an der Küste und in Bergen/Gebirgen.

Preisspanne

Preisspanne 125-500 Dinar. € 5-20. [BB] inc 🖵.

Zimmer und Reservierungen

(R) während Jan-Mär, Jul-Sept. (Alle Zimmer). Reservierungen über Herberge per ❶ ❻. Es gibt Zimmer für Raucher.

Gäste

Reisepass/Personalausweis erforderlich. ⫯⫯⫯ willkommen. Gruppenbuchungen über Herberge per ❶ ❻.

Öffnungszeiten

Hauptherbergen: Zugang 📧, ☍. Rezeption ☍. Herbergsmanager wohnt im Haus. **Andere Herbergen:** Zugang 📧, ☍. Rezeption zwischen 07:00-23:00Uhr. Herbergsmanager wohnt im Haus. **Saison-Herbergen** sind normalerweise Mai-Sept geöffnet.

Mahlzeiten

🍽 BLD (R) Für Einzelreisende & für ⫯⫯⫯.

Reisen im Land

Reisen ist einfach mit 🚐.

Reise-/Aktivitäten-Packages

Touren/sightseeing, Wintersport, Wassersport, wandern/trekking und Unterkunft/Transport-Packages erhältlich. Package-Buchungen über Herberge per ❶ ❻.

Reisepässe und Visa

Reisepass/Einreisevisum erforderlich.

Gesundheit

Nur im Notfall sind medizinische Behandlungen kostenlos.

Español

Los albergues están situados en las ciudades, el campo, la costa y la montaña.

Tarifas mínima y máxima

Tarifas mínima y máxima 125-500 Dinar. € 5-20. [BB] inc 🖵.

Habitaciones y Reservas

(R) en ene-mar, jul-sep. (Todas las habitaciones). Reservas a través del albergue por ❶ ❻. Los albergues disponen de habitaciones para fumadores.

Huéspedes

Los huéspedes deben presentar su pasaporte o carnet de identidad. Se admiten ⫯⫯⫯. Reservas de grupo a través del albergue por ❶ ❻.

Horarios y fechas de apertura

Albergues principales - abiertos 📧, ☍. Horario de recepción: ☍. Gerente residente. **Otros albergues** - abiertos 📧, ☍. Horario de recepción: 07:00-23:00h. Gerente residente. **Albergues de temporada** suelen abrir: may-sep.

Comidas

🍽 BLD (R) Para individuales y para ⫯⫯⫯.

Desplazamientos

Transportes recomendados: 🚐.

Viajes Combinados con Actividades

Viajes combinados con visitas turísticas, deportes de invierno, deportes náuticos, senderismo y alojamiento/transporte. Reserva de viajes combinados a través del albergue por ❶ ❻.

Pasaportes y Visados

Pasaporte y visado obligatorios.

Información Sanitaria

Asistencia médica de urgencia gratuita.

Belgrade (Beograd) -
M' Beograd

Bulevar JNA 56a,
Beograd 11000.
☎ (11) 3972560, (11) 3972561
f (11) 461236

Open Dates: 🗓

Open Hours: 🕐

Reservations: **R** **CC**

Price Range: $15.00-22.00 BB|inc 🖵

Beds: 382 - 10x^1🛏 120x^2🛏 30x^3🛏 2x^4🛏 2x^5🛏 4x^6🛏

Facilities: 👫 👫 🍽 ⚲ 🚺 📺 3 x ⛵ 🔲 📷 🎰 🛗 💲 P ℹ 🛝 🐾 🌐

Directions: 5SE from city centre

✈ Belgrade 25km

A🚌 Terminal "Slavia" JAT 5km

⛴ Port Belgrade 6km

🚊 Belgrade 5km

🚌 47,48 50m ap "Kovač"

🚋 9,10, 14 200m ap Vojvode Stepe Street

Attractions: ⛳ ∪6km ⚲200m ⚓200m

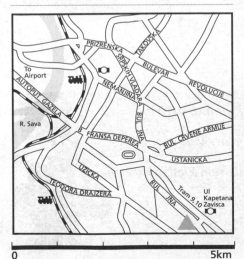

To Airport

PRIZRENSKA — RAKOVSKA
SRPSKIH VLADARA — BULEVAR REVOLUCIJE
NEMANJINA — BUL JNA
AUTOPUT GAZELA
R. Sava
FRANSA DEPEREA — BUL CRVENE ARMIJE
USTANICKA
UZICKA
TEODORA DRAJZERA
BUL JNA — Tram 9,10 — Ul Kapetana Zavisca

0   5km

"Travel only with thy equals or thy betters; if there are none, travel alone."

"Ne voyage qu'avec tes égaux ou tes supérieurs; si tu n'en as pas, voyage tout seul."

„Reise nur mit deinesgleichen oder Höherstehenden; wenn es keine gibt, reise allein."

"Viaja solamente con tus iguales o con tus superiores; si no tienes ninguno, viaja solo."

The Dhammapada

Location/Address	Telephone No. Fax No.	Beds	Opening Dates	Facilities
▲ Belgrade (Beograd) - M' Beograd Bulevar JNA 56a, Beograd 11000.	☎ (11) 3972560, (11) 3972561 ☎ (11) 461236	382	🛏	ⅢⅠ ⅰ⊙ⅼ Ⓡ 5SE ⊂CC⊃ ⚲ Ⓟ ⊡
△ Belgrade (Beograd) - Lipovička Šuma Lipovica-Barajevo, Beograd.	☎ (11) 8302184 ☎ (11) 8302134	40	🛏	ⅢⅠ ⅰ⊙ⅼ Ⓡ 20S Ⓟ ⎁
△ Belgrade (Beograd) - SRC "Pionirski Grad" Kneza Višeslava 27, 11000 Belgrade.	☎ (11) 542166 ☎ (11) 559538	40	🛏	ⅢⅠ ⅰ⊙ⅼ Ⓡ 5S Ⓟ ⎁
▲ Bijela Hotel "Delfin", 85343 Bijela.	☎ (88) 72215, (88) 72219 ☎ (88) 71730	460	🛏	ⅢⅠ ⅰ⊙ⅼ Ⓡ Ⓟ ⊡ ⎁
▲ Brus - Junior Kopaonik, 37220 Brus.	☎ (37) 823344 ☎ (37) 823033	150	🛏	ⅢⅠ ⅰ⊙ⅼ Ⓡ 2SW Ⓟ ⎁
△ Buljarice "Toplica", 81352 Buljarice.	☎ (86) 61479 ☎ (27) 321035	200	01.07–30.08	ⅰ⊙ⅼ 0.5E Ⓟ ⎁
▲ Kladovo Omladinski Kamp "Djerdap" 19320 Kladovo.	☎ (19) 87577, (19) 87983 ☎ (19) 81394	350	01.07–30.08	ⅢⅠ ⅰ⊙ⅼ Ⓡ 2W Ⓟ ⊡ ⎁
▲ Sutomore - "Lovćen" Hotel - "Lovćen", 85000 Sutomore.	☎ (85) 74444, (85) 74111 ☎ (85) 73468	175	🛏	ⅢⅠ ⅰ⊙ⅼ Ⓡ 0.3NW Ⓟ ⊡ ⎁
△ Sutomore Odmaralište Crvenog Krsta, 85000 Sutomore.	☎ (85) 73124, (85) 73608 ☎ (85) 73124	200	01.06–31.08	ⅢⅠ ⅰ⊙ⅼ Ⓡ 0.3W Ⓟ ⊡ ⎁

"To travel hopefully is a better thing than to arrive."

"Voyager avec espoir est mieux que d'arriver."

„Mit Hoffnung zu reisen ist besser, als sein Ziel zu erreichen."

"Viajar con esperanza es mejor que llegar."

Robert Louis Stevenson

AFFILIATED ORGANIZATIONS

The International Youth Hostel Federation also has Affiliated Organizations in a number of other countries. These are not listed in the main body of the Guide, as they do not fulfil the minimum requirements for full membership, and hostel standards may be outside the assured standards scheme. In some instances, approval has been given for the inclusion of details on their hostel network and/or other relevant information.

Those organizations which are in Europe are as follows:-

ORGANISATIONS AFFILIEES

La Fédération Internationale des Auberges de Jeunesse a également des organisations affiliées dans un certain nombre d'autres pays. Celles-ci ne figurent pas sur la liste des pays dans la partie principale du Guide, car elles ne répondent pas aux exigences minimales régissant l'adhésion de membre à part entière et la conformité de leurs établissements aux Normes Minimales n'est pas garantie. Dans certains cas, la publication de renseignements concernant leurs auberges de jeunesse et/ou d'autres informations utiles a été approuvée.

Les organisations en question en Europe sont les suivantes:-

ANGESCHLOSSENE ORGANISATIONEN

Der Internationale Jugendherbergsverband steht ebenso in Verbindung mit angeschlossenen Organisationen in verschiedenen anderen Ländern. Diese sind jedoch nicht im Hauptverzeichnis angegeben, weil sie zum einen keine vollberechtigten Mitgliedsverbände sind und zum anderen der Standard dieser Herbergen nicht den zugesicherten Normen entspricht. In einigen Fällen konnten jedoch Angaben über JH solcher Verbände sowie andere wesentliche Angaben ins Verzeichnis aufgenommen werden.

Es handelt sich dabei um folgende Organisationen in Europa:-

ORGANIZACIONES AFILIADAS

La Federación Internacional de Albergues Juveniles (IYHF) también posee Organizaciones Afiliadas en otros países. Estas no han sido incluidas en la parte principal de la Guía, ya que no cumplen con los requisitos mínimos necesarios para ser miembros de pleno derecho y es posible que el nivel de calidad de sus albergues no corresponda al garantizado por nuestras normas. En algunos casos, se ha aprobado la publicación de información sobre su red de albergues y/u otros datos pertinentes.

En Europa, estas organizaciones son las siguientes:

BULGARIA

USIT Colours
35 Vassil Levski Blvd, Sofia 1000.
- (359) (2) 9811900
- (359) (2) 9819991
- sofia@usitcolours.bg
- www.usitcolours.bg

ESTONIA

Eesti Noortehostelite Ühendus, Estonian Youth Hostels Association,
Tatati 39-310, 10134 Tallinn.
- (372) 6461 455
- (372) 6461 595
- eyha@online.ee
- http://eyha.jg.ee

LATVIA:

Latvian Youth Hostel Association,
8 Aldaru Str, Riga, LV 1050.
- (371) 9218560 (international), 7227207 (local)
- (371) 7224030
- lyha@navigators.lv

LITHUANIA:

Lithuanian Youth Hostels,
Filaretai Youth Hostel, Filaretų St 17, 2007 Vilnius.
- (370) (2) 254627, 262660
- (370) (2) 220149, 262660
- filaretai@post.omnitel.net

MACEDONIA:

Macedonian Youth Hostel Association,
PO Box 499, Prolet 25, 91000 Skopje.
- (389) (91) 239947, 235029
- (389) (91) 235029

ROMANIA:

Youth Hostel Association Romania,
3400 Cluj-Napoca,
Clabucet Street Nr 2 Bloc P4, Ap 69 Jud. Cluj.
- (40) (64) 186616
- (40) (64) 186616
- yhr@mail.dntcj.ro
- www.dntcj.ro/yhr

RUSSIA:

Russian Youth Hostels Association,
St Petersburg International Hostel,
3rd Sovetskaya Ulitsa, St Petersburg 193036.
- (7) (812) 3298018
- (7) (812) 3298019
- ryh@ryh.ru
- www.ryh.ru

Blue Chip Travel,
Chistoprudny Blvd 12a, Suite 628, 101000 Moscow.
- (7) (095) 9169364, 9169365
- (7) (095) 9244968, 9563438

STAR Travel,
3rd Floor, Leningradski Prospect, 80/21, 125178 Moscow.
- (7) (095) 7979555
- (7) (095) 7979554
- help@startravel.ru
- www.startravel.ru

SLOVAKIA:

CKM SYTS
Vysoka 32, 814 45 Bratislava.
- (421) (7) 52731024
- (421) (7) 52731025
- ckmhostels@ckm.sk
- www.ckm.sk

TURKEY:

Gençtur Tourism & Travel Agency Ltd,
Prof K Ismail Gurkan Cad No.14 K.4,
Cagaloglu-Sultanahmet, Istanbul.
- (90) (212) 5205274/5
- (90) (212) 5190864
- info@genctur.com
- www.genctur.com

Yücelt Interyouth Hostel,
Caferiye Sok No 6/1, Sultanahmet 34400, Istanbul.
- (90) (212) 5136150, 5136151
- (90) (212) 5127628
- info@yucelthostel.com
- www.yulcelthostel.com

ESTONIA

Eesti Noortehostelite Ühendus - Estonian Youth Hostels Association,
Tatari 39-310, 10134 Tallinn.
☎ (372) 6461 455, ✆ (372) 6461 595
✉ eyha@online.ee 🖳 http://eyha.jg.ee

Visas:
A visa may be required for entering Estonia, which in most cases will be valid for Latvia and Lithuania also. A visa is obtainable from an Estonian Embassy. For updated information see our Internet http://eyha.jg.ee or Ministry for Foreign Affairs of Estonia http://www.vm.ee. If you need any visa support we will be happy to provide you with any relevant information or documentation.

Bookings:
If possible, visit our WWW page for update information and/or bookings. Please allow at least a week for dealing with fax/mail bookings. Booking conditions may change - current information on the Internet. When requesting information by mail-enclosing IPRC is essential. To make secure, fast and guaranteed bookings please book through our website at http://eyha.jg.ee. If booking through Internet is not possible please contact hostel directly. Groups must book through EYHA office. Credit cards are accepted.

Travel Section:
Balti Puhkemajad,Tatari 39-310, 10134 Tallinn, Estonia
☎ (372) 6461 457 ✆ (372) 6461 595
✉ puhkemajad@online.ee 🖳 http://bpm.jg.ee

Budget travel services for incoming individuals or groups. Accommodation bookings for Estonia, Russia, Latvia, Lithuania and Finland.

Location/Address	Telephone No. Fax No.	Beds	Opening Dates	Facilities
▲ **Tallinn** - "Merevaik" Söpruse Str 182, Tallinn 13424.	☎ 6553767 ✆ 6561127	60	🖾	⛹ 🍴 Ⓡ 2SW Ⓟ ☕

YOUTH HOSTEL ACCOMMODATION
OUTSIDE THE ASSURED STANDARDS SCHEME

Haapsalu - Paralepa Paralepa, Lääne County.	☎ (5) 106735 ✆ (47) 55849	56	01.05–30.08	⛹ 🍴 Ⓡ ⚓ Ⓟ 🔲 ☕
Harju County - Nelijärve Nelijärve 4, Aegviidu, Harju County.	☎ (2) 767382, 6 304350 ✆ 6 304500	150	🖾	⛹ 🍴 Ⓡ Ⓟ 🔲 ☕
Kohtla-Järve - Ontika Ontika, Kohtla Parish, 41541 Ida-Viru County.	☎ (33) 73738 ✆ (33) 73679	42	🖾	⛹ 🍴 Ⓡ 5N Ⓟ ☕
Kuressaare - Ühishümnaasium Hariduse 13, Kuressaare, Saaremaa.	☎ (45) 54388 ✆ (45) 57226	48	🖾	⛹ 🍴 Ⓡ Ⓟ ☕
Otepää - Pikajärve Valgjärve Parish, 63402 Põlva County.	☎ (79) 74413 ✆ (79) 74439	20	🖾	⛹ 🍴 Ⓡ 7SW ⚓ Ⓟ
Pärnu - Kalevi Pansionaat Ranna 2, 80030 Pärnu.	☎ (44) 43008 ✆ (44) 59683	82	🖾	⛹ 🍴 Ⓡ 1.3S ⚓ Ⓟ 🔲 ☕

Location/Address	Telephone No. Fax No.	Beds	Opening Dates	Facilities
Põlva - Taevaskoja Taevaskoja puhkemaja, Taevaskoja sjk, Põlva County.	☎ (79) 92 067	40	🍴	⛹ 🍴 ⓡ 6S P 🖨
Tallinn - Mahtra Mahtra 44, Tallinn.	☎ 6218828 ☎ 6586765	40	🍴	⛹ 🍴 ⓡ ☛ P 🖨
Tartu - Salimo Guesthouse Kopli 1, Tartu.	☎ (7) 470888 ☎ (7) 470888	78	🍴	⛹ 🍴 ⓡ 4S ♿ P ☛
Võsu - Sinikorall Mere 3, Võsu, Lääne-Viru County.	☎ (32) 99455 ☎ (32) 61124	24	01.05–30.09	⛹ ⓡ 0.5W ♿ ☛ P 🖨

LITHUANIA

Lithuanian Youth Hostels, Filaretai Youth Hostel, Filaretų St 17, 2007 Vilnius.
☎ (370) (2) 254627, 262660 ☎ (370) (2) 220149, 262660
📧 filaretai@post.omnitel.net

Visas:
Visa free entrance for all main Western countries (Australia, USA, Canada, UK, Sweden, Finland, Norway, Croatia, Hungary, Japan, Poland, Slovenia, Portugal).

Need for visas: Russia & CIS countries, Romania, all African & Asian countries, Latin America (with exception of Ecuador, Venezuela, Columbia).

Location/Address	Telephone No. Fax No.	Beds	Opening Dates	Facilities
▲ Vilnius - Filaretai IBN Filaretų str 17, Vilnius. 📧 filaretai@post.omnitel.net	☎ (3702) 254627 ☎ (3702) 220149	54	01.01–23.12	ⓡ 1.2E CC ☛ P 🖨

YOUTH HOSTEL ACCOMMODATION OUTSIDE THE ASSURED STANDARDS SCHEME

Klaipeda - Travellers Guesthouse Turgaus 3-4, Klaipeda. 📧 oldtown@takas.lt	☎ (3706) 214935, (37085) 33104 ☎ (3706) 214935	10	🍴	ⓡ
Vilnius - Old Town YH Aušros Vartu, 20-15A, Vilnius. 📧 livijus@pub.osf.lt	☎ (3702) 625357 ☎ (3702) 262660	21	🍴	0.8S CC ☛ 🖨
Zarasai - Zarasai Youth Hostel Šiaulių 26, Zárasai.		8	15.05–15.09	ⓡ
Zervynos - Svirnelis YH Zervynos km, Varėnos raj. 📧 svirnelis@hotmail.com	☎ (37060) 52720	12	15.05–15.09	ⓡ

ROMANIA:

Youth Hostel Association Romania, 3400 Cluj-Napoca, Clabucet Street Nr 2,
Bloc P4, Ap 69 Jud. Cluj.
📞 (40) (64) 186616 📞 (40) (64) 186616
📧 yhr@mail.dntcj.ro 🖳 www.dntcj.ro/yhr

YOUTH HOSTEL ACCOMMODATION
OUTSIDE THE ASSURED STANDARDS SCHEME

Location/Address	Telephone No. Fax No.	Beds	Opening Dates	Facilities
Aiud - Casa Helvetica Strada Gheorghe Doja nr. 53/A.	📞 (94) 635655 📠 (58) 861258	38	🗒	🍴 ® ⅙ ♂ Ⓟ ☕ 🐾
Baişoara - Hostel BTT Strada Principala.	📞 (64) 198067 📠 (64) 197879	26	🗒	👫 🍴 ® ♂ Ⓟ
Belis - Popas Turistic Bradet Strada Principala.	📞 (64) 147206	20	01.05–30.09	👫 ® ♂
Bucureşti-Bucharest - Hostel Helga Strada Salcâmilor nr.2. 📧 helga@rotravel.com	📞 (01) 6102214 📠 (01) 6102214	32	🗒	🍴 ® ♂ 🖨 ☼
Buşteni - Vila Maximilian Strada Pescariei nr.8.	📞 (44) 323297; (92) 879355 📠 (44) 323297	26	🗒	👫 🍴 ® Ⓟ ☕
Cluj Mapoca - Hotel Continental Strada Napoca nr.1. 📧 conticj@codec.ro	📞 (64) 193977 📠 (64) 193977	40	🗒	🍴 ® ⌐CC⌐ ☕ ☼
Cluj Mapoca - Hostel Doremi Strada Brasov nr.2-4. 📧 yhr@mail.dntcj.ro	📞 (64) 186616 📠 (64) 186616	25	01.07–31.08	® ♂ ☼
Cornu - Hotel Sport Strada Principală 747.	📞 (44) 367110 📠 (44) 121060	25	🗒	🍴 ® ☕
Izvorul Muresului - Vila Closca Strada Principală.	📞 (66) 171925 📠 (66) 171925	46	🗒	🍴 ® Ⓟ ☕
Lunca Ariesului - Vila Ramona Strada Principală. 📧 vpeteanu@ciasce.logicnet.ro	📞 (64) 147742	16	01.06–30.09	👫 ® ♂
Lunca Ilvei Strada Principală. 📧 mail@pantravel.ro	📞 (64) 420516 📠 (64) 420516	9	🗒	👫 🍴 ® ♂ Ⓟ
Praid Strada Principală nr.21. 📧 transtur@netsoft.ro	📞 (65) 570484; (66) 240272 📠 (65) 570484	24	01.05–15.09	🍴 ® Ⓟ ☕
Sighişoara - Bobby's Hostel Strada Tache Ionescu nr.18.	📞 (65) 772232	30	01.07–31.08	® 🖨

RUSSIA

Russian Youth Hostels Association, St. Petersburg International Hostel,
3rd Sovetskaya Ulitsa, 28, St. Petersburg, 193036, Russia.
☎ (7) (812) 3298018 ✆ (7) (812) 3298019
📧 ryh@ryh.ru 🖥 www.ryh.ru

Visas:
Visa is required. IBN voucher not sufficient to receive visa. Only RYH visa support allows guest to obtain a tourist visa from the Russian consulate. Consulate requires passport, 3 passport photos and consular fees. Visa Support is valid for in-transit and reserved hostel dates + 2 weeks to allow travel flexibility. We can extend tourist visas for 3 days only. For more information see the Internet: www.ryh.ru.

Bookings & Visa Support:
Fax or e-mail each guest's full legal name; citizenship; birth date; passport number and expiration date; hostel dates; date of entry/exit - into/from Russia; IBN voucher number and fax number. Booking confirmation and/or visa support will be faxed to you next working day. If using IBN, visa support and fax fees are payable upon arrival.

International Bookings For All Hostels:
Russian Youth Hostels, (to Russia via Finnish post), PO Box 8, SF-53501, Lappeenranta, Finland.
☎ (7) (812) 3298018 ✆ (7) (812) 3298019
📧 ryh@ryh.ru

Travel Services:
Sindbad Travel, 3rd Sovetskaya Ulitsa, 28, St. Petersburg, 193036, Russia.
☎ (7) (812) 3278384, ✆ (7) (812) 3298019
📧 sindbad@sindbad.ru

IBN booking center for hostels in Russia and worldwide; full-service student and youth budget travel agency; discounted air, rail, bus and sea tickets.

Location/Address	Telephone No. Fax No.	Beds	Opening Dates	Facilities
▲ **Moscow** - Traveller's Guest House Bolshaya Pereyaslavskaya Vl.,50, 10th Floor, Moscow 129041. 📧 tgh@startravel.ru	☎ (095) 971-4059 ✆ (095) 280-7686	100	🗓	👬 🍴 R ✆ P 🔒 ☕ ☼
▲ **St Petersburg** - International Hostel (IBN) 3rd Sovetskaya Ul., 28, St. Petersburg, 193036. 📧 ryh@ryh.ru	☎ (812) 329-8018 ✆ (812) 329-8019	50	🗓	👬 🍴 R 0.5 SE ✆ P 🔒 ☼

YOUTH HOSTEL ACCOMMODATION
OUTSIDE THE ASSURED STANDARDS SCHEME

Moscow - G & R Hostel Asia Zelenodolskaya 3/2, 1410, Moscow 109377. 📧 hostel-asia@mtu-net.ru	☎ (095) 378-0001 ✆ (095) 378-2866	70	🗓	👬 🍴 R CC ✆ P ☕ ☼
Novgorod - Roza Vetrov Hostel Novoluchanskaya, 27A, Novgord.	☎ (816) 227-2033 ✆ (816) 227-1570	150	🗓	👬 R ✆ P 🔒 ☕
St. Petersburg - Puppet Theatre Hostel Nekrasova Vl.12, St. Petersburg 191014. 📧 ryh@ryh.ru	☎ (812) 272-5401 ✆ (812) 329-8019	22	🗓	👬 🍴 R P ☕ ☼

ADDITIONAL HOSTEL INFORMATION

At the time of printing, no information has been received from the country listed below for this 2001 Edition. We have, therefore reprinted information available from the 2000 edition for reference purposes only.

MACEDONIA

Macedonian Youth Hostel Association, PO Box 499, Prolet 25, 91000 Skopje.
☎ (389) (91) 239947, 235029   ☏ (389) (91) 235029

YOUTH HOSTEL ACCOMMODATION
OUTSIDE THE ASSURED STANDARDS SCHEME

Location/Address	Telephone No. Fax No.	Beds	Opening Dates	Facilities
Ferijalen Dom-Skopje Prolet 25, 91000 Skopje	☎ (91) 114849 ☏ (91) 235029	46	📷	👥 🍽 🅿

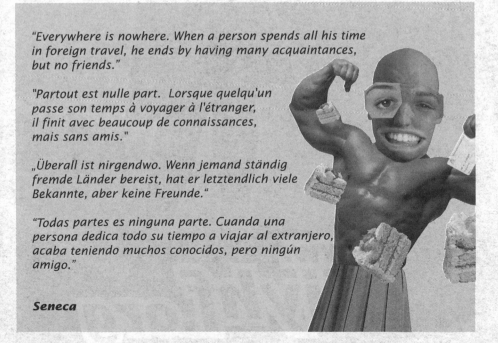

"Everywhere is nowhere. When a person spends all his time in foreign travel, he ends by having many acquaintances, but no friends."

"Partout est nulle part. Lorsque quelqu'un passe son temps à voyager à l'étranger, il finit avec beaucoup de connaissances, mais sans amis."

„Überall ist nirgendwo. Wenn jemand ständig fremde Länder bereist, hat er letztendlich viele Bekannte, aber keine Freunde."

"Todas partes es ninguna parte. Cuanda una persona dedica todo su tiempo a viajar al extranjero, acaba teniendo muchos conocidos, pero ningún amigo."

Seneca

WHAT IS FIYTO ?

Ever since its inception in 1951, the aim of FIYTO (Federation of International Youth Travel Organisations) has been to promote educational, cultural and social travel among young people.

In its fifty year history, FIYTO has become the largest and most influential organisation in the youth travel industry. Towards the mainstream travel and tourism community, international, governmental and non-governmental organisations, FIYTO advocates the special identity of young travellers and their right to affordable travel and travel-related services.

FIYTO is today the premier trade association for youth travel and tourism, a rapidly growing segment of the travel industry. Today we represent the unique interests of an estimated 20% of the tourism population. Our nearly 400 Members account for a turn-over of more than 8 billion US Dollars, serve some 16 million young travellers annually and sell over 9 million air- and surface tickets. FIYTO Members can be found in over 70 countries on all continents.

FIYTO is an open, world-wide, non-political and non-sectarian organisation. Non-profit and for-profit companies, public and private, retailers, wholesalers, buyers, sellers and suppliers are all represented in the FIYTO membership.

FIYTO is an affiliate member of the World Tourism Organisation (WTO) and a member of the Pacific Asia Travel Association (PATA). FIYTO enjoys operational relations with UNESCO, the United Nations Educational, Scientific and Cultural Organisation.

For qualified companies, actively engaged in incoming or outgoing youth travel, FIYTO provides the pre-eminent professional forum to trade, exchange information and advance the interests of the young traveller.

For more information on FIYTO please contact:

FIYTO, Bredgade 25H
1260 Copenhagen K, Denmark
E-mail: mailbox@fiyto.org
www.fiyto.org

International Student Travel Confederation (ISTC)

ISTC

THE WORLD OF
STUDENT TRAVEL
SINCE 1949

In 1949 a group of emerging student travel organisations formed the International Student Travel Confederation (ISTC). They shared a common goal - "to increase international understanding through travel and exchange opportunities for students, young people and the academic community".

Today, ISTC members continue to lead in the development of specialised products and services for the student travel community. Students recognise these organisations as "the source" for reliable products and sound advice. Through a network of 17,000 locations in more than 90 countries, ISTC members provide a truly global network for student and youth travellers.

To better develop products and services for today's student and youth travellers, and negotiate benefits on their behalf, the ISTC is a confederation of five associations active in specialised areas of student and youth travel services - surface travel, international identity cards, student flights, insurance and work exchange programs. The Associations include:

IAEWEP   International Association for Educational and Work Exchange Programmes
IASIS   International Association for Student Insurance Services
ISIC   International Student Identity Card Association
ISSA   International Student Surface Travel Association
SATA   Student Air Travel Association

As the world-wide administrator of the International Student Identity Card (ISIC), the ISTC oversees the distribution and promotion of over 4 million cards annually. UNESCO endorses the ISIC and recognises it as the unique document for student mobility.

The ISTC maintains relationships with UNESCO, the IYHF, the World Tourism Organisation and other international organisations.

For more information contact:

ISTC
PO Box 15857
1001 NJ Amsterdam
The Netherlands
E-mail: istcinfo@istc.org
www.istc.org

... help us to implement our assurance of standards at hostels by writing to us or by using the reply slip in this Guide to tell us what you think of our hostels.

Just tick the boxes to indicate how well the hostel did in the five areas, and remember to let us have your comments on how you found your stay.

Simply put your reply in an envelope and post to us at the address shown on the slip.

NOUS AIMERIONS CONNAITRE VOTRE OPINION...

... aidez-nous à mettre en place les normes garanties dans nos auberges en nous faisant part de ce que vous pensez d'elles, soit en nous écrivant, soit en remplissant la fiche prévue à cet effet que vous trouverez dans ce guide.

Il vous suffira de cocher les cases pour évaluer la performance de l'auberge dans les cinq domaines indiqués, sans oublier d'ajouter vos observations sur votre séjour.

Envoyez-nous votre fiche sous enveloppe, à l'adresse indiquée dessus.

WIR MÖCHTEN IHRE MEINUNG HÖREN...

... helfen Sie uns, unsere zugesicherten Standards zu gewährleisten, indem Sie uns wissen lassen, was Sie von unseren Herbergen halten. Bitte schreiben Sie uns oder benutzen Sie dazu die am Ende dieses Führers beigefügte Antwortkarte.

Kreuzen Sie bitte Ihre Beurteilung für die jeweilige Kategorie in dem entsprechenden Kästchen an, und vergessen Sie nicht, uns Ihren Kommentar über Ihren Aufenthalt mitzuteilen.

Ihre Antwort ganz einfach in einen Umschlag stecken und an die auf der Antwortkarte angegebene Adresse schicken.

QUEREMOS SABER LO QUE USTED OPINA...

... ayúdenos a implementar nuestras normas garantizadas en los albergues. Escríbanos, o haga uso de las hojas provistas en la Guía, para comunicarnos lo que piensa de nuestros albergues.

Sólo tiene que marcar las casillas según la opinión que le merezca el albergue en lo que respecta a los cinco apartados de consulta. No olvide añadir comentarios sobre su estancia en el recuadro de las observaciones.

Envíe su comunicación en un sobre dirigido a la dirección indicada.

We want to hear from YOU....

TELL US WHAT YOU THINK!

DITES-NOUS CE QUE VOUS EN PENSEZ!
SAGEN SIE UNS IHRE MEINUNG!
¡DIGANOS LO QUE OPINA!

Hostel Name-Address/
Nom de l'Auberge-Adresse/
Name der Jugendherberge
Anschrift/
Nombre y Dirección del Albergue

*City/Ville/*Stadt/*Ciudad*

Country/*Pays*/Land/*País*

Date(s) stayed/*Dates du séjour/*
Daten des Aufenthaltes/
Fechas de la Estancia

Please return to:
INTERNATIONAL YOUTH HOSTEL FEDERATION,
1st Floor, Fountain House, Parkway, Welwyn Garden City,
Hertfordshire AL8 6JH. ENGLAND

Welcome/*Accueil/*
Aufnahme/*Recibimiento*

Comfort/*Confort/*
Komfort/*Comodidad*

Cleanliness/*Propreté/*
Sauberkeit/*Limpieza*

Security/*Sécurité/*
Sicherheit/*Seguridad*

Privacy/*Intimité,*
Privatsphäre/*Intimidad*

COMMENTS/*COMMENTAIRES*/BEMERKUNGEN/*OBSERVACIONES*

Name/*Nom/*
Name/*Nombre*

Address/*Adresse/*
Anschrift/*Dirección*

... help us to implement our assurance of standards at hostels by writing to us or by using the reply slip in this Guide to tell us what you think of our hostels.

Just tick the boxes to indicate how well the hostel did in the five areas, and remember to let us have your comments on how you found your stay.

Simply put your reply in an envelope and post to us at the address shown on the slip.

NOUS AIMERIONS CONNAITRE VOTRE OPINION...

... aidez-nous à mettre en place les normes garanties dans nos auberges en nous faisant part de ce que vous pensez d'elles, soit en nous écrivant, soit en remplissant la fiche prévue à cet effet que vous trouverez dans ce guide.

Il vous suffira de cocher les cases pour évaluer la performance de l'auberge dans les cinq domaines indiqués, sans oublier d'ajouter vos observations sur votre séjour.

Envoyez-nous votre fiche sous enveloppe, à l'adresse indiquée dessus.

WIR MÖCHTEN IHRE MEINUNG HÖREN...

... helfen Sie uns, unsere zugesicherten Standards zu gewährleisten, indem Sie uns wissen lassen, was Sie von unseren Herbergen halten. Bitte schreiben Sie uns oder benutzen Sie dazu die am Ende dieses Führers beigefügte Antwortkarte.

Kreuzen Sie bitte Ihre Beurteilung für die jeweilige Kategorie in dem entsprechenden Kästchen an, und vergessen Sie nicht, uns Ihren Kommentar über Ihren Aufenthalt mitzuteilen.

Ihre Antwort ganz einfach in einen Umschlag stecken und an die auf der Antwortkarte angegebene Adresse schicken.

QUEREMOS SABER LO QUE USTED OPINA...

... ayúdenos a implementar nuestras normas garantizadas en los albergues. Escríbanos, o haga uso de las hojas provistas en la Guía, para comunicarnos lo que piensa de nuestros albergues.

Sólo tiene que marcar las casillas según la opinión que le merezca el albergue en lo que respecta a los cinco apartados de consulta. No olvide añadir comentarios sobre su estancia en el recuadro de las observaciones.

Envíe su comunicación en un sobre dirigido a la dirección indicada.

We want to hear from YOU....

TELL US WHAT YOU THINK!

DITES-NOUS CE QUE VOUS EN PENSEZ!
SAGEN SIE UNS IHRE MEINUNG!
¡DIGANOS LO QUE OPINA!

Hostel Name-Address/
Nom de l'Auberge-Adresse/
Name der Jugendherberge
Anschrift/
Nombre y Dirección del Albergue

City/Ville/Stadt/Ciudad

Country/*Pays*/Land/*País*

Date(s) stayed/*Dates du séjour/*
Daten des Aufenthaltes/
Fechas de la Estancia

Please return to:
INTERNATIONAL YOUTH HOSTEL FEDERATION,
1st Floor, Fountain House, Parkway, Welwyn Garden City,
Hertfordshire AL8 6JH. ENGLAND

Welcome/*Accueil/*
Aufnahme/*Recibimiento*

Comfort/*Confort/*
Komfort/*Comodidad*

Cleanliness/*Propreté/*
Sauberkeit/*Limpieza*

Security/*Sécurité/*
Sicherheit/*Seguridad*

Privacy/*Intimité,*
Privatsphäre/*Intimidad*

COMMENTS/*COMMENTAIRES*/BEMERKUNGEN/*OBSERVACIONES*

Name/*Nom/*
Name/*Nombre*

Address/*Adresse/*
Anschrift/*Dirección*

DISCOUNTS & CONCESSIONS

Hostelling International Membership enables you to claim discounts and concessions on everything from travel and museums, to eating and entertainment! The top discounts are included here – for the full story check out the Global Discounts Database at **www.iyhf.org**. Simply present your Hostelling International Membership Card to claim a discount – and begin recovering the cost of Membership!

Discounts are sorted by **Country**. Within each country, discounts are listed alphabetically by **City** – national discounts are listed first. Within each city, discounts are listed by **Discount Category** – Entertainment ♔, General ☺, Museums and Culture ▥, Retail ▦, or Travel ✈. For each discount, we list: discount provider's name, address and telephone number, along with a brief description of the discount available.

Please note: The information about discounts has been supplied by the Youth Hostel Association of each country represented. Every effort has been made to ensure that this information is correct, and Hostelling International can accept no responsibility for any inaccuracies or for changes subsequent to publication.

REMISES ET RÉDUCTIONS

Votre adhésion à Hostelling International vous permet de profiter de nombreuses remises et réductions sur presque tout, des transports aux entrées de musées en passant par la restauration et les spectacles! Seuls les avantages les plus importants sont cités ci-après – pour la liste complète, faites donc un tour sur notre site Internet, **www.iyhf.org**, où vous trouverez notre base de données mondiale des remises. Présentez votre carte d'adhérent Hostelling International pour bénéficier d'une réduction et commencez à amortir le coût de votre adhésion!

Les différents avantages que l'on vous propose sont d'abord répertoriés par **Pays** puis en ordre alphabétique par **Ville** – les offres qui sont valables à l'échelle nationale sont en tête de liste. Elles sont ensuite classées par **Catégorie** – Voyages ✈ *(Travel)*, Magasins et Restaurants ▦ *(Retail)*, Spectacles et Activités ♔ *(Entertainment)*, Musées et Culture ▥ *(Museums and Culture)* ou Général ☺. Pour chaque remise, nous fournissons le nom de l'entité qui la propose, son adresse et numéro de téléphone, ainsi qu'un bref descriptif de l'offre en question.

Remarque: Les renseignements sur ces remises nous sont communiqués par l'Association d'Auberges de Jeunesse de chaque pays représenté. Tout a été mis en oeuvre pour s'assurer que ces données sont correctes mais Hostelling International ne peut accepter aucune responsabilité pour toute inexactitude ou tout changement intervenant ultérieurement à la publication du présent ouvrage.

RABATTE & ERMÄßIGUNGEN

Die Mitgliedschaft bei Hostelling International sichert Ihnen Anspruch auf Rabatte und Ermäßigungen bei Reisen und Museen, in der Gastronomie und Unterhaltung! Die Top-Preisnachlässe sind hier enthalten – für einen kompletten Überblick schauen Sie in die Datenbank für internationale Rabatte *(Global Discounts Database)* unter **www.iyhf.org**. Legen Sie einfach Ihre Hostelling International Mitgliedskarte vor, um einen Nachlaß in Anspruch zu nehmen – und fangen Sie an, den Mitgliedsbeitrag wieder einzuholen!

Die Rabatte sind nach **Ländern** *(Country)* und innerhalb jedes Landes nach **Städten** *(City)* in alphabetischer Reihenfolge geordnet. Die nationalen Preisnachlässe *(National)* sind zuerst aufgeführt. Sie sind für jede Stadt nach **Rabattkategorien** *(Discount Category)* – Unterhaltung ▼ *(Entertainment)*, Allgemeines ☺ *(General)*, Museen und Kultur ▥ *(Museum and Culture)*, Einzelhandel ▥ *(Retail)* sowie Reisen ✦ *(Travel)* – systematisiert. Für jeden Nachlaß ist, neben dem Namen des Anbieters, dessen Adresse und Telefonnummer, eine kurze Beschreibung des verfügbaren Rabattes *(Discount Discription)* aufgeführt.

Bitte beachten Sie: Die Informationen über die Rabatte wurden von den Jugendherbergsverbänden jedes aufgeführten Landes zur Verfügung gestellt. Wir haben alles unternommen, um sicherzugehen, daß diese Informationen korrekt sind. Hostelling International kann keine Verantwortung für jegliche Ungenauigkeiten oder Änderungen im Anschluß an die Veröffentlichung übernehmen.

OFERTAS Y DESCUENTOS

Su afiliación a Hostelling International le permite disfrutar de ofertas y descuentos de todo tipo: en los transportes y entradas de museo, restaurantes y espectáculos – ¡la lista es interminable! A continuación se relacionan los descuentos más importantes solamente. Si desea verlos todos, consulte nuestra Base de Datos Mundial de Descuentos *(Global Discounts Database)* en Internet en **www.iyhf.org**. Para conseguir un descuento, no tiene más que presentar su tarjeta de socio de Hostelling International – y así ir amortizando el coste de la misma.

Los descuentos están clasificados en primer lugar por **país** y en segundo lugar por **ciudad o población**, ambos en orden alfabético. Los que son válidos a nivel nacional aparecen primero y todos están ordenados por **categoría**, a saber: Viajes ✦ *(Travel)*, Tiendas y Restaurantes ▥ *(Retail)*, Actividades Recreativas ▼ *(Entertainment)*, Museos y Cultura ▥ *(Museums and Culture)*, y General ☺. Para cada uno de ellos, se indica el nombre de la organización o compañía que concede el descuento, su dirección y número de teléfono, y una breve descripción del mismo.

Importante: La información sobre estos descuentos nos ha sido suministrada por la Asociación de Albergues Juveniles de cada país representado. Hemos hecho todo lo posible por asegurarnos de que los datos son correctos y Hostelling International no se responsabiliza de ninguna inexactitud ni de ningún cambio que se produzca en fecha posterior a la publicación de la presente guía.

Explanation of Symbols

☺ General	☺ Général	☺ Allgemeines	☺ General
▼ Entertainment	▼ Spectacles et Activités	▼ Unterhaltung	▼ Actividades Recreativas
▥ Retail	▥ Magasins et Restaurants	▥ Einzelhandel	▥ Tiendas y Restaurantes
▥ Museums and Culture	▥ Musées et Culture	▥ Museen und Kultur	▥ Museos y Cultura
✦ Travel	✦ Voyages	✦ Reisen	✦ Viajes

GLOBAL

✛ **Budget Rent a Car**
🖳 www.budget.com

15% OFF STANDARD CAR RENTAL RATES - A SPECIAL OFFER FOR HOSTELLING INTERNATIONAL MEMBERS. Budget Rent a Car - The world's third largest car and truck rental company, offers Hostelling International Members 15% off standard rental rates. To claim your discount simply quote **BCD G514400** when making a reservation. See www.iyhf.org for a full list of countries. Conditions apply

Ⓖ **Travelex**
🖳 www.travelexgrp.com

COMMISSION FREE CURRENCY EXCHANGE - A SPECIAL OFFER FOR HOSTELLING INTERNATIONAL MEMBERS. TRAVELEX - the world's largest airport and passenger terminal bureau de change - has offered Hostelling International members a very special service to reduce the cost of international travel. By showing your membership card and quoting "Hostelling International" or "IYHF" you can enjoy Commission Free Currency exchange at any of the 300 Travelex offices world-wide. The list of their offices can be found on the Travelex website at www.travelexgrp.com. Conditions apply

✛ **Greyhound International**
🖳 www.greyhound-uk.co.uk

10% discount on the purchase of any Ameripass or Canada Coach Pass purchased before you travel to North America. To see the list of agents in your area please visit www.greyhound-uk.co.uk. Please note that this offer only applies to pass products. It does not apply to single/return journey tickets (point to point)

✛ **Greyhound Pioneer Australia**
❶ 13 20 30 (Australia)

15% discount on passes when purchased outside Australia. 10% discount on passes and point to point tickets purchased in Australia

Ⓖ **Lonely Planet Guide Books**
🖳 www.lonelyplanet.com

Lonely Planet, the world's leading publisher of independent travel information, offer various discounts to Hostelling International members around the world. Please check the global discount database at www.iyhf.org for further details.

EUROPEAN

✛ **Hertz**
❶ Call one of the following Reservation Hotlines or contact your local reservation office:
Belgium: 02 717 3200,
France: 0803 861 861,
Germany: 01 805 000 768,
Italy: 199 11 77 11,
The Netherlands: 020 504 0584,
Spain: 902 303 230,
UK: 0870 844 4 844.
General reservations:
Switzerland: 0848 822020,
Austria: 0800 20 1111.
🖳 www.hertz.com

Hertz are offering Hostelling International members a discount of between 10-25% (sometimes more) on standard car rental rates depending on the make and model of the car and length of time. The discount is available on both business and leisure rentals in Europe and when travelling from Europe to North America, Australia, Asia and South Africa. Simply quote **CDP number 532239** when making your booking. You may be asked to show your membership card upon collection of vehicle. Normal restrictions apply.

ARGENTINA

BUENOS AIRES

🍴 **Hard Rock Café-Buenos Aires**
Av. Pueyrredon 2501, Piso 2
☎ +54 11 4807 7625
✆ +54 11 4807 7625
15% discount on food & beverages except special offers

🍴 **World Sport Café**
Junin 1745
☎ +54 11 4807 3800
✉ info@worldsport-café.com.ar
🖥 www.worldsport-café.com.ar
50% discount everyday from 1700-2100. 20% discount from Sunday-Thursday after 2100h. Conditions apply.

SAN RAFAEL - MENDOZA

✝ **Turismo Iselin**
Cnel Suarez 255
☎ +54 2627 424 618
10% discount on local excursions

USHUAIA

✝ **Excursiones Isla Verde S.A.**
San Martin 1295
☎ +54 2901 437 606
10% discount on local excursions

AUSTRALIA

National

🎭 **Dendy Cinemas**
🖥 www.dendy.com.au
$10 entry at all Dendy locations in Sydney, Melbourne and Brisbane

Ⓖ **YHA Travel Insurance**
5-10% nationwide discount on all Australian and overseas travel insurance policies at all YHA Membership and Travel Centres

Ⓖ **Travelex Money Exchange**
Commission free transactions of foreign currency to all HI members at any Travelex location

Ⓖ **Australian Council of National Trusts**
☎ 1800 246 766
$20 off national membership rates. Membership gives you free entry into hundreds of heritage properties in Australia and 17 other countries around the world - over 700 properties in the UK

Ⓖ **Lonely Planet Guides**
10% off when purchased at YHA Membership and Travel Centres

Ⓖ **The Travel Clinic**
☎ 1300 369 359
10% off travel health care products and a free pocket guide and vaccination certificate (value $6.95) with first consultation

Ⓖ **Travel Health Service - HSA**
☎ 1300 361 046
10% discount on travel vaccines. Conveniently located in every Australian capital city

Ⓖ **Travellers Medical & Vaccination Centre (TMVC)**
☎ 1300 658 844
10% discount on TMVC vaccines, products and medical kits. Free copy of Travelling Well, essential travel health handbook valued at $14.95 with travel health consultation. Clinics all over Australia

🎒 **Paddy Pallin**
☎ 1800 805 398
10% discount for cash, 7% for credit card purchases over $50 for all outdoor and travel equipment (does not apply to sales items). Stores all over Australia. Mail order available

🎒 **Snowgum**
10% off normal price of all outdoor and travel equipment

🎒 **Mountain Designs**
☎ 07 3252 8894
🖥 www.mountaindesigns.com
10% off all outdoor and travel equipment (already discounted items excluded)

🎒 **Kathmandu**
☎ 1800 333 484
25% off Kathmandu packs, tents and Goosedown sleeping bags, plus 10% off all full-priced stock (outdoor and travel equipment). Stores in Victoria, New South Wales and Queensland. Mail order available

✝ McCafferty's Coaches
10% discount on all McCafferty's passes and point-to-point tickets. 15% discount on passes and point-to-point tickets when purchased outside Australia

✝ AAT King's Tours
10% discount on one day sightseeing tours

✝ Oz Experience
5% discount on selected passes in Australia and New Zealand (Kiwi Experience)

✝ Great Southern Rail
☎ 132147
10% discount on rail content in all classes of travel on the Ghan, Indian Pacific and Overland

✝ Countrylink Rail
10% off New South Wales Discovery Pass

✝ Hertz Australia
☎ 13 30 39
Hertz is pleased to offer YHA members up to 35% off standard car hire rates. To access these rates quote Customer Discount Program (CDP) number 317961. Drive safely

✝ Budget Rent a Car
☎ 1300 362 848
Special rates with an average discount of 30%. Rent a small manual car for 7 days for $55 per day with unlimited kilometres. Please quote BCD (Budget Customer Discount) number E013609

✝ Network Rentals
☎ 1800 2077
Nationwide discount from Network car and truck rentals - corporate rate (approximately 20% off). Contact YHA Membership and Travel Centres or Network offices nationally

✝ Avis Australia
☎ 1800 255 533
A minimum of 30% off standard rates, and if applicable, a further 5% off promotional rates (excludes commercial vehicles). Conditions apply. To ensure members receive discounts, quote discount number P081600 when making a reservation

✝ Delta
☎ 1300 362 848
15% discount if this ad is mentioned. Quote YHA Delta corporate discount number DC161200

ADELAIDE

✝ Kangaroo Island Ferry Connections
☎ 08 8231 5583
5% off all tours

ALICE SPRINGS

✝ Sahara Outback Tours
☎ 08 8952 8855
5% discount on all tours

✝ Ballooning Downunder
☎ 08 8952 8855
20% discount on all flights

BLUE MOUNTAINS

✝ Blue Mountains Adventure Co.
☎ 02 4782 1271
10% off various abseiling tours

CAIRNS

✝ Sunlover Cruises
☎ 07 4051 1368
10% off

DARWIN, KAKADU & LITCHFIELD

✝ Crocodylus Park
☎ 08 8981 2561
15% off entry

✝ The Blue Banana
☎ 08 8981 2560
10% off all tours

HOBART

✝ Tasmania Tours and Travel
☎ 1300 653 633
10% off day and half-day sightseeing tours

MELBOURNE

✝ Eco Adventure Tours
☎ 03 9670 9611
10% off Yarra Valley Tours

PERTH

✝ Oceanic Cruises
☎ 08 9325 1616
15% discount on Rottnest Island Ferry and Swan River Cruises

✝ West Australia Travel and Dive
☎ 08 9421 1883
5% discount

PORT CAMPBELL
✝ **Port Campbell Boat Charters**
  ☎ 03 5598 6411
  33% off scenic tours

PORT MACQUARIE
✝ **Beach to Bush Eco Tours**
  ☎ 0428 667 913
  6% off Sydney-Byron Bay Eco Tours

QUEENSLAND
✝ **Queensland Rail**
  ☎ 07 3236 1680
  10% off adult economy seat, economy and first class booths

SYDNEY
✝ **Gray Line**
  ☎ 02 9261 1111
  20% off Sydney day tours

TASMANIA
✝ **Tasmanian Redline Tours**
  ☎ 1300 360 000
  20% off main road route services

WHITSUNDAYS
✝ **Southern Cross Sailing Adventures**
  ☎ 07 4946 6312
  $10 off 3 day sailing adventures

AUSTRIA

INNSBRUCK
🏛 **Tiroler Volkskunstmuseum**
  Universitätsstraß2 2
  ☎ 0512 58 43 02
  🖷 0512 58 43 70
  Admission at student's discount for ATS 35 instead of 60

SALZBURG
🏛 **Mozart's Geburtshaus**
  Getreidegasse 9
  ☎ 0662 84 43 13
  🖷 0662 84 06 93
  Membership card holder gets group discount

✝ **Salzburg VELOactive**
  Willibald Hauthaler Straße 10
  ☎ 0662 43 55 95-0
  🖷 0662 43 55 95-22
  10% discount on bike hire

WIEN
🏛 **Beethoven Gedenkstätte**
  Probusgasse 6
  ☎ 01 402 12 60
  🖷 01 408 80 83
  Admission ATS 10 instead of 25

🏛 **Schubert Geburtshaus**
  Nußdorferstraße 54
  ATS 10 instead of 25

✝ **DDSG Blue Danube Schiffahrt GmbH**
  Friedrichstraße 7
  ☎ 01 588 80-0
  🖷 01 588 80-440
  10% discount on round trips within Vienna and Wachau

BELGIUM

National
✝ **Eurolines**
  10% discount

🏢 **Grote Routepaden**
  15% discount on maps and guidebooks for long distance walking and cycling

CANADA

GARIBALDI HIGHLANDS
✝ **Ocean West Expeditions Ltd**
  PO Box 3322, V0N 1T0
  ☎ 604 688 5770
  10% off

SALTSPRING ISLAND
✝ **Saltspring Kayaking**
  521 Isabella Point Road, V8K 1V3
  ☎ 250 653 4222
  20% off all kayak tours and rentals

SQUAMISH
✝ **Ecomountain Tours Ltd**
  PO Box 1803, V0N 3G0
  ☎ 1800 925 4453
  20% off

TOFINO

✝ **Cypre Prince Tours**
PO Box 149, V0R 1Z0
☎ 250 725 2202
10% off all boat trips

✝ **Jamie's Whaling Station**
Box 129 "B"
☎ 250 725 3919
10% off all boat tours

✝ **Tofino Sea Kayaking Co.**
PO Box 620, 300 Main Street, V0R 2Z0
☎ 250 725 2070
10% off all tours, 5% off outdoor gear rental

TORONTO

✝ **Skydome Tours**
$2.00 off

VICTORIA

✝ **Blackfish Wilderness Expeditions**
2886 Ilene Terrace, V8R 4P1
☎ 250 216 2389
20% discount

✝ **Midnight Sun Adventure Travel**
843 Yates Street, V8W 1M1
☎ 250 480 9409
HI members who book 2 Island tours receive one free night's accommodation at either the Nanaimo, or the Victoria Hostel

✝ **Nature Calls Eco-Tours**
12 Falstaff Place
☎ 250 361 4453
10% discount to HI members and Victoria hostel guests

✝ **Seacoast Expeditions**
45 Songhees Road
☎ 250 383 2254
30% discount on regular 3 hour adult fare

✝ **Seagull Expeditions Ltd**
213-451 Topaz Avenue, V8T 2M2
☎ 250 360 0893
60% off on T-shirt purchase

CZECH REPUBLIC
PRAGUE

🏛 **Národni Museum/National Museum & Branch offices**
35% discount for members under 26 years especially groups booked via KMC

CHILE
SANTIAGO

✝ **Ansa Rent A Car**
Av. Eliodoro Yañez 1198
☎ +56-2 251 0256
📠 +56-2 2510425
15% discount on car rental

✝ **Cascada Expediciones**
Orrego Luco 054 20 Piso
☎ +56-2 2327214
📠 +56-2 2339768
✉ info@cascada-expediciones.com
🖥 www.cascada-expediciones.com
10% discount on all services

COSTA RICA
SAN JOSÉ

Ⓖ **Academia Latinoamericana de Español**
Ave. 8 Calles 31-33, #3113
☎ +506 2249917
📠 +506 2258125
✉ espalesa@sol.racsa.co.cr
15% discount on all Spanish courses

DENMARK
AALBORG

✝ **Eurolines**
J.F Kennedys plads 1, 9000 Aalborg
☎ +45 9934 4488
10% discount on all tickets

🏛 **Nordjyllands Kuntsmuseum**
Kong Christians Allé 50, 9000 Aalborg
☎ +45 9813 8088
50% discount

ESBJERG

🏛 **Esbjerg Museum**
Torvegade 45, 6700 Esbjerg
☎ +45 7512 7811
20% discount

FREDERIKSVÆRK

Frederiksværk Bymuseum
Torvet 18-20, 3300 Frederiksværk
☎ +45 4772 0605
50% discount

HERNING

Danmarks Fotomuseum
Museumsgade 28, 7400 Herning
☎ +45 9722 5322
Two for the price of one

KOPENHAVN K

Guiness World of Records museum
Ostergade 16, 1100 Kobenhavn K
☎ +45 3332 3183
DKK5.00 discount

ODENSE

Jernbanemuseet
Dannebrogsgade 24, 5000 Odense
☎ +45 6612 3265
25% discount

ENGLAND & WALES

ASHBOURNE

Carsington Sports and Leisure Ltd
Carsington Water, Ashbourne, Derbyshire DE6 1ST
☎ +44 1629 540478
✆ +44 1629 540666
✉ carsington@ryh-online.net
10% off watersports and cycle hire including tuition

BATH

The Jane Austen Centre
40 Gay Street, Bath, BA1 2NT
☎ +44 1225 443000
✆ +44 1225 443000
✉ info@janeausten.co.uk
🖳 www.janeausten.co.uk
20% discount

BRIGHTON

Newhaven Fort
Fort Road, Newhaven, East Sussex BN9 9DL
☎ +44 1273 517622
✆ +44 1273 512059
✉ enquiries@newhavenfort.org.uk
🖳 www.newhavenfort.org.uk
2 for the price of 1

BRISTOL

John Nike Leisure Sport- Bristol Ice Rink
Frogmore Street, Bristol, BS1 5NA
☎ +44 117 9292148
✆ +44 117 9259736
🖳 www.nikegroup.co.uk
£3.30 admission including skate hire

CAMBRIDGE

Geoff's Bike Hire
65 Devonshire Road, Cambridge, Cambridgeshire
☎ +44 1223 365629
10% off cycle hire and guided cycle tours

CANTERBURY

Dickens House Museum
Victoria Parade, Broadstairs, Kent CT10 1QS
☎ +44 1843 862853
30% discount

CAPEL-Y-FFIN

Black Mountain Holidays
Castle Farm, Capel-y-Ffin, Abergavenny, Wales
☎ +44 1873 890961
✆ +44 1497 821058
✉ bmholidays@cma-int.demon.co.uk
🖳 www.hay-on-wye.co.uk/bmholidays
15% discount

CARDIFF

Rhondda Heritage Park
Lewis Merthyr Colliery, Coed Cae Road, Trehafod,
Rhondda Cynon Taff, CF37 7NP
☎ +44 1443 682036
✆ +44 1443 687420
✉ rhonpark@netwales.co.uk
🖳 www.netwales.co.uk/rhondda-
heritage
20% off admissions (not special event days)

Techniquest
Stuart Street, Cardiff CF10 5BW
☎ +44 29 2047 5475
✆ +44 29 2048 2517
✉ gen@techniquest.org
🖳 www.techniquest.org
10% discount on adult, child and family admission

CHESTER

Chester Gateway Theatre
Hamilton Place, Chester, Cheshire CH1 2BH
- **☎** +44 1244 344238
- **✆** +44 1244 341296
- 🖰 www.gateway-theatre.org
£2 off all seat prices

Sygun Copper Mine
Beddgelert, Caernarfon, Gwynedd LL55 4NE
- **☎** +44 1766 510100
- **✆** +44 1766 510100
- **e** sygunmine@cs.com
- 🖰 http://ourworld.compuserve.com/
homepages/snowdoniamine
10% discount

EXETER

BikeTrail Cycle Hire
Unit 6, Estuary Business Park, Yelland, Barnstaple
EX31 3EZ
- **☎** +44 1271 861424
- **e** info@biketrail.co.uk
- 🖰 www.biketrail.co.uk
10% discount on cycle hire

LAKE DISTRICT

Windermere Steamboat Museum
Rayrigg Road, Windermere, Cumbria LA23 1BN
- **☎** +44 15394 45565
- **✆** +44 15394 48769
- 🖰 www.steamboat.co.uk
2 for the price of 1

The Climbers Shop
Compston Corner, Ambleside, Cumbria LA22 9DS
- **☎** +44 15394 32297
- **✆** +44 15394 34165
- **e** info@climbersshop.demon.co.uk
10% off full price items except publications and
electricals

Windermere Lake Cruises
Waterhead Pier, Ambleside, Cumbria LA22 0EY
- **☎** +44 15395 31188
- **✆** +44 15395 31947
- **e** w.lakes@virgin.net
10% off sailings between Ambleside Bowness,
Lakeside & Brockhole

LIVERPOOL

The Boat Museum
South Pier Head, Ellesmere Port, CH65 4FW
- **☎** +44 151 955 5017
- **✆** +44 151 355 4079
20% discount

Blue Planet
Cheshire Oaks, Ellesmere Port, Cheshire CH65 9LF
- **☎** +44 151 357 8800
- **✆** +44 151 356 7288
- **e** info@blueplanetaquarium.co.uk
- 🖰 www.blueplanetaquarium.co.uk
10% discount

LONDON

Florence Nightingale Museum
2 Lambeth Palace Road, London SE1 7EW
- **☎** +44 20 7620 0374
- **✆** +44 20 7928 1760
- 🖰 www.florence-nightingale.co.uk
£1 off all admission prices for individuals

BBC Experience
Rm 319 Egton House, 8 Langham Street, London
W1A 1AA
- **☎** +44 20 77651109
- **✆** +44 20 7765 0540
- 🖰 www.bbc.co.uk/experience
£1 off admission price for adults; 50p off admission
price for children

MANCHESTER

Museum of Science and Industry
Liverpool Road, Castlefield, Manchester M3 4FP
- **☎** +44 161 832 2244
- **✆** +44 161 833 1471
- 🖰 www.msim.org.uk
Group rate for individuals

NEWCASTLE

Outdoor World
49 Ilfracombe Gardens, Whitley Bay, Tyne and Wear
NE26 3LZ
- **☎** +44 191 2514388
- **✆** +44 191 2514388
10% discount

OXFORD

Oxford Campus Stores
various addresses in Oxford
☎ +44 1865 727517
📠 +44 1865 248160
10% discount on all purchases

Upton House
Near Banbury, Oxfordshire
☎ +44 1295 670266
📠 +44 1295 670266
🖥 www.ntrustsevern.org.uk
2 non members of National Trust get in for the price of 1

Wycombe Summit Ski and Snowboard Centre
Abbey Barn Lane, High Wycombe, Buckinghamshire HP10 9QQ
☎ +44 1494 474711
📠 +44 1494 443757
✉ wycombesummit@skico.uk
🖥 www.ski.co.uk/wycombesummit
20% discount on open practice and group lessons

PEAK DISTRICT

The Bass Museum
Box 220, Horninnglow Street, Burton upon Trent, Staffordshire
☎ +44 1283 511000
📠 +44 1283 516316
🖥 www.bass-museum.com
2 for the price of 1

Peak Rail PLC
Matlock Station, Matlock, Derbyshire DE4 3NA
☎ +44 1629 580381
📠 +44 1629 760645
10% discount on adult and childrens tickets

PENZANCE

Harry Safari
Tamarisk, Fore Street, Penzance TR20 9LL
☎ +44 1736 711427
📠 +44 1736 711427
✉ harrysafari@compuserve.com
£2.50 discount on normal prices

ROCHESTER

Royal Engineers Museum
Prince Arthur Road, Gillingham, Kent ME4 4UG
☎ +44 1634 406397
📠 +44 1634 822371
✉ remuseum.rhqre@gtnet.gov.uk
🖥 www.army.mod.uk/museums
£1 off adults; 50p off children

World Naval Base - The Historic Dockyard
Chatham, Kent ME4 4TZ
☎ +44 1634 823800
📠 +44 1634 823801
✉ info@worldnavalbase.org.uk
£1 off entry

STRATFORD UPON AVON

National Waterways Museum
Llanthony Warehouse, Gloucester Docks, Gloucester GL1 2BH
☎ +44 1452 318054
📠 +44 1452 318066
✉ infor@nwm.deom.co.uk
🖥 www.nwm.org.uk
20% discount for adults on museum entry

Winchcombe Railway Museum & Gardens
23 Gloucester Street, Winchcombe, Gloucestershire Gl54 5LX
☎ +44 1242 602257
20% off admissions

TREFDRAETH (NEWPORT)

Cenarth Paintball Games
Swiss Cottage, Pentrecagal, Newcastle Emlyn, Carmathenshire SA38 9HT
☎ +44 1559 371621
✉ fun@cenarthpaintball.fsnet.co.uk
🖥 www.cenarthpaintball.fsnet.co.uk
10% off game fee for each player

TREYARNON BAY

Harlyn Surf School
16 Boyd Avenue, Padstow, Cornwall PL28 8ER
☎ +44 1841 533076
📠 +44 1841 533076
🖥 www.harlynsurf.co.uk
10% discount on all surfing courses and beach hire

YORK

📷 **Royal Armouries Museum**
Armouries Drive, Leeds, Yorkshire LS10 1LT
☎ +44 113 2201895
🖷 +44 113 2201955
✉ enquiries@armouries.org.uk
🖳 www.armouries.org.uk
2 for the price of 1

📷 **National Railway Museum**
Leeman Road, York, Yorkshire YO26 4XJ
☎ +44 1904 621261
🖷 +44 1904 611112
✉ nrm@nmsi.ac.uk
🖳 www.nrm.org.uk
£1 off full adult price; children under 17 & over 60's free

ESTONIA

TALLINN

✛ **Balti Puhkemajad**
Tatari 39-310
☎ 372 6461 457
🖷 372 6461 595
✉ puhkemajad@online.ee
🖳 www.bmp.jg.ee
5% discount on travel services. 5-10% discount on airfare tickets

✛ **Inges Kindlustus**
☎ 372 6410 436
🖳 www.inges.ee
5% discount on travel insurance

FINLAND

National

✛ **Cruises to the Coast**
☎ 400 840 591
10-20% discount on normal rates on most cruises off the coast and on most lake routes and cruises. Season in summertime. Tickets usually on board

✛ **Transvell Car Rental**
☎ 9 350 5590 (Helsinki)
15% discount on car hire

FRANCE

National

✛ **Eurolines**
3% discount

BOURGES

📷 **Bourge's museums**
All museums in Bourges - Free entrance

MONTPELLIER

📀 **Le Comptoir du disque (CD, Music)**
20% discount

PARIS

✛ **Tour Montparnasse**
5% discount

✛ **Vedettes de Pont Neuf (Cruises on La Seine)**
5% discount

VERDUN

📷 **World Peace Center (museum)**
30% discount

INDIA

NEW DELHI

✛ **Travel Corporation (India) Ltd**
C-35, Connaught Place, New Delhi 110 001
☎ 91 11 3319992
🖷 91 11 3328363
🖳 www.tcindia.com
10% discount on Eurail, Eurostar and Greyhound and 5% discount on Amtrak (American Railway system)

🍴 **Lazeez Affaire**
Malcha Marg Shopping Centre, Chanakyapuri, New Delhi 110 021
☎ 6114380
10% discount on food

IRELAND, NORTHERN

BELFAST

✛ **Carriageway Cars**
92 Bloomfield Road
10% discount on car hire

✛ **TIC Walking Tours**
N.I.T.B, St Annes Court, 59 North Street
£1.00 off

IRELAND, REP OF

There are discounts available on Transport, Tours, Tourism and Cultural activities for Hostelling International members on production of a current membership card. For details check the National or IYHF web pages under discounts or enquire to the National Office.

ISRAEL

EILAT

🏨 **Eilat Youth Hostel**
Ha'atava St.
 ☎ 972 7 6370088
 📠 972 7 6375835
 ✉ eilat@iyha.org.il
 🖥 www.youth-hostels.org.il
Coral Sea Divers. 10% discount. Tickets available for Youth Hostel guests

EIN GEDI

🏨 **Ein Gedi Youth Hostel**
 ☎ 972 7 6584165
 📠 972 7 6584445
Ein Gedi Spa - 10% discount. Purchase tickets at the Youth Hostel

🏨 **Ein Gedi Youth Hostel**
 ☎ 972 7 6584165
 📠 972 7 6584445
Mineral Beach - 10% discount. Purchase tickets at the Youth Hostel

JERUSALEM

🏨 **Yitzhak Rabin Youth Hostel**
1 Nahman Avigad St.
 ☎ 972 2 6780101
 📠 972 2 6796566
 ✉ rabin@iyha.org.il
 🖥 www.youth-hostels.org.il
Israel Museum. 10% discount. Purchase tickets at the Youth Hostel

ITALY

National

✚ **Italian Railways**
 ☎ +39 06 4871152
 🖥 www.hostels-aig.org
HI Members aged under 26 can obtain a 50% discount on the Carta Verde (Green Card) which entitles them to 20% discount on 2nd class, and 30% discount on 1st class travel.

✚ **Sixt Agency (Rent a Car)**
 ☎ 800 900686 (toll free)
Special rates for HI members. Contact the AIG National Office for the code to access the concession

Ⓖ **Didattica e Metodo**
 ☎ +39 06 5781141
Special price for the Italian Language course on CD "The Italian Treasure".

📖 **Mondadori and Mel Bookstores**
10% off all books

📖 **Calderini and Edagricole Bookshops**
20% off all books

📖 **Modi e Moda Visa Gina Lebole Department stores**
 🖥 www.hostels-aig.org
Free admission to stores that are not normally open to the public. See www.hostels-aig.org for full list of the stores

📖 **Cisalfa Sportswear Network**
Various discounts on purchasing

✚ **Bike and Moto rental**
 🖥 www.hostels-aig.org
Various discounts on bike and moto rental in Rome and other towns in Italy.

🏨 **Italian Theatres**
 🖥 www.hostels-aig.org
Discounted entrance tickets in several Italian Theatres. See www.hostels-aig.org for full list

🏨 **Amusement Parks**
 🖥 www.hostels-aig.org
Discounted entrance tickets to the best amusement parks in Italy such as Genoa Aquarium, Safari park, Fantasy World and much more

MILAN, ROME & TURIN

🄖 **Vacupan Dental Care**
🕿 800 861104
Special rates for Dental Care

ROME

📧 **Planet Hollywood**
Via Del Tritone 118
🕿 +39 06 42818909
💻 www.hostels-aig.org
Various discounts. See www.hostels-aig.org for
further details

🏰 **Rome Biopark**
P.L.E. del Giardino Zoologie 1
🕿 +39 06 3608211
20% discount on the entrance fee

JAPAN

National

✚ **Japan Rent-a-Car**
🕿 03 3580-3410 (head office)
20% discount off the basic rate (except for "joyful
JSS, JS" class car)

✚ **Nissan Rent-a-Car**
🕿 03 5424-4123 (Tokyo)
5% discount off the basic rate (except for at Station
Rent-a-Car & Service cars)

📧 **Sanyo-do**
🕿 03 3580-3410 (head office)
Suitcases 20% off, Backpacks 15% off, Small travel
goods 5% off

📧 **Sogo department stores**
🕿 03 3284-6711 (Tokyo -
Yurakuo-cho)
5% discount for over ¥1,000 purchase. "Shopping
ticket" should be purchased in advance at
GAISHO-salon. (As for Osaka & Kobe Sogo, they are
available at YH information center)

NARA

📧 **Nara Bank (headquarters & all 23
branches)**
🕿 0120 39 3800 (Nara headquarters -
free dial)
50% discount off travellers check issue commission

SOUTH KOREA

SEOUL

🏰 **Lotte World**
40-1, Zamsil-dong, Songpa-ku
🕿 +82 2 411 2000
🄵 +82 2 419 1767
💻 www.lotteworld.com
20% off entrance ticket. Free ticket, BIG 5 ticket
(Possible for HI member to buy 5 tickets at one
time)

YONGIN-SI

🏰 **Samsung Everland**
310, Jeondae-ri, Pokok-myun, Yongin-shi,
Kyonggi-do
🕿 +82 31 320 9747
🄵 +82 31 320 9727
💻 www.everland.co.kr
15-30% off entrance ticket. (possible for HI
member to buy 5 tickets at one time)

LUXEMBOURG

BEAUFORT

🏰 **Castle Beaufort "Amis de l'Ancien
Château"**
L-6313 Beaufort
🕿 +352 83 60 02
Normal price: LUF80-, Reduced price LUF30.50-

LAROCHETTE

🏰 **Castle Larochette "Amis de la Ville
Larochette"**
33 Chemin J.A. Zinnen, L-7626 Larochette
🕿 +352 83 74 97
Normal price: LUF60-, Reduced price LUF40-

LUXEMBOURG

🏰 **Casino Luxembourg**
41 Rue Notre-Dame, L-2013 Luxembourg
🕿 +352 22 50 45
🄵 +352 22 95 95
Normal price LUF150-, Reduced price LUF100-

🏰 **Castle Vianden "Amis du Château"**
Montée du Château, L-9408 Vianden
🕿 +352 84 9291
🄵 +352 849284
Normal price LUF 180-, Reduced price LUF130-

MACEDONIA

SKOPJE

☪ **Olimpiski Bazen**
bul. Koco Racin bb
☎ +389 91 114 143
30% discount

🏛 **Muzej na Makedonija**
Kurliska bb
☎ +389 91 221 973
60% discount

THE NETHERLANDS

National

✛ **Budget Rent a Car**
☎ 0800 0537 (toll free in The Netherlands)
🖳 www.budget.nl
10% discount on car rental. Ask for Budget traveller (1 or 2 days) or Budget World Travel Plan (from 3 days)

✛ **Eurolines**
☎ See below
10% discount by showing your membership card at the following Eurolines offices:
Amsterdam Rokin: +31 20 560 87 88,
Amsterdam Julianaplein 5: +31 20 560 87 88,
Rotterdam Conradstraat 20: +31 10 412 44 44

🅖 **GWK**
🖳 www.gwk.nl
25% discount on transaction costs for cash currency exchange at any of the 65 GWK outlets, situated at main railway stations and border crossings

NEW ZEALAND

National

✛ **Air New Zealand**
☎ 0800 737 000
50% off full economy fare when flying standby on domestic flights. Available only to international visitors to New Zealand. Conditions apply

✛ **Ansett NZ**
☎ 0800 267 388
50% off full domestic economy fare when flying standby. Available to international visitors. Conditions apply

✛ **Trans Scenic Unique Train Journeys**
☎ 0800 802 802
30% off standard adult fares. Cannot be used in conjunction with any other offer

✛ **Mt Cook Landline**
30% off standard adult fares exceeding NZ$20 one way. Cannot be used in conjunction with any other offer

✛ **Intercity Coachlines**
☎ 09 913 6100 (Auckland)
20% off standard adult fares. Cannot be used in conjunction with any other offer

✛ **Kiwi Experience**
☎ 09 366 9830
5% off NZ adventure transport network. Cannot be used in conjunction with any other offer

✛ **Magic Travellers Network**
☎ 09 358 5600
🅔 info@magicbus.co.nz
5% off NZ's transport network for the independent traveller. Cannot be used in conjunction with any other offer

NORWAY

National

✛ **Hertz Car rental**
☎ +47 671680 00
Call for special rates. Remember to give the agreement number CDP 85 83 59. You must be aged 25 or more to qualify

BERGEN

☪ **Bergen**
Floeybanen - (The Funicular Railway). 10% discount when you buy a ticket at the Montana hostel or the YMCA Hostel

✛ **Bergen**
Fjord sightseeing on MS Bruvik: 20% discount, 8-9 hours fjord sightseeing around Osterøy Island between 1st July and 31st August

DOMBÅS

☪ **Dovrefjell Aktivitetssenter**
15% on canoeing, rafting, musk ox tours, elk safaris, mountain-climbing etc

EVJE

Troll Mountain AS
10% discount on rafting and safaris

LAKSELV

Lakselv Youth Hostel
P.B. 74, N-9700 Lakselv
☎ +47 78 46 14 76
✆ +47 78 46 19 96
Free hire of canoe, boat and fishing rod. Free use of sauna and Sami barbeque hut

LILLEHAMMER

Lillehammer Youth Hostel
Jernbanetorget 2, N 2609 Lillehammer
☎ +47 61 24 87 00
✆ +47 61 26 25 66
✉ lillehammer.vandrerhjem@c2i.net
Free rental of cross country skis for guests of the hostel

MO I RANA

Mo Youth Hostel Fageråsen
Postboks 1227, N-8602, Mo
☎ +47 75 15 09 63
✆ +47 90 16 21 35
✉ mo.vandrerhjem@c2i.net
Arctic Circle Centre - 15% discount

MJOELFJELL

Mjoelfjell Youth Hostel
Mjoelfjell, N-5700, Voss
☎ +47 56 52 31 50
✆ +47 56 52 31 51
✉ muhas@online.no
💻 www.bgif.no/netcon/mjfjell
Heated outdoor swimming pool from 23 June to Mid September

OSLO

Oslo Youth Hostel Haraldsheim
Haraldsheimveien 4, P.B. 41 Grefsen, N-0409 Oslo
☎ +47 22 22 29 65
✆ +47 22 22 10 25
✉ booking@haraldsheim.oslo.no
💻 www.haraldsheim.oslo.no
Oslo Promotion card. Oslo card can be purchased here. The card gives you discounts and benefits all over Oslo city

SJOA

Heidal Rafting AS
10% discount on rafting, glaciering, canyoning etc.

STAMSUND

Stamsund Youth Hostel
Justad Rorbuer Og Vandrerhjem, P.B. 110, N-8378 Stamsund
☎ +47 76 08 93 34
✆ +47 76 08 97 39
Free loan of boat and fishing tackle (deposit required)

STRYN

Stryn Sommerski (summer skiing centre)
10-15% discount on ski pass for downhill, snowboarding and cross country skiing

SCOTLAND

National

✚ Arnold Clarke Car Rental
10% off basic tariffs (except economy class)

Ⓖ National Trust for Scotland
30% off site entrance fees

✚ Stena Sealink Services
10% off (except Friday and Saturday sailings during July and August). Tickets only available from port sailing office

Ⓖ Wildfowl Trust
Reduction on entry fees

AYR

Burns Cottage
Two for the price of one. One free child admission per paying adult

INVERNESS

Inverness Traction
☎ +44 1463 239292
Student rate for members. Loch Ness Tours, Inverness-Durness and Inverness-Gairloch

SOUTH AFRICA

National

✛ **Intercape Mainliner Buses/Coaches**
  ℮ info@intercape.co.za
  🖵 www.intercape.co.za
  15% discount to all HI card holders on all Southern African Routes. Discount available when booked at any location nationally

CAPE TOWN

🏛 **Two Oceans Aquarium**
  🖵 www.aquarium.co.za
  All HI card holders receive student rates on admission and adventure diving

DURBAN, KWAZULU-NATAL

🏛 **Gibela Safaris**
  ℮ gibela@gibela.co.za
  🖵 www.gibela.co.za
  10% discount on all products when booked directly with Gibela

PRETORIA

✛ **Packer Tours**
  ℮ ptaback@hotmail.com
  10% discount when booking any of 7 day tours. These bookings can be nationally. The choice of tours: Pretoria City Tour, Soweto Tour, Suncity Tour, Pilansberg Tour, Ndebele Village Tour, Cullinan Diamond mine Tour, De Wildt Cheetah Centre Tour

SWITZERLAND

BASEL

✛ **Youth Hostel Basel**
  St. Alban—Kirchrain 10, CH-4052 Basel
  ☎ +41 61 272 05 72
  📠 +41 61 272 08 33
  ℮ basel@youthhostel.ch
  🖵 www.youthhostel.ch/basel
  Checked in guests receive a "Mobility Ticket" for free transportation in Basel

BÖNIGEN

🏛 **Youth Hostel Bönigen-Interlaken**
  Aareweg 21, Am See, 3806 Bönigen
  ☎ +41 33 822 43 53
  📠 +41 33 823 20 58
  ℮ boenigen@youthhostel.ch
  🖵 www.youthhostel.ch/boenigen
  50% discount on cow craving

ZERMATT

🚁 **Air Taxi**
  M.D.Bahling, CH-3920 Zermatt
  ☎ +41 27 967 67 44
  📠 +41 27 967 67 45
  Reduced price for paragliding tandem flight

THAILAND

BANGKOK

🏠 **Bangkok International Youth Hostel**
  25/2 Phitsanulok Road, Thaywej Market, Dusit, Bangkok 10300
  ☎ 2 2810361
  Free guided tours by local university students for checked in guests. A look into the Thai lifestyle and cultural sights of Bangkok

UNITED STATES OF AMERICA

National

✛ **Alamo Rental Cars**
  5-15% off the daily rate for rental cars from all U.S. domestic locations

✛ **Hertz Car Rental**
  5-15% off the daily rate for rental cars from all U.S. domestic locations

For a more complete listing of local discounts in U.S.A., visit our website at www.hiayh.org